Public Policy

Contents

PART TWO

Making Public Policy   **86**
The process, structure, and context of policy making

PART THREE

The Players   **201**
Institutional and noninstitutional actors

PART FOUR

The Policy Game   *333*

Rules, strategies, culture, and resources

Preface

What exactly is public policy, and is the policy-making process a truly rational one through which effective policy is made in the public interest? Although these are apparently simple questions to those of us who do research and teach in the field of public policy, such questions confuse many students. Understanding the policy process necessitates an understanding of the environment within which policy is being made. The purpose of this reader is to help students comprehend both the environment and the actual policy-making process.

The text provides key classic and contemporary readings on public policy that introduce readers to the underpinnings and current practices of the policy-making arena. The selected readings have been classified as "essential" in that they are among the most influential in the field. Either they are among the most frequently cited, or they highlight the link between theory and practice particularly well, making public policy intelligible.

We believe that the reader supplements existing textbooks by providing extra insight into issues and concepts covered in such standard texts. At the same time, due to its organization, the book is suitable for use as a core text for both the beginner and more advanced student of policy and public administration.

The readings are grouped into four broad sections, which parallel both the majority of policy texts and the way many courses are designed. The first section introduces material that deals with the nature of public policy, defining what is meant by public policy. The section ends with readings that illustrate theories and models of public policy making. The second section deals with the making of policy from a process perspective by identifying the sequential stages that policies pass through. Section three presents material on the players, both institutional and noninstitutional, who are involved with policy making. The last section treats policy making as a game. The readings in this section deal with the rules, strategies, and culture of the policy game. We have begun each section with an overview essay that sums up the overall focus of the section and also provides summaries of the focuses of the remaining authors.

Finally we would like to express our thanks and appreciation to Ben Ventura, our research assistant; our editors; the reviewers Patricia Freeman, University of Tennessee, Michael E. Kraft, University of Wisconsin at Green Bay, and Stephen Percy, University of Wisconsin at Milwaukee; and Danielle Owens, our Prentice Hall field representative.

Stella Z. Theodoulou
Matthew A. Cahn

Public Policy

PART ONE

The Nature of Public Policy

1

The Contemporary Language of Public Policy: A Starting Point

Stella Z. Theodoulou

In recent years there has been a substantial transformation in the way public policy is studied. The student of policy making is faced not only with a diversity of theoretical approaches but also, at times, with rival vocabularies and specialist terminologies. Nowhere is this better illustrated than in the definitions of public policy. Such discussions frequently use a specialized language, indeed often jargon, which often confuses and muddles an understanding of public policy. The one thing, however, that all authors on public policy do agree on is that public policy deeply affects the daily lives of every individual in society.

THE CONCEPT OF PUBLIC POLICY

Rather than look at how individual authors define public policy, it is far more advantageous to discuss a composite of the ideas and elements that are present in the vast majority of definitions. The purpose of doing so is to allow for a less restrictive meaning of public policy.

The first idea one encounters is that public policy should distinguish between what governments intend to do and what, in fact, they actually do; that governmental inactivity is as important as governmental activity. The second element is the notion that public policy ideally involves all levels of government and is not necessarily restricted to formal actors; informal actors are also extremely important. Third, public policy is pervasive and is not solely limited to legislation, executive orders, rules, and regulations. Fourth, public policy is an intentional course of action with an accomplished end goal as its objective. A fifth idea describes public policy as both long term and short term. Policy is an ongoing process; it involves not only the decision to enact a law but also the subsequent actions of implementation, enforcement, and evaluation.

We cannot divorce politics from public policy or the environment in which it is made. Public policy generally does one or more of the following: it reconciles conflicting claims on scarce resources; it establishes incentives for cooperation and collective action that would be irrational without government influence; it prohibits morally unacceptable behavior; it protects the activity of a group or an individual, promoting activities that are essential or important to government. Finally, policy provides direct benefits to citizens.

WHY STUDY PUBLIC POLICY

On a simplistic level, researchers and students are interested in studying public policy because it concerns issues and decisions that affect them. Beyond this, studying policy allows for an overview of the workings of the whole political system, including a concern with political institutions and the informal elements of the political process, such as interest groups and public opinion. Thus the study of public policy allows one to view the entirety of the political system, including its output. As Thomas Dye concludes, policy study

> Involves a description of the content of public policy; an assessment of the impact of environmental forces on the content of public policy; an analysis of the effect of various institutional arrangements and political processes on public policy; an inquiry into the consequences of various public policies for the political system; and an evaluation of the impact of public policies on society, both in terms of expected and unexpected consequences.[1]

In sum, students of public policy are concerned with the question posed over fifty years ago by Harold Lasswell, "Who gets what, when, and how?"[2]

There are additional theoretical, practical, and political considerations in studying policy making. Such study allows for the testing and development of explanations and generalizations that form the basis of many of the theories that contemporary political scientists have formulated about the very nature of politics in modern industrialized societies. On a practical level, by studying existing policy it is hoped that future problems may be handled in a much more efficient and rational manner, so that the process of formulating and implementing new policies will be more effective and appropriate. To argue that policy making is value free is naive: one cannot ignore the ideological debate that surrounds the creation of public policy. Concurrently, it is also true that many of the individuals who study policy are not value free in their recommendations. In a perfect world it would be admirable if as Duncan MacRae and James Wilde argue public policy analysis was "the use of reason and evidence to choose the best policy among a number of alternatives."[3]

However, this ignores the agenda of many who study policy. Such researchers contend that their goal is aiding in the adoption of policies that will accomplish the "right" goals. In short, they have taken on the role of policy advocates. For such individuals "right" equals "correct" policy solutions. Such an argument views the policy-making arena as an inherently political process involving conflict and struggle among competing actors—both formal and informal—with conflicting interests, values, and desires on policy issues.

A word of warning to new students of public policy; it is beneficial to realize that one should distinguish between a basic understanding of the policy-making process and the reasons for studying it. The two are inextricably linked, but they should be very separate undertakings. The primary goal should be the explanation of policy rather than the prescription of "good" policy. Thus the emphasis should be on analysis rather than advocacy. Next, the causes and consequences of public policy should be searched through the application of social scientific methodology rather than through political agendas. From this, reliable theories concerning policies and their politics can be developed, thus allowing policy studies to be both theoretical and practical.

APPROACHES TO STUDYING PUBLIC POLICY

Political scientists have utilized many theoretical approaches in their analysis of policy making. The approaches discussed here are not exhaustive but are examples of the most commonly used. It is also not the intention here to compare or evaluate the usefulness of such approaches but rather to outline each so that students may recognize the various ones they will encounter in their reading.

The first group have in common the concept of cycle and process: one image of political activity is to see it as phased behavior leading from stimulus to new or adapted policy. Who dominates, controls, and benefits from policy is the basis for the second group of approaches.

CYCLE–PROCESS APPROACHES

The common assumption that each of these approaches shares about political society is that policy makers respond to the demands put on them. The focus is upon the process of policy making.

1. Systems Theory

Systems theory is best exemplified by the work of David Easton and his adherents. Easton's approach is suggested by the base model (see Figure 1) that he offers in *A Systems Analysis of Political Life*.[4] He views public policy as a political system's response to demands arising from the environment. The political system is thus a mechanism by which popular demands and popular support for the state are combined to produce those policy outputs that best ensure the long-term stability of the political system. Policy outputs may produce new demands that lead to further outputs, and so on in a never-ending flow of public policy. The basic idea is that political systems should be seen as analogues to operating mechanical systems with feedback loops and clear goals.

Systems theory has often been seen as innately conservative because of its stress on stability rather than change. However, this does not negate the usefulness of the approach in allowing students to see the interrelationship of the various actors and institutions in the policy process. The basic weakness of the systems model, in analyzing policy, is that it says little about how decisions are determined or how they arrive into the decision-making structures.

2. Structural Functionalism

This is an attempt to find a way of comparing both the structures and the operations of all social systems by finding necessary elements common to any stable social system.[5] Much of its origins depends on analogies with biological systems. In the way that biologists might study the role of some physiological aspect in the maintenance of life, functionalists have tried to understand (1) the necessary "functions" that must be carried out in any political system if it is to cope with its environment and achieve its goals and (2) the location of the "structures"—political parties and socializing agencies—that facilitate that functioning. This is an acknowledgment that the structures, arrangements, and procedures of political institutions have important consequences for the adoption and content of public

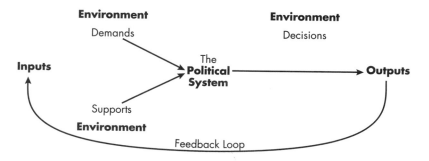

FIGURE 1   A Simplified Model of a Political System. Source: David Easton, *A Systems Analysis*, 1965, p. 32.

policy. Those who concentrate on institutions focus on the relationship of the various governmental institutions with each other in the policy-making process. As James Anderson concludes: "Institutions provide part of the context for policy making which must be considered along with the more dynamic aspects of politics, such as political parties, groups and public opinion."[6] In the same way that its related theory, the systems model, is criticized for being conservative for stressing stability, so has structural-functionalism. The real weakness of this approach is that it tends to fragment the study of policy making by focusing on the various structures, thus making it difficult to concisely draw all of the different elements involved in the policy process together. Concentrating on the institutional functions will give only a partial perspective. However, the approach is useful in that it does acknowledge the role of institutional structures and procedures in policy making.

3. The Policy Cycle

This approach views the policy process as a cycle that is deliberative, staged, recursive, and administrative.[7] Policy making is thus seen as a dynamic ongoing process confirming the importance of policy as a learning system. Policies are described in two different but important senses: how they are made and how they can be made better.

MODELS OF WHO MAKES PUBLIC POLICY

These models look at how the policy process operates and, most importantly, who controls or dominates the process and who benefits from it. In other words, who rules? It is not the purpose here to critique or compare the models in terms of their usefulness but rather to outline each of them to prepare students for the relevant readings.

1. Group Theory

The tenet here is that public policy is a product of group struggle. Group theory is largely associated with the work of David Truman and in various formulations with pluralist writers such as Robert Dahl.[8] The central argument of both group theory and pluralism is that societies consist of a large number of social, ethnic, or economic groups, who are more or less well organized. These groups, in political competition with each other, put pressure on the government to produce policies favorable to them. The public interest thus tends to emerge out of the struggle of competing individual and group claims. Specific policies reflect the relative influence of the different interests on any given issue. Therefore, each policy area involves a distinctive set of problems and separate sets of political agents and forces. Public policy is the result of a unique process of interaction.

The basic elements of pluralism and group theory are multiple centers of powers and optimum policy developments through competing interests.

2. Elite Theory

This model holds that policies are made by a relatively small group of influential leaders who share common goals and outlooks. The theory is most associated with the work of writers such as C. Wright Mills and Ralph Miliband.[9] Such theorists do not see policy as the product of group conflict and demands but rather as determined by the preferences of the power elite or ruling class. Thus it is the preferences of the elite that are adopted by policy makers; policies reflect their values and serve their interests. Public policy is not then determined by the masses but by a minority who have political and economic power.

3. Corporatism

A significant challenge in recent years to group theory as an approach has come from the corporatism of Philippe Schmitter.[10] The concept assumes that interest groups do not merely attempt to influence policy but themselves become part of the decision-making and implementation system. In return for this participation in policy making the groups—through the control of their members—make society more manageable for the state or government.

4. Subgovernments[11]

This model argues that the government alone does not make policy choices but endorses decisions made by sections of the government in alliance with interest groups. This partnership has been referred to as subgovernments, which are coalitions of members of Congress, the bureaucracy, and interest groups.[12] All those involved in a subgovernment have similar interests. Such structures develop around particular policy areas and involve the relevant legislators, bureaucrats, and interest groups. Thus, policy outcomes are determined by various subgovernments and revolve around their interests. Subgovernments, therefore, tend to develop around those specialized areas of policy that have a low level of general public interest and awareness. This perspective has in recent years become outmoded among political scientists, who argue that there are now much larger numbers of interested actors than the three posited by the subgovernment model.[13] For example, Hugh Heclo argues that one should view the process as being dominated by issue networks, all of whom have substantial expertise in the policy area.[14]

TYPES OF PUBLIC POLICY

Since the advent of the New Deal and the grudging acceptance that government—national, state, and local—will intrude into society's day-to-day operation, there has been a proliferation of public policies to deal with the problems that arise in a complex industrialized society. In order to come to grips with the huge task of understanding the nature of policy enactment, political scientists have developed several typologies to categorize public policy.[15]

The classic typology, constantly referred to, is that of Theodore Lowi.[16] This author classifies policies according to whether they are regulatory, distributive, or redistributive in nature. Such a typology differentiates policies on the basis of their impact on society and the relationship among those involved in policy formation.

A second typology is that of Murray Edelman, who views policy as being either material or symbolic.[17] Material policies provide tangible resources or substantive power to their beneficiaries, and they may also impose costs on those who may be adversely affected. On the other hand, symbolic policies provide little material impact on individuals and no real tangible advantages or disadvantages. Rather, they appeal to the values held in common by individuals in society, values that could include social justice, equality, and patriotism. Symbolic policies can be used to either divert public attention or to satisfy public demand when no substantive benefits are being provided.

James Anderson argues that policies may also be classified as either substantive or procedural.[18] Substantive policies are what government intends to do (actual plans of action), and they provide individuals with advantages and disadvantages, costs and benefits. In contrast, procedural policies are how something will be done or who will do it.

A further way to classify policies is to ask whether a policy provides collective goods or private goods.[19] Collective policy may be viewed as providing indivisible goods, in that if they are given to one individual or group, then they must be provided to all individuals or groups. In contrast, private policy may be seen as including divisible goods. Such policies are broken into units and charged for on an individual beneficiary basis. Michael O'Hare recently conceptualized various policies by the types of action that government might take.[20] He argues that there are direct and indirect actions that governments may take to address issues when the private or public sectors do not allocate goods efficiently or when there are equity or distributional problems.[21]

Finally, because of the political nature of policy making, policies may be classified as either liberal or conservative.[22] Liberal policies seek government intervention to bring about social change while conservative policies oppose such intervention. It could be argued that this distinction has become blurred in recent years and that the division is not about whether government should intervene but in what areas, in what form, and on whose behalf.

CONCLUSION

The concern here has been to summarize for readers the debate on what public policy has come to mean, why it should be studied, and how such study has been done. An attempt has been made to link the study of policy to the larger study of government and politics. There has been no real venture to critique any of the definitions, approaches, or models that are commonly found in the literature. It is hoped that such critiques will be provoked by the reading selections. From this discussion it should become clear that there is no simple way to view public policy. This point is clearly supported by Paul Sabatier who traces the development of public policy as a subfield of the political science discipline. Sabatier acknowledges there are many sources of tension between political scientists and public policy scholars.[23]

The readings that follow represent a cross-section of the literature and have been selected because they are generally considered by political scientists to form the benchmark from which the discipline looks at policy making. What should emerge is the recognition that there exists a cycle and process of public policy and that it involves interaction among a wide spread of participants.

NOTES

1. Thomas R. Dye, *Understanding Public Policy* (5th ed.) (Englewood Cliffs, N.J.: Prentice-Hall, 1984), pp. 5–7.

2. Harold Lasswell, *Politics: Who Gets What, When, and How* (New York: St. Martin's Press, 1988). (Originally published 1936.)

3. Duncan MacRae, Jr. and James A. Wilde, *Policy Analysis for Public Decisions* (North Scituate, Mass.: Duxbury Press, 1979), p. 4.

4. David Easton, *A Systems Analysis of Political Life* (New York: Wiley, 1965).

5. Gabriel Almond and J. S. Coleman, *The Politics of Developing Areas* (Princeton, N.J.: Princeton University Press, 1960).

6. James E. Anderson, *Public Policymaking: An Introduction* (Boston: Houghton Mifflin, 1990), p. 31.

7. R. Mack, *Planning and Uncertainty* (New York: Wiley, 1971), p. 136; also see B. W. Hogwood and L. A. Gunn, *Policy Analysis for the Real World* (Oxford: Oxford University Press, 1984); B. W. Hogwood and B. Guy Peters, *Policy Dynamics* (New York: St. Martin's Press, 1983); and W. Jenkins, *Policy Analysis* (Oxford: Martin Robertson, 1978).

8. See Robert Dahl, "With the Consent of All" (this reader, part 1, reading 6); also "Pluralism Revisited," *Comparative Politics*, 10, no. 2 (January 1978), 191–204; and David B. Truman, "Group Politics and Representative Democracy" (this reader, part 1, reading 9).

9. See Ralph Miliband, "Imperfect Competition" (this reader, part 1, reading 8); and C. Wright Mills, "The Power Elite" (this reader, part 1, reading 10).

10. Philippe Schmitter and G. Lehmbruch (eds.), *Trends towards Corporatist Intermediation* (Newbury Park, Calif.: Sage, 1979).

11. Subgovernments are also referred to as iron triangles.

12. J. Leiper Freeman, *The Political Process: Executive Bureau-Legislative Committee Relations* (New York: Norton, 1979); T. L. Gais and others, "Interest Groups, Iron Triangles and Representative Institutions in American National Government," *British Journal of Political Science*, 14 (April 1984), 161–186; and A. G. Jordan, "Iron Triangles, Woolly Corporatism and Elastic Nets: Images of the Policy Process," *Journal of Public Policy*, 1 (February 1981), 95–123.

13. Jack Walker, *Mobilizing Interest Groups in America* (Ann Arbor: University of Michigan Press, 1991).

14. See Hugh Heclo (this reader, part 1, reading 7).

15. Issue areas have also been used to classify types of policy, for example, welfare, foreign, en-

vironment, labor policy; or institutional categories such as judicial policy; also legislative policy or time period, for example, pre–World War II. See Robert Salisbury, "The Analysis of Public Policy: A Search for Theories and Roles" (this reader, part 1, reading 5).

    16. See Theodore J. Lowi, "Distribution, Regulation, Redistribution" (this reader, part 1, reading 3).

    17. See Murray Edelman, "Symbols and Political Quiescence" (this reader, part 1, reading 4).

    18. Anderson, *Public Policymaking*, p. 10.

    19. L. L. Wade and R. L. Curry, Jr., *A Logic of Public Policy* (Belmont, Calif.: Heath, 1979), chapter 5.

    20. Michael O'Hare, "A Typology of Governmental Action," *Journal of Policy Analysis and Management*, 8 (Fall 1989), 670–672.

    21. O'Hare, "A Typology," p. 670.

    22. Theodore E. Lowi, *The End of Liberalism* (2nd ed.) (New York: Norton, 1979), chapter 3.

    23. See Paul A. Satatier, "Political Science and Public Policy" (this reader part 1, reading 2).

ADDITIONAL SUGGESTED READING

CHAMPNEY, LEONARD. "Public Goods and Policy Types." *Public Administration Review*, 48 (November/December 1988), 988–994.

CIGLER, ALLAN J., and BURDETT, A. LOOMIS. *Interest Group Politics* (2nd ed.). Washington, D.C.: CQ Press, 1986.

COCHRAN, CLARKE E., MAYER, LAWRENCE C., CARR, T. R., and CAYER, N. JOSEPH. *American Public Policy* (4th ed.). New York: St Martin's Press, 1993.

DANEKE, GREGORY A. "On Paradigmatic Progress in Public Policy and Administration." *Policy Studies Journal*, 17 (Winter 1988/1989), 277–296.

DOMHOFF, G. W. *Who Rules America?* Englewood Cliffs, N.J.: Prentice-Hall, 1967.

DYE, THOMAS R. *Who's Running America: The Conservative Years* (4th ed.). Englewood Cliffs, N.J.: Prentice-Hall, 1986.

EYESTONE, ROBERT E. *The Threads of Public Policy*. Indianapolis, Ind.: Bobbs-Merrill, 1971.

GOLEMBIEWSKI, R. "The Group Basis of Politics." *American Political Science Review*, 54 (December 1960), 962–971.

HEIDENHEIMER, ARNOLD J., HECLO, HUGH, and ADAMS, CAROLYN TEICH, *Comparative Public Policy* (3rd ed.). New York: St. Martin's Press, 1990.

HEISLER, M. "Corporate Pluralism Revisited." *Scandinavian Political Studies*, new series, 2 (1979), 277–297.

KOENIG, LOUIS W. *An Introduction to Public Policy*. Englewood Cliffs, N.J.: Prentice-Hall, 1986.

OLSON, MANCUR. *The Logic of Collective Action*. Cambridge, Mass.: Harvard University Press, 1965.

PETERS, B. GUY. *American Public Policy: Promise and Performance* (3rd ed.). Chatham, N.J.: Chatham House, 1993.

PETERSON, PAUL E. "The Rise and Fall of Special Interest Politics." *Political Science Quarterly*, 105 (Winter 1990/1991), 539–556.

PRESTHUS, ROBERT. *Elites in the Policy Process*. New York: Cambridge University Press, 1974.

RANNEY, AUSTIN (ed.). *Political Science and Public Policy*. Chicago: Markham, 1968.

REICH, ROBERT B. (ed.). *The Power of Public Ideas*. Cambridge, Mass.: Ballinger, 1988.

ROURKE, FRANCIS B. E. *Bureaucracy, Politic, and Public Policy* (3rd ed.). Boston: Little, Brown, 1984.

SCHATTSCHNEIDER, E. E. *The Semi-Sovereign People*. New York: Holt, Rinehart & Winston, 1969.

SCHUMPETER, J. *Capitalism, Socialism and Democracy*. London: Allen & Unwin, 1943.

SUNDQUIST, JAMES L. "Political Scientists and Public Policy Research." *PS*, 24 (September 1991), 531–535.

WILSON. GRAHAM K. *Special Interests and Policy-Making*. London: Wiley, 1977.

Political Science and Public Policy

Paul A. Sabatier

Political scientists who are policy scholars often trace their lineage back to the pioneering work of Lerner and Lasswell (1951). But public policy did not emerge as a significant subfield within the discipline of political science until the late 1960s or early 70s. This resulted from at least three important stimuli: (1) social and political pressures to apply the profession's accumulated knowledge to the pressing social problems of racial discrimination, poverty, the arms race, and environmental pollution; (2) the challenge posed by Dawson and Robinson (1963), who argued that governmental policy decisions were less the result of traditional disciplinary concerns such as public opinion and party composition than of socioeconomic factors such as income, education, and unemployment levels; and (3) the efforts of David Easton, whose *Systems Analysis of Political Life* (1965) provided an intellectual framework for understanding the entire policy process, from demand articulation through policy formulation and implementation, to feedback effects on society.

Over the past twenty years, policy research by political scientists can be divided into four types, depending upon the principal focus:

1. *Substantive area research.* This seeks to understand the politics of a specific policy area, such as health, education, transportation, natural resources, or foreign policy. Most of the work in this tradition has consisted of detailed, largely atheoretical, case studies. Examples would include the work of Derthick (1979) on social security, Moynihan (1970) on antipoverty programs, and Bailey and Mosher (1968) on federal aid to education. Such studies are useful to practitioners and policy activists in these areas, as well as providing potentially useful information for inductive theory building. In terms of the profession as a whole, however, they are probably less useful than theoretical case studies—such as Pressman and Wildavsky (1973) on implementation or Nelson (1984) on agenda-setting—which use a specific case to illustrate or test theories of important aspects of the policy process.

2. *Evaluation and impact studies.* Most evaluation research is based on contributions from other disciplines, particularly welfare economics (Stokey and Zeckhauser 1978; Jenkins-Smith 1990). Policy scholars trained as political scientists have made several contributions. They have broadened the criteria of evaluation from traditional social welfare functions to include process criteria, such as opportunities for effective citizen participation (Pierce and Doerksen 1976). They have focused attention on distributional effects (MacRae 1989). They have criticized traditional techniques of benefit-cost analysis on many grounds (Meier 1984; MacRae and Whittington 1988).

From Paul A. Sabatier, "Political Science and Public Policy," *PS: Political Science & Politics* (June 1991), pp. 143–146. Reprinted by permission.

Most importantly, they have integrated evaluation studies into research on the policy process by examining the use and non-use of policy analysis in the real world (Wildavsky 1966; Dunn 1980; Weiss 1977).

3. *Policy process.* Two decades ago, both Ranney (1968) and Sharkansky (1970) urged political scientists interested in public policy to focus on the policy process, i.e. the factors affecting policy formulation and implementation, as well as the subsequent effects of policy. In their view, focusing on substantive policy areas risked falling into the relatively fruitless realm of atheoretical case studies, while evaluation research offered little promise for a discipline without clear normative standards of good policy. A focus on the policy process would provide opportunities for applying and integrating the discipline's accumulated knowledge concerning political behavior in various institutional settings. That advice was remarkably prescient; the first paper in this symposium attempts to summarize what has been learned.

4. *Policy design.* With roots in the policy sciences tradition described by deLeon (1988), this approach has recently focused on such topics as the efficacy of different types of policy instruments (Salamon 1989; Linder and Peters 1989). Although some scholars within this orientation propose a quite radical departure from the behavioral traditions of the discipline (Bobrow and Dryzek 1987), others build upon work by policy-oriented political scientists over the past twenty years (Schneider and Ingram 1990) while Miller (1989) seeks to integrate political philosophy and the behavioral sciences.

While all have made some contributions, the third has been the most fruitful.

Before turning to a preview of the symposium, some mention should be made of tensions that have emerged between political scientists and the subfield of policy scholars.

SOURCES OF STRAIN

The first, and most subtle, concerns a difference in the fundamental conception of the purpose of government and political life (Hofferbert 1986). Virtually all policy scholars view government in *instrumental* terms: Governments are there to improve the welfare of members of society—to protect public health, provide for the common defense, correct externalities and other market failures, improve public safety, etc. Many political scientists are uncomfortable with this view. Having been schooled in Plato, Aristotle, Locke, and Mill, there is a tendency to view citizenship and political participation as ends in themselves rather than as a means of influencing policy decisions.

Fortunately, this strain need not be serious. Policy scholars can certainly acknowledge the value of solidary incentives and a sense of political efficacy arising from political participation, even if these topics hold no intrinsic interest for them. Likewise most political scientists would admit that people participate in political life at least in part to influence governmental decisions and ultimately improve social welfare. Thus both sides should be able to agree on the importance of developing theories of the policy process which focus on ascertaining the factors which affect the extent to which governmental policy decisions and their social effects are consistent with popular preferences. This is, in fact, a well-established tradition within many subfields of political science, including public opinion (Luttbeg 1968; Page and Shapiro 1983), legislative representation (Miller and Stokes 1963; Ingram et al. 1980), and administrative agencies (Meier 1975; 1987).

The second strain also involves a difference in normative assumptions which need not impede close relations. Most policy scholars have an activist bent, i.e. at some point they wish to influence policy in the area(s) in which they are specialists. Conversely, political scientists probably tend to be preoccupied with better understanding the way the world operates within their areas of specialization, with a smaller percentage seeking to use their expertise to influence political behavior. That percentage, however, is far from trivial: Henry Kissinger and Jeane Kirkpatrick are obvious exceptions, while voting scholars often serve as campaign consultants and many other political scientists have sought to improve the performance of various governmental institutions (Huntington 1988).

The third, and probably most serious, source of strain is that, in the eyes of many political scientists, policy scholars have made only modest contributions to developing reasonably clear, generalizable, and empirically verified theories of the policy process. See, for example, Eulau (1977) and Landau (1977), as well as the relatively poor performance of policy proposals in NSF's Political Science Program (Sigelman and Scioli 1987). In some respects, this indictment strikes me as quite valid. Much of what passes as policy research—particularly by substantive area specialists—shares all the defects of traditional case studies in public administration: descriptive analyses of specific institutions or decisions relying upon very subjective methods of data acquisition and analysis, virtually no attention to the theoretical assumptions underlying the research or the theoretical implications of the findings, and very little concern with the potential generalizability of those findings.

In addition, the dominant paradigm of the policy process—the stages heuristic of Jones (1970), Anderson (1975), and Peters (1986)—is not really a causal theory. Instead, it divides the policy process into several stages (agenda setting, formulation and adoption, implementation, and evaluation), but contains no coherent assumptions about what forces are driving the process from stage to stage and very few falsifiable hypotheses.[1] While the stages heuristic has helped to divide the policy process into manageable units of analysis, researchers have tended to focus exclusively on a single stage with little recognition of work in other stages. The result is weakened theoretical coherence across stages. Even within stages, such as implementation, where there has been a great deal of empirical research, disagreement exists as to how much has been learned over the past 20 years (see Sabatier 1986 and O'Toole 1986 for contrasting reviews). Finally, Nakamura (1987) and others have noted that the real world process often does not fit the sequence of stages envisaged.

On the other hand, a great deal of policy research—particularly in the policy process tradition—has been methodologically sophisticated and guided by explicit theory. Examples would include Kingdon (1984) and Nelson (1984) on agenda-setting; Pressman and Wildavsky (1973), Rodgers and Bullock (1976), Mazmanian and Sabatier (1981; 1989), and Goggin (1987) on implementation; Browning et al. (1984) on long-term policy change; and Ostrom (1990) on institutional arrangements for managing common property resources. In short, while the criticisms of Eulau and Landau were largely justified in the 1970s, they are less valid today.

None of these sources of strain should pose serious obstacles to close collaboration between "mainline" political scientists and the subfield of policy scholars. Both groups share an overwhelming common interest in developing a better understanding of the policy process, i.e. the range of factors which affect governmental policy decisions and the impacts of those decisions on society. Since at least the first part of that process has traditionally been the domain of political science, the subfield of policy scholars clearly have an interest in keeping abreast of developments in the rest of the discipline. By the same token, policy scholars can take pride in having made major contributions to our understanding of the functioning of governmental institutions which should be of interest to all political scientists, even those with no particular concerns with policy impacts.

NOTES

The participants would like to express their thanks to Robert Hauck for shepherding this symposium to publication and to Ken Meier for accepting responsibility for all errors of fact, interpretation, and logic.

1. This criticism is less valid for Anderson (1975). His first two chapters discuss a variety of socio-economic conditions and types of actors which affect the policy process, and he briefly reviews several approaches. But nowhere does he elaborate one or more frameworks and then seek to apply it/them throughout the book. Ripley (1985) proposes a somewhat similar framework, although his arguments derive primarily from Lowi's arenas of power.

On the other hand, the stages heuristic—which distinguishes a major policy decision, such as a statute, from what emerges in the implementation and reformulation stages—is one means of dealing with several of the problems mentioned by Greenberg et al. (1977).

REFERENCES

ANDERSON, JAMES. 1975. *Public Policy-Making*. N.Y.: Praeger.

BAILEY, STEPHEN and MOSHER, EDITH. 1968. *ESEA: The Office of Education Administers a Law*. Syracuse: Syracuse University Press.

BOBROW, DAVIS and DRYZEK, JOHN. 1987. *Policy Analysis by Design*. Pittsburgh: University of Pittsburgh Press.

BROWNING, RUFUS, MARSHALL, DALE ROGERS, and TABB, DAVID. 1984. *Protest Is Not Enough: The Struggle of Blacks and Hispanics for Equality in Urban Politics*. Berkeley: University of California Press.

DAWSON, RICHARD and ROBINSON, JAMES. 1963. "Interparty Competition, Economic Variables, and Welfare Policies in the American States," *Journal of Politics* 25 (May): 265–289.

DELEON, PETER. 1988. *Advice and Consent*. New York: Russell Sage.

DERTHICK, MARTHA. 1979. *Policymaking for Social Security*. Washington: Brookings.

DUNN, WILLIAM. 1980. "The Two-Communities Metaphor and Models of Knowledge Use," *Knowledge* 1 (June): 515–536.

EASTON, DAVID. 1965. *A Systems Analysis of Political Life*. N.Y.: John Wiley and Sons.

EULAU, HEINZ. 1977. "The Interventionist Synthesis," *American Journal of Political Science* 21 (May): 419–423.

GOGGIN, MALCOLM. 1987. *Policy Design and the Politics of Implementation.* Knoxville: University of Tennessee Press.

GREENBERG, GEORGE, JEFFREY MILLER, LAWRENCE MOHR, and BRUCE VLADECK. 1977. "Developing Public Policy Theory Perspectives from Empirical Research," *American Political Science Review* 71 (December): 1532–1543.

HOFFERBERT, RICHARD. 1974. *The Study of Public Policy.* Indianapolis: Bobbs Merrill.

———. 1986. "Policy Evaluation, Democratic Theory, and the Division of Scholarly Labor," *Policy Studies Review* 5 (Feb.): 511–519.

HUNTINGTON, SAMUEL. 1988. "One Soul at a Time: Political Science and Reform," *American Political Science Review* 82 (March): 3–10.

INGRAM, HELEN, NANCY LANEY, and JOHN MCCAIN. 1980. *A Policy Approach to Political Representation: Lessons from the Four Corners States.* Baltimore: Johns Hopkins University Press.

JENKINS-SMITH, HANK. 1990. *Democratic Politics and Policy Analysis.* Pacific Grove, CA: Brooks/Cole.

JONES, CHARLES. 1970. *An Introduction to the Study of Public Policy.* Belmont, CA: Wadsworth.

KINGDON, JOHN. 1984. *Agendas, Alternatives, and Public Policies.* Boston: Little, Brown & Co.

KISER, LARRY and OSTROM, ELINOR. 1982. "The Three Worlds of Action," in *Strategies of Political Inquiry*, ed. E. Ostrom. Beverly Hills: Sage, pp. 179–222.

LANDAU, MARTIN. 1977. "The Proper Domain of Policy Analysis," *American Journal of Political Science* 21 (May): 423–427.

LERNER, DANIEL and LASSWELL, HAROLD, eds. 1951. *The Policy Sciences.* Stanford: Stanford University Press.

LINDER, STEPHEN and PETERS, B. GUY. 1989. "Instruments of Government: Perceptions and Contexts," *Journal of Public Policy* 9 (1): 35–58.

LUTTBEG, NORMAN, ed. 1968. *Public Opinion and Public Policy: Models of Political Linkages.* Homewood, IL: Dorsey.

MACRAE, DUNCAN. 1989. "Social Science and Policy Advice," Paper presented at the PSO/APSA Conference, "Advances in Policy Studies." Atlanta.

———. and WHITTINGTON, DALE. 1988. "Assessing Preferences in Cost-Benefit Analysis," *Journal of Policy Analysis and Management* 7 (Winter): 246–263.

MAZMANIAN, DANIEL and SABATIER, PAUL, eds. 1981. *Effective Policy Implementation.* Lexington, Mass.: D.C. Heath.

———. 1989. *Implementation and Public Policy*, rev. ed. Lanham, MD: University Press of America.

MEIER, KENNETH. 1975. "Representative Bureaucracy: An Empirical Analysis," *American Political Science Review* 69 (June): 526–542.

———. 1984. "The Limits of Cost-Benefit Analysis," *Decision-Making in the Public Sector*, ed. Lloyn Nigro. N.Y.: Marcel Dekker, pp. 43–63.

———. 1987. *Politics and the Bureaucracy*, 2d. ed. Monterey, CA: Brooks/Cole.

MILLER, TRUDI. 1989. "Design Science as a Unifying Paradigm," Paper presented at the PSO/APSA Conference, "Advances in Policy Studies." Atlanta.

MILLER, WARREN and STOKES, DONALD. 1963. "Constituency Influence on Congress," *American Political Science Review* 57 (March): 45–56.

MOYNIHAN, DANIEL. 1970. *Maximum Feasible Misunderstanding.* N.Y.: Free Press.

NAKAMURA, ROBERT. 1987. "The Textbook Policy Process and Implementation Research," *Policy Studies Review* 7 (1): 142–154.

NELSON, BARBARA J. 1984. *Making an Issue of Child Abuse.* Chicago: University of Chicago Press.

OSTROM, ELINOR. 1989. *Governing the Commons.* Cambridge: Cambridge University Press.

O'TOOLE, LAURENCE. 1986. "Policy Recommendations for Multi-Actor Implementation: An Assessment of the Field," *Journal of Public Policy* 6 (April): 181–210.

PAGE, BENJAMIN and SHAPIRO, ROBERT. 1983. "Effects of Public Opinion on Policy," *American Political Science Review* 77 (March): 175–190.

PETERS, B. GUY. 1986. *American Public Policy: Promise and Performance*, 2d ed. Chatham, NJ: Chatham House.

PIERCE, JOHN and DOERKSEN, eds. 1976. *Water Politics and Public Involvement.* Ann Arbor: Ann Arbor Science.

PRESSMAN, JEFFREY and WILDAVSKY, AARON. 1973. *Implementation.* Berkeley: University of California Press.

RANNEY, AUSTIN, ed. 1968. *Political Science and Public Policy.* Chicago: Markham.

RIPLEY, RANDALL. 1985. *Policy Analysis in Political Science*. Chicago: Nelson-Hall.
RODGERS, HARRELL and BULLOCK, CHARLES. 1976. *Coercion to Compliance*. Lexington, Mass: D.C. Heath.
SABATIER, PAUL. 1986. "Top-Down and Bottom-Up Models of Policy Implementation: A Critical Analysis and Suggested Synthesis," *Journal of Public Policy* 6 (January): 21–48.
————. 1988. "An Advocacy Coalition Framework of Policy Change and the Role of Policy-Oriented Learning Therein," *Policy Sciences* 21 (Fall): 129–168.
SALAMON, LESTER, ed. 1989. *Beyond Privatization: The Tools of Government*. Washington, DC: The Urban Institute.
SCHNEIDER, ANNE and INGRAM, HELEN. 1990. "Behavioral Assumptions of Policy Tools," *Journal of Politics* 52 (May): 510–529.
SHARKANSKY, IRA, ed. 1970. *Policy Analysis in Political Science*. Chicago: Markham.
STOKEY, EDITH and ZECKHAUSER, RICHARD. 1978. *A Primer for Policy Analysis*. NY: W. W. Norton.
WEISS, CAROL. 1977. *Using Social Research in Public Policy Making*. Lexington, MA: D. C. Heath.
WILDAVSKY, AARON. 1966. "The Political Economy of Efficiency: Cost-Benefit Analysis, Systems Analysis, and Program Budgeting," *Public Administration Review* 26 (December): 292–310.

3

Distribution, Regulation, Redistribution: The Functions of Government

Theodore J. Lowi

In the long run, all governmental policies may be considered redistributive, because in the long run some people pay in taxes more than they receive in services. Or, all may be thought regulatory because, in the long run, a governmental decision on the use of resources can only displace a private decision about the same resource or at least reduce private alternatives about the resource. But politics works in the short run, and in the short run certain kinds of government decisions can be made without regard to limited resources. Policies of this kind are called "distributive," a term first coined for nineteenth-century land policies, but easily extended to include most contemporary public land and resource policies; rivers and harbors ("pork barrel") programs; defense procurement and research and development programs; labor, business, and agricultural "clientele" services; and the traditional tariff. Distributive policies are characterized by the ease with which they can be disaggregated and dispensed unit by small unit, each unit more or less in isolation from other units and from any general rule. "Patronage" in the fullest meaning of the word can be taken as a synonym for "distributive." These are policies that are virtually not policies at all but are highly individualized decisions that

From Theodore J. Lowi, "American Business, Public Policy Case Studies and Political Theory," World Politics, xvi (July 1964), 677–715. Reprinted by permission.

only by accumulation can be called a policy. They are policies in which the indulged and the deprived, the loser and the recipient, need never come into direct confrontation. Indeed, in many instances of distributive policy, the deprived cannot as a class be identified, because the most influential among them can be accommodated by further disaggregation of the stakes.

Regulatory policies are also specific and individual in their impact, but they are not capable of the almost infinite amount of disaggregation typical of distributive policies. Although the laws are stated in general terms ("Arrange the transportation system artistically." "Thou shalt not show favoritism in pricing."), the impact of regulatory decisions is clearly one of directly raising costs and/or reducing or expanding the alternatives of private individuals ("Get off the grass!" "Produce kosher if you advertise kosher!"). Regulatory policies are distinguishable from distributive in that in the short run the regulatory decision involves a direct choice as to who will be indulged and who deprived. Not all applicants for a single television channel or an overseas air route can be propitiated. Enforcement of an unfair labor practice on the part of management weakens management in its dealings with labor. So, while implementation is firm-by-firm and case-by-case, policies cannot be disaggregated to the level of the individual or the single firm (as in distribution), because individual decisions must be made by application of a general rule and therefore become interrelated within the broader standards of law. Decisions cumulate among all individuals affected by the law in roughly the same way. Since the most stable lines of perceived common impact are the basic sectors of the economy, regulatory decisions are cumulative largely along sectoral lines; regulatory policies are usually disaggregable only down to the sector level.

Redistributive policies are like regulatory policies in the sense that relations among broad categories of private individuals are involved and, hence, individual decisions must be interrelated. But on all other counts there are great differences in the nature of impact. The categories of impact are much broader, approaching social classes. They are, crudely speaking, haves and have-nots, bigness and smallness, bourgeoisie and proletariat. The aim involved is not use of property but property itself, not equal treatment but equal possession, not behavior but being. The fact that our income tax is in reality only mildly redistributive does not alter the fact of the aims and the stakes involved in income tax policies. The same goes for our various "welfare state" programs, which are redistributive only for those who entered retirement or unemployment rolls without having contributed at all. The nature of a redistributive issue is not determined by the outcome of a battle over how redistributive a policy is going to be. Expectations about what it *can* be, what it threatens to be, are determinative.

ARENAS OF POWER

Once one posits the general tendency of these areas of policy or governmental activity to develop characteristic political structures, a number of hypotheses become compelling. And when the various hypotheses are accumulated, the general contours of each of the three arenas begin quickly to resemble, respectively, the three "general" theories of political process. The arena that develops around distributive policies is best characterized in the terms of E. E. Schattschneider's findings on the politics of tariff legislation in the nineteen-twenties. The regulatory arena corresponds to the pluralist school, and the school's general notions are found to be limited pretty much to this one arena. The redistributive arena most closely approximates, with some adaptation, an elitist view of the political process.

(1) The distributive arena can be identified in considerable detail from Schattschneider's case-study alone.[1] What he and his pluralist successors did not see was that the traditional structure of tariff politics is also in largest part the structure of politics of all those diverse policies identified earlier as distributive. The arena is "pluralistic" only in the sense that a large number of small, intensely organized interests are operating. In fact, there is even greater multiplicity of participants here than the pressure-group model can account for, because essentially it is a politics of every man for himself. The single person and the single firm are the major activists.

Although a generation removed, Schattschneider's conclusions about the politics of the Smoot-Hawley Tariff are almost one-for-one applicable to rivers and harbors and land development policies, tax exemptions, defense procurement, area redevelopment, and government "services." Since there is no real basis for discriminating between those who should and those who should not be protected [indulged], says Schattschneider, Congress seeks political support by "giving a limited protection [indulgence] to all interests strong enough to furnish formidable resistance." Decision-makers become "responsive to considerations of equality, consistency, impartiality, uniformity, precedent, and moderation, however formal and insubstantial these may be." Furthermore, a "policy that is so hospitable and catholic . . . disorganizes the opposition."

When a billion-dollar issue can be disaggregated into many millions of nickel-dime items and each item can be dealt with without regard to the others, multiplication of interests and of access is inevitable, and so is reduction of conflict. All of this has the greatest bearing on the relations among participants and, therefore, the "power structure." Indeed, coalitions must be built to pass legislation and "make policy," but what of the nature and basis of the coalitions? In the distributive arena, political relationships approximate what Schattschneider called "mutual noninterference"—"a mutuality under which it is proper for each to seek duties [indulgences] for himself but improper and unfair to oppose duties [indulgences] sought by others." In the area of rivers and harbors, references are made to "pork barrel" and "log-rolling," but these colloquialisms have not been taken sufficiently seriously. A log-rolling coalition is not one forged of conflict, compromise, and tangential interest but, on the contrary, one composed of members who have absolutely nothing in common; and this is possible because the "pork barrel" is a container for unrelated items. This is the typical form of relationship in the distributive arena.

The structure of these log-rolling relationships leads typically, though not always, to Congress; and the structure is relatively stable because all who have access of any sort usually support whoever are the leaders. And there tend to be "elites" of a peculiar sort in the Congressional committees whose jurisdictions include the subject-matter in question. Until recently, for instance, on tariff matters the House Ways and Means Committee was virtually the government. Much the same can be said for Public Works on rivers and harbors. It is a broker leadership, but "policy" is best understood as cooptation rather than conflict and compromise.

Distributive issues individualize conflict and provide the basis for highly stable coalitions that are virtually irrelevant to the larger policy outcomes; thousands of obscure decisions are merely accumulated into a "policy" of protection or of natural-resources development or of defense subcontracting. Congress did not "give up" the tariff; as the tariff became a matter of regulation (see below), committee elites lost their power to contain the participants because obscure decisions became interrelated, therefore less obscure, and more controversy became built in and unavoidable.

(2) The regulatory arena could hardly be better identified than in the thousands of pages written for the whole polity by the pluralists. But, unfortunately, some translation is necessary to accommodate pluralism to its more limited universe. The regulatory arena appears to be composed of a multiplicity of groups organized around tangential relations or David Truman's "shared attitudes." Within this narrower context of regulatory decisions, one can even go so far as to accept the most extreme pluralist statement that policy tends to be a residue of the interplay of group conflict. This statement can be severely criticized only by use of examples drawn from non-regulatory decisions.

As I argued before, there is no way for regulatory policies to be disaggregated into very large numbers of unrelated items. Because individual regulatory decisions involve direct confrontations of indulged and deprived, the typical political coalition is born of conflict and compromise among tangential interests that usually involve a total sector of the economy. Thus, while the typical basis for coalition in distributive politics is uncommon interests (log-rolling), an entirely different basis is typical in regulatory politics.

Owing to the unrelatedness of issues in distributive politics, the activities of single participants need not be related but rather can be specialized as the situation warrants it. But the relatedness of regulatory issues, at least up to the sector level of the trade association, leads to the containment of all these within the association. When all the stakes are contained in one organization, constituents have no alternative but to fight against each other to shape the policies of that organization or actually to abandon it.

What this suggests is that the typical power structure in regulatory politics is far less stable than that in the distributive arena. Since coalitions form around shared interests, the coalitions will shift as the interests change or as conflicts of interest emerge. With such group-based and shifting patterns of conflict built into every regulatory issue, it is in most cases impossible for a Congressional committee, an administrative agency, a peak association governing board, or a social elite to contain all the participants long enough to establish a stable power elite. Policy outcomes seem inevitably to be the residue remaining after all the reductions of demands by all participants have been made in order to extend support to majority size. But a majority-sized coalition of shared interests on one issue could not possibly be entirely appropriate for some other issue. In regulatory decision-making, relationships among group leadership elements and between them on any one or more points of governmental access are too unstable to form a single policy-making elite. As a consequence, decision-making tends to pass from administrative agencies and Congressional committees to Congress, the place where uncertainties in the policy process have always been settled. Congress as an institution is the last resort for breakdowns in bargaining over policy, just as in the case of parties the primary is a last resort for breakdowns in bargaining over nominations. No one leadership group can contain the conflict by an almost infinite subdivision and distribution of the stakes. In the regulatory political process, Congress and the "balance of power" seem to play the classic role attributed to them by the pluralists.

Beginning with reciprocity in the 1930's, the tariff began to lose its capacity for infinite disaggregation because it slowly underwent redefinition, moving away from its purely domestic significance towards that of an instrument of international politics. In brief, the tariff, especially following World War II and our assumption of peacetime international leadership, became a means of regulating the domestic economy for international purposes. The significant feature here is not the international but the regulatory part of the redefinition. As the process of redefinition took place, a number of significant shifts in power relations took place as well, because it was no longer possible to deal with each dutiable item in isolation. Everything in Bauer, Pool, and Dexter points toward the expansion of relationships to the level of the sector. The political problem of the South was the concentration of textile industry there. Coal, oil, and rails came closer and closer to coalition. The final shift came with the 1962 Trade Expansion Act, which enabled the President for the first time to deal with broad categories (to the sector) rather than individual commodities.

Certain elements of distributive politics remain, for two obvious reasons. First, there are always efforts on the part of political leaders to disaggregate policies because this is the best way to spread the patronage and to avoid conflict. (Political actors, like economic actors, probably view open competition as a necessary evil or a last resort to be avoided at almost any cost.) Second, until 1962, the basic tariff law and schedules were still contained in the Smoot-Hawley Act. This act was amended by Reciprocal Trade but only to the extent of allowing negotiated reductions rather than reductions based on comparative costs. Until 1962, tariff politics continued to be based on commodity-by-commodity transactions, and thus until then tariff coalitions could be based upon individual firms (or even branches of large and diversified firms) and log-rolling, unrelated interests. The escape clause and peril point were maintained in the 1950's so that transactions could be made on individual items even within reciprocity. And the coalitions of strange bedfellows continued: "Offered the proper coalition, they both [New England textiles and Eastern railroads] might well have been persuaded that their interest was in the opposite direction."

But despite the persistence of certain distributive features, the true nature of tariff in the 1960's emerges as regulatory policy with a developing regulatory arena. Already we can see some changes in Congress even more clearly than the few already observed in the group structure. Out of a committee (House Ways and Means) elite, we can see the emergence of Congress in a pluralist setting. Even as early as 1954–1955, the compromises eventually ratified by Congress were worked out, not in committee through direct cooptation of interests, but in the Randall Commission, a collection of the major interests in conflict. Those issues that could not be thrashed out through the "group process" also could not be thrashed out in committee but had to pass on to Congress and the floor. After 1954 the battle centered on major categories of goods (even to the extent of a textile management-union entente) and the battle took place more or less openly on the floor. The weakening of the Ways and Means Committee as the tariff elite is seen in the fact that in 1955 Chairman Jere Cooper was unable to push a closed rule through. The Rules Committee, "in line with tradition," granted a closed rule but the House voted it down 207–178. Bauer, Pool, and Dexter saw this as a victory for protectionism, but it is also evidence of the emerging regulatory arena—arising from the difficulty of containing conflict and policy within the governing committee. The last effort to keep the tariff as a traditional instrument of distributive politics—a motion by Daniel Reed to recommit, with instructions to write in a provision that Tariff Commission rulings under the escape clause be final except where the President finds the national security to be involved—was voted down 206–199. After that, right up to 1962, it was clear that tariff decisions would not be made piecemeal. Tariff became a regulatory policy in 1962; all that remains of distributive politics now are quotas and subsidies for producers of specific commodities injured by general tariff reductions.

(3) Compared particularly with the regulatory area, very few case-studies of redistributive decisions have ever been published. This in itself is a significant datum—which C. Wright Mills attributes to the middle-level character of the issues that have gotten attention. But, whatever the reasons, it reduces the opportunities for elaborating upon and testing the scheme. Most of the propositions to follow are illustrated by a single case, the "welfare state" battle of the 1930's. But this case is a complex of many decisions that became one of the most important acts of policy ever achieved in the United States. A brief review of the facts of the case will be helpful. Other cases will be referred to in less detail from time to time.

As the 1934 mid-term elections approached, pressures for a federal social security system began to mount. The Townsend Plan and the Lundeen Bill had become nationally prominent and were gathering widespread support. Both schemes were severely redistributive, giving all citizens access to government-based insurance as a matter of right. In response, the President created in June of 1934 a Committee on Economic Security (CES) composed of top cabinet members with Secretary of Labor Perkins as chairman. In turn, they set up an Advisory Council and a Technical Board, which held hearings, conducted massive studies, and emerged on January 17, 1935, with a bill. The insiders around the CES were representatives of large industries, business associations, unions, and the most interested government bureaucracies. And the detailed legislative histories reveal that virtually all of the debate was contained within the CES and its committees until a mature bill emerged. Since not all of the major issues had been settled in the CES's bill, its members turned to Congress with far from a common front. But the role of Congress was still not what would have been expected. Except for a short fight over committee jurisdiction (won by the more conservative Finance and Ways and Means committees) the legislative process was extraordinarily quiet, despite the import of the issues. Hearings in both Houses brought forth very few witnesses, and these were primarily CES members supporting the bill, and Treasury Department officials, led by Morgenthau, opposing it with "constructive criticism."

The Congressional battle was quiet because the real struggle was taking place elsewhere, essentially between the Hopkins-Perkins bureaucracies and the Treasury. The changes made in the CES bill had all been proposed by Morgenthau (the most important one being the principle of contribution, which took away the redistributive sting). And the final victory for Treasury and mild redistribution came with the removal of administrative responsibility from both Labor and Hopkins's Federal Emergency Relief Administration. Throughout all of this some public expressions of opinion were to be heard from the peak associations, but their efforts were mainly expended in the quieter proceedings in the bureaucracies. The Congress's role seems largely to have been one of ratifying agreements that arose out of the bureaucracies and the class agents represented there. Revisions attributable to Congress concerned such matters as exceptions in coverage, which are part of the distributive game that Congress plays at every opportunity. The *principle* of the Act was set in an interplay involving (quietly) top executives and business and labor leaders.

With only slight changes in the left-right positions of the participants, the same pattern has been observed in income tax decisions. Professor Stanley S. Surrey notes: "The question, 'Who speaks for tax equity and tax fairness?,' is answered today largely in terms of only the Treasury Department." "Thus, in tax bouts . . . it is the Treasury versus percentage legislation, the Treasury versus capital gains, the Treasury versus this constituent, the Treasury versus that private group. . . . As a consequence, the congressman . . . [sees] a dispute . . . only as a contest between a private group and a government department." Congress, says Surrey, "occupies the role of mediator between the tax views of the executive and the demands of the pressure groups." And when the tax issues "are at a major political level, as are tax rates or personal exemptions, then pressure groups, labor organizations, the Chamber of Commerce, the National Association of Manufacturers, and the others, become concerned." The "average congressman does not basically believe in the present income tax in the upper brackets," but rather than touch the principle he deals in "special hardship" and "penalizing" and waits for decisions on principle to come from abroad. Amidst the 1954–1955 tax controversies, for example, Ways and Means members decided to allow each member one bill to be favorably reported if the bill met with unanimous agreement.

Issues that involve redistribution cut closer than any others along class lines and activate interests in what are roughly class terms. If there is ever any cohesion within the peak associations, it occurs on redistributive issues, and their rhetoric suggests that they occupy themselves most of the time with these. In a ten-year period just before and after, but not including, the war years, the Manufacturers' Association of Connecticut, for example, expressed itself overwhelmingly more often on redistributive than on any other types of issues. Table 1 summarizes the pattern, showing that expressions on generalized issues involving basic relations between bourgeoisie and proletariat outnumbered expressions on regulation of business practices by 870 to 418, despite the larger number of issues in the latter category. This pattern goes contrary to the one observed by Bauer, Pool, and Dexter in tariff politics, where they discovered, much to their surprise, that self-interest did not activate both "sides" equally. Rather, they found, the concreteness and specificity of protectionist interests activated them much more often and intensely than did the general, ideological position of the liberal-traders. This was true in tariff, as they say, because there the "structure of the communications system favored the propagation of particular demands." But there is also a structure of communications favoring generalized and ideological demands; this structure consists of the peak associations, and it is highly effective when the issues are gen-

TABLE 1   Published Expressions of Manufacturers' Association of Connecticut on Selected Issues

	Number of References in Ten-year Period (1934–40, 1946–48)		Per Cent of Favorable References
1. Unspecified regulation	378		7.7
2. Labor relations, general	297		0.0
3. Wages and hours	195		0.5
Total expressions, redistribution		870	
4. Trade practices	119		13.8
5. Robinson-Patman	103		18.4
6. Antitrust	72		26.4
7. Basing points	55		20.0
8. Fair-Trade (Miller-Tydings)	69		45.5
Total expressions, regulation		418	

Source: Lane, *The Regulation of Businessmen* (New Haven, 1953), 388. The figures are his; their arrangement is mine.

eralizable. This is the case consistently for redistributive issues, almost never for distributive issues, and only seldom for regulatory issues.

As the pluralists would argue, there will be a vast array of organized interests for any item on the policy agenda. But the relations among the interests and between them and government vary, and the nature of and conditions for this variation are what our political analyses should be concerned with. Let us say, in brief, that on Monday night the big associations meet in agreement and considerable cohesion on "the problem of government," the income tax, the Welfare State. On Tuesday, facing regulatory issues, the big associations break up into their constituent trade and other specialized groups, each prepared to deal with special problems in its own special ways, usually along subject-matter lines. On Wednesday night still another fission takes place as the pork barrel and the other forms of subsidy and policy patronage come under consideration. The parent groups and "catalytic groups" still exist, but by Wednesday night they have little identity. As Bauer, Pool, and Dexter would say, they have preserved their unanimity through overlapping memberships. They gain identity to the extent that they can define the issues in redistributive terms. And when interests in issues are more salient in sectoral or geographic or individual terms, the common or generalized factor will be lost in abstractness and diffuseness. This is what happened to the liberal trade groups in the tariff battles of the 1950's, when "the protectionist position was more firmly grounded in direct business considerations and . . . the liberal-trade position fitted better with the ideology of the times . . ."

Where the peak associations, led by elements of Mr. Mills's power elite, have reality, their resources and access are bound to affect power relations. Owing to their stability and the impasse (or equilibrium) in relations among broad classes of the entire society, the political structure of the redistributive arena seems to be highly stabilized, virtually institutionalized. Its stability, unlike that of the distributive arena, derives from shared interests. But in contrast to the regulatory arena, these shared interests are sufficiently stable and clear and consistent to provide the foundation for ideologies. Table 2 summarizes the hypothesized differences in political relationships drawn above.

Many of the other distinctive characteristics of this arena are related to, perhaps follow from, the special role of the peak associations. The cohesion of peak associations means that the special differences among related but competing groups are likely to be settled long before the policies reach the governmental agenda. In many respects the upperclass directors perform the functions in the redistributive arena that are performed by Congressional committees in the distributive arena and by committees and Congress in the regulatory arena. But the differences are crucial. In distributive policies there are as many "sides" as there are tariff items, bridges and dams to be built, parcels of public land to be given away or leased, and so on. And there are probably as many elites as there are Congressional committees and subcommittees which have jurisdiction over distributive policies. In redistribution, there will never be more than two sides and the sides are clear, stable, and consistent. Negotiation is possible, but only for the pur-

TABLE 2 Arenas and Political Relationships: A Diagrammatic Survey

Arena	Primary Political Unit	Relation among Units	Power Structure	Stability of Structure	Primary Decisional Locus	Implementation
Distribution	Individual, firm, corporation	Log-rolling, mutual non-interference, uncommon interests	Non-conflictual elite with support groups	Stable	Congressional committee and/or agency**	Agency centralized to primary functional unit ("bureau")
*Regulation**	Group	"The coalition," shared subject-matter interest, bargaining	Pluralistic, multi-centered "theory of balance"	Unstable	Congress, in classic role	Agency decentralized from center by "delegation," mixed control
Redistribution	Association	The "peak association," class, ideology	Conflictual elite, i.e., elite and counterelite	Stable	Executive and peas associa-tions	Agency centralized toward top (above bureau"), elaborate standards

*Given the multiplicity of organized interests in the regulatory arena, there are obviously many cases of successful log-rolling coalitions that resemble the coalitions prevailing in distributive politics. In this respect, the difference between the regulatory and the distributive arenas is thus one of degree. The *predominant* form of coalition in regulatory politics is deemed to be that of common or tangential interest. Although the difference is only one of degree, it is significant because this prevailing type of coalition makes the regulatory arena so much more unstable, unpredictable, and non-elitist ("balance of power"). When we turn to the redistributive arena, however, we find differences of principle in every sense of the word.

**Distributive politics tends to stabilize around an institutional unit. In most cases, it is the Congressional committee (or subcommittee). But in others, particularly in the Department of Agriculture, the focus is the agency or the agency *and* the committee. In the cities, this is the arena where machine domination continues, if machines were in control in the first place.

pose of strengthening or softening the impact of redistribution. And there is probably one elite for each side. The elites do not correspond directly to bourgeoisie and proletariat; they are better understood under Wallace Sayre's designation of "money-providing" and "service-demanding" groups. Nonetheless, the basis for coalition is broad, and it centers around those individuals most respected and best known for worth and wealth. If the top leaders did not know each other and develop common perspectives as a result of common schooling, as Mills would argue, these commonalities could easily develop later in life because the kinds of stakes involved in redistributive issues are always the same. So institutionalized does the conflict become that governmental bureaucracies themselves begin to reflect them, as do national party leaders and Administrations. Finally, just as the nature of redistributive policies influences politics towards the centralization and stabilization of conflict, so does it further influence the removal of decision-making from Congress. A decentralized and bargaining Congress can cumulate but it cannot balance, and redistributive policies require complex balancing on a very large scale. What William H. Riker has said of budget-making applies here: ". . . legislative governments cannot endure a budget. Its finances must be totted up by party leaders in the legislature itself. In a complex fiscal system, however, haphazard legislative judgments cannot bring revenue into even rough alignment with supply. So budgeting is introduced—which transfers financial control to the budget maker. . . ." Congress can provide exceptions to principles and it can implement those principles with elaborate standards of implementation as a condition for the concessions that money-providers will make. But the makers of principles of redistribution seem to be the holders of the "command posts."

None of this suggests a power elite such as Mills would have had us believe existed, but it does suggest a type of stable and continual conflict that can only be understood in class terms. The foundation upon which the social-stratification and power-elite school rested, especially when dealing with national power, was so conceptually weak and empirically unsupported that its critics were led to err in the opposite direction by denying the direct relevance of social and institutional positions and the probability of stable decision-making elites. But the relevance of that approach becomes stronger as the scope of its application is reduced and as the standards for identifying the scope are clarified. But this is equally true of the pluralist school and of those approaches based on a "politics of this-or-that policy."

NOTE

1. E. E. Schattschneider, *Politics, Pressures, and the Tariff* (Hamden, Conn.: Shoe String, 1935).

Symbols
and Political Quiescence

Murray Edelman

If the regulatory process is examined in terms of a divergence between political
and legal promises on the one hand and resource allocations and group reactions
on the other hand, the largely symbolic character of the entire process becomes
apparent. What do the studies of government regulation of business tell us of the
role and functions of that amorphous group who are affected by these policies,
but who are not organized to pursue their interests? The following generalizations
would probably be accepted by most students, perhaps with occasional changes of
emphasis:

(1) Tangible resources and benefits are frequently not distributed to unorganized political group interests as promised in regulatory statutes and the propaganda attending their enactment.

This is true of the values held out to (or demanded by) groups which regard
themselves as disadvantaged and which presumably anticipate benefits from a
regulatory policy. There is virtually unanimous agreement among students of the
antitrust laws, the Clayton and Federal Trade Commission acts, the Interstate
Commerce acts, the public utility statutes and the right-to-work laws, for example, that through much of the history of their administration these statutes have
been ineffective in the sense that many of the values they promised have not in
fact been realized. The story has not been uniform, of course; but the general
point hardly needs detailed documentation at this late date. Herring,[1] Leiserson,[2]
Truman,[3] and Bernstein[4] all conclude that few regulatory policies have been pursued unless they proved acceptable to the regulated groups or served the interests
of these groups. Redford,[5] Bernstein,[6] and others have offered a "life cycle" theory of regulatory history, showing a more or less regular pattern of loss of vigor by
regulatory agencies. For purposes of the present argument it need not be assumed that this always happens but only that it frequently happens in important
cases.[7]

(2) When it does happen, the deprived groups often display little tendency
to protest or to assert their awareness of the deprivation.

The fervent display of public wrath, or enthusiasm, in the course of the initial legislative attack on forces seen as threatening "the little man" is a common
American spectacle. It is about as predictable as the subsequent lapse of the same

From Murray Edelman, *The Symbolic Uses of Politics*. Copyright © 1964 The University of Illinois.
(Urbana: University of Illinois Press, 1964), chapter 2. Reprinted by permission.

fervor. Again, it does not always occur, but it happens often enough to call for thorough explanation. The leading students of regulatory processes have all remarked upon it; but most of these scholars, who ordinarily display a close regard for rigor and full exploration, dismiss this highly significant political behavior rather casually. Thus, Redford declares that, "In the course of time the administrator finds that the initial public drive and congressional sentiment behind his directive has wilted and that political support for change from the existing pattern is lacking."[8]

Although the presumed beneficiaries of regulatory legislation often show little or no concern with its failure to protect them, they are nevertheless assumed to constitute a potential base of political support for the retention of these statutes in the law books. The professional politician is probably quite correct when he acts on the assumption that his advocacy of this regulatory legislation, in principle, is a widely popular move, even though actual resource allocations inconsistent with the promise of the statutes are met with quiescence. These responses (support of the statute together with apathy toward failure to allocate resources as the statute promises) define the meanings of the law so far as the presumed beneficiaries are concerned.[9] It is the frequent inconsistency between the two types of response that is puzzling.

(3) The most intensive dissemination of symbols commonly attends the enactment of legislation which is most meaningless in its effects upon resource allocation. In the legislative history of particular regulatory statutes the provisions least significant for resource allocation are most widely publicized and the most significant provisions are least widely publicized.

The statutes listed under Proposition 1 as having promised something substantially different from what was delivered are also the ones which have been most intensively publicized as symbolizing protection of widely shared interests. Trustbusting, "Labor's Magna Carta" (the Clayton Act), protection against price discrimination and deceptive trade practices, protection against excessive public utility charges, tight control of union bureaucracies (or, by other groups, the "slave labor law"), federal income taxation according to "ability to pay," are the terms and symbols widely disseminated to the public as descriptive of much of the leading federal and state regulation of the last seven decades, and they are precisely the descriptions shown by careful students to be most misleading. Nor is it any less misleading if one quotes the exact language of the most widely publicized specific provisions of these laws: Section 1 of the Sherman Act, Sections 6 and 20 of the Clayton Act, or the closed shop, secondary boycott, or emergency strike provisions of Taft-Hartley, for example. In none of these instances would a reading of either the text of the statutory provision or the attendant claims and publicity enable an observer to predict even the direction of future regulatory policy, let alone its precise objectives.

Other features of these statutes also stand as the symbols of threats stalemated, if not checkmated, by the forces of right and justice. Typically, a preamble (which does not pretend to be more than symbolic, even in legal theory) includes strong assurances that the public or the public interest will be protected, and the most widely publicized regulatory provisions always include other nonoperational standards connoting fairness, balance, or equity.

If one asks, on the other hand, for examples of changes in resource allocations that have been influenced substantially and directly by public policy, it quickly appears that the outstanding examples have been publicized relatively little. One thinks of such legislation as the silver purchase provisions, the court definitions of the word "lawful" in the Clayton Act's labor sections, the procedural provisions of Taft-Hartley and the Railway Labor Act, the severe postwar cuts in grazing service appropriations, and changes in the parity formula requiring that such items as interest, taxes, freight rates, and wages be included as components of the index of prices paid by farmers.

Illuminating descriptions of the operational meaning of statutory mandates are found in Truman's study and in Earl Latham's *The Group Basis of Politics*.[10] Both emphasize the importance of contending groups and organizations in day-to-day decision-making as the dynamic element in policy formation; and both distinguish this element from statutory language as such.[11]

We are only beginning to get some serious studies of the familiarity of voters with current public issues and of the intensity of their feelings about issues; but successful political professionals have evidently long acted on the assumption that there is in fact relatively little familiarity, that expressions of deep concern are rare, that quiescence is common, and that, in general, the congressman can count upon stereotyped reactions rather than persistent, organized pursuit of material interests on the part of most constituents.[12]

(4) Policies severely denying resources to large numbers of people can be pursued indefinitely without serious controversy.

The silver purchase policy, the farm policy, and a great many other subsidies are obvious examples. The antitrust laws, utility regulations, and other statutes ostensibly intended to protect the small operator or the consumer are less obvious examples, though there is ample evidence, some of it cited below, that these usually support the proposition as well.

The federal income tax law offers a rather neat illustration of the divergence between a widely publicized symbol and actual resource allocation patterns. The historic constitutional struggle leading up to the Sixteenth Amendment, the warm defenses of the principle of ability to pay, and the frequent attacks upon the principle through such widely discussed proposals as that for a 25 per cent limit on rates have made the federal tax law a major symbol of justice. While the fervent rhetoric from both sides turns upon the symbol of a progressive tax and bolsters the assumption that the system is highly progressive, the bite of the law into people's resources depends upon quite other provisions and activities that are little publicized and that often seriously qualify its progressive character. Special tax treatments arise from such devices as family partnerships, gifts inter vivos, income-splitting, multiple trusts, percentage depletion, and deferred compensation.

Tax evasion alone goes far toward making the symbol of "ability to pay" hollow semantically though potent symbolically. While 95 per cent of income from wages and salaries is taxed as provided by law, taxes are actually collected on only 67 per cent of taxable income from interest, dividends, and fiduciary investments and on only about 36 per cent of taxable farm income.[13] By and large, the recipients of larger incomes can most easily benefit from exemptions, avoidance, and evasions. This may or may not be desirable public policy, but it certainly marks a disparity between symbol and effect upon resources. . . .

Two broad patterns of group interest activity vis-à-vis public regulatory policy are evidently identifiable on the basis of these various modes of observing the social scene. The two patterns may be summarized in the following shorthand fashion:

(1) Pattern A: a relatively high degree of organization—rational, cognitive procedures—precise information—an effective interest in specifically identified, tangible resources—a favorably perceived strategic position with respect to reference groups—relatively small numbers.

(2) Pattern B: shared interest in improvement of status through protest activity—an unfavorably perceived strategic position with respect to reference groups—distorted, stereotyped, inexact information and perception—response to symbols connoting suppression of threats—relative ineffectiveness in securing tangible resources through political activity—little organization for purposeful action—quiescence—relatively large numbers.

It is very likely misleading to assume that some of these observations can be regarded as causes or consequences of others. That they often occur together is both a more accurate observation and more significant. It is also evident that each of the patterns is realized in different degrees at different times.

While political scientists and students of organizational theory have gone far toward a sophisticated description and analysis of Pattern A, there is far less agreement and precision in describing and analyzing Pattern B and in explaining how it intermeshes with Pattern A.

The most common explanation of the relative inability of large numbers of people to realize their economic aspirations in public policy is in terms of invisibility. The explanation is usually implicit rather than explicit, but it evidently assumes that public regulatory policy facilitating the exploitation of resources by knowledgeable organized groups (usually the "regulated") at the expense of taxpayers, consumers, or other unorganized groups is possible only because the latter do not know it is happening. What is invisible to them does not arouse interest or political sanctions.

On a superficial level of explanation this assumption is no doubt valid. But it is an example of the danger to the social scientist of failure to inquire transactionally: of assuming, in this instance, (1) that an answer to a questioner, or a questionnaire, about what an individual "knows" of a regulatory policy at any point in time is in any sense equivalent to specification of a group political interest; and (2) that the sum of many individual knowings (or not knowings) as reported to a questioner is a *cause* of effective (or ineffective) organization, rather than a consequence of it, or simply a concomitant phase of the same environment. If one is interested in policy formation, what count are the assumptions of legislators and administrators about the determinants of future political disaffection and political sanctions. Observable political behavior, as well as psychological findings, reveal something of these assumptions.

There is, in fact, persuasive evidence of the reality of a political interest in continuing assurances of protection against economic forces understood as powerful and threatening. The most relevant evidence lies in the continuing utility of old political issues in campaigns. Monopoly and economic concentration, antitrust policy, public utility regulation, banking controls, and curbs on management and labor are themes that party professionals regard as good for votes in one campaign after another, and doubtless with good reason. They know that these are areas in which concern is easily stirred. In evaluating allegations that the public has lost "interest" in these policies the politician has only to ask himself how much apathy would remain if an effort were made formally to repeal the antitrust, public utility, banking, or labor laws. The answers and the point become clear at once.

The laws may be repealed in effect by administrative policy, budgetary starvation, or other little publicized means; but the laws as symbols must stand because they satisfy interests that are very strong indeed: interests that politicians fear will be expressed actively if a large number of voters are led to believe that their shield against a threat has been removed.

More than that, it is largely as symbols of this sort that these statutes have utility to most of the voters. If they function as reassurances that threats in the economic environment are under control, their indirect effect is to permit greater claims upon tangible resources by the organized groups concerned than would be possible if the legal symbols were absent.

To say this is not to assume that everyone objectively affected by a policy is simply quiescent rather than apathetic or even completely unaware of the issue. It is to say that those who are potentially able and willing to apply political sanctions constitute the politically significant group. It is to suggest as well that incumbent or aspiring congressmen are less concerned with individual constituents' familiarity or unfamiliarity with an issue as of any given moment than with the possibility that the interest of a substantial number of them *could* be aroused and organized if he should cast a potentially unpopular vote on a bill or if a change in their economic situation should occur. The shrewder and more effective politicians probably appreciate intuitively the validity of the psychological finding noted earlier: that where public understanding is vague and information rare, interests in reassurance will be all the more potent and all the more susceptible to manipulation by political symbols.

We have already noted that it is one of the demonstrable functions of symbolization that it induces a feeling of well-being: the resolution of tension. Not only is this a major function of widely publicized regulatory statutes, but it is also a major function of their administration. Some of the most widely publicized administrative activities can most confidently be expected to convey a sense of well-being to the onlooker because they suggest vigorous activity while in fact signifying inactivity or protection of the "regulated."

One form this phenomenon takes is noisy attacks on trivia. The Federal Trade Commission, for example, has long been noted for its hit-and-miss attacks on many relatively small firms involved in deceptive advertising or unfair trade practices while it continues to overlook much of the really significant activity it is ostensibly established to regulate: monopoly, interlocking directorates, and so on.[14]

Another form it takes is prolonged, repeated, well-publicized attention to a significant problem which is never solved. A notable example is the approach of the Federal Communications Commission to surveillance of program content in general and to discussions of public issues on the air in particular. In the postwar period we have had the Blue Book, the Mayflower Policy, the abolition of the Mayflower Policy, and the announcement of a substitute policy; but the radio or television licensee is in practice perfectly free, as he has been all along, to editorialize, with or without opportunity for opposing views to be heard, or to avoid serious discussion of public affairs entirely.

The most obvious kinds of dissemination of symbolic satisfactions are to be found in administrative dicta accompanying decisions and orders, in press releases, and in annual reports. It is not uncommon to give the rhetoric to one side and the decision to the other. Nowhere does the FCC wax so emphatic in emphasizing public service responsibility, for example, as in decisions permitting greater concentration of control in an area, condoning license transfers at inflated prices, refusing to impose sanctions for flagrantly sacrificing program quality to profits, and so on.[15]

The integral connection is apparent between symbolic satisfaction of the disorganized, on the one hand, and the success of the organized, on the other, in using governmental instrumentalities as aids in securing the tangible resources they claim.

Public policy may usefully be understood as the resultant of the interplay among groups.[16] But the political and socio-psychological processes discussed here mean that groups which present claims upon resources may be rendered quiescent by their success in securing nontangible values. Far from representing an obstacle to organized producers and sellers, they become defenders of the very system of law which permits the organized to pursue their interests effectively.

Thurman Arnold has pointed out how the antitrust laws perform precisely this function:

> The actual result of the antitrust laws was to promote the growth of great industrial organizations by deflecting the attack on them into purely moral and ceremonial channels . . . every scheme for direct control broke to pieces on the great protective rock of the antitrust laws. . . .
>
> The antitrust laws remained as a most important symbol. Whenever anyone demanded practical regulation, they formed an effective moral obstacle, since all the

liberals would answer with a demand that the antitrust laws be enforced. Men like Senator Borah founded political careers on the continuance of such crusades, which were entirely futile but enormously picturesque, and which paid big dividends in terms of personal prestige.[17]

Arnold's subsequent career as chief of the antitrust division of the Department of Justice did as much to prove his point as his writings. For a five-year period he instilled unprecedented vigor into the division, and his efforts were widely publicized. He thereby unquestionably made the laws a more important symbol of the protection of the public; but despite his impressive intentions and talents, monopoly, concentration of capital, and restraint of trade were not seriously threatened or affected.

This is not to suggest that signs or symbols in themselves have any magical force as narcotics. They are, rather, the only means by which groups not in a position to analyze a complex situation rationally may adjust themselves to it, through stereotypization, oversimplification, and reassurance.

There have, of course, been many instances of effective administration and enforcement of regulatory statutes. In each such instance it will be found that organized groups have had an informed interest in effective administration. Sometimes the existence of these groups is explicable as a holdover from the campaign for legislative enactment of the basic statute; and often the initial administrative appointees are informed, dedicated adherents of these interests. They are thus in a position to secure pertinent data and to act strategically, helping furnish "organization" to the groups they represent. Sometimes the resources involved are such that there is organization on both sides; or the more effective organization may be on the "reform" side. The securities exchange legislation is an illuminating example, for after Richard Whitney's conviction for embezzlement, key officials of the New York Stock Exchange recognized their own interest in supporting controls over less scrupulous elements. This interest configuration doubtless explains the relative popularity of the SEC in the thirties both with regulated groups and with organized liberal groups.

NOTES

1. E. Pendleton Herring, *Public Administration and the Public Interest* (New York, 1936), p. 213.

2. Avery Leiserson, *Administrative Regulation: A Study in Representation of Interests* (Chicago, 1912), p. 14.

3. David Truman, *The Governmental Process* (New York, 1951), Chap. 5.

4. Marver Bernstein, *Regulating Business by Independent Commissions* (New York, 1955), Chap. 3.

5. Emmette S. Redford, *Administration of National Economic Control* (New York, 1952), pp. 385–386.

6. Bernstein, *op. cit.*

7. In addition to the statements in these analytical treatments of the administrative process, evidence for the proposition that regulatory statutes often fail to have their promised consequences in

terms of resource allocation are found in general studies of government regulation of business and in empirical research on particular statutes. As an example of the former see Clair Wilcox, *Public Policies Toward Business* (Chicago, 1955). As examples of the latter see Frederic Meyers, *"Right to Work" in Practice* (New York, 1959); Walton Hamilton and Irene Till, *Antitrust in Action*, TNEC Monograph 16 (Washington, D.C., GPO, 1940).

8. Redford, *op. cit.*, p. 383. Similar explanations appear in Herring, *op. cit.*, p. 227, and Bernstein, *op. cit.*, pp. 82–83. Some writers have briefly suggested more rigorous explanations, consistent with the hypotheses discussed in this paper, though they do not consider the possible role of interests in symbolic reassurance. Thus Truman calls attention to organizational factors, emphasizing the ineffectiveness of interest groups "whose interactions on the basis of the interest are not sufficiently frequent or stabilized to produce an intervening organization and whose multiple memberships, on the same account, are a constant threat to the strength of the claim." Truman, *op. cit.*, p. 441. Multiple group memberships are, of course, characteristic of individuals in all organizations, stable and unstable; and "infrequent interactions" is a phenomenon that itself calls for explanation if a common interest is recognized. Bernstein, *loc. cit.*, refers to the "undramatic nature" of administration and to the assumption that the administrative agency will protect the public.

9. Compare the discussion of meaning in George Herbert Mead, *Mind, Self and Society* (Chicago, 1934), pp. 78–79.

10. Truman, *op. cit.*, pp. 439–446; Earl Latham, *The Group Basis of Politics* (Ithaca, N.Y., 1952), Chap. 1.

11. I have explored this effect in labor legislation in "Interest Representation and Labor Law Administration," *Labor Law Journal*, Vol. 9 (1958), pp. 218–226.

12. See Lewis A. Dexter, "Candidates Must Make the Issues and Give Them Meaning," *Public Opinion Quarterly*, Vol. 10 (1955–56), pp. 408–414.

13. Randolph E. Paul, "Erosion of the Tax Base and Rate Structure," in Joint Committee on the Economic Report, *Federal Tax Policy for Economic Growth and Stability*, 84th Congress, 1st Session, 1955, pp. 123–138.

14. Cf. Wilcox, *op. cit.*, pp. 281, 252–255.

15. Many examples may be found in the writer's study entitled *The Licensing of Radio Services in the United States, 1927 to 1947* (Urbana, Ill., 1950).

16. For discussions of the utility of this view to social scientists, see Arthur F. Bentley, *The Process of Government* (1908; New York, reprint 1949); Truman, *op. cit.*

17. *The Folklore of Capitalism* (New Haven, Conn., 1937), pp. 212, 215, 216.

The Analysis of Public Policy: A Search for Theories and Roles

Robert H. Salisbury

I. WHAT WE MEAN BY POLICY

It is commonplace to lament the absence of clear understanding concerning the basic terms of political analysis, but it appears that the range of disagreement concerning the notion of "policy" is not so very great. One may distinguish three major positions on the question, sometimes taken separately and sometimes in combination. The most common usage of the term "policy," surely, is derived from some version of David Easton's definition of the proper object of political analysis: "the authoritative allocation of values for the whole society."[1] Public policy consists in authoritative or sanctioned decisions by governmental actors. It refers to the "substance" of what government does and is to be distinguished from the processes by which decisions are made. Policy here means the outcomes or outputs of governmental processes.[2]

A second view of policy would confine the usage to "broad" or general questions, and use another term for detailed choices made within the framework of "policy." Thus policy consists of a general frame of authoritative rules, and, while the precise boundary between policy and nonpolicy is nearly always debatable in the particular situation, the distinction crops up over and over. Dichotomies like "discretionary versus ministerial acts," "political versus nonpolitical," "controversial versus routine," and, of course, "policy versus administration" suggest the manifold permutations on the theme and remind us of the wide currency of the usage.[3]

A third way of talking about policy is rooted in the assumption that political behavior is goal-oriented or purposive. Policy here means those actions calculated to achieve the goal or purpose. Thus one may speak of "policy orientations," or "the policy of the AFL-CIO." Lasswell and Kaplan define policy as "a projected program of goal values and practices."[4] Closely related would be the Bentleyan conception that political behavior is always to be understood in terms of its interest or purposive orientation. According to this view, all political activity should be viewed as policy-oriented, and one must logically encompass the policy substance if one is to comprehend the behavior directed toward that set of goals.

From Robert H. Salisbury, "The Analysis of Public Policy: A Search for Theories and Roles." In Austin Ranney (ed.), *Political Science and Public Policy* (Chicago: Markham, 1968), pp. 151–178. Reprinted by permission.

These conceptions of policy are combined in Friedrich's definition:

> a proposed course of action of a person, group or government within a given environment providing obstacles and opportunities which the policy was proposed to utilize and overcome in an effort to reach a goal or realize an objective or a purpose. . . . It is essential for the policy concept that there be a goal, objective or purpose.[5]

Friedrich and most other writers agree that there is a difference between specific decisions or actions and a program or course of action, and that it is the latter to which the term "policy" refers.[6] Policy is necessarily an abstraction, therefore, to be approached through aggregative or summarizing analytic procedures. It is *patterns* of behavior rather than separate, discrete acts which constitute policy. The concept of policy is thus anti–case study in its implications for research strategy and encourages controlling for idiosyncratic variables.

Unless one wishes to contend that policy refers only to broad decisional rules and that implementation or other subsequent behavior is to be examined in terms of some other focus, it follows from these conceptions that political science can hardly avoid being policy-centered. That is, if authoritative outputs of the political system, actions aimed at affecting those outputs, and the goals or purposes or interests at stake in authoritative decisions are what we mean by policy, we cannot logically escape dealing with it.

The apparent paradox is, of course, that so much political science inquiry has escaped this logical necessity, or at least seemed to do so. I believe the answer lies in two directions at once. One is revealed in the recent literature suggesting that variations in political processes, with which political scientists have undoubtedly been concerned, may have relatively little explanatory value in accounting for variations in policy outputs. We shall examine these findings later, but, insofar as they are valid, it follows that we may have spent so much time investigating process factors of relatively minor importance that it has been easy to ignore the substance of public policy, for which our research has little relevance.

A second part of the explanation, however, is that in fact political scientists have long been concerned, and vitally so, with policy analysis, but only of a particular kind of policy, namely, *constitutional policy.* That is, we have spent much labor analyzing authoritative decisions that prescribe the rules and specify the structural characteristics of the authoritative decisional system, i.e., government. That these questions are policy issues is obvious, and that political scientists have invested heavily in their analysis is even more so. Whether the investment has turned an explanatory profit may be debated, but in consequence of this work I think we are richer in what Froman calls "policy theory"[7] than we may realize. . . .

Policy typologies may be based on data that are composed of perceptions of the actors. Thus whether a particular policy is classified as zero sum or non-zero sum may depend on how the relevant actors perceive it, and similarly with the distinction between symbolic and material policies. Lowi, in a different approach, attempts to classify policies as distributive, redistributive, or regulatory in part according to their "impact on the society." Or one might classify according to the internal structure of the decisions, using such criteria as amount, complexity, or self-execution. Froman's areal-versus-segmental distinction appears to involve some combination of internal characteristics of the policies with their impact on the system. In evaluating the utility of the alternatives we must go immediately to the operational problem, and this appreciably narrows the real research alternatives. "Impact on the society" appears to me beyond our present capacity to measure in any way that goes beyond the plausible hunch. If this is so, then the criterion itself is really a special case of the criterion of actor's perceptions, with observers replacing decision-makers as the active parties. We know, at least in principle, how to approach the data of perception, and if we recognize the accessible data as largely of this kind, we may enhance our abilities even more. From this point of view, whether a policy is classified as distributive or redistributive depends on how it is seen by the actors, and I suggest that any hypotheses we might advance relating process variables to policy types would, in fact, assume that policy types were so derived. It would be odd, I think, if actors very often behaved in systematically variable ways without perceiving some parallel variations in the substance of their actions.

This still leaves an option in the form of internal decision structures as the classification criterion. Where observers can agree on variations in decision form—as they obviously can when using nominal categories, and also probably by using distinctions in amount or complexity of policy—this criterion is especially valuable because it shortcuts the necessity of interviewing the actors.[8] But there are many potentially interesting questions that are not yet amenable to such shortcuts and which do take advantage of unambiguous features of the public record. Moreover, as Froman's effort has illustrated, categories invented by the observer may create as many problems as they solve.

From the array of extant possibilities, I propose to employ a typology that is adapted from Lowi's formulation and uses data derived from actor perceptions.[9] The typology differentiates four possible main types: distributive, redistributive, regulatory, and self-regulatory. Distributive policies are those perceived to confer direct benefits upon one or more groups. Typically such policies are determined with little or no conflict over the passage of the legislation, but only over the size and specific distribution of the shares. Redistributive policies likewise confer benefits, but also are perceived to take benefits away from other groups. They therefore involve more intense conflict over passage itself, over the legitimacy of the action as well as the specific content. Regulatory policies impose constraints on subsequent behavior of particular groups and thus indirectly deny or confirm potentially beneficial options in the future. Conflict over regulatory policy is likely to be ambiguous and shifting, since the specific content and direction of benefits and costs is not known; only, so to speak, the "guidelines."[10]

Self-regulatory policies also impose constraints upon a group, but are perceived only to increase, not decrease, the beneficial options to the group. The relevant perceptions in each case are those of the active participants in the policy-making process. This would include all those making explicit demands on the decisional system, as well as those taking an active part in it. In the self-regulatory policy situation, only a small group, such as lawyers or oil companies, makes demands, and typically there is little or no opposition.[11]

A question that immediately arises is how this formulation fits the distinction between zero-sum and non-zero-sum policies. The argument may be advanced that none of the four types necessarily implies zero-sum conditions. Distributive and self-regulatory policies are, one would suppose, invariably non-zero sum, since there is comparatively little implication of conflict or even of overt self-perceived losers in such situations. Redistributive and regulatory policies, on the other hand, may approach zero-sum conditions. But if side payments are permitted, these conditions are mitigated, and I shall argue that in American politics even redistributive policies are generally decided in distinctly positive-sum games. . . .

NOTES

1. David Easton, *The Political System* (New York: Alfred A. Knopf, Inc., 1953), pp. 129ff.

2. In a more recent statement Easton defines policy as "decision rules adopted by authorities as a guide to behavior. . . . In this sense, policies would be just a term for a kind of authoritative verbal output" (*A Systems Analysis of Political Life* [New York: John Wiley & Sons, 1965], p. 358). See also pp. 6–9 and 27–29, above.

3. Thus Easton: "But the term [policy] is used in a second and broader sense to describe the more general intentions of the authorities of which any specific binding output might be a partial expression" (*ibid.*). From the days of Frank Goodnow on the distinction is a familiar one.

4. Harold D. Lasswell and Abraham Kaplan, *Power and Society* (New Haven: Yale University Press, 1950), p. 71.

5. Carl J. Friedrich, *Man and His Government* (New York: McGraw-Hill Book Co., 1963), p. 79.

6. Reitzel, Kaplan, and Coblentz suggest rather the reverse, however: that policy refers to specific actions designed to achieve objectives or realize interests (*United States Foreign Policy, 1945–1955* [Washington: Brookings Institution, 1956], p. 473).

7. Theodore J. Lowi, "American Business, Public Policy, Case-Studies, and Political Theory," *World Politics*, 16 (July 1964): 677–715. Lowi actually seems to go both ways; he conceptualizes policies in "terms of their impact or expected impact on the society" (p. 689), but in discussing redistributive policy he says, "Expectations about what it *can* be . . . are determinative" (p. 691).

8. It would seem to me appropriate to subject, for example, agricultural policy decisions and bills of the past thirty years to content analysis. My hypothesis would be that over time the structure of policy has grown increasingly complex, especially in its treatment of commodities. This change would, I think, be more or less systematically related to the "commodityization" of agricultural production. See John P. Heinz, "The Political Impasse in Farm Support Legislation," *Yale Law Journal*, 71 (April 1962): 952–78.

9. I propose to beg the question, important though it be, of how to get at the appropriate perceptual data. I suspect much of it can be taken and ordered from the public record, but much would depend too on sophisticated interviewing instruments whose shape is beyond the scope of this paper.

10. This is why the conversion of a dispute over substance to one over procedure may be expected to reduce the intensity of the conflict. I should also note that what Lowi means by regulation may be somewhat different. He stresses the "sector" level at which regulatory policy operates, an indicator that would be compatible with my argument. Beyond that, however, either he or I remain unclear as to the precise meaning of his usage.

11. Good examples of self-regulation policy include not only professional licensing (see V. O. Key, *Politics, Parties and Pressure Groups*, 5th ed. [New York: Thomas Y. Crowell Co., 1964], pp. 122–23), but the successful quest of the National Association of Retail Druggists for fair-trade legislation (see Joseph Palamountain, *The Politics of Distribution* [Cambridge: Harvard University Press, 1955], chap. 8).

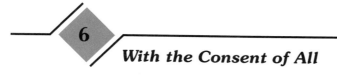

6

With the Consent of All

Robert A. Dahl

There are at least four reasons for insisting that governments ought, ideally, to derive their just powers from the consent of the governed. First, government without consent is inconsistent with personal freedom. To the extent that I am compelled to obey man-made rules that do not have my moral approval, I am not a free man. To be sure, personal freedom is an exacting demand; complete personal freedom is probably impossible to achieve. Nonetheless, one who believes in the value of individual freedom may reasonably hold that so far as possible no adult human being should ever be governed without his consent.

Second, government without one's consent can be an affront to human dignity and respect. We see this most vividly in extreme cases—the hapless victim in a concentration camp, who is subjected to the utmost humiliation, degradation, deprivation, and torture, loses thereby a part of his humanity.

Third, one may demand solely out of self-interest that a government rest on consent. For one might reason as follows: Certainly I do not want the government to act without my approval. But since I am not nor am I likely to be a dictator or even a member of a ruling oligarchy, perhaps the safest way to insure that the government will have my approval is to insist that it must have the approval of everyone. Reasoning from self-interest is not generally thought to be quite as noble as reasoning from general principles of freedom and dignity. Nonetheless we should rejoice, I believe, whenever freedom and dignity are supported by wide-spread self-interest; for nothing is quite so strong a buttress to social institutions as a firm foundation in self-interest.

Finally, one may insist on consent because one thinks that governments "deriving their just powers from the consent of the governed" are more likely to be stable and durable. There are innumerable reasons why one may want stable government, including the fact that revolutions are very uncertain affairs; with a few exceptions, among which, happily, the American Revolution may be counted, those who start the first fires of a revolution are consumed in the holocaust. To control the course of a revolution is almost as difficult as to direct the path of a tornado. Whatever the reasons why one may want stability in government, it is reasonable to suppose that a government is less likely to create hostility, frustration, and resentment—sentiments that breed revolution—if it acts with the approval of its citizens than if it does not. Common sense and modern history both lend substance to this judgment; in the past century the most durable governments in the

From Robert A. Dahl, *Pluralist Democracy in the United States* (Chicago: Rand McNally, 1967), pp. 14–24. Reprinted by permission.

world have rested on widespread suffrage and other institutions for popular control.

But if it is relatively easy to say *why* governments should derive their just powers from the consent of the governed, it is very much more difficult to say *how* they can do so. The difficulty stems from that inescapable element of conflict in the human condition: People living together simply will not always agree. When people disagree, how can a decision be based on the consent of all? Since political philosophers, like architects, sometimes conceal their failures behind a handsome façade, the unwary student may conclude that the solution would be clear if he only understood the philosophers better. In this case, however, modesty may be misplaced; although political philosophers have long wrestled with the problem, the disagreeable fact remains that they have not been able to prescribe a perfect solution except under certain highly improbable circumstances.

The obvious way out, of course, is to eliminate conflict. This happy solution is characteristic of many literary Utopias, where social life is downright inhuman in its lack of conflict. Utopianism of this genre appears in unsuspected places: Karl Marx was a militant critic of the Utopian socialists of an earlier generation, yet he evidently thought that his famous dialectic—"All history is the history of class conflict"—would for all practical purposes come to an end in a communist society: there would be no need for a state because there would be no significant conflicts.

If one concludes that complete agreement is a hopeless objective and not necessarily a very desirable one, then one must search elsewhere for a solution to the problem of consent. A second way out is to search for specific policies that every citizen approves of, even though he may have disagreed, initially, with his fellow citizens. It is not absurd, surely, to suppose that conflict can sometimes be transmuted into decisions that have the approval of everyone. Perhaps all of us have had experiences of this kind, particularly when we try to arrive at decisions within some group where everyone else shares our fundamental values, even though we may differ on specific questions. There is something of this idea behind Rousseau's much disputed notion of a General Will that bespeaks more truly what we believe than we always do ourselves. Yet the difficulty with all solutions along these lines is that decisions rarely do receive unanimous approval. Do I consent to decisions with which I disagree? Who is a better judge than I of what my 'will', my policy, really is? Should anyone else have the authority to proclaim that a policy really has my consent? Although a distinction can be made between what I really believe is best and what I momentarily think or say is best, a good deal of experience suggests that to allow someone else to make this distinction for me is very dangerous. A tyrant might insist that he has my consent for all he does, though I deny it, because he knows better than I what I really want. When an individual says he disapproves of the policies of the government, even when they have the blessings of an enlightened dictator or an enlightened majority, the safest course in practise, I believe, is to postulate that he knows his own mind. Otherwise, government by consent is likely to degenerate into a mere ritualistic formula.

Even if people cannot always agree on specific policies, however, a third solution is to gain their consent for a *process*. It is perfectly reasonable of me to say that I approve of the process by which certain kinds of decisions are made, even if I do not always like the specific results. Thus the consent of the governed may be interpreted to mean their approval of the processes by which decisions are arrived at and their willingness to abide by these decisions even when these seem wrong.

But what kind of a process shall I require? If I hold that no one can, as a general matter, know my goals and values better than I myself, then no doubt I will insist that the process of making decisions must provide me with a full opportunity to make my views known; and even if I am willing to leave details to experts, I do not want anyone else to have more power over the decision, in the last say, than I do. A solution along these lines might well appeal to me as the best attainable, given the inescapable conditions mentioned earlier: that my need for human fellowship impels me to live in a society, that I cannot live with others without sometimes disagreeing with them, and that I must therefore find some way to adjust our conflicts that will appeal to all of us as fair.

This solution is, in fact, what links consent with democracy. In the real world, of course, democracies never quite satisfy all the conditions implied by this solution; but it serves as one standard against which to measure their success and failure.

THE SOVEREIGN MAJORITY

But how is this solution to be applied? What kind of process will insure that I shall have a full opportunity to make my views known, and that no one else will have more power over decisions, in the last say, than I do?

There are a number of different answers to these questions, and it is with two of these that we are concerned. Purely as a matter of abstract theory, the one is admirably clear and explicit; this is decision-making by the sovereign majority. Yet no country seems to have adopted this method in entirety. The other is in greater or lesser degree the pattern that seems to have evolved in the countries we usually call 'democratic.' Yet the pattern is so blurred and chaotic—and there are so many variations from country to country—that it is difficult to describe.

Does the difference between these two kinds of answers reflect a conflict of ideals or only the familiar conflict between ideals and reality? Perhaps a bit of both. What an 'ideal democracy' would be is a subject of interminable dispute. One is tempted to say that there are as many different visions of what democracy ought to be as there are individuals who think about the matter. Because the advocates of each vision shape their definitions to fit their ideals, the world of political thought and political rhetoric is over-populated with definitions of the term 'democracy.'

I want to refrain here from adding to this definitional explosion. I shall speak of the American political system with terms that Americans themselves have used for generations—a democracy, a republic, or a democratic republic. One may if he chooses quarrel with my use of these terms, but he will find me an unwilling contestant, for I do not wish to argue overmuch about terms in this book. Without trying to decide, then, which of the different visions of democracy is more truly democratic, let me nonetheless describe two of these: decision-making by the sovereign majority, and pluralistic democracy.

In the vision of democracy as decision-making by the sovereign majority, the citizens of a given country all approve of the principle of majority rule, according to which all conflicts over the policies of government are settled, sooner or later, by a majority of citizens or voters—either directly in a public assembly or in a referendum, or indirectly through elected representatives. A person who approves of the principle of majority rule need not go so far as to assume, as Rousseau is often interpreted as saying, that a majority mysteriously reveals the 'real' will even of the minority who would prefer a different policy. Nor does one need to assume that every policy preferred by a majority is bound to be morally right. One need not even believe that the principle of majority rule is the best principle for every political system. Although people sometimes lay down these exaggerated requirements, none of them seems to be demanded either by strict logic or by inference from actual experience. To approve of a system that applies the principle of majority rule, evidently one needs only to believe that during this historical period and in this particular society the principle represents the fullest attainable achievement of one's values. An American is not logically inconsistent if he holds that majority rule is not the best principle to apply in the Congo. For it would be entirely consistent to argue that the workability and acceptability of majority rule depends upon the existence of conditions that may or may not be present in a specific society.

In fact, the straightforward application of the principle of the sovereign majority to all questions of public significance is, as a practical matter, not likely to receive everyone's continuing approval—except under unusual circumstances. While a citizen may make certain allowances for majority decisions that displease him, the more frequently he expects to be in a minority, the less likely he is to accept the principle of majority rule. One can, perhaps, accept calmly the prospect of being in a minority so long as the issues are trivial. But the more important the issues, the more difficult it is to accept defeat by a hostile majority. The more I expect that majorities are going to insist on policies that conflict with my most cherished values, the more likely I am to oppose the principle of majority rule. Surely few people would be so loyal to the abstract principle as to approve of it even if they expected it to lead regularly to repugnant policies. At some point even the most convinced adherent of majority rule will give up in despair. In a nation of convinced anti-Semites and religious bigots, a modern Jefferson might be compelled to oppose the principle of the sovereign majority. In short, continuing and universal approval of the principle of majority rule requires a high degree of consensus among all the citizens as to what the policies of government should be.

It seems reasonable to conjecture that the more diverse the beliefs held among a body of people, the less likely it is that they will approve of the idea of making decisions by majority rule. To the extent that this conjecture is valid, it is a severe restriction on the principle of rule by a sovereign majority, particularly in modern heterogeneous societies. For it seems entirely reasonable to hold that diversity of beliefs is likely to be greater the larger the number of citizens, the bigger the territory over which they are spread, and the greater the distinctions of race, ethnic group, regional culture, occupation, social class, income, property, and so on. Some advocates of rule by the sovereign majority have therefore argued, as Rousseau did, that majority decisions would be acceptable only among very small and highly homogeneous bodies of people, groups no larger perhaps than a town or a very small city. According to this view, nations even as small as Norway, and certainly as large as the United States, are unsuitable for democracy.

One possible way to maintain homogeneity would be to eliminate all dissenting minorities who would object to the decisions of a majority. In Athens the Ecclesia—the sovereign town meeting composed theoretically of all adult citizens—had the power of *ostracism,* by which it could banish an unpopular citizen from Athens for ten years. Rousseau evidently believed that homogeneity would be maintained if dissident citizens had the right to emigrate—presumably to a more sympathetic community. Another possibility, a painful one to Americans, is secession. Yet all of these solutions entail serious practical and moral difficulties, particularly in the modern world. Emigration, for example, can be a staggering price to pay simply for being in a minority; must the price of one's beliefs depend solely on the numbers who happen to share them? Yet if emigration is purely optional, who would emigrate? Many dissenters would remain to deny the legitimacy of majority rule as it applies to them. Shall we then expel these dissenters in order to maintain consensus? To expel an individual from a community is not difficult; American communities have often done so, sometimes with the aid of tar and feathers. But to expel a significant minority that does not choose to depart in peace can mean civil war. It might be said that a discontented minority can be permitted to separate amicably by the simple expedient of redrawing the boundary lines and thus creating a new and independent state. But should every minority that wishes to do so be allowed to secede in full possession of the territory in which they happen to reside, even if this has been so integrated into the economy, transportation system, defenses, and sense of nationhood of the larger country that its loss would be a serious blow? Such forbearance and generosity are unlikely. In any case, what is to be the fate of a minority within a minority, as in the case of Negroes in the South? And of minorities that are not geographically separated but intermixed, like Jehovah's Witnesses?

For Americans these questions are more than rhetorical; here, secession was proposed and rejected as a practical solution by a civil war. Lincoln's first inaugural address pierced the logic of secession:

> Plainly, the central idea of secession is the essence of anarchy. A majority held in restraint by constitutional checks and limitations, and always changing easily with deliberate changes of popular opinions and sentiments, is the only true sovereign of a

free people. Whoever rejects it does, of necessity, fly to anarchy or to despotism. Unanimity is impossible; the rule of a minority, as a permanent arrangement, is wholly inadmissible; so that, rejecting the majority principle, anarchy or despotism in some form is all that is left.[1]

But even civil war did not finally settle the debate about the proper scope and limits of rule by majorities in the United States.

There is one further difficulty in the application of majority rule that is of special significance to Americans. That some people may have voted in the distant past to accept the Constitution of the United States—as a rather small proportion of the population did in 1787–8, and as the people or their representatives did in the territories prior to entering the Union—is surely no reason why we, today, should feel bound to accept their verdict: not, at any rate, if we demand continuing 'consent' to the processes of government. Ideally, then, every new generation must be free to refuse its consent to the old rules and to make new ones. The Declaration of Independence contains these ringing phrases:

> That whenever any Form of Government becomes destructive of these ends, (Life, Liberty, and the pursuit of Happiness) it is the Right of the People to alter or to abolish it, and to institute a new Government, laying its foundation on such principles and organizing its powers in such form, as to them shall seem most likely to effect their Safety and Happiness.

Seventy years later, confronted by secession, and on the eve of war, in the inauguration speech from which I quoted a moment ago, Lincoln reaffirmed this principle:

> This country, with its institutions, belongs to the people who inhabit it. Whenever they shall grow weary of the existing government, they can exercise their constitutional right of amending it, or their revolutionary right to dismember or overthrow it.[2]

But "the People" is an ambiguous phrase. Do these famous words mean that whenever a majority is discontented with the government it should be free to change it? If they are not permitted to do so, then can we say that they have given their approval, in any realistic sense, to the processes of government? Yet if every majority must be free to alter the rules of government, what is the significance of a "Constitution"? How can a constitution be more binding than ordinary law? Is there no legitimate way by which groups smaller than a majority can receive guarantees that the rules they agree to abide by will be more or less permanent and will not change at the whim of the next legislature?

These are difficult questions to answer, and no answers seem to command universal agreement.[3] To gain "the consent of all" consistently applying the principle that the majority should be sovereign gives rise to serious problems, both logical and practical. Perhaps under certain unusual conditions, such as a very high degree of homogeneity, among a very small body of citizens, these problems could be solved.

In practise, however, popular governments have moved toward a rather different solution.

A PLURALISTIC SOLUTION

The practical solutions that democratic countries have evolved are a good deal less clear than a straightforward application of the principle of majority rule. These solutions seem less 'logical,' less coherent, more untidy, and a good deal more attainable. Patterns of democratic government do not reflect a logically conceived philosophical plan so much as a series of responses to problems of diversity and conflict, by leaders who have sought to build and maintain a nation, to gain the loyalty and obedience of citizens, to win general and continuing approval of political institutions, and at the same time to conform to aspirations for democracy. However, some common elements can be discovered.

For one thing, in practise, countries with democratic regimes use force, just as other regimes do, to repel threats to the integrity of the national territory. Consequently secession is, as a practical matter, usually either impossible or extremely costly. (Colonies thought to lie outside the territory of the 'nation' may, of course, be granted independence.) To a considerable extent, then, large minorities are virtually 'compelled' to remain within the territorial limits of the nation. To make compulsory citizenship tolerable, great efforts are made to create and sustain a common sense of nationhood, so that minorities of all kinds will identify themselves with the nation. Hence secession or mass emigration are not usually thought of as practical alternatives.

Second, many matters of policy—religious beliefs and practises, for example—are effectively outside the legal authority of any government. Often they are placed beyond the legal authority of government through understandings and agreements widely shared and respected. In many cases these understandings and agreements are expressed in written constitutions that cannot be quickly or easily amended. Such a constitution is regarded as peculiarly binding; and ordinary laws that run counter to the constitution will be invalid, or, at the very least, subject to special scrutiny.

Third, a great many questions of policy are placed in the hands of private, semi-public, and local governmental organizations such as churches, families, business firms, trade unions, towns, cities, provinces, and the like. These questions of policy, like those left to individuals, are also effectively beyond the reach of national majorities, the national legislature, or indeed any national policymakers acting in their legal and official capacities. In fact, whenever uniform policies are likely to be costly, difficult, or troublesome, in pluralistic democracies the tendency is to find ways by which these policies can be made by smaller groups of like-minded people who enjoy a high degree of legal independence.

Fourth, whenever a group of people believe that they are adversely affected by national policies or are about to be, they generally have extensive opportunities for presenting their case and for negotiations that may produce a more acceptable alternative. In some cases, they may have enough power to delay, to obstruct, and even to veto the attempt to impose policies on them.

Now in addition to all these characteristics, the United States has limited the sovereignty of the majority in still other ways. In fact, the United States has gone so far in this direction that it is sometimes called a pluralistic system, a term I propose to use here.

The fundamental axiom in the theory and practise of American pluralism is, I believe, this: Instead of a single center of sovereign power there must be multiple centers of power, none of which is or can be wholly sovereign. Although the only legitimate sovereign is the people, in the perspective of American pluralism even the people ought never to be an absolute sovereign; consequently no part of the people, such as a majority, ought to be absolutely sovereign.

Why this axiom? The theory and practise of American pluralism tend to assume, as I see it, that the existence of multiple centers of power, none of which is wholly sovereign will help (may indeed be necessary) to tame power, to secure the consent of all, and to settle conflicts peacefully:

> Because one center of power is set against another, power itself will be tamed, civilized, controlled, and limited to decent human purposes, while coercion, the most evil form of power, will be reduced to a minimum.
>
> Because even minorities are provided with opportunities to veto solutions they strongly object to, the consent of all will be won in the long run.
>
> Because constant negotiations among different centers of power are necessary in order to make decisions, citizens and leaders will perfect the precious art of dealing peacefully with their conflicts, and not merely to the benefit of one partisan but to the mutual benefit of all the parties to a conflict.

These are, I think, the basic postulates and even the unconscious ways of thought that are central to the American attempt to cope with the inescapable problems of power, conflict, and consent.

NOTES

1. Carl Sandburg, *Abraham Lincoln, The War Years*, vol. I, New York, Harcourt Brace & Co., 1939, p. 132.

2. *Ibid.*, p. 133.

3. Cf. Hanna Pitkin, "Obligations and Consent," *American Political Science Review*, December, 1965, 990–1000; March, 1966, 39–52.

Issue Networks
and the Executive Establishment

Hugh Heclo

The connection between politics and administration arouses remarkably little interest in the United States. The presidency is considered more glamorous, Congress more intriguing, elections more exciting, and interest groups more troublesome. General levels of public interest can be gauged by the burst of indifference that usually greets the announcement of a new President's cabinet or rumors of a political appointee's resignation. Unless there is some White House "tie-in" or scandal (preferably both), news stories about presidential appointments are usually treated by the media as routine filler material.

This lack of interest in political administration is rarely found in other democratic countries, and it has not always prevailed in the United States. In most nations the ups and downs of political executives are taken as vital signs of the health of a government, indeed of its survival. In the United States, the nineteenth-century turmoil over one type of connection between politics and administration—party spoils—frequently overwhelmed any notion of presidential leadership. Anyone reading the history of those troubled decades is likely to be struck by the way in which political administration in Washington registered many of the deeper strains in American society at large. It is a curious switch that appointments to the bureaucracy should loom so large in the history of the nineteenth century, when the federal government did little, and be so completely discounted in the twentieth century, when government tries to do so much.

Political administration in Washington continues to register strains in American politics and society, although in ways more subtle than the nineteenth-century spoils scramble between Federalists and Democrats, Pro- and Anti-tariff forces, Nationalists and States-Righters, and so on. Unlike many other countries, the United States has never created a high level, government-wide civil service. Neither has it been favored with a political structure that automatically produces a stock of experienced political manpower for top executive positions in government. How then does political administration in Washington work? More to the point, how might the expanding role of government be changing the connection between administration and politics?

From Hugh Heclo, "Issue Networks and the Executive Establishment," in Anthony King (ed.) *The New American Political System* (Washington: American Enterprise Institute, 1978), pp. 87–124. Reprinted with the permission of The American Enterprise Institute for Public Policy Research, Washington, D.C.

Received opinion on this subject suggests that we already know the answers. Control is said to be vested in an informal but enduring series of "iron triangles" linking executive bureaus, congressional committees, and interest group clienteles with a stake in particular programs. A President or presidential appointee may occasionally try to muscle in, but few people doubt the capacity of these subgovernments to thwart outsiders in the long run.

Based largely on early studies of agricultural, water, and public works policies, the iron triangle concept is not so much wrong as it is disastrously incomplete. And the conventional view is especially inappropriate for understanding changes in politics and administration during recent years. Preoccupied with trying to find the few truly powerful actors, observers tend to overlook the power and influence that arise out of the configurations through which leading policy makers move and do business with each other. Looking for the closed triangles of control, we tend to miss the fairly open networks of people that increasingly impinge upon government. . . .

Obviously questions of power are still important. But for a host of policy initiatives undertaken in the last twenty years it is all but impossible to identify clearly who the dominant actors are. Who is controlling those actions that go to make up our national policy on abortions, or on income redistribution, or consumer protection, or energy? Looking for the few who are powerful, we tend to overlook the many whose webs of influence provoke and guide the exercise of power. These webs, or what I will call "issue networks," are particularly relevant to the highly intricate and confusing welfare policies that have been undertaken in recent years.

The notion of iron triangles and subgovernments presumes small circles of participants who have succeeded in becoming largely autonomous. Issue networks, on the other hand, comprise a large number of participants with quite variable degrees of mutual commitment or of dependence on others in their environment; in fact it is almost impossible to say where a network leaves off and its environment begins. Iron triangles and subgovernments suggest a stable set of participants coalesced to control fairly narrow public programs which are in the direct economic interest of each party to the alliance. Issue networks are almost the reverse image in each respect. Participants move in and out of the networks constantly. Rather than groups united in dominance over a program, no one, as far as one can tell, is in control of the policies and issues. Any direct material interest is often secondary to intellectual or emotional commitment. Network members reinforce each other's sense of issues as their interests, rather than (as standard political or economic models would have it) interests defining positions on issues.

Issue networks operate at many levels, from the vocal minority who turn up at local planning commission hearings to the renowned professor who is quietly telephoned by the White House to give a quick "reading" on some participant or policy. The price of buying into one or another issue network is watching, reading, talking about, and trying to act on particular policy problems. Powerful interest groups can be found represented in networks but so too can individuals in or out of government who have a reputation for being knowledgeable. Particular professions may be prominent, but the true experts in the networks are those who are issue-skilled (that is, well informed about the ins and outs of a particular policy debate) regardless of formal professional training. More than mere technical experts, network people are policy activists who know each other through the issues. Those who emerge to positions of wider leadership are policy politicians—experts in using experts, victuallers of knowledge in a world hungry for right decisions.

In the old days—when the primary problem of government was assumed to be doing what was right, rather than knowing what was right—policy knowledge could be contained in the slim adages of public administration. Public executives, it was thought, needed to know how to execute. They needed power commensurate with their responsibility. Nowadays, of course, political administrators do not execute but are involved in making highly important decisions on society's behalf, and they must mobilize policy intermediaries to deliver the goods. Knowing what is right becomes crucial, and since no one knows that for sure, going through the process of dealing with those who are judged knowledgeable (or at least continuously concerned) becomes even more crucial. Instead of power commensurate with responsibility, issue networks seek influence commensurate with their understanding of the various, complex social choices being made. Of course some participants would like nothing better than complete power over the issues in question. Others seem to want little more than the security that comes with being well informed. As the executive of one new group moving to Washington put it, "We didn't come here to change the world; we came to minimize our surprises."[1]

Whatever the participants' motivation, it is the issue network that ties together what would otherwise be the contradictory tendencies of, on the one hand, more widespread organizational participation in public policy and, on the other, more narrow technocratic specialization in complex modern policies. Such networks need to be distinguished from three other more familiar terms used in connection with political administration. An issue network is a shared-knowledge group having to do with some aspect (or, as defined by the network, some problem) of public policy. It is therefore more well-defined than, first, a shared-attention group or "public"; those in the networks are likely to have a common base of information and understanding of how one knows about policy and identifies its problems. But knowledge does not necessarily produce agreement. Issue networks may or may not, therefore, be mobilized into, second, a shared-action group (creating a coalition) or, third, a shared-belief group (becoming a conventional interest organization). Increasingly, it is through networks of people who regard each other as knowledgeable, or at least as needing to be answered, that public policy issues tend to be refined, evidence debated, and alternative options worked out—though rarely in any controlled, well-organized way.

What does an issue network look like? It is difficult to say precisely, for at any given time only one part of a network may be active and through time the various connections may intensify or fade among the policy intermediaries and the executive and congressional bureaucracies. For example, there is no single health policy network but various sets of people knowledgeable and concerned about cost-control mechanisms, insurance techniques, nutritional programs, prepaid plans, and so on. At one time, those expert in designing a nationwide insurance system may seem to be operating in relative isolation, until it becomes clear that previous efforts to control costs have already created precedents that have to be accommodated in any new system, or that the issue of federal funding for abortions has laid land mines in the path of any workable plan.

The debate on energy policy is rich in examples of the kaleidoscopic interaction of changing issue networks. The Carter administration's initial proposal was worked out among experts who were closely tied in to conservation-minded networks. Soon it became clear that those concerned with macroeconomic policies had been largely bypassed in the planning, and last-minute amendments were made in the proposal presented to Congress, a fact that was not lost on the networks of leading economists and economic correspondents. Once congressional consideration began, it quickly became evident that attempts to define the energy debate in terms of a classic confrontation between big oil companies and consumer interests were doomed. More and more policy watchers joined in the debate, bringing to it their own concerns and analyses: tax reformers, nuclear power specialists, civil rights groups interested in more jobs; the list soon grew beyond the wildest dreams of the original energy policy planners. The problem, it became clear, was that no one could quickly turn the many networks of knowledgeable people into a shared-action coalition, much less into a single, shared-attitude group believing it faced the moral equivalent of war. Or, if it was a war, it was a Vietnam-type quagmire.

It would be foolish to suggest that the clouds of issue networks that have accompanied expanding national policies are set to replace the more familiar politics of subgovernments in Washington. What they are doing is to overlay the once stable political reference points with new forces that complicate calculations, decrease predictability, and impose considerable strains on those charged with government leadership. The overlay of networks and issue politics not only confronts but also seeps down into the formerly well-established politics of particular policies and programs. Social security, which for a generation had been quietly managed by a small circle of insiders, becomes controversial and politicized. The Army Corps of Engineers, once the picturebook example of control by subgovernments, is dragged into the brawl on environmental politics. The once quiet "traffic safety establishment" finds its own safety permanently endangered by the consumer movement. Confrontation between networks and iron triangles in the Social and Rehabilitation Service, the disintegration of the mighty politics of the Public Health Service and its corps—the list could be extended into a chronicle of American national government during the last generation.[2] The point is that a somewhat new and difficult dynamic is being played out in the world of politics and administration. It is not what has been feared for so long: that technocrats and other people in white coats will expropriate the policy process. If there is to be any expropriation, it is likely to be by the policy activists, those who care deeply about a set of issues and are determined to shape the fabric of public policy accordingly.

THE TECHNOPOLS

The many new policy commitments of the last twenty years have brought about a play of influence that is many-stranded and loose. Iron triangles or other clear shapes may embrace some of the participants, but the larger picture in any policy area is likely to be one involving many other policy specialists. More than ever, policy making is becoming an intramural activity among expert issue-watchers, their networks, and their networks of networks. In this situation any neat distinction between the governmental structure and its environment tends to break down.

Political administrators, like the bureaucracies they superintend, are caught up in the trend toward issue specialization at the same time that responsibility is increasingly being dispersed among large numbers of policy intermediaries. The specialization in question may have little to do with purely professional training. Neither is it a matter of finding interest group spokesmen placed in appointive positions. Instead of party politicians, today's political executives tend to be policy politicians, able to move among the various networks, recognized as knowledgeable about the substance of issues concerning these networks, but not irretrievably identified with highly controversial positions. Their reputations among those "in the know" make them available for presidential appointments. Their mushiness on the most sensitive issues makes them acceptable. Neither a craft professional nor a gifted amateur, the modern recruit for political leadership in the bureaucracy is a journeyman of issues.

Approximately 200 top presidential appointees are charged with supervising the bureaucracy. These political executives include thirteen departmental secretaries, some half a dozen nondepartmental officials who are also in the cabinet, several dozen deputy secretaries or undersecretaries, and many more commission chairmen, agency administrators, and office directors. Below these men and women are another 500 politically appointed assistant secretaries, commissioners, deputies, and a host of other officials. If all of these positions and those who hold them are unknown to the public at large, there is nevertheless no mistaking the importance of the work that they do. It is here, in the layers of public managers, that political promise confronts administrative reality, or what passes for reality in Washington.

At first glance, generalization seems impossible. The political executive system in Washington has everything. Highly trained experts in medicine, economics, and the natural sciences can be found in positions where there is something like guild control over the criteria for a political appointment. But one can also find the most obvious patronage payoffs; obscure commissions, along with cultural and inter-American affairs, are some of the favorite dumping grounds. There are highly issue-oriented appointments, such as the sixty or so "consumer advocates" that the Ralph Nader groups claimed were in the early Carter administration. And there are also particular skill groups represented in appointments devoid of policy content (for example, about two-thirds of the top government public relations positions were filled during 1977 with people from private media organizations). In recent years, the claims of women and minorities for executive positions have added a further kind of positional patronage, where it is the number of positions rather than any agreed policy agenda that is important. After one year, about 11 percent of President Carter's appointees were women, mainly from established law firms, or what is sometimes referred to as the Ladies' Auxiliary of the Old Boys' Network.

How to make sense of this welter of political executives? Certainly there is a subtlety in the arrangements by which top people become top people and deal with each other. For the fact is that the issue networks share information not only about policy problems but also about people. Rarely are high political executives people who have an overriding identification with a particular interest group or credentials as leading figures in a profession. Rather they are people with recognized reputations in particular areas of public policy. The fluid networks through which they move can best be thought of as proto-bureaucracies. There are subordinate and superordinate positions through which they climb from lesser to greater renown and recognition, but these are not usually within the same organization. It is indeed a world of large-scale bureaucracies but one interlaced with loose, personal associations in which reputations are established by word of mouth. The reputations in question depend little on what, in Weberian terms, would be bureaucratically rational evaluations of objective performance or on what the political scientist would see as the individual's power rating. Even less do reputations depend on opinions in the electorate at large. What matters are the assessments of people like themselves concerning how well, in the short term, the budding technopol is managing each of his assignments in and at the fringes of government. . . .

The emergence of the policy politicians in our national politics goes back many years, at least to the new policy commitments of the New Deal era. Policy initiatives undertaken in the last generation have only intensified the process. For example, since 1960 the selection process for presidential appointees has seen important changes.[3] Using somewhat different techniques, each White House staff has struggled to find new ways of becoming less dependent on the crop of job applicants produced by normal party channels and of reaching out to new pools of highly skilled executive manpower. The rationale behind these efforts is always that executive leadership in the bureaucracy requires people who are knowledgeable about complex policies and acceptable to the important groups that claim an interest in the ever growing number of issue areas. Not surprisingly, the policy experts within the various networks who are consulted typically end by recommending each other. Thus over half of the people President-elect Carter identified as his outside advisers on political appointments ended up in executive jobs themselves. Similarly, while candidate Carter's political manager promised to resign if establishment figures such as Cyrus Vance and Zbigniew Brzezinski were given appointments after the election, at least half of the candidate's expert foreign policy advisers (including Vance and Brzezinski) wound up in major political positions with the administration. . . .

What are the implications for American government and politics? The verdict cannot be one-sided, if only because political management of the bureaucracy serves a number of diverse purposes. At least three important advantages can be found in the emerging system.

First, the reliance on issue networks and policy politicians is obviously consistent with some of the larger changes in society. Ordinary voters are apparently less constrained by party identification and more attracted to an issue-based style of politics. Party organizations are said to have fallen into a state of decay and to have become less capable of supplying enough highly qualified executive manpower. If government is committed to intervening in more complex, specialized areas, it is useful to draw upon the experts and policy specialists for the public management of these programs. Moreover, the congruence between an executive leadership and an electorate that are both uninterested in party politics may help stabilize a rapidly changing society. Since no one really knows how to solve the policy puzzles, policy politicians have the important quality of being disposable without any serious political ramifications (unless of course there are major symbolic implications, as in President Nixon's firing of Attorney General Elliot Richardson).

Within government, the operation of issue networks may have a second advantage in that they link Congress and the executive branch in ways that political parties no longer can. For many years, reformers have sought to revive the idea of party discipline as a means of spanning the distance between the two branches and turning their natural competition to useful purposes. But as the troubled dealings of recent Democratic Presidents with their majorities in Congress have indicated, political parties tend to be a weak bridge.

Meanwhile, the linkages of technocracy between the branches are indeliberately growing. The congressional bureaucracy that has blossomed in Washington during the last generation is in many ways like the political bureaucracy in the executive branch. In general, the new breed of congressional staffer is not a legislative crony or beneficiary of patronage favors. Personal loyalty to the congressman is still paramount, but the new-style legislative bureaucrat is likely to be someone skilled in dealing with certain complex policy issues, possibly with credentials as a policy analyst, but certainly an expert in using other experts and their networks.

None of this means an absence of conflict between President and Congress. Policy technicians in the two branches are still working for different sets of clients with different interests. The point is that the growth of specialized policy networks tends to perform the same useful services that it was once hoped a disciplined national party system would perform. Sharing policy knowledge, the networks provide a minimum common framework for political debate and decision in the two branches. For example, on energy policy, regardless of one's position on gas deregulation or incentives to producers, the policy technocracy has established a common language for discussing the issues, a shared grammar for identifying the major points of contention, a mutually familiar rhetoric of argumentation. Whether in Congress or the executive branch or somewhere outside, the "movers and shakers" in energy policy (as in health insurance, welfare reform, strategic arms limitation, occupational safety, and a host of other policy areas) tend to share an analytic repertoire for coping with the issues. Like experienced party politicians of earlier times, policy politicians in the knowledge networks may not agree; but they understand each other's way of looking at the world and arguing about policy choices.

A third advantage is the increased maneuvering room offered to political executives by the loose-jointed play of influence. If appointees were ambassadors from clearly defined interest groups and professions, or if policy were monopolized in iron triangles, then the chances for executive leadership in the bureaucracy would be small. In fact, however, the proliferation of administrative middlemen and networks of policy watchers offers new strategic resources for public managers. These are mainly opportunities to split and recombine the many sources of support and opposition that exist on policy issues. Of course, there are limits on how far a political executive can go in shopping for a constituency, but the general tendency over time has been to extend those limits. A secretary of labor will obviously pay close attention to what the AFL-CIO has to say, but there are many other voices to hear, not only in the union movement but also minority groups interested in jobs, state and local officials administering the department's programs, consumer groups worried about wage-push inflation, employees faced with unsafe working conditions, and so on. By the same token, former Secretary of Transportation William Coleman found new room for maneuver on the problem of landings by supersonic planes when he opened up the setpiece debate between pro- and anti-Concorde groups to a wider play of influence through public hearings. Clearly the richness of issue politics demands a high degree of skill to contain expectations and manage the natural dissatisfaction that comes from courting some groups rather than others. But at least it is a game that can be affected by skill, rather than one that is predetermined by immutable forces.

These three advantages are substantial. But before we embrace the rule of policy politicians and their networks, it is worth considering the threats they pose for American government. Issue networks may be good at influencing policy, but can they govern? Should they?

The first and foremost problem is the old one of democratic legitimacy. Weaknesses in executive leadership below the level of the President have never really been due to interest groups, party politics, or Congress. The primary problem has always been the lack of any democratically based power. Political executives get their popular mandate to do anything in the bureaucracy secondhand, from either an elected chief executive or Congress. The emerging system of political technocrats makes this democratic weakness much more severe. The more closely political administrators become identified with the various specialized policy networks, the farther they become separated from the ordinary citizen. Political executives can maneuver among the already mobilized issue networks and may occasionally do a little mobilizing of their own. But this is not the same thing as creating a broad base of public understanding and support for national policies. The typical presidential appointee will travel to any number of conferences, make speeches to the membership of one association after another, but almost never will he or she have to see or listen to an ordinary member of the public. The trouble is that only a small minority of citizens, even of those who are seriously attentive to public affairs, are likely to be mobilized in the various networks.[4] Those who are not policy activists depend on the ability of government institutions to act on their behalf.

If the problem were merely an information gap between policy experts and the bulk of the population, then more communication might help. Yet instead of garnering support for policy choices, more communication from the issue networks tends to produce an "everything causes cancer" syndrome among ordinary citizens. Policy forensics among the networks yield more experts making more sophisticated claims and counterclaims to the point that the nonspecialist becomes inclined to concede everything and believe nothing that he hears. The ongoing debates on energy policy, health crises, or arms limitation are rich in examples of public skepticism about what "they," the abstruse policy experts, are doing and saying. While the highly knowledgeable have been playing a larger role in government, the proportion of the general public concluding that those running the government don't seem to know what they are doing has risen rather steadily.[5] Likewise, the more government has tried to help, the more feelings of public helplessness have grown.

No doubt many factors and events are linked to these changing public attitudes. The point is that the increasing prominence of issue networks is bound to aggravate problems of legitimacy and public disenchantment. Policy activists have little desire to recognize an unpleasant fact: that their influential systems for knowledgeable policy making tend to make democratic politics more difficult. There are at least four reasons.

Complexity. Democratic political competition is based on the idea of trying to simplify complexity into a few, broadly intelligible choices. The various issue networks, on the other hand, have a stake in searching out complexity in what might seem simple. Those who deal with particular policy issues over the years recognize that policy objectives are usually vague and results difficult to measure. Actions relevant to one policy goal can frequently be shown to be inconsistent with others. To gain a reputation as a knowledgeable participant, one must juggle all of these complexities and demand that other technocrats in the issue networks do the same.

Consensus. A major aim in democratic politics is, after open argument, to arrive at some workable consensus of views. Whether by trading off one issue against another or by combining related issues, the goal is agreement. Policy activists may commend this democratic purpose in theory, but what their issue networks actually provide is a way of processing dissension. The aim is good policy— the right outcome on the issue. Since what that means is disputable among knowledgeable people, the desire for agreement must often take second place to one's understanding of the issue. Trade-offs or combinations—say, right-to-life groups with nuclear-arms-control people; environmentalists and consumerists; civil liberties groups and anti-gun controllers—represent a kind of impurity for many of the newly proliferating groups. In general there are few imperatives pushing for political consensus among the issue networks and many rewards for those who become practiced in the techniques of informed skepticism about different positions.

Confidence. Democratic politics presumes a kind of psychological asymmetry between leaders and followers. Those competing for leadership positions are expected to be sure of themselves and of what is to be done, while those led are expected to have a certain amount of detachment and dubiety in choosing how to give their consent to be governed. Politicians are supposed to take credit for successes, to avoid any appearance of failure, and to fix blame clearly on their opponents; voters weigh these claims and come to tentative judgments, pending the next competition among the leaders.

The emerging policy networks tend to reverse the situation. Activists mobilized around the policy issues are the true believers. To survive, the newer breed of leaders, or policy politicians, must become well versed in the complex, highly disputed substance of the issues. A certain tentativeness comes naturally as ostensible leaders try to spread themselves across the issues. Taking credit shows a lack of understanding of how intricate policies work and may antagonize those who really have been zealously pushing the issue. Spreading blame threatens others in the established networks and may raise expectations that new leadership can guarantee a better policy result. Vagueness about what is to be done allows policy problems to be dealt with as they develop and in accord with the intensity of opinion among policy specialists at that time. None of this is likely to warm the average citizen's confidence in his leaders. The new breed of policy politicians are cool precisely because the issue networks are hot.

Closure. Part of the genius of democratic politics is its ability to find a nonviolent decision-rule (by voting) for ending debate in favor of action. All the incentives in the policy technocracy work against such decisive closure. New studies and findings can always be brought to bear. The biggest rewards in these highly intellectual groups go to those who successfully challenge accepted wisdom. The networks thrive by continuously weighing alternative courses of action on particular policies, not by suspending disbelief and accepting that something must be done.

For all of these reasons, what is good for policy making (in the sense of involving well-informed people and rigorous analysts) may be bad for democratic politics. The emerging policy technocracy tends, as Henry Aaron has said of social science research, to "corrode any simple faiths around which political coalitions ordinarily are built."[6] Should we be content with simple faiths? Perhaps not; but the great danger is that the emerging world of issue politics and policy experts will turn John Stuart Mill's argument about the connection between liberty and popular government on its head. More informed argument about policy choices may produce more incomprehensibility. More policy intermediaries may widen participation among activists but deepen suspicions among unorganized nonspecialists. There may be more group involvement and less democratic legitimacy, more knowledge and more Know-Nothingism. Activists are likely to remain unsatisfied with, and nonactivists uncommitted to, what government is doing. Superficially this cancelling of forces might seem to assure a conservative tilt away from new, expansionary government policies. However, in terms of undermining a democratic identification of ordinary citizens with their government, the tendencies are profoundly radical.

A second difficulty with the issue networks is the problem that they create for the President as ostensible chief of the executive establishment. The emerging policy technocracy puts presidential appointees outside of the chief executive's reach in a way that narrowly focused iron triangles rarely can. At the end of the day, constituents of these triangles can at least be bought off by giving them some of the material advantages that they crave. But for issue activists it is likely to be a question of policy choices that are right or wrong. In this situation, more analysis and staff expertise—far from helping—may only hinder the President in playing an independent political leadership role. The influence of the policy technicians and their networks permeates everything the White House may want to do. Without their expertise there are no option papers, no detailed data and elaborate assessments to stand up against the onslaught of the issue experts in Congress and outside. Of course a President can replace a political executive, but that is probably merely to substitute one incumbent of the relevant policy network for another. . . .

Where does all this leave the President as a politician and as an executive of executives? In an impossible position. The problem of connecting politics and administration currently places any President in a classic no-win predicament. If he attempts to use personal loyalists as agency and department heads, he will be accused of politicizing the bureaucracy and will most likely put his executives in an untenable position for dealing with their organizations and the related networks. If he tries to create a countervailing source of policy expertise at the center, he will be accused of aggrandizing the Imperial Presidency and may hopelessly bureaucratize the White House's operations. If he relies on some benighted idea of collective cabinet government and on departmental executives for leadership in the bureaucracy (as Carter did in his first term), then the President does more than risk abdicating his own leadership responsibilities as the only elected executive in the national government; he is bound to become a creature of the issue networks and the policy specialists. It would be pleasant to think that there is a neat way out of this trilemma, but there is not.

Finally, there are disturbing questions surrounding the accountability of a political technocracy. The real problem is not that policy specialists specialize but that, by the nature of public office, they must generalize. Whatever an influential political executive does is done with all the collective authority of government and in the name of the public at large. It is not difficult to imagine situations in which policies make excellent sense within the cloisters of the expert issue watchers and yet are nonsense or worse seen from the viewpoint of ordinary people, the kinds of people political executives rarely meet. Since political executives themselves never need to pass muster with the electorate, the main source of democratic accountability must lie with the President and Congress. Given the President's problems and Congress's own burgeoning bureaucracy of policy specialists, the prospects for a democratically responsible executive establishment are poor at best.

Perhaps we need not worry. A case could be made that all we are seeing is a temporary commotion stirred up by a generation of reformist policies. In time the policy process may reenter a period of detumescence as the new groups and networks subside into the familiar triangulations of power.

However, a stronger case can be made that the changes will endure. In the first place, sufficient policy-making forces have now converged in Washington that it is unlikely that we will see a return to the familiar cycle of federal quiescence and policy experimentation by state governments. The central government, surrounded by networks of policy specialists, probably now has the capacity for taking continual policy initiatives. In the second place, there seems to be no way of braking, much less reversing, policy expectations generated by the compensatory mentality. To cut back on commitments undertaken in the last generation would itself be a major act of redistribution and could be expected to yield even more turmoil in the policy process. Once it becomes accepted that relative rather than absolute deprivation is what matters, the crusaders can always be counted upon to be in business.

A third reason why our politics and administration may never be the same lies in the very fact that so many policies have already been accumulated. Having to make policy in an environment already crowded with public commitments and programs increases the odds of multiple, indirect impacts of one policy on another, of one perspective set in tension with another, of one group and then another being mobilized. This sort of complexity and unpredictability creates a hostile setting for any return to traditional interest group politics.

Imagine trying to govern in a situation where the short-term political resources you need are stacked around a changing series of discrete issues, and where people overseeing these issues have nothing to prevent their pressing claims beyond any resources that they can offer in return. Imagine too that the more they do so, the more you lose understanding and support from public backers who have the long-term resources that you need. Whipsawed between cynics and true believers, policy would always tend to evolve to levels of insolubility. It is not easy for a society to politicize itself and at the same time depoliticize government leadership. But we in the United States may be managing to do just this.

NOTES

1. Steven V. Roberts, "Trade Associations Flocking to Capital as U.S. Role Rises," *New York Times*, March 4, 1978, p. 44.

2. For a full account of particular cases, see for example Martha Derthick, *Policy-Making for Social Security* (Washington, D.C.: Brookings Institution, 1979); Daniel Mazmanian and Jeanne Nienaber, *Environmentalism, Participation and the Corps of Engineers: A Study of Organizational Change* (Washington, D.C.: Brookings Institution, 1978). For the case of traffic safety, see Jack L. Walker, "Setting the Agenda in the U.S. Senate," *British Journal of Political Science*, vol. 7 (1977), pp. 432–45.

3. Changes in the presidential personnel process are discussed in Hugh Heclo, *A Government of Strangers* (Washington, D.C.: Brookings Institution, 1977), pp. 89–95.

4. An interesting recent case study showing the complexity of trying to generalize about who is "mobilizable" is James N. Rosenau, *Citizenship Between Elections* (New York: The Free Press, 1974).

5. Since 1964 the Institute for Social Research at the University of Michigan has asked the question, "Do you feel that almost all of the people running the government are smart people, or do you think that quite a few of them don't seem to know what they are doing?" The proportions choosing the latter view have been 28 percent (1964), 38 percent (1968), 45 percent (1970), 42 percent (1972), 47 percent (1974), and 52 percent (1976). For similar findings on public feelings of lack of control over the policy process, see U.S. Congress, Senate, Subcommittee on Intergovernmental Relations of the Committee on Government Operations, *Confidence and Concern: Citizens View American Government*, committee print, 93d Cong., 1st sess., 1973, pt. 1, p. 30. For a more complete discussion of recent trends see the two articles by Arthur H. Miller and Jack Citrin in the *American Political Science Review* (September 1974).

6. Henry J. Aaron, *Politics and the Professors* (Washington, D.C.: Brookings Institution, 1978), p. 159.

Imperfect Competition

Ralph Miliband

Democratic and pluralist theory could not have gained the degree of ascendancy which it enjoys in advanced capitalist societies if it had not at least been based on one plainly accurate observation about them, namely that they permit and even encourage a multitude of groups and associations to organise openly and freely and to compete with each other for the advancement of such purposes as their members may wish. With exceptions which mainly affect the Left, this is indeed the case.

What is wrong with pluralist-democratic theory is not its insistence on the fact of competition but its claim (very often its implicit assumption) that the major organised 'interests' in these societies, and notably capital and labour, compete on more or less equal terms, and that none of them is therefore able to achieve a decisive and permanent advantage in the process of competition. This is where ideology enters, and turns observation into myth. In previous chapters, it was shown that business, particularly large-scale business, did enjoy such an advantage *inside* the state system, by virtue of the composition and ideological inclinations of the state elite. In this chapter, we shall see that business enjoys a massive superiority *outside* the state system as well, in terms of the immensely stronger pressures which, as compared with labour and any other interest, it is able to exercise in the pursuit of its purposes.

I

One such form of pressure, which pluralist 'group theorists' tend to ignore, is more important and effective than any other, and business is uniquely placed to exercise it, without the need of organisation, campaigns and lobbying. This is the pervasive and permanent pressure upon governments and the state generated by the private control of concentrated industrial, commercial and financial resources. The existence of this major area of independent economic power is a fact which no government, whatever its inclinations, can ignore in the determination of its policies, not only in regard to economic matters, but to most other matters as well. The chairman of the editorial board of *Fortune* magazine said in 1952 that 'any president who wants to seek a prosperous country depends on the corporation at least as much—probably more than—the corporation depends on him. His dependence is not unlike that of King John on the landed barons at Runnymede, where Magna Carta was born'.[1] The parallel may not be perfect but the stress on the independent power of business, and on the dependence of government upon it, is altogether justified, not only for the United States but for all other advanced capitalist countries.

Of course, governments do have the formal power to impose their will upon business, to prevent it, by the exercise of legitimate authority, from doing certain things and to compel it to do certain other things. And this is in fact what governments have often done. But this, though true and important, is not at all the point at issue. Quite obviously, governments are not *completely* helpless in the face of business power, nor is it the case that businessmen, however large the concerns which they run, can openly defy the state's command, disregard its rules and flout the law. The point is rather that the control by business of large and crucially important areas of economic life makes it extremely *difficult* for governments to impose upon it policies to which it is firmly opposed. Other interests, it may well be said, are by no means helpless *vis-à-vis* their government either; they too may oppose, sometimes successfully, the purposes and policies of the state. But business, in the very nature of a capitalist system of economic organisation, is immeasurably better placed than any other interest to do so effectively, and to cause governments to pay much greater attention to its wishes and susceptibilities than to anybody else.

Writing about the United States, Professor Hacker has noted in this connection that:

> what Parsons and other liberals like to think of as business regulation is, despite the predictable complaints of businessmen, more a paper tiger than an effective system of economic controls in the public interest . . . [and, he goes on] a few questions may be asked about these supposed powers of the national government. Can any public agency determine the level of wages, of prices, of profits? Can it perhaps, more important, specify the level and direction of capital investment? Can any government bureau allocate raw materials or control plant location? Can it in any way guarantee full employment or the rate of economic growth? Has any writ of the Anti-Trust Division actually broken up one of our larger corporations in any appreciable way? The simple answer is that measures such as these are neither possible under the laws nor do we know what the reaction to them would be.[2]

Even for the United States this may well underestimate the influence which governments do have, by direct and indirect intervention, on economic life; and in many other capitalist countries, where a more positive philosophy of intervention has generally come to prevail, governments have been able to do rather more than what is here suggested as possible.

Nevertheless, the *limits* of intervention, at least in relation to business, and particularly *against* it, are everywhere much more narrow and specific than insistence on the formal powers of government would tend to suggest; and the area of decision-making which is left to private enterprise is correspondingly greater than is usually conveyed by the assiduously propagated image of a 'business community' cribbed and confined by bureaucratically meddlesome governments and their agents.

Even governments which *are* determined to 'control' private enterprise soon find that the mechanisms of intervention which they seek to super-impose upon business are extremely cumbersome and almost impossible to operate without the collaboration and help of business itself. But that collaboration and help are unlikely to be forthcoming unless a price is paid for them—the price being that governments should not be too determined in the pursuit of policies which business itself deems detrimental to it, and of course to the 'national interest'.

What is involved here is not necessarily or at all the active resistance of the controllers of economic power to the law, or the deliberate evasion of duly promulgated regulations, though there may be that as well. More important than such defiance, which may be politically damaging and even dangerous, is the *inert* power of business, the failure to do such things as are not positively commanded by the state but merely asked for, and the doing of other things which are not strictly illegal. Much is possible on this basis, and would be sufficient to present a reforming government with formidable problems, so long as it chose to operate within the framework of a capitalist regime. As Professor Meynaud notes, in a reference to Italy which is of more general application, private ownership and control makes it very difficult to undertake a policy of reform within the framework of established economic structures. Any government concerned to engineer a certain redistribution of economic power and of the social product without bringing into question the foundations of the system rapidly comes up, in the medical sense of the word, against a kind of intolerance of the regime to such changes.

This 'intolerance', it must be stressed, is not such as to prevent *any* kind of economic policy of which business disapproves. The veto power of business, in other words, is not absolute. But it is very large, and certainly larger than that of any other interest in capitalist society.

It has sometimes been argued that governments have now come to possess one extremely effective weapon in relation to business, namely the fact that they are now by far the largest customer of private enterprise and have thus an important and speedy instrument for influencing the decisions of private industry and commerce in such a way as to enable the government to achieve *on time* its major national industrial objectives. . . .

In the abstract, governments do indeed have vast resources and powers at their command to "wield the big stick" against business. In practice, governments which are minded to use these powers and resources—and most of them are not—soon find, given the economic and political context in which they operate, that the task is fraught with innumerable difficulties and perils.

These difficulties and perils are perhaps best epitomised in the dreaded phrase "loss of confidence." It is an implicit testimony to the power of business that all governments, not least reforming ones, have always been profoundly concerned to gain and retain its "confidence". Nor certainly is there any other interest whose "confidence" is deemed so precious, or whose "loss of confidence" is so feared.

The presidency of John F. Kennedy provides some illuminating instances of this concern. Soon after he came to office, President Kennedy found himself engaged in a "spectacular power struggle" with the Business Advisory Council, "an exclusive and self-perpetuating club of top corporate executives that had enjoyed a private and special relationship with the government since 1933" and which 'from Administration to Administration . . . had a continuous privilege to participate in government decisions with no public record or review.'[3] The Secretary of Commerce, Luther Hartwell Hodges, though hardly a fiery radical, entertained the odd notion that the manner of appointment of BAC members, and its procedures, ought to be modified. In the event, the difficulties this produced led the BAC itself to sever its official connections and to rename itself the Business Council. "Hodges drew plans for a new BAC, one that would include a broad cross-section of American business—big, medium and small-sized. It would include representatives as well of labor, agriculture, and education".[4]

But these plans never materialised: faced with many problems which appeared to him to require business support, "and sensitive to the growing insistence that he was 'anti-business', the President turned full circle from his earlier, firm and bold posture toward the Business Advisory Council'.[5] A rapprochement was engineered and arrangements were made for 'small committees of the BC to be assigned to each of several government departments and agencies—and to the White House itself.'6 For their part, "labor leaders complained about the Kennedy campaign against 'inflationary wage increases', itself part of Kennedy's assurance to business that he was playing no favorites. But the President wanted to restore a good working relationship with the Business Council *regardless of labor's concerns.*'7

It was only a few months later that the President found himself 'at war' with no less a member of the business establishment than Roger Blough, the chairman of U.S. Steel, who announced a substantial increase in the price of steel produced by his company and who was soon followed by other steel giants. On this occasion, the mobilisation of various forms of presidential pressure,8 including a spectacular display of presidential anger on television, succeeded in causing the rescinding of the increases—though only for a year. However, the episode was no loss to business in general, since it merely enhanced the President's almost obsessional concern to earn and enjoy its "confidence." Indeed, Governor Connally, who was riding in the President's car at the time of the assassination, has recalled that at least part of Kennedy's purpose in undertaking the trip to Texas was to reassure its "business community" as to his intentions; "I think it galled him," Governor Connally writes, "that conservative business people would suspect that he, a wealthy product himself of our capitalistic system, would do anything to damage that system."9 . . .

Given the degree of economic power which rests in the "business community" and the decisive importance of its actions (or of its non-actions) for major aspects of economic policy, any government with serious pretensions to radical reform must either seek to appropriate that power or find its room for radical action rigidly circumscribed by the requirements of business "confidence." So far, no government in any Western-type political system, whatever its rhetoric before assuming office, has taken up the first of these options. Instead, reform-minded governments have, sometimes reluctantly, sometimes not, curbed their reforming propensities (though never enough for the men they sought to appease) or adapted their reforms to the purposes of business (as happened in the case of the nationalisation proposals of the 1945 Labor government), and turned themselves into the allies of the very forces they had promised, while in opposition, to counter and subdue. Politics, in this context, is indeed the art of the possible. But what is possible is above all determined by what the 'business community' finds acceptable.

Nowadays, however, it is not only with the power of their own business class that reform-minded and "left-wing" governments have to reckon, or whose 'confidence' they must try and earn. Such governments must also reckon, now more than ever before, with the power and pressure of outside capitalist interests and forces—large foreign firms, powerful and conservative foreign governments, central banks, private international finance, official international credit organizations like the International Monetary Fund and the World Bank, or a formidable combination of all these. Economic and financial orthodoxy, and a proper regard for the prerogatives and needs of the free enterprise system, is not only what internal business interests expect and require from their office-holders; these internal interests are now powerfully seconded by outside ones, which may easily be of greater importance.

Capitalism, we have already noted, is now more than ever an international system, whose constituent economies are closely related and interlinked. As a result, even the most powerful capitalist countries depend, to a greater or lesser extent, upon the good will and cooperation of the rest, and of what has become, notwithstanding enduring and profound national capitalist rivalries, an interdependent international capitalist "community." The disapproval by that 'community' of the policies of one of its members, and the withdrawal of good will and co-operation which may follow from it, are obviously fraught with major difficulties for the country concerned. And so long as a country chooses to remain part of the 'community', so long must the wish *not* to incur its disapproval weigh very heavily upon its policy decisions and further reduce the impulses of reform-minded governments to stray far from the path of orthodoxy. Central bankers, enjoying a high degree of autonomy from their governments, have come to assume extraordinary importance as the guardians of that orthodoxy, and as the representatives *par excellence* of 'sound finance'. A *conservative* government in a relatively strong economic and financial position, such as the government of President de Gaulle long enjoyed, may play rogue elephant without undue risk of retribution. A radical government, on the other hand, would be unlikely to be given much shrift by these representatives of international capitalism.

Moreover, radical governments, as was also noted earlier, normally come to office in circumstances of severe economic and financial crisis, and find that credits, loans and general financial support are only available on condition that they pursue economic and foreign policies which are acceptable to their creditors and bankers and which are only marginally distinguishable, if at all, from the conservative policies they had previously denounced. . . .

This kind of dependence and surveillance has always been characteristic of the relations between the world of advanced capitalism and those governments of the 'Third World' which have sought aid and credits from it; and the price of such aid and credits has always been the pursuit by the governments concerned of policies designed to favour, or at least not to hinder, foreign capitalist enterprise, and the adoption in international affairs of policies and attitudes not likely, at the least, to give offence to the creditors and donors.

But these external pressures do not only now affect the underdeveloped countries of the 'Third World'. They can also be directed, with considerable effect, upon the governments of advanced capitalist countries; and here, obviously, is a great source of additional strength to national capitalist interests faced with governments bent on policies unacceptable to these interests. Class conflict, in these countries, has always had an international dimension, but this is now even more directly and specifically true than in the past.

II

In the light of the strategic position which capitalist enterprise enjoys in its dealings with governments, simply by virtue of its control of economic resources, the notion, which is basic to pluralist theory, that here is but one of the many 'veto groups' in capitalist society, on a par with other 'veto groups', must appear as a resolute escape from reality.

Of these other groups, it is labour, as an 'interest' in society, whose power is most often assumed to equal (when it is not claimed to surpass) the power of capital. But this is to treat as an accomplished fact what is only an unrealised potentiality, whose realisation is beset with immense difficulties.

For labour has nothing of the power of capital in the day-to-day economic decision-making of capitalist enterprise. What a firm produces; whether it exports or does not export; whether it invests, in what, and for what purpose; whether it absorbs or is absorbed by other firms—these and many other such decisions are matters over which labour has at best an indirect degree of influence and more generally no influence at all. In this sense, labour lacks a firm basis of economic power, and has consequently that much less pressure potential *vis-à-vis* the state. This is also one reason why governments are so much less concerned to obtain the 'confidence' of labour than of business.

Moreover, labour does not have anything, by way of exercising pressure, which corresponds to the foreign influences which are readily marshalled on behalf of capital. There are no labour 'gnomes' of Zurich, no labour equivalent of the World Bank, the International Monetary Fund, or the OECD, to ensure that governments desist from taking measures detrimental to wage-earners and favourable to business, or to press for policies which are of advantage to 'lower income groups' and which are opposed to the interests of economic elites. For wage-earners in the capitalist world, international solidarity is part of a hallowed rhetoric which seldom manifests itself concretely and effectively; for business, it is a permanent reality.

The one important weapon which labour, as an 'interest', does have is the strike; and where it has been used with real determination its effectiveness as a means of pressure has often been clearly demonstrated. Again and again, employers and governments have been forced to make concessions to labour because of the latter's resolute use of the strike weapon, or even because of the credible threat of its use. On innumerable occasions, demands which, the unions and the workers were told, could not conceivably be granted since they must inevitably mean ruin for a firm or industry or inflict irreparable damage to the national economy, have somehow become acceptable when organised labour has shown in practice that it would not desist.

Determination, however, is the problem. For labour, as a pressure group, is extremely vulnerable to many internal and external influences calculated to erode its will and persistence. Because of the effectiveness of these influences, governments have generally found it unnecessary to treat labour with anything like the deference which they have accorded to business. . . .

One important weakness which affects labour as a pressure group, as compared to business, is that the latter's national organisations are able to speak with considerably more authority than can their labour counterparts.

There are a number of reasons for this. One of them is that business organisations can truly claim to 'speak for business', either because they include a very high percentage of individual business units or because the firms which they do represent are responsible for a crucial part of economic activity. The equivalent labour organisations on the other hand nowhere include a majority of wage-earners, and mostly include far less. Business associations, in this sense, are much more representative than trade unions.

Secondly, and more important, business is nowhere as divided as labour. The point has been made before that business is neither an economic nor an ideological monolith, speaking always or even normally with one single voice on all issues. Indeed, its separate interests find everywhere expression in the different national associations which represent different sectors of the 'business community'. These divisions, notably the division between large-scale enterprise and medium or small business, are by no means negligible, either in specific or in general terms. But they do not prevent a basic ideological consensus, which is of fundamental importance in the representation and impact of business. Thus the policies advocated by the Diet of German Industry and Commerce may well be more 'moderate and liberal' than those of the Federation of German Industry;[10] and similar shades of difference may also be found among national business associations in other countries. But these differences obviously occur within a fairly narrow *conservative* spectrum of agreement which precludes major conflict. Business, it could be said, is tactically divided but strategically cohesive; over most of the larger issues of economic policy, and over other large national issues as well, it may be expected to present a reasonably united front.

This is certainly not the case for trade union movements anywhere. *Their* outstanding characteristic, in fact, is division, not unity; and the divisions from which they suffer, far from being tactical and superficial, are more often than not deep and fundamental.

Trade unions have of course always been divided from each other (and often, indeed, within themselves) in terms of the particular functions and skills of their members, sometimes by geography, often by religious, ethnic or racial factors. But, whether because of these factors or for other reasons, they are above all divided by ideology and attitudes from each other and within themselves.

In some countries, for instance France and Italy, these divisions find institutional expression in the existence of separate, distinct and often bitterly antagonistic federations—Communist, social-democratic and Christian, whose conflicts are a profoundly inhibiting factor in their encounter both with employers and with the state, and in their effectiveness as pressure groups. Nowhere does business suffer anything remotely comparable to these divisions.

Moreover, even in countries where ideological cleavages have not found institutional expression, trade union movements have still been subject to profound divisions, which may be contained within one organisation, but which are scarcely less debilitating. . . .

NOTES

1. Mills, *The Power Elite*, p. 169. Or, as Alfred de Grazia puts it, 'whoever controls the great industries will have awful political power' (*Politics and Government*, 1962, vol. 2, p. 56).

2. A. Hacker, 'Sociology and Ideology,' in M. Black (ed.), *The Social Theories of Talcott Parsons*, 1961, p. 302.

3. Rowen, *The Free Enterprisers. Kennedy, Johnson and the Business Establishment*, pp. 61–62. Another writer has described the Council as follows: 'Although nominally a private organisation, the BAC is publicly influential in a way in which pressure groups without the same case of access to the federal government can never be. It is apparent, for instance, that it serves as a recruiting and placement agency for personnel in many of the federal agencies. More significantly, it prepares elaborate "studies" and "reports". Although the specific import of such advisory reports is often hard to gauge, the Justice Department has found it necessary to inform the Secretary of the Interior that "fundamental questions of basic policy" are being initially settled by industry advisory committees, with the result that government action amounts to no more than giving effect to decisions already made by such committees' (Kariel, *The Decline of American Pluralism*, p. 99).

4. Rowen, op cit., p. 70.

5. *Ibid.*, p. 71.

6. *Ibid.*, p. 71.

7. *Ibid.*, p. 73 (my italics).

8. For which see *ibid.*, chapter 6.

9. J. Connally, 'Why Kennedy went to Texas', *Life*, 24 November 1967, p. 100.

10. Braunthal, *The Federation of German Industry in Politics*, p. 27.

Group Politics
and Representative Democracy

David B. Truman

"Group organization," said the late Robert Luce, momentarily dropping his usually cautious phrasing, "is one of the perils of the times."[1] The scholarly Yankee legislator's opinion has been echoed and re-echoed, sometimes in qualified and sometimes in categorical terms, by an impressive number of journalists, academicians, and politicians. The common themes running through most of these treatments are: alarm at the rapid multiplication of organized groups; an explicit or,

From David B. Truman, *The Governmental Process* (New York: Knopf, 2nd edition, 1971), pp. 501–508. Reprinted by permission.

more frequently, an implicit suggestion that the institutions of government have no alternative but passive submission to specialized group demands; and an admonition that the stability or continuance of democracy depends upon a spontaneous, self-imposed restraint in advancing group demands. Thus we are told that "there is no escape from the pressure of organized power. . . ," that the pitiful plight of American government is that "there is nothing it can do to protect itself from pressures. . . ," and that unless these groups "face the kind of world they are living in. . . ." it will be only a matter of time "until somebody comes riding in on a white horse."[2]

We have seen earlier that the vast multiplication of interests and organized groups in recent decades is not a peculiarly American phenomenon. The causes of this growth lie in the increased complexity of techniques for dealing with the environment, in the specializations that these involve, and in associated disturbances of the manifold expectations that guide individual behavior in a complex and interdependent society. Complexity of technique, broadly conceived, is inseparable from complexity of social structure. This linkage we observe in industrialized societies the world over. In the United States the multiplicity of interests and groups not only has been fostered by the extent of technical specialization but also has been stimulated by the diversity of the social patterns that these changes affect and by established political practices such as those that permit ease and freedom of association. Diversity of interests is a concomitant of specialized activity, and diversity of groups is a means of adjustment.

We have also seen that the institutions of government in the United States have reflected both the number and the variety of interests in the society and that this responsiveness is not essentially a modern feature of our politics. We have argued, in fact, that the behaviors that constitute the process of government cannot be adequately understood apart from the groups, especially the organized and potential interest groups, which are operative at any point in time. Whether we look at an individual citizen, at the executive secretary of a trade association, at a political party functionary, at a legislator, administrator, governor, or judge, we cannot describe his participation in the governmental institution, let alone account for it, except in terms of the interest with which he identifies himself and the groups with which he affiliates and with which he is confronted. These groups may or may not be interest groups, and all the interests he holds may not be represented at a given point in time by organized units. Organized interest groups, however, from their very nature bulk large in the political process. Collections of individuals interacting on the basis of shared attitudes and exerting claims upon other groups in the society usually find in the institutions of government an important means of achieving their objectives. That is, most interest groups become politicized on a continuing or intermittent basis. In this respect, therefore, such organized groups are as clearly a part of the governmental institution as are the political parties or the branches formally established by law or constitution.

The activities of political interest groups imply controversy and conflict, the essence of politics. For those who abhor conflict in any form, who long for some past or future golden age of perfect harmony, these consequences of group activity are alone sufficient to provoke denunciation. Such people look upon any groups or activities, except those to which they are accustomed, as signs of degeneration, and they view with alarm the appearance upon the political scene of new and insistent claimants. Objections from these sources are part of the peripheral data of politics, but they offer little to an understanding of the process. There are other people, however, who do not shrink from controversy and who are ready to assume that politics inevitably emerges out of men's specialized experiences and selective perceptions. For many of these observers the kinds of activity described in the preceding sections of this book are a source of concern. They listen receptively if not with pleasure to alarms like those quoted at the opening of this chapter. They see a possibility that the pursuits of organized interest groups may produce a situation of such chaos and indecision that representative government and its values may somehow be lost. With such concerns we may appropriately reckon.

INTEREST GROUPS AND THE NATURE OF THE STATE

Predictions concerning the consequences of given political activities are based upon conceptions of the governmental process. Predictions of any sort, of course, are outgrowths of understandings concerning the process to which the anticipated events are related. When the physiologist predicts that the consumption of a quantity of alcohol will have certain effects upon an individual's reflexes, when the chemist predicts that the application of heat to a particular mixture of substances will produce an explosion, and when the astronomer predicts that on a certain date there will occur an eclipse of the sun that will be visible from particular points on the earth's surface, each is basing his anticipation on a conception or an understanding of the respective somatic, chemical, and astronomical processes. Political prediction is no different. When an observer of the governmental scene says that the activities of organized political interest groups will result in the eclipse of certain behaviors subsumed under the heading of representative government, his statement reflects a conception of the dynamics of human relationships. Other elements enter into his prediction, but some such conception is basic to it.

A major difficulty in political prediction is that, in part because the relevant processes are extremely complex, our understanding of them is often not adequate; that is, the conceptions do not always account for all the variables and specify their relative importance. Such conceptions being inadequate in these respects, predictions based upon them are not reliable. Their accuracy is in large measure a matter of chance.[3] There are many people, both laymen and professional students of government, who argue that the complexity and irregularity of the political process are such that the reliability of predictions in this area will always be of a low order. We need not enter this controversy in these pages; one's position on the issue is in any case largely a matter of faith. We cannot, however, escape the necessity to predict. Government officials and private citizens must anticipate as best they can the consequences of political actions with which they are involved, though such predictions may have to rely heavily upon hunch, intuition, or calculated risk. In a good many cases our largely unformulated conceptions of the political process in America are adequate for prediction. For example, in every presidential election except that of 1860 one could have predicted, and many people tacitly did predict, that, whichever candidate was successful, his opponents and their supporters would not appeal from the decision of the ballot box to that of open violence. In many controversial areas of political behavior, however, our conceptions are almost completely lacking in predictive value.

A second handicap in political prediction is that the underlying conceptions are often almost completely implicit. They involve an array of partial and mutually contradictory assumptions of which the prophet is only dimly aware and of which many are derived from uncritically accepted myths and folklore concerning the political process in America. Predictions that are based upon such ill-formed, incomplete, and inaccurate premises are bound to be highly unreliable. Except as these unarticulated conceptions by chance happen to conform adequately to reality, they are a treacherous foundation for predictive statements. Many, if not most, predictions about the significance and implications of organized interest groups on the American scene rest on unreliable, implicit conceptions. To the extent that such statements are intended merely as a means of increasing or reducing the relative strength of competing interest groups, they may be evaluated wholly in terms of their effectiveness for that purpose. If they are presented, however, as systematic and responsible prognostications, they must be examined as such. In a large proportion of cases they will be found to rely on a flimsy conceptual structure, on a hopelessly inadequate and unacknowledged theory of the political process. . . .

Men, wherever they are observed, are creatures participating in those established patterns of interaction that we call groups. Excepting perhaps the most casual and transitory, these continuing interactions, like all such interpersonal relationships, involve power. This power is exhibited in two closely interdependent ways. In the first place, the group exerts power over its members; an individual's group affiliations largely determine his attitudes, values, and the frames of reference in terms of which he interprets his experiences. For a measure of conformity to the norms of the group is the price of acceptance within it. Such power is exerted not only by an individual's present group relationships; it also may derive from past affiliations such as the childhood family as well as from groups to which the individual aspires to belong and whose characteristic shared attitudes he also holds. In the second place, the group, if it is or becomes an interest group, which any group in a society may be, exerts power over other groups in the society when it successfully imposes claims upon them.

Many interest groups, probably an increasing proportion in the United States, are politicized. That is, either from the outset or from time to time in the course of their development they make their claims through or upon the institutions of government. Both the forms and functions of government in turn are a reflection of the activities and claims of such groups. The constitution-writing proclivities of Americans clearly reveal the influence of demands from such sources, and the statutory creation of new functions reflects their continuing operation. Many of these forms and functions have received such widespread acceptance from the start or in the course of time that they appear to be independent of the overt activities of organized interest groups. The judiciary is such a form. The building of city streets and the control of vehicular traffic are examples of such a function. However, if the judiciary or a segment of it operates in a fashion sharply contrary to the expectations of an appreciable portion of the community or if its role is strongly attacked, the group basis of its structure and powers is likely to become apparent. Similarly, if street construction greatly increases tax rates or if the control of traffic unnecessarily inconveniences either pedestrians or motorists, the exposure of these functions to the demands of competing interests will not be obscure. Interests that are widely held in the society may be reflected in government without their being organized in groups. They are what we have called potential groups. If the claims implied by the interests of these potential groups are quickly and adequately represented, interaction among those people who share the underlying interests or attitudes is unnecessary. But the interest base of accepted governmental forms and functions and their potential involvement in overt group activities are ever present even when not patently operative.

The institutions of government are centers of interest-based power; their connections with interest groups may be latent or overt and their activities range in political character from the routinized and widely accepted to the unstable and highly controversial. In order to make claims, political interest groups will seek access to the key points of decision within these institutions. Such points are scattered throughout the structure, including not only the formally established branches of government but also the political parties in their various forms and the relationships between governmental units and other interest groups.

The extent to which a group achieves effective access to the institutions of government is the resultant of a complex of interdependent factors. For the sake of simplicity these may be classified in three somewhat overlapping categories: (1) factors relating to a group's strategic position in the society; (2) factors associated with the internal characteristics of the group; and (3) factors peculiar to the governmental institutions themselves. In the first category are: the group's status or prestige in the society, affecting the ease with which it commands deference from those outside its bounds; the standing it and its activities have when measured against the widely held but largely unorganized interests or "rules of the game"; the extent to which government officials are formally or informally "members" of the group; and the usefulness of the group as a source of technical and political knowledge. The second category includes: the degree and appropriateness of the group's organization; the degree of cohesion it can achieve in a given situation, especially in the light of competing group demands upon its membership; the skills of the leadership; and the group's resources in numbers and money. In the third category are: the operating structure of the government institutions, since such established features involve relatively fixed advantages and handicaps; and the effects of the group life of particular units or branches of the government.

The product of effective access, of the claims of organized and unorganized interests that achieve access with varying degrees of effectiveness, is a governmental decision. Note that these interests that achieve effective access and guide decisions need not be "selfish," are not necessarily solidly unified, and may not be represented by organized groups. Governmental decisions are the resultant of effective access by various interests, of which organized groups may be only a segment. These decisions may be more or less stable depending on the strength of supporting interests and on the severity of disturbances in the society which affect that strength.

A characteristic feature of the governmental system in the United States is that it contains a multiplicity of points of access. The federal system establishes decentralized and more or less independent centers of power, vantage points from which to secure privileged access to the national government. Both a sign and a cause of the strength of the constituent units in the federal scheme is the peculiar character of our party system, which has strengthened parochial relationships, especially those of national legislators. National parties, and to a lesser degree those in the States, tend to be poorly cohesive leagues of locally based organizations rather than unified and inclusive structures. Staggered terms for executive officials and various types of legislators accentuate differences in the effective electorates that participate in choosing these officers. Each of these different, often opposite, localized patterns (constituencies) is a channel of independent access to the larger party aggregation and to the formal government. Thus, especially at the national level, the party is an electing-device and only in limited measure an integrated means of policy determination. Within the Congress, furthermore, controls are diffused among committee chairmen and other leaders in both chambers. The variety of these points of access is further supported by relationships stemming from the constitutional doctrine of the separation of powers, from related checks and balances, and at the State and local level from the common practice of choosing an array of executive officials by popular election. At the Federal level the formal simplicity of the executive branch has been complicated by a Supreme Court decision that has placed a number of administrative agencies beyond the removal power of the president. The position of these units, however, differs only in degree from that of many that are constitutionally within the executive branch. In consequence of alternative lines of access available through the legislature and the executive and of divided channels for the control of administrative policy, many nominally executive agencies are at various times virtually independent of the chief executive.

Although some of these lines of access may operate in series, they are not arranged in a stable and integrated hierarchy. Depending upon the whole political context in a given period and upon the relative strength of contending interests, her of the centers of power in the formal government or in the parties ...; become the apex of a hierarchy of controls. Only the highly routinized governmental activities show any stability in this respect, and these may as easily be subordinated to elements in the legislature as to the chief executive. Within limits, therefore, organized interest groups, gravitating toward responsive points of decision, may play one segment of the structure against another as circumstances and strategic considerations permit. The total pattern of government over a period of time thus presents a protean complex of crisscrossing relationships that change in strength and direction with alterations in the power and standing of interests, organized and unorganized. . . .

NOTES

1. Luce: *Legislative Assemblies*, p. 421.

2. These three quotations, taken somewhat unfairly from their contexts, are, respectively, from Harvey Fergusson: *People and Power* (New York: William Morrow & Company, 1947), p. 101; J. H. Spigelman: "The Protection of Society," *Harper's Magazine* (July, 1946), p. 6; and Stuart Chase: *Democracy Under Pressure: Special Interests vs. the Public Welfare* (New York: The Twentieth Century Fund, 1945), p. 8. Cf. Robert C. Angell: *The Integration of American Society* (New York: McGraw-Hill Book Company, 1941); Brady: *Business as a System of Power*; and John Maurice Clark: *Alternative to Serfdom* (New York: Alfred A. Knopf, Inc., 1948).

3. Cf. David B. Truman: "Political Behavior and Voting," in Mosteller *et al.: The Pre-election Polls of 1948*, pp. 225–50.

The Power Elite

C. Wright Mills

The powers of ordinary men are circumscribed by the everyday worlds in which they live, yet even in these rounds of job, family, and neighborhood they often seem driven by forces they can neither understand nor govern. 'Great changes' are beyond their control, but affect their conduct and outlook none the less. The very framework of modern society confines them to projects not their own, but from every side, such changes now press upon the men and women of the mass society, who accordingly feel that they are without purpose in an epoch in which they are without power.

But not all men are in this sense ordinary. As the means of information and of power are centralized, some men come to occupy positions in American society from which they can look down upon, so to speak, and by their decisions mightily affect, the everyday worlds of ordinary men and women. They are not made by their jobs; they set up and break down jobs for thousands of others; they are not confined by simple family responsibilities; they can escape. They may live in many hotels and houses, but they are bound by no one community. They need not merely 'meet the demands of the day and hour'; in some part, they create these demands, and cause others to meet them. Whether or not they profess their power, their technical and political experience of it far transcends that of the underlying population. What Jacob Burckhardt said of 'great men,' most Americans might well say of their elite: 'They are all that we are not.'[1]

The power elite is composed of men whose positions enable them to transcend the ordinary environments of ordinary men and women; they are in positions to make decisions having major consequences. Whether they do or do not make such decisions is less important than the fact that they do occupy such pivotal positions: their failure to act, their failure to make decisions, is itself an act that is often of greater consequence than the decisions they do make. For they are in command of the major hierarchies and organizations of modern society. They rule the big corporations. They run the machinery of the state and claim its prerogatives. They direct the military establishment. They occupy the strategic command posts of the social structure, in which are now centered the effective means of the power and the wealth and the celebrity which they enjoy.

The power elite are not solitary rulers. Advisers and consultants, spokesmen and opinion-makers are often the captains of their higher thought and decision. Immediately below the elite are the professional politicians of the middle levels of power, in the Congress and in the pressure groups, as well as among the new and old upper classes of town and city and region. Mingling with them, in curious ways which we shall explore, are those professional celebrities who live by being continually displayed but are never, so long as they remain celebrities, displayed enough. If such celebrities are not at the head of any dominating hierarchy, they do often have the power to distract the attention of the public or afford sensations to the masses, or, more directly, to gain the ear of those who do occupy positions of direct power. More or less unattached, as critics of morality and technicians of power, as spokesmen of God and creators of mass sensibility, such celebrities and consultants are part of the immediate scene in which the drama of the elite is enacted. But that drama itself is centered in the command posts of the major institutional hierarchies.

The truth about the nature and the power of the elite is not some secret which men of affairs know but will not tell. Such men hold quite various theories about their own roles in the sequence of event and decision. Often they are uncertain about their roles, and even more often they allow their fears and their hopes to affect their assessment of their own power. No matter how great their actual power, they tend to be less acutely aware of it than of the resistances of others to its use. Moreover, most American men of affairs have learned well the rhetoric of public relations, in some cases even to the point of using it when they are alone, and thus coming to believe it. The personal awareness of the actors is only one of the several sources one must examine in order to understand the higher circles. Yet many who believe that there is no elite, or at any rate none of any consequence, rest their argument upon what men of affairs believe about themselves, or at least assert in public.

There is, however, another view: those who feel, even if vaguely, that a compact and powerful elite of great importance does now prevail in America often base that feeling upon the historical trend of our time. They have felt, for example, the domination of the military event, and from this they infer that generals and admirals, as well as other men of decision influenced by them, must be enormously powerful. They hear that the Congress has again abdicated to a handful of men decisions clearly related to the issue of war or peace. They know that the bomb was dropped over Japan in the name of the United States of America, although they were at no time consulted about the matter. They feel that they live in a time of big decisions; they know that they are not making any. Accordingly, as they consider the present as history, they infer that at its center, making decisions or failing to make them, there must be an elite of power.

On the one hand, those who share this feeling about big historical events assume that there is an elite and that its power is great. On the other hand, those who listen carefully to the reports of men apparently involved in the great decisions often do not believe that there is an elite whose powers are of decisive consequence.

Both views must be taken into account, but neither is adequate. The way to understand the power of the American elite lies neither solely in recognizing the historic scale of events nor in accepting the personal awareness reported by men of apparent decision. Behind such men and behind the events of history, linking the two, are the major institutions of modern society. These hierarchies of state and corporation and army constitute the means of power; as such they are now of a consequence not before equaled in human history—and at their summits, there are now those command posts of modern society which offer us the sociological key to an understanding of the role of the higher circles in America.

Within American society, major national power now resides in the economic, the political, and the military domains. Other institutions seem off to the side of modern history, and, on occasion, duly subordinated to these. No family is as directly powerful in national affairs as any major corporation; no church is as directly powerful in the external biographies of young men in America today as the military establishment; no college is as powerful in the shaping of momentous events as the National Security Council. Religious, educational, and family institutions are not autonomous centers of national power; on the contrary, these decentralized areas are increasingly shaped by the big three, in which developments of decisive and immediate consequence now occur.

Families and churches and schools adapt to modern life; governments and armies and corporations shape it; and, as they do so, they turn these lesser institutions into means for their ends. Religious institutions provide chaplains to the armed forces where they are used as a means of increasing the effectiveness of its morale to kill. Schools select and train men for their jobs in corporations and their specialized tasks in the armed forces. The extended family has, of course, long been broken up by the industrial revolution, and now the son and the father are removed from the family, by compulsion if need be, whenever the army of the state sends out the call. And the symbols of all these lesser institutions are used to legitimate the power and the decisions of the big three.

The life-fate of the modern individual depends not only upon the family into which he was born or which he enters by marriage, but increasingly upon the corporation in which he spends the most alert hours of his best years; not only upon the school where he is educated as a child and adolescent, but also upon the state which touches him throughout his life; not only upon the church in which on occasion he hears the word of God, but also upon the army in which he is disciplined.

If the centralized state could not rely upon the inculcation of nationalist loyalties in public and private schools, its leaders would promptly seek to modify the decentralized educational system. If the bankruptcy rate among the top five hundred corporations were as high as the general divorce rate among the thirty-seven million married couples, there would be economic catastrophe on an international scale. If members of armies gave to them no more of their lives than do believers to the churches to which they belong, there would be a military crisis.

Within each of the big three, the typical institutional unit has become enlarged, has become administrative, and, in the power of its decisions, has become centralized. Behind these developments there is a fabulous technology, for as institutions, they have incorporated this technology and guide it, even as it shapes and paces their developments.

The economy—once a great scatter of small productive units in autonomous balance—has become dominated by two or three hundred giant corporations, administratively and politically interrelated, which together hold the keys to economic decisions.

The political order, once a decentralized set of several dozen states with a weak spinal cord, has become a centralized, executive establishment which has taken up into itself many powers previously scattered, and now enters into each and every cranny of the social structure.

The military order, once a slim establishment in a context of distrust fed by state militia, has become the largest and most expensive feature of government, and, although well versed in smiling public relations, now has all the grim and clumsy efficiency of a sprawling bureaucratic domain.

In each of these institutional areas, the means of power at the disposal of decision makers have increased enormously; their central executive powers have been enhanced; within each of them modern administrative routines have been elaborated and tightened up.

As each of these domains becomes enlarged and centralized, the consequences of its activities become greater, and its traffic with the others increases.
The decisions of a handful of corporations bear upon military and political as well
as upon economic developments around the world. The decisions of the military
establishment rest upon and grievously affect political life as well as the very level
of economic activity. The decisions made within the political domain determine
economic activities and military programs. There is no longer, on the one hand, an
economy, and, on the other hand, a political order containing a military establishment unimportant to politics and to money-making. There is a political economy
linked, in a thousand ways, with military institutions and decisions. On each side
of the world-split running through central Europe and around the Asiatic rim-
lands, there is an ever-increasing interlocking of economic, military, and political
structures.[2] If there is government intervention in the corporate economy, so is
there corporate intervention in the governmental process. In the structural sense,
this triangle of power is the source of the interlocking directorate that is most important for the historical structure of the present.

The fact of the interlocking is clearly revealed at each of the points of crisis
of modern capitalist society—slump, war, and boom. In each, men of decision are
led to an awareness of the interdependence of the major institutional orders. In
the nineteenth century, when the scale of all institutions was smaller, their liberal
integration was achieved in the automatic economy, by an autonomous play of
market forces, and in the automatic political domain, by the bargain and the vote.
It was then assumed that out of the imbalance and friction that followed the limited decisions then possible a new equilibrium would in due course emerge. That
can no longer be assumed, and it is not assumed by the men at the top of each of
the three dominant hierarchies.

For given the scope of their consequences, decisions—and indecisions—in
any one of these ramify into the others, and hence top decisions tend either to become co-ordinated or to lead to a commanding indecision. It has not always been
like this. When numerous small entrepreneurs made up the economy, for example, many of them could fail and the consequences still remain local; political and
military authorities did not intervene. But now, given political expectations and
military commitments, can they afford to allow key units of the private corporate
economy to break down in slump? Increasingly, they do intervene in economic affairs, and as they do so, the controlling decisions in each order are inspected by
agents of the other two, and economic, military, and political structures are inter-
locked.

At the pinnacle of each of the three enlarged and centralized domains, there
have arisen those higher circles which make up the economic, the political, and
the military elites. At the top of the economy, among the corporate rich, there are
the chief executives; at the top of the political order, the members of the political
directorate; at the top of the military establishment, the elite of soldier-statesmen
clustered in and around the Joint Chiefs of Staff and the upper echelon. As each
of these domains has coincided with the others, as decisions tend to become total

in their consequence, the leading men in each of the three domains of power—the warlords, the corporation chieftains, the political directorate—tend to come together, to form the power elite of America.

The higher circles in and around these command posts are often thought of in terms of what their members possess: they have a greater share than other people of the things and experiences that are most highly valued. From this point of view, the elite are simply those who have the most of what there is to have, which is generally held to include money, power, and prestige—as well as all the ways of life to which these lead.[3] But the elite are not simply those who have the most, for they could not 'have the most' were it not for their positions in the great institutions. For such institutions are the necessary bases of power, of wealth, and of prestige, and at the same time, the chief means of exercising power, of acquiring and retaining wealth, and of cashing in the higher claims for prestige.

By the powerful we mean, of course, those who are able to realize their will, even if others resist it. No one, accordingly, can be truly powerful unless he has access to the command of major institutions, for it is over these institutional means of power that the truly powerful are, in the first instance, powerful. Higher politicians and key officials of government command such institutional power; so do admirals and generals, and so do the major owners and executives of the larger corporations. Not all power, it is true, is anchored in and exercised by means of such institutions, but only within and through them can power be more or less continuous and important.

Wealth also is acquired and held in and through institutions. The pyramid of wealth cannot be understood merely in terms of the very rich; for the great inheriting families, as we shall see, are now supplemented by the corporate institutions of modern society: every one of the very rich families has been and is closely connected—always legally and frequently managerially as well—with one of the multi-million dollar corporations.

The modern corporation is the prime source of wealth, but, in latter-day capitalism, the political apparatus also opens and closes many avenues to wealth. The amount as well as the source of income, the power over consumer's goods as well as over productive capital, are determined by position within the political economy. If our interest in the very rich goes beyond their lavish or their miserly consumption, we must examine their relations to modern forms of corporate property as well as to the state; for such relations now determine the chances of men to secure big property and to receive high income.

Great prestige increasingly follows the major institutional units of the social structure. It is obvious that prestige depends, often quite decisively, upon access to the publicity machines that are now a central and normal feature of all the big institutions of modern America. Moreover, one feature of these hierarchies of corporation, state, and military establishment is that their top positions are increasingly interchangeable. One result of this is the accumulative nature of prestige. Claims for prestige, for example, may be initially based on military roles, then expressed in and augmented by an educational institution run by corporate executives, and cashed in, finally, in the political order, where, for General Eisenhower and those he represents, power and prestige finally meet at the very peak. Like wealth and power, prestige tends to be cumulative: the more of it you have, the more you can get. These values also tend to be translatable into one another: the wealthy find it easier than the poor to gain power; those with status find it easier than those without it to control opportunities for wealth.

If we took the one hundred most powerful men in America, the one hundred wealthiest, and the one hundred most celebrated away from the institutional positions they now occupy, away from their resources of men and women and money, away from the media of mass communication that are now focused upon them—then they would be powerless and poor and uncelebrated. For power is not of a man. Wealth does not center in the person of the wealthy. Celebrity is not inherent in any personality. To be celebrated, to be wealthy, to have power requires access to major institutions, for the institutional positions men occupy determine in large part their chances to have and to hold these valued experiences.

The people of the higher circles may also be conceived as members of a top social stratum, as a set of groups whose members know one another, see one another socially and at business, and so, in making decisions, take one another into account. The elite, according to this conception, feel themselves to be, and are felt by others to be, the inner circle of 'the upper social classes.'⁴ They form a more or less compact social and psychological entity; they have become self-conscious members of a social class. People are either accepted into this class or they are not, and there is a qualitative split, rather than merely a numerical scale, separating them from those who are not elite. They are more or less aware of themselves as a social class and they behave toward one another differently from the way they do toward members of other classes. They accept one another, understand one another, marry one another, tend to work and to think if not together at least alike.

Now, we do not want by our definition to prejudge whether the elite of the command posts are conscious members of such a socially recognized class, or whether considerable proportions of the elite derive from such a clear and distinct class. These are matters to be investigated. Yet in order to be able to recognize what we intend to investigate, we must note something that all biographies and memoirs of the wealthy and the powerful and the eminent make clear: no matter what else they may be, the people of these higher circles are involved in a set of overlapping 'crowds' and intricately connected 'cliques.' There is a kind of mutual attraction among those who 'sit on the same terrace'—although this often becomes clear to them, as well as to others, only at the point at which they feel the need to draw the line; only when, in their common defense, they come to understand what they have in common, and so close their ranks against outsiders.

The idea of such ruling stratum implies that most of its members have similar social origins, that throughout their lives they maintain a network of informal connections, and that to some degree there is an interchangeability of position between the various hierarchies of money and power and celebrity. We must, of course, note at once that if such an elite stratum does exist, its social visibility and its form, for very solid historical reasons, are quite different from those of the noble cousinhoods that once ruled various European nations.

That American society has never passed through a feudal epoch is of decisive importance to the nature of the American elite, as well as to American society as a historic whole. For it means that no nobility or aristocracy, established before the capitalist era, has stood in tense opposition to the higher bourgeoisie. It means that this bourgeoisie has monopolized not only wealth but prestige and power as well. It means that no set of noble families has commanded the top positions and monopolized the values that are generally held in high esteem; and certainly that no set has done so explicitly by inherited right. It means that no high church dignitaries or court nobilities, no entrenched landlords with honorific accouterments, no monopolists of high army posts have opposed the enriched bourgeoisie and in the name of birth and prerogative successfully resisted its self-making.

But this does *not* mean that there are no upper strata in the United States. That they emerged from a 'middle class' that had no recognized aristocratic superiors does not mean they remained middle class when enormous increases in wealth made their own superiority possible. Their origins and their newness may have made the upper strata less visible in America than elsewhere. But in America today there are in fact tiers and ranges of wealth and power of which people in the middle and lower ranks know very little and may not even dream. There are families who, in their well-being, are quite insulated from the economic jolts and lurches felt by the merely prosperous and those farther down the scale. There are also men of power who in quite small groups make decisions of enormous consequence for the underlying population.

The American elite entered modern history as a virtually unopposed bourgeoisie. No national bourgeoisie, before or since, has had such opportunities and advantages. Having no military neighbors, they easily occupied an isolated continent stocked with natural resources and immensely inviting to a willing labor force. A framework of power and an ideology for its justification were already at hand. Against mercantilist restriction, they inherited the principle of *laissez-faire*; against Southern planters, they imposed the principle of industrialism. The Revolutionary War put an end to colonial pretensions to nobility, as loyalists fled the country and many estates were broken up. The Jacksonian upheaval with its status revolution put an end to pretensions to monopoly of descent by the old New England families. The Civil War broke the power, and so in due course the prestige, of the ante-bellum South's claimants for the higher esteem. The tempo of the whole capitalist development made it impossible for an inherited nobility to develop and endure in America.

No fixed ruling class, anchored in agrarian life and coming to flower in military glory, could contain in America the historic thrust of commerce and industry, or subordinate to itself the capitalist elite—as capitalists were subordinated, for example, in Germany and Japan. Nor could such a ruling class anywhere in the world contain that of the United States when industrialized violence came to decide history. Witness the fate of Germany and Japan in the two world wars of the twentieth century; and indeed the fate of Britain herself and her model ruling class, as New York became the inevitable economic, and Washington the inevitable political capital of the western capitalist world.

The elite who occupy the command posts may be seen as the possessors of power and wealth and celebrity; they may be seen as members of the upper stratum of a capitalistic society. They may also be defined in terms of psychological and moral criteria, as certain kinds of selected individuals. So defined, the elite, quite simply, are people of superior character and energy.

The humanist, for example, may conceive of the 'elite' not as a social level or category, but as a scatter of those individuals who attempt to transcend themselves, and accordingly, are more noble, more efficient, made out of better stuff. It does not matter whether they are poor or rich, whether they hold high position or low, whether they are acclaimed or despised; they are elite because of the kind of individuals they are. The rest of the population is mass, which, according to this conception, sluggishly relaxes into uncomfortable mediocrity.[5]

This is the sort of socially unlocated conception which some American writers with conservative yearnings have recently sought to develop. But most moral and psychological conceptions of the elite are much less sophisticated, concerning themselves not with individuals but with the stratum as a whole. Such ideas, in fact, always arise in a society in which some people possess more than do others of what there is to possess. People with advantages are loath to believe that they just happen to be people with advantages. They come readily to define themselves as inherently worthy of what they possess; they come to believe themselves 'naturally' elite; and, in fact, to imagine their possessions and their privileges as natural extensions of their own elite selves. In this sense, the idea of the elite as composed of men and women having a finer moral character is an ideology of the elite as a privileged ruling stratum, and this is true whether the ideology is elite-made or made up for it by others.

In eras of equalitarian rhetoric, the more intelligent or the more articulate among the lower and middle classes, as well as guilty members of the upper, may come to entertain ideas of a counter-elite. In western society, as a matter of fact, there is a long tradition and varied images of the poor, the exploited, and the oppressed as the truly virtuous, the wise, and the blessed. Stemming from Christian tradition, this moral idea of a counter-elite, composed of essentially higher types condemned to a lowly station, may be and has been used by the underlying population to justify harsh criticism of ruling elites and to celebrate utopian images of a new elite to come.

The moral conception of the elite, however, is not always merely an ideology of the overprivileged or a counter-ideology of the underprivileged. It is often a fact: having controlled experiences and select privileges, many individuals of the upper stratum do come in due course to approximate the types of character they claim to embody. Even when we give up—as we must—the idea that the elite man or woman is born with an elite character, we need not dismiss the idea that their experiences and trainings develop in them characters of a specific type.

Nowadays we must qualify the idea of elite as composed of higher types of individuals, for the men who are selected for and shaped by the top positions have many spokesmen and advisers and ghosts and make-up men who modify their self-conceptions and create their public images, as well as shape many of their decisions. There is, of course, considerable variation among the elite in this respect, but as a general rule in America today, it would be naïve to interpret any major elite group merely in terms of its ostensible personnel. The American elite often seems less a collection of persons than of corporate entities, which are in great part created and spoken for as standard types of 'personality.' Even the most apparently free-lance celebrity is usually a sort of synthetic production turned out each week by a disciplined staff which systematically ponders the effect of the easy ad-libbed gags the celebrity 'spontaneously' echoes.

Yet, in so far as the elite flourishes as a social class or as a set of men at the command posts, it will select and form certain types of personality, and reject others. The kind of moral and psychological beings men become is in large part determined by the values they experience and the institutional roles they are allowed and expected to play. From the biographer's point of view, a man of the upper classes is formed by his relations with others like himself in a series of small intimate groupings through which he passes and to which throughout his lifetime he may return. So conceived, the elite is a set of higher circles whose members are selected, trained and certified and permitted intimate access to those who command the impersonal institutional hierarchies of modern society. If there is any one key to the *psychological* idea of the elite, it is that they combine in their persons an awareness of impersonal decision-making with intimate sensibilities shared with one another. To understand the elite as a social class we must examine a whole series of smaller face-to-face milieux, the most obvious of which, historically, has been the upper-class family, but the most important of which today are the proper secondary school and the metropolitan club.[6]

*   *   *

The power elite is composed of political, economic, and military men, but this instituted elite is frequently in some tension: it comes together only on certain coinciding points and only on certain occasions of 'crisis.' In the long peace of the nineteenth century, the military were not in the high councils of state, not of the political directorate, and neither were the economic men—they made raids upon the state but they did not join its directorate. During the 'thirties, the political man was ascendant. Now the military and the corporate men are in top positions.

Of the three types of circle that compose the power elite today, it is the military that has benefited the most in its enhanced power, although the corporate circles have also become more explicitly intrenched in the more public decision-making circles. It is the professional politician that has lost the most, so much that in examining the events and decisions, one is tempted to speak of a political vacuum in which the corporate rich and the high warlord, in their coinciding interests, rule.

It should not be said that the three 'take turns' in carrying the initiative, for the mechanics of the power elite are not often as deliberate as that would imply. At times, of course, it is—as when political men, thinking they can borrow the prestige of generals, find that they must pay for it, or, as when during big slumps, economic men feel the need of a politician at once safe and possessing vote appeal. Today all three are involved in virtually all widely ramifying decisions. Which of the three types seems to lead depends upon 'the tasks of the period' as they, the elite, define them. Just now, these tasks center upon 'defense' and international affairs. Accordingly, as we have seen, the military are ascendant in two senses: as personnel and as justifying ideology. That is why, just now, we can most easily specify the unity and the shape of the power elite in terms of the military ascendancy.

*   *   *

The conception of the power elite and of its unity rests upon the corresponding developments and the coincidence of interests among economic, political, and military organizations. It also rests upon the similarity of origin and outlook, and the social and personal intermingling of the top circles from each of these dominant hierarchies. This conjunction of institutional and psychological forces, in turn, is revealed by the heavy personnel traffic within and between the big three institutional orders, as well as by the rise of go-betweens as in the high-level lobbying. The conception of the power elite, accordingly, does *not* rest upon the assumption that American history since the origins of World War II must be understood as a secret plot, or as a great and co-ordinated conspiracy of the members of this elite. The conception rests upon quite impersonal grounds.

There is, however, little doubt that the American power elite—which contains, we are told, some of 'the greatest organizers in the world'—has also planned and has plotted. The rise of the elite, as we have already made clear, was not and could not have been caused by a plot; and the tenability of the conception does not rest upon the existence of any secret or any publicly known organization. But, once the conjunction of structural trend and of the personal will to utilize it gave rise to the power elite, then plans and programs did occur to its members and indeed it is not possible to interpret many events and official policies of the fifth epoch without reference to the power elite. 'There is a great difference,' Richard Hofstadter has remarked, 'between locating conspiracies *in* history and saying that history *is*, in effect, a conspiracy . . .[7]

The structural trends of institutions become defined as opportunities by those who occupy their command posts. Once such opportunities are recognized, men may avail themselves of them. Certain types of men from each of the dominant institutional areas, more far-sighted than others, have actively promoted the liaison before it took its truly modern shape. They have often done so for reasons not shared by their partners, although not objected to by them either; and often the outcome of their liaison has had consequences which none of them foresaw, much less shaped, and which only later in the course of development came under explicit control. Only after it was well under way did most of its members find themselves part of it and become gladdened, although sometimes also worried, by this fact. But once the co-ordination is a going concern, new men come readily into it and assume its existence without question.

So far as explicit organization—conspiratorial or not—is concerned, the power elite, by its very nature, is more likely to use existing organizations, working within and between them, than to set up explicit organizations whose membership is strictly limited to its own members. But if there is no machinery in existence to ensure, for example, that military and political factors will be balanced in decisions made, they will invent such machinery and use it, as with the National Security Council. Moreover, in a formally democratic polity, the aims and the powers of the various elements of this elite are further supported by an aspect of the permanent war economy: the assumption that the security of the nation supposedly rests upon great secrecy of plan and intent. Many higher events that would reveal the working of the power elite can be withheld from public knowledge under the guise of secrecy. With the wide secrecy covering their operations and decisions, the power elite can mask their intentions, operations, and further consolidation. Any secrecy that is imposed upon those in positions to observe high decision-makers clearly works for and not against the operations of the power elite.

There is accordingly reason to suspect—but by the nature of the case, no proof—that the power elite is not altogether 'surfaced.' There is nothing hidden about it, although its activities are not publicized. As an elite, it is not organized, although its members often know one another, seem quite naturally to work together, and share many organizations in common. There is nothing conspiratorial about it, although its decisions are often publicly unknown and its mode of operation manipulative rather than explicit.

It is not that the elite 'believe in' a compact elite behind the scenes and a mass down below. It is not put in that language. It is just that the people are of necessity confused and must, like trusting children, place all the new world of foreign policy and strategy and executive action in the hands of experts. It is just that everyone knows somebody has got to run the show, and that somebody usually does. Others do not really care anyway, and besides, they do not know how. So the gap between the two types gets wider. . . .

NOTES

1. Jacob Burckhardt, *Force and Freedom* (New York: Pantheon Books, 1943), pp. 303 ff.

2. Cf. Hans Gerth and C. Wright Mills, *Character and Social Structure* (New York: Harcourt, Brace, 1953), pp. 457 ff.

3. The statistical idea of choosing some value and calling those who have the most of it an elite derives, in modern times, from the Italian economist, Pareto, who puts the central point in this way: 'Let us assume that in every branch of human activity each individual is given an index which stands as a sign of his capacity, very much the way grades are given in the various subjects in examinations in school. The highest type of lawyer, for instance, will be given 10. The man who does not get a client will be given 1—reserving zero for the man who is an out-and-out idiot. To the man who has made his millions—honestly or dishonestly as the case may be—we will give 10. To the man who has earned his thousands we will give 6; to such as just manage to keep out of the poor-house, 1, keeping zero for those who get in . . . So let us make a class of people who have the highest indices in their branch of activity, and to that class give the name of *elite.*' Vilfredo Pareto, *The Mind and Society* (New York: Harcourt, Brace, 1935), par. 2027 and 2031. Those who follow this approach end up not with one elite, but with a number corresponding to the number of values they select. Like many rather abstract ways of reasoning, this one is useful because it forces us to think in a clear-cut way. For a skillful use of this approach, see the work of Harold D. Lasswell, in particular, *Politics: Who Gets What, When, How* (New York: McGraw-Hill, 1936); and for a more systematic use, H. D. Lasswell and Abraham Kaplan, *Power and Society* (New Haven: Yale University Press, 1950).

4. The conception of the elite as members of a top social stratum, is, of course, in line with the prevailing common-sense view of stratification. Technically, it is closer to 'status group' than to 'class,' and has been very well stated by Joseph A. Schumpeter, 'Social Classes in an Ethically Homogeneous Environment,' *Imperialism and Social Classes* (New York: Augustus M. Kelley, Inc., 1951), pp. 133 ff., especially pp. 137–47. Cf. also his *Capitalism, Socialism and Democracy*, 3rd ed. (New York: Harper, 1950), Part II. For the distinction between class and status groups, see *From Max Weber: Essays in Sociology* (trans. and ed. by Gerth and Mills; New York: Oxford University Press, 1946). For an analysis of Pareto's conception of the elite compared with Marx's conception of classes, as well as data on France, see Raymond Aron, 'Social Structure and Ruling Class,' *British Journal of Sociology*, vol. I, nos. 1 and 2 (1950).

5. The most popular essay in recent years which defines the elite and the mass in terms of a morally evaluated character-type is probably José Ortega y Gasset's, *The Revolt of the Masses*, 1932 (New York: New American Library, Mentor Edition, 1950), esp. pp. 91 ff.

6. 'The American elite' is a confused and confusing set of images, and yet when we hear or when we use such words as Upper Class, Big Shot, Top Brass, The Millionaire Club, The High and The Mighty, we feel at least vaguely that we know what they mean, and often do. What we do not often do, however, is connect each of these images with the others; we make little effort to form a coherent picture in our minds of the elite as a whole. Even when, very occasionally, we do try to do this, we usually come to believe that it is indeed no 'whole'; that, like our images of it, there is no one elite, but many, and that they are not really connected with one another. What we must realize is that until we *do* try to see it as a whole, perhaps our impression that it may not be is a result merely of our lack of analytic rigor and sociological imagination.

The first conception defines the elite in terms of the sociology of institutional position and the social structure these institutions form; the second, in terms of the statistics of selected values; the third, in terms of membership in a clique-like set of people; and the fourth, in terms of the morality of certain personality types. Or, put into inelegant shorthand: what they head up, what they have, what they belong to, who they really are.

In this chapter, as in this book as a whole, I have taken as generic the first view—of the elite defined in terms of institutional position—and have located the other views within it. This straightforward conception of the elite has one practical and two theoretical advantages. The practical advantage is that it seems the easiest and the most concrete 'way into' the whole problem—if only because a good deal of information is more or less readily available for sociological reflection about such circles and institutions.

But the theoretical advantages are much more important. The institutional or structural definition, first of all, does not force us to prejudge by definition that we ought properly to leave open for investigation. The elite conceived morally, for example, as people having a certain type of character is not an ultimate definition, for apart from being rather morally arbitrary, it leads us immediately to ask *why* these people have this or that sort of character. Accordingly, we should leave open the type of characters which the members of the elite in fact turn out to have, rather than by definition select them in terms of one type or another. In a similar way, we do not want, by mere definition, to prejudge whether or not the elite are conscious members of a social class. The second theoretical advantage of defining the elite in terms of major institutions, which I hope this book as a whole makes clear, is the fact that it allows us to fit the other three conceptions of the elite into place in a systematic way: (1) The institutional positions men occupy throughout their lifetime determine their chances to get and to hold selected values. (2) The kind of psychological beings they become is in large part determined by the values they thus experience and the institutional roles they play. (3) Finally, whether or not they come to feel that they belong to a select social class, and whether or not they act according to what they hold to be its interests—these are also matters in large part determined by their institutional position, and in turn, the select values they possess and the characters they acquire.

7. As in the case, quite notably, of Gaetano Mosca, *The Ruling Class* (New York: McGraw-Hill, 1939). For a sharp analysis of Mosca, see Fritz Morstein Marx, 'The Bureaucratic State,' *Review of Politics*, vol. I, 1939, pp. 457 ff. Cf. also Mills, 'On Intellectual Craftsmanship,' April 1952, mimeographed, Columbia College, February 1955.

P A R T T W O

Making Public Policy

How Public Policy Is Made

Stella Z. Theodoulou

Political scientists who study the policy process attempt to provide a framework that will guide students from the emergence of a problem to the final enactment of a policy to address that problem. Such a framework for policy development shows the process to be one of sequential stages of activity. A survey of the literature shows that there is little disagreement about what the stages are, though some political scientists are attempting to move beyond the traditional framework of stages.[1] Where most scholars disagree is on the impact each stage has upon the next, and on what should and should not occur at each stage. The commonly agreed-on stages are

1. *Problem Recognition and Issue Identification*: This stage draws the attention of policy makers to a problem that might require governmental action; problems, if legitimate, then become issues.
2. *Agenda Setting*: The issue is given the status of a serious matter.
3. *Policy Formulation*: Proposals are developed for dealing with issues.
4. *Policy Adoption*: Efforts are made to obtain enough support for a proposal to make it to the government's stated policy.
5. *Policy Implementation*: The policy mandate is aimed at through public programs and the federal bureaucracy, often with citizen, state, and local government cooperation.

6.   *Policy Analysis and Evaluation*: This involves examining the consequences of policy actions, including whether the policy has worked.

The process should be viewed as a dynamic ongoing cycle. That is to say, once policy has been enacted to deal with a problem the process does not stop; that policy should be constantly monitored in order to see not only how it is operating but whether it is in fact doing what it is supposed to. The following discusses the process, context, and structure of public policy development.

THE PROCESS OF POLICY MAKING: ISSUE IDENTIFICATION AND AGENDA FORMATION

Where do issues come from? Why are some issues ignored? How does an issue gain access to the political system? These are crucial questions to answer when looking at the first stages of the policy process cycle. Before we see how the issue agenda is set, we must determine exactly what is meant by the term "agenda." Generally the issue agenda is the list of subjects or problems to which governmental and nongovernmental actors are paying serious attention at any given point in time.[2] Agenda setting is the narrowing of the set of issues that the actors will focus on and address.

There are different types of agendas. They can be highly general, such as a list of items that occupy the attention of the president, or they can be highly specialized, such as the agendas of congressional subcommittees. According to Cobb and Elder, agendas can be classified into two main types.[3] The first such agenda is the systemic agenda. This covers all issues that are generally recognized to deserve public attention and are matters within the government's legitimate jurisdiction. An example of such a matter would be education. The second type of agenda is the institutional agenda. Cobb and Elder state that this involves all issues explicitly up for active and serious consideration by the authoritative decision makers, for example, actual congressional bills.[4] The institutional agenda is less abstract and narrower in scope than the systemic agenda, and the priorities of both do not necessarily correspond. Often there is considerable discrepancy between the two agendas.

The "normal" agenda sequence is for issues to arrive on the systemic agenda before they are put onto the institutional agenda. This creates a problem for policy makers and other involved actors in that, if the lag time between moving from the systemic to the institutional agenda is too great, the issue could fall apart and prove critical to the political system. The viability of the political system is a function of its ability to cope with the lag between these two agendas. It is also important to note that both agendas have their own sets of biases and are therefore subject to conflict.

Why do some issues move onto the agenda while other issues are ignored? The chances of an issue proceeding to the agenda depends on how it is generally perceived within the political system. If an issue is thought to be a conflict or a crisis, if an issue is advocated by a visible interest group, or if an issue is backed by the bureaucracy, there is a good chance that the issue will move on to the agenda. Such perceptions act as triggers.[5] Thus agenda setting begins when decision makers first recognize a problem, feel the need for government to address it, and start to search for a solution.

The agenda-setting process is complex and multifaceted. In order to comprehend it, one must look not only at the dynamics of the process but also at the interactions and roles of the various governmental and nongovernmental participants. John Kingdon is an author who provides such a framework,[6] using four organizing concepts to form a model of agenda building. First, agenda setting should be viewed as a garbage can that consists of the coupling of streams of problems, politics, solutions, participants, and choice opportunities.[7] Next, policy ideas are recombined and incubated over the years in "policy communities" of specialists and experts. Third, "policy entrepreneurs" provide the linkage between ideas and decision makers. Such individuals are advocates who are willing to spend their resources in the promotion of an idea; they might be elected officials, civil servants, lobbyists, academics, or journalists. Finally, there are structures of opportunity for ideas to become part of the agenda. Kingdon refers to such structures as "policy windows," which "policy entrepreneurs" must take advantage of. In Kingdon's model, policy windows open and close as a result of changes in the problem and political streams.

POLICY FORMULATION AND ADOPTION

Policy formulation is the creation of relevant and supportable courses of action for dealing with problems and does not always result in the adoption of policy.[8] Because a problem or issue arrives on the agenda, it does not necessarily mean that the government will act effectively to resolve it.[9] Various actors are involved in policy formulation, including legislators, the president and his advisors, the various departments and agencies of the executive branch, and interest groups.[10] Similarly, at the state and local level of policy making, legislators, executives, agency staff, and interest groups are involved.

Formulation is a two-step process. First, a general decision has to be made about what, if anything, is to be done about a problem. Second, if something is to be done, a policy has to be drafted that, if adopted, will carry out identified objectives. For policy formulation to be successful, it is essential that policy proposals be adoptable. In other words, policy proposals have to be formulated that will be acceptable not only to the people who make policy decisions but also to most other actors. Thus, it is often the case that decision makers are influenced by what they need to win policy adoption. Certain provisions will be included and others dropped, depending upon what builds support for the proposed policy. The more actors involved in the adoption process, the more difficult it is to get an "acceptable" proposal. The process of building support for adoption can be understood as policy legitimation.[11] Policy adoption is the act of choosing which policy alternative will be finally chosen as the preferred course of action to meet the problem.

POLICY IMPLEMENTATION

Implementation starts after the decision to adopt a particular course of action is made and ends successfully when the goals sought by the policy are achieved and the costs are within reasonable expectations. Thus implementation can be defined as the directed change that follows a policy adoption. Often a decision by government to "do something" is seen by the general public as the end of the matter. However, in practice, the policy decision that emerges from the formulation and adoption stages sets off a long and complex chain—the implementation process—where any multitude of things can go wrong, including, for example, judicial constraints, abandonment by the public, and resistance by those who must alter their patterns of behavior so as to comply with the policy.[12] Moreover, there is a tendency for implementation to become largely bureaucratic and rule laden.[13] Thus it is not uncommon for the original policy to be distorted, for the original goals to be forgotten, and for bureaucrats to substitute their own objectives as they implement policies. Thus public policies often fail to have their intended effects due to the dynamics of the implementation process.

Until quite recently relatively little attention was paid to the process of implementation by governments and academics; this neglect, however, is being altered by an increasing body of literature that can be referred to as implementation theory.[14] Much of the theory attempts to build "perfect" models of implementation that outline the conditions that must be met for successful actualization of policy.[15] One can also find in the literature various perspectives as to what implementation involves. Political scientists may differ in their perceptions but all agree that implementation is, in many respects, an opaque phenomenon, as its most consequential characteristics are difficult to detect and as it is a pliant process that can undergo rapid transformation.

Majone and Wildavsky argue that implementation should be seen as evolution.[16] They conclude that it is shaped by the original policy making from which it springs; therefore, policies consist of a variety of goals, ideas, and dispositions, each connected in some disarray. On the other hand, Sabatier and Mazmanian see implementation as a composite of statutory structures, problem tractability, and nonstatutory forces.[17] These authors argue that there are several categories of variables embedded in the implementation process and these affect the achievement of policy objectives. The variables include social, economic, and technological conditions and the target groups that are involved. According to another group of theorists, implementation should be viewed as planning, hierarchy, and control.[18] This requires that administrative structures must be hierarchically organized to ensure that the higher levels of administration can ensure effective implementation by not allowing the actual day-to-day administrators to implement as they see fit; rather they must implement as they are told to. This necessitates organizational control, which is accountable to the "creators" of policy. One final way to see implementation is, as Bardach argues, the playing out of many loosely interrelated games,[19] in which the players all have goals and strategies and the arena is uncertain and therefore so is the outcome. This perspective views implementation as political with a backdrop of constant accommodation and bargaining.

Just as there are different types of agendas, different types of implementation can also occur.[20] The first such type is programmed implementation, which tries to eliminate or control the problems and pitfalls that await implementation by thorough, explicit programming of implementation procedures. Programmed implementation places high value on clarity and rationality and rests on the assumption that the problems that plague implementation are the result of (1) ambiguities of policy goals, (2) the involvement of an excessive number of actors, (3) overlapping jurisdictions of authorities, (4) misperceived interests, and (5) conflicts. The second type of implementation that can occur is adaptive implementation, which tries to improve the process by allowing for adjustments to the original policy mandate as events unfold. In contrast to programmed implementation, clarity and specification are seen as barriers to implementation, for they produce rigidity in the face of shifting political realities.

The last type of implementation that can occur is premeditated nonimplementation: behavior deliberately aimed at preventing implementation from occurring. Such behavior ensures that the policy will never be more than partially accomplished. Usually, because of the multidimensional nature of the policy process, implementation is a combination of the programmed and adaptive types, though premeditated nonimplementation often occurs because policy goals and objectives are vague.

When asking who is responsible for implementation, one should realize that it is not the focus of policy makers, who are in reality only moderately interested in it. Their level of interest is dictated by the fact that they perceive implementation to be (1) too costly—politically, timewise, and electorally; and (2) too low in visibility and never living up to its promises. Thus the major actor in implementation is the bureaucracy; indeed, implementation can be viewed as the bureaucratization of policy.

POLICY ANALYSIS AND EVALUATION

From the discussion here it is evident that policy does not always achieve its intended objectives and at times even produces unintended consequences. The reasons why policy does not always do what it is supposed to are multiple. Some have already been discussed, but briefly, we can cite additional reasons, including unclear goals, an inability to see how to achieve those goals, adversarial conditions within the system, and ambiguous criteria for success. What this dictates is that policies be examined to see how they are working. It should be noted that evaluation does not have to wait until an actual policy has been implemented; it can and does occur throughout the policy process. Evaluation can be undertaken by a variety of governmental actors as well as nongovernmental actors, including the media, academics, and interest groups.

Michael Patton has concluded that there are over one hundred types of evaluation approaches.[21] All of these, however, can basically be categorized as one of two distinct but interrelated categories of evaluation. The first, process evaluation, looks at the extent to which a particular policy is implemented according to its stated guidelines. This type acknowledges that a policy and its impact may be modified, elaborated upon, or even negated during implementation. The second, impact evaluation, is concerned with examining the extent to which a policy causes a change in the intended direction. This requires the specification of operationally defined policy goals, delineation of criteria of success, and measurement of progress toward the stated goals. Various methodological tools have been developed to carry out evaluation research.[22]

When evaluation decisions are made, it is usually through the consideration of all the available information. One of the ways to deal with this information and to make decisions as to which course of action to take is through a special form of evaluation, policy analysis. The analysis of a policy takes place through the analysis and comparison of a set of criteria.[23] It provides decision makers with a technique to help weigh the relative merits of one policy over another. Analysis can be conducted before or after a policy has been implemented.[24] It can be done to anticipate alternative policies' possible results so that a choice can be made between the various options or it can be used to describe the results and impact of existing policies.

Thus policy analysis is basically a process by which decision makers can identify and evaluate alternative policies. The term was first used by Charles Lindblom in 1958 and in subsequent years has been redefined in various ways.[25] One can differentiate policy analysis from both policy formulation and evaluation.

Policy analysis differs from policy formulation in its emphasis on evaluating alternative policies rather than on concentrating on how policies should be formulated. Policy formulation is, however, relevant to policy analysis, because good analysis requires an awareness of how policies are adopted. Without such an awareness there is a tendency to recommend policies that stand little chance of adoption. In relation to policy evaluation, policy analysis differs mainly in its emphasis on evaluating decisions before they are reached rather than afterwards. Also, policy analysis takes policy goals as givens and discusses how they can best be achieved, rather than taking, as evaluation does, the policy as a given and discussing its effects.

THE CONTEXT OF POLICY

Like so much of politics, the process of policy making cannot be divorced from the context in which it is made. It is crucial to an understanding of how certain policies prevail over others. The overall context of contemporary public policy is made up of a number of individual contexts.[26]

The first such individual context is the history of past policies. In short, the policy history in a specific issue area is an important contextual limit on new policy options because policy changes take place in a context provided by past policies. Environmental factors form the second context. From the environment come demands for policy action, support for both the overall political system and individual policy proposals, and limitations upon what policy makers can do. The environmental context is a composite of cultural, demographic, economic, social, and ideological factors. Common values and beliefs help to determine the demands made upon policy makers, and if such values and beliefs are commonly held then greater public acceptance for policies can be won by decision makers. Public opinion lays the boundaries and direction of policy while the social system attunes policy makers to the social forces that are salient in terms of both demands and supports. The interaction and interrelationship between the political arena and the economic system are given. Those who possess economic power through their control of economic resources also possess undeniable political power, which raises their demands and support for policies to a level of priority. The institutional context, which involves both the formal governmental institutions and structural arrangements of the system, also affects the formulation, implementation, and substance of public policies. Finally, the ideological conflict between liberals and conservatives over the nature of governmental action affects policy debates in all areas. The level and type of government intervention is the framework of all policy.

A final context is the budgetary process, for few public policies can be implemented without public expenditure. In turn, public expenditure cannot take place unless governments raise finance through taxation charges or through borrowing. This fact of life is the basis for the complicated political process of deciding resource allocation, which in turn gives rise to an equally complex process of bargaining and compromise between government and groups within society. One need only tune in to any daily news broadcast to recognize the pressure put upon government by various societal groups to spend more public money on their particular policy area. The demand for spending is eternal, although the willingness to pay for it through taxation is not. Pliatzky argues that on top of this the process cannot ignore ideological concerns and economic theory.[27]

The budgetary process is a highly politicized one in which bargains are struck, targets are not met, deviations are made, and large numbers of actors are involved. Additionally, it is heavily influenced by the need to control public sector borrowing requirements and the deficit.[28] Heclo and Wildavsky note the importance of the "political climate" over spending policies.[29]

THE STRUCTURE OF POLICY MAKING

The debate over structure can be seen as a discussion on how decisions are made. It is essentially a choice between rationality and incrementalism. Rationality is a major concern within the study of policy making.[30] One of the basic axioms of the rational choice approach is that issues and problems are approached in a well-ordered sequence. Problems are identified and isolated; then the goals, values, and objectives of pertinent solutions to the problems are identified and ranked according to saliency. Next, various alternative solutions are formulated and weighted, and finally an alternative is chosen by decision makers that will be the most appropriate means to secure described ends.

Incrementalism as an approach is summarized in Lindblom's *"The 'Science' of Muddling Through."*[31] The title given to the piece underlies that while "muddling through" is usually seen as a criticism of policy making, as a process it may have its own intrinsic merits. Lindblom outlines incrementalism as present oriented and frequently remedial in nature, focusing on making necessary changes and adaptations in the existing practices. Therefore, incrementalism can be viewed as a fine-tuning of existing policy. It is decision making through what Lindblom refers to as small or incremental steps. The incremental approach is seen as a simpler and more realistic way of making policy, for it is not a comprehensive and synoptic type of response, as rationalist decision making is viewed. In his subsequent article *"Still Muddling, Not Yet Through,"* Lindblom argues that it is now textbook orthodoxy to accept that in policy making only small or incremental steps are ordinarily possible.[32] He goes on to argue:

> But most people, including many policy analysts and policy makers, want to separate the "ought" from the "is." They think we should try to do better. So do I. What remains then? . . . Many critics of incrementalism believe that doing better usually means turning away from incrementalism. Incrementalists believe that for complex problem solving it usually means practicing incrementalism more skillfully and turning away from it only rarely.[33]

This is a defense for the designed, deliberate, and conscious incompleteness of analysis that is incrementalism over the rationalist approach. Dempster and Wildavsky, who support incrementalism, also spell out that different types of incrementalism can occur.[34]

The major difference between rationality and incrementalism is that the rationality approach views policy making as comprehensive. A further difference is that incrementalism has built into it the allowance for multiple actors with competing values. In *"The 'Science' of Muddling Through,"* Lindblom stresses that one of the features of "successive" limited comparisons—incrementalism—is that the test of a good policy is that analysts can agree on it, without having to agree on ultimate goals. Some twenty years later Lindblom was still arguing that social "decisions" arise out of someone's particular understanding.

CONCLUSION

The discussion here has tried to outline what the literature commonly perceives to be the process, context, and structure of contemporary policy making. The process should be viewed as one of struggle and accommodation among many actors. Ultimately decisions will be made and differences among competing interests resolved by authoritative decision makers in a process of accommodation, bargaining, and compromise.

NOTES

1. See Paul Sabatier, "Toward Better Theories of the Policy Process," *PS: Political Science and Politics* (June 1991), pp. 147–156.

2. James E. Anderson, *Public Policymaking* (Boston: Houghton Mifflin, 1986), chapter 3; Lawrence G. Brewster, *The Public Agenda* (New York: St Martin's Press, 1984), pp. 1–12; Robert Eyestone, *From Social Issues to Public Policy* (New York: Wiley, 1978), chapter 1.

3. See Roger W. Cobb and Charles D. Elder "Issues and Agendas" (this reader, part 2, reading 12).

4. Cobb and Elder, "Issues and Agendas" (this reader, part 2, reading 12).

5. Cobb and Elder refer to such mechanisms as triggering devices (this reader, part 2, reading 12).

6. See John W. Kingdon, "Agenda Setting" (this reader, part 2, reading 13).

7. This is a modification of the model described by M. Cohen and others. "A Garbage Can Model of Organizational Choice," *Administrative Science Quarterly*, 17 (March 1972), 1–25.

8. Anderson, *Public Policy Making*, p. 93.

9. Peter Bachrach and Morton S. Baratz refer to this as nondecisions. *Power and Poverty* (New York: Oxford University Press, 1970), p. 44.

10. Anderson, *Public Policy Making*, pp. 94–98.

11. Peters, *American Public Policy* (3rd ed.) (Chatham, N.J.: Chatham House, 1993), chapter 4.

12. L. A. Gunn, "Why Is Implementation So Difficult?" *Management Services in Government*, 33, no. 4 (November 1978), 169–176.

13. Anthony Downs, *Inside Bureaucracy* (Boston: Little, Brown, 1967).

14. S. Barrett and C. Fudge (eds.), *Policy and Action* (London: Methuen, 1981); C. C. Hood, *The Limitations of Administration* (London: Wiley, 1976); R. S. Montjoy and L. J. O'Toole, "Toward a Theory of Policy Implementation," *Public Administration Review*, 34, no. 5 (1979), 465–476; Jeffrey Pressman and Aaron Wildavsky, *Implementation* (Berkley: University of California Press, 1973); Paul A. Sabatier and Daniel A. Mazmanian, *Implementation and Public Policy* (Chicago: Scott, Foresman, 1983); Clarence N. Stone, "Efficiency versus Social Learning: A Reconsideration of the Implementation Process," *Policy Studies Review*, 4, no. 3 (February 1985), 484–495; D. S. Van Meter and C. E. Van Horn, "The Implementation Process; A Conceptual Framework," *Administration Science Quarterly*, 6, no. 4 (1975), 445–488.

15. Brian Hogwood and others, *Policy Analysis for the Real World* (Oxford: Oxford University Press, 1984), pp. 199–206. These authors draw upon several writers on implementation to list ten preconditions that have to be satisfied for successful implementation.

16. Giandomenico Majone and Aaron Wildavsky, "Implementation as Evolution" (this reader, part 2, reading 17).

17. Paul Sabatier and Daniel Mazmanian, "A Conceptual Framework of the Implementation Process"(this reader, part 2, reading 18).

18. Rufus Marshall Browning and others, "Implementation and Political Change In Effective Policy Implementation," in *Effective Policy Implementation*, eds. Daniel Mazmanian and Paul Sabatier, (Lexington Mass.: D. C. Heath, 1981); James G. March and Zuv Shapira, "Behavioral Decision Theory and Organizational Decision Theory," in G. Ungson and D Braunstein (eds.), *Decision Making: An Interdisciplinary Inquiry* (Boston: Kent, 1982).

19. Eugene Bardach, "The Implementation Game" (this reader, part 2, reading 16).

20. Paul Berman, "Thinking about Programmed and Adaptive Implementation," in *Why Policies Succeed or Fail*, ed. Helen Ingram and Dean Mann (Newbury Park, Calif.: Sage, 1980).

21. Michael Quinn Patton, *Creative Evaluation* (Newbury Park, Calif.: Sage, 1981).

22. See David Nachmias, "The Role of Evaluation in Public Policy" (this reader, part 2, reading 19); Peter H. Rossi and Howard E. Freeman, *Evaluation: A Systematic Approach* (4th ed.) (Newbury Park, Calif.: Sage, 1989); Carol H. Weiss, *Evaluation Research: Methods for Assessing Program Effectiveness* (Englewood Cliffs, N.J.: Prentice-Hall, 1972).

23. See Stuart Nagel, "Trends in Policy Analysis" (this reader, part 2, reading 20).

24. For a discussion of the various types of policy analysis, see Carl V. Patton and David Sawicki, *Basic Methods of Policy Analysis and Planning* (2nd ed.) (Englewood Cliffs, N.J.: Prentice-Hall, 1993), pp. 23–25.

25. Charles E. Lindblom, "Policy Analysis," *American Economic Review*, 48 (June 1958), 298–312.

26. This discussion of the institutional, historical, and environmental contexts draws extensively upon the work of Clarke E. Cochran and others, *American Public Policy* (4th ed.) (New York: St. Martin's Press, 1993), chapter 1; and James Anderson and others, *Public Policy and Politics in America* (Monterey: Brooks/Cole, 1984), pp. 7–16.

27. See L. Pliatzky, *Getting and Spending: Public Expenditure, Employment and Inflation* (2nd ed.) (Oxford: Basil Blackwell, 1984).

28. Irene S. Rubin, "The Politics of Public Budgets" (this reader, part 2, reading 21).

29. Hugh Heclo and Aaron Wildavsky, *The Private Government of Public Money* (2nd ed.) (London: Macmillan, 1981), pp. 35–36.

30. See Paul R. Schulman, "Nonincremental Policy Making" (this reader, part 2, reading 15).

31. See Charles E. Lindblom, "The Science of 'Muddling Through'" (this reader, part 2, reading 14).

32. Charles E. Lindblom, "Still Muddling, Not Yet Through," *Public Administration Review*, 39 (1979) 517–526.

33. Lindblom, "Still Muddling, Not Yet Through," p 517.

34. M. A. H. Dempster and Aaron Wildavsky, "On Change: Or There Is No Magic Size for Increment," *Political Studies*, 27, no. 3 (September 1979), 371–389.

ADDITIONAL SUGGESTED READING

ANDERSON, CHARLES W. "The Place of Principles in Policy Analysis." *American Political Science Review*, 73 (September 1979), 711–723.

BAUER, RAYMOND A., and GERGEN, KENNETH J. (eds.). *The Study of Policy Formation*. New York: Free Press, 1968.

BERKOWITZ, EDWARD D. "History, Public Policy and Reality." *Journal of Social History*, 16 (Fall 1984), 79–89.

BOVBJERG, RANDALL R. "Nurturing Policy Ideas." *Journal of Policy Analysis and Management*, 8 (Spring 1989), 329–332.

BREWER, G. D., and DE LEON, P. *The Foundations of Policy Analysis*. Homewood, Ill.: Dorsey Press, 1983.

BURSTEIN, PAUL. "Policy Domains: Organization, Culture, and Public Policy Outcomes." *Annual Review of Sociology*, 17 (1991), 327–350.

DYE, THOMAS R. *Policy Analysis*. University: University of Alabama Press, 1976.

EDWARDS, GEORGE C. III. *Implementing Public Policy*. Washington, D.C.: CQ Press, 1980.

ELDER, CHARLES D., and COBB, ROGER W. *The Political Use of Symbols*. New York: Longman, 1983.

FROHOCK, FRED M. *Public Policy: Scope and Logic*. Englewood Cliffs, N.J.: Prentice-Hall, 1979.

GOGGIN, MALCOLM L. *Policy Design and the Politics of Implementation*. Knoxville: University of Tennessee Press, 1988.

HAM, C., and HILL, M. *The Policy Process in the Modern Capitalist State*. Brighton, Sussex, England: Wheatsheaf, 1984.

JENKINS, B., and GRAY, A. "Bureaucratic Politics and Power," *Political Studies*, 31, no. 2 (June 1980), 177–193.

JONES, CHARLES O. *An Introduction to the Study of Public Policy*. Monterey, Calif.: Brooks/Cole, 1984.

LINDBLOM, CHARLES E. *The Intelligence of Democracy*. New York: Free Press, 1965.

———, and Woodhouse, L. G. *The Policy-Making Process* (3rd ed.). Englewood Cliffs, N.J.: Prentice-Hall, 1993.

LINDER, STEPHEN H., and Peters, B. Guy. "Implementation as a Guide to Policy Formulation." *International Review of Administrative Services*, 55 (1989), 631–652.

LINEBERRY, ROBERT L. *American Public Policy: What Government Does and What Difference It Makes*. New York: HarperCollins, 1977.

MCCONNELL, GRANT. *Private Power and American Democracy*. New York: Knopf, 1966.

NACHMIAS, DAVID. *Public Policy Evaluation: Approaches and Methods*. New York: St. Martin's Press, 1979.

NATHAN, RICHARD P. *Social Science in Government: Uses and Misuses*. New York: Basic Books, 1989.

PETERS, B. GUY, and HOGWOOD, BRIAN W. "In Search of the Issue-Attention Cycle." *The Journal of Politics*, 47 (1985), 238–253.

RIPLEY, RANDAL B., and FRANKLIN, GRACE E. *Bureacracy and Policy Implementation* (2nd ed.). Homewood, Ill.: Dorsey Press, 1986.

RODRIK, DANI, and ZECKLIAUSER, RICHARD. "The Dilemma of Government Responsiveness." *Journal of Policy Analysis and Management*, 7 (1988), 601–620.

SIMON, HERBERT. *Models of Bounded Rationality, Vols. 1 and 2*. Cambridge, Mass.: MIT Press, 1982.

SMITH, T. ALEXANDER. "A Phenomenology of the Policy Process." *International Journal of Comparative Sociology*, 23 (March/June 1982), 1–16.

STONE, ALAN E., and HARPHAM, EDWARD J. *The Political Economy of Public Policy*. Newbury Park, Calif.: Sage, 1982.

STONE, DEBRA. *Policy Paradox and Political Reason*. Boston: Little, Brown, 1988.

WADE, LARRY L. *The Elements of Public Policy*. Columbus, Ohio: Merrill, 1972.

WILDAVSKY, AARON. *The Art and Craft of Policy Analysis*. London: Macmillan, 1980.

WILLIAM, WALTER L. *Social Policy Analysis and Research*. New York: American Elsevier, 1971.

---

12 Issues and Agendas

Roger W. Cobb and Charles D. Elder

WHAT IS AN ISSUE? WHAT MAKES AN ISSUE?

. . . An issue is a conflict between two or more identifiable groups over procedural or substantive matters relating to the distribution of positions or resources. Generally, there are four means by which issues are created. The most common method is the manufacturing of an issue by one or more of the contending parties who perceive an unfavorable bias in the distribution of positions or resources. For example, in 1950 truckers in Pennsylvania thought the railroads had an inherent advantage in carrying freight over long distances and sought to create an issue to redress this imbalance.[1] Such initiators are labeled "readjustors."

From Roger W. Cobb and Charles D. Elder, *Participation in American Politics: the Dynamics of Agenda Building* (Baltimore/London: Johns Hopkins University Press, 1983), pp. 82–93. Reprinted by permission.

Another form of issue creation can be traced to a person or group who man-ufacture an issue for their own gain; for example, individuals who want to run for public office and are looking for an issue to advance their cause. Such individuals may be labeled "exploiters." As Herbert Blumer has written:

> The gaining of sympathizers or members rarely occurs through a mere combination of a pre-established appeal and a pre-established individual psychological bent on which it is brought to bear. Instead the prospective sympathizer has to be aroused, nurtured and directed.[2]

Hans Toch echoes a similar sentiment when he writes:

> People are brought into social movements through the skills of leaders and agitators rather than because of pre-existing problems. . . . Appeals seem to originate with people who are primarily interested in other ends than the solution of the problems of potential members.[3]

Another means of issue initiation is through an unanticipated event. Such events could be called "circumstantial reactors." Examples include the develop-ment of an oil slick off the California coast near Santa Barbara in early 1969 that led to a reconsideration of the whole question of offshore drilling regulations. Other examples are the assassination of President Kennedy, which led to the gun control issue, and Eisenhower's heart attack in the mid-1950's, which raised the question of presidential disability.

Issues can be generated by persons or groups who have no positions or re-sources to gain for themselves. Often, they merely acquire a psychological sense of well-being for doing what they believe is in the public interest. These initiators might be called "do-gooders." The efforts to support Biafran relief programs fall in this category.

The above categories are not mutually exclusive, as an individual or group may have more than one motive for a particular action. For example, some people supported civil rights legislation because they felt it was humanitarian, while oth-ers supported it because they sought personal or collective gains.

Triggering devices.   At least two classes of triggering mechanisms, or un-foreseen events, help shape issues that will be defined by the initiators. These can be subdivided into internal and external events that correspond to the domestic and foreign spheres.

Within the internal subdivision, there are five types of triggering devices. The first is a natural catastrophe, such as a mine cave-in, air inversion, flooding, and fire. The second is an unanticipated human event, such as a spontaneous riot, assassination of public officials, air hijackings, and murder of private individuals. The third is a technological change in the environment that creates heretofore undiscussed questions. It might involve mass transportation, air and water pollu-tion, or air travel congestion. The fourth category is an actual imbalance, or bias, in the distribution of resources leading to such things as civil rights protest and union strikes.[4] A fifth type is ecological change, such as population explosion and black migration to Northern cities.

There are four types of external trigger mechanisms. The first is an act of war or military violence involving the United States as a direct combatant. Examples include the Vietnam war, the Pueblo seizure, and the dropping of atomic bombs on Hiroshima. The second category includes innovations in weapons technology involving such things as arms control, the Hotline between the Kremlin and the White House, and the deployment of an anti-ballistic system. The third type is an international conflict in which the United States is not a direct combatant, such as the conflicts in the Middle East and the Congo. The final category involves changing world alignment patterns that may affect American membership in the United Nations, troop commitments in the North Atlantic Treaty Organization, and the American role in the Organization of American States.

Issue initiation and trigger mechanisms.   The formation of an issue is dependent on the dynamic interplay between the initiator and the trigger device. This can be seen in the following diagram:

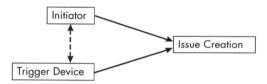

For example, a mine disaster itself does not create an issue. Many times in the past such an event has occurred with no ameliorative action. A link must be made between a grievance (or a triggering event) and an initiator who converts the problem into an issue for a private or a public reason.

In a system perspective, the inputs consist of the initiator and the event, or triggering mechanism, that transform the problem into an issue. The output is the agenda, which will be the focus of the next section. Transforming an issue into an agenda item will be the focus of succeeding chapters.

AGENDAS: WHAT ARE THEY?

In general terms, we have identified two basic types of political agendas. The first of these is the systemic agenda for political controversy. *The systemic agenda consists of all issues that are commonly perceived by members of the political community as meriting public attention and as involving matters within the legitimate jurisdiction of existing governmental authority.* Every local, state, and national political community will have a systemic agenda. The systemic agenda of the larger community may subsume items from the systemic agendas of subsidiary communities, but the two agendas will not necessarily correspond. For example, the systemic agenda of Boston may include items on the national agenda of controversy, such as pollution and crime in the streets, but will also include such items as the need for a new sports arena.

There are three prerequisites for an issue to obtain access to the systemic agenda: (1) widespread attention or at least awareness; (2) shared concern of a sizeable portion of the public that some type of action is required; and (3) a shared perception that the matter is an appropriate concern of some governmental unit and falls within the bounds of its authority. The terms "shared concern" and "shared perception" refer to the prevailing climate of opinion, which will be conditioned by the dominant norms, values, and ideology of a community. An issue requires the recognition of only a major portion of the polity, not the entire citizenry.

For an item or an issue to acquire public recognition, its supporters must have either access to the mass media or the resources necessary to reach people. They may require more than money and manpower; often the use of action rhetoric is essential. For example, use of terms such as *communist-inspired* or *anti-American* is a useful verbal ploy in attracting a larger audience than the original adherents of a cause.

In addition to gaining popular recognition, the issue must be perceived by a large number of people as both being subject to remedial action and requiring such action. In other words, action must be considered not only possible, but also necessary for the resolution of the issue. To foster such popular conviction, the mobilization of a significant number of groups or persons will normally be required.

Often, the fate of an issue in gaining systemic agenda status will hinge on whether or not it can be defined as being within the purview of legitimate governmental action. Perhaps one of the most devastating tactics that may be used to prevent an issue from reaching the systemic agenda is to deny that it falls within the bounds of governmental authority. For example, equal access to public accommodations was kept off the systemic agenda for some time because opponents successfully argued that the grievance fell outside the proper bounds of governmental authority.

The second type of agenda is the institutional, governmental, or formal agenda, which may be defined as *that set of items explicitly up for the active and serious consideration of authoritative decision-makers*. Therefore, any set of items up before any governmental body at the local, state, or national level will constitute an institutional agenda.

Two clarifications are in order regarding key terms in the above definition of a formal agenda. "Explicitly" refers to an issue involving action or policy alternatives or involving simply the identification of a problem requiring some action. An example of the former would be a proposal to raise the minimum wage to a specific level per hour. An illustration of the latter would be a reconsideration of certain restrictive loan practices of savings and loan institutions in the ghetto.

"Active and serious" are used to distinguish formal agenda items from what might be called "pseudo-agenda items." By pseudo-agenda, we mean any form of registering or acknowledging a demand without explicitly considering its merit. Decision-makers will often use such an agenda to assuage frustrations of constituency groups and to avoid political ramifications of a failure to acknowledge the demand. This typically occurs in a legislature where bills are placed in the hopper to placate some groups of activists with no real chance of action being taken.

Policy-makers will participate in the building of both systemic and institutional agendas. However, the natures of the two agendas are substantially different. The systemic agenda will be composed of fairly abstract and general items that do little more than identify a problem area. It will not necessarily suggest either the alternatives available or the means of coping with the problem. For example, it might include a vague item like "ending discrimination."

An institutional agenda will tend to be more specific, concrete, and limited in the number of items. It will identify, at least implicitly, those facets of a problem that are to be seriously considered by a decision-making body. An example would be a city council's consideration of alternative forms of local taxation for the support of public schools. It is possible for an item to get onto the formal agenda without having been a part of the systemic agenda. Each year, Congress considers many private bills of little social import or concern. However, it is unlikely that any issue involving substantial social consequences will gain standing on a governmental agenda unless it has first attained systemic agenda status.

Content of formal agendas. Formal agenda items can be divided into two major categories: *old items* and *new items. Old items* are those that have action alternatives delineated. They are predefined in most instances, except in specific cases (for example, the issue may not be whether workers will receive a 5 percent or a 10 percent raise, but whether they will get a raise at all).

There are two agenda components under the general heading of *old items.* Habitual items include those that come up for regular review. Examples would be budget items such as personnel pay and fights between existing agencies for a larger slice of the federal budget.

Recurrent items are those that occur with some periodicity, but need not appear at regular intervals. Examples would include governmental reorganization and regulation arising from a concern for efficiency or economy or both, rules changes in the legislature (for example, the filibuster in the Senate), Congressional reform, tariff items, tax reform, and social security increases or extensions.

The second general heading, *new items,* refers to those components that have no predetermined definitions, but are flexible in their interpretation or development. The first subdivision would include automatic or spontaneous issues appearing as an action or reaction of a key decision-maker in a specific situation. Examples include public employee or major industry strikes with a substantial impact on the economy or our military strength, the steel crisis under President Truman during the Korean War, foreign policy crises (e.g., Korea, Cuba, and the

Dominican Republic), and innovations in foreign policy (e.g., American entrance into the United Nations, the test ban treaty, and the nuclear proliferation treaty).

A second component of *new items* is channeled items, those issues channeled to the agenda by the mobilization of mass support or by the activation of significant public groups (e.g., unions). Examples of issues with mass support include the civil rights issues of the 1960's and the gun control issue. Illustrations of issues backed by significant public groups include the Taft-Hartley repeal effort and the farm parity program.

An issue need not be static or confined to one category throughout its existence. At any point in time, it may be redefined. An example of a dynamic issue is the Vietnam policy. Initially, it became a spontaneous issue when President Eisenhower committed several hundred advisers in the late 1950's. The issue of expanded commitment became recurrent under Presidents Kennedy and Johnson. By 1963, the dispute appeared on the docket with great regularity. It continued in this form until opposition to the war—a channelized item begun by peace groups—raised the question of the legitimacy of American involvement. The peace groups expanded concern with American involvement until it became the policy stance of a major presidential candidate in 1968.

The form of an institutional agenda.   The explicit form of the formal agenda may be found in the calendar of authoritative decision-making bodies such as legislatures, high courts, or regulatory agencies.[5] Unless an item appears on some docket, it will not be considered to be an agenda item. Agenda composition will vary over time. However, recurrent or habitual items will be the most numerous. They tend to receive priority from the decision-makers, who constantly find that their time is limited and that their agenda is overloaded. Spontaneous, or automatic, items take precedence over channeled items, so it is very difficult to get new issues on the agenda. Decision-makers presume that older problems warrant more attention because of their longevity and the greater familiarity officials have with them.

DIFFERENTIAL ACCESS TO INSTITUTIONAL GATEKEEPERS

The content of a formal agenda will tend to reflect structural and institutional biases found within the system. These biases arise from differential resources among individuals and groups and concomitant differences in access. For an issue to attain agenda status, it must command the support of at least some key decision-makers, for they are the ultimate guardians of the formal agenda.

Political leaders are active participants in the agenda-building process, not simply impartial arbiters of issue disputes. As Bauer, Pool, and Dexter note:

> Congress is not a passive body, registering already-existent public views forced on its attention by public pressures. Congress, second only to the president, is, rather the major institution for initiating and creating political issues and projecting them into a national civic debate.[6]

The strategic location of these leaders assures them of media visibility when they want to promote an issue and places them in an excellent position to bargain with other decision-makers over formal agenda content. Because they have fairly direct control over what will appear on the formal agenda and considerable freedom to choose among the plethora of issues competing for attention, they can insist that an issue of concern to them be considered in return for agreement to consider an issue that is salient to another decision-maker or set of decision-makers.

It is easy then to understand why access to one or more key officials is so important to political groups. As one commentator noted,

> The development and improvement of such access is a common denominator of the tactics of all of them, frequently leading to efforts to exclude competing groups from equivalent access or to set up new decision points access to which can be monopolized by a particular group.[7]

Some groups have a greater ease of access than others, and are thus more likely to get their demands placed on an agenda.

This differential responsiveness arises from a variety of factors. First, the decision-maker may be indebted to a particular group or identify himself as a member of that group. Second, some groups have more resources than others or are better able to mobilize their resources. Third, some groups are located so strategically in the social or economic structure of society that their interests cannot be ignored (for example, big business and agriculture). Fourth, some groups (such as doctors, lawyers and church leaders) are held in greater esteem by the public than others and thus can command greater access to decision-makers. As a consequence, certain groups are more likely than others to receive attention from decision-makers when they come up with new demands. Farmers have an inherent advantage over many other groups in obtaining action on their needs because there are many decision-makers who identify themselves with farm groups and because agriculture occupies a pivotal position in the American economy.

A group may encounter different types of responses from different levels or branches of the government. When the National Association for the Advancement of Colored People first started to press its demands, it focused on the Congress and the presidency, but received no support. However, the group was much more effective when it focused on a judicial strategy of making gains in civil rights through a series of court cases. Thus, differential responsiveness may result from the type of governmental unit petitioned as well as from differences among groups themselves.

Political parties also play an important part in translating issues into agenda items.[8] To assure support, they will often seek out and identify themselves with issues that are salient to large portions of the populace. Typically, these issues are identified in the party platform in general terms and with considerable ambiguity. However, as Truman notes:

> The significance of preparing a platform lies primarily in the evidence that the negotiations provide concerning what groups will have access to the developing national

party organization. . . . Interest group leaders are aware that the real settlement of the issues they are concerned with . . . will take place later; in the platform, they seek tentative assurance of a voice in that settlement. To maximize this assurance, political interest groups normally seek recognition in the platforms of both major parties.[9]

Certainly recognition on a party platform is at least indicative of an issue attaining standing on the systemic agenda of political controversy.[10]

The media can also play a very important role in elevating issues to the systemic agenda and increasing their chances of receiving formal agenda consideration. Certain personages in the media can act as opinion leaders in bringing publicity to a particular issue. Examples of individuals who have gained a larger audience for a dispute include Walter Lippmann, Jack Anderson, and Drew Pearson. Individuals who have acquired an audience simply by constantly appearing in the news can also publicize an issue. Ralph Nader has a ready-made constituency stemming from his many attacks on various inefficient and unscrupulous business practices.

DIFFERENTIAL LEGITIMACY

While most observers grant that there are inequalities in access to decision-makers, they argue that the existence of multiple points of access owing to different levels and branches of government has the net effect of insuring widespread contacts. Further, the existence of dispersed inequalities (that is, the fact that groups having great resources in one area may not have comparable resources in other areas) supposedly assures that no group will be without political influence in some areas. However, this argument fails to consider the relatively stable pattern of differential legitimacy accorded various social groupings. Differences in accessibility to decision-makers are a function of the relative legitimacy of various groups. For example, a proposal advanced by a group of businessmen to improve traffic flows into the downtown business area is more likely to receive the attention of decision-makers than a counterproposal by ghetto residents to develop more extensive and effective mass transit systems.

The problem confronted by any newly formed group is often how to legitimize the group and the interest represented rather than how to legitimize a particular issue position. The legitimacy of the group will be greatly enhanced by the status and community standing of its members. In other words, people without resources (for example, lower-income groups) will have greater difficulty attaining legitimacy than their higher-income counterparts. For example, the anti-war movement initially promoted by student groups who traditionally have little political standing received little public support until more socially prominent persons and groups entered the fray on their behalf (for example, business groups, military leaders, clergymen, and senators).

SYSTEMIC CONSTRAINTS ON AGENDA ENTRANCE

Even if an issue is promoted by a group that is perceived to be legitimate, its appearance on a formal agenda may be problematic owing to cultural constraints on the range of issues that are considered legitimate topics for governmental action. Any institutional agenda will be restricted by the prevailing popular sentiment as to what constitutes appropriate matters for governmental attention. For example, federal aid to education was long considered by many to be an inappropriate area for federal governmental action, a fact that precluded active and serious consideration of the merits of the issue for decades. Legitimizing issues that are considered outside of the governmental realm is difficult and normally takes a long time. The net effect of this is that new demands of particularly disadvantaged or deprived groups are the least likely to receive attention on either the systemic agenda of controversy or the institutional agenda. . . .

NOTES

1. For a case study of this conflict, see Andrew Hacker, "Pressure Politics in Pennsylvania: The Truckers vs. The Railroads," in Alan Westin. (ed.), *The Uses of Power: 7 Cases in American Politics* (New York: Harcourt, 1962), pp. 323–76.

2. Herbert Blumer, "Collective Behavior," in J. B. Gittler (ed.), *Review of Sociology* (New York: Wiley, 1957), 148.

3. Hans Toch, *The Psychology of Social Movements* (Indianapolis: Bobbs-Merrill, 1965), 87.

4. Here the focus is on *actual* maldistribution of resources. A *perceived* maldistribution is covered by the "readjustor" type of issue initiator.

5. Calendars normally provide predefined agendas for both the legislature and the court. However, most legislatures have some procedure to allow items to be entered on the agenda at the request of one decision-maker without going through the normal procedures of agenda specification. For example, in the Congress, this procedure involves the private calendar. That calendar will be excluded from our analysis, which focuses on the public and union calendars, where most issues of public import will be found.

6. Raymond Bauer, Ithiel Pool and Lewis Dexter, *American Business and Public Policy* (New York: Atherton Press, 1963), p. 478.

7. David Truman, *The Governmental Process* (New York: Knopf, 1964), p. 264.

8. See, for example, Everett C. Ladd, Jr., *American Political Parties* (New York: W. W. Norton and Company, 1970).

9. Truman, *op. cit.*, p. 285.

10. Significant differences in the platforms of the two major parties may portend a major alteration in the national systemic agenda. This change may be realized through what Key called "a critical election." Certainly a critical, or realigning, election may be taken as an indicator of a major shift in the systemic agenda. See V. O. Key, *Politics, Parties and Pressure Groups*. 5th ed. (New York: Thomas Crowell Company, 1964), pp. 520–36.

Agenda Setting

John W. Kingdon

. . . Why do some subjects rise on agendas while others are neglected? Why do some alternatives receive more attention than others? Some of our answers to these questions concentrate on participants: We uncover who affects agendas and alternatives, and why they do. Other answers explore the processes through which these participants affect agendas and alternatives. We have conceived of three streams of processes: problems, policies, and politics. People recognize problems, they generate proposals for public policy changes, and they engage in such political activities as election campaigns and pressure group lobbying. Each participant—president, members of Congress, civil servants, lobbyists, journalists, academics, etc.—can in principle be involved in each process (problem recognition, proposal formation, and politics). Policy is not the sole province of analysts, for instance, nor is politics the sole province of politicians. In practice, though, participants usually specialize in one or another process to a degree. Academics are more involved in policy formation than in politics, for instance, and parties are more involved in politics than in drafting detailed proposals. But conceptually, participants can be seen as different from processes.

Each of the participants and processes can act as an impetus or as a constraint. As an impetus, the participant or process boosts a subject higher on an agenda, or pushes an alternative into more active consideration. A president or congressional committee chair, for instance, decides to emphasize a subject. Or a problem is highlighted because a disaster occurs or because a well-known indicator changes. As a constraint, the participant or process dampens consideration of a subject or alternative. Vigorous pressure group opposition to an item, for instance, moves it down the list of priorities or even off the agenda. As an administration emphasizes its priorities, for another example, it limits people's ability to attend to other subjects. Concerns over budgetary costs of an item can also make its serious consideration quite unlikely.

AGENDA SETTING

How are governmental agendas set? Our answer has concentrated on three explanations: problems, politics, and visible participants.

Problems

Why do some problems come to occupy the attention of governmental officials more than other problems? The answer lies both in the means by which
those officials learn about conditions and in the ways in which conditions become
defined as problems. As to means, we have discussed indicators, focusing events,
and feedback. Sometimes, a more or less systematic indicator simply shows that
there is a condition out there. Indicators are used to assess the magnitude of the
condition (e.g., the incidence of a disease or the cost of a program), and to discern
changes in a condition. Both large magnitude and change catch officials' attention. Second, a focusing event—a disaster, crisis, personal experience, or powerful
symbol—draws attention to some conditions more than to others. But such an
event has only transient effects unless accompanied by a firmer indication of a
problem, by a preexisting perception, or by a combination with other similar
events. Third, officials learn about conditions through feedback about the operation of existing programs, either formal (e.g., routine monitoring of costs or program evaluation studies) or informal (e.g., streams of complaints flowing into
congressional offices).

There is a difference between a condition and a problem. We put up with all
kinds of conditions every day, and conditions do not rise to prominent places on
policy agendas. Conditions come to be defined as problems, and have a better
chance of rising on the agenda, when we come to believe that we should do something to change them. People in and around government define conditions as
problems in several ways. First, conditions that violate important values are transformed into problems. Second, conditions become problems by comparison with
other countries or other relevant units. Third, classifying a condition into one category rather than another may define it as one kind of problem or another. The
lack of public transportation for handicapped people, for instance, can be classified as a transportation problem or as a civil rights problem, and the treatment of
the subject is dramatically affected by the category.

Problems not only rise on governmental agendas, but they also fade from
view. Why do they fade? First, government may address the problem, or fail to address it. In both cases, attention turns to something else, either because something has been done or because people are frustrated by failure and refuse to
invest more of their time in a losing cause. Second, conditions that highlighted a
problem may change—indicators drop instead of rise, or crises go away. Third,
people may become accustomed to a condition or relabel a problem. Fourth,
other items emerge and push the highly placed items aside. Finally, there may
simply be inevitable cycles in attention; high growth rates level off, and fads come
and go.

Problem recognition is critical to agenda setting. The chances of a given
proposal or subject rising on an agenda are markedly enhanced if it is connected
to an important problem. Some problems are seen as so pressing that they set
agendas all by themselves. Once a particular problem is defined as pressing,

whole classes of approaches are favored over others, and some alternatives are highlighted while others fall from view. So policy entrepreneurs invest considerable resources bringing their conception of problems to officials' attention, and trying to convince them to see problems their way. The recognition and definition of problems affect outcomes significantly.

Politics

The second family of explanations for high or low agenda prominence is in the political stream. Independently of problem recognition or the development of policy proposals, political events flow along according to their own dynamics and their own rules. Participants perceive swings in national mood, elections bring new administrations to power and new partisan or ideological distributions to Congress, and interest groups of various descriptions press (or fail to press) their demands on government.

Developments in this political sphere are powerful agenda setters. A new administration, for instance, changes agendas all over town as it highlights its conceptions of problems and its proposals, and makes attention to subjects that are not among its high priorities much less likely. A national mood that is perceived to be profoundly conservative dampens attention to costly new initiatives, while a more tolerant national mood would allow for greater spending. The opposition of a powerful phalanx of interest groups makes it difficult—not impossible, but difficult—to contemplate some initiatives.

Consensus is built in the political stream by bargaining more than by persuasion. When participants recognize problems or settle on certain proposals in the policy stream, they do so largely by persuasion. They marshal indicators and argue that certain conditions ought to be defined as problems, or they argue that their proposals meet such logical tests as technical feasibility or value acceptability. But in the political stream, participants build consensus by bargaining—trading provisions for support, adding elected officials to coalitions by giving them concessions that they demand, or compromising from ideal positions to positions that will gain wider acceptance.

The combination of national mood and elections is a more potent agenda setter than organized interests. Interest groups are often able to block consideration of proposals they do not prefer, or to adapt to an item already high on a governmental agenda by adding elements a bit more to their liking. They less often initiate considerations or set agendas on their own. And when organized interests come into conflict with the combination of national mood and elected politicians, the latter combination is likely to prevail, at least as far as setting an agenda is concerned.

Visible Participants

Third, we made a distinction between visible and hidden participants. The visible cluster of actors, those who receive considerable press and public attention, include the president and his high-level appointees, prominent members of

Congress, the media, and such elections-related actors as political parties and campaigners. The relatively hidden cluster includes academic specialists, career bureaucrats, and congressional staffers. We have discovered that the visible cluster affects the agenda and the hidden cluster affects the alternatives. So the chances of a subject rising on a governmental agenda are enhanced if that subject is pushed by participants in the visible cluster, and dampened if it is neglected by those participants. The administration—the president and his appointees—is a particularly powerful agenda setter, as are such prominent members of Congress as the party leaders and key committee chairs.

At least as far as agenda setting is concerned, elected officials and their appointees turn out to be more important than career civil servants or participants outside of government. To those who look for evidences of democracy at work, this is an encouraging result. These elected officials do not necessarily get their way in specifying alternatives or implementing decisions, but they do affect agendas rather substantially. To describe the roles of various participants in agenda setting, a fairly straightforward top-down model, with elected officials at the top, comes surprisingly close to the truth.

ALTERNATIVE SPECIFICATION

How is the list of potential alternatives for public policy choices narrowed to the ones that actually receive serious consideration? There are two families of answers: (1) Alternatives are generated and narrowed in the policy stream; and (2) Relatively hidden participants, specialists in the particular policy area, are involved.

Hidden Participants: Specialists

Alternatives, proposals, and solutions are generated in communities of specialists. This relatively hidden cluster of participants includes academics, researchers, consultants, career bureaucrats, congressional staffers, and analysts who work for interest groups. Their work is done, for instance, in planning and evaluation or budget shops in the bureaucracy or in the staff agencies on the Hill.

These relatively hidden participants form loosely knit communities of specialists. There is such a community for health, for instance, which includes analogous subcommunities for more specialized areas like the direct delivery of medical services and the regulation of food and drugs. Some of these communities, such as the one for transportation, are highly fragmented, while others are more tightly knit. Each community is composed of people located throughout the system and potentially of very diverse orientations and interests, but they all share one thing: their specialization and acquaintance with the issues in that particular policy area.

Ideas bubble around in these communities. People try out proposals in a variety of ways: through speeches, bill introductions, congressional hearings, leaks to the press, circulation of papers, conversations, and lunches. They float their ideas, criticize one another's work, hone and revise their ideas, and float new versions. Some of these ideas are respectable, while others are out of the question. But many, many ideas are possible and are considered in some fashion somewhere along the line.

The Policy Stream

The generation of policy alternatives is best seen as a selection process, analogous to biological natural selection. In what we have called the policy primeval soup, many ideas float around, bumping into one another, encountering new ideas, and forming combinations and recombinations. The origins of policy may seem a bit obscure, hard to predict and hard to understand or to structure.

While the origins are somewhat haphazard, the selection is not. Through the imposition of criteria by which some ideas are selected out for survival while others are discarded, order is developed from chaos, pattern from randomness. These criteria include technical feasibility, congruence with the values of community members, and the anticipation of future constraints, including a budget constraint, public acceptability, and politicians' receptivity. Proposals that are judged infeasible—that do not square with policy community values, that would cost more than the budget will allow, that run afoul of opposition in either the mass or specialized publics, or that would not find a receptive audience among elected politicians—are less likely to survive than proposals that meet these standards. In the process of consideration in the policy community, ideas themselves are important. Pressure models do not completely describe the process. Proposals are evaluated partly in terms of their political support and opposition, to be sure, but partly against logical or analytical criteria as well.

There is a long process of softening up the system. Policy entrepreneurs do not leave consideration of their pet proposals to accident. Instead, they push for consideration in many ways and in many forums. In the process of policy development, recombination (the coupling of already-familiar elements) is more important than mutation (the appearance of wholly new forms). Thus entrepreneurs, who broker people and ideas, are more important than inventors. Because recombination is more important than invention, there may be "no new thing under the sun" at the same time that there may be dramatic change and innovation. There is change, but it involves the recombination of already-familiar elements.

The long softening-up process is critical to policy change. Opportunities for serious hearings, the policy windows we explored in Chapter 8, pass quickly and are missed if the proposals have not already gone through the long gestation process before the window opens. The work of floating and refining proposals is not wasted if it does not bear fruit in the short run. Indeed, it is critically important if the proposal is to be heard at the right time.

COUPLING AND WINDOWS

The separate streams of problems, policies, and politics each have lives of their own. Problems are recognized and defined according to processes that are different from the ways policies are developed or political events unfold. Policy proposals are developed according to their own incentives and selection criteria, whether or not they are solutions to problems or responsive to political considerations. Political events flow along on their own schedule and according to their own rules, whether or not they are related to problems or proposals.

But there come times when the three streams are joined. A pressing problem demands attention, for instance, and a policy proposal is coupled to the problem as its solution. Or an event in the political stream, such as a change of administration, calls for different directions. At that point, proposals that fit with that political event, such as initiatives that fit with a new administration's philosophy, come to the fore and are coupled with the ripe political climate. Similarly, problems that fit are highlighted, and others are neglected.

Decision Agendas

A complete linkage combines all three streams—problems, policies, and politics—into a single package. Advocates of a new policy initiative not only take advantage of politically propitious moments but also claim that their proposal is a solution to a pressing problem. Likewise, entrepreneurs concerned about a particular problem search for solutions in the policy stream to couple to their problem, then try to take advantage of political receptivity at certain points in time to push the package of problem and solution. At points along the way, there are partial couplings: solutions to problems, but without a receptive political climate; politics to proposals, but without a sense that a compelling problem is being solved; politics and problems both calling for action, but without an available alternative to advocate. But the complete joining of all three streams dramatically enhances the odds that a subject will become firmly fixed on a decision agenda.

Governmental agendas, lists of subjects to which governmental officials are paying serious attention, can be set solely in either problems or political streams, and solely by visible actors. Officials can pay attention to an important problem, for instance, without having a solution to it. Or politics may highlight a subject, even in the absence of either problem or solution. A decision agenda, a list of subjects that is moving into position for an authoritative decision, such as legislative enactment or presidential choice, is set somewhat differently. The probability of an item rising on a decision agenda is dramatically increased if all three elements—problem, policy proposal, and political receptivity—are linked in a single package. Conversely, partial couplings are less likely to rise on decision agendas. Problems that come to decisions without solutions attached, for instance, are not as likely to move into position for an authoritative choice as if they did have solutions attached. And proposals that lack political backing are less likely to move into position for a decision than ones that do have that backing. . . .

Policy Windows

An open policy window is an opportunity for advocates to push their pet solutions or to push attention to their special problems. Indeed, advocates in and around government keep their proposals and their problems at hand, waiting for these opportunities to occur. They have pet solutions, for instance, and wait for problems to float by to which they can attach their solutions, or for developments in the political stream that they can use to their advantage. Or they wait for similar opportunities to bring their special problems to the fore, such as the appearance of a new administration that would be concerned with these problems. That administration opens a window for them to bring greater attention to the problems about which they are concerned.

Windows are opened by events in either the problems or political streams. Thus there are problems windows and political windows. A new problem appears, for instance, creating an opportunity to attach a solution to it. Or such events in the political stream as turnover of elected officials, swings of national mood, or vigorous lobbying might create opportunities to push some problems and proposals to the fore and dampen the chances to highlight other problems and proposals.

Sometimes, windows open quite predictably. Legislation comes up for renewal on a schedule, for instance, creating opportunities to change, expand, or abolish certain programs. At other times, windows open quite unpredictably, as when an airliner crashes or a fluky election produces an unexpected turnover in key decision makers. Predictable or unpredictable, open windows are small and scarce. Opportunities come, but they also pass. Windows do not stay open long. If a chance is missed, another must be awaited.

The scarcity and the short duration of the opening of a policy window create a powerful magnet for problems and proposals. When a window opens, problems and proposals flock to it. People concerned with particular problems see the open window as their opportunity to address or even solve these problems. Advocates of particular proposals see the open window as the opportunity to enact them. As a result, the system comes to be loaded down with problems and proposals. If participants are willing to invest sufficient resources, some of the problems can be resolved and some of the proposals enacted. Other problems and proposals drift away because insufficient resources are mobilized.

Open windows present opportunities for the complete linkage of problems, proposals, and politics, and hence opportunities to move packages of the three joined elements up on decision agendas. One particularly crucial coupling is the link of a solution to something else. Advocates of pet proposals watch for developments in the political stream that they can take advantage of, or try to couple their solution to whatever problems are floating by at the moment. Once they have made the partial coupling of proposal to either problem or politics, they attempt to join all three elements, knowing that the chances for enactment are considerably enhanced if they can complete the circle. Thus they try to hook packages of problems and solutions to political forces, packages of proposals and political incentives to perceived problems, or packages of problems and politics to some proposal taken from the policy stream.

ENTREPRENEURS

Policy entrepreneurs are people willing to invest their resources in return for future policies they favor. They are motivated by combinations of several things: their straightforward concern about certain problems, their pursuit of such self-serving benefits as protecting or expanding their bureaucracy's budget or claiming credit for accomplishment, their promotion of their policy values, and their simple pleasure in participating. We have encountered them at three junctures: pushing their concerns about certain problems higher on the agenda, pushing their pet proposals during a process of softening up the system, and making the couplings we just discussed. These entrepreneurs are found at many locations; they might be elected officials, career civil servants, lobbyists, academics, or journalists. No one type of participant dominates the pool of entrepreneurs.

As to problems, entrepreneurs try to highlight the indicators that so importantly dramatize their problems. They push for one kind of problem definition rather than another. Because they know that focusing events can move subjects higher on the agenda, entrepreneurs push to create such things as personal viewings of problems by policy makers and the diffusion of a symbol that captures their problem in a nutshell. They also may prompt the kinds of feedback about current governmental performance that affect agendas: letters, complaints, and visits to officials.

As to proposals, entrepreneurs are central to the softening-up process. They write papers, give testimony, hold hearings, try to get press coverage, and meet endlessly with important and not-so-important people. They float their ideas as trial balloons, get reactions, revise their proposals in the light of reactions, and float them again. They aim to soften up the mass public, specialized publics, and the policy community itself. The process takes years of effort.

As to coupling, entrepreneurs once again appear when windows open. They have their pet proposals or their concerns about problems ready, and push them at the propitious moments. In the pursuit of their own goals, they perform the function for the system of coupling solutions to problems, problems to political forces, and political forces to proposals. The joining of the separate streams described earlier depends heavily on the appearance of the right entrepreneur at the right time. In our case study of Health Maintenance Organizations in Chapter I, Paul Ellwood appeared on the scene to link his pet proposal (HMOs) to the problem of medical care costs and to the political receptivity created by the Nixon administration casting about for health initiatives. The problems and political streams had opened a window, and Ellwood cleverly took advantage of that opportunity to push his HMO proposal, joining all three streams in the process.

The appearance of entrepreneurs when windows are open, as well as their more enduring activities of trying to push their problems and proposals into prominence, are central to our story. They bring several key resources into the fray: their claims to a hearing, their political connections and negotiating skills, and their sheer persistence. An item's chances for moving up on an agenda are enhanced considerably by the presence of a skillful entrepreneur, and dampened considerably if no entrepreneur takes on the cause, pushes it, and makes the critical couplings when policy windows open. . . .

The 'Science' of Muddling Through

Charles E. Lindblom

Suppose an administrator is given responsibility for formulating policy with respect to inflation. He might start by trying to list all related values in order of importance, e.g., full employment, reasonable business profit, protection of small savings, prevention of a stock market crash. Then all possible policy outcomes could be rated as more or less efficient in attaining a maximum of these values. This would of course require a prodigious inquiry into values held by members of society and an equally prodigious set of calculations on how much each value is equal to how much of each other value. He could then proceed to outline all possible policy alternatives. In a third step, he could undertake systematic comparison of his multitude of alternatives to determine which attains the greatest amount of values.

In comparing policies, he would take advantage of any theory available that generalized about classes of policies. In considering inflation, for example, he would compare all policies in the light of the theory of prices. Since no alternatives are beyond his investigation, he would consider strict central control and the abolition of all prices and markets on the one hand and elimination of all public controls with reliance completely on the free market on the other, both in the light of whatever theoretical generalizations he could find on such hypothetical economies.

Finally, he would try to make the choice that would in fact maximize his values.

From Charles E. Lindblom, "The 'Science' of Muddling Through", *Public Administration Review*, 19 (1959), 79–88. Reprinted with permission from *Public Administration Review* © by the American Society for Public Administration (ASPA), 1120 G Street NW, Suite 700, Washington DC 20005. All rights reserved.

An alternative line of attack would be to set as his principal objective, either explicitly or without conscious thought, the relatively simple goal of keeping prices level. This objective might be compromised or complicated by only a few other goals, such as full employment. He would in fact disregard most other social values as beyond his present interest, and he would for the moment not even attempt to rank the few values that he regarded as immediately relevant. Were he pressed, he would quickly admit that he was ignoring many related values and many possible important consequences of his policies.

As a second step, he would outline those relatively few policy alternatives that occurred to him. He would then compare them. In comparing his limited number of alternatives, most of them familiar from past controversies, he would not ordinarily find a body of theory precise enough to carry him through a comparison of their respective consequences. Instead he would rely heavily on the record of past experience with small policy steps to predict the consequences of similar steps extended into the future.

Moreover, he would find that the policy alternatives combined objectives or values in different ways. For example, one policy might offer price level stability at the cost of some risk of unemployment; another might offer less price stability but also less risk of unemployment. Hence, the next step in his approach—the final selection—would combine into one the choice among values and the choice among instruments for reaching values. It would not, as in the first method of policy-making, approximate a more mechanical process of choosing the means that best satisfied goals that were previously clarified and ranked. Because practitioners of the second approach expect to achieve their goals only partially, they would expect to repeat endlessly the sequence just described, as conditions and aspirations changed and as accuracy of prediction improved.

BY ROOT OR BY BRANCH

For complex problems, the first of these two approaches is of course impossible. Although such an approach can be described, it cannot be practiced except for relatively simple problems and even then only in a somewhat modified form. It assumes intellectual capacities and sources of information that men simply do not possess, and it is even more absurd as an approach to policy when the time and money that can be allocated to a policy problem is limited, as is always the case. Of particular importance to public administrators is the fact that public agencies are in effect usually instructed not to practice the first method. That is to say, their prescribed functions and constraints—the politically or legally possible—restrict their attention to relatively few values and relatively few alternative policies among the countless alternatives that might be imagined. It is the second method that is practiced.

Curiously, however, the literatures of decision-making, policy formulation, planning, and public administration formalize the first approach rather than the second, leaving public administrators who handle complex decisions in the position of practicing what few preach. For emphasis I run some risk of overstatement. True enough, the literature is well aware of limits on man's capacities and of the inevitability that policies will be approached in some such style as the second. But attempts to formalize rational policy formulation—to lay out explicitly the necessary steps in the process—usually describe the first approach and not the second.[1]

The common tendency to describe policy formulation even for complex problems as though it followed the first approach has been strengthened by the attention given to, and success enjoyed by, operations research,[*] statistical decision theory,[†] and systems analysis.[‡] The hallmarks of these procedures, typical of the first approach, are clarity of objective, explicitness of evaluation, a high degree of comprehensiveness of overview, and, wherever possible, quantification of values for mathematical analysis. But these advanced procedures remain largely the appropriate techniques of relatively small-scale problem-solving where the total number of variables to be considered is small and value problems restricted. Charles Hitch, head of the Economics Division of RAND Corporation, one of the leading centers for application of these techniques, has written:

> I would make the empirical generalization from my experience at RAND and elsewhere that operations research is the art of sub-optimizing, i.e., of solving some lower-level problems, and that difficulties increase and our special competence diminishes by an order of magnitude with every level of decision making we attempt to ascend. The sort of simple explicit model which operations researchers are so proficient in using can certainly reflect most of the significant factors influencing traffic control on the George Washington Bridge, but the proportion of the relevant reality which we can represent by any such model or models in studying, say, a major foreign-policy decision, appears to be almost trivial.[2]

Accordingly, I propose in this paper to clarify and formalize the second method, much neglected in the literature. This might be described as the method of *successive limited comparisons*. I will contrast it with the first approach, which might be called the rational-comprehensive method.[3] More impressionistically and briefly—and therefore generally used in this article—they could be characterized as the branch method and root method, the former continually building out from the current situation, step-by-step and by small degrees; the latter starting from fundamentals anew each time, building on the past only as experience is embodied in a theory, and always prepared to start completely from the ground up.

[*]*Operations research*: type of analysis, based on mathematical models, used to determine the most efficient use of resources for a set of goals.

[†]*Statistical decision theory*: theory that allows one to make choices between alternatives by objectifying problems and analyzing them quantitatively. Also called Bayesian decision theory after Thomas Bayes (1702–1761), who developed the mathematical foundation of inference, the method of using information on a sample to infer characteristics about a population.

[‡]*Systems analysis*: analysis of systemic data by means of advanced quantitative techniques to aid in selecting the most appropriate course of action among a series of alternatives.

Let us put the characteristics of the two methods side by side in simplest terms.

Rational-Comprehensive (Root)

1. Clarification of values or objectives distinct from and usually prerequisite to empirical analysis of alternative policies.
2a. Policy-formulation is therefore approached through means-end analysis: First the ends are isolated, then the means to achieve them are sought.
3a. The test of a "good" policy is that it can be shown to be the most appropriate means to desired ends.
4a. Analysis is comprehensive; every important relevant factor is taken into account.
5a. Theory is often heavily relied upon.

Assuming that the root method is familiar and understandable, we proceed directly to clarification of its alternative by contrast. In explaining the second, we shall be describing how most administrators do in fact approach complex questions, for the root method, the "best" way as a blueprint or model, is in fact not workable for complex policy questions, and administrators are forced to use the method of successive limited comparisons.

INTERTWINING EVALUATION AND EMPIRICAL ANALYSIS (1B)

The quickest way to understand how values are handled in the method of successive limited comparisons is to see how the root method often breaks down in *its* handling of values or objectives. The idea that values should be clarified, and in advance of the examination of alternative policies, is appealing. But what happens when we attempt it for complex social problems? The first difficulty is that on many critical values or objectives, citizens disagree, congressmen disagree, and public administrators disagree. Even where a fairly specific objective is prescribed for the administrator, there remains considerable room for disagreement on sub-objectives. Consider, for example, the conflict with respect to locating public housing, described in Meyerson and Banfield's study of the Chicago Housing Authority[4]—disagreement which occurred despite the clear objective of providing a certain number of public housing units in the city. Similarly conflicting are objectives in highway location, traffic control, minimum wage administration, development of tourist facilities in national parks, or insect control.

Successive Limited Comparisons (Branch)

1b. Selection of value goals and empirical analysis of the needed action are not distinct from one another but are closely intertwined.
2b. Since means and ends are not distinct, means-end analysis is often inappropriate or limited.

3b. The test of a "good" policy is typically that various analysts find themselves directly agreeing on a policy (without their agreeing that it is the most appropriate means to an agreed objective).

4b. Analysis is drastically limited: i) Important possible outcomes are neglected. ii) Important alternative potential policies are neglected. iii) Important affected values are neglected.

5b. A succession of comparison greatly reduces or eliminates reliance on theory.

Administrators cannot escape these conflicts by ascertaining the majority's preference, for preferences have not been registered on most issues; indeed, there often *are* no preferences in the absence of public discussion sufficient to bring an issue to the attention of the electorate. Furthermore, there is a question of whether intensity of feeling should be considered as well as the number of persons preferring each alternative. By the impossibility of doing otherwise, administrators often are reduced to deciding policy without clarifying objectives first.

Even when an administrator resolves to follow his own values as a criterion for decisions, he often will not know how to rank them when they conflict with one another, as they usually do. Suppose, for example, that an administrator must relocate tenants living in tenements scheduled for destruction. One objective is to empty the buildings fairly promptly, another is to find suitable accommodation for persons displaced, another is to avoid friction with residents in other areas in which a large influx would be unwelcome, another is to deal with all concerned through persuasion if possible, and so on.

How does one state even to himself the relative importance of these partially conflicting values? A simple ranking of them is not enough; one needs ideally to know how much of one value is worth sacrificing for some of another value. The answer is that typically the administrator chooses—and must choose—directly among policies in which these values are combined in different ways. He cannot first clarify his values and then choose among policies.

A more subtle third point underlies both the first two. Social objectives do not always have the same relative values. One objective may be highly prized in one circumstance, another in another circumstance. If, for example, an administrator values highly both the dispatch with which his agency can carry through its projects *and* good public relations, it matters little which of the two possibly conflicting values he favors in some abstract or general sense. Policy questions arise in forms which put to administrators such a question as: Given the degree to which we are or are not already achieving the values of dispatch and the values of good public relations, is it worth sacrificing a little speed for a happier clientele, or is it better to risk offending the clientele so that we can get on with our work? The answer to such a question varies with circumstances.

The value problem is, as the example shows, always a problem of adjustments at a margin. But there is no practicable way to state marginal objectives or values except in terms of particular policies. That one value is preferred to another in one decision situation does not mean that it will be preferred in another decision situation in which it can be had only at great sacrifice of another value. Attempts to rank or order values in general and abstract terms so that they do not shift from decision to decision end up by ignoring the relevant marginal preferences. The significance of this third point thus goes very far. Even if all administrators had at hand an agreed set of values, objectives, and constraints, and an agreed ranking of these values, objectives, and constraints, their marginal values in actual choice situations would be impossible to formulate.

Unable consequently to formulate the relevant values first and then choose among policies to achieve them, administrators must choose directly among alternative policies that offer different marginal combinations of values. Somewhat paradoxically, the only practicable way to disclose one's relevant marginal values even to oneself is to describe the policy one chooses to achieve them. Except roughly and vaguely, I know of no way to describe—or even to understand—what my relative evaluations are for, say, freedom and security, speed and accuracy in governmental decisions, or low taxes and better schools than to describe my preferences among specific policy choices that might be made between the alternatives in each of the pairs.

In summary, two aspects of the process by which values are actually handled can be distinguished. The first is clear: evaluation and empirical analysis are intertwined; that is, one chooses among values and among policies at one and the same time. Put a little more elaborately, one simultaneously chooses a policy to attain certain objectives and chooses the objectives themselves. The second aspect is related but distinct: the administrator focuses his attention on marginal or incremental values. Whether he is aware of it or not, he does not find general formulations of objectives very helpful and in fact makes specific marginal or incremental comparisons. Two policies, X and Y, confront him. Both promise the same degree of attainment of objectives *a, b, c, d,* and *e.* But X promises him somewhat more of *f* than does Y, while Y promises him somewhat more of *g* than does X. In choosing between them, he is in fact offered the alternative of a marginal or incremental amount of *f* at the expense of a marginal or incremental amount of *g.* The only values that are relevant to his choice are these increments by which the two policies differ; and, when he finally chooses between the two marginal values, he does so by making a choice between policies.[5]

As to whether the attempt to clarify objectives in advance of policy selection is more or less rational than the close intertwining of marginal evaluation and empirical analysis, the principal difference established is that for complex problems the first is impossible and irrelevant, and the second is both possible and relevant. The second is possible because the administrator need not try to analyze any values except the values by which alternative policies differ and need not be concerned with them except as they differ marginally. His need for information on values or objectives is drastically reduced as compared with the root method; and his capacity for grasping, comprehending, and relating values to one another is not strained beyond the breaking point.

RELATIONS BETWEEN MEANS AND ENDS (2B)

Decision-making is ordinarily formalized as a means-ends relationship: means are conceived to be evaluated and chosen in the light of ends finally selected independently of and prior to the choice of means. This is the means-ends relationship of the root method. But it follows from all that has just been said that such a means-ends relationship is possible only to the extent that values are agreed upon, are reconcilable, and are stable at the margin. Typically, therefore, such a means-ends relationship is absent from the branch method, where means and ends are simultaneously chosen.

Yet any departure from the means-ends relationship of the root method will strike some readers as inconceivable. For it will appear to them that only in such a relationship is it possible to determine whether one policy choice is better or worse than another. How can an administrator know whether he has made a wise or foolish decision if he is without prior values or objectives by which to judge his decisions? The answer to this question calls up the third distinctive difference between root and branch methods: how to decide the best policy.

THE TEST OF "GOOD" POLICY (3B)

In the root method, a decision is "correct," "good," or "rational" if it can be shown to attain some specified objective, where the objective can be specified without simply describing the decision itself. Where objectives are defined only through the marginal or incremental approach to values described above, it is still sometimes possible to test whether a policy does in fact attain the desired objectives; but a precise statement of the objectives takes the form of a description of the policy chosen or some alternative to it. To show that a policy is mistaken one cannot offer an abstract argument that important objectives are not achieved; one must instead argue that another policy is more to be preferred.

So far, the departure from customary ways of looking at problem-solving is not troublesome, for many administrators will be quick to agree that the most effective discussion of the correctness of policy does take the form of comparison with other policies that might have been chosen. But what of the situation in which administrators cannot agree on values or objectives, either abstractly or in marginal terms? What then is the test of "good" policy? For the root method, there is no test. Agreement on objectives failing, there is no standard of "correctness." For the method of successive limited comparisons, the test is agreement on policy itself, which remains possible even when agreement on values is not.

It has been suggested that continuing agreement in Congress on the desirability of extending old age insurance stems from liberal desires to strengthen the welfare programs of the federal government and from conservative desires to reduce union demands for private pension plans. If so, this is an excellent demonstration of the ease with which individuals of different ideologies often can agree on concrete policy. Labor mediators report a similar phenomenon: the contestants cannot agree on criteria for settling their disputes but can agree on specific proposals. Similarly, when one administrator's objective turns out to be another's means, they often can agree on policy.

Agreement on policy thus becomes the only practicable test of the policy's correctness. And for one administrator to seek to win the other over to agreement on ends as well would accomplish nothing and create quite unnecessary controversy.

If agreement directly on policy as a test for "best" policy seems a poor substitute for testing the policy against its objectives, it ought to be remembered that objectives themselves have no ultimate validity other than they are agreed upon. Hence agreement is the test of "best" policy in both methods. But where the root method requires agreement on what elements in the decision constitute objectives and on which of these objectives should be sought, the branch method falls back on agreement wherever it can be found.

In an important sense, therefore, it is not irrational for an administrator to defend a policy as good without being able to specify what it is good for.

NON-COMPREHENSIVE ANALYSIS (4B)

Ideally, rational-comprehensive analysis leaves out nothing important. But it is impossible to take everything important into consideration unless "important" is so narrowly defined that analysis is in fact quite limited. Limits on human intellectual capacities and on available information set definite limits to man's capacity to be comprehensive. In actual fact, therefore, no one can practice the rational-comprehensive method for really complex problems, and every administrator faced with a sufficiently complex problem must find ways drastically to simplify.

An administrator assisting in the formulation of agricultural economic policy cannot in the first place be competent on all possible policies. He cannot even comprehend one policy entirely. In planning a soil bank program, he cannot successfully anticipate the impact of higher or lower farm income on, say, urbanization—the possible consequent loosening of family ties, possible consequent eventual need for revisions in social security and further implications for tax problems arising out of new federal responsibilities for social security and municipal responsibilities for urban services. Nor, to follow another line of repercussions, can he work through the soil bank program's effects on prices for agricultural products in foreign markets and consequent implications for foreign relations, including those arising out of economic rivalry between the United States and the U.S.S.R.

In the method of successive limited comparisons, simplification is systematically achieved in two principal ways. First, it is achieved through limitation of policy comparisons to those policies that differ in relatively small degree from policies presently in effect. Such a limitation immediately reduces the number of alternatives to be investigated and also drastically simplifies the character of the investigation of each. For it is not necessary to undertake fundamental inquiry into an alternative and its consequences; it is necessary only to study those respects in which the proposed alternative and its consequences differ from the status quo. The empirical comparison of marginal differences among alternative policies that differ only marginally is, of course, a counterpart to the incremental or marginal comparison of values discussed above.[6]

RELEVANCE AS WELL AS REALISM

It is a matter of common observation that in Western democracies public administrators and policy analysts in general do largely limit their analyses to incremental or marginal differences in policies that are chosen to differ only incrementally. They do not do so, however, solely because they desperately need some way to simplify their problems; they also do so in order to be relevant. Democracies change their policies almost entirely through incremental adjustments. Policy does not move in leaps and bounds.

The incremental character of political change in the United States has often been remarked. The two major political parties agree on fundamentals; they offer alternative policies to the voters only on relatively small points of difference. Both parties favor full employment, but they define it somewhat differently; both favor the development of water power resources, but in slightly different ways; and both favor unemployment compensation, but not the same level of benefits. Similarly, shifts of policy within a party take place largely through a series of relatively small changes, as can be seen in their only gradual acceptance of the idea of government responsibility for support of the unemployed, a change in party positions beginning in the early 30's and culminating in a sense in the Employment Act of 1946.*

Party behavior is in turn rooted in public attitudes, and political theorists cannot conceive of democracy's surviving in the United States in the absence of fundamental agreement on potentially disruptive issues, with consequent limitation of policy debates to relatively small differences in policy.

Since the policies ignored by the administrator are politically impossible and so irrelevant, the simplification of analysis achieved by concentrating on policies that differ only incrementally is not a capricious kind of simplification. In addition, it can be argued that, given the limits on knowledge within which policy-makers are confined, simplifying by limiting the focus to small variations from present policy makes the most of available knowledge. Because policies being considered are like present and past policies, the administrator can obtain information and claim some insight. Non-incremental policy proposals are there-

---

Employment Act of 1946: act mandating federal responsibility for promoting full employment and for stabilizing the economy. The act created the Council of Economic Advisers, a unit of the Executive Office of the President.

fore typically not only politically irrelevant but also unpredictable in their consequences.

The second method of simplification of analysis is the practice of ignoring important possible consequences of possible policies, as well as the values attached to the neglected consequences. If this appears to disclose a shocking shortcoming of successive limited comparisons, it can be replied that, even if the exclusions are random, policies may nevertheless be more intelligently formulated than through futile attempts to achieve a comprehensiveness beyond human capacity. Actually, however, the exclusions, seeming arbitrary or random from one point of view, need be neither.

Achieving a Degree of Comprehensiveness

Suppose that each value neglected by one policy-making agency were a major concern of at least one other agency. In that case, a helpful division of labor would be achieved, and no agency need find its task beyond its capacities. The shortcomings of such a system would be that one agency might destroy a value either before another agency could be activated to safeguard it or in spite of another agency's efforts. But the possibility that important values may be lost is present in any form of organization, even where agencies attempt to comprehend in planning more than is humanly possible.

The virtue of such a hypothetical division of labor is that every important interest or value has its watchdog. And these watchdogs can protect the interests in their jurisdiction in two quite different ways: first, by redressing damages done by other agencies; and second, by anticipating and heading off injury before it occurs.

In a society like that of the United States in which individuals are free to combine to pursue almost any possible common interest they might have and in which government agencies are sensitive to the pressures of these groups, the system described is approximated. Almost every interest has its watchdog. Without claiming that every interest has a sufficiently powerful watchdog, it can be argued that our system often can assure a more comprehensive regard for the values of the whole society than any attempt at intellectual comprehensiveness.

In the United States, for example, no part of government attempts a comprehensive overview of policy on income distribution. A policy nevertheless evolves, and one responding to a wide variety of interests. A process of mutual adjustment among farm groups, labor unions, municipalities and school boards, tax authorities, and government agencies with responsibilities in the fields of housing, health, highways, national parks, fire, and police accomplishes a distribution of income in which particular income problems neglected at one point in the decision process become central at another point.

Mutual adjustment is more pervasive than the explicit forms it takes in negotiation between groups; it persists through the mutual impacts of groups upon each other even where they are not in communication. For all the imperfections and latent dangers in this ubiquitous process of mutual adjustment, it will often accomplish an adaptation of policies to a wider range of interests than could be done by one group centrally.

Note, too, how the incremental pattern of policy-making fits with the multiple pressure pattern. For when decisions are only incremental—closely related to known policies—it is easier for one group to anticipate the kind of moves another might make and easier for it to make correction for injury already accomplished.[7]

Even partisanship and narrowness, to use pejorative terms, will sometimes be assets to rational decision-making, for they can doubly insure that what one agency neglects, another will not; they specialize personnel to distinct points of view. The claim is valid that effective rational coordination of the federal administrator, if possible to achieve at all, would require an agreed set of values[8]—if "rational" is defined as the practice of the root method of decision-making. But a high degree of administrative coordination occurs as each agency adjusts its policies to the concerns of the other agencies in the process of fragmented decision-making I have just described.

For all the apparent shortcomings of the incremental approach to policy alternatives with its arbitrary exclusion coupled with fragmentation, when compared to the root method, the branch method often looks far superior. In the root method, the inevitable exclusion of factors is accidental, unsystematic, and not defensible by any argument so far developed, while in the branch method the exclusions are deliberate, systematic, and defensible. Ideally, of course, the root method does not exclude; in practice it must.

Nor does the branch method necessarily neglect long-run considerations and objectives. It is clear that important values must be omitted in considering policy, and sometimes the only way long-run objectives can be given adequate attention is through the neglect of short-run considerations. But the values omitted can be either long-run or short-run.

SUCCESSION OF COMPARISONS (5B)

The final distinctive element in the branch method is that the comparisons, together with the policy choice, proceed in a chronological series. Policy is not made once and for all; it is made and re-made endlessly. Policy-making is a process of successive approximation to some desired objectives in which what is desired itself continues to change under reconsideration.

Making policy is at best a very rough process. Neither social scientists, nor politicians, nor public administrators yet know enough about the social world to avoid repeated error in predicting the consequences of policy moves. A wise policy-maker consequently expects that his policies will achieve only part of what he hopes and at the same time will produce unanticipated consequences he would have preferred to avoid. If he proceeds through a *succession* of incremental changes, he avoids serious lasting mistakes in several ways.

In the first place, past sequences of policy steps have given him knowledge about the probable consequences of further similar steps. Second, he need not attempt big jumps toward his goals that would require predictions beyond his or anyone else's knowledge, because he never expects his policy to be a final resolution of a problem. His decision is only one step, one that if successful can quickly be followed by another. Third, he is in effect able to test his previous predictions as he moves on to each further step. Lastly, he often can remedy a past error fairly quickly—more quickly than if policy proceeded through more distinct steps widely spaced in time.

Compare this comparative analysis of incremental changes with the aspiration to employ theory in the root method. Man cannot think without classifying, without subsuming one experience under a more general category of experiences. The attempt to push categorization as far as possible and to find general propositions which can be applied to specific situations is what I refer to with the word "theory." Where root analysis often leans heavily on theory in this sense, the branch method does not.

The assumption of root analysis is that theory is the most systematic and economical way to bring relevant knowledge to bear on a specific problem. Granting the assumption, an unhappy fact is that we do not have adequate theory to apply to problems in any policy area, although theory is more adequate in some areas—monetary policy, for example—than in others. Comparative analysis, as in the branch method, is sometimes a systematic alternative to theory.

Suppose an administrator must choose among a small group of policies that differ only incrementally from each other and from present policy. He might aspire to "understand" each of the alternatives—for example, to know all the consequences of each aspect of each policy. If so, he would indeed require theory. In fact, however, he would usually decide that, *for policy-making purposes*, he need know, as explained above, only the consequences of each of those aspects of the policies in which they differed from one another. For this much more modest aspiration, he requires no theory (although it might be helpful, if available), for he can proceed to isolate probable differences by examining the differences in consequences associated with past differences in policies, a feasible program because he can take his observations from a long sequence of incremental changes.

For example, without a more comprehensive social theory about juvenile delinquency than scholars have yet produced, one cannot possibly understand the ways in which a variety of public policies—say on education, housing, recreation, employment, race relations, and policing—might encourage or discourage delinquency. And one needs such an understanding if he undertakes the comprehensive overview of the problem prescribed in the models of the root method. If, however, one merely wants to mobilize knowledge sufficient to assist in a choice among a small group of similar policies—alternative policies on juvenile court procedures, for example—he can do so by comparative analysis of the results of similar past policy moves.

THEORISTS AND PRACTITIONERS

This difference explains—in some cases at least—why the administrator often feels that the outside expert or academic problem-solver is sometimes not helpful and why they in turn often urge more theory on him. And it explains why an administrator often feels more confident when "flying by the seat of his pants" than when following the advice of theorists. Theorists often ask the administrator to go the long way round to the solution of his problems, in effect ask him to follow the best canons of the scientific method, when the administrator knows that the best available theory will work less well than more modest incremental comparisons. Theorists do not realize that the administrator is often in fact practicing a systematic method. It would be foolish to push this explanation too far, for sometimes practical decision-makers are pursuing neither a theoretical approach nor successive comparisons, not any other systematic method.

It may be worth emphasizing that theory is sometimes of extremely limited helpfulness in policy-making for at least two rather different reasons. It is greedy for facts; it can be constructed only through a great collection of observations. And it is typically insufficiently precise for application to a policy process that moves through small changes. In contrast, the comparative method both economizes on the need for facts and directs the analyst's attention to just those facts that are relevant to the fine choices faced by the decision-maker.

With respect to precision of theory, economic theory serves as an example. It predicts that an economy without money or prices would in certain specified ways misallocate resources, but this finding pertains to an alternative far removed from the kind of policies on which administrators need help. On the other hand, it is not precise enough to predict the consequences of policies restricting business mergers, and this is the kind of issue on which the administrators need help. Only in relatively restricted areas does economic theory achieve sufficient precision to go far in resolving policy questions; its helpfulness in policy-making is always so limited that it requires supplementation through comparative analysis.

SUCCESSIVE COMPARISON AS A SYSTEM

Successive limited comparisons is, then, indeed a method or system; it is not a failure of method for which administrators ought to apologize. None the less, its imperfections, which have not been explored in this paper, are many. For example, the method is without a built-in safeguard for all relevant values, and it also may lead the decision-maker to overlook excellent policies for no other reason than that they are not suggested by the chain of successive policy steps leading up to the present. Hence, it ought to be said that under this method, as well as under some of the most sophisticated variants of the root method—operations research, for example—policies will continue to be as foolish as they are wise.

Why then bother to describe the method in all the above detail? Because it is in fact a common method of policy formulation, and is, for complex problems, the principal reliance of administrators as well as of other policy analysts.[9] And because it will be superior to any other decision-making method available for complex problems in many circumstances, certainly superior to a futile attempt at superhuman comprehensiveness. The reaction of the public administrator to the exposition of method doubtless will be less a discovery of a new method than a better acquaintance with an old. But by becoming more conscious of their practice of this method, administrators might practice it with more skill and know when to extend or constrict its use. (That they sometimes practice it effectively and sometimes not may explain the extremes of opinion on "muddling through," which is both praised as a highly sophisticated form of problem-solving and denounced as no method at all. For I suspect that in so far as there is a system in what is known as "muddling through," this method is it.)

One of the noteworthy incidental consequences of clarification of the method is the light it throws on the suspicion an administrator sometimes entertains that a consultant or adviser is not speaking relevantly and responsibly when in fact by all ordinary objective evidence he is. The trouble lies in the fact that most of us approach policy problems within a framework given by our view of a chain of successive policy choices made up to the present. One's thinking about appropriate policies with respect, say, to urban traffic control is greatly influenced by one's knowledge of the incremental steps taken up to the present. An administrator enjoys an intimate knowledge of his past sequences that "outsiders" do not share, and his thinking and that of the "outsider" will consequently be different in ways that may puzzle both. Both may appear to be talking intelligently, yet each may find the other unsatisfactory. The relevance of the policy chain of succession is even more clear when an American tries to discuss, say, antitrust policy with a Swiss, for the chains of policy in the two countries are strikingly different and the two individuals consequently have organized their knowledge in quite different ways.

If this phenomenon is a barrier to communication, an understanding of it promises an enrichment of intellectual interaction in policy formulation. Once the source of difference is understood, it will sometimes be stimulating for an administrator to seek out a policy analyst whose recent experience is with a policy chain different from his own.

This raises again a question only briefly discussed above on the merits of likemindedness among government administrators. While much of organization theory argues the virtues of common values and agreed organizational objectives, for complex problems in which the root method is inapplicable, agencies will want among their own personnel two types of diversification: administrators whose thinking is organized by reference to policy chains other than those familiar to most members of the organization and, even more commonly, administrators whose professional or personal values or interests create diversity of view (perhaps coming from different specialties, social classes, geographical areas) so that, even within a single agency, decision-making can be fragmented and parts of the agency can serve as watchdogs for other parts.

NOTES

1. James G. March and Herbert A. Simon similarly characterize the literature. They also take some important steps, as have Simon's recent articles, to describe a less heroic model of policy-making. See *Organizations* (John Wiley and Sons, 1958), p. 137.

2. "Operations Research and National Planning—A Dissent," 5 *Operations Research* 718 (October, 1957). Hitch's dissent is from particular points made in the article to which his paper is a reply; his claim that operations research is for low-level problems is widely accepted. For examples of the kind of problems to which operations research is applied, see C. W. Churchman, R. L. Ackoff, and E. L. Arnoff, *Introduction to Operations Research* (John Wiley and Sons, 1957); and J. F. McCloskey and J. M. Coppinger (eds.), *Operations Research for Management*, Vol. II (The Johns Hopkins Press, 1956).

3. I am assuming that administrators often make policy and advise in the making of policy and am treating decision-making and policy-making as synonymous for purposes of this paper.

4. Martin Meyerson and Edward C. Banfield, *Politics, Planning and the Public Interest* (The Free Press, 1955).

5. The line of argument is, of course, an extension of the theory of market choice, especially the theory of consumer choice, to public policy choices.

6. A more precise definition of incremental policies and a discussion of whether a change that appears "small" to one observer might be seen differently by another is to be found in my "Policy Analysis," 48 *American Economic Review* 298 (June, 1958).

7. The link between the practice of the method of successive limited comparisons and mutual adjustment of interests in a highly fragmented decision-making process adds a new facet to pluralist theories of government and administration.

8. Herbert Simon, Donald W. Smithburg, and Victor A. Thompson, *Public Administration* (Alfred A. Knopf, 1950), p. 434.

9. Elsewhere I have explored this same method of policy formulation as practiced by academic analysts of policy ("Policy Analysis," 48 *American Economic Review* 298 [June 1958]). Although it has been here presented as a method for public administrators, it is no less necessary to analysts more removed from immediate policy questions, despite their tendencies to describe their own analytical efforts as though they were the rational-comprehensive method with an especially heavy use of theory. Similarly, this same method is inevitably resorted to in personal problem-solving, where means and ends are sometimes impossible to separate, where aspirations or objectives undergo constant development, and where drastic simplification of the complexity of the real world is urgent if problems are to be solved in the time that can be given to them. To an economist accustomed to dealing with the marginal or incremental concept in market processes, the central idea in the method is that both evaluation and empirical analysis are incremental. Accordingly, I have referred to the method elsewhere as "the incremental method."

Nonincremental Policy Making

Paul R. Schulman

Two major paradigms have come to dominate the scholarly analysis of public policy and quite possibly, the policy-making process itself. One is the decision model of incrementalism; the other a "divisibility" model of piecemeal public programs with negotiated and specialized pay-offs.

Incrementalism, described by Charles E. Lindblom, is a decision model which asserts the propensity of organizations to move in small steps.[1] Because of (1) disagreement on primary values and policy objectives, and (2) the difficulty of gathering and processing information on which to evaluate a wide range of potential policy options, policy makers typically arrive at their decisions by assessing only "limited comparisons to those policies that differ in relatively small degree from policies presently in effect."[2] The strategy of incrementalism is one of continual policy readjustments in pursuit of marginally redefined policy goals. Long-term plans are abandoned in favor of short-term political implementation.

The divisibility paradigm is not unrelated to incrementalism. It asserts, basically, that any large policy undertaking is simply the aggregation of many politically self-contained subprograms and activities. Policy is the distribution of discrete goods in portions—in line with prevailing configurations of power or publicized need.[3] This divisibility assumption, of course, lies behind the concept of "pluralism" invariably applied to the analysis of industrialized democracies.[4] It is implicit in the emerging "public choice" school of policy analysis.[5]

The divisibility paradigm supports the perception of the public interest as simply the sum total of countless individual interests.[6] As Anthony Downs has aptly described the paradigm in practice: "Each decision-maker or actor makes whatever choices seem to him to be the most appropriate at that moment, in light of his own interests and his own view of the public welfare."[7]

These two paradigms, as mentioned, enjoy a currency both in policy analysis and policy practice. Few critiques of these outlooks have appeared, and those criticisms which are offered suffer from inflated normative judgments and anemic descriptive insights.[8]

Yet the breadth of application accorded incremental and divisibility outlooks has not been without its costs. In particular, these paradigms have deprived policy analysis and public administration of attention to a class of policy enterprises which fit into neither framework. This essay is about that class of policies.

From Paul R. Schulman, "Nonincremental Policy Making," *American Political Science Review*, 69 (1975), 1354–1370. Reprinted by permission.

These are enterprises distinguished by their demand for *comprehensive* rather than incremental decisions; synoptic rather than piecemeal outlooks and vision. These policies are characterized by an *indivisibility* in the political commitment and resources they require for success.

This class of nonincremental, indivisible policies is perhaps small but is nonetheless significant. It consists of large-scale government undertakings commanding major shares of the public budget. Frequently these undertakings involve the application of new technologies to major political or social problems. Nonincremental policies must be cast within large-scale and risk-taking frameworks if they are even to approximate acceptable levels of goal-seeking performance. Again, as we shall see, these are characteristics for which conventional analytical models are inadequate.

In order to explore adequately the implications of nonincremental, indivisible policy, one case has been selected from this class for explication. Its analysis, supplemented by references to additional policy examples, will illustrate three primary characteristics of major significance—characteristics which elude the present coverage of policy-making models. The policy is U.S. manned space exploration—a large and revealing public undertaking.

THE NONINCREMENTAL POLICY START-UP

The first characteristic associated with this special class of policies to which we have been referring is important. *Nonincremental, indivisible policy pursuits are beset by organizational thresholds or "critical mass" points closely associated with their initiation and subsequent development.* These policies must rely for their success upon factors which come into play only at high levels of political and resource commitment. . . .

As pressure builds for government action within a specific issue setting it is likely to confront a partial vacuum in ongoing public policy. The beginnings of the ecology "movement" amply illustrate this phase—where increased public concern over problems of environmental quality quickly overbalanced the minimal regulatory standards of the federal government. This initial stage is one of *underscaling* in public policy. Such an underscaling also characterized the organizational insufficiencies of the space program in the period on which we have so far been concentrating.

Eventually, of course, public policies are generated in response to escalating public pressure. But, again, the discontinuous nature of policy expansion makes it difficult to match appropriately government performance with fluctuations in public "demand." Frequently, the appearance of government activity itself can contribute to the dissipation of public arousal. Secure in the symbolic reassurance that "something is being done," the public shifts its fleeting attentions to other issues of greater currency and fashion.[9] This decay in public concern can lead ultimately to a condition in which policy performance actually exceeds public demand, which might well be termed an *overscaling* dimension to public policy. At this extreme of the policy-pressure relationship, bureaucratic programs can persist long after generalized support for such pursuits has subsided. In regulatory policy making this is typically the stage at which the "capture" of the agency by a specialized constituency can occur. Because public arousal has waned, the regulatory agency must turn for its support to the one social component whose attention and watchfulness remain unwavering—the very interest which the agency seeks to regulate. Should policies in general fail to locate steadfast constituencies during this period of overscaling, the result must invariably be that saddest of administrative spectacles—the politically orphaned agency, an object (in Norton Long's words) "of contempt to its enemies and despair to its friends."[10] The overscaling dimension too has become an important part of the manned space exploration story.

In essence the expansion-support "game" is one at which the nonincremental, indivisible policy enterprise is considerably disadvantaged. This is so because of the extreme start-up lags to which it is subject. Nonincremental policy is beset by substantial discontinuities in both enlargement and payoff. Continuing the description of manned space exploration will illustrate this point more fully.

INSTABILITY IN NONINCREMENTAL POLICY

Apart from the problem of start-up thresholds, another major characteristic besets the nonincremental, indivisible policy pursuit: *nonincremental policy is in essence unstable—devoid of middle ground between self-generating states of growth and decay. . . .*

PUBLIC POLICY AND INDIVISIBILITY

A final, summary trait of nonincremental policy now presents itself. *Nonincremental policies are beset by an indivisibility which defies disaggregation into piecemeal decisions or additive partial advancements.* This means simply that for nonincremental policies a "self-containment" demand must be observed. Policy requirements as well as outputs must be provided at high levels or they cannot be provided at all.

Space exploration required elaborate and expensive start-up investments before it really got under way. Because of the delayed pay-off of the policy, a major political commitment was essential in order that these initial start-up costs would be judged worthwhile. *No short-term, piecemeal, or incremental commitment* could have mobilized the support and generated the expectations that space exploration required to surpass its start-up thresholds.

Perhaps this "threshold effect" lies at the heart of nonincremental policy.

Thresholds themselves are highly important to the understanding of a great many social processes. As Kenneth Boulding has observed:

> [Social] depreciation and appreciation are not continuous functions of use or load, but exhibit threshold or overload phenomena, which is what causes crises. . . . Continuous functions, which are fine for celestial mechanics, are characteristic of social mechanics only over small ranges of variation, and most social problems arise because of discontinuous functions—the road that suddenly jams up as one more car appears on it, the river that refuses to clean itself under a single addition of sewage, the international system that breaks down into war, or the city that erupts into riot when some small straw is laid onto some existing back.[12]

Thresholds make it exceedingly difficult for a series of small incremental steps to add up in cumulative fashion to one big comprehensive step. *They detach piecemeal decisions or resource commitments from corresponding or proportionate policy pay-offs.* This is a critical oversight in incrementalism and the divisible goods model of policy making, and an area to which a great deal of corrective attention should be directed.

In examining this last trait of nonincremental policy it is appropriate to offer additional examples of public enterprises which might fit into this class. Consider urban renewal undertakings, for instance. In urban areas it is becoming increasingly apparent that the rejuvenation of the inner city is an operation to which thresholds or critical masses are attached. Slums represent resource and structural "sinks"—downward cycles of dilapidation and capital depreciation. The influx of limited recovery-inducing elements into the slum environment—in the form of public housing projects, piecemeal slum clearance efforts and private capital investment—is rarely sufficient to overcome the "sink" effect which characterizes the slum. The decay rate of public housing, as well as shrinking inner-city investment returns testify to the failure of small-scale, incremental policy interventions to effect slum rejuvenation.[13]

Perhaps only massive efforts, commitments or expenditures will result in a cycle of rejuvenation which would overcome the sink effect and establish itself as self-sustaining. Major capital inflows will begin to justify private inner-city investment. This investment will in turn enlarge the urban job market, providing resources and incentives for the repair and rebuilding of slum housing. The subsequent appreciation of this housing will add to the supply of inner-city capital, and so on.[14]

If this were so, an urban redevelopment policy, unless cast on a scale approaching its critical resource thresholds, has little chance of realizing—*or even approximately realizing*—its ends. The potential challenge here to a strategy of incrementalism is unmistakable. A series of small decisions or steps, below a policy threshold, will not advance the policy even incrementally in the direction of its goals. Yet at a critical point of personnel or resource commitment, a "take-off" can occur in policy output—yielding vastly multiplied gains in goal-seeking performance.

The need to breach thresholds and to maintain an organizational transcendence of these limiting factors, places severe constraints on the "divisibility" of the nonincremental policy enterprise. It is likely that urban transportation policies frequently fall victim to their own indivisibility requirements. Rapid transit systems in particular possess underlying scale demands—they must attain a requisite coverage or they simply cannot cope with traffic densities in sufficient degree to justify their costs. Additionally, these systems require firm commitments to detailed plans, and an early construction start-up before labor and materials costs rise prohibitively, and before land acquisition and rezoning resistance coalesces.

Given these requirements, it is easy to understand why, despite feasibility studies, campaign promises, and the establishment of urban transportation planning agencies, urban transport policy remains underdeveloped. Rapid transit systems, because of their indivisibility characteristics, acquire a rigidity which will not permit them to surmount successfully the compromise, delay, and reduction processes of urban political bargaining. These are essentially processes of *disaggregation*, and they push transportation ventures below those critical thresholds upon which they rely for success.

Indivisibility of the same type can also afflict large-scale planning efforts in general. Plans, after all, create their own support requirements and must generate political commitments and public aspiration in order to fulfill them. Disaggregation can undermine the base of support required for adequate plan implementation. It can seriously disrupt the internal "logic" upon which the plan must rely for its persuasiveness. In this connection Gerhard Colm has argued that "it is very important to recognize that a one-year plan cannot be obtained merely by dividing, say, a five-year plan into five equal parts."[15]

Indivisibility, of course, leads to a major vulnerability in the nonincremental policy enterprise. To a large extent its success depends on the degree to which it can be shielded from the ever-present forces of political disaggregation. Yet this very shielding requirement contains enormous political implications.

NONINCREMENTAL POLICY AND ITS POLITICAL CONSEQUENCES

It often happens that nonincremental policy managers, painfully aware of the vulnerabilities to which their programs are subject, will go to great lengths to establish congenial political environments. Frequently, a nonincremental policy will be "oversold" to the public in order to gain the support and resources deemed essential in the overcoming of thresholds. Once oversold, it becomes difficult to modify the basic objectives of the policy without threatening the political foundations upon which its support has been based. For manned space exploration the Kennedy lunar landing commitment became the major sustaining but at the same time the major constraining factor with which space policy makers had to deal.

Yet this overselling effect is not confined to space exploration alone.

Theodore Lowi has noted an identical tendency in large-scale foreign policy undertakings as well. The war in Vietnam, Lowi argues, was rigidified by the very way in which it was sold to the public:

> No policy has escaped injury to itself and to national interests and international stability in the years since American statesmen have felt the need to oversell policies *in order to avoid coming up with a partial decision.* The war in Vietnam has been just another instance of the point. The fighting in the South was not of our making. The crisis was. The escalation was. The involvement in Vietnam was sold by American image-makers as a case of unambiguous aggression and therefore of the need for military victory. Perhaps it was both of these things, but to sell it on the front pages that way in order to ensure support at home left world diplomats, including our own, *with almost no options.*[16]

If Lowi's point is true, it hints strongly at major rigidities implicit in nonincremental foreign policies. The perceived need to accommodate thresholds (i.e., to avoid "partial decisions") can lock foreign policy makers into unyielding, "all-or-nothing" commitments.

This rigidity has major consequences for all policies of a nonincremental nature. It renders them resistant to the compromise and adjustment processes of political bargaining—frequently the major means by which public accountability is imposed. At the same time, their rigidity places nonincremental policies at a disadvantage in responding to shifting political coalitions—a demand essential to the maintenance of public support.

Compounding these difficulties is the instability of nonincremental policy itself. As mentioned earlier, policies in this class are unable to balance themselves within resource or aspirational steady-states. Because of this, a twofold political problem presents itself. In what way besides overselling are policy makers to ensure the requisite support for their undertakings? Without overselling, thresholds can render nonincremental policy so vulnerable to political "adjustments" that it exceeds existing capacities for bureaucratic support. Policy managers, in this case, are likely to experience a continuing frustration in starting up their programs and in mobilizing sufficient resources to offer an adequate chance of goal attainment.

The second half of the political dilemma is that of *disengaging* from rigid, nonincremental policy endeavors which have entered into a self-escalating spiral of growth. Disengagement is difficult to accomplish because of heightened aspirations and bureaucratic forces which support such spirals. (It is also likely if accomplished to lead to serious organizational perturbations as a concomitant retrenchment cycle sets in.) The war in Vietnam would appear to illustrate this disengagement dilemma to a frightening degree.

THE INAPPLICABILITY OF TRIAL PROGRAMS

Another policy implication attached to nonincremental, indivisible undertakings is their challenge to the ever-popular limited-scope trial program. These programs are frequently employed in policy settings because, in the event of failure, not too much in the way of prestige or organizational resources has been risked in them. If they succeed, they provide a blueprint for adjustments in design and an enlargement of application. These advantages have led many policy makers to urge that we "expand the area of governmental and public affairs activity in which new ideas can be tried out as limited-scale programs."[17]

If nothing else, this analysis of nonincremental policy suggests that trial programs can have severe limitations. It suggests that small-scale policy efforts may not necessarily replicate larger ones. Trial programs cannot hope to duplicate those critical commitment and resource thresholds upon which nonincremental, indivisible policy pursuits must rely.

As a result, limited-scale programs are likely to be seriously misleading indicators of nonincremental policy performance. Such programs may indicate a potential for success which is really mythical where larger forces must come into play. Perhaps more importantly, they may project failure where success is possible, given resource commitments on the requisite scale.

All of these policy implications hint strongly at the need for new analytical attention to nonincremental policy, and particularly the need to identify, prior to policy commitment, *which public undertakings are likely to have thresholds attached*. This identification might allow for more enlightened political decisions and the subsequent design of more congenial organizational environments should commitments to nonincremental policies be undertaken. In the meantime, however, no such analytical imagination appears likely until alternatives to the incremental and divisibility paradigms which dominate policy analysis are presented.

NONINCREMENTAL POLICY: THE CONCEPTUAL CHALLENGE

To review briefly, this essay has described a class of policy undertakings which elude much of the analytical weaponry of political science. Nonincremental policies require large start-up investments unfulfillable by incremental or piecemeal commitments. They are policies which are nonequilibrating with respect to growth—that is, they are devoid of middle ground between expansion and decay. Lindblom, in his description of incrementalism, stresses the importance of marginal and continuous decisional refinements to the policy process. Yet the policies of which we have been speaking are precisely those for which this strategy is inappropriate. They cannot attain the equilibrium *which would allow these adjustive actions to be successful*.

It is important to recognize the extent to which incremental and equilibrating outlooks dominate political science. Policy analysis repeatedly stresses the degree to which marginal balances are struck between bureaucrat and client, between policy goals and public pressure, and between bureaucratic decisions of the present and organizational routines of the past.

In addition, many of the emerging trends in the analysis of public policy lead in the direction of further elevating decentralized, divisible processes as the "stuff" of policy making. The "public choice" school of policy analysis applies economic models to its assessment of policy activity. In effect, this approach assumes the existence of a decision "market" in which the disaggregated forces of competition, bargaining, and exchange are the determining factors in policy output. Related to this analytical outlook is a developing political persuasion which endorses the increased decentralization of public decision making.

Perhaps the best argument for this public policy "approach" has been presented by Alan Altshuler. Altshuler asserts that it is now necessary "to think more systematically about the virtues of disaggregation versus integration, pluralism versus coordination, and the free market versus regulation in social life."[18] Altshuler calls for a "debureaucratization" in public policy—wherein bureaucratic decisions are supplanted by popular decisions (as in citizen participation and community control) and by market decisions (in which a market adjustment of individual preferences, such as in voucher plans, replaces centralized efforts at planning or control).

There is obviously a great deal to be said in behalf of the public choice and decentralization movements in public policy. Yet there is a real danger, again, that such outlooks will command a disproportionate amount of both analytical attention *and* political support—at the expense of important nonincremental and indivisible policy objectives to which thresholds are attached. This is a problem of theoretical and practical dimensions.

In political theory at present, decision-making models as well as most models of the political system itself, describe deviance-minimizing, self-stabilizing, and equilibrating operations exclusively. Yet as we have seen, nonincremental policy frequently entails a high-level, unstable process of deviance *amplification*—a performance "take-off" based upon systems of mutual causation.[19] Entirely new models must be fashioned to account for deviance-amplifying processes before we can hope to analyze enterprises like manned space exploration adequately.

Meanwhile, a deep disillusionment has come to surround the public's assessment of nonincremental political commitments to large-scale policy. In this era of skepticism little support exists for ambitious and expensive undertakings in the public sector. Peculiarly, however, interest in large-scale *goals* remains; and herein lies a major dilemma. Solutions are still urgently sought to problems of poverty, unemployment, and urban decay. Demands continue for major improvements in transportation, housing, energy supply, and environmental quality. These are large-scale demands. Yet the decentralization movement may force us to rely for their resolution upon small-scale, disaggregated policy efforts.

It may well be that many of these efforts will be successful. But the danger exists that in a number of problem areas, incremental policy attempts will fail repeatedly as each falls below some critical effectiveness threshold. Perhaps only nonincremental modes of policy making will prove appropriate in satisfying many of our implicit societal aspirations. The decentralization movement threatens to undercut seriously the political support upon which such nonincremental enterprises would have to depend.

The point of this essay is not to attack the public choice or decentralization movements in public administration, nor even to challenge the utility of the incremental model of policy making. The purpose of this essay is to argue for *additional* analytical frameworks to account for phenomena which lie outside present theoretical coverage. New departures in policy analysis are called for if we are to understand many large-scale public undertakings and their problems. Such understanding is important—both to the development of political science and to the success of public policy.

NOTES

1. See Charles E. Lindblom, "The 'Science' of Muddling Through," *Public Administration Review*, 19 (Spring, 1959), 79–88; Lindblom and David Braybrooke, *A Strategy of Decision* (New York: The Free Press, 1963); and Lindblom, *The Intelligence of Democracy: Decision-Making Through Mutual Adjustment* (New York: The Free Press, 1965).

2. Lindblom, "The 'Science' of Muddling Through," p. 84.

3. For a description of "divisible" policy making see Robert A. Dahl and Charles E. Lindblom, *Politics, Economics and Welfare* (New York: Harper and Brothers, 1953); E. E. Schattschneider, *The Semi-Sovereign People* (New York: Holt, Rinehart and Winston, 1960); and Robert A. Dahl, *Pluralist Democracy in the United States* (Chicago: Rand McNally, 1967). A more critical appraisal of the same phenomenon can be found in Theodore J. Lowi, *The End of Liberalism: Ideology, Policy and the Crisis of Public Authority* (New York: W. W. Norton and Company, 1969).

4. For the classic statement regarding pluralism see, of course, David B. Truman, *The Governmental Process* (New York: Alfred A. Knopf, 1951).

5. The public choice or economic market models of the policy process are presented in such works as James M. Buchanan and Gordon Tullock, *The Calculus of Consent* (Ann Arbor: University of Michigan Press, 1962); Warren F. Ilchman and Norman T. Uphoff, *The Political Economy of Change* (Berkeley: University of California Press, 1969); Robert L. Curry and L. L. Wade, *A Theory of Political Exchange* (Englewood Cliffs, New Jersey: Prentice-Hall, 1968); and William C. Mitchell, *Public Choice in America* (Chicago: Markham Publishing Company, 1971).

6. An excellent description of this "realist" approach to the public interest can be found in Glendon A. Schubert, *The Public Interest* (Glencoe, Illinois: The Free Press, 1961), ch. 4.

7. Anthony Downs, *Urban Problems and Prospects* (Chicago: Markham Publishing Company, 1970), p. 37.

8. See, for example, Yehezkel Dror, "Muddling Through—'Science' or Inertia?" *Public Administration Review*, 24 (September, 1964), 153–157; Dror, *Public Policymaking Reexamined* (San Francisco: Chandler Publishing Company, 1968); and Amitai Etzioni, "Mixed Scanning: A 'Third' Approach to Decision-Making," *Public Administration Review*, 27 (December, 1967), 385–392.

9. In this context see Murray Edelman, *The Symbolic Uses of Politics* (Urbana, Illinois: University of Illinois Press, 1964).

10. Norton E. Long, "Power and Administration," *Public Administration Review*, 9 (Autumn 1949), 257.

11. Richard S. Lewis, "The Kennedy Effect," *Bulletin of the Atomic Scientists*, 24 (March, 1968), 2.

12. Kenneth Boulding, "Discussion," in "The Political Economy of Environmental Quality," *American Economic Review*, 61 (May, 1971), 167.

13. For a discussion of the urban decay spiral see William J. Baumol, "Macroeconomics and Unbalanced Growth: The Anatomy of Urban Crisis," *American Economic Review*, 57 (June, 1967), 415–426. Also, Harry W. Richardson, *Urban Economics* (London: Penguin Books, 1971), pp. 133–145.

14. For an analysis of these potential "accelerator effects" in urban renewal see Wilbur R. Thompson, *A Preface to Urban Economics* (Baltimore: The Johns Hopkins Press, 1965), pp. 299–302.

15. Gerhard Colm, *Integration of National Planning and Budgeting* (Washington, D.C.: National Planning Association, 1965), p. 24.

16. Theodore J. Lowi, *The End of Liberalism*, p. 179 (emphasis added).

17. Adam Yarmolinsky, "Ideas Into Programs," in *The Presidential Advisory System*, ed. Thomas E. Cronin and Sanford D. Greenberg (New York: Harper and Row, 1969), p. 99. For a further discussion of experimental policy making see Alice M. Rivlin, *Systematic Thinking for Social Action* (Washington, D.C.: The Brookings Institution, 1971), pp. 108–119.

18. Alan Altshuler, "New Institutions to Serve the Individual," in *Environment and Policy: The Next Fifty Years*, ed. William R. Ewald (Bloomington: Indiana University Press, 1968), p. 425.

19. For an excellent discussion of the deviance-amplification process see Margoroh Maruyama, "The Second Cybernetics: Deviance-Amplifying Mutual Causal Processes," in *Modern Systems, Research for the Behavioral Scientist*, ed. Walter Buckley (Chicago: Aldine Press, 1968), pp. 304–313.

16

The Implementation Game

Eugene Bardach

Indeed, it is precisely because Pressman and Wildavsky have identified so many of the numerous features of the process that tend to *aggravate and exaggerate* underlying conflicts that their study is so worthwhile.[1] They lead us to a critical insight about the implementation process: the maneuvers of the several parties both express conflict and create it—and with every maneuver aimed at reducing it there is an associated risk of actually making matters worse. In an important sense, therefore, much of the implementation process moves along "out of control," driven by complex forces not of any party's making. . . .

Pressman and Wildavsky have attempted a dynamic interpretation of the implementation process, that is, an interpretation that takes the passage of time into account.[2] Consider, for instance, their implied proposition that, under certain conditions, the longer players continue their maneuvering the worse the prospects for program success. Consider also their attempt to quantify what they call "the anatomy of delay"[3] by assigning differential clearance times to each separate agreement requirement and summing them. Given seventy clearances and "arbitrarily assigning a value of one week for minimal delay, three weeks for minor delay, and six weeks for moderate delay," they come up with a total of 233-1/3

From Eugene Bardach, *The Implementation Game: What Happens after a Bill Becomes a Law*. Copyright © 1977 MIT. (Cambridge, Mass.: MIT Press, 1977), chapter 1. Reprinted by permission.

weeks. "Under these assumptions the delay thus far would come out to approximately four and a half years, which is not far off the mark."[4] . . .

The main problem with the Pressman-Wildavsky approach is that it does not go far enough. It suggests that typologies might be important, for example, their three or four types of delay processes, but stops short of suggesting a conceptual basis for such typologies. It is also limited, when it does discuss typologies, to one specialized topic, delay. It does not explicitly identify and analyze implementation processes that result in the perversion or subversion of policy goals or the processes that lead to excessive financial costs. Nor does it attempt to characterize in a moderately abstract and systematic way the interactions that routinely link the different kinds of institutions or roles normally involved in a process of program assembly.

It is a felt need for a usable typology that has led me to the metaphor of "games." Games can be classified according to the nature of their stakes. As a simple organizing device, if nothing else, this classification principle is quite effective. This is not the only way one might attempt to classify games, to be sure. Mathematical game theorists have invented, for their own purposes, much more elegant schemes contained in a vast literature that we shall ignore. For our own, basically descriptive, purposes, relying on the idea of stakes appears far more useful. Readers who can think of a better method are encouraged to try their own hands at it. As a description of the basic activities of the implementation process, it is a helpful refinement of the original idea of "control," which we said in the introduction was at the heart of the "implementation problem." We have seen that "control" is exercised through bargaining, persuasion, and maneuvering under conditions of uncertainty. "Control," therefore, resolves into strategies and tactics—hence the appropriateness of "games" as the characterization of the "control" aspects of the process.

The idea of "games," therefore, will serve principally as a master metaphor that directs attention and stimulates insight.[5] It directs us to look at the players, what they regard as the stakes, their strategies and tactics, their resources for playing, the rules of play (which stipulate the conditions for winning), the rules of "fair" play (which stipulate the boundaries beyond which lie fraud or illegitimacy), the nature of the communications (or lack of them) among the players, and the degree of uncertainty surrounding the possible outcomes. The game metaphor also directs our attention to who is not willing to play and for what reasons, and to who insists on changes in some of the game's parameters as a condition for playing.

By "system" I mean simply a collection of structural elements related to one another through ongoing processes. The elements are games, and their interrelationships are so manifold and convoluted that it is impossible to say much about the system as a whole except that the constituent elements, the games, are on the whole only loosely interrelated.[6]

Consider, for instance, the interrelationships depicted in the case study of the EDA project in Oakland. Within the EDA, the Washington office, the Seattle office, and the Oakland office were all involved in a game among themselves, and the continually changing outcomes of that game affected "the agency's" resources and strategies in its games with the Port of Oakland and with World Airways. Games that the agency was playing with the U.S. General Accounting Office, the Congress, and the Nixon Administration (beginning, of course, only in 1969), constrained its choices of strategy in dealing with the port and with World. The port was constrained by its ongoing game with the city of Oakland, as World Airways was constrained by its games with its business competitors, its stockholders, its customers, and so on.

These relations exemplify cases where different games do in fact interact with each other. The outcomes of certain games set the conditions for the play of other games. Resources committed to one game, and the maneuvering within its rules, affect a player's ability to maneuver in other games being played simultaneously. Yet the illustrations above can suggest weak or absent interactions as well, for example, between the General Accounting Office and the competitors of World Airways, or between the Seattle office of EDA and the Nixon White House. As we list, describe, and analyze the following series of different implementation games, we shall attempt to delineate the plausible interrelationships among them. Of all possible two-way interrelationships, only a minority seem to me plausibly connected with any degree of either strength or regularity, however. The political and institutional relationships in an implementation process on any but the smallest scale are simply too numerous and diverse to admit of our asserting lawlike propositions about them. It is the fragmentary and disjunctive nature of the real world that makes "a general theory of the implementation process" (which has been urged upon me by some readers of the draft manuscript) unattainable and, indeed, unrealistic.

To summarize, then, the "implementation process" is: (1) a process of assembling the elements required to produce a particular programmatic outcome, and (2) the playing out of a number of loosely interrelated games whereby these elements are withheld from or delivered to the program assembly process on particular terms. . . .

NOTES

1. Jeffrey L. Pressman and Aaron Wildavsky, *Implementation* (Berkeley: University of California Press, 1973).

2. Pressman and Wildavsky, *Implementation*, p. 93.

3. Pressman and Wildavsky, *Implementation*, p. 93.

4. Pressman and Wildavsky, *Implementation*, pp. 106–107.

5. See Allison's comparable usage and his justification, "Conceptual Models," p. 708, esp. fn 79. See also the usage in Norton Long's classic article, "The Local Community as an Ecology of Games," *American Sociological Review* 64 (November 1968): 251–261.

6. As with "game theory," we shall ignore the large body of literature on "systems theory."

Implementation As Evolution

Giandomenico Majone and Aaron Wildavsky

The study of implementation is becoming a growth industry; tens, perhaps hundreds, of studies are underway now. Yet researchers are visibly uneasy. It is not so much that they expect to discover all the right answers; they are not even sure they are asking the right questions. Amidst the flurry of activity is an underlying suspicion that the phenomenon to be studied—implementation—eludes understanding. But this uneasiness is not surprising, for the attempt to study implementation raises the most basic question about the relation between thought and action: How can ideas manifest themselves in a world of behavior?

"WHO'S ON FIRST?"

Let us begin with the initial source of enlightenment (or, if you prefer, confusion) in defining the domain of implementation, the effort in the first edition of *Implementation* to distinguish a stage of implementation from a stage of policy when these are intertwined. Is it appropriate to separate objectives and actions when, analytically, language and behavior have joined them together? Having said that there must be a goal against which to judge implementation, Pressman and Wildavsky went on to say that the goal and the implementing actions are part of a process of interaction. What comes first, then, the chicken of the goal or the egg of implementation? The authors answer that "each element is dependent on the other," so that "program implementation thus becomes a seamless web." Now you see it (implementation of course); now you don't. Having just indicated that implementation involves forging a causal chain from objectives to results, the authors immediately reverse the direction of causality. "We oversimplify . . . once a program is underway implementers become responsible both for the initial conditions and for the objectives toward which they are supposed to lead."[1]

If implementation is everywhere, as one of the authors suggested in another connection,[2] is it *ipso facto* nowhere? Indeed, the authors warn that "the separation of policy design from implementation is fatal." Yet if they cannot be separated, what place is there for policy analysis or, indeed, for anything but action? "Though we can't isolate policy and implementation for separate discussion," the authors of *Implementation* continue, "the purpose of our analysis is to bring them into closer correspondence with one another." It just possibly may be reasonable to separate in the mind subjects that must be joined in action. To what purpose? To improve policy design. But aren't policies always being redesigned? Yes, there's the rub. No doubt this is why students of implementation complain that the subject is so slippery; it does depend on what one is trying to explain, from what point of view, at what point in its history.

IMPLEMENTATION AS CONTROL

One way to conceptualize the split between policy and implementation is to merge them into each other. One may absorb implementation into planning and design; what is supposed to be, will be, when the grand design unfolds; some may deny the existence of anything preceding implementation so that implementation is absorbed into interaction. Which position one takes depends on how one answers the question: What sort of entity is a "policy" before it is implemented? Is policy a fully articulated plan, needing only enforcement, or is policy the necessary premise for everything that follows? Or is the preimplementation stage a limbo where policy ghosts await the arrival of a merciful implementer? In the following pages we shall argue that both positions—reification and nullification—discount important features of policy development.

In the planning-and-control model of implementation, the initial plan, call it P_0, and its realization, call it P_1, are on the same logical level. The implementation problem, as the users of the model see it, is to transform one into the other by a suitable theory or "production function." Barring design errors P_1 is logically implied by P_0 and good implementation is the irresistible unfolding of a tautology. The model prescribes clearly stated goals, detailed plans, tight controls and—to take care of the human side of the equation—incentives and indoctrination.

This view of implementation—which we have caricatured just enough to make its main features stand out—has the intuitive appeal of all teleological or means-end theories, which seem to embody the very essence of rational action. As description, it leaves out the detours, the blind alleys, the discarded hypotheses, the constraints tightened and loosened, the lumpy stuff of life in favor of a predigested formula consisting of a ranking of objectives, a considering of alternatives, and a criterion that chooses among them. Presentation of the end of inquiry provides prescription for its beginning and its middle. No one does (or should) think like that if only because divorcing available resources from desirable objectives stultifies policy analysis. As prescription, this prevailing paradigm of rationality encourages consistency in ranking objectives at the expense of effectiveness in making policy preferences live in the world. But, at least in the area of public policy, it is neither descriptively nor prescriptively adequate. In this view, for instance, implementers must know what they are supposed to do in order to be effective. Yet, "street-level" bureaucrats are notorious for being too busy coping with their day-to-day problems to recite to themselves the policies they are supposed to apply. Even high-level officials do not seem to be particularly committed to the idea of making correct deductions from firmly established principles. Writing about the administrative process in the regulatory commissions of the New Deal era, James Landis recalls how "one of the ablest administrators that it was my good fortune to know, I believe, never read, at least more than casually, the statutes that he translated into reality. He assumed that they gave him power to deal with the broad problems of an industry and, upon that understanding, he sought his own solutions."[3]

The planning model recognizes that implementation may fail because the original plan was infeasible. But it does not recognize the important point that many, perhaps most, constraints remain hidden in the planning stage, and are only discovered in the implementation process. Moreover, feasibility conditions keep changing over time: old constraints disappear or are overcome (e.g., through learning), while new ones emerge. The solution space undergoes continuous transformations, shrinking in one direction, expanding in another. Consequently, the implementer's left hand must be probing constantly the feasibility boundary, while his right hand tries to assemble the various program components.

This sort of ad hoc, trial-and-error searching for a feasible solution is a far cry from the deliberate procedures suggested by the planning model. The complicated flowcharts purporting to "structure" the implementation process only show how close implementation analysts of this stripe can come to the same infinite regress that has plagued all other planners: since there is good and bad implementation (as there is good and bad planning), it is not enough simply to "implement"; one must choose the *right* implementation plan. But then, by the same logic, one must know the *right* way to implement the implementation plan, so that there is no way to tell where the implied regress ends. In practice, implementing a policy is a unitary process or procedure, not a tandem operation of setting a goal and then enforcing the plan that embodies it.

IMPLEMENTATION AS INTERACTION

The second major model in implementation analysis minimizes the importance of goals and plans. An authoritatively adopted policy is "only a collection of words" prior to implementation.[4] At most it is a point of departure for bargaining among implementers. Policy standards—establishing requirements for how policy goals shall be implemented—"represent no more than exhortations: they are inanimate messages that must be communicated to those in charge of executing the policy."[5] The more consistent analysts of this school actually deny any meaning to expressions such as: "the implementation process translates a policy mandate into action"; "implementation realizes policy goals"; or "implementation transforms prescriptions into results." For, as Bardach carefully points out, such locutions suggest that words can somehow become deeds (he concedes, however, that these "words" can create expectations and thereby influence behavior).[6]

These analysts correctly sense that a yet-to-be implemented policy and an implemented one do not belong to the same logical category, but their words/deeds dichotomy is too crude, in our opinion, to be useful analytically. This dichotomy implies, among other things, that in success or failure, implementation is completely divorced from policy success or failure. The process is the purpose. The next logical step, which in fact has been taken by some writers, is to assert that the central problem of implementation is not whether implementers conform to prescribed policy, but whether the implementation process results in consensus on goals, individual autonomy, and commitment to policy on the part of those who must carry it out. But these problems are pervasive; they are not the product of functional distinctions among different groups of actors in a policy problem.

At a deeper level, we disagree with the idea that the function of the implementation process is to satisfy the psychological and social needs of the participants, regardless of the actual policy results. This view is strangely reminiscent of old syndicalist doctrines summarized in once-popular slogans like "The Railroads to the Railroadmen," and "The Mines to the Miners." The syndicalists' demand for "industrial democracy" actually concealed a view of production as an end in itself rather than as a means of satisfying consumers' wants. We feel the emphasis on consensus, bargaining, and political maneuvering can easily lead (and has, in fact, led) to the conception that implementation is its own reward.

The interaction model of implementation carries interesting evolutionary overtones. The results are not predictable, an element of surprise is maintained, and the outcomes are likely to be different from those sought by any single participant. Does an evolutionary conception of implementation imply that any path, any product of a number of active forces, is appropriate so that, as Hegel said, the real is right? Certainly not, but that is the impression one often gets from the writings of advocates of the interaction model. The model is inadequate for assessing the intrinsic worth of policy ideas and their significance for policy evolution. Hence, interpretations based on it are, at best, partial. Consider, for example, the "capture theory" of governmental regulation in the United States. The theory holds that regulatory commissions inevitably become captured by the interests—truckers, airlines, drug companies—they are supposed to regulate because these are the forces that care most about what the commissions do. With the understanding that this capture may ebb and flow according to the political seasons, this scenario appears to be a reasonable description of reality. However, the economic critique of regulation is more parsimonious and, at the same time, more fundamental. For the economist argues that the policy idea is defective at its roots: compared to market adjustments, government regulations are inevitably ill-informed, slow to respond, and detrimental to consumers because they reduce competition. Explaining policy failure in terms of the quality of the policy idea seems to work at least as well as explaining it in terms of social forces capturing and corrupting the implementation process.

POLICIES AS DISPOSITIONS

Having rejected the idea of reifying goals and programs (policies do not grow from small but true replicas of their mature form) as well as the idea of reducing them to mere "words" (evolution presupposes a genetic basis), it is appropriate for us to propose an alternative viewpoint.

We begin by observing that the essential constituents of any policy are objectives and resources. In most policies of interest, objectives are characteristically multiple (because we want many things, not just one), conflicting (because we want different things), and vague (because that is how we can agree to proceed without having to agree also on exactly what to do). So if the objectives are not uniquely determined, neither are the modes of implementation for them.

Because of cognitive limitations and the dynamic quality of our environment, moreover, there is no way for us to understand at first all the relevant constraints on resources. We can discover and then incorporate them into our plans only as the implementation process unfolds. As long as we cannot determine what is feasible, we cannot carry out any well-defined policy univocally; all we can do is carry along a cluster of potential policies. Implementation begins neither with words nor deeds, but with multiple dispositions to act or to treat certain situations in certain ways.

Plans, programs, judicial decisions, and administrative regulations may be evaluated as specific occurrences or results by the legislative draftsman, the lawyer, the administrative expert, or the historian. As far as the implementation analyst is concerned, these exist only as potentialities, and their realization depends both on intrinsic qualities and on external circumstances. If we want to think of a plan as a tool in the hands of the implementer, we must bear in mind that even a tool is only a cluster of dispositions. To say that something is a tool is to say that it can produce certain results under appropriate circumstances; it is not to say that it is drilling, sawing, or welding at any particular moment.

Now Webster's definition of disposition ("the tendency of something to act in a certain manner under given circumstances") obscures the important point that many dispositions—and certainly those relevant to the present discussion—are generic rather than specific. They do not find expression in a unique function or activity, and it may even be impossible to determine, a priori, the specific forms in which they will be realized. Even a highly specialized tool can be employed for uses other than the normal ones: *faute de mieux*, one can hit a nail with a shoe or with a fat dictionary. Dispositional terms like "skillful," "intelligent," "fair," "knowledgeable" (and their opposites) imply wide ranges of possible actions and types of behavior rather than tendencies toward, or capabilities of, specific achievements.

Policies grow out of ideas, and ideas are inexhaustible. What can be done with them depends as much on their intrinsic richness as on the quality of the minds and the nature of their environment. As problems are truly understood only after they have been solved, so the full implications of an idea can often be seen only from hindsight, only after the idea has been used and adapted to a variety of circumstances. Hence the beginnings of an idea are, generally speaking, an insufficient measure of its capabilities or its scope. Any new idea, Cardinal Newman once observed, has unknown amplitude:

> It will, in proportion of its native vigour and subtlety, introduce itself into the framework and details of social life, changing public opinion and supporting or undermining the foundations of established order. Thus in time it has grown into an ethical code, or into a system of government, or into a theology, or into a ritual, according to its capabilities; and this system, or body of thought, theoretical and practical . . . will after all be only the adequate representation of the original idea, *being nothing else than what that very idea meant from the first—its exact image as seen in a combination of the most diversified aspects, with the suggestions and corrections of many minds, and the illustration of many trials.*[7]

Is the policy idea, then, what it was or what it became or what it might have been? And how do we credit the contributions of those "many minds" and "many trials"?

IMPLEMENTATION SHAPES POLICY

Policies are continuously transformed by implementing actions that simultaneously alter resources and objectives. Varying the amount of resources need not require doing more or less of the same thing: one might do quite different things with $1 million than if one had $10 million. Altering objectives may change the significance of behaviors that are seemingly the same. Suppose the actual purpose of a system of effluent charges gradually shifts from pollution control to raising general revenue. The fiscal and administrative mechanisms may remain the same, but the policy would change significantly. When social security changes from insurance to income redistribution, the same name covers very different realities.

Which objectives are to be implemented, in what order, with what proportion of available resources? Constraints are also objectives. There is no such thing as "the objective"—reducing poverty or improving health. There are always constraints as to time allowed, money permitted, procedures allowable, liberties held inviolable, and so on. That we focus our attention on a particular one, singling it out as our objective, does not mean there are not others within which we must also operate or, at least, find ways to relax or overcome. Knowing only the avowed programmatic objective without being aware of other constraints is insufficient for predicting or controlling outcomes. When we are able to confront the multiplicity of objectives and constraints—so little inflation versus so much unemployment—or to observe the juggling acts of ill-fated commissions on national goals, in which the early objectives are likely to catch the worm of scarce resources, then the necessity to continuously readjust the means and ends becomes evident.

The goal of the British National Health Service Act of 1946 was the "improvement in the physical and mental health of the people of England and Wales, and the prevention, diagnosis, and treatment of illness." "The services so provided," the Act continues, "shall be free of charge, except where provision of this act expressly provides for the making and recovery of charges." But how is the government to provide, at no cost to users, services whose demand elasticity is on the average quite high, and whose costs keep rapidly rising? No independent economist or government adviser seems to have raised this question at the time the National Health Service was created. Instead, the advocates of the new system relied on three implicit assumptions: (1) that health needs could be determined on the basis of purely medical criteria; (2) that it was possible to meet those needs without placing too heavy a burden on the national resources; and (3) that by reducing ill health, the Service would contribute to increased production, and would in fact become "a wealth-producing as well as health-producing Service."

Experience has shown that the first two assumptions were incorrect, and the third one is still highly doubtful.[8] The costs of the Service soon proved much higher than initial estimates. It became necessary to introduce charges for drug prescriptions, dentures, spectacles, replacement of surgical appliances and equipment, and for hospital treatment following road accidents. Because the prevailing ideology has prevented the development of a coherent system for rationing medical services, unplanned rationing took place, resulting in congestion, and, in the opinion of many observers, a decrease in quality of services. Since available resources were not even sufficient to meet current demands, very little investment in new facilities was possible, and the goal of prevention kept receding into the distant future. In sum, the goals of the National Health Service had to be adjusted and readjusted as the impossibility of efficiently providing "free" services with high elasticity of demand became increasingly clear.

Conversely, the discovery that some constraints are no longer binding can suggest to implementers possibilities that the original planners did not envisage or desire. Significant developments in social security in the United States since 1935 (in particular, the repeated extensions of coverage to new groups) appear to be due not only to political pressures, but even more to organizational breakthroughs in data collection and information handling.[9]

How well policies respond to opportunities, how well they facilitate adaptation and error correction, are qualities insufficiently discussed. For our purposes, however, it is more important to observe that keeping things going rather than getting things started is the ordinary condition of administration. It is not policy design but redesign that occurs most of the time. Who is to say, then, whether implementation consists of altering objectives to correspond with available resources (as social welfare spending decreases, inflation increases), or of mobilizing new resources to accomplish old objectives (as the United States buys foreign currencies to defend the dollar)? Indeed, old patterns of behavior are often retrospectively rationalized to fit new notions about appropriate objectives. We do not always decide what to do and succeed or fail at it; rather, we observe what we have done and try to make it consistent in retrospect.[10] If Head Start finds it difficult to demonstrate lasting improvement in children's reading abilities, it may stress its clear capacity for increasing parents' involvement, which in turn may lead to educational improvement in their children. We choose after the act as well as before. For example, policymakers often come to certain conclusions under the pressure of events, or previous commitments, or the force of their own convictions. A policy may come into being still lacking a doctrine capable of explaining it, and yet gaining support and finding an ecological niche in a crowded policy space. Though they have seldom been discussed, such late doctrinal developments are part of the implementation process and exert a considerable influence on policy evolution.

BUT DOES POLICY SHAPE IMPLEMENTATION?

Biologists tell us that embryonic tissue of the fruitfly *Drosophila* is capable of developing into a wing, a leg, or an antenna, according to the influences brought to bear on it. Also, the tissues of the flank of a newt are capable of developing into a leg, but it would be impossible to induce a fish to develop a leg, or a horse to develop a wing. Whereas policies can assume marvelous new forms during implementation, in order to understand policy evolution (or indeed any type of evolution), it is as important to understand what cannot happen as what can.

Although the literature is rich in examples of implementation failures (or, at least, of outcomes that do not meet certain standards, though they may be considered functional on other grounds), implementation monsters—policy outcomes bearing no recognizable relationship to the original idea—seem to be rare. As Bardach writes, most participants in the implementation process "act within a context of expectations that *something will happen* that bears at least a passing resemblance to whatever was mandated by the initial policy decision."[11] This expectation, it seems to us, is precisely what needs to be explained. Why is it reasonable to assume that the final results will be genetically related, however indirectly, to the original policy idea? And why does implementing policy decisions appear to be so much more problematic in some areas than in others?

In discussing the "capture theory" of governmental regulation we have already pointed out that some implementation failures can be explained satisfactorily by inadequacies in the theory. This suggests that such objective properties of a policy as its substantive content and its theory ought to be included among the variables used to explain implementation results. We would argue, for example, that the difficulties of implementing federal pollution control programs cannot be ascribed only to the destabilizing effects of the federal intrusion into a delicately balanced political situation,[12] but must also be related to the technical and scientific inadequacies of current environmental policies. Enforcement would be easier if more were known about the health and other effects of pollution and about methods of controlling particular types of pollutants. Environmental standards, for instance, could be based on generally accepted scientific evidence. In a situation in which controversy over questions of fact was greatly reduced, conflicting interests would probably prefer to fight their battles during the policy adoption stage rather than during implementation. Similarly, the implementation of innovative educational policies is much more difficult because of a widespread lack of confidence in the underlying cognitive theories.

Some of the ways in which policy affects implementation are fairly obvious. Policy content shapes implementation by defining the arena in which the process takes place, the identity and role of the principal actors, the range of permissible tools for action, and of course by supplying resources. The underlying theory provides not only the data, information, and hypotheses on which subsequent debate and action will rely, but also, and most importantly, a conceptualization of the policy problem. For instance, the mode of implementing a large-scale program of multiphasic health screening (MHS) would depend significantly on which of two alternative philosophies of MHS were adopted: MHS can be seen merely as a multiple screening program, or as the basis of an alternative method of delivering primary care, one in which prevention is considered an important factor.

Is the empirical evidence supplied by the growing number of case studies sufficient to indicate systematic relationships between different policy characteristics and classes of implementation problems? Although we can do little more than open up the question at present, this seems to be one of the most promising approaches to the study of implementation. Armed with such knowledge, the analyst would be able to work out the set, large but not unbounded, of possible policy developments.

EVOLUTIONARY IMPLEMENTATION

In the interaction model, implementation is the continuation of politics by other means. According to the planning model, implementation is an extension of organizational design. To say that implementation should be part of design is to suggest that policy theory be formulated with a view toward its execution. This may mean at least two things: policy relevance—the variables in the theory should be manipulable by those with authority; and the specification of a variety of conditions that might occur, with instructions as to what to do under different circumstances. In view of our limited knowledge, this list would be relatively short and inevitably insufficient. Although it is usual to speak of making authority commensurate with responsibility, it is rare for an official to coerce all others, both because the political system divides authority and because it is costly to use up persuasiveness for this purpose. Additional authority therefore must be acquired along the way without necessarily being able to anticipate objections from all interested actors.

Since administrative discretion can be used as a cover for arbitrary behavior that is unrelated to policy intentions, some authors feel that the problem of administration is, purely and simply, one of controlling discretion. Controlling it how? Unless one is willing to assume that policies spring fully armed from the forehead of an omniscient policymaker, discretion is both inevitable and necessary. Unless administration is programmed—a robot comes to mind—discretion can be controlled only by indirect means. Again, we must rely on learning and invention rather than on instruction and command. In punishing his generals for failing to execute his orders faithfully even when their disobedience brought him victory, Frederick the Great of Prussia was at least consistent. We require the impossible when we expect our bureaucrats to be at the same time literal executors and successful implementers of policy mandates. Something has to be left to chance. In a world of uncertainty, success is only loosely correlated with effort, and chance can never be ruled out as the main cause of either success or failure. To the extent that success *is* related to effort, it depends more on "knowing how" than on "knowing that," on the ability to select appropriate types of behavior and rules of conduct, more than on abstract knowledge of decision rules or on blind obedience to directives.

When problems are puzzles for which unique solutions exist, technicians can take over. But when problems are defined through the process of attempting to draft acceptable solutions, then analysts become creators as well as implementers of policy. "This particular problem may not be solvable," they tell their clients, "but how about substituting one that can be solved?" In other words, if problems are best understood through solutions, then implementation includes not only finding answers, but also framing questions. Reformulating problems means changing solutions. Policy ideas in the abstract (assuming only minimal logical coherence) are subject to an infinite variety of contingencies, and they contain worlds of possible practical applications. What is in them depends on what is in us, and vice versa. They have no resting point, no final realization; they are endlessly evolving. How then, and why then, separate analytically what life refuses to tear apart?

Reducing, bounding, limiting contingencies is the analytic function. Discovering the constraints under which policy ideas may be expected to operate—applying negative knowledge, if you will—is the main task of analysis. Fixed prescriptions—"knowing that"—give way to "knowing how"—adopting the right rule at the right moment as events unfold, in order to bring out one potential result over many others. Knowing how is a craft, not a science.

How effectively can implementation bring out one rather than another range of results? The more general an idea and the more adaptable it is to a range of circumstances, the more likely it is to be realized in some form, but the less likely it is to emerge as intended in practice. The more restricted the idea, and the more it is constrained, the more likely it is to emerge as predicted, but the less likely it is to have a significant impact. At one extreme we have the ideal type of the perfectly preformed policy idea; it only requires execution, and the only problems it raises are those of control. At the other extreme, the policy idea is only an expression of basic principles and aspirations, a matter for philosophical reflection and political debate. In between, where we live, is a set of more or less developed potentialities embedded in pieces of legislation, court decisions, and bureaucratic plans. This land of potentiality we claim as the territory of implementation analysis.

Implementation is evolution. Since it takes place in a world we never made, we are usually right in the middle of the process, with events having occurred before and (we hope) continuing afterward. At each point we must cope with new circumstances that allow us to actualize different potentials in whatever policy ideas we are implementing. When we act to implement a policy, we change it. When we vary the amount or type of resource inputs, we also intend to alter outputs, even if only to put them back on the track where they were once supposed to be. In this way, the policy theory is transformed to produce different results. As we learn from experience what is feasible or preferable, we correct errors. To the degree that these corrections make a difference at all, they change our policy ideas as well as the policy outcomes, because the idea is embodied in the action.

EVALUATING IMPLEMENTATION

In the world of what Herbert Simon calls programmed decisions—a world in which objectives are known, agreed upon, and singular, so that all that remains is to make the required calculations—people supposedly know how to distinguish the quality of an implementation from the quality of a decision. The four possibilities can be represented in tabular form:

Implementation in a Preprogrammed World

		Decision	
		Good	Bad
Execution	Good	1. No problem (too good to be true)	3. The policy problem
	Bad	2. The control problem	4. No problem (or: how two bads = one good)

If both the decision and the execution are good (#1), then evidently there is no problem; if both are bad (#4), then we can only be grateful that poor decisions are made ineffective by worse actions. If the decision is good but the execution is bad (#2), then the problem can only be one of control (ineptitude, laziness, or whatever) in connecting premises to conclusions. Here the implementation problem is indistinguishable from the control problem. If implementation is good but the decision is bad (because the result is suboptimal or even infeasible) (#3), the there is, in this pre-programmed world, nothing the implementer can do about it. Since decision is the only active element, the only place to go is back to the drawing board.

Outside the static world of programmed decisions, "good" and "bad" take on multiple meanings. In an evolutionary context "good" means "faithful," but interestingly enough, it might also mean "faithless." A faithful translation of an ill-formed policy idea or theory would bring into being all the inconsistencies, inadequacies, and/or unfortunate consequences inherent in the pristine conception. A faithless interpretation would straighten out logical defects and/or alter elements so that the consequences were more desirable than those in the original plan. But immediately an objection springs to mind: this is not the original policy idea at all, but a new one transformed into something quite different. Quite right! If the implementation were faithful, then an imperfect idea would have been nursed along only to produce unsatisfactory effects. Evidently then, if imperfect policy ideas can be compatible with good implementation, it must be possible for implementation to alter policy. Indeed, if all activity is composed entirely of behaviors that incorporate inseparable ideas and actions, then any change in implementation must bring about a change in policy.

Consider government subsidies for medical care, such as Medicaid for the poor. The policy is designed to increase access to medical services for the poor by reducing the cost to them, but it is also designed to raise the quality of service without raising the cost of care for others. In practice, however, since the medical system absorbs all monies, the entry of additional funds paid essentially on a cost plus basis has raised the price of medical care for everyone. Equal access, higher quality, and lower cost seem to be incompatible. What are we to do? The conflict between cost and quality is most acute in the hospital sector, where prices have been rising at a phenomenal rate. Government could try to specify allowable treatment for all ailments, ruling out more expensive methods and monitoring each individual transaction. Access to care would still be independent from the patient's ability to pay, but the problem of administrative calculation would be virtually insuperable. Or government could work out a formula to give each hospital a lump sum which it could allocate among services and patients. Calculations might become manageable, costs might be contained, but quality and equality would probably suffer because it would be no longer possible to mandate the precise services that had to be performed for each potential patient. Or government might give poor people a direct subsidy, a medical voucher, allowing them to buy services up to a specified level. Cost containment would be more certain but the chances for equal access and high quality would fall.

Clearly, none of the available alternatives meets all the criteria for the original policy. Any change in implementation—lump sums to hospitals or vouchers to patients—changes what the policy does, alters the mix of values, and shifts the relationships among quality, cost, and access. How then should we evaluate the implementation of this policy?

Or how should we evaluate the implementation of the British National Health Service Act? Is this a case of implementation failure (because no efficient system of rationing was used), of policy failure (because the theory proved inadequate), or no failure at all (since, as a British economist puts it, "there is now a consensus among all segments of British society and among all shades of political opinion that health should be distributed in accordance with need rather than ability-to-pay, in other words 'Communism in health'").[13]

Is what has been said of successful scientific theories also true of policies, that they never prove to be "right," but only gain increasing acceptance? One cannot discount the possibility that successful implementation may be made possible only by a lowering of standards, a reformulation of evaluative criteria, or a shift in viewpoints (from the goals of the U.S. Office of Education or of federal granting agencies to those of local school districts and states receiving grants-in-aid).

Faithful implementation is not a vacuous notion: it may be tested in several different ways. But there is no need to feel guilty about failing to carry out a mandate inherent in a policy in a literal way, because literal implementation is literally impossible. Unless a policy matter is narrow and uninteresting (i.e., preprogrammed), the policy will never be able to contain its own consequences. Implementation will always be evolutionary; it will inevitably reformulate as well as carry out policy. Perhaps implementation angers as well as intrigues us because, after the deeds have been done, we wish that implementation had been cowardly or courageous, killing off the idea or making it successful, so that either way, without specifying which way in advance, the blame would not be ours.

Implementation is worth studying precisely because it is a struggle over the realization of ideas. It is the analytical equivalent of original sin; there is no escape from implementation and its attendant responsibilities. What has policy wrought? Having tasted of the fruit of the tree of knowledge, the implementer can only answer, and with conviction, it depends. . . .

NOTES

1. See Preface to First Edition.

2. Aaron Wildavsky, "If Planning Is Everything, Maybe It's Nothing," in *Policy Sciences*, vol. 4, no. 2 (Amsterdam: Elsevier Scientific Publishing Co., June 1973).

3. James M. Landis, *The Administrative Process* (New Haven: Yale University Press, 1966 [1938]), p. 75.

4. Eugene Bardach, "On Designing Implementable Programs," to appear in *Pitfalls of Analysis*, ed. G. Majone and E. Quade (London and New York: John Wiley and Sons, 1979).

5. Carl E. Van Horn and Donald S. Van Meter, "The Implementation of Intergovernmental Policy," now in *Policy Studies Review Annual*, vol. 1, ed. Stuart S. Nagel (Beverly Hills and London: Sage Publications, 1977), p. 108.

6. Bardach, "On Designing Implementable Programs."

7. John Henry Newman, *An Essay on the Development of Christian Doctrine* (Harmondsworth, Middlesex, England: Penguin Books Ltd., 1974 [1845]), pp. 98–99; our italics.

8. Walter Hagenbuch, *Social Economics* (Cambridge: Cambridge University Press, 1958), pp. 282–283.

9. Eveline Burns, *Social Security and Public Policy* (New York: McGraw-Hill, 1956).

10. Karl Weick, *The Social Psychology of Organizing* (Reading, Mass.: Addison-Wesley Publishing Co., 1969); and Aaron Wildavsky, *Speaking Truth to Power: The Art and Craft of Policy Analysis* (Boston: Little, Brown, 1979).

11. Eugene Bardach, *The Implementation Game* (Cambridge: MIT Press, 1977), p. 50.

12. J. Clarence Davies 3rd and Barbara S. Davies, *The Politics of Pollution*, 2nd ed. (Indianapolis: Pegasus, 1975).

13. Mark Blaugh, *Economics of Education* (Harmondsworth, Middlesex, England: Penguin Books Ltd., 1972), p. 324.

18

A Conceptual Framework of the Implementation Process

Paul A. Sabatier and Daniel Mazmanian

Implementation is the carrying out of a basic policy decision, usually made in a statute (although also possible through important executive orders or court decisions). Ideally that decision identifies the problem(s) to be addressed, stipulates the objective(s) to be pursued, and, in a variety of ways, "structures" the implementation process. In the case of a statute regulating private economic behavior, the implementation process normally runs through a number of stages beginning with passage of the basic statute, followed by the policy outputs (decisions) of the implementing agencies, the compliance of target groups with those decisions, the *actual* impacts—both intended and unintended—of those outputs, the *perceived* impacts of agency decisions, and, finally, important revisions (or attempted revisions) in the basic statute.

In our view, the crucial role of implementation analysis is to identify the factors that affect the achievement of statutory objectives throughout this entire process. These can be divided into three broad categories: (1) the tractability of the problem(s) being addressed by the statute; (2) the ability of the statute to favorably structure the implementation process; and (3) the net effect of a variety of "political" variables on the balance of support for statutory objectives. In the remainder of this section, we shall examine each of the component variables and their potential effects.

The entire framework is presented in very skeletal form in figure 1. It distinguishes the three categories of (independent) variables from the stages of implementation, which constitute the dependent variables. It should be noted, however, that each of the stages can affect subsequent ones; for example, the degree of target-group compliance with the policy decisions of implementing agencies certainly affects the actual impacts of those decisions.

From Paul A. Sabatier and Daniel Mazmanian, "The Implementation of Public Policy: A Framework for Analysis," *Policy Studies Journal*, 8 (1980), pp. 538–560. Reprinted by permission.

TRACTABILITY OF THE PROBLEM(S) ADDRESSED BY A STATUTE

Totally apart from the difficulties universally associated with the implementation of governmental programs, some social problems are much easier to deal with than others. Preserving neighborhood tranquility from noise disturbances in Davis, California, is inherently a far more manageable or tractable problem than the safe generation of electrical power from nuclear energy. In the former, unlike the latter, there is a clear understanding of the behavioral changes necessary to resolve the problem; the behavior to be regulated is not very varied (primarily fraternity parties) and involves only a small subset of the town's population; and the amount of behavioral change required among target groups is quite modest. The specific aspects of a social problem that affect the ability of governmental institutions to achieve statutory objectives are discussed here. While each is a separate

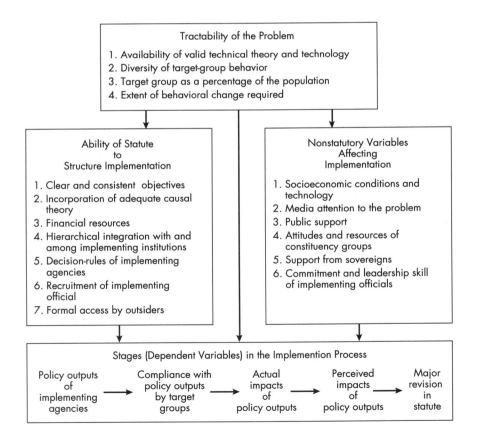

FIGURE 1   Skeletal Flow Diagram of the Variables Involved in the Implementation Process

variable, the aspects can be aggregated—at least conceptually—into a summary index of (inherent) tractability.[1]

Difficulties in handling change. There are difficulties in measuring changes in the seriousness of the problem, in relating such changes back to modifications in the behavior of target groups, and in developing the technology to enable target groups to institute such changes. Any regulatory program assumes that by modifying the behavior of target groups the problem will be ameliorated. For example, reducing sulfur emissions from power plants will reduce the ambient-air levels of sulfur dioxide and thereby improve public health. But this implies that ambient-air levels can be measured relatively inexpensively and that a causal model exists that relates emissions from specific sources to ambient-air levels and, in turn, to health effects on specific subsets of the population.

Moreover, many programs are predicated on the availability of technologies without which changes in target-group behavior will not achieve the desired objectives. For example, reduction in sulfur emissions from power plants is contingent on finding a reliable and relatively inexpensive technology for removing sulfur from coal either before or after it is used in power generation—with considerable dispute between utilities and the Environmental Protection Agency over whether such a technology is presently available. Other social problems beset by serious technological difficulties include pollution emissions from automobiles, the storage of nuclear wastes, and agricultural pest control.

The absence of a valid causal theory and/or the requisite technology in turn poses a number of difficulties for the successful implementation of statutory objectives. First, any program poses costs to taxpayers (in the form of program administration) and to target groups. To the extent that these costs cannot be justified by measurable improvements in the problem being addressed, political support for the program will almost surely decline and thus statutory objectives will be either ignored or modified. Second, disputes over the availability of the requisite technology will produce strong pressures for delaying deadlines for achieving statutory objectives and/or considerable uncertainty over the most effective means of encouraging technological innovation—as the very problematic implementation of the "technology-forcing" provisions of the 1970 Federal Clean Air amendments amply demonstrates.

Diversity of proscribed behavior. The more diverse the behavior being regulated, the more difficult it becomes to frame clear regulations and thus the less likely that statutory objectives will be attained. For example, one of the major obstacles confronting the implementation of the 1972 Federal Water Pollution Control amendments has been the extreme diversity in the type and seriousness of discharges from the nation's estimated 62,000 point sources. Such variation makes the writing of precise overall regulations essentially impossible, with the result that regulations for each industry and firm have to be negotiated on an ad hoc basis with considerable discretion left to field personnel. On the other hand, there is some indication that this aspect of tractability can sometimes be ameliorated through greater emphasis on economic incentives, for example, effluent taxes, rather than detailed regulations.[2]

Percentage of population within a political jurisdiction whose behavior needs to be changed.   In general, the smaller and more definable (isolatable) the target group whose behavior needs to be changed, the more likely that political support can be mobilized in favor of the program and thus the more probable that the statutory objectives can be achieved. For example, the successful implementation of the 1965 Voting Rights Act derived in large part from the fact that it applied to a fairly specific set of abuses among voting registrars in only seven southern states. This facilitated the formation of a strong constituency in support of the legislation. In contrast, civil-rights measures have been notably less successful when dealing with country-wide problems, such as housing discrimination and de facto school segregation.

Extent of behavioral change required of target groups.   The amount of behavioral modification required to achieve statutory objectives is a function of the (absolute) number of people in the ultimate target groups and the amount of change required of them. The basic hypothesis is, of course, that the greater the amount of behavioral change, the more problematic successful implementation.

In short, some problems are far more tractable than others. Programs that address the former are much more likely to be effective in producing the desired changes in the behavior of target groups and, in turn, in ameliorating the problem being addressed. This brief review of the variables involved suggests that problems are most tractable if (1) there is a valid theory connecting behavioral change to problem amelioration; the requisite technology exists; and, measurement of change in the seriousness of the problem is inexpensive; (2) there is minimal variation in the behavioral practices that cause the problem; (3) the target group constitutes an easily identifiable minority of the population within a political jurisdiction; and (4) the amount of behavioral change is modest. For example, the success of the 1965 Voting Rights Act in drastically improving the percentage of blacks voting in the South can ultimately be traced largely to the first and third reasons, even though the amount of behavioral change among southern voting officials was considerable. In contrast, the implementation of federal occupational health and safety legislation has been exacerbated by the extreme diversity of the practices being regulated, the extensive amount of behavioral change required (particularly in small manufacturing establishments), and, to a lesser extent, problems in actually measuring health and safety benefits.

Nevertheless one should be cautious about placing too much emphasis on the tractability of the problem being addressed. After all, one of the goals of policy analysis is to develop better tools, for example, a greater reliance on economic incentives, for addressing heterogeneous problems that demand substantial behavioral change. It is also conceivable that more adequate causal theories, better methods of measurement, and the requisite technologies can be developed during the course of program implementation. Finally, one of the purposes of our framework is to show how even relatively difficult problems can be ameliorated through a more adequate understanding of the manner in which statutory and political variables affect the mobilization of support necessary to bring about rather substantial behavioral change. We now turn to an examination of these variables.

EXTENT TO WHICH THE STATUTE COHERENTLY STRUCTURES THE IMPLEMENTATION PROCESS

From the perspective of our framework, a statute constitutes the fundamental policy decision being implemented in that it indicates the problem(s) being addressed and stipulates the objective(s) to be pursued. It also has the capacity to "structure" the entire implementation process through its selection of the implementing institutions; through providing legal and financial resources to those institutions; through biasing the probable policy orientations of agency officials; and through regulating the opportunities for participation by nonagency actors in the implementation process. To the extent that the statute stipulates a set of clear and consistent objectives, incorporates a sound theory relating behavioral change to those objectives, and then structures the implementation process in a fashion conducive to obtaining such behavioral change, the possibilities for attaining statutory objectives are enhanced—even if the amount of behavioral change sought in target groups is considerable.

Precision and clear ranking of statutory objectives.   Statutory objectives that are precise and clearly ranked in importance serve as an indispensable aid in program evaluation, as unambiguous directives to implementing officials, and as a resource available to supporters of those objectives.[3] With respect to the last, for example, implementing officials confronted with objections to their programs can sympathize with the aggrieved party but nevertheless respond that they are only following the legislature's instructions. Clear objectives can also serve as a resource to actors within and external to the implementing institutions who perceive discrepancies between agency outputs and those objectives (particularly if the statute also provides them formal access to the implementation process, for example, via citizen suit provisions).

While the desirability of unambiguous policy directives within a given statute is normally understood, it is also important that a statute assigned for implementation to an already existing agency clearly indicate the relative priority that the new directives are to play in the totality of the agency's programs. If this is not done, the new directives are likely to undergo considerable delay and be accorded low priority as they struggle for incorporation into the agency's operating procedures. In short, to the extent that a statute provides precise and clearly ranked instructions to implementing officials and other actors—controlling for required departure from the status quo ante—the more likely that the policy outputs of the implementing agencies and ultimately the behavior of target groups will be consistent with those directives.

Validity of the causal theory incorporated into the statute. Every major reform contains, at least implicitly, a causal theory of the manner in which its objectives are to be attained. In fact, one of the major contributions of implementation analysis—as opposed to simply public administration and organization theory—is its emphasis on the overall theory for obtaining the desired changes.

An adequate causal theory requires (1) that the principal causal linkages between governmental intervention and the attainment of program objectives be understood[4] and (2) that the officials responsible for implementing the program have jurisdiction over a sufficient number of the critical linkages to actually attain the objectives. For example, if one assumes that the major objective of southern school desegregation was simply the elimination of dual schools, then the causal theory was relatively simple and basically involved bringing sufficient incentives and sanctions on southern school boards. But to the extent that the objective was to provide equal educational opportunity to children regardless of race, the theory became much more problematic both in its cognitive and jurisdictional aspects. On the one hand, there is considerable dispute over the factors affecting—and indeed the means of measuring—educational achievement. On the other, the implementing agencies (principally the Office of Education and local school boards) had practically no jurisdiction over the host of factors outside the schools affecting educational achievement.

In fact, inadequate causal theories lie behind many of the cases of implementation failure. For example, the chapter by Goodwin and Moen in this volume examines welfare policy in terms of our lack of understanding of many of the factors affecting the work incentives of the poor, to say nothing of the lack of jurisdiction by welfare agencies over the macroeconomic factors affecting the number of jobs available to the poor.

Financial resources available to the implementing agency. Money is obviously critical in any program involving conditional grants in aid. It is also important in classical regulatory programs to hire the staff and to conduct the technical analyses involved in the development of regulations, the administration of permit programs, and the monitoring of compliance. Moreover, we subsequently argue that there are tremendous pressures for regulatory programs to gradually substitute side-payments for police-power decisions over time, for example, to purchase public easements rather than try to force land-developers to provide at their own expense public rights-of-way to beaches. In general, a threshold level of funding is necessary for there to be any possibility of achieving statutory objectives, and the level of funding above this threshold is (up to some saturation point) proportional to the probability of achieving those objectives.[5]

The extent of hierarchical integration within and among implementing institutions. Numerous studies of the implementation of regulatory and social-service programs have demonstrated that one of the principal obstacles is the difficulty of obtaining coordinated action within any given agency and among the numerous semiautonomous agencies involved in most implementation efforts. The problem is particularly acute in federal statutes that rely on state and local agencies for carrying out the details of program delivery in a very heterogeneous system. Thus one of the most important attributes of any statute is the extent to which it hierarchically integrates the implementing agencies. To the extent that the system is only loosely integrated, there will be considerable variation in the degree of behavioral compliance among implementing officials and target groups—as each responds to the incentive for modification within his local setting.

The degree of hierarchical integration among implementing agencies is determined by (1) the number of veto/clearance points involved in the attainment of statutory objectives and (2) the extent to which supporters of statutory objectives are provided with inducements and sanctions sufficient to assure acquiescence among those with a potential veto. Veto/clearance points involve those occasions in which an actor has the capacity (quite apart from the question of legal authority) to impede the achievement of statutory objectives.[6] Resistance from specific veto points can, however, be overcome if the statute provides sufficient sanctions and/or inducements to convince the actor (whether implementing officials or target groups) to alter their behavior. In short, if these sanctions and inducements are great enough, the number of veto points can delay—but probably never ultimately impede—compliance by target groups. In practice, however, the compliance incentives are usually sufficiently modest that the number of veto/clearance points become extremely important, and thus the most direct route to a statutory objective, for example, a negative income tax to provide a minimum income, may be preferable to complex programs administered by numerous semiautonomous bureaucracies.

Extent to which decision-rules of implementing agencies are supportive of statutory objectives.   In addition to providing clear and consistent objectives, few veto points, and adequate incentives for compliance, a statute can further bias the implementation process by stipulating the formal decision-rules of the implementing agencies.[7] To the extent, for example, that the burden of proof in permit/licensing cases is placed on the applicant and agency officials are required to make findings fully consistent with statutory objectives, the decisions of implementing institutions fall to those officials who are most likely to support statutory objectives. Finally, when multi-membered commissions are involved, the statute can stipulate the majority required for specific actions. In the case of regulatory agencies that operate primarily through the granting of permits or licenses, decision-rules which make the granting of a permit contingent on substantial consensus, for example, a two-thirds majority, are obviously conducive to stringent regulation.

Assignment to implementing agencies/officials committed to statutory objectives.   No matter how well a statute structures the formal decision process, the attainment of statutory objectives that seek to significantly modify target-group behavior is unlikely unless officials in the implementing agencies are strongly committed to the achievement of those objectives. Any new program requires implementors who are not merely neutral but sufficiently persistent to develop new regulations and standard operating procedures, and to enforce them in the face of resistance from target groups and from public officials reluctant to make the mandated changes.

In principle, a number of mechanisms are available to statutory framers to reasonably assure that implementing officials have the requisite commitment to statutory objectives. First, the responsibility for implementation can be assigned to agencies whose policy orientation is consistent with the statute and that will accord the new program high priority.[8] This is most likely when a new agency is created specifically to administer the statute, as the program will necessarily be its highest priority and the creation of new positions opens the door to a vast infusion of statutory supporters. Alternatively, implementation can be assigned to a prestigious existing agency that perceives the new mandate to be compatible with its traditional orientation and is looking for new programs. Second, the statute can often stipulate that top implementing officials be selected from social sectors that generally support the legislation's objectives. For example, several studies of state and regional land-use agencies have shown that local elected officials are generally more likely to approve developments than appointees of state officials.[9]

The choice of implementing officials is, however, often severely constrained in practice. In many situations there is little option but to assign implementation to existing agencies that may be ambivalent or even hostile. In fact, the generally limited ability of program designers to assign, through statutory provisions, implementation to agency officials who are committed to its objectives probably lies behind many cases of suboptimal accomplishment of statutory objectives.

Extent to which opportunities for participation by actors external to the implementing agencies are biased toward supporters of statutory objectives. Just as a statute can bias the implementation process through design characteristics of implementing agencies, it can also affect the participation of two groups of actors external to those institutions: (1) the potential beneficiaries and target groups of the program and (2) the legislative, executive, and judicial sovereigns of the agencies.

In most regulatory programs, for example, the target groups do not have problems with legal standing nor do they generally lack the financial incentives to pursue their case in court if they are displeased with agency decisions. In contrast, the beneficiaries of most consumer- and environmental-protection legislation *individually* do not have a sufficiently direct and salient interest at stake to obtain legal standing and to bear the costs of petitioning adverse agency decisions to judicial and legislative sovereigns. Thus statutes that provide liberal rules of standing for citizen participation as formal interveners in agency proceedings and as petitioners in judicial review (in the form of mandamus actions requiring agency officials to comply with statutory provisions) are more likely to have their objectives attained.[10]

Statutes can also affect the scope and the direction of oversight by agency sovereigns. On the one hand, requirements for formal evaluation studies and provisions that centralize formal legislative oversight in the hands of the statute's chief sponsor (for example, via a select committee of which he is chairman) are probably conducive to the achievement of statutory objectives. On the other hand, provisions for legislative veto of administrative regulations are probably inimical to the achievement of those objectives simply because the target groups are likely to be much better organized and to have more incentives for appealing to legislators than are the beneficiaries of regulation.

In sum, a carefully drafted statute can substantially affect the extent to which its objectives are attained. More precisely, legislation that seeks to significantly change target-group behavior in order to achieve its objectives is most likely to succeed if (1) its objectives are precise and clearly ranked; (2) it incorporates a valid causal theory; (3) it provides adequate funds to the implementing agencies; (4) the number of veto points in the implementation process is minimized and sanctions/inducements are provided to overcome resistance; (5) the decision-rules of the implementing agencies are biased toward the achievement of statutory objectives; (6) implementation is assigned to agencies that support the legislation's objectives and will give the program high priority; and (7) the provisions for outsider participation are similarly biased through liberalized rules of standing and by centralizing oversight in the hands of statutory supporters.

We recognize, of course, that statutes often do not structure the implementation process very coherently. This is particularly true at the federal level, where the heterogeneity of interests effectively represented, the diversity in proscribed activities and the sheer magnitude of behavioral change envisaged by most programs, the multiple vetoes and weak party system in Congress, and the constitutional and political incentives toward implementation by state and local agencies make it extremely difficult to develop clear goals, to minimize the number of veto points, and to assign implementation to sympathetic agencies. Moreover, adequate causal theories are often either unavailable or unincorporated into legislation. But this is only to say that many programs may, from their inception, be doomed to very modest achievements by the intractability of the problems they address and/or the inability of the legislature to coherently structure the implementation process. In any case, the potential importance of tractability and statutory variable in explaining program success and failure needs to be more adequately examined than often has been the case in implementation research.

NONSTATUTORY VARIABLES AFFECTING IMPLEMENTATION

While a statute establishes the basic legal structure in which the politics of implementation take place, implementation also has an inherent dynamism driven by at least two important processes: (1) the need for any program that seeks to change behavior to receive constant and/or periodic infusions of political support if it is to overcome the inertia and delay inherent in seeking cooperation and acquiescence among large numbers of people, many of whom perceive their interest to be adversely affected by successful implementation of statutory objectives; and (2) the effect of continuous changes in socioeconomic and technological conditions on the reservoir of support for those objectives among the general public, interest groups, and sovereigns. In addition to these changes over time, there is usually enormous variation in crucial independent variables, for example, the seriousness of the problem being addressed, relevant socioeconomic conditions, public opinion, among governmental jurisdictions in which the same statute is being implemented.

The policy outputs of implementing agencies are essentially a function of the interaction between legal structure and political process. Whereas a statute that provides little institutionalized bias leaves implementing officials very dependent on variations in political support over time and among local settings, a well-drafted statute can provide them with sufficient policy direction and legal resources to withstand short-term changes in public opinion and considerable capacity to bring about the desired behavioral changes in widely different local jurisdictions.

This section discusses the major nonlegal variables affecting the policy outputs of implementing agencies, target-group compliance with those decisions, and ultimately the achievement of statutory objectives. It begins with clearly exogenous variables, for example, changes in socioeconomic conditions; moves through essentially intervening variables, for example, attitudes of sovereigns and constituency groups; and finally deals with the variable most directly affecting the policy outputs of implementing agencies, namely the commitment and leadership skill of agency officials.

Variation over time and among governmental jurisdictions in social, economic, and technological conditions affecting the attainability of statutory objectives. There are at least four ways in which variation in such conditions over time and among local settings can substantially affect the political support for statutory objectives and, hence, the policy outputs of implementing agencies and eventually the achievement of statutory objectives.

First, variation in socioeconomic conditions can affect perceptions of the relative importance of the problem addressed by a statute. To the extent that other social problems become relatively more important over time, political support for allocating scarce resources to the original statute is likely to diminish.[11] Second, successful implementation is rendered more difficult by local variation in socioeconomic conditions and, as indicated previously, in the seriousness of the problem being addressed. Such variation produces enormous pressures for "flexible" regulations and considerable administrative discretion to local units. But such discretion increases the probability of variation in the extent to which the policy outputs of implementing agencies are consistent with statutory objectives. On the other hand, the imposition of uniform standards on jurisdictions with widely different situations almost inevitably increases opposition from those who must bear costs that appear unjust. In either case, statutory objectives are less likely to be achieved.

Third, support for regulation aimed at environmental or consumer protection or worker safety seems to be correlated with the economic viability of target groups and their relative importance in the total economy.[12] Thus the more diverse an economy and the more prosperous the target groups, the more probable the effective implementation of statutes imposing nonproductive costs on them. The lower the diversity and prosperity, the more likely the substitution of subsidies for police power regulation. Finally, in the case of policies (such as pollution control) that are directly tied to technology, changes or lack of changes in the technological state of the art over time is obviously crucial.

In short, social, economic, and technological conditions are some of the principal exogenous variables affecting the policy outputs of implementing agencies and ultimately the attainment of statutory objectives. The primary linkage is through changes in interest-group and public support for statutory objectives and/or through the legislative and executive sovereigns of the implementing agencies. Alternatively, implementing officials may respond directly (that is, without any intervening variables) to changes in environmental conditions, particularly if they perceive those changes to be supportive of their programs or preferences.

The amount and continuity of media attention to the problem addressed by a statute.   The mass media are important in the implementation process for at least two reasons. First, they are generally a crucial intervening variable between changes in socioeconomic conditions and perceptions of those changes by the general public and, to a lesser extent, political elites. This is particularly true for events beyond the local political arena, where most individuals have little direct experience.

Second, the tendency for most television stations and newspapers to play an issue to the hilt and then go on to something else is a real obstacle to the constant infusion of political support from the very diffuse beneficiaries of most environmental and consumer protection programs.[13] This tendency of the media to have a short "issue-attention span" is, in turn, a function of many factors, one of the most important of which is the tendency of most communications organizations to rely on general assignment reporters rather than topic specialists. This suggests that programs that are monitored by specialist reporters will receive above-normal media attention over a sustained period of time and—given media support or at least neutrality—are more likely to be effectively implemented.[14]

Variations over time and jurisdiction in public support for statutory objectives.   The previous discussion has suggested that interest among the general public in a statute or the problem it addresses tends to be cyclical, which, in turn, makes it difficult for any program to receive sustained political support. Similarly, variation among political jurisdictions in support for a particular program is likely to result in pressures for ambiguous regulation and considerable discretion to local officials, both of which probably make behavioral change more difficult to achieve.

The general public can influence the implementation process in at least three ways: (1) public opinion (and its interaction with the mass media) can strongly affect the political agenda, that is, the issues to be discussed by legislatures; (2) there is substantial evidence that legislators are influenced by their general constituents on issues of salience to those constituents, particularly when opinion within the district is relatively homogenous;[15] and (3) public opinion polls are often employed by administrators and sovereigns to support particular policy positions. For example, the Environmental Protection Agency sponsored a survey in 1973–1974 to refute the conventional wisdom that the Arab oil embargo had substantially undermined public support for pollution control measures; when the poll essentially confirmed the agency's position, it used this information extensively in an effort to convince Congress not to emasculate the 1970 clean air amendments.[16]

Changes in the resources and attitudes of constituency groups toward statutory objectives and the policy outputs of implementing institutions. The basic dilemma confronting proponents of any regulatory program seeking a change in the behavior of one or more target groups is that public support for their position will almost invariably decline over time. Normally such statutes are the result of very heightened public concern with a general problem, such as environmental quality, consumer protection, or gross disparities in school district revenues. Such concern soon wanes as the public and the media turn to other issues and as the costs of such programs on specific segments of the population draw away previous supporters and intensify opposition.[17] The essential—and very problematic—task confronting proponents is to translate the diffuse support that helped pass the initial legislation into viable organizations with sufficient membership, cohesion, and expertise to be accepted as legitimate and necessary participants in important policy decisions by both implementing officials and their legislative/executive sovereigns.

On the other hand, the opponents of the mandated change generally have the resources and incentives to intervene actively in the implementation process. Their organizational resources and access to expertise enable them to make an effective case before administrative agencies and, if displeased with their decisions, to initiate appeals to the legislative sovereigns, to the courts, and to public opinion. Because opponents can generally intervene more actively over a longer period of time than proponents, it long has been noted that most regulatory agencies eventually recognize that survival in an unbalanced political environment necessitates some accommodation with the interests of target groups and thus less departure from the status quo than envisaged by the original statutory mandate.[18]

Constituency groups interact with the other variables in our framework in a number of ways.[19] First, their membership and financial resources are likely to vary with public support for their position and with the amount of behavioral change mandated by statutory objectives. Second, constituency groups can intervene directly in the decisions of the implementing agencies both through commenting on proposed decisions and through supplementing the agency's resources. Finally, such groups have the capacity to affect agency policy indirectly through publishing studies critical of the agency's performance, through public opinion campaigns, and through appeals to its legislative and judicial sovereigns.

Continued support for statutory objectives among sovereigns of implementing institutions.   This can be accomplished via (1) amount and direction of oversight and (2) extent of new (that is, after original statute) and conflicting legal mandates. The sovereigns of an implementing agency are those institutions which control its legal and financial resources. They will normally include the legislature (and, more specifically, the relevant policy and fiscal committees); the chief executive; the courts; and, in intergovernmental programs, hierarchically superior agencies.

One major difficulty in implementing intergovernmental programs is that implementing agencies are responsible to different sovereigns who wish to pursue different policies. In such situations, we would suggest that, when an intergovernmental subordinate is faced with conflicting directives from its intergovernmental superiors and its coordinate sovereigns, it will ultimately lean toward the directives of the sovereigns who will most affect its legal and financial resources over the longest period of time. For example, when a state agency is faced with conflicting directives from a federal agency and the state legislature, institutional survival requires that it give its primary loyalty to the sovereign most likely to affect its vital resources, which, in almost any conceivable case, will be the state legislature. In relations between a local agency and its state superiors, however, the situation is not nearly so predictable, in large part because local governments generally have less constitutional autonomy vis-à-vis states than do the states vis-à-vis the federal government.

These difficulties in intergovernmental programs aside, sovereigns can affect the policies pursued by implementing agencies through both informal oversight and formal changes in the agency's legal and financial resources. Oversight refers to the continuous interaction between an agency and its legislative (and executive) sovereigns in the form of formal oversight hearings, consultation with staff and legislators on the key committees, routine requests from legislators concerning constituent complaints, and so on. On the one hand, there appear to be rather strong reasons for legislative policy committees to become increasingly sympathetic to target groups over time, in part as a reflection of changes in the balance of interest-group support, in part because constituency casework appears to be weighted toward complaints. On the other hand, legislative sovereigns supportive of a stringent regulatory program can play a crucial role in the successful implementation of such statutes if they have the resources and the desire to do so. Here we come to Eugene Bardach's extremely interesting concept of a *fixer*, an important legislator or executive official who controls resources important to crucial actors and who has the desire and the staff resources to closely monitor the implementation process and to intervene on an almost continuous basis.

On a more formal level, sovereigns have the authority to alter and/or undermine the legal and financial resources of implementing agencies. There have, for example, been statutes that have been essentially emasculated by the courts or through the appropriations process.[20] Legislatures also have the authority to substantially revise and even revoke statutes; in fact, the first major effort to do so marks the end of what we have termed the short-term implementation process. But the most frequent effects may well be of a more indirect nature. As indicated previously, almost any statute is affected by policies outside its specific domain. Changes in any of these can strongly affect support for statutory objectives and/or the number of veto points involved in statutory implementation. The role of an agency and its legislative supporters is to be aware of these ramifications and to make sure that they are explicitly addressed by subsequent legislation. In short, the very interrelatedness of policy areas in any complex society enormously increases the monitoring responsibility of the protectors of any particular statute and thus the probability that the statute will gradually be undermined through subsequent tangential legislation.

Commitment and leadership skill of supportive implementing officials. We finally come to the variable most directly affecting the policy outputs of implementing agencies, namely, the commitment of agency officials to the realization of statutory objectives. This comprises at least two components: first, the direction and ranking of the statutory objectives in officials' preference orderings; and, second, their skill in realizing those preferences, that is, their ability to go beyond what could reasonably be expected in using the available resources. The importance of both attitudes and skill, of course, varies with the amount of discretion afforded administrators.

The commitment of agency officials will partially, and in some cases largely, be a function of the capacity of the statute to institutionalize a bias in the implementing agencies through its selection of institutions and top officials. It will also be a function of professional norms, personal values, and support for statutory objectives among interest groups and sovereigns in the agencies' political environment. In general, the commitment of agency officials to statutory objectives, and the consequent probability of their successful implementation, will be highest in a new agency with high visibility that was created after an intense political campaign. After the initial period, however, the degree of commitment will probably decline over time as the most committed people become burned out and disillusioned with bureaucratic routine, to be replaced by officials much more interested in security than in taking risks to attain policy goals.[21]

But commitment to statutory objectives contributes little to their attainment unless accompanied by skill in using available resources to that end. Usually discussed under the rubric of "leadership," this comprises both political and managerial elements. The former refers to the ability to develop good working relationships with sovereigns in the agency's subsystems, to convince opponents and target groups that they are being treated fairly, to mobilize support among latent supportive constituencies, to adroitly present the agency's case through the mass media, and so on. Managerial skill involves developing adequate controls so that the program is not subject to charges of fiscal mismanagement, to maintaining high morale among agency personnel, and to managing internal dissent in such a way that outright opponents are shunted off to noncrucial positions.

On the whole, however, leadership skill remains a rather elusive concept. While everyone acknowledges its importance, its attributes vary from situation to situation and thus it is extremely difficult to predict whether specific individuals will go beyond what could reasonably be expected in using the available resources in support of statutory objectives.

STAGES (OR DEPENDENT VARIABLES) IN THE IMPLEMENTATION PROCESS

The discussion thus far has focused on the generic factors affecting the implementation process as a whole. But that process must be viewed in terms of its several stages: (1) the policy outputs (decisions) of the implementing agencies; (2) the compliance of target groups with those decisions; (3) the actual impacts of agency decisions; (4) the perceived impacts of those decisions; and finally, (5) the political system's evaluation of a statute in terms of major revisions (or attempted revisions) in its content. All of these stages are often lumped together under the rubric of "feedback loop," but one must distinguish two separate processes. If one is concerned only with the extent to which actual impacts conform to statutory objectives, then only the first three stages are pertinent. In our view, however, one should also consider the political system's summary evaluation of a statute, which necessarily involves the latter two stages as well.

Each of these stages can be thought of as an endpoint or dependent variable. Each is also, however, an input into successive stages. For example, compliance of target groups with the policy decisions of the implementing agencies clearly affects the actual impacts of those decisions. Likewise, the perceived impacts of agency decisions are probably the crucial variable affecting (attempted) revisions in the agency's statutory mandate.

Policy outputs of the implementing agencies: conformity with statutory objectives.   Statutory objectives must be translated into substantive regulations, standard operating procedures for processing individual cases, specific adjudicatory (permit, licensing) decisions, and enforcement of those adjudicatory decisions. This process normally requires considerable effort on the part of officials in one or more implementing agencies in the form of technical analyses of the manner in which general rules apply to successively more concrete situations and then the actual application of those rules in thousands of specific cases. While most administrative officials can generally be expected to follow legal mandates, some discretion is invariably involved. Into this realm flow officials' personal and professional conceptions of what constitutes sound public policy.[22] Moreover, the implementation of most programs involves the hiring of new personnel and changes in the behavior of existing officials. Such changes are likely to meet some resistance, as they require alterations in interpersonal relationships and work habits, as well as the loss of sunk costs. Finally, as the implementation of most statutes involves several implementing agencies with varying degrees of commitment to the achievement of statutory objectives, problems of coordination and communication can be expected.[23] For these and many other reasons, the translation of statutory objectives into the policy decisions of implementing agencies in individual cases is an exceedingly problematic process.

While some slippage is almost inevitable (if for no other reason than legitimate disagreements about how general rules apply to specific cases), it is our contention that such slippage can be minimized if the statute stipulates unambiguous objectives; assigns implementation to sympathetic agencies who will give it high priority; minimizes the number of veto points and provides sufficient incentives to overcome resistance among recalcitrant officials; provides sufficient financial resources to conduct the technical analyses and process individual cases; and biases the decision-rules and access points in favor of statutory objectives. Conformity of policy decisions with statutory objectives is also very dependent on the ability of supportive constituency groups and legislative/executive sovereigns to intervene actively in the process to supplement the agency's resources and to counter resistance from target groups.

Even under such favorable conditions, however, implementing agencies and the entire political system find it difficult to sustain the tension and conflict inherent in a stringent regulatory program over an extended period of time (for example, more than five years). Moreover, as indicated previously, the balance of constituency group support for such a program almost invariably declines over time. For these reasons, in regulatory programs that mandate a substantial change in target-group behavior, within five to seven years the sovereigns and/or the implementing officials will (1) change, delay, or ignore the statutory objectives so as to require less change in target group behavior and/or (2) reduce opposition through side-payments of various sorts (for example, subsidies, tax breaks). In fact, it is probably only through supplementing police-power regulation with such side-payments that the policy outputs of implementing agencies can be maintained consistent with stringent statutory objectives over an extended period of time.[24]

Target group compliance with policy outputs of implementing agency(s). Although the vast majority of Americans affirms a general commitment to law-abidingness, a number of studies of compliance with judicial and administrative decisions have demonstrated that, in practice, behavioral compliance is generally a function of individuals' assessment of the relative costs and benefits to them of following legal directives. These same studies have suggested that the decision to comply is, in turn, a function of (1) the probability that noncompliance will be detected and successfully prosecuted; (2) the sanctions available to penalize noncompliance; (3) target group attitudes concerning the fundamental legitimacy of the rules; and (4) the costs to target groups of compliance.[25]

In the context of our framework, the probability that severe sanctions will follow from noncompliance is affected by the variety and magnitude of sanctions provided by statute; the resources available to implementing agencies to monitor noncompliance; the ability of constituency groups to supplement agency resources in monitoring compliance and bringing enforcement cases; the commitment of agency officials to prosecuting noncompliance; and the number of veto points involved in actually bringing enforcement actions. With respect to the perceived legitimacy of the rules, the entire literature on civil disobedience certainly indicates that some individuals will risk jail rather than submit to fundamentally unjust laws. On the whole, however, most individuals modify even behavior based on deeply held beliefs if the probability that severe sanctions will be invoked is sufficiently high.[26]

Apart from such instances of rule-rejection, however, any regulatory program that seeks to substantially modify target-group behavior will involve cases of extreme hardship in which the regulated will engage in all-out opposition rather than comply. It is precisely to minimize the incidence of such debilitating battles—and the possibility that they will result in court suits which endanger the entire program—that police-power programs need to be supplemented by the provision of side-payments.

Actual impacts of policy outputs: conformity to statutory objectives. Throughout this discussion we have been concerned with the achievement of statutory objectives. It should now be clear that a statute will achieve its desired impacts if (1) the policy outputs of the implementing agencies are consistent with statutory objectives; (2) the ultimate target groups comply with those outputs; (3) there is no serious "subversion" of policy outputs or impacts by conflicting statutes; and (4) the statute incorporates a valid causal theory linking behavioral change in target groups to the achievement of mandated goals.

Although our major concern is the conformity of impacts to statutory objectives, two other aspects of this stage of the implementation process merit brief mention. First, the implementation of a statute may—perhaps because of changing socioeconomic conditions or technologies—have substantive impacts not envisaged in the statutory objectives. A second important category of impacts concerns long-term changes in the political strength of competing interests. For example, the mobilization of constituencies associated with stringent regulatory statutes can result in viable local political organizations, which then elect some of their members to local office and eventually change a wide variety of local programs.[27]

Perceived impacts: conformity with statutory objectives and the values of relevant political elites.   While academic policy scientists and professionally oriented administrative officials may be primarily interested in the *actual* impacts of the policy outputs of implementing agencies, these are often very difficult to measure in any comprehensive and systematic fashion. Moreover, what is of most concern in the evaluation of the program by the political system (and eventually changes in the statutory mandate) are the impacts *perceived* by constituency groups and sovereigns in the policy subsystem.

It is our contention that perceived impacts will be a function of actual impacts as mediated by the values of the perceivor. In general, we expect a high correlation between an actor's initial evaluation of a statute and his perception and evaluation of its impacts.[28] More specifically an actor who does not approve of the (perceived) impacts of a statute will (1) view those impacts as being inconsistent with statutory objectives, (2) view the statute as illegitimate, and/or (3) question the validity of the impact data. This is based on the theory of cognitive dissonance and, specifically, on the corollary that an actor tends to reject any suggestion that the impacts of a legitimate statute might be undesirable.[29]

The amount and direction of ultimate policy feedback—changes in the statute.   Just as the passage of a statute should be viewed as the starting point for an analysis of implementation, so the revision of that statute (or major attempts at revision) should be viewed as the culminating stage of the process (which may, however, be repeated several times). The amount and direction of such changes, or attempted changes, in the statutory mandates of implementing agencies will be a function of the perceived impacts of past agency activities, changes in policy priorities among the general public and policy elites as a result of changing socioeconomic conditions, the political resources of competing groups, and the strategic positions of supportive and opposing sovereigns.

In this regard, a few observations are pertinent. First, in the five to seven years after passage of the basic statute, a "fixer" (to use Bardach's term) can play an absolutely crucial role in preventing emasculation, although not necessarily revisions, in an agency's statute. But after ten to fifteen years, it is the balance of constituency forces and, behind them, changes in social, economic, and technological conditions that prevail. The reason is simply that any particular fixer, no matter what his resources or his skill in employing them is, after all, subject to electoral defeat, retirement, and death. In view of our hypotheses concerning the declining balance of constituency support for stringent regulation over time and the inability of our political system to tolerate intense opposition from legitimate interests over sustained periods, we conclude that stringent regulatory statutes will invariably be revised to, at the very least, substitute side-payments for some of the more onerous police-power decisions. It is our contention, then, that only by mixing distributive with regulatory policies can substantial changes in target-group behavior be achieved. . . .

NOTES

1. By *inherent* we mean inherent in the nature of the problem itself, given technical and practical constraints that cannot be removed through human effort (at least not in the short term). Hence our focus on the availability of a valid causal theory, variation in target group behavior, and so on. We do *not* include the political resources of target groups, as these are discussed later under "political resources of constituency groups." For an excellent discussion of intractable problems, see Richard Nelson, "Intellectualizing about the Moon-Ghetto Metaphor," *Policy Sciences* 5 (December 1974): 375–414.

2. See, for example, Charles Schultze, *The Public Use of Private Interest* (Washington, D.C.: Brookings Institution, 1976).

3. We would like to suggest that the clarity and consistency of statutory objectives be conceptualized along the following ordinal scale:

1. Ambiguous objectives. These include both meaningless injunctions to regulate "in the public interest" and mandates to balance potentially conflicting objectives, e.g., air quality and industrial employment, without establishing priorities among them.

2. Definite "tilt." This involves a relatively clear ranking of potentially conflicting rather general objectives, for example, "improve air quality even if it results in some unemployment."

3. Qualitative objectives. These involve a rather precise qualitative mandate to, for example, "protect air quality so as to maintain the public health, including that of susceptible populations." Note that this qualitative objective is considerably more precise than that under a "tilt."

4. Quantitative objectives, e.g., reduce automotive emissions from 1970 levels by 90 percent by December 31, 1975.

Clearly, the last objective constitutes a greater resource to proponents of change than the first.

4. In their analysis of the implementation of the Public Works and Economic Development Act in Oakland, for example, Pressman and Wildavsky argue persuasively that the underlying technical theory that minority employment can be improved through subsidizing capital was simply invalid—or certainly very inefficient—in a generally healthy economy such as Oakland's. A far more valid strategy would have been a direct labor subsidy to businesses that hired minority workers (Pressman and Wildavsky, *Implementation*, pp. 149–159).

5. Determining what constitutes adequate financial resources is, however, extremely difficult, except to note that it must be related to the seriousness of the problem(s) to be addressed (with per capita expenditures often used as a very crude indicator).

6. In calculating the total number of such points, one must sum those involved in the development of general rules and operating procedures, the disposition of specific cases, and the enforcement of those decisions. One must also consider the possibility that implementing agencies are not given adequate legal authority to achieve mandated objectives.

7. On the importance of decision rules, see James Buchanan and Gordon Tullock, *The Calculus of Consent* (Ann Arbor: University of Michigan Press, 1962), and Charles Wright, "A Note on the Decision Rules of Public Regulatory Agencies," *Public Choice* 31 (Fall 1977): 151–155.

8. Anthony Downs, *Inside Bureaucracy* (Boston: Little, Brown, 1967), chapter 3. For an example in which choice of the principal implementing agency was a major issue, see Zigurd Zile, "A Legislative-Political History of the Coastal Zone Management Act of 1972," *Coastal Zone Management Journal* 1 (1974): 235–274.

9. Judy Rosener with Sally Russell and Dennis Brehn, *Environmental vs. Local Control: A Study of the Voting Behavior of Some California Coastal Commissions* (Irvine: University of California, 1977).

10. James Q. Wilson, "The Politics of Regulation," in James McKie, ed., *Social Responsibility and the Business Predicament* (Washington, D.C.: Brookings Institution, 1974), 135–168; Paul Sabatier, "Social Movements and Regulatory Agencies," *Policy Science* 6 (Fall 1975): 301–342; Karen Orren, "Standing to Sue: Interest Group Conflict in the Federal Courts," *American Political Science Review* 70 (September 1976): 723–741.

11. For example, the Arab oil boycott of 1973–1974 undermined support for implementation of the 1970 Clean Air amendments as both the general public and political elites became more aware of the effects of air pollution control measures on, for example, increased consumption of natural gas by utilities and the adverse impacts of automotive emission control on gasoline mileage.

12. For the relationship between economic diversity and an ability to withstand perturbations (or, in the case of regulation, nonproductive costs), see Jane Jacobs, *The Economy of Cities* (New York: Vintage, 1970).

13. Anthony Downs, "Up and Down with Ecology—The Issue-Attention Cycle," *Public Interest* (Summer 1972): 38–50.

14. The crucial role of specialist reporters is illustrated by the role of Morton Mintz of the *Washington Post* in monitoring the Food and Drug Administration and Casey Buckro of the *Chicago Tribune* on water pollution in Lake Michigan.

15. Warren Miller and Donald Stokes, "Constituency Influence in Congress," *American Political Science Review* 57 (March 1963): 45–56; Charles Backstrom, "Congress and the Public," *American Politics Quarterly* 4 (October 1977): 411–435.

16. Joseph Viladas Co., *The American People and Their Environment*, A Report to the Environmental Protection Agency (Springfield, Va.: NTIS, 1973).

17. Downs, "The Issue-Attention Cycle"; Riley Dunlap and Dan Dillman, "Decline in Public Support for Environmental Protection," *Rural Sociology* 41 (Fall 1976): 382–390.

18. For the general argument, see Marver H. Bernstein, *Regulating Business by Independent Commission* (Princeton: Princeton University Press, 1955), chapters 3–8.

19. Constituency groups can supplement the agency's resources by providing technical data and by helping to monitor compliance. See B. Guy Peters, "Insiders and Outsiders: The Politics of Pressure Group Influence on Bureaucracy," *Administration and Society* 9 (August 1977): 191–218.

20. Peter Woll, *American Bureaucracy* (New York: Norton, 1963), pp. 39–40. In general, however, courts are reluctant to overturn agency decisions.

21. For discussions of leadership and illustrations of its importance, see Frances Rourke, *Bureaucracy, Politics, and Public Policy*, 2d ed. (Boston: Little, Brown, 1976), pp. 94–101.

22. To the extent that an agency is staffed by professionals, sufficient discretion to enable individuals to exercise their professional training and judgment is crucial if they are to perform their tasks with any enthusiasm—even if such discretion conflicts with hierarchical control. Rein and Rabinovitz, *Implementation*, pp. 11–14; Wilbert Moore, *The Professions* (New York: Russell Sage, 1970), chapter 11; Donald Pelz and Frank Andrews, *Scientists in Organizations*, rev. ed. (Ann Arbor: Institute for Social Research, 1976).

23. See Van Meter and Van Horn, "The Policy Implementation Process"; Helen Ingram, "Policy Implementation Through Bargaining: The Case of Federal Grants-In-Aid," *Public Policy* 25 (Fall 1977): 499–526; Christa Altenstetter and James Bjorkman, *Implementation of a Federal-State Health Program* (Berlin: International Institute of Management, 1977); Robert Thomas, "Intergovernmental Coordination in the Implementation of National Air and Water Pollution Policies," in *Public Policy-Making in the Federal System*, ed. Charles Jones and Robert Thomas (Beverly Hills, Calif.: Sage, 1976), pp. 129–148.

24. The response to the 1970 Clean Air amendment has, for example, involved both actions: the deadlines for achieving the auto emission reductions have been repeatedly delayed, while side-payments have included tax credits and low-interest loans for the purchase of pollution control equipment. Although such subsidies are generally criticized by economists for their inefficient allocation of resources, they are also fully in keeping with what Charles Schultze has termed the "no direct harm" rule of American politics. Schultze, *The Public Use of Private Interest*, pp. 70–72.

25. Rodgers and Bullock, *Coercion to Compliance*, chapter 1; Nelson Rosenbaum and Michael Fix, *Enforcing State Land Use Controls* (Washington, D.C.: Urban Institute Working Paper 1236-01,

September 1977); Don Brown and Robert Stover, "Court Directives and Compliance: A Utility Approach," *American Politics Quarterly* 5 (October 1977): 465–480.

26. For example, after years of massive noncompliance with desegregation orders by southern school districts, compliance was achieved in a short period of time when administrative authority was vested in a specific agency and when the 1964 Civil Rights Act and a 1969 court decision enabled those officials to bring very severe sanctions to bear on local districts—specifically, loss of about 67 percent of the funding (Rodgers and Bullock, *Coercion to Compliance*, chapters 2–4). Moreover, individual parents complied even though many continued to view desegregation rules as illegitimate; Douglas Gatlin, Michael Giles, and Everett Cataldo, "Policy Support Within a Target Group: The Case of School Desegregation," *American Political Science Review* 72 (September 1978): 985–995.

27. Browning and Marshall, "Implementation of Model Cities and Revenue Sharing."

28. For evidence in support of this position, see Daniel Mazmanian and Paul Sabatier, "The Role of Attitudes and Perceptions in Policy Evaluation by Attentive Elites: The California Coastal Commissions," in *Why Policies Succeed or Fail*, by Helen Ingram and Dean Mann, Vol. VIII of Sage Yearbook in Politics and Public Policy (Beverly Hills, Calif.: 1980).

29. For example, about 60 percent of southern school officials who viewed the anticipated impacts of school desegregation as undesirable justified their noncompliant behavior on the grounds that the federal court orders were illegitimate (Rodgers and Bullock, *Coercion to Compliance*, pp. 70–74). For a general review of cognitive dissonance, see Roger Brown, *Social Psychology* (New York: Macmillan, 1965), pp. 584–604.

The Role of Evaluation in Public Policy

David Nachmias

"That's a great deal to make one word mean," Alice said in a thoughtful tone.

"When I make a word do a lot of work like that," said Humpty Dumpty, "I always pay it extra."

Much recent concern has been expressed about the impact of evaluation research on public policy. Does evaluation make a difference? Do policymakers make decisions based upon evaluation information that in the absence of such information they would not make? Are evaluation findings utilized when decisions to terminate, expand or markedly alter policies and programs are made?

Commitments and expectations. Such questions were of little concern in the past. Little over a decade ago, the prevailing belief was that questions concerning the utilization of evaluation research were mute, or at best, of secondary

From David Nachmias, "The Role of Evaluation in Public Policy," *Policy Studies Journal*, 8 (1980), pp. 1163–1169. Reprinted by permission.

importance because policymakers would obviously incorporate scientific information into the policy making process. Policymakers habitually complain that they lack the relevant information they need to make more effective polices; were they to have relevant and timely information the public could have been served better. Ineffective programs would be terminated or modified, and effective ones would be continued and, if resources permit, expanded. Ultimately, informed policy decisions would enhance the general public interest.

Tangible and symbolic manifestations of the policymakers' commitments to evaluation, and by implication to utilization, were the appropriations for evaluation research and the creation of evaluation offices and positions in the various levels and branches of government. Congress, for example, has not only approved hundreds of millions of dollars for program evaluation by executive agencies but has also strengthened its own evaluation capability by creating and expanding evaluation staffs in the General Accounting Office, the Congressional Budget Office, the House and Senate Budget Committees, and the legislative and appropriations committees.

Concomitant with the policymakers' commitments to evaluation have been the high expectations of the academic community about the contributions that it could make to the rationalization of public policy making. In the words of Carol Weiss (1977), "There is much hoopla about the rationality that social science would bring to the untidy world of government. It would provide hard data for planning, evidence of need and resources. It would give cause-and-effect theories for policymaking, so that statesmen would know which variables to alter in order to effect the desired outcomes. It would bring to the assessment of alternative policies a knowledge of relative costs and benefits, so that decision makers could select the options with the highest payoff. And once policies were in operation, it would provide objective evaluation of their effectiveness so that necessary modifications could be made to improve performance."

Indicators of the scope and magnitude of the academic community's commitment are the number of evaluation studies actually conducted, the number of books and articles published, and the number of evaluation courses, seminars and workshops offered by universities and research institutes. Thus, in the early 1970s about two hundred evaluation studies were begun each year with direct federal support and with average budgets of about $100,000 each. By now the number of evaluations started each year has more than doubled and the costs have risen sharply. The 1976 congressional sourcebook on federal program evaluation contains 1,700 citations of evaluation reports issued by 18 executive branch agencies and the General Accounting Office during fiscal years 1973 through 1975.

Coupled with the growth of evaluation as a scientific undertaking has been the evaluators' *expectations* that their findings would immediately and dramatically impact public policy. Many still share the following scenario: The evaluator constructs a theoretical model explicating the assumptions of the policymakers, the target and program variables and their interrelations. He or she develops the best possible research design (preferably an experimental one), and the data yield conclusive results at a probability level of .001. If the findings indicate that the program is effective, and as soon as they become public knowledge, policymakers from all over the country request assistance in establishing replicas of the program in their own settings; in a short period of time the program ameliorates the problem it was designed to address. On the other hand, if the findings indicate that the program is ineffective it is immediately dropped or drastically modified. In fact, such a scenario is closely related to idealized conceptualizations of the policy process in which feedback directly and freely flows from the evaluation stage (the last stage of the policy sequence) to the policy formation stage—where it all begins.

The idealized model of utilization.   In the idealized model of utilization the evaluation community is portrayed as one that continuously, systematically and rigorously produces relevant and timely information on the implementation, impact and cost-effectiveness of policies and programs. Based upon their theoretical and empirical investigations, evaluators can explain systematic variations in program performance and predict the effects of altering program variables. Furthermore, once evaluators come to understand the policy problem, they assist in designing new programs or redesigning ineffective ones. The policy goals are always agreed upon, clear and measurable; the theoretical foundations are sound; the resources committed to the implementation of the program are adequate; the agents of implementation straightforwardly execute the policymakers' intents; the program's target population is willing to participate in the program; the evaluators have the skills, expertise, incentives and resources to conduct the best possible evaluation.

In the idealized model, policymakers—the consumers of evaluation information—realize the need for utilization and actively search for information. Evaluation research is an integral component of the decision making process. The policy objectives are known, clear and consistent. Whenever possible "Trade-offs among these objectives would be known and decision makers would seek in all their decisions to equate the marginal benefit of achieving any one of the objectives with that of achieving any other" (Haveman, 1977, p. 580). Once programs are activated, there is a minimum of stability in their duration in order to make sound evaluation possible and useful. The motivational structure of policymakers is one in which the public interest serves as the criterion for making policy decisions. The self-interest of policymakers is enhanced as the general public interest is advanced. The structure of the political market is identical to that of the free economic market, and since producers and consumers of evaluation information share a mutual interest, the "invisible hand" frames the conditions for optimizing utilization.

The criterion for assessing utilization is built into the definition of evaluation: Evaluation research is meant for immediate direct use in improving policy decisions. Evaluation is assessing the worth of a policy; once worth is established, discrete policy decisions either conform to the assessed worth (utilization), or else they contradict the value relations (nonutilization). If this does not occur (and in fact it rarely does under this view), another medium of exchange is needed to bring producers and consumers into optimum exchange relations. Mann (1972), for example, used this conceptualization and concluded that ". . . evaluation research presents a specific blind alley. It has failed to validate itself in practice and the sooner its failure is accepted and recognized, the easier will be a transition to another approach to the same problem."

Actual utilization of evaluation.   Given the idealized model of evaluation it should not be too surprising that the evaluation community is undergoing a crisis of unfulfilled expectations. Indeed, the least ambiguous evidence we have so far concerning the utilization of evaluation information is that the high expectations of policymakers and evaluators alike have not been met.

There are only a few documented case studies in which the evaluation information dramatically and immediately impacted discrete policy decisions. There are more documented case studies showing that the evaluation findings did not impact discrete decisions. The little systematic and empirical research available suggests that utilization occurs but not with the frequency, magnitude and manner envisioned.

With respect to the first situation, that is, a dramatic, instantaneous impact, two examples will suffice. At the national level, Richardson (1972) reports that "A study of the National Defense Education Act loans to students who undertake a career in teaching suggested that this had not been a significant incentive. It was possible to conclude, with the concurrence of the Congress, that the feature should be eliminated, and it was." In this case the evaluation findings were conclusive, and the termination of the program was not expected to trigger a political controversy: the policy issue was of low political salience. At the local level, Alkin, Daillack and White (1979) evaluated a program funded under ESEA Title I in Rockland. The evaluation results were negative and the program was dropped. The decision to drop the program rested with one person: the Rockland Title I director. The termination of the program was not expected to trigger controversy; it did not displace personnel, and it did not involve the loss of any capital expenditures. Rockland is a textbook case of utilization: "A specific identifiable program was evaluated; comparison groups were established; students were tested in both the experimental program and in comparison programs; an evaluation report was written; the findings were negative; and the program was dropped."

With respect to nonutilization the case of the New Jersey Income Maintenance Experiments is instructive. The evaluations were commissioned by OEO in 1968. The purpose of the experiments was to determine the amount of work reduction that would result from the adoption of the controversial negative-income-tax policy. The experiments were designed to produce findings after five years of field observation. After less than a year of field work, a proposal for the nationwide implementation of the policy, the Family Assistance Plan, was put forward. This created a sense of urgency on the part of the policymakers to obtain evidence from the experiments. Reacting to pressures from OEO officials, the investigators released preliminary results based on one year's work. Even though the findings indicated an increase in work effort by those receiving a negative income tax, Congress did not enact the proposal. Subsequent interviews with members of the relevant congressional committees elicited a common response: the tax experiments provided only tentative and inconclusive evidence (Boeckmann, 1976).

The very few published systematic empirical studies of evaluation utilization tend to support the proposition that utilization in the sense of influencing program decision making and management occurs, but not in the manner proposed in the early evaluation literature. Patton et al. (1975), looked at twenty evaluations of national health programs and for each program studied, interviewed the evaluator and a major program decision maker. Based upon these interviews the authors suggest that ". . . evaluation research is used by decision makers but not in the clear-cut and organization-shaking ways that social scientists sometimes believe research should be used" (p. 119). Similarly, Alkin et al. (1974) studied forty-two ESEA Title VII programs and concluded that the project directors used information from evaluations for local program decision making. Caplan et al. (1975) interviewed 204 persons from the White House, federal departments and research institutes, and cited 450 separate instances of utilization. The authors concluded: "Many of the reported instances involved creative and strategically important applications of policy-relevant social science information and would suggest reason for modest satisfaction rather than despair and cynicism so prevalent in the literature" (p. 4). Lynn gives additional examples of HEW's utilization of evaluation studies of major programs, ranging from evaluations of the use of health-care services to an array of educational assistance programs (Lynn, 1972, pp. 24–28). Finally, but not exhaustively, in studying 350 policy and program changes at mental hospitals, Roberts and Larsen (1972) found that 60 percent of them were stimulated by research reports, with another 15 percent using research findings to refine decisions already made.

Utilization and public policy.   Not even in the best of all possible worlds can we expect all the suppositions of the idealized model of utilization to represent reality. Elsewhere, I discussed the immense methodological difficulties involved in conducting evaluation research; these, of course, are reflected in the quality of evaluation information (Nachmias, 1979). In fact, the variability in the quality of information is so great that in many cases policymakers are better off ignoring the information altogether. Bernstein and Freeman (1975), for example, report that of 382 evaluations funded by federal agencies only about three-quarters included impact measurement, and about one-half of these are ". . . deficient either in design, sampling or validity measures" (p. 97). But even if the quality of evaluation information improves, and I believe it will, the fact that it constitutes only one component of a typically fragmented public policy process in which the incentives of policymakers are diverse, conflicting, and always congruent with the public interest hinges on more effective utilization.

Evaluation research is a scientific but also a political act. It may indicate that policymakers consider the issues the evaluation will address to be worthy of serious consideration. But it may also be a symbolic act, or even a ritual ". . . whose function is to calm the anxieties of the citizenry and to perpetuate the image of government rationality" (Floden and Weimer, 1978, p. 16). Indeed, evaluation became the law of the land as a political response to discontent and demands for government accountability and efficiency. By legislating evaluation, policymakers responded to pressures generated by the political process. The legislation, of course, does not mandate utilization although the intent of the political demands was to formalize and institutionalize the transformation of knowledge into public policy.

Not only is evaluation a political act, but it also serves functions other than the assessment of worth. Thus, evaluation may be a means for conflict management, a tactic used to reduce conflict by narrowing its scope. An evaluation may be an indication that the policy is subject to negotiation and modification once the research findings become available. Indeed, the New Jersey Income Maintenance Experiments served the function of transforming an ideological debate into a specific policy agenda. Yet, whatever the data show, the political climate places constraints on what kinds of policy changes will be taken, how fast, and at what cost.

Evaluation may also serve the function of complacency reduction: "The very fact of participating in an evaluation may spur the consideration of new practices by practitioners. . . . Participation in evaluative efforts can promote both the clarification of standard operating procedures and their revision" (Floden and Weimer, 1978, p. 14). In such cases utilization will be manifested perhaps in program administration, a very demanding situation to measure. But the fact that it is hard to measure and detect utilization should not mean that the evaluation has not been utilized.

Since evaluation serves varied functions, utilization should be assessed with respect to the function it serves for specific policymakers. This, of course, is a formidable task given the fragmentation of the policy process. Who makes income maintenance policy, or crime control policy, or energy conservation policy? There is no single, authoritative policymaker. The power to make public policies is fragmented among all branches and levels of government. Fragmentation is further enhanced by functional and administrative specialization. For example, 11 committees in the U.S. House of Representatives, 10 in the U.S. Senate, and 9 executive agencies have some jurisdiction over income maintenance programs. These actors have different roles, interests, values, attitudes and constituencies, and indeed their commitments to evaluation and utilization differ. Some will make the best possible use of the information, others will attempt to use the findings for partisan or legitimizing purposes, and still others will ignore the information all together.

If utilization has any general meaning, it means relevance to a great number of actors in a complex and fragmented policy process. From the point of view of policymakers, evaluation is research that can help them to carry out their roles and achieve goals *they* (not the evaluators) consider important. From the evaluator's perspective, this means that his or her findings are evaluated within the framework of an adversary political process in which policy decisions are reached through bargaining, compromise and trade-offs. In this process the evaluation information has to compete with a host of nonscientific factors that policymakers consider relevant in making policy decisions. If these factors will be interpreted by the policymakers to reinforce the evaluation findings, the chances for utilization will dramatically increase. If these factors will stand in the way of the research findings, the chances for utilization will decrease. In most cases, neither the evaluation findings nor the factors that induce policymakers to act the way they do are crystal clear; this in turn, makes both the detection of utilization instances and the study of policy formation extremely difficult.

Public policy making is not only highly fragmented but it is also incremental. Policy making is not a discrete, single act or event. Rather, policies are shaped incrementally over time in a series of measures and along a number of phases; the measures are partial and not necessarily cumulative.

This has several implications for utilization. First, and perhaps most important, utilization can occur throughout the policy cycle, not necessarily in certain stages. For example, utilization can occur in the implementation stage but not in the policy formation stage. The higher the likelihood for conflict and the more fragmented the policy formation stage, the greater the chances for utilization to occur in the implementation stage. In such cases, utilization would be unobtrusive and carried out by program personnel rather than program formulators. The fact that utilization can occur throughout the policy cycle implies that instances of nonutilization at a given point of time cannot be interpreted adequately. Furthermore, it takes time for the evaluation findings to be internalized by policymakers. This is especially true when normative convictions or common sense are contradicted by scientific findings. In such cases, the evaluation findings cannot be expected to impact the policy process in a nonincremental way.

The incremental nature of the policy process makes the detection and measurement of utilization very difficult. Davis and Salasin (1978) exemplify this point with the following episode: After participating for many months in the development of the portion of the regulations dealing with the evaluation of mental health programs, a minor bureaucrat is about to sign a document when his eye catches these words: "Client outcome will be evaluated by assessment of the client's adjustment at a pre-determined follow-up point." The official marks out this statement, substituting: "Client outcome will be measured by assessing the reduction of the client's presenting problem." The change is so slight, incremental and unobtrusive that it would hardly be noticed as a policy change or utilization. But if it would be successfully implemented, it will influence the practice of community mental health centers throughout the nation in serving some 5 million clients each year. Such incremental utilization may or may not be cumulative, but that is the nature of public policy making.

A final note.   We have little systematic knowledge on the impact of evaluation research on public policy. This is a new and difficult area of investigation. It is hard to define utilization; it is extremely difficult to measure it, and it is a formidable task to systematically account for its antecedents. Furthermore, the early evaluation literature separated utilization from politics and evaluation from policy making. But both evaluation and utilization take place in a complex, fragmented and incremental policy process. Awareness of this observation should at the minimum reduce the gap between our expectations from evaluation and its past performance.

REFERENCES

ALKIN, M. C., DAILLACK, R., and WHITE, P., *Using Evaluations*, Beverly Hills, Calif.: Sage, 1979, p. 224.

ALKIN, M. C. et al., "Evaluation and Decision Making: The Title VII Experience," *CSE Monograph Series in Evaluation*, Center for the Study of Evaluation, University of California, Los Angeles, 1974.

BERNSTEIN, I. L. and FREEMAN, H. E., *Academic and Entrepreneurial Research*, New York: Russell Sage Foundation, 1975, p. 97.

BOECKMANN, M. E., "Policy Impacts of the New Jersey Income Maintenance Experiment," *Policy Sciences*, 7 (March, 1976), p. 53.

CAPLAN, N., MORRISON, A., and STAMBAUGH, R. J., *The Use of Social Science Knowledge in Policy Decisions of the National Level*, Ann Arbor: Institute for Social Research, 1975, p. 4.

DAVIS, H. R. and SALASIN, S. E., "Strengthening the Contribution of Social R&D to Policy Making," in L. E. Lynn (ed.), *Knowledge and Policy*, Washington, D.C.: National Academy of Sciences, 1978, pp. 93–125.

FLODEN, R. E. and WEIMER, S. S., "Rationality to Ritual: The Multiple Roles of Evaluation in Governmental Processes," *Policy Sciences*, 9 (1978), p. 16.

Ibid., p. 14.

HAVEMAN, R. H., "Policy Analysis and Congress: An Economist's View," in R. H. Haveman and J. Margolis (eds.), *Public Expenditures and Policy Analysis*, Chicago: Rand McNally, 1977, p. 580.

LYNN, E. L., "Notes from HEW," *Evaluation*, 1(1) (1972), pp. 24–28.

MANN, J., "The Outcome of Evaluative Research," in C. H. Weiss (ed.), *Evaluating Action Research*, Boston: Allyn and Bacon, 1972, p. 278.

NACHMIAS, DAVID, *Public Policy Evaluation*, New York: St. Martin's, 1979.

OFFICE OF PROGRAM ANALYSIS, GENERAL ACCOUNTING OFFICE, *Federal Program Evaluations: A Directory for the Congress*, Washington, D.C.: U.S. Government Printing Office, 1976.

PATTON, M. O. et al., *In Search of Impact: An Analysis of Utilization of Federal Health Evaluation Research*, Minneapolis: University of Minnesota, 1975, p. 119.

RICHARDSON, R. E., "Conversational Contact," *Evaluation*, 1(1), (1972), pp. 9–16.

ROBERTS, A. AND LARSEN, J., "Effective Use of Mental Health Research Information," Final Report, NIMH Grant No. RO1-MH-15445, 1972.

WEISS, C. H., "Introduction," in C. H. Weiss (ed.), *Using Social Research and Public Policy Making*, Lexington, Mass.: D.C. Heath, 1977, p. 4.

Trends in Policy Analysis

Stuart Nagel

Policy analysis can be defined as the study of nature, causes, and effects of ways in which governments attempt to deal with social problems. Systematically evaluating the effects of alternative policies involves processing a set of goals to be achieved, alternative policies for achieving them, and relations between goals and alternatives in order to arrive at or explain the best alternative, combination, allocation, or predictive decision-rule.

Looking over the 20th century and especially over the past 40 years from 1950 to 1990, one can observe various trends in policy analysis regarding those key elements of goals, means, methods of analysis, and analytic institutions, as well as public policy substance and perspectives.

GOALS TO BE ACHIEVED

There is a trend toward higher goals for society in economic, social, political, and science policy. This can be seen in the redefining of concepts like poverty, equality, fair procedure, free speech, good government, adequate education, adequate health, and a clean environment.

There have been major changes in almost all fields of public policy, which have resulted in increased benefits for the less privileged groups in society, but also increased benefits simultaneously for the more privileged groups. In the fields of labor policy and consumer policy, for example, there are now more rights for workers and consumers, but those rights have provided a stimulus to labor-saving technology and a stimulus to generating better products. Those effects have promoted greater productivity, sales, and profits.

MEANS FOR ACHIEVING POLICY GOALS

There is a trend toward the use of positive incentives like subsidies, tax breaks, and low-interest loans for encouraging socially desired behavior. This can be contrasted with an emphasis on negative incentives associated with jail, fines, and injunctions.

From Stuart Nagel, "Trends in Policy Analysis," *Policy Studies Journal*, 18 (1990), pp. 802–807. Reprinted by permission.

There is a trend toward more policy making on the part of the national government relative to the states and cities, and more policy making on the part of the executive branch relative to the legislative and judicial. One should, however, note that policy making is increasing among all levels and branches, as governments are given more responsibility to deal with various social problems.

There is a trend toward a more pragmatic, mixed approach in dividing responsibility between the public and private sectors for public functions. This can be contrasted with a more ideological approach that allocates between the public and private sectors by determining what would be capitalistic or socialistic.

METHODS FOR ANALYZING ALTERNATIVE PUBLIC POLICIES

The key overall trend is toward new ideas that combine both simplicity and validity. There is a trend toward the use of microcomputer software that facilitates systematic trial-and-error experimentation. There is also a trend toward an expert systems perspective that seeks to develop methods by analyzing how good decision makers implicitly decide, rather than trying to deduce how they should decide in light of unrealistic and/or unfeasible premises that relate to calculus optimization or mathematical programming.

More specific trends relate to how to deal with each of the six trends toward systematic evaluation mentioned in the methods column of Table 1. Separate rate trends involve moving toward (1) MCDM, rather than single objective functions, (2) variations on breakeven analysis to determine critical values of missing information, rather than trying to devise expensive ways of not having missing information, (3) the use of percentaging methods to deal with allocation problems, (4) an expansionist philosophy to deal with conflicting constraints, (5) variations on if-then analysis for multiple prediction, and (6) spreadsheet analysis as the most popular decision-aiding software.

TABLE 1   The Elements of Policy Analysis in Four Recent Time Periods

	Goals	Means	Methods	Institutions
Pre-1960	Good government	Describing policies	Journalism, history, and philosophy	The APSA and the APSR
1960–1975	Goals as being unscientific	Correlating policies	Statistical analysis	Behavioral and regional journals
1975–1985	Goals as variables	Feasible and inter-disciplinary policies	Benefit-cost analysis	Policy journals and courses
Post-1985	Questioning goals	Incentives, multiple government foci and pragmatism	MCDM spread-sheet analysis	Design science

INSTITUTION FOR CONDUCTING AND COMMUNICATING PUBLIC POLICY ANALYSIS

There has been a substantial growth and now a plateauing out at a high level of activity with regard to policy evaluation (1) training programs, (2) research centers, (3) funding sources, (4) publishing outlets, and (5) scholarly associations.

The Policy Studies Organization has been active in helping to develop all five kinds of policy evaluation institutions. It has conducted workshop training programs for national meetings, government agencies, and developing nations. It has stimulated research by offering numerous publication outlets for policy evaluation research. It has facilitated finding funding for symposia and other projects. It has provided such publication outlets as the *Policy Studies Journal, Policy Studies Review*, PSO Directories, PSO-JAI Research Annuals, and the PSO Book Series with Greenwood, Macmillan, Nelson-Hall, Lexington, Sage, Kennikat, Associated Faculty Press, Marcel Dekker, University Press of America, and others. As a scholarly association, PSO has provided opportunities for networking, presenting papers, conferences, and other forms of scholarly interaction.

SOME OVERALL TRENDS

The post-1985 period can be characterized as one in which (1) there are higher goals for public policy, including the goal of satisfying both liberals and conservatives, (2) there are more positive incentives, more sources of ideas among government levels and branches, and more pragmatic relations between the public and private sectors for achieving those goals, and (3) there is a trend toward MCDM and spreadsheet analysis (see Table 1).

Instead of talking in terms of goals, means, and methods, one could discuss the trends in policy studies in terms of substance and process. With regard to substance, there has been a trend from a concern for how to allocate resources to a greater concern for how to increase the resources to allocate. This trend can be seen in supply-side economics, industrial policy, win-win mediation, and non-zero-sum games. With regard to process, there has been a trend from talking so much about the process of policy formation to talking more about the process of policy implementation. Along with implementation goes a concern for impact and how to improve impact or goal achievement.

ALTERNATING BETWEEN PRODUCTIVITY AND EQUALITARIANISM

Public policy seems to proceed through a series of time periods that alternate between a push for greater societal productivity and then a push for greater equalitarian division of the results of the increased productivity. That may imply productivity precedes equalitarianism, which is partly true. It is difficult to be equalitarian if societal resources are especially scarce as in times of recession, famine, or losing a war. On the other hand, equal opportunity is essential to fully realizing societal productivity. The productivity of many countries of the world has increased substantially in recent years as a result of providing greater job opportunities to women, ethnic minorities, the elderly, the disabled, and others who have been qualified for more productive jobs than they were previously in.

Another defect in the implications of the analysis is the idea that those alternating periods can continue indefinitely. That may be so regarding increased productivity. New technologies do generate other new technologies at an expanding rate rather than with diminishing returns. There may be diminishing returns or plateauing out in a given technology (such as automobiles), but not in a broad field (such as transportation) or in technology in general. On the other hand, equality of opportunity can eventually reach the point where there is almost no major discrimination against groups of people. We do seem to be approaching that desirable limit, while not approaching a technological saturation.

SUPER-OPTIMUM SOLUTIONS

One result of the continuing concern for productivity growth and decreasing need for concern about nonmerit discrimination is a changing of ideological divisions. The past divisions have mainly related to conservatives (who tend to emphasize the interests of those who are relatively well off in a society) versus liberals (who tend to emphasize the interests of those who are not so relatively well off). The present and future divisions are increasingly related to those who seek to expand the total societal product through industrial policy and supply-side economics versus those who still think in terms of fixed pies, zero-sum games, and the idea that the main way to benefit the poor is to take from the rich. The new expansionist philosophy emphasizes solutions to public policy problems that benefit categories of rich-poor, whites-blacks, males-females, urban-rural, north-south, and other groups that were formerly considered inherently in conflict over scarce resources.

Some policy analysts are even advocating and predicting the idea of super-optimum solutions (SOS) where all sides in traditional policy conflicts can come out ahead of their original best expectations. An example is the American national debt. Traditional conservatives argue the need to cut domestic spending. Traditional liberals argue the need to cut defense spending. They may reluctantly compromise by cutting both and even by raising some taxes. The new expansionist thinkers look for ways to increase the gross national product so there can be increased revenue even with a constant tax rate and without cutting needed expenditures.

If there is going to be more emphasis on super-optimum solutions that can simultaneously achieve otherwise conflicting goals or trade-offs, then we are in for an exciting future in the development of public policy substance and methods. It is trite to say that these are exciting times. It has not yet become trite to say that we may be entering into super-optimum times. That does not mean that the solutions reached will necessarily be super-optimum. It does mean that policy makers and policy analysts may be expanding their thinking away from trade-offs and split-the-difference compromises toward thinking about ways in which we can have our expanded pie and eat it too. The future looks good for creative thinkers, systematic policy analysts, and insightful futures researchers.[1]

NOTE

1. For literature dealing with trends and the future of policy analysis and public policy, see Franklin Tugwell (ed.), *Search for Alternatives: Public Policy and the Study of the Future* (Winthrop, 1973); Thomas Jones, *Options for the Future: A Comparative Analysis of Policy-Oriented Forecasts* (Praeger, 1980); Albert Somit (ed.), *Political Science and the Study of the Future* (Dryden, 1974); and S. Nagel, "Policy Studies and Futures Research," 14 *World Futures Society Bulletin* 1–10 (1980).

21

The Politics of Public Budgets

Irene S. Rubin

Public budgets describe what governments do by listing how governments spend money. A budget links tasks to be performed with the amount of resources necessary to accomplish those tasks, ensuring that money will be available to wage war, provide housing, or maintain streets. Budgets limit expenditures to the revenues available, to ensure balance and prevent overspending. Most of the work in drawing up a budget is technical, estimating how much it will cost to feed a thousand shut-ins with a Meals-on-Wheels program or how much revenue will be produced from a 1 percent tax on retail sales. But public budgets are not merely technical managerial documents; they are also intrinsically and irreducibly political.

☐ Budgets reflect choices about what government will and will not do. They reflect general public consensus about what kinds of services governments should provide and what citizens are entitled to as members of society. Should government provide services that the private sector could provide, such as water, electricity, transportation, and housing? Do all citizens have a guarantee of health care, regardless of ability to pay? Are all insured against hunger? Are they entitled to some kind of housing?

From Irene S. Rubin, *The Politics of Public Budgeting* (2nd ed.) (Chatham, N.J.: Chatham House, 1993), pp. 1–6; 10–20. Reprinted by permission.

☐ Budgets reflect priorities—between police and flood control, day care and defense, the Northeast and the Southwest. The budget process mediates between groups and individuals who want different things from government and determines who gets what. These decisions may influence whether the poor get job training or the police get riot training, both as a response to an increased number of unemployed.

☐ Budgets reflect the relative proportion of decisions made for local and constituency purposes, and for efficiency, effectiveness, and broader public goals. Budgets reflect the degree of importance legislators put on satisfying their constituents and the legislators' willingness to listen to interest-group demands. For example, the Defense Department may decide to spend more money to keep a military base open because the local economy depends on it and to spend less money to improve combat readiness.

☐ Budgets provide a powerful tool of accountability to citizens who want to know how the government is spending their money and if government has generally followed their preferences. Budgeting links citizen preferences and governmental outcomes.

☐ Budgets reflect citizens' preferences for different forms of taxation and different levels of taxation, as well as the ability of specific groups of taxpayers to shift tax burdens to others. The budget reflects the degree to which the government redistributes wealth upward or downward through the tax system.

☐ At the national level, the budget influences the economy, so fiscal policy affects the level of employment—how many people are out of work at any time.

☐ Budgets reflect the relative power of different individuals and organizations to influence budget outcomes. Budgetary decision making provides a picture of the relative power of budget actors within and between branches of government, as well as the importance of citizens in general and specific interest groups.

In all these ways, public budgeting is political. But budgeting is not typical of other political processes and hence one example among many. It is both an important and a unique arena of politics. It is important because of the specific policy issues reflected in the budget: the scope of government, the distribution of wealth, the openness of government to interest groups, and the accountability of government to the public at large. It is unique because these decisions have to take place in the context of budgeting, with its need for balance, its openness to the environment, and its requirements for timely decisions so that government can carry on without interruption.

Public budgets clearly have political implications, but what does it mean to say that key political decisions are made in the context of budgeting? The answer has several parts. First, what is budgeting? Second, what is public budgeting, as opposed to individual or family budgeting or the budgeting of private organizations? Third, what does *political* mean in the context of public budgeting?

WHAT IS BUDGETING?

The essence of budgeting is that it allocates scarce resources and hence implies choice between potential objects of expenditure. Budgeting implies balance, and it requires some kind of decision-making process.

Making Budgetary Choices

All budgeting, whether public or private, individual or organizational, involves choices between possible expenditures. Since no one has unlimited resources, people budget all the time. A child makes a budget (a plan for spending, balancing revenues and expenditures) when she decides to spend money on a marshmallow rabbit rather than a chocolate one, assuming she has money enough for only one rabbit. The air force may choose between two different airplanes to replace current bombers. These examples illustrate the simplest form of budgeting because they involve only one actor, one resource, one time, and two straightforward and comparable choices.

Normally, budgeting does not take place by comparing only two reasonably similar items. There may be a nearly unlimited number of choices. Budgeting usually limits the options to consider by grouping together similar things that can be reasonably compared. When I go to the supermarket, I do not compare all the possible things I could buy, not only because I cannot absorb that number of comparisons, but because the comparisons would be meaningless and a waste of time. I do not go to the supermarket and decide to get either a turkey or a bottle of soda pop. I compare main dishes with main dishes, beverages with beverages, desserts with desserts. Then I have a common denominator for comparison. For example, I may look at the main course and ask about the amount of protein for the dollar. I may compare the desserts in terms of the amount of cholesterol or the calories.

There is a tendency, then, to make comparisons within categories where the comparison is meaningful. This is as true for governmental budgeting as it is for shoppers. For example, weapons might be compared with weapons or automobiles with automobiles. They could be compared in terms of speed, reliability, availability of spare parts, and so on, and the one that did the most of what you wanted it to do at the least cost would be the best choice. As long as there is agreement on the goals to be achieved, the choice should be straightforward.

Sometimes, budgeting requires comparison of different, and seemingly incomparable things. If I do not have enough money to buy a whole balanced meal, I may have to make choices between main dishes and desserts. How do I compare the satisfaction of a sweet tooth to the nourishment of a turkey? Or, in the public sector, how do I compare the benefits of providing shelters for the homeless with buying more helicopters for the navy? I may then move to more general comparisons, such as how clearly were the requests made and the benefits spelled out; who got the benefits last time and whose turn is it this time; are there any specific contingencies that make one choice more likely than the other? For example, will we be embarrassed to show our treatment of the homeless in front of a visiting dignitary? Or, are disarmament negotiations coming up in which we need to display strength or make a symbolic gesture of restraint? Comparing dissimilar items may require a list of priorities. It may be possible to do two or more important things if they are sequenced properly.

Budgeting often allocates money, but it can allocate any scarce resource, for example, time. A student may choose between studying for an exam or playing softball and drinking beer afterward. In this example, it is time that is at a premium, not money. Or it could be medical skills that are in short supply, or expensive equipment, or apartment space, or water.

Government programs often involve a choice of resources and sometimes involve combinations of resources, each of which has different characteristics. For example, some federal farm programs involve direct cash payments plus loans at below-market interest rates, and welfare programs often involve dollar payments plus food stamps, which allow recipients to pay less for food. Federal budgets often assign agencies money, personnel, and sometimes borrowing authority, three different kinds of resources.

Balancing and Borrowing

Budgets have to balance. A plan for expenditures that pays no attention to ensuring that revenues cover expenditures is not a budget. That may sound odd in view of huge federal deficits, but a budget may technically be balanced by borrowing. Balance means only that outgo is matched or exceeded by income. The borrowing, of course, has to be paid off. Borrowing means spending more now and paying more in the future in order to maintain balance. It is a balance over time.

To illustrate the nature of budget balance, consider me as shopper again. Suppose I spend all my weekly shopping money before I buy my dessert. I have the option of treating my dollar limit as if it were more flexible, by adding the dimension of time. I can buy the dessert and everything else in the basket, going over my budget, and then eat less at the end of the month. Or I can pay the bill with a credit card, assuming I will have more money in the future with which to pay off the bill when it comes due. The possibility of borrowing against the future is part of most budget choices.

Process

Budgeting cannot proceed without some kind of decision process. Even in the simplest cases of budgeting, there has to be some limit set to spending, some order of decision making, some way to structure comparisons among alternatives, and some way to compare choices. Budget processes also regulate the flow of decisions so they are made in a timely manner.

Back to my shopping example: If I shop for the main course first, and spend more money than I intended on it because I found some fresh fish, there will be less money left for purchasing the dessert. Hence, unless I set a firm limit on the amount of money to spend for each segment of the meal, the order in which I do the purchasing counts. Of course, if I get to the end of my shopping and do not have enough money left for dessert, I can put back some of the items already in the cart and squeeze out enough money for dessert.

Governmental budgeting is also concerned with procedures for managing tradeoffs between large categories of spending. Budgeters may determine the relative importance of each category first, attaching a dollar level in proportion to the assigned importance, or they may allow purchasing in each area to go on independently, later reworking the choices until the balance between the parts is acceptable.

The order of decisions is important in another sense. I can determine how much money I am likely to have first and then set that as an absolute limit on expenditures, or I can determine what I must have, what I wish to have, and what I need to set aside for emergencies and then go out and try to find enough money to cover some or all of those expenditures. Especially in emergencies, such as accidents or other health emergencies, people are likely to obligate the money first and worry about where it will come from later. Governmental budgeting, too, may concentrate first on revenues and later on expenditures, or first on expenditures and later on income. Like individuals or families, during emergencies such as floods or hurricanes or wars, governments will commit the expenditures first and worry about where the money will come from later.

GOVERNMENTAL BUDGETING

Public budgeting shares the characteristics of budgeting in general but differs from household and business budgeting in some key ways. First, in public budgeting, there are always people and organizations with different perspectives and different goals trying to get what they want out of the budget. In individual budgets, there may be only one person involved; and in family and business budgets, there may be only a limited number of actors and they may have similar views of what they want to achieve through the budget.

Second, public budgets are more open to the environment than budgets of families or businesses are. Not only are public budgets open to the economy but also to other levels of government, to citizens, to interest groups, to the press, and to politicians.

Third, budgets form a crucial link between citizen taxpayers and government officials. The document itself may be a key form of accountability. This function does not apply to businesses, families, or individuals.

Fourth, public budgeting is characterized by a variety of constraints, legal limits, perceived limits imposed by public opinion, rules and regulations about how to carry out the budget, and many more. Public budgeting is far more constrained in this sense than budgets of individuals or businesses. . . .

More formally, public budgeting has five particular characteristics that differentiate it from other kinds of budgeting. First, public budgeting is characterized by a variety of budgetary actors who often have different priorities and different levels of power over budget outcomes. These actors have to be regulated and orchestrated by the budget process. Second, in government there is a distinction between those who pay taxes and those who decide how money will be spent—the citizens and the elected politicians. Public officials can force citizens to pay taxes for expenditures they do not want, but citizens can vote politicians out of office. Third, the budget document is important as a means of public accountability. Fourth, public budgets are very vulnerable to the environment—to the economy, to changes in public opinion, to elections, to local contingencies such as natural disasters like floods, or political disasters such as the police bombing of MOVE headquarters in Philadelphia, which burned down part of a neighborhood. Fifth, public budgets are incredibly constrained. Although there is a built-in necessity to make budgets adaptable to contingencies, there are many elements of public budgets that are beyond the immediate control of those who draw up budgets.

A Variety of Actors

The first characteristic of public budgeting was the variety of actors involved in the budget and their frequently clashing motivations and goals. On a regular basis, bureau chiefs, executive budget officers, and chief executives are involved in the budget process, as are legislators, both on committees and as a whole group. Interest groups may be involved at intervals, sometimes for relatively long stretches of time, sometimes briefly. Sometimes citizens play a direct or indirect role in the budget process. Courts may play a role in budgets at any level of government at unpredictable intervals. When they do play a role in budgetary decisions, what are these actors trying to achieve?

Bureau chiefs.   Many students of budgeting assume that agency heads always want to expand their agencies, that their demands are almost limitless, and that it is up to other budget actors to curtail and limit their demands. The reasons given for that desire for expansion include prestige, more subordinates, more space, larger desks, more secretaries, and not incidentally, more salary. The argument presumes that agency heads judge their bureaucratic skills in terms of the satisfaction of their budget requests. Successful bureaucrats bring back the budget. Agency expansion is the measure of success.

Recent research has suggested that while some bureaucrats may be motivated by salaries, many feel that one of their major rewards is the opportunity to do good for people—to house the homeless, feed the hungry, find jobs for the unemployed, and send out checks to the disabled.[1] For these bureaucrats, efforts to expand agency budgets are the result of their belief in the programs they work for.

Recent research has also suggested that the bureaucracy has become more professional, which introduces the possibility of another motivation, the desire to do a good job, to do it right, to put in the best machinery that exists or build the biggest, toughest engineering project or the most complicated weapons.

The generalization that bureaucrats always press for budget increases appears to be too strong. Some agencies are much more aggressive in pushing for growth than others. Some are downright moribund. Sometimes agency heads refuse to expand when given the opportunity,[2] suggesting there are some countervailing values to growth. One of these countervailing values is agency autonomy. Administrators may prefer to maintain autonomy rather than increase the budget if it comes down to a choice between the two. A second countervailing value to growth is professionalism, the desire to get the job done, and do it quickly and right. Administrators generally prefer to hire employees who have the ability to get the job done, plus a little, a spare amount of intelligence, motivation, and energy just in case they need to get some extra work done or do it fast in response to a political request.[3] Administrators may refuse to add employees if the proposed employees do not add to the agency's capacity to get things done.

A third countervailing value is program loyalty. Expansion may be seen as undesirable if the new mission swamps the existing mission, if it appears contradictory to the existing mission, or if the program requires more money to carry out than is provided, forcing the agency to spend money designated for existing programs on new ones or do a poor job.

A fourth countervailing value is belief in the chain of command. Many, if not all, bureaucrats believe that their role is to carry out the policies of the chief executive and the legislature. If those policies mean cutting back budgets, agency heads cut back the agencies. Agency heads may be appointed precisely because they are willing to make cuts in their agencies.[4]

Bureaucrats, then, do not always try to expand their agencies' budgets. They have other, competing goals, which sometimes dominate. Also, their achievements can be measured by other than expanded budgets. They may go for some specific items in the budget without raising totals, or may try for changes in the wording of legislation. They may strive to get a statutory basis for the agency and security of funding. They may take as a goal providing more efficient and effective service, rather than expanded or more expensive service.

The executive budget office.   The traditional role of the budget office has been to scrutinize requests coming up from the agencies, to find waste and eliminate it, and to discourage most requests for new money. The executive budget office has been perceived as the naysayer, the protector of the public purse. Most staff members in the budget office are very conscious of the need to balance the budget, to avoid deficits, and to manage cash flow so that there is money on hand to pay bills. Hence they tend to be skeptical of requests for new money.

In recent years, however, there has been a change in the role of the budget office. At the national level under President Ronald Reagan, budgeting became much more top-down, with the director of the Office of Management and Budget

(OMB) proposing specific cuts and negotiating them directly with Congress, without much scrutiny of requests coming up from departments or bureaus. OMB became more involved in trying to accomplish the policy goals of the President through the budget.[5] At state levels too, there has been an evolution of budget staff from more technical to more political and more policy-related goals. When the governor is looking for new spending proposals these may come from the budget office.

Chief executive officers.   The role of chief executive officers (the mayor or city manager, the governor, the President) is highly variable, and hence these executives' goals in the budget process cannot be predicted without knowledge of the individuals. Some chief executives have been expansive, proposing new programs; others have been economy minded, cutting back proposals generated by the legislatures. Some have been efficiency oriented, reorganizing staffs and trying to maintain service levels without increases in taxes or expenditures.

Legislators.   Legislators have sometimes been described as always trying to increase expenditures.[6] Their motivation is viewed as getting reelected, which depends on their ability to provide constituents services and deliver "pork"—jobs and capital projects—to their districts. Norms of reciprocity magnify the effects of these spending demands because legislators are reluctant to cut others' pork lest their own be cut in return. At the city level, a council member described this norm of reciprocity, "There is an unwritten rule that if something is in a councilman's district, we'll go along and scratch each other's back."[7]

For some legislators, however, getting reelected is not a high priority. They view elected office as a service they perform for the community rather than a career, and while they may be responsive to constituents' needs, they are simply not motivated to start new projects or give public employees a raise in order to get reelected. Also, some legislators feel secure about the possibility of reelection, and hence have no urgent need to deliver pork in order to increase their chances of reelection.[8]

Even assuming the motivation to get reelected, holding down taxes may be as important to reelection as spending on programs and projects. The consequence of tax reduction is usually curtailed expenditures. Legislators are bound to try to balance the budget, which puts some constraints on the desire to spend.

The tendency to provide pork is real, but there are counterbalancing factors. Some legislators are more immune to pressures from constituents because they are secure electorally, and legislators can organize themselves in such a way as to insulate themselves somewhat from these pressures. They can, for example, select more electorally secure representatives for key positions on appropriations committees; they can separate committees that deal extensively with interest groups from those that deal with expenditures; they can set up buffer groups to deal with interest groups; they can structure the budget process so that revenue limits precede and guide spending proposals.

Moreover, legislators have interests other than providing pork. Some legislators are deeply concerned about solving social problems, designing and funding defense and foreign aid systems, and monitoring the executive branch. The proportion of federal budget spent on pork-type projects has declined in recent years, despite reforms in Congress that decentralized control and allowed pressure for pork to increase.[9] "Congressmen are not single-minded seekers of local benefits, struggling feverishly to win every last dollar for their districts. However important the quest for local benefits may be, it is always tempered by other competing concerns."[10] The pull for local benefits depends on the program. Some, like water projects, are oriented to local payoffs; others, like entitlement programs for large numbers of people, are not. Programs with local pull account for smaller and smaller proportions of the budget[11] and the trend has accelerated since 1978.[12]

Interest groups.   Interest groups, too, have often been singled out as the driving force behind budget increases. They are said to want more benefits for their members and to be undeterred by concerns for overall budget balance or the negative effects of tax increases. Moreover, their power has been depicted as great. Well-funded interest groups reportedly wine and dine legislators and provide campaign funding for candidates who agree with their positions.

There is some truth to this picture, but it is oversimplified. Interest groups have other policy goals besides budget levels. In fact, most probably deal with the budget only when a crisis occurs, such as a threat to funding levels. Because they can be counted on to come to the defense of a threatened program, they reduce the flexibility of budget decision makers, who find it difficult to cut programs with strong interest-group backing. But many areas of the budget do not have strong interest-group backing. For example, foreign aid programs have few domestic constituencies. Agencies may even have negative constituencies, that is, interest groups that want to reduce their funding and terminate their programs. The American Medical Association sought for years to eliminate the Health Planning Program.

Often when there are interest groups, there are many rather than one, and these interest groups may have conflicting styles or conflicting goals, canceling one another out or absorbing energy in battles among themselves. A coalition of interest groups representing broad geographic areas and a variety of constituencies is likely to be more effective at lobbying.

Hence coalitions may form, but individual members of the coalition may not go along with measures supported by others, so the range of items lobbied for as a unified group may be narrow. Extensive negotiations and continual efforts are required to get two or more independent groups together for a lobbying effort, and the arrangement can then fall apart. In short, interest groups are often interested in maintaining their autonomy.

Individuals.   Individuals seldom have a direct role in the budget process, as they did in the DeKalb case, but they often have an indirect role. They may vote on referenda to limit revenues, forbid some forms of taxation, or require budgetary balance. They voice their opinions also in public opinion polls, and more informally by calling or writing their elected representatives and giving their opinions. Their knowledge of the budget is not usually detailed, but their feelings about the acceptability of taxation are an important part of the constraints of public budgeting. Their preferences for less visible taxes and for taxes earmarked for specific approved expenditures have been an important factor in public budgeting.

The courts.   Another budget actor that plays an intermittent role in determining expenditures is the courts.[13] The courts get involved when other actors, often interest groups, bring a case against the government. Suits that affect the budget may involve service levels or the legality of particular forms of taxation. If a particular tax is judged unconstitutional, the result is usually lost revenues. If there are suits concerning levels of service, governments may be forced to spend more money on that service. There can also be damage suits against governments that affect expenditures. These suits are usually settled without regard to the government agencies' ability to pay. The result may be forced cuts in other areas of the budget, tax increases, or even bankruptcy. When the courts get involved, they may determine budget priorities. They introduce a kind of rigidity into the budget that says do this, or pay this, first.

Typical areas in which courts have gotten involved and mandated expenditures for state and local governments are prison overcrowding (declared cruel and unusual punishment) and deinstitutionalization of mentally ill and mentally handicapped patients. In each case, the rights of the institutionalized population required more services or more space, often involving expenditures of additional funds. From the perspective of the courts, the priority of rights outweighs immediate concerns for budget balances, autonomy of governmental units, and local priorities.

Power differentials.   These various actors not only have different and potentially clashing budgetary goals, but they typically have different levels of power. Thus, at times, the budget office may completely dominate the agencies; at times, the Congress may differ from the President on budgetary policy and pass its own preferences. The courts may preempt the decision making of the executive and the legislature. Some particular interest groups may always be able to get tax breaks for themselves.

The combination of different preferences and different levels of power has to be orchestrated by the budget process in such a way that agreement is reached, and the players stay in the game, continuing to abide by the rules. If some actors feel too powerless over the budget, they may cease to participate or become obstructionist, blocking any agreements or imposing rigid, nonnegotiable solutions. Why participate in negotiations and discussions if the decision will go against you regardless of what you do? If some actors lose on important issues, they may try to influence budget implementation to favor themselves. Or the actors with less budget power may try to change the budget process so that they have a better chance of influencing the outcomes.

The Separation of Payer and Decider

The second feature of public budgeting is that decisions about how money will be spent are made not by those providing the money but by their representatives. The payers and the deciders are two distinct groups. The payers are not given a choice about whether they want to pay or how much they want to pay. The power of the state may force them to pay. They may protest if they do not like how their money is being spent, and elect new representatives. They cannot, generally, take their money and do something else with it.

The distinction between the payers and the deciders leads to two crucial characteristics of public budgeting: public *accountability* and political *acceptability*. *Accountability* means to make sure that every penny of public money is spent as agreed, and to report accurately to the public on how money was spent. *Acceptability* means that public officials who make budget decisions are constrained by what the public wants. Sometimes they will do precisely what they think the public wants, even if the results are inefficient or inequitable, and sometimes they will present the budget so that it will be accepted by the public, even if they have not precisely followed public will. This effort may involve persuasion or deception.

Since public demands may not be clearly expressed, and since different segments of the public may make different and competing demands, and since public officials themselves may have priorities, officials may not be able or willing to be bound tightly to public opinion. Nevertheless, if politicians knowingly make decisions that differ from what the public wants, there is pressure to present the budget in a way that makes it appear acceptable. That pressure creates a tension between accountability, which requires nearly complete openness, and acceptability, which sometimes involves hiding or distorting information or presenting it in an unclear fashion.

The Budget Document and Accountability

Because of the separation of payer and decider, the budget document itself becomes an important means of public accountability. How did the public's representatives actually decide to spend taxpayer money? Did they waste it? Did they spend it on defense or police or on social services? The streets are in terrible shape—how much money did they spend on street repair? Citizens do not typically watch the decision making, but they and the press have access to the budget document and can look for the answers. They can hold the government accountable through the budget, to see that what officials promised them was actually delivered.

But budgets do not always present a complete and accurate picture. One example of how budgets can lose information happened recently in a state university. A university president decided to expand the big-time sports program, in an environment of overall financial scarcity. While some faculty members undoubtedly favored the action, many would have opposed it if they had been asked. The president did not ask their opinions, however; instead, the full costs of the program were disguised to make the budget appear acceptable. Because of progressive underestimates of costs in the sports program, some pundits labeled the sports program the case of the disappearing budget.

To obscure the real costs, the president broke up the costs for the program and scattered them among different portions of the budget. To complicate the picture further, he drew on different pockets of revenue, including student athletic fees, bond revenues, and voluntary donations. When asked, he said money going to the athletic programs was earmarked and could not be spent on other programs, so that professors trying to get more money to teach history or biology would look elsewhere than to sports. The amount of money showing as costs in the athletic program remained constant every year, although the program costs were expanding. Fearing conflict and disapproval, the president hid the costs in the budget.

The more complicated the budget, the more different activities and accounts, the greater the discretion of the administrators. As one university president offered, "Not a day goes by when we do not wish we had a more complex budget." The complexity allows for choice of where to report expenditures, and which revenues to use, to highlight some expenditures and gloss over others.

It would be misleading to suggest that the tension between accountability and acceptability always leads to more distortion or more secrecy. Sometimes the balance tends toward more accountability and budgets become clearer and more representative of true costs. The federal budget, for example, has moved toward clearer and more comprehensive portraits of public expenditures in recent years. But the tension is always present, and each budget represents some degree of selectivity about what it will present and how. The art of selective revelation is part of public budgeting.

Openness to the Environment

Public budgets are open to the environment. The environment for budgeting includes a number of different factors including the overall level of resources available (the amount of taxable wealth, the existing tax structure, current economic conditions); the degree of certainty of revenues; and a variety of emergencies such as very heavy snowfall, tornadoes, wars, bridge collapses, droughts, chemical explosions, and water pollution. The environment also includes rigidities resulting from earlier decisions, which may now be embodied in law. For example, rapid inflation in housing prices in California resulted in a citizen referendum to protect themselves from rapidly rising property taxes. The result of the referendum was incorporated in the state constitution, limiting the taxing options of local governments. Constitutional restrictions to maintain a balanced budget or limit expenditures or put a ceiling on borrowing operate in a similar manner. Prior borrowing creates a legal obligation for future budgets, an obligation that may press other possible expenditures out of consideration or require higher levels of taxation. The environment in this sense may frame policy issues and limit alternatives. Public opinion is also part of the budgetary environment, and the perception of change in public opinion will be reflected in changing budgets.

The intergovernmental system is also a key part of the environment for budget actors. The legal sources of revenues, limits on borrowing, strings attached to grants, and mandated costs are but a few of the budgetary implications of the intergovernmental system. The requirement that some grants be spent on particular items or that a recipient match expenditures on grants may result in a pattern of spending different from what the state or local government would have preferred.

Budget Constraints

Openness to the environment creates the need for budgets to be flexible. Public officials have to be able to adapt quickly, reallocating funds to meet emergencies, spending more now and making up the difference later, cutting back expenditures during the year to meet sudden declines in revenues or increases in expenditures. But the same openness to the environment that creates the need for flexibility may simultaneously subject budgeting to numerous constraints.

For example, in California, a statewide referendum limited the rate of growth of local assessments, restraining the growth of property tax revenues. Federal grants provide budgetary constraints when they can be spent only on particular programs. The courts may create budgetary constraints by declaring programs inadequate or taxes illegal. Legal obligations to repay debt and maintain public businesses separate from the rest of the budget also create constraints.

The need for flexibility and the number of budgetary constraints contest with one another, creating patterns typical of public budgeting. For example, local officials may press for home rule, which gives more independence and autonomy to local governments to manage their own affairs and adapt to changing conditions. But state officials may erode home rule through continually mandating local costs. State universities may try to squirrel away contingency funds outside those appropriated by the legislature so that they can respond to emergencies; the legislature may then try to appropriate and hence control this new local source of revenues.

THE MEANING OF *POLITICS* IN PUBLIC BUDGETING

Public budgets have a number of special characteristics. These characteristics suggest some of the ways that the budget is political. Political is a word that covers a number of meanings, even when narrowed to the context of budgetary decision making. The purpose of this book is to clarify the meaning of politics in the context of budgeting by sorting out some key meanings and showing how these meanings apply to different parts of budgetary decision making.

Concepts of Politics in the Budget

The literature suggests at least five major ways of viewing politics in the budget: reformism, incrementalist bargaining, interest-group determinism, process, and policy making.

☐ The first is a reform orientation, which argues that politics and budgeting are or should be antithetical, that budgeting should be primarily or exclusively technical, and that comparison between items should be technical and efficiency based. Politics in the sense of the opinions and priorities of elected officials and interest groups is an unwanted intrusion that reduces efficiency and makes decision making less rational. The politics of reform involves a clash of views between professional staff and elected officials over the boundary between technical budget decisions and properly political ones.

☐ The second perspective is the incrementalist view, which sees budgeting as negotiations among a group of routine actors, bureaucrats, budget officers, chief executives, and legislators, who meet each year and bargain to resolution. To the extent that interest groups are included at all in this view, they are conceived of in the pluralist model. The process is open, anyone can play and win, and the overall outcome is good; conflict is held down because everyone wins something and no one wins too much.

☐ The third view is that interest groups are dominant actors in the budget process. In its extreme form this argument posits that richer and more powerful interest groups determine the budget. Some interests are represented by interest groups and others are not, or are represented by weaker interest groups; the outcome does not approximate democracy. There may be big winners and big losers in this model. Conflict is more extensive than in the incrementalist model. This view of politics in budgeting raises the questions whether these interest groups represent narrow or broad coalitions, or possibly even class interest. To what extent do these interest groups represent oil or banking or the homeless, and to what extent do they represent business and labor more broadly?

☐ The fourth view of politics in the budget is that the budget process itself is the center and focus of budget politics. Those with particular budget goals try to change the budget process to favor their goals. Branches of government struggle with one another over budgetary power through the budget process; the budget process becomes the means of achieving or denying separation and balance between the branches of government. The degree of examination of budget requests, and the degree to which review is technical or political, cursory or detailed, is regulated by the budget process. The ability of interest groups to influence the budget, the role of the public in budget decisions, the openness of budget decision making—all these are part of the politics of process. In this view of politics, the individual actors and their strategies and goals may or may not be important, depending on the role assigned to individual actors in the budget process, and depending on whether the external environment allows any flexibility.

☐ The fifth view is that the politics of budgeting centers in policy debates, including debates about the role of the budget. Spending levels, taxing policies, and willingness to borrow to sustain spending during recessions are all major policy issues that have to be resolved one way or another during budget deliberations. Budgets may reflect a policy of moderating economic cycles or they may express a policy of allowing the economy to run its course. Each is a policy. Similarly, budgets must allocate funding to particular programs, and in the course of doing so, decide priorities for federal, state, and local governments. This view of politics in the budget emphasizes tradeoffs, especially those that occur between major areas of the budget, such as social services and defense or police. This view also emphasizes the role of the budget office in making policy and the format of the budget in encouraging comparisons between programs.

These five views of politics have been developed over time, and like an ancient document, the messages have been written over one another. Surely they are not all equally true, and certainly they often contradict each other. Parts of each may still be true, and they may be true of different parts of budgetary decision making, or true of budgetary decision making at different times or at different levels of government. . . .

NOTES

1. Patricia Ingraham and Charles Barrilleaux, "Motivating Government Managers for Retrenchment: Some Possible Lessons from the Senior Executive Service," *Public Administration Review* 43, no. 3 (1983): 393–402. They cite the Office of Personnel Management Federal Employee Attitude Surveys of 1979 and 1980, extracting responses from those in the Senior Executive Service, the upper ranks of the civil service and appointed administrators. In 1979, 99 percent of the senior executives said that they considered accomplishing something worthwhile was very important; 97 percent said the same in 1980. By contrast, in response to the question "How much would you be motivated by a cash award," only 45 percent said either to a great extent or a very great extent.

2. Twelve percent of LeLoup and Moreland's Department of Agriculture requests between 1946 and 1971 were for decreases. See Lance LeLoup, *Budgetary Politics*, 3d ed. (Brunswick, Ohio: King's Court, 1986), 83. For a more recent case study of an agency requesting decreases, see the case study of the Office of Personnel Management, in Irene Rubin, *Shrinking the Federal Government* (New York: Longman, 1985). See Irene Rubin, *Running in the Red: The Political Dynamics of Urban Fiscal Stress* (Albany: State University of New York Press, 1982), for an example of a department refusing additional employees.

3. For a good discussion of this phenomenon, see Frank Thompson, *The Politics of Personnel in the City* (Berkeley: University of California Press, 1975).

4. See Rubin, *Shrinking the Federal Government*, for examples during the Reagan administration.

5. U.S. Senate, Committee on Governmental Affairs, *Office of Management and Budget:*

Evolving Roles and Future Issues, Committee Print 99–134, 99th Cong., 2d sess., prepared by the Congressional Research Service of the Library of Congress, February 1986.

6. See, for example, Kenneth Shepsle and Barry Weingast, "Legislative Politics and Budget Outcomes," in *Federal Budget Policy in the 1980s*, ed. Gregory Mills and John Palmer (Washington, D.C.: Urban Institute Press, 1984), 343–67.

7. Rubin, *Running in the Red*, 56.

8. For a vivid account of the relationship between pork-barrel spending and building political coalitions, see Martin Shefter, "New York City's Fiscal Crisis: The Politics of Inflation and Retrenchment," *Public Interest* 48 (Summer 1977): 99–127.

9. See John Ellwood, "Comments," in Mills and Palmer, *Federal Budget Policy in the 1980s*, 368–78.

10. Douglas Arnold, "The Local Roots of Domestic Policy," in *The New Congress*, ed. Thomas Mann and Norman Ornstein (Washington, D.C.: American Enterprise Institute, 1981), 252, quoted by Ellwood, in Mills and Palmer.

11. Arnold, "Local Roots," 282.

12. Ellwood, in Mills and Palmer, 370.

13. Linda Harriman and Jeffrey Straussman, "Do Judges Determine Budget Decisions? Federal Court Decisions in Prison Reform and State Spending for Corrections," *Public Administration Review* 43, no. 4 (1983): 343–51.

PART THREE

The Players

The Players: Institutional and Noninstitutional Actors in the Policy Process

Matthew A. Cahn

As discussed earlier, public policy has been defined in different ways by different observers. Peters defines policy as "the sum of government activities . . . (that have) an influence on the lives of citizens."[1] Lasswell pointed out that public policy determines "who gets what, when, and how."[2] Contemporary policy analysts might also include "why?" Ripley and Franklin define policy and the policy process more specifically:

> Policy is what the government says and does about perceived problems. Policy making is how the government decides what will be done about perceived problems. Policy making is a process of interaction among governmental and nongovernmental actors; policy is the outcome of that interaction.[3]

In a real world context, public policy can be understood as the public solutions that are implemented in an effort to solve public problems. Policy actors, or "players," are those individuals and groups, both formal and informal, that seek to influence the creation and implementation of these public solutions.

This chapter explores the function and influence that policy actors exert in the policy process. It begins with an overview of the policy process and then moves on to explore each actor within the process, including the institutional actors—Congress, the president, executive agencies, and the courts—and the non-institutional actors—the media, political parties, interest groups, and political consultants.

The policy process is significantly more subtle than many realize. While the Constitution provides for a legislature that makes laws, an executive that enforces laws, and a judiciary that interprets laws, the policy process has evolved into a confusing web of state and federal departments, agencies, and committees that make up the institutional policy bureaucracy. In addition, the vast network of organized citizen groups (parties, interest groups, and PACs), as well as the rise of the electronic media, political consultants, and other image-making professionals, further complicates the process. The role each actor plays, in combination with the relationship between actors in both policy bureaucracies, is ultimately what determines policy outcomes.

INSTITUTIONAL ACTORS

Congress

Congress is a central institution in the policy process because of its legislative authority. Article I section 8 of the Constitution defines the various powers of Congress, including the power to

- tax
- borrow money on the credit of the United States
- regulate interstate commerce
- regulate commerce with other nations
- produce currency and determine its value
- fix and regulate weights and measures
- establish a postal system
- establish a network of roads
- issue patents and copyrights
- declare war
- make any law that is "necessary and proper" in the implementation of the other powers.

While congressional power is diffused among the 435 voting members of the House and 100 voting members of the Senate, there are specific points where power is focused. It is these points that are points of access for those seeking policy influence.

The vast majority of legislative decisions are made in committees. With standing committees, special committees, joint committees, conference committees, and all of their associated subcommittees, there are several hundred committees in a typical congressional session. As Fenno[4] describes, committees and subcommittees are responsible for the initial review of draft legislation. Committees can report positively or negatively on any bill, or they can report amended bills. Rather than report negatively on bills, however, committees typically ignore bills that lack favor. This precludes the necessity of debating and voting on the bill on the full floor, since bills that are not acted upon die at the close of the congressional session.[5]

Committee chairs have disproportionate influence over policy as a consequence of their power to determine committee agendas. Similarly, certain committees have more policy influence than others. The House Rules Committee, for example, is responsible for determining which bills will be heard and in what order. The Appropriation Committees in both the House and Senate are responsible for reviewing any legislation that requires funding. The power that members of such committees hold, and the powers of committee chairs, make them key players in the policy process.

Congressional staffers are another source of influence that is often overlooked. In *The Power Game* Hedrick Smith describes staffers as "policy entrepreneurs."[6] Staffers are important in two areas. First, as Fiorina points out, the increasing use of staff in district offices to service constituents strengthens the congress member's position among local voters, perhaps explaining in part the strength of incumbency.[7] Second, staffers are the real expertise behind the legislator. With over six thousand bills introduced in an average session, legislators rely more and more on staff to analyze legislation, negotiate compromises, research issues, and meet with lobbyists.[8] In their roles as legislative analysts and policy negotiators, as well as their roles as political confidants and counselors, senior staffers have significant policy influence.

There are several explanations of congressional behavior. What appears to be consistent between analyses is the observation that members of Congress are primarily concerned with achieving reelection. Mayhew[9] argues that the organization of Congress itself evolved to maximize the reelectability of members. Since congressional power is tied to seniority, this is not surprising. But it does have negative policy implications. If members are acting to maximize their individual political futures, their ability to govern in the national interest is severely limited. The need to satisfy constituent interests over national interests has led to dangerously high levels of pork in legislative outcomes.

The election connection has other impacts that are similarly troubling. The average cost to run a successful congressional campaign is $400,000 for a House seat and over $3.5 million dollars for a Senate seat.[10] As a consequence, members of Congress are in a constant state of fundraising. Those interests with greater financial resources may thus achieve greater access. With limited time to meet with members of the public, legislators have a built-in incentive to meet with those individuals who can best benefit their reelection efforts.

Committee decisions, compromises between committees and executive agencies, the influence of staffers, and the cozy relationships between legislators and deep pocket lobbyists have even greater policy importance because they all take place outside of the public eye. Although as a consequence of political reform in the 1970s committee meetings are open, staff reports are available for public review, lobbyists are required to register with the government, and all financial contributions are public record, few people have the time to closely follow the intricacies of the policy process. Consequently, members of Congress and those whose business it is to influence them are generally free to act without concern for public attention.

The President and the Executive Bureaucracy

Like Congress, the president is mandated by the Constitution as a partner in the policy process, but, unlike Congress, the president can only approve or disapprove legislation; he or she has no power to amend. Thus, the policy priorities of the president cannot be directly legislated. Rather, presidents must rely on legislative partners in both houses, and on what Neustadt called the power to persuade.[11]

In "The Presidential Policy Stream" Paul Light suggests that presidential policy is a result of the "stream of people and ideas that flow through the White House."[12] If public policy is a process of identifying problems, identifying solutions, and implementing those solutions, the identification of problems and solutions, Light argues, is tied to the assumptions held by players in that stream. The policy stream must accommodate the issues that percolate up through the systemic agenda, as well as those issues that may be on the presidential agenda.

In addition to balancing the demands of the systemic agenda with presidential policy objectives, the president also must balance domestic policy concerns with foreign policy concerns. Wildavsky[13] suggests that there are in fact two presidencies, the domestic presidency and the foreign policy presidency, each with different responsibilities and different policy objectives. The foreign policy president has much more power, Wildavsky argues, than the domestic president. As Richard Neustadt suggests, the domestic president may have to rely more on his or her ability to persuade Congress and members of the executive bureaucracy to implement presidential policy objectives than on any specific domestic power. The foreign policy president, on the other hand, has the power to move troops into combat and to negotiate executive agreements and treaties, and controls a vast international intelligence network.

The implementation of presidential policy objectives involves a different set of problems than those of Congress. While Congress makes laws, the president can only recommend laws. Yet the president, as chief executive, may do whatever is necessary to enforce legislation, an enforcement that typically involves discretionary policy decisions. Article II, sections 2 and 3, define the powers of the president:

- to recommend policy proposals to Congress
- to act as commander-in-chief of the armed services (the power to move and control troops, but not to declare war)

- to grant pardons and reprieves for federal offenses except in cases of impeachment
- to make treaties with advice and consent of the Senate
- to appoint federal judges, ambassadors and consuls, and the heads of cabinet level departments and regulatory agencies with the advice and consent of the Senate
- to "faithfully" enforce all laws

While the president is often looked upon to set the national policy agenda, he or she can only do so as long as he or she holds an ability to persuade. With the expressed powers of the president limited to specific areas, effective presidents must rely on their power to persuade members of Congress, the bureaucracy, the media, and the public.

When expressed powers are insufficient, presidents can rely upon executive prerogative. Executive orders have the power of law but have no statutory basis. Roosevelt's 1942 executive order number 9066 authorized the incarceration of 110,000 Japanese Americans without warrants, indictments, or hearings. Submitting to anti-Asian hysteria following the bombing of Pearl Harbor, Roosevelt lifted the constitutional protections of a specific class of American citizens.

Reagan's 1981 executive order number 12291 required that a benefit-cost calculation be performed prior to implementing any policy. If the costs outweighed the benefits, the policy would not be implemented. Aside from the obvious problem in quantifying benefits—what is the value of clean air, for example?—EO 12291 redefines the policy relationship between the executive and the legislature. Rather than fulfilling the constitutional imperative to "faithfully execute all laws," EO 12291 claims for the executive the right to evaluate whether laws should be enforced, and how extensively.

Effective presidents use the powers and perks of their office to maximize their policy agendas. Appointments are a major source of policy influence. By appointing individuals who share his or her political perspective and agenda, a president is able to extend influence throughout the executive and judicial bureaucracies. Cabinet officers and heads of regulatory agencies establish policy priorities within their agencies. And, since most legislation allows for a significant measure of discretion among implementing and enforcement agencies, the cabinet officers and agency heads have wide latitude in defining, implementing, and enforcing policy.

This is best illustrated by Reagan's appointment of Anne Burford as EPA administrator. Burford, a corporate attorney who often represented clients in suits against the government over environmental regulations, sought to bring Reagan's antiregulatory philosophy into the EPA. In order to sidestep the legislative mandate that defined EPA's mission, Burford instituted a variety of mechanisms intended to reduce environmental enforcement. She held unannounced meetings with regulated industries, effectively precluding public participation.[14] Further, she centralized all decision making in her office, effectively paralyzing staff activities.[15] Ultimately, discretionary policy enforcement fell to an all-time low.[16]

The ability to control the executive bureaucracy is critical for the development and maintenance of presidential power. The tendency to organize bureaucratically is best described by Max Weber, who suggests that "modern officialdom" seeks the efficiency of specificity and hierarchy.[17] Bureaucratic government incorporates a vast network of interrelated offices, each of which has a specific jurisdiction and a specific task (task differentiation), there is a set hierarchy, and authority is subservient to the rule of law. In "The Rise of the Bureaucratic State" Wilson explores the evolution of the American bureaucracy.[18] While bureaucratic organization is necessary to administer a society of 250 million people, the size of the bureaucracy itself represents certain hazards. Weber warned that bureaucracies inevitably become insensitive to individual concerns. With the executive bureaucracy employing over five million people, it may often appear sluggish and unresponsive. Still, specialization is critical for effective government; the Department of Defense clearly has different needs and concerns than the Department of Agriculture. There may, as a result, be little alternative to bureaucratic organization.

The policy influence of regulatory agencies within the executive bureaucracy is substantial. Meier[19] describes the regulatory process as a combination of regulatory bureaucracies (values, expertise, agency subculture, bureaucratic entrepreneurs) and public interaction (interest groups, economic issues, legislative committees and subcommittees). Regulatory outcomes are a consequence of subsystem interaction among all of these influences. Those who are best able to influence these subsystems are best able to maximize their interests. As a result, policy subsystems are major points of access for policy influence.

The Courts

The influence of judges in interpreting laws has an equally significant impact on policy. The *Brown* v. *Topeka Board of Education* decision in 1955, for example, initiated antisegregation policies and acted as a catalyst for the voting rights acts of the 1960s and civil rights policies through the 1980s. Similarly, the 1973 *Roe* v. *Wade* decision virtually defined abortion policy thereafter. But judicial policy influence is not restricted to Supreme Court decisions. As Lawrence Baum[20] points out, appellate courts are significant, if often ignored, partners in policy making. Appellate courts have had critical policy influence in several areas, including abortion and civil rights policy.

The policy role of the judiciary is not universally appreciated. The current debate over judicial activism and judicial restraint is only the most recent in a long discourse. In "Towards an Imperial Judiciary"[21] Nathan Glazer argues that judicial activism infringes on democratic policy institutions, and that an activist court erodes the respect and trust people hold for the judiciary. Still, whether a court is active or passive, there are significant policy implications. While the Brown decision may be considered "activist," for example, had the Court chosen to remain passive, civil rights policy might have remained nonexistent for many more years. Nonaction is in itself a policy decision with substantial policy implications.

NONINSTITUTIONAL ACTORS

Public policy is not merely the result of independent policy-making institutions. Noninstitutional actors also play a significant role: the public elects legislators and executives; the media influences policy through its inherent agenda-setting function; parties, in their role in drafting and electing candidates, influence policy through influencing the composition of legislative and executive bodies; and organized interest groups lobby elected officials and nonelected policy makers (for example, agency staff). Policy, then, is a result of institutional processes influenced by noninstitutional actors.

Media

The media are influential to policy outcomes because they help define social reality.[22] The work of McCombs and Shaw[23] supports the assertion that the media influence the salience of issues. As Lippmann[24] observed in 1922, perceptions of reality are based on a tiny sampling of the world around us. No one can be everywhere; no one can experience everything. Thus, to a greater or lesser extent, all of us rely on media portrayals of reality.

Graber[25] argues that the way people process information makes them especially vulnerable to media influence. First, people tend to pare down the scope of information they confront. Second, people tend to think schematically; when confronted with information, individuals will fit that information into preexisting schema. And, since news stories tend to lack background and context, schemata allow the individual to give the information meaning. In such a way, individuals recreate reality in their minds.

The data collected by Iyengar and Kinder[26] show that television news, to a great extent, defines which problems the public considers most serious. Iyengar and Kinder refine the agenda-setting dynamic to include what they call "priming." Priming refers to the selective coverage of only certain events, and the selective way in which those events are covered. Because there is no way to cover all events, or cover any event completely, selective decisions must be made. There are consequences, however.

> By priming certain aspects of national life while ignoring others, television news sets the terms by which political judgements are rendered and political choices made (Iyengar and Kinder, 1987, p. 4).

The implications for public policy are serious. If policy is a result of the problem recognition model that Theodoulou[27] summarized earlier, then the problems that gain media recognition are much more likely to be addressed.

Parties

Political parties are distinct from other citizen organizations. Rather than attempting to influence existing policy makers, parties seek to get their own members elected to policy-making positions. While interest groups seek influence on specific policy issues, parties seek influence on a wide spectrum of policy issues. Parties develop issue platforms, draft candidates, campaign on behalf of candidates, and work to get out the vote. In short, parties work to bring together citizens under a common banner.

Most people may think of parties only during election cycles, but their policy influence extends beyond campaigns. While the rise of the media over the last thirty years has deemphasized the power of parties in electoral politics, Eldersveld[28] accurately points out that parties continue to play a dominant role in policy outcomes. First and foremost, the party that emerges dominant determines the direction policy will take.

The president is responsible to the party that got him or her elected and therefore must pursue at least some of the policy objectives articulated at the party convention. Congress continues to distribute committee membership and chairmanships according to party affiliation. Although negotiation and compromise are typically necessary, the general direction of congressional policy is directly tied to the ideology of the larger party. The strength of political parties has waned over the past three decades, but parties maintain policy influence in critical areas. Elections, patronage appointments, legislative committees, and national policy discourses all reflect the influence of parties.

Interest Groups

Interest groups are fundamental partners in policy making. Citizens participate in the policy process through communication with policy makers. Such communication takes place individually (for example, letters to elected representatives) and collectively. Interest groups facilitate collective communication. James Madison recognized the propensity for individuals to factionalize in an effort to maximize political influence.[29] Robert Dahl further refined the analysis of Madisonian democracy, arguing that in an open society all persons have the right to press their interests. To the extent others share these interests, collective pressure may allow greater policy influence. Indeed, Dahl argued, those issues that have greater salience have greater interest group representation.[30]

The interest group dynamic, however, is not so simple. While it may be true that many salient issues have interest group representation, the strength of that representation is not tied to the strength of the issue salience. Further, the salience itself may be a consequence of interest group action. When studying policy outcomes, it is necessary to identify the policy actors and the political resources they use. Maximizing policy interests—winning the policy game—requires specific political resources. The most common resources include bureaucratic knowledge, a network of contacts, citizen backing (size of constituency), an ability to make political contributions, and an ability to mount a public relations (media) campaign. Clearly, no group utilizes all of these resources, but the ability of an organized group to make use of one or more is critical for policy influence.

The pluralist model of counterbalancing elites mediating interests is inadequate. The theoretical work done by Mills, and empirical work done by Dye, Domhoff, and Presthus, among others, suggest that rather than competing, the interests of economic elites tend to cohere in key policy areas.[31] Lowi's *The End of Liberalism*[32] argues that this interest group influence threatens the democratic basis of government. If interest groups provide the framework for government-citizen interaction, and these groups are based on individual self-interest, there is little opportunity for pursuing a meaningful national interest.

Not only is the influence of corporate interest groups and PACs at an all-time high, but the structure of the policy-making establishment has come to accept private think tanks as democratic institutions. The Brookings Institution, RAND Corporation, Council for Economic Development (CED), Council on Foreign Relations (CFR), and others form a bridge between corporate interests and government. The think tanks are considered by many policy makers to be neutral policy consultants and are thus extended great access to the policy-making arena, yet virtually all of them have strong foundations in the corporate community. The RAND Corporation was created as a joint venture between the U.S. Air Force and the aerospace industry as a think tank devoted to the theory and technology of deterrence. The CED was founded in the early 1940s by a consortium of corporate leaders to influence specific policy formation. The CFR was founded in 1921 by corporate executives and financiers to help shape foreign policy. As a result, economic elites are able to influence policy through what are essentially interest group think tanks.[33]

Political Consultants

Increasingly, political expertise is purchased by those with the need and the resources. In reviewing the rise and structure of the political consulting industry, Sabato[34] exposes the fragile relationship between articulating ideas in a political marketplace and manipulating public opinion. It is virtually impossible to win at the policy game without the marketing skills held by consultants and strategists. Like many other policy resources, political consultants are costly. As a consequence, those with greater economic resources enjoy a policy advantage.

CONCLUSION

This chapter has explored the role and influence of actors in the policy process—both institutional (Congress, the president and executive bureaucracy, and the courts) and noninstitutional (media, parties, interest groups, and political consultants). From the discussion it can be seen that policy outcomes are typically a result of institutional processes and noninstitutional influence.

NOTES

1. B. Guy Peters, *American Public Policy: Promise and Performance* (3rd ed.) (Chatham, N.J.: Chatham House, 1993), p. 4.

2. Harold Lasswell, *Politics: Who Gets What, When, and How* (New York: St. Martin's Press, 1988). (Originally published 1936.)

3. Randall B. Ripley and Grace A. Franklin, *Congress, the Bureaucracy, and Public Policy* (4th ed.) (Chicago: Dorsey Press, 1987), p. 1.

4. Richard Fenno, Jr., *Congressmen in Committees* (Boston: Little, Brown, 1973).

5. Barbara Hinckley and Sheldon Goldman, *American Politics and Government: Structure, Processes, Institutions, and Policies* (Glenview, Ill.: Scott, Foresman, 1990).

6. Hedrick Smith, *The Power Game: How Washington Works* (New York: Ballantine Books, 1988).

7. Morris P. Fiorina, *Congress: Keystone of the Washington Establishment* (New Haven, Conn.: Yale University Press, 1977).

8. James Q. Wilson, *American Government* (5th ed.) (Lexington, Mass.: D.C. Heath, 1992).

9. David Mayhew, *Congress: The Electoral Connection* (New Haven, Conn.: Yale University Press, 1974).

10. James Q. Wilson, *American Government*.

11. Richard Neustadt, *Presidential Power: The Politics of Leadership* (New York: Wiley, 1960).

12. Paul Light, "The Presidential Policy Stream," in *The Presidency and the Political System*, ed. Michael Nelson (Washington, D.C.: CQ Press, 1984).

13. Aaron Wildavsky, "The Two Presidencies," *Transaction*, 4, no. 2 (1966).

14. Walter Rosenbaum, *Environmental Politics and Policy* (2nd ed.) (Washington, D.C.: CQ Press, 1991).

15. Steven Cohen, "EPA: A Qualified Success," in *Controversies in Environmental Policy*, eds. Sheldon Kamieniecki, Robert O'Brien, and Michael Clark (Albany, N.Y.: State University of New York Press, 1986).

16. Matthew A. Cahn, *Environmental Deceptions: The Tension between Liberalism and Environmental Policymaking in the United States* (Albany, N.Y.: SUNY Press, 1995).

17. Max Weber, "Bureaucracy," in *From Max Weber: Essays in Sociology*, eds. H. H. Gerth and C. Wright Mills (New York: Oxford University Press, 1946).

18. James Q. Wilson, "The Rise of the Bureaucratic State," *Public Interest*, 41 (Fall 1975).

19. Kenneth J. Meier, *Regulation: Politics, Bureaucracy, and Economics* (New York: St. Martin's Press, 1985).

20. Lawrence Baum, *American Courts: Process and Policy* (Boston: Houghton Mifflin, 1990).

21. Nathan Glazer, "Towards an Imperial Judiciary," *Public Interest* (Fall 1975).

22. Denis McQuail, "The Influence and Effects of Mass Media," in *Mass Communication and Society*, eds. J. Curran, M. Gurevitch, and J. Woolacott (Newbury Park, Calif.: Sage, 1979).

23. Maxwell E. McCombs and Donald L. Shaw, *The Emergence of American Political Issues: The Agenda Setting Function of the Press* (St. Paul, Minn.: West, 1977).

24. Walter Lippman, *Public Opinion* (New York: Free Press, 1922).

25. Doris Graber, *Processing the News: How People Tame the Information Tide* (2nd ed.) (New York: Longman, 1988).

26. Shanto Iyengar and Donald Kinder, *News That Matters: Television and American Opinion* (Chicago: University of Chicago Press, 1987).

27. See Stella Z. Theodoulou, "How Public Policy Is Made" (this reader, part 2, reading 11).

28. Samuel J. Eldersveld, *Political Parties in American Society* (New York: Basic Books, 1982).

29. James Madison, "Federalist #10," in Alexander Hamilton, James Madison, and John Jay, *The Federalist Papers* (New York: New American Library, 1961).

30. Robert Dahl, *Who Governs* (New Haven, Conn.: Yale University Press, 1961).

31. See C. Wright Mills, *The Power Elite* (Oxford: Oxford University Press, 1956); Thomas Dye, *Who's Running America? The Conservative Years* (4th ed.) (Englewood Cliffs, N.J.: Prentice-Hall, 1986); G. William Domhoff, *Who Rules America Now?* (New York: Simon and Schuster, 1983); Robert Presthus, *Elites in the Policy Process* (Cambridge: Cambridge University Press, 1974).

32. Theodore Lowi, *The End of Liberalism* (2nd ed.) (New York: Norton, 1979).

33. Matthew A. Cahn, *Environmental Deceptions*.

34. Larry J. Sabato, *The Rise of Political Consultants: New Ways of Winning Elections* (New York: Basic Books, 1981).

ADDITIONAL SUGGESTED READING

BARBER, JAMES DAVID. *The Presidential Character* (3rd ed.). (Englewood Cliffs, N.J.: Prentice-Hall, 1985).
CORWIN, EDWARD. *The Presidency: Office and Powers*. New York: NYU Press, 1957.
CRONIN, THOMAS. *The State of the Presidency* (2nd ed.). Boston: Little, Brown, 1980.
FENNO, RICHARD. *Homestyle: House Members in their Districts*. Boston: Little, Brown, 1978.
HECLO, HUGH. *A Government of Strangers*. Washington, D.C.: Brookings Institution, 1977.
HERMAN, EDWARD, and CHOMSKY, NOAM. *Manufacturing Consent: The Political Economy of the Mass Media*. New York: Pantheon Books, 1988.
JACOBSON, GARY. *The Politics of Congressional Elections* (3rd ed.). New York: HarperCollins, 1992.
LASSER, WILLIAM. *The Limits of Judicial Power*. Chapel Hill: University of North Carolina Press, 1988.
LAWSON, KAY, and MERKL, PETER. *When Parties Fail: Emerging Alternative Organizations*. Princeton, N.J.: Princeton University Press, 1988.
LINSKY, MARTIN. *How the Press Affects Federal Policymaking*. New York: Norton, 1986.
MILLS, C. WRIGHT. *The Power Elite*. New York: Oxford University Press, 1956.
O'BRIEN, DAVID M. *Storm Center: The Supreme Court and American Politics*. New York: Norton, 1986.
RIPLEY, RANDALL. *Congress: Process and Policy*. New York: Norton, 1983.
ROURKE, FRANCIS. *Bureaucracy, Politics, and Public Policy* (3rd ed.). Boston: Little, Brown, 1984.
SCHATTSCHNEIDER, E. E. *The Semi-Sovereign People*. New York: Holt, Rinehart & Winston, 1969.
WATTENBERG, MARTIN. *The Decline of American Political Parties*. Cambridge, Mass.: Harvard University Press, 1986.

Congress: Keystone
of the Washington Establishment

Morris Fiorina

In this chapter, the heart of the book, I will set out a theory of the Washington establishment(s). The theory is quite plausible from a commonsense standpoint, and it is consistent with the specialized literature of academic political science. Nevertheless, it is still a theory, not proven fact. Before plunging in let me bring out in the open the basic axiom on which the theory rests: the self-interest axiom.

I assume that most people most of the time act in their own self-interest. This is not to say that human beings seek only to amass tangible wealth but rather to say that human beings seek to achieve their own ends—tangible and intangible—rather than the ends of their fellow men. I do not condemn such behavior nor do I condone it (although I rather sympathize with Thoreau's comment that "if I knew for a certainty that a man was coming to my house with the conscious design of doing me good, I should run for my life.").[1] I only claim that political and economic theories which presume self-interested behavior will prove to be more widely applicable than those which build on more altruistic assumptions.

What does the axiom imply when used in the specific context of this book, a context peopled by congressmen, bureaucrats, and voters? I assume that the primary goal of the typical congressman is reelection. Over and above the $45,000 salary plus "perks" and outside money, the office of congressman carries with it prestige, excitement, and power. It is a seat in the cockpit of government. But in order to retain the status, excitement, and power (not to mention more tangible things) of office, the congressman must win reelection every two years. Even those congressmen genuinely concerned with good public policy must achieve reelection in order to continue their work. Whether narrowly self-serving or more publicly oriented, the individual congressman finds reelection to be at least a necessary condition for the achievement of his goals.[2]

Moreover, there is a kind of natural selection process at work in the electoral arena. On average, those congressmen who are not primarily interested in reelection will not achieve reelection as often as those who are interested. We, the people, help to weed out congressmen whose primary motivation is not reelection. We admire politicians who courageously adopt the aloof role of the disinterested statesman, but we vote for those politicians who follow our wishes and do us favors.

What about the bureaucrats? A specification of their goals is somewhat more controversial—those who speak of appointed officials as public servants obviously take a more benign view than those who speak of them as bureaucrats. The literature provides ample justification for asserting that most bureaucrats wish to protect and nurture their agencies. The typical bureaucrat can be expected to seek to expand his agency in terms of personnel, budget, and mission. One's status in Washington (again, not to mention more tangible things) is roughly proportional to the importance of the operation one oversees. And the sheer size of the operation is taken to be a measure of importance. As with congressmen, the specified goals apply even to those bureaucrats who genuinely believe in their agency's mission. If they believe in the efficacy of their programs, they naturally wish to expand them and add new ones. All of this requires more money and more people. The genuinely committed bureaucrat is just as likely to seek to expand his agency as the proverbial empire-builder.[3]

And what of the third element in the equation, us? What do we, the voters who support the Washington system, strive for? Each of us wishes to receive a maximum of benefits from government for the minimum cost. This goal suggests maximum government efficiency, on the one hand, but it also suggests mutual exploitation on the other. Each of us favors an arrangement in which our fellow citizens pay for our benefits.

With these brief descriptions of the cast of characters in hand, let us proceed.

TAMMANY HALL GOES TO WASHINGTON

What should we expect from a legislative body composed of individuals whose first priority is their continued tenure in office? We should expect, first, that the normal activities of its members are those calculated to enhance their chances of reelection. And we should expect, second, that the members would devise and maintain institutional arrangements which facilitate their electoral activities. These general propositions are the focus of the remainder of this book.

For most of the twentieth century, congressmen have engaged in a mix of three kinds of activities: lawmaking, pork barreling, and casework. Congress is first and foremost a lawmaking body, at least according to constitutional theory. In every postwar session Congress "considers" thousands of bills and resolutions, many hundreds of which are brought to a record vote (over 500 in each chamber in the 93rd Congress). Naturally the critical consideration in taking a position for the record is the maximization of approval in the home district. If the district is unaffected by and unconcerned with the matter at hand, the congressman may then take into account the general welfare of the country. (This sounds cynical, but remember that "profiles in courage" are sufficiently rare that their occurrence inspires books and articles.) Abetted by political scientists of the pluralist school, politicians have propounded an ideology which maintains that the good of the country on any given issue is simply what is best for a majority of congressional districts. This ideology provides a philosophical justification for what congressmen do while acting in their own self-interest.

A second activity favored by congressmen consists of efforts to bring home the bacon to their districts. Many popular articles have been written about the pork barrel, a term originally applied to rivers and harbors legislation but now generalized to cover all manner of federal largesse.[4] Congressmen consider new dams, federal buildings, sewage treatment plants, urban renewal projects, etc. as sweet plums to be plucked. Federal projects are highly visible, their economic impact is easily detected by constituents, and sometimes they even produce something of value to the district. The average constituent may have some trouble translating his congressman's vote on some civil rights issue into a change in his personal welfare. But the workers hired and supplies purchased in connection with a big federal project provide benefits that are widely appreciated. The historical importance congressmen attach to the pork barrel is reflected in the rules of the House. That body accords certain classes of legislation "privileged" status: they may come directly to the floor without passing through the Rules Committee, a traditional graveyard for legislation. What kinds of legislation are privileged? Taxing and spending bills, for one: the government's power to raise and spend money must be kept relatively unfettered. But in addition, the omnibus rivers and harbors bills of the Public Works Committee and public lands bills from the Interior Committee share privileged status. The House will allow a civil rights or defense procurement or environmental bill to languish in the Rules Committee, but it takes special precautions to insure that nothing slows down the approval of dams and irrigation projects.

A third major activity takes up perhaps as much time as the other two combined. Traditionally, constituents appeal to their congressman for myriad favors and services. Sometimes only information is needed, but often constituents request that their congressman intervene in the internal workings of federal agencies to affect a decision in a favorable way, to reverse an adverse decision, or simply to speed up the glacial bureaucratic process. On the basis of extensive personal interviews with congressmen, Charles Clapp writes:

> Denied a favorable ruling by the bureaucracy on a matter of direct concern to him, puzzled or irked by delays in obtaining a decision, confused by the administrative maze through which he is directed to proceed, or ignorant of whom to write, a constituent may turn to his congressman for help. These letters offer great potential for political benefit to the congressman since they affect the constituent personally. If the legislator can be of assistance, he may gain a firm ally; if he is indifferent, he may even lose votes.[5]

Actually congressmen are in an almost unique position in our system, a position shared only with high-level members of the executive branch. Congressmen possess the power to expedite and influence bureaucratic decisions. This capability flows directly from congressional control over what bureaucrats value most: higher budgets and new program authorizations. In a very real sense each congressman is a monopoly supplier of bureaucratic unsticking services for his district.

Every year the federal budget passes through the appropriations committees of Congress. Generally these committees make perfunctory cuts. But on occasion they vent displeasure on an agency and leave it bleeding all over the Capitol. The most extreme case of which I am aware came when the House committee took away the entire budget of the Division of Labor Standards in 1947 (some of the budget was restored elsewhere in the appropriations process). Deep and serious cuts are made occasionally, and the threat of such cuts keeps most agencies attentive to congressional wishes. Professors Richard Fenno and Aaron Wildavsky have provided extensive documentary and interview evidence of the great respect (and even terror) federal bureaucrats show for the House Appropriations Committee.[6] Moreover, the bureaucracy must keep coming back to Congress to have its old programs reauthorized and new ones added. Again, most such decisions are perfunctory, but exceptions are sufficiently frequent that bureaucrats do not forget the basis of their agencies' existence. For example, the Law Enforcement Assistance Administration (LEAA) and the Food Stamps Program had no easy time of it this last Congress (94th). The bureaucracy needs congressional approval in order to survive, let alone expand. Thus, when a congressman calls about some minor bureaucratic decision or regulation, the bureaucracy considers his accommodation a small price to pay for the goodwill its cooperation will produce, particularly if he has any connection to the substantive committee or the appropriations subcommittee to which it reports.

From the standpoint of capturing voters, the congressman's lawmaking activities differ in two important respects from his porkbarrel and casework activities. First, programmatic actions are inherently controversial. Unless his district is homogeneous, a congressman will find his district divided on many major issues. Thus when he casts a vote, introduces a piece of nontrivial legislation, or makes a speech with policy content he will displease some elements of his district. Some constituents may applaud the congressman's civil rights record, but others believe integration is going too fast. Some support foreign aid, while others believe it's money poured down a rathole. Some advocate economic equality, others stew over welfare cheaters. On such policy matters the congressman can expect to make friends as well as enemies. Presumably he will behave so as to maximize the excess of the former over the latter, but nevertheless a policy stand will generally make some enemies.

In contrast, the pork barrel and casework are relatively less controversial. New federal projects bring jobs, shiny new facilities, and general economic prosperity, or so people believe. Snipping ribbons at the dedication of a new post office or dam is a much more pleasant pursuit than disposing of a constitutional amendment on abortion. Republicans and Democrats, conservatives and liberals, all generally prefer a richer district to a poorer one. Of course, in recent years the river damming and stream-bed straightening activities of the Army Corps of Engineers have aroused some opposition among environmentalists. Congressmen happily reacted by absorbing the opposition and adding environmentalism to the pork barrel: water treatment plants are currently a hot congressional item.

Casework is even less controversial. Some poor, aggrieved constituent becomes enmeshed in the tentacles of an evil bureaucracy and calls upon Congressman St. George to do battle with the dragon. Again Clapp writes;

> A person who has a reasonable complaint or query is regarded as providing an opportunity rather than as adding an extra burden to an already busy office. The party affiliation of the individual even when known to be different from that of the congressman does not normally act as a deterrent to action. Some legislators have built their reputations and their majorities on a program of service to all constituents irrespective of party. Regularly, voters affiliated with the opposition in other contests lend strong support to the lawmaker whose intervention has helped them in their struggle with the bureaucracy.[7]

Even following the revelation of sexual improprieties, Wayne Hays won his Ohio Democratic primary by a two-to-one margin. According to a *Los Angeles Times* feature story, Hays's constituency base was built on a foundation of personal service to constituents:

> They receive help in speeding up bureaucratic action on various kinds of federal assistance—black lung benefits to disabled miners and their families, Social Security payments, veterans' benefits and passports.
>
> Some constituents still tell with pleasure of how Hays stormed clear to the seventh floor of the State Department and into Secretary of State Dean Rusk's office to demand, successfully, the quick issuance of a passport to an Ohioan.[8]

Practicing politicians will tell you that word of mouth is still the most effective mode of communication. News of favors to constituents gets around and no doubt is embellished in the process.

In sum, when considering the benefits of his programmatic activities, the congressman must tote up gains and losses to arrive at a net profit. Pork barreling and casework, however, are basically pure profit.

A second way in which programmatic activities differ from casework and the pork barrel is the difficulty of assigning responsibility to the former as compared with the latter. No congressman can seriously claim that he is responsible for the 1964 Civil Rights Act, the ABM, or the 1972 Revenue Sharing Act. Most constituents do have some vague notion that their congressman is only one of hundreds and their senator one of an even hundred. Even committee chairmen may have a difficult time claiming credit for a piece of major legislation, let alone a rank-and-file congressman. Ah, but casework, and the pork barrel. In dealing with the bureaucracy, the congressman is not merely one vote of 435. Rather, he is a nonpartisan power, someone whose phone calls snap an office to attention. He is not kept on hold. The constituent who receives aid believes that his congressman and his congressman alone got results. Similarly, congressmen find it easy to claim credit for federal projects awarded their districts. The congressman may have instigated the proposal for the project in the first place, issued regular progress reports, and ultimately announced the award through his office. Maybe he can't claim credit for the 1965 Voting Rights Act, but he can take credit for Littletown's spanking new sewage treatment plant.

Overall then, programmatic activities are dangerous (controversial), on the one hand, and programmatic accomplishments are difficult to claim credit for, on the other. While less exciting, casework and pork barreling are both safe and profitable. For a reelection-oriented congressman the choice is obvious.

The key to the rise of the Washington establishment (and the vanishing marginals) is the following observation: *the growth of an activist federal government has stimulated a change in the mix of congressional activities*. Specifically, a lesser proportion of congressional effort is now going into programmatic activities and a greater proportion into pork-barrel and casework activities. As a result, today's congressmen make relatively fewer enemies and relatively more friends among the people of their districts.

To elaborate, a basic fact of life in twentieth-century America is the growth of the federal role and its attendant bureaucracy. Bureaucracy is the characteristic mode of delivering public goods and services. Ceteris paribus, the more the government attempts to do for people, the more extensive a bureaucracy it creates. As the scope of government expands, more and more citizens find themselves in direct contact with the federal government. Consider the rise in such contacts upon passage of the Social Security Act, work relief projects and other New Deal programs. Consider the millions of additional citizens touched by the veterans' programs of the postwar period. Consider the untold numbers whom the Great Society and its aftermath brought face to face with the federal government. In 1930 the federal bureaucracy was small and rather distant from the everyday concerns of Americans. By 1975 it was neither small nor distant.

As the years have passed, more and more citizens and groups have found themselves dealing with the federal bureaucracy. They may be seeking positive actions—eligibility for various benefits and awards of government grants. Or they may be seeking relief from the costs imposed by bureaucratic regulations—on working conditions, racial and sexual quotas, market restrictions, and numerous other subjects. While not malevolent, bureaucracies make mistakes, both of commission and omission, and normal attempts at redress often meet with unresponsiveness and inflexibility and sometimes seeming incorrigibility. Whatever the problem, the citizen's congressman is a source of succor. The greater the scope of government activity, the greater the demand for his services.

Private monopolists can regulate the demand for their product by raising or lowering the price. Congressmen have no such (legal) option. When the demand for their services rises, they have no real choice except to meet that demand—to supply more bureaucratic unsticking services—so long as they would rather be elected than unelected. This vulnerability to escalating constituency demands is largely academic, though. I seriously doubt that congressmen resist their gradual transformation from national legislators to errand boy-ombudsmen. As we have noted, casework is all profit. Congressmen have buried proposals to relieve the casework burden by establishing a national ombudsman or Congressman Reuss's proposed Administrative Counsel of the Congress. One of the congressmen interviewed by Clapp stated:

> Before I came to Washington I used to think that it might be nice if the individual states had administrative arms here that would take care of necessary liaison between citizens and the national government. But a congressman running for reelection is interested in building fences by providing personal services. The system is set to reelect incumbents regardless of party, and incumbents wouldn't dream of giving any of this service function away to any subagency. As an elected member I feel the same way.[9]

In fact, it is probable that at least some congressmen deliberately stimulate the demand for their bureaucratic fixit services. (See the exhibit at the end of this chapter.) Recall that the new Republican in district A travels about his district saying:

> I'm your man in Washington. What are your problems? How can I help you?

And in district B, did the demand for the congressman's services rise so much between 1962 and 1964 that a "regiment" of constituency staff became necessary? Or, having access to the regiment, did the new Democrat stimulate the demand to which he would apply his regiment?

In addition to greatly increased casework, let us not forget that the growth of the federal role also greatly expanded the federal pork barrel. The creative pork barreler need not limit himself to dams and post offices—rather old-fashioned interests. Today, creative congressmen can cadge LEAA money for the local police, urban renewal and housing money for local politicians, educational program grants for the local education bureaucracy. And there are sewage treatment plants, worker training and retraining programs, health services, and programs for the elderly. The pork barrel is full to overflowing. The conscientious congressman can stimulate applications for federal assistance (the sheer number of programs makes it difficult for local officials to stay current with the possibilities), put in a good word during consideration, and announce favorable decisions amid great fanfare.

In sum, everyday decisions by a large and growing federal bureaucracy bestow significant tangible benefits and impose significant tangible costs. Congressmen can affect these decisions. Ergo, the more decisions the bureaucracy has the opportunity to make, the more opportunities there are for the congressman to build up credits.

The nature of the Washington system is now quite clear. Congressmen (typically the majority Democrats) earn electoral credits by establishing various federal programs (the minority Republicans typically earn credits by fighting the good fight). The legislation is drafted in very general terms, so some agency, existing or newly established, must translate a vague policy mandate into a functioning program, a process that necessitates the promulgation of numerous rules and regulations and, incidentally, the trampling of numerous toes. At the next stage, aggrieved and/or hopeful constituents petition their congressman to intervene in the complex (or at least obscure) decision processes of the bureaucracy. The cycle closes when the congressman lends a sympathetic ear, piously denounces the evils of bureaucracy, intervenes in the latter's decisions, and rides a grateful electorate to ever more impressive electoral showings. Congressmen take credit coming and going. They are the alpha and the omega.

The popular frustration with the permanent government in Washington is partly justified, but to a considerable degree it is misplaced resentment. *Congress is the linchpin of the Washington establishment.* The bureaucracy serves as a convenient lightning rod for public frustration and a convenient whipping boy for congressmen. But so long as the bureaucracy accommodates congressmen, the latter will oblige with ever larger budgets and grants of authority. Congress does not just react to big government—it creates it. All of Washington prospers. More and more bureaucrats promulgate more and more regulations and dispense more and more money. Fewer and fewer congressmen suffer electoral defeat. Elements of the electorate benefit from government programs, and all of the electorate is eligible for ombudsman services. But the general, long-term welfare of the United States is no more than an incidental by-product of the system.

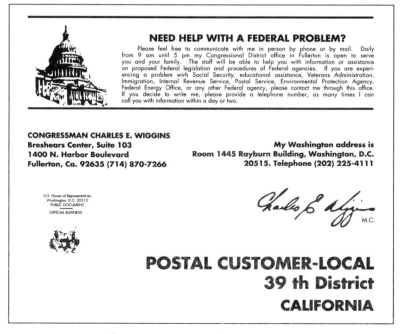

EXHIBIT: How the Congressman-as-Ombudsman Drums up Business

NOTES

1. Henry David Thoreau, *Walden* (London: Walter Scott Publishing Co., no date) p. 72.

2. For a more extended discussion of the electoral motivation see Fiorina, *Representatives, Roll Calls, and Constituencies*, chap. 2; David R. Mayhew, *Congress: The Electoral Connection* (New Haven: Yale University Press, 1974).

3. For a discussion of the goals of bureaucrats see William Niskanen, *Bureaucracy and Representative Government* (Chicago: Aldine-Atherton, 1971).

4. The traditional pork barrel is the subject of an excellent treatment by John Ferejohn. See his *Pork Barrel Politics: Rivers and Harbors Legislation 1947–1968*, (Stanford: Stanford University Press, 1974).

5. Charles Clapp, *The Congressman: His Job As He Sees It* (Washington: Brookings Institution, 1963), p. 84.

6. Richard Fenno, *The Power of the Purse* (Boston: Little, Brown, 1966); Aaron Wildavsky, *The Politics of the Budgetary Process*, 2d ed. (Boston: Little, Brown, 1974).

7. Clapp, *The Congressman: His Job As He Sees It*, p. 84.

8. "Hays Improves Rapidly from Overdose," *Los Angeles Times*, June 12, 1976, part I, p. 19. Similarly, Congressman Robert Leggett (D., Calif.) won reelection in 1976 even amid revelations of a thirteen-year bigamous relationship and rumors of other affairs and improprieties. The *Los Angeles Times* wrote:

> Because of federal spending, times are good here in California's 4th Congressional District, and that is a major reason why local political leaders in both parties, as well as the man on the street, believe that Leggett will still be their congressman next year. . . .
> Leggett has concentrated on bringing federal dollars to his district and on acting as an ombudsman for constituents having problems with their military pay or Social Security or GI benefit checks. He sends out form letters to parents of newborn children congratulating them.

Traditionally, personal misbehavior has been one of the few shoals on which incumbent congressmen could founder. But today's incumbents have so entrenched themselves by personal service to constituents that even scandal does not harm them mortally. See David Johnson, "Rep. Leggett Expected to Survive Sex Scandal," *Los Angeles Times*, July 26, 1976, part I, p. 1.

9. Clapp, *The Congressman: His Job As He Sees It*, p. 94.

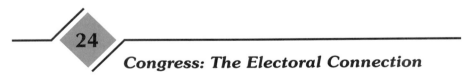

Congress: The Electoral Connection

David Mayhew

How to study legislative behavior is a question that does not yield a consensual answer among political scientists. An ethic of conceptual pluralism prevails in the field, and no doubt it should. If there is any consensus, it is on the point that scholarly treatments should offer explanations—that they should go beyond descriptive accounts of legislators and legislatures to supply general statements about why both of them do what they do. What constitutes a persuasive explanation? In their contemporary quest to find out, legislative students have ranged far and wide, sometimes borrowing or plundering explanatory styles from the neighboring social sciences.

The most important borrowing has been from sociology. In fact it is fair to say that legislative research in the 1950s and 1960s had a dominant sociological tone to it. The literature abounded in terms like *role, norm, system,* and *socialization.* We learned that some United States senators adopt an "outsider" role;[1] that the House Appropriations Committee can usefully be viewed as a self-maintaining system;[2] that legislators can be categorized as "trustees," "politicos," or "delegates";[3] that the United States Senate has "folkways."[4] These findings and others like them grew out of research based for the first time on systematic elite interviewing.

From no other social science has borrowing been so direct or so important. But it is possible to point to writings that have shared—or partly shared—a root assumption of economics. The difference between economic and sociological explanation is sharp. As Niskanen puts it, "the 'compositive' method of economics, which develops hypotheses about social behavior from models of purposive behavior by individuals, contrasts with the 'collectivist' method of sociology, which develops hypotheses about social behavior from models of role behavior by aggregative ideal types."[5] To my knowledge no political scientist has explicitly anchored his legislative research in economics, but a number have in one way or another invoked "purposive behavior" as a guide to explanation. Thus there are three articles by Scher in which he posits the conditions under which congressmen will find it in their interest to engage in legislative oversight.[6] Other examples are Wildavsky's work on bargaining in the budgetary process[7] and Riker's general work on coalition building with its legislative applications.[8] More recently Manley and Fenno have given a clear purposive thrust to their important committee studies.[9] Fenno's thinking has evolved to the point where he now places a strong emphasis on detecting why congressmen join specific committees and what they get out of being members of them.

There is probably a disciplinary drift toward the purposive, a drift, so to speak, from the sociological toward the economic. If so, it occurs at a time when some economists are themselves edging over into the legislative field. There is Lindblom's writing on the politics of partisan mutual adjustment, with its legislative ramifications.[10] More generally there are recent writings of economists in the public finance tradition.[11] Public finance has its normative and empirical sides, the former best exemplified here in the discussion of legislative decision making offered by Buchanan and Tullock.[12] Niskanen develops the empirical side in his work positing bureaus as budget maximizers—an effort that leads him to hypothesize about the relations between bureaus and legislative committees.[13] Public finance scholars seem to have become interested in legislative studies as a result of their abandoning the old idea of the Benthamite legislator; that is, they have come to display a concern for what public officials actually do rather than an assumption that officials will automatically translate good policy into law once somebody finds out what it is.[14] With political scientists exploring the purposive and economists the legislative, there are at least three forms that future relations between writers in the two disciplines could take. First, scholars in both could continue to disregard each other's writings. Second, they could engage in an unseemly struggle over turf. Third, they could use each other's insights to develop collectively a more vigorous legislative scholarship in the style of political economy.

All this is an introduction to a statement of what I intend to do in the following essay. Mostly through personal experience on Capitol Hill, I have become convinced that scrutiny of purposive behavior offers the best route to an understanding of legislatures—or at least of the United States Congress. In the fashion of economics, I shall make a simple abstract assumption about human motivation and then speculate about the consequences of behavior based on that motivation. Specifically, I shall conjure up a vision of United States congressmen as single-minded seekers of reelection, see what kinds of activity that goal implies, and then speculate about how congressmen so motivated are likely to go about building and sustaining legislative institutions and making policy. At all points I shall try to match the abstract with the factual.

I find an emphasis on the reelection goal attractive for a number of reasons. First, I think it fits political reality rather well. Second, it puts the spotlight directly on men rather than on parties and pressure groups, which in the past have often entered discussions of American politics as analytic phantoms. Third, I think politics is best studied as a struggle among men to gain and maintain power and the consequences of that struggle. Fourth—and perhaps most important—the reelection quest establishes an accountability relationship with an electorate, and any serious thinking about democratic theory has to give a central place to the question of accountability. The abstract assumption notwithstanding, I regard this venture as an exercise in political science rather than economics. Leaving aside the fact that I have no economics expertise to display, I find that economists who study legislatures bring to bear interests different from those of political scientists. Not surprisingly the public finance scholars tend to look upon government as a device for spending money. I shall give some attention to spending, but also to other governmental activities such as the production of binding rules. And I shall touch upon such traditional subjects of political science as elections, parties, governmental structure, and regime stability. Another distinction here is that economics research tends to be infused with the normative assumption that policy decisions should be judged by how well they meet the standard of Pareto optimality. This is an assumption that I do not share and that I do not think most political scientists share. There will be no need here to set forth any alternative assumption. I may say, for the record, that I find the model of proper legislative activity offered by Rawls a good deal more edifying than any that could be built on a foundation of Pareto optimality.[15]

My subject of concern here is a single legislative institution, the United States Congress. In many ways, of course, the Congress is a unique or unusual body. It is probably the most highly "professionalized" of legislatures, in the sense that it promotes careerism among its members and gives them the salaries, staff, and other resources to sustain careers.[16] Its parties are exceptionally diffuse. It is widely thought to be especially "strong" among legislatures as a checker of executive power. Like most Latin American legislatures but unlike most European ones, it labors in the shadow of a separately elected executive. My decision to focus on the Congress flows from a belief that there is something to be gained in an intensive analysis of a particular and important institution. But there is something general to be gained as well, for the exceptionalist argument should not be carried too far. In a good many ways the Congress is just one in a large family of legislative bodies. I shall find it useful at various points in the analysis to invoke comparisons with European parliaments and with American state legislatures and city councils. I shall ponder the question of what "functions" the Congress performs or is capable of performing—a question that can be answered only with the records of other legislatures in mind. Functions to be given special attention are those of legislating, overseeing the executive, expressing public opinion, and servicing constituents. No functional capabilities can be automatically assumed.[17] Indeed the very term *legislature* is an unfortunate one because it confuses structure and function. Accordingly I shall from here on use the more awkward but more neutral term *representative assembly* to refer to members of the class of entities inhabited by the United States House and Senate. Whatever the noun, the identifying characteristics of institutions in the class have been well stated by Loewenberg: it is true of all such entities that (1) "their members are formally equal to each other in status, distinguishing parliaments from hierarchically ordered organizations," and (2) "the authority of their members depends on their claim to representing the rest of the community, in some sense of that protean concept, representation."[18] . . .

NOTES

1. Ralph K. Huitt, "The Outsider in the Senate: An Alternative Role," ch. 4 in Huitt and Robert L. Peabody (eds.), *Congress: Two Decades of Analysis* (New York: Harper and Row, 1969).

2. Richard F. Fenno, Jr., *The Power of the Purse* (Boston: Little, Brown and Co., 1966), ch. 5.

3. John C. Wahlke et al., *The Legislative System* (New York: Wiley, 1962), ch. 12; Roger H. Davidson, *The Role of the Congressman* (New York: Pegasus, 1969), ch. 4.

4. Donald R. Matthews, *U.S. Senators and Their World* (Chapel Hill: University of North Carolina Press, 1960), ch. 5.

5. William A. Niskanen, *Bureaucracy and Representative Government* (New York: Aldine-Atherton, 1971), p. 5.

6. Seymour Scher, "Congressional Committee Members as Independent Agency Overseers: A Case Study," 54 *American Political Science Review* 911–20 (1960); "The Politics of Agency Organization," 15 *Western Political Quarterly* 328–44 (1962); "Conditions for Legislative Control," 25 *Journal of Politics* 526–51 (1963).

7. Aaron Wildavsky, *The Politics of the Budgetary Process* (Boston: Little, Brown and Co., 1964).

8. William H. Riker, *The Theory of Political Coalitions* (New Haven: Yale University Press, 1962), with ch. 7 specifically on Congress; also William H. Riker and Donald Niemi, "The Stability of Coalitions in the House of Representatives," 56 *American Political Science Review* 58–65 (1962).

9. John F. Manley, *The Politics of Finance: The House Committee on Ways and Means* (Boston: Little, Brown and Co., 1970); Richard F. Fenno, Jr., *Congressmen in Committees* (Boston: Little, Brown and Co., 1973).

10. Charles E. Lindblom, *The Intelligence of Democracy* (New York: Free Press, 1965).

11. A suitable characterization of this tradition: "The theory of public finance has addressed itself to the questions of how much money should be spent on public expenditures, how these expenditures should be distributed among different public wants, and how the costs should be distributed between present and future, and among the members of the society." James S. Coleman, "Individual Interests and Collective Action," in Gordon Tullock (ed.), *Papers on Non-Market Decision-Making* (Charlottesville: Thomas Jefferson Center for Political Economy, University of Virginia, 1966).

12. James M. Buchanan and Gordon Tullock, *The Calculus of Consent* (Ann Arbor: University of Michigan Press, 1967), part III.

13. Niskanen, *Bureaucracy and Representative Government*.

14. There is a discussion of this point in Nathan Rosenberg, "Efficiency in the Government Sector: Discussion," 54 *American Economic Review* 251–52 (May 1954); and in James M. Buchanan, *Public Finance in Democratic Process* (Chapel Hill: University of North Carolina Press, 1967), p. 173.

15. John Rawls, *A Theory of Justice* (Cambridge: Harvard University Press, 1971), chs. 4 and 5, and especially pp. 274–84.

16. The term is from H. Douglas Price, "Computer Simulation and Legislative 'Professionalism': Some Quantitative Approaches to Legislative Evolution," paper presented to the annual convention of the American Political Science Association, 1970.

17. "But it is equally true, though only of late and slowly beginning to be acknowledged, that a numerous assembly is as little fitted for the direct business of legislation as for that of administration." John Stuart Mill, *Considerations on Representative Government* (Chicago: Regency, 1962), p. 104.

18. Gerhard Loewenberg, "The Role of Parliaments in Modern Political Systems," in Loewenberg (ed.), *Modern Parliaments: Change or Decline?* (Chicago: Aldine-Atherton, 1971), p. 3.

25

The Presidential Policy Stream

Paul Light

Presidential policy is the product of a stream of people and ideas that flows through the White House. At the start of the term, the stream is often swollen with campaign promises and competing issues. The president's major task is to narrow the stream into a manageable policy agenda. By the end of the term, the stream is reduced to a trickle and the president's major task is to pass the initial programs and get re-elected.

From Paul Light, "The Presidential Policy Stream," in Michael Nelson (ed.), *The Presidency and the Political System* (Washington, D.C.: CQ Press, 1984), pp. 423–448. Reprinted by permission.

The stream itself is composed of four currents that come together in the White House. The first current carries the *problems* that confront an administration during its term: budget deficits, energy shortages, international crises. The second current carries the different *solutions* that emerge as answers to the problems: tax and spending cuts, solar energy research, summit diplomacy. The third current carries the *assumptions* that define the problems and solutions: economic forecasts, missile tests, guesses about Soviet intentions. The fourth current carries the *players* who participate in the presidential policy debate: presidents, their staffs, cabinet members, commissions.

Although these four currents carry the essential ingredients of presidential policy, they are narrowed into final decisions by two filters: *resources* and *opportunities*. Resources are needed to make and market the president's agenda; they include time and energy to make decisions, information and expertise to evaluate choices, public approval and party seats in Congress to win passage, and money and bureaucrats to implement final legislation. Opportunities are needed to present the national agenda to Congress and the public; these depend upon the ebb and flow of the major policy calendars and upon presidential cycles of increasing effectiveness and decreasing influence.

The four currents—problems, solutions, assumptions, and players—often flow together before they reach the presidency: problems find players; solutions find assumptions; problems find solutions, and so on. In theory, all potential problems, solutions, players, and assumptions exist somewhere in the presidential policy stream. In reality, presidents see only a fraction of the problems and solutions that merit attention. Most presidents deliberately structure the policy stream to limit the flow of problems and solutions to a manageable level, leaving the filtering decisions to the White House staff. Presidents who will not delegate (Jimmy Carter) or do not watch the evolving process (Ronald Reagan) are sometimes overwhelmed. The key to narrowing the policy stream to a final agenda of presidential priorities—and to winning reelection or a place in history—is to combine the "right" problems with the "right" solutions, assumptions, and players. Presidents differ, of course, in their ability to make these matches.

Before looking at each policy current separately, it is important to recognize that, like a stream, the policy process is extremely fluid. A change of problems— from economics to defense, from foreign affairs to domestic programs—has a rippling effect on the rest of the stream. A change of players—from Alexander Haig to George Shultz, from Edwin Meese to James Baker—significantly affects the kinds of problems and solutions that emerge from the filtering process. A change of assumptions—from optimistic to pessimistic, from best-case to worst-case— has a major influence on players who control the winnowing decisions. And a change of solutions—from supply-side to tax-side, from MX race-track to MX dense-pack—affects assumptions and problems.

Moreover, because the process is so fluid, few fixed rules apply. There is no required sequence for channeling the four currents into a policy agenda; no rule on where to start. Although the filtering process generally begins with the selection of a problem and continues with a search for a solution, some decisions start with a solution and only then move to the problem. Still other decisions start with a pessimistic forecast or an ambitious staff player. The presidential policy stream often transcends constitutional and legal boundaries, taking on a life of its own. The very notion that there is a presidential policy stream suggests a dynamic, often unpredictable process that is much less mechanical and orderly than our civics books have led us to believe.

CURRENTS OF PRESIDENTIAL POLICY

Problems

Over time, the current of problems changes, and different issues merit presidential attention. The current includes old problems that have been discussed for decades and new problems that have just been noticed, large problems that appear to be virtually unsolvable and small problems that border on the routine. Although some problems seem to demand presidential action because of their seriousness, presidents retain considerable discretion over the choice of issues for their policy agendas. In 1969, Richard Nixon concentrated on foreign problems—détente with the Soviet Union, the Vietnam War, a new China policy—while largely ignoring domestic policy. In 1977, Jimmy Carter concentrated on domestic problems—energy, hospital cost containment, electoral reform, welfare reform—at the expense of foreign policy. In 1981, Ronald Reagan concentrated on economic problems—inflation, budget deficits, tax rates—while largely avoiding foreign and domestic policy.

Although presidents have wide leeway, some problems move through the presidential policy stream with more visibility than others. Medical care for the aged was a prominent problem long before President John F. Kennedy selected it for his domestic agenda in 1961; welfare reform was a problem on at least two presidential agendas before Carter tackled it in 1977. The rise and fall of problems within the presidential policy stream involves the combined interests of Congress, lobbyists, bureaucrats, and presidents, all looking for problems that match their political and policy goals.

Once a problem is "discovered," it may produce intense activity for several years. But hot issues usually cool off quickly. During the past decade, civil rights and education virtually disappeared from the domestic problem list, only to return as campaign issues for 1984. They were replaced by energy, welfare reform, social security deficits, and deregulation—issues that were not in the current 20 years ago.

The movement of problems within the presidential policy stream involves two simple patterns.[1] First, some problems surface so quickly and involve such controversy that all other issues are submerged. In 1981, Reagan's tax and spending cuts dominated the presidential agenda; little room was left for competing issues, including school prayer and abortion, until 1982. Other issues may dominate the problem current, not because of their controversial nature, but because of their appeal as easy targets for presidential success. In the late 1970s and early 1980s, economic deregulation greatly interested presidents: first railroad, then airline and trucking, now telecommunications. Second, some problems exhaust themselves over time, dropping from the policy currents. Often a problem proves so difficult that presidents and other policy makers finally let it drop. Richard Nixon, Gerald Ford, and Jimmy Carter all tried to tackle welfare reform and all eventually gave up.

On the other hand, some problems disappear from the presidential agenda because they appear to be resolved. One reason education dropped from the problem current is that Kennedy and Lyndon B. Johnson were remarkably successful in winning passage of their legislative agenda. Between 1961 and 1968, Congress passed a long string of education programs: aid to primary and secondary education, aid to higher education, Headstart, the Teacher Corps, library and school construction, school lunches, teacher education. For a decade after Johnson, many policy makers believed that the problems were solved. When education returned to the agenda in 1977, the problem was to build an executive department to house the programs as well as to find the money in a tight budget to pay for them. When education returned once more in 1983, however, the problem was defined as a decline in school quality, an implicit criticism of the Kennedy and Johnson programs. Perhaps some problems can never be completely resolved, returning at uncertain intervals in the policy stream.

Although individual problems come and go within the current, presidents generally think in terms of problem clusters: domestic, economic, defense and foreign affairs. Domestic and economic issues concern what happens *inside* the nation—even if the causes are international—while defense and foreign problems are about what happens *outside* the nation—even if the results are felt within the United States. These problem clusters are treated differently in the institutional presidency. Domestic problems usually move through the Office of Policy Development (known as the Domestic Council under Nixon and Ford, then as the Domestic Policy Staff under Carter); economic problems through the Council of Economic Advisers and the Office of Management and Budget; and foreign and defense problems through the National Security Council. The players in each cluster are generally separate (domestic policy aides rarely interact with national security staff), and the lines of communication radiate to different corners of the executive branch. Yet even if presidents think in terms of these "subpresidencies,"[2] the distinctions frequently are blurred in reality. Foreign crises may cause severe economic problems at home; defense problems outside the United States may cause domestic problems, particularly if the solutions call for deep domestic spending cuts (Reagan) or draft registration (Carter).

Once the problem current enters the White House policy stream, the critical question is why some problems are selected and others ignored. Why did Carter pick energy shortages and welfare reform but neglect national health insurance? Why did Kennedy choose education and medical care for the aged but delay civil rights? Why did Reagan mention school prayer and tuition tax credits in his 1983 State of the Union address but not abortion? All problems carry some level of benefits that make them attractive to presidents. Although the levels vary from problem to problem, president to president, and year to year, they exist nonetheless. Theoretically, presidents could assign specific values to every problem in the policy stream, then choose the problems with the highest returns. Realistically, they can estimate only the rough rewards of one problem over another, either through public opinion or their own political instincts.

Ultimately, then, benefits are in the eye of the beholder. School prayer was an inviting problem for Ronald Reagan but of no interest to liberal Democrats; equal rights for women was an attractive problem for Gerald Ford but not for more conservative Republicans. The reason why one president will see value in a problem when another does not is goals. Presidents want to be reelected, because they care about their place in history, or because they truly believe the problems are important. . . .

Solutions

Solutions to problems take the form of legislation, executive orders, regulations, symbolic maneuvers, vetoes, or commissions. Even doing nothing is a possible solution in the presidential policy stream. . . .

The solution current has two basic features. First, each problem can have a number of potential solutions. As one Carter domestic policy aide told me: "There's never any shortage of people telling you what to do. They come out from under every rock with their own answer to the problems. Energy is a great example. We got ideas ranging from solar to geothermal to coal gasification to offshore drilling to conservation. It was more an exercise in picking the right ones."

Second, and more important, most solutions are designed to answer more than one problem. Indeed, when solutions are designed to solve multiple problems, the chances for legislative passage increase. Carter's hospital cost containment plan was advertised as a solution to four different problems: inflation, by holding down medical costs; deficits, by holding down Medicare and Medicaid spending; social security bankruptcy, by freeing up room for higher payroll taxes; and urban health shortages, by providing more doctors for inner cities. That the program did not pass is a tribute to the combined efforts of the American Medical Association and the hospital lobbies, who did not agree that hospital cost containment was the proper solution to the various problems. . . .

Solutions are actually the product of a string of decisions. First, presidents must decide whether to act. A president may understand the importance of a problem but still be unable or unwilling to propose a solution. A president may want the acclaim that comes from finding the problem but not the costs of winning a solution. Second, presidents then must decide just what to put into the solution. The choices are many. Should it involve legislation or executive action;

include a specific proposal to Congress or an effort to veto a bill already passed; be new and innovative or a simple modification of past legislation; center on a large, complicated package or a small, modest bill; rely on spending or regulation to accomplish its ends; be short-term or leave more time for full implementation; be sent to Congress as a "take-it-or-leave-it" omnibus package or as a series of smaller, self-contained proposals? Although the list of questions is rarely so straightforward, each choice must be made at some point in the current of solutions.

Once the president decides to act, costs determine why some solutions are adopted and others ignored. Just as presidents weigh benefits in selecting problems, they measure costs in adopting solutions. First, presidents are very aware of *budget costs*. In an era of tight budgets and high deficits, new programs must pass the budget test before presidents will adopt them. Second, presidents assess *political costs*. Although presidents are interested in public reactions, they are concerned most directly with the question "Will it fly on Capitol Hill?" Presidents try to reduce their political costs in Congress by bargaining over pet projects, trading votes on other bills, assigning credit or blame, timing their requests to avoid overloading in important committees, lobbying to direct congressional attention to their priorities, and using the power of the presidency to stimulate public pressure. Certainly, trips to Camp David and invitations to White House dinners do not sway votes on major bills, but they do make it easier for members of Congress to stay in the habit of supporting the president longer.

Third, presidents are aware—sometimes only dimly—of *technical costs*. Unfortunately, the question "Will it work?" is asked only occasionally. Presidents appear much less concerned with workability than with budget and political costs. According to Martin Anderson, a domestic policy aide under Nixon and director of the Office of Policy Development under Reagan, Nixon's 1969 welfare reform plan never passed the technical hurdle: "No one seemed to clearly comprehend that there was, in fact, no way out of the dilemma presented by the conflicting goals of reasonably high welfare payments, low tax rates, and low cost. To some it seemed that the plan was 'such a good thing' that the possibility of it not being possible was never seriously considered."[3]

Presidents view costs, like benefits, differently. Among recent presidents, Reagan may be the most preoccupied with budget costs, while Johnson may have been overconcerned with politics. Since 1970, however, budget costs have become the dominant influence in the search for solutions. This major change in presidential policy making was evident in the Ford, Carter, and Reagan administrations: if a solution could not pass the budget hurdle, it was dropped. Concern with budgetary effects is, of course, a product of staggering deficits since the early 1970s. Yet, as the budget has grown in importance, the attention to technical issues has declined. Reagan's supply-side economic program and defense expansion surmounted both the budget and political hurdles, but as Office of Management and Budget Director David Stockman acknowledged in an interview in *The Atlantic*, they never passed the test of workability.[4] The critical issue is whether the three costs can ever be compatible. Do budget questions rule out potentially workable solutions? Do political costs conflict with budget considerations? And, if they are incompatible, which cost should come first?

Assumptions

Assumptions tell presidents what the world is like. They help presidents to understand the causes of problems and the effects of solutions. Some assumptions are based on complicated models of how the economy behaves; others are simple guesses about what the Soviets believe. Because there is always some uncertainty about how the world works, presidents often must make choices among competing assumptions. The president must decide, for example, whether the Soviets are basically evil (Reagan's assumption in a 1983 speech to evangelical Christians) or somewhat more humane (Carter's assumption until the invasion of Afghanistan).

As presidents make choices among competing problems and solutions, they must rely on the best available assumptions, which are themselves the results of subjective and sometimes conflicting estimates: How bad is the problem? Can it be solved? What are the benefits? How much will it cost? Will it work? What will the public think? When will the economy improve? Most of these questions cannot be answered in any objective sense. Presidents are no more gifted at fortunetelling than other human beings; they must rely on the best assumptions available. In early 1983, for example, Reagan was forced to choose between an optimistic economic forecast backed by supply-siders and a pessimistic forecast supported by more traditional advisers.

Assumptions may be the most important but least understood current in the presidential policy stream. Assumptions help presidents to predict the future, understand the present, and analyze the past. They help players recognize problems and work out solutions. Because assumptions are not always based on a complete knowledge of objective reality, conflict in the White House over which assumptions should be made can be intense. Indeed, assumptions are sometimes designed after the fact to build support or undermine opposition. Presidents may select a problem and adopt a solution for political, philosophical, or personal reasons, and only then prepare the evidence of need. Moreover, because presidents often see the world as they want it to be, not as it actually is, assumptions can become the critical flaw in a presidential program. For example, Reagan's overly optimistic assumption of economic recovery early in his term made change more difficult later on.

The role of assumptions in the presidential policy stream has become increasingly important during the last decade. In the 1970s, spending on federal programs, including Social Security, was increased automatically with rises in the Consumer Price Index (CPI). Thus, assumptions about future inflation became crucial for forecasting budget deficits. Much of what government now does is "uncontrollable" in the normal legislative process; thus assumptions have become the central element in telling policy makers when and where to act.

Players

Several thousand people actively engage in presidential policy making: White House staffers, cabinet secretaries, OMB analysts, bureaucrats, old friends, pollsters, the first lady, the vice president, and a host of lesser lights. Certainly the most important player is the president. As Abraham Lincoln once said to his cabinet after a heated debate: "One Aye, Seven Nays. The Ayes have it." Yet the mix of players can have an important bearing on the president's final decisions. When Shultz replaced Haig as Reagan's secretary of state, the constellation of advice changed immediately. As a former director of OMB and secretary of the Treasury, Shultz brought a much stronger economic background to his foreign policy views. Suddenly international trade was elevated as a problem in the Reagan White House. Shultz also began to participate in White House debates on the economy. He was widely seen as a powerful force in persuading Reagan of the need for a pessimistic budget forecast in 1983, as well as deeper defense cuts. There is no question that Shultz changed the direction of the Reagan agenda. Nor is there any doubt that Shultz had to compete with and against other players for the president's support.

At least four major offices fight to influence the president's policy agenda. The largest is the *Office of Management and Budget*, which has primary control over the president's annual budget and the legislative clearance process. Each year federal departments are required to submit detailed budgets and legislative priorities to OMB, which reviews all of the requests, makes "final" budget decisions, and assigns priorities to each piece of legislation. Budget and clearance responsibilities give OMB considerable leverage in dealing with the president and the executive branch, and in Stockman's first months as Reagan's budget director they were skillfully manipulated.

The second major policy office is the *Council of Economic Advisers*, which is responsible for preparing the president's annual economic report and thereby has an important role in developing the most important set of forecasts and projections. However, unlike OMB, CEA has no formal power over the budget or legislation. The OMB director is guaranteed access to the White House, but the CEA chairman must battle for a chance to speak. Reagan's first CEA chairman, Murray Weidenbaum, was unable to crack Stockman's control of economic advice; his replacement, Martin Feldstein, was initially more successful.

The third major policy agency is the *Office of Policy Development*, which originally was named the Domestic Council in 1970. OPD is primarily responsible for the review of domestic policy issues for possible elevation to the president's agenda. Unlike OMB, which reviews all executive branch requests, OPD can be more selective, performing an important role in bringing major problems and solutions to the president's attention. OPD is the domestic counterpart of the fourth major policy office, the *National Security Council*. The NSC staff acts as a much smaller version of the departments of State and Defense and has evolved into a powerful alternative source of advice.[5]

Perhaps the most important feature of these four offices is their competition *against* the executive branch for White House influence. CEA competes with the Treasury Department; OPD competes with Health and Human Service, Housing and Urban Development, and Transportation, among others; NSC competes with State and Defense; OMB competes with almost all of the departments. Although departments sometimes gain a measure of influence through a skillful secretary, the White House policy offices have an important advantage in their proximity to the president. In the "us-versus-them" mentality that often dominates the White House, presidents frequently conclude that the executive branch simply cannot be trusted to follow the presidential point of view faithfully.

Within the White House, however, the four policy offices are not the only competitors. The Congressional Relations Office, Public Liaison Office, Vice President's Office, Office of the Trade Representative, Counsel's Office, and Press Office participate in the policy debate, usually through the device of a "paper loop" that circulates proposals within the White House. At the very top, the president's chief of staff exercises the ultimate control over the movement of ideas in and out of the Oval Office. H. R. Haldeman (Nixon), Donald Rumsfeld (Ford), Hamilton Jordan (Carter), and Edwin Meese, James Baker, and Michael Deaver (Reagan) all became powerful "gate keepers" in the presidential policy stream. . . .

THE FILTERING PROCESS

As the policy stream flows through the White House, presidents must choose among the competing problems, solutions, assumptions, and players that make up the policy agenda. Because presidents cannot do everything, they must narrow the stream to a rather short list of priorities.

This presidential filtering process must serve two often competing demands in the policy stream. First, the filtering process must *merge* problems, solutions, assumptions, and players into final decisions. When the process fails, presidential proposals may face immediate defeat. Reagan's 1981 Social Security package, rejected by the Senate 96 to 0, is an example of a decision that moved through the filtering process without being matched with the political players. Second, the filtering process must *regulate* the flow of problems and solutions into the Oval Office. If too few items reach the president, important problems, solutions, assumptions, and players may be neglected. If too many items come to his attention, serious overloading may result. . . .

In the search for the best match of problems, solutions, assumptions, and players, the policy stream expands to include a wider current of ideas. In regulating the flow into the president, however, the stream must narrow. Here the important question is "How much is enough?" How many problems should a president tackle? How many solutions should be reviewed? How many players should be involved? While Carter spread himself over too many problems, perhaps Reagan limited himself to too few. While Kennedy opened the stream to too many players, perhaps Nixon did not listen to enough . . .

As presidents try to both merge and regulate the policy stream, they rely on two filters: resources and opportunities. As problems, solutions, assumptions, and players pass through these two filters, final decisions are set.

Resources

Resources "pay" for the final decisions presidents make. Some resources pay the costs of arriving at the decisions; others pay the costs of winning congressional passage; still others pay the costs of implementing the policies. Three basic kinds of resources are used for decision making, political marketing, and program implementation. These resources finance the presidential agenda.

Decision-making resources.   The most basic decision-making resource is *time*. Players need time to digest new ideas, form coalitions to influence the president, and review solutions. Similarly, problems need time to find sponsors, build public support, and locate solutions. In theory, each presidential term starts with 1,461 days. In reality, the start of the reelection campaign early in the third year limits the available policy time to approximately 700 days. For particular policies, time can be much shorter. According to Stockman, there were only 20 to 25 days to build the Reagan economic program at the start of 1981.

Energy is a second decision-making resource. One only has to look at the "before" and "after" pictures of presidents to notice the wearing effect of the office on the individual. Similarly, some problems, solutions, and assumptions consume more energy than others. Few Carter staff members would equate the stress of the Iranian hostage crisis with the lesser demands of routine domestic policy.

A third decision-making resource is *information*. Knowledge about problems, solutions, and assumptions often varies significantly. Presidents can predict the accuracy of an MX missile within 200 yards on a normal East-to-West flight range but do not know the accuracy on the North-South arctic path to the Soviet Union. What would the magnetic fields at the North Pole do to the complex MX-guidance system? Presidents still have few proven theories on how the Social Security program affects the economy. As one economist warned the National Commission on Social Security Reform, "relatively little good evidence" is available to policy makers on the subject. Using the "best that economic theory and statistical techniques have to offer," economists "have produced a series of studies that can be selectively cited by the true believers of conflicting hunches or by people with political agendas that they seek to advance."[6]

A final decision-making resource is *expertise*. This resource applies specifically to the players, who must know how to bring problems, solutions, and assumptions together into final decisions. Policy expertise is more than the sum of an individual's experience in government. It is the skill that comes from learning.

Political resources.   The policy stream also absorbs political resources. As Vice President Mondale noted on leaving office, "a president . . . starts out with a bank full of good will and slowly checks are drawn on that, and it's very rare that it's replenished. It's a one-time deposit."[7] This political capital is composed of public approval and seats in Congress. For several reasons, among them the simple decay of support and presidential mistakes, capital is depleted during the term. At least since 1960, all presidents have experienced a loss in public support over time; since 1934, all presidents have lost party seats in Congress in every midterm election. Like Mondale, many White House players see political capital as a finite resource that is spent with each choice of a problem, solution, or assumption. Clearly, some problems, solutions, and assumptions are more "expensive" politically than others.

Program resources.   Just as presidents need resources to make and sell final decisions, they need them for implementation, that is, for converting legislation into actual government activity. The most basic program resources are federal dollars and employees. However, program resources also can include supplies, land, computer time, and new equipment. Carter's MX missile "racetrack" plan had a staggering list of resource needs. Designed as an elaborate shell game in the Nevada-Utah desert, the program required 200 MX missiles, numerous decoy missiles, 4,600 hardened concrete shelters, 8,500 miles of heavy-duty roadbed, huge new trucks to carry the missiles, new launchers, new computers, and 40,000 square miles of land. Each of the 200 missiles cost $50 million in the Carter budget, but construction and maintenance expenses of the entire program would have boosted the final price tag to $500 million per missile. Moreover, construction required 50,000 workers, 190 billion gallons of water, and 100 million tons of concrete—all to be transported somehow to the desert. Critics argued that construction alone would have caused a decade-long concrete shortage. . . .

Opportunities

Once the filtering process has merged a problem with a solution, a set of assumptions, and a collection of players, and has found the decision-making, political, and program resources to pay for the combination, the White House must decide when to present the idea to Congress and the public. With the steady increase in its workload, in particular more committee and subcommittee meetings and greater constituency demands, Congress offers fewer opportunities for presidential influence. Indeed, one of Carter's critical mistakes in filtering his legislative agenda was to flood the congressional tax-writing committees with proposals. Most of Carter's program had to move through the Senate Finance Committee and House Ways and Means Committee. His economic stimulus package (January 1977), hospital cost containment plan (April 1977), Social Security financing proposal (May 1977), welfare reform bill (August 1977), urban assistance plan (January 1978), and tax reform measure (January 1978) all moved through Congress with little thought of the opportunities for legislative review.

Policy calendar.   The timing of the president's requests to Congress is critical to their success. According to John Kessel, there is a presidential policy cycle that begins sometime "after Labor Day when programs to be proposed to Congress are readied. Fall is probably the time of the heaviest work load for the policy-staffer in the White House, because work is still progressing on Capitol Hill on the present year's program at the same time preparations for the next year are being made."[8] The calendar continues with basic choices on the budget in December, major messages to Congress in January and February (including the State of the Union address, the budget message, and the economic report), congressional decision making in the spring and summer, vacations in August, and a return to planning in September and October. . . .

Cycles of influence.   Although presidents are guaranteed a certain number of opportunities to introduce policy when they enter office—four State of the Unions, four budgets, etc.—they can create additional opportunities through the *cycle of increasing effectiveness*. Whatever the initial level of information and expertise, presidents and their staffs learn over time, becoming more effective in managing their scarce opportunities. Carter, for example, became more adept at handling Congress as his term wore on and he learned how to use his limited policy opportunities. Presidents can create opportunities for new ideas through carefully staged public events or through skillful manipulation of the press. A president's effectiveness in using these informal opportunities always grows over time, as a simple byproduct of learning the ropes.

Just as presidents can create opportunities through the cycle of increasing effectiveness, they can lose opportunities through the *cycle of decreasing influence*. As public approval and party seats drop during the term—one month-to-month, the other at the midterm election—presidents lose opportunities for influence. Even though they become more effective at finding opportunities for ideas, Congress and the public become less interested. Moreover, even the formal opportunities lose effectiveness later in the term. Major messages, televised addresses, and press conferences carry less weight.

Filtering and Policy

Why are resources and opportunities so important as policy filters? The reason is that presidents enter office with different amounts of each. Ford had only two years in his brief term, Johnson had five. Ford had fewer than 150 party faithful in the House, Johnson once had more than 290. Carter and Reagan had little expertise in national policy making, Nixon had little in domestic affairs. Carter's Georgia staff had little background in national policy, too, which left considerable room for learning, while Reagan's legislative staff had considerable expertise in legislative lobbying. These kinds of differences tell a great deal about the policy stream as it flows through an administration. The resources and opportunities at the start of a term determine both the quantity and quality of the president's policy agenda.

CONCLUSION

If presidential policy is the product of a highly dynamic stream, the final issue is whether the stream has changed its course during the past decades. The problems have changed, but have they become more difficult? Is cutting government spending more difficult than increasing it? Kennedy and Johnson selected problems that seemed to demand expanded government, while Carter and Reagan picked problems that seemed to require contracted government. Nor did Kennedy and Johnson have to tackle any of the new "single issues" such as abortion and school prayer. Perhaps the most important change in the past 20 years has been the rise of a new class of "constituentless" issues—problems, such as energy conservation, which have few supporters but many potential enemies.

The solutions also have changed. Spending and regulation are no longer the popular response to national problems, but it is not yet clear what kinds of solutions will replace them. The players have changed, too. The rise of the National Security Council staff and the Office of Policy Development has shaped a new pool of players who compete for the president's attention and support. Moreover, most White House aides argue that interest groups are penetrating further into the policy process in recent years. As presidents reach out to interest groups to help pass their programs, interest groups reach further in to draft legislation and influence decisions.

Perhaps the most important area of change—or lack of change—is in assumptions. Despite new methods of forecasting and computer analysis, presidents do not seem much closer to being able to predict problems or solutions accurately. Much of the policy process still rests on best guesses about what will or will not happen. Even in the very short-term, players have difficulty predicting what will happen. Stockman was willing to admit in early 1983 that we cannot predict even the next year, let alone five years out. That may be the most serious obstacle to presidents as they continue to search for problems and solutions. If problems are more controversial in this era of single-issue politics, if solutions are more constrained by tight budgets and personnel shortages, if players are more competitive for presidential influence, there is even greater need for accurate assumptions. Unfortunately, presidents still look into their crystal balls and see pretty much what they want to see.

NOTES

1. See Jack L. Walker, "Setting the Agenda in the U.S. Senate: A Theory of Problem Selection," *British Journal of Political Science* (1977): 438.

2. Thomas E. Cronin, *The State of the Presidency* (Boston: Little, Brown & Co., 1980), 143–186.

3. Martin Anderson, *Welfare: The Political Economy of Welfare Reform in the United States* (Stanford, Cal.: Hoover Institution Press, 1978), 143–144.

4. William Greider, "The Education of David Stockman," *The Atlantic*, 248 (December 1981): 38, 44–47.

5. I. M. Destler, "National Security II: The Rise of the Assistant (1961–1981)," in *The Illusion of Presidential Government*, ed. Hugh Heclo and Lester M. Salamon (Boulder, Colo.: Westview Press, 1982.)

6. Henry Aaron, *Economic Effects of Social Security* (Washington: The Brookings Institution, 1983), 51, 82.

7. *Washington Post*, January 21, 1981, A-24.

8. John Kessel, *The Domestic Presidency* (Boston: Duxbury Press, 1975), 9.

26

The Two Presidencies

Aaron Wildavsky

The United States has one President, but it has two presidencies; one presidency is for domestic affairs, and the other is concerned with defense and foreign policy. Since World War II, Presidents have had much greater success in controlling the nation's defense and foreign policies than in dominating its domestic policies. Even Lyndon Johnson has seen his early record of victories in domestic legislation diminish as his concern with foreign affairs grows.

What powers does the President have to control defense and foreign policies and so completely overwhelm those who might wish to thwart him?

The President's normal problem with domestic policy is to get congressional support for the programs he prefers. In foreign affairs, in contrast, he can almost always get support for policies that he believes will protect the nation—but his problem is to find a viable policy.

Whoever they are, whether they begin by caring about foreign policy like Eisenhower and Kennedy or about domestic policies like Truman and Johnson, Presidents soon discover they have more policy preferences in domestic matters than in foreign policy. The Republican and Democratic parties possess a traditional roster of policies, which can easily be adopted by a new President—for example, he can be either for or against Medicare and aid to education. Since existing domestic policy usually changes in only small steps, Presidents find it relatively simple to make minor adjustments. However, although any President knows he supports foreign aid and NATO,* the world outside changes much more

From Aaron Wildavsky, "The Two Presidencies," *Transaction*, 4, no. 2 (1966). Reprinted by permission.

North Atlantic Treaty Organization, or NATO: alliance uniting North America and Western Europe in a commitment to collective defense aimed primarily at preventing Soviet expansion in Europe.

rapidly than the nation inside—Presidents and their parties have no prior policies on Argentina and the Congo. The world has become a highly intractable place with a whirl of forces we cannot or do not know how to alter.

THE RECORD OF PRESIDENTIAL CONTROL

It takes great crises, such as Roosevelt's hundred days in the midst of the depression, or the extraordinary majorities that Barry Goldwater's candidacy willed to Lyndon Johnson, for Presidents to succeed in controlling domestic policy. From the end of the 1930's to the present (what may roughly be called the modern era), Presidents have often been frustrated in their domestic programs. From 1938, when conservatives regrouped their forces, to the time of his death, Franklin Roosevelt did not get a single piece of significant domestic legislation passed. Truman lost out on most of his intense domestic preferences, except perhaps for housing. Since Eisenhower did not ask for much domestic legislation, he did not meet consistent defeat, yet he failed in his general policy of curtailing governmental commitments. Kennedy, of course, faced great difficulties with domestic legislation.

In the realm of foreign policy there has not been a single major issue on which Presidents, when they were serious and determined, have failed. The list of their victories is impressive: entry into the United Nations, the Marshall Plan,[†] NATO, the Truman Doctrine,[‡] the decisions to stay out of Indochina in 1954 and to intervene in Vietnam in the 1960's, aid to Poland and Yugoslavia, the test-ban treaty, and many more. Serious setbacks to the President in controlling foreign policy are extraordinary and unusual.

Table 1, compiled from the Congressional Quarterly Service tabulation of presidential initiative and congressional response from 1948 through 1964, shows that Presidents have significantly better records in foreign and defense matters than in domestic policies. When refugees and immigration—which Congress considers primarily a domestic concern—are removed from the general foreign policy area, it is clear that Presidents prevail about 70 per cent of the time in defense and foreign policy, compared with 40 per cent in the domestic sphere.

WORLD EVENTS AND PRESIDENTIAL RESOURCES

Power in politics is control over governmental decisions. How does the President manage his control of foreign and defense policy? The answer does not reside in the greater constitutional power in foreign affairs that Presidents have possessed

---

[†]*Marshall Plan*: common name for the European Recovery Program proposed by George C. Marshall, President Harry S. Truman's secretary of state. Implemented in 1948 under the Economic Cooperation Administration, the plan provided funds to European nations to aid in reconstructing their economies and bolster their resistance to communism.

[‡]*Truman Doctrine*: a 1947 "containment" policy of President Truman's that provided aid to countries trying to resist Communist takeover. Truman lobbied Congress to provide $400 million to support Greece and Turkey in their struggles against leftist movements when Great Britain ended its aid program after World War II.

TABLE I   Congressional Action on Presidential Proposals from 1948–1964

Policy Area	Congressional Action		Number of Proposals
	% Pass	% Fail	
Domestic policy (natural resources, labor, agricultural, taxes, etc.)	40.2	59.8	2499
Defense policy (defense, disarmament, manpower, misc.)	73.3	26.7	90
Foreign policy	58.5	41.5	655
Immigration, refugees	13.2	86.0	129
Treaties, general foreign relations, State Department, foreign aid	70.8	29.2	445

Source: Congressional Quarterly Service, *Congress and the Nation*, 1945–1964 (Washington, 1965).

since the founding of the Republic. The answer lies in the changes that have taken place since 1945.

The number of nations with which the United States has diplomatic relations has increased from 53 in 1939 to 113 in 1966. But sheer numbers do not tell enough; the world has also become a much more dangerous place. However remote it may seem at times, our government must always be aware of the possibility of nuclear war.

Yet the mere existence of great powers with effective thermonuclear weapons would not, in and of itself, vastly increase our rate of interaction with most other nations. We see events in Assam or Burundi as important because they are also part of a larger worldwide contest, called the cold war, in which great powers are rivals for the control or support of other nations. Moreover, the reaction against the blatant isolationism of the 1930's has led to a concern with foreign policy that is worldwide in scope. We are interested in what happens everywhere because we see these events as connected with larger interests involving, at the worst, the possibility of ultimate destruction.

Given the overriding fact that the world is dangerous and that small causes are perceived to have potentially great effects in an unstable world, it follows that Presidents must be interested in relatively "small" matters. So they give Azerbaijan or Lebanon or Vietnam huge amounts of their time. Arthur Schlesinger, Jr., wrote of Kennedy that "in the first two months of his administration he probably spent more time on Laos than on anything else." Few failures in domestic policy, Presidents soon realize, could have as disastrous consequences as any one of dozens of mistakes in the international arena.

The result is that foreign policy concerns tend to drive out domestic policy. Except for occasional questions of domestic prosperity and for civil rights, foreign affairs have consistently higher priority for Presidents. Once, when trying to talk to President Kennedy about natural resources, Secretary of the Interior Stewart Udall remarked, "He's imprisoned by Berlin."

The importance of foreign affairs to Presidents is intensified by the increasing speed of events in the international arena. The event and its consequences follow closely on top of one another. The blunder at the Bay of Pigs is swiftly followed by the near catastrophe of the Cuban missile crisis.[†] Presidents can no longer count on passing along their most difficult problems to their successors. They must expect to face the consequences of their actions—or failure to act—while still in office.

Domestic policy-making is usually based on experimental adjustments to an existing situation. Only a few decisions, such as those involving large dams, irretrievably commit future generations. Decisions in foreign affairs, however, are often perceived to be irreversible. This is expressed, for example, in the fear of escalation or the various "spiral" or "domino" theories[‡] of international conflict.

If decisions are perceived to be both important and irreversible, there is every reason for Presidents to devote a great deal of resources to them. Presidents have to be oriented toward the future in the use of their resources. They serve a fixed term in office, and they cannot automatically count on support from the populace, Congress, or the administrative apparatus. They have to be careful, therefore, to husband their resources for pressing future needs. But because the consequences of events in foreign affairs are potentially more grave, faster to manifest themselves, and less easily reversible than in domestic affairs, Presidents are more willing to use up their resources.

THE POWER TO ACT

Their formal powers to commit resources in foreign affairs and defense are vast. Particularly important is their power as Commander-in-Chief to move troops. Faced with situations like the invasion of South Korea or the emplacement of missiles in Cuba, fast action is required. Presidents possess both the formal power to act and the knowledge that elites and the general public expect them to act. Once they have committed American forces, it is difficult for Congress or anyone else to alter the course of events. The Dominican venture is a recent case in point.

Presidential discretion in foreign affairs also makes it difficult (though not impossible) for Congress to restrict their actions. Presidents can use executive agreements instead of treaties, enter into tacit agreements instead of written ones, and otherwise help create *de facto* situations not easily reversed. Presidents also have far greater ability than anyone else to obtain information on developments

---

[†]*Cuban missile crisis*: incident in 1962 during which President Kennedy ordered a naval quarantine of Cuba until the Soviet Union dismantled long-range nuclear missile launch it was building there. The Soviets soon complied on condition that the United States pledge not to invade Cuba.

[‡]*Domino theory*: concept, first popularized by President Eisenhower in 1954, that if one country became Communist, neighboring countries would also fall in an inevitable chain reaction. The metaphor was used to gain support for U.S. military policy in Indochina, especially during the Vietnam War.

abroad through the Departments of State and Defense. The need for secrecy in some aspects of foreign and defense policy further restricts the ability of others to compete with Presidents. These things are all well known. What is not so generally appreciated is the growing presidential ability to *use* information to achieve goals.

In the past Presidents were amateurs in military strategy. They could not even get much useful advice outside of the military. As late as the 1930's the number of people outside the military establishment who were professionally engaged in the study of defense policy could be numbered on fingers. Today there are hundreds of such men. The rise of the defense intellectuals has given the President of the United States enhanced ability to control defense policy. He is no longer dependent on the military for advice. He can choose among defense intellectuals from the research corporations and the academies for alternative sources of advice. He can install these men in his own office. He can play them off against each other or use them to extend spheres of coordination.

Even with these advisers, however, Presidents and Secretaries of Defense might still be too bewildered by the complexity of nuclear situations to take action—unless they had an understanding of the doctrine and concept of deterrence.* But knowledge of doctrine about deterrence has been widely diffused; it can be picked up by any intelligent person who will read books or listen to enough hours of conversation. Whether or not the doctrine is good is a separate question; the point is that civilians can feel they understand what is going on in defense policy. Perhaps the most extraordinary feature of presidential action during the Cuban missile crisis was the degree to which the Commander-in-Chief of the Armed Forces insisted on controlling even the smallest moves. From the positioning of ships to the methods of boarding, to the precise words and actions to be taken by individual soldiers and sailors, the President and his civilian advisers were in control.

Although Presidents have rivals for power in foreign affairs, the rivals do not usually succeed. Presidents prevail not only because they may have superior resources but because their potential opponents are weak, divided, or believe that they should not control foreign policy. Let us consider the potential rivals—the general citizenry, special interest groups, the Congress, the military, the so-called military-industrial complex, and the State Department.

COMPETITORS FOR CONTROL OF POLICY

The Public. The general public is much more dependent on Presidents in foreign affairs than in domestic matters. While many people know about the impact of social security and Medicare, few know about politics in Malawi. So it is

---

*Deterrence: prevention of military aggression by persuading enemies that the price of aggression would be unacceptably high. American defense policy is based on the idea that an unsurpassed military capacity is the best guarantor of national security because the consequences of engaging the United States in hostilities would be too great.

not surprising that people expect the President to act in foreign affairs and reward him with their confidence. Gallup Polls consistently show that presidential popularity rises after he takes action in a crisis—whether the action is disastrous as in the Bay of Pigs or successful as in the Cuban missile crisis. Decisive action, such as the bombing of oil fields near Haiphong, resulted in a sharp (though temporary) increase in Johnson's popularity.

The Vietnam situation illustrates another problem of public opinion in foreign affairs: it is extremely difficult to get operational policy directions from the general public. It took a long time before any sizable public interest in the subject developed. Nothing short of the large scale involvement of American troops under fire probably could have brought about the current high level of concern. Yet this relatively well developed popular opinion is difficult to interpret. While a majority appear to support President Johnson's policy, it appears that they could easily be persuaded to withdraw from Vietnam if the administration changed its line. Although a sizable majority would support various initiatives to end the war, they would seemingly be appalled if this action led to Communist[†] encroachments elsewhere in Southeast Asia. (See "The President, the Polls, and Vietnam" by Seymour Martin Lipset, *Trans-Action*, Sept/Oct 1966.)

Although Presidents lead opinion in foreign affairs, they know they will be held accountable for the consequences of their actions. President Johnson has maintained a large commitment in Vietnam. His popularity shoots up now and again in the midst of some imposing action. But the fact that a body of citizens do not like the war comes back to damage his overall popularity. We will support your initiatives, the people seem to say, but we will reserve the right to punish you (or your party) if we do not like the results.

Special interest groups.   Opinions are easier to gauge in domestic affairs because, for one thing, there is a stable structure of interest groups that covers virtually all matters of concern. The farm, labor, business, conservation, veteran, civil rights, and other interest groups provide cues when a proposed policy affects them. Thus people who identify with these groups may adopt their views. But in foreign policy matters the interest group structure is weak, unstable, and thin rather than dense. In many matters affecting Africa and Asia, for example, it is hard to think of well-known interest groups. While ephemeral groups arise from time to time to support or protest particular policies, they usually disappear when the immediate problem is resolved. In contrast, longer-lasting elite groups like the Foreign Policy Association and Council on Foreign Relations are composed of people of diverse views; refusal to take strong positions on controversial matters is a condition of their continued viability.

The strongest interest groups are probably the ethnic associations whose

---

[†]*Communist*: In the modern context, as discussed by Marx and Engels, a communist is one who supports a society characterized by the absence of private property, distribution of goods and services based on individuals' needs, and the withering away of the state.

members have strong ties with a homeland, as in Poland or Cuba, so they are rarely activated simultaneously on any specific issue. They are most effective when most narrowly and intensely focused—as in the fierce pressure from Jews to recognize the state of Israel. But their relatively small numbers limit their significance to Presidents in the vastly more important general foreign policy picture—as continued aid to the Arab countries shows. Moreover, some ethnic groups may conflict on significant issues such as American acceptance of the Oder-Neisse line separating Poland from what is now East Germany.

The Congress.   Congressmen also exercise power in foreign affairs. Yet they are ordinarily not serious competitors with the President because they follow a self-denying ordinance. They do not think it is their job to determine the nation's defense policies. Lewis A. Dexter's extensive interviews with members of the Senate Armed Services Committee, who might be expected to want a voice in defense policy, reveal that they do not desire for men like themselves to run the nation's defense establishment. Aside from a few specific conflicts among the armed services which allow both the possibility and desirability of direct intervention, the Armed Services Committee constitutes a sort of real estate committee dealing with the regional economic consequences of the location of military facilities.

The congressional appropriations power is potentially a significant resource, but circumstances since the end of World War II have tended to reduce its effectiveness. The appropriations committees and Congress itself might make their will felt by refusing to allot funds unless basic policies were altered. But this has not happened. While Congress makes its traditional small cuts in the military budget, Presidents have mostly found themselves warding off congressional attempts to increase specific items still further.

Most of the time, the administration's refusal to spend has not been seriously challenged. However, there have been occasions when individual legislators or committees have been influential. Senator Henry Jackson in his campaign (with the aid of colleagues on the Joint Committee on Atomic Energy) was able to gain acceptance for the Polaris weapons system and Senator Arthur H. Vandenberg played a part in determining the shape of the Marshall Plan and so on. The few congressmen who are expert in defense policy act, as Samuel P. Huntington says, largely as lobbyists with the executive branch. It is apparently more fruitful for these congressional experts to use their resources in order to get a hearing from the executive than to work on other congressmen.

When an issue involves the actual use or threat of violence, it takes a great deal to convince congressmen not to follow the President's lead. James Robinson's tabulation of foreign and defense policy issues from the late 1930's to 1961 (Table 2) shows dominant influence by Congress in only one case out of seven— the 1954 decision not to intervene with armed force in Indochina. In that instance President Eisenhower deliberately sounded out congressional opinion and, finding it negative, decided not to intervene—against the advice of Admiral Radford,

TABLE 2   Congressional Involvement in Foreign and Defense Policy Decisions

Issue	Congressional Involvement (High, Low, None)	Initiator (Congress or Executive)	Predominant Influence (Congress or Executive)	Legislation or Resolution (Yes or No)	Violence at Stake (Yes or No)	Decision Time (Long or Short)
Neutrality Legislation, the 1930's	High	Exec	Cong	Yes	No	Long
Lend-Lease, 1941	High	Exec	Exec	Yes	Yes	Long
Aid to Russia, 1941	Low	Exec	Exec	No	No	Long
Repeal of Chinese Exclusion, 1943	High	Cong	Cong	Yes	No	Long
Fullbright Resolution, 1943	High	Cong	Cong	Yes	No	Long
Building the Atomic Bomb, 1944	Low	Exec	Exec	Yes	Yes	Long
Foreign Services Act of 1946	High	Exec	Exec	Yes	No	Long
Truman Doctrine, 1947	High	Exec	Exec	Yes	No	Long
The Marshall Plan, 1947–48	High	Exec	Exec	Yes	No	Long
Berlin Airlift, 1948	None	Exec	Exec	No	Yes	Long
Vandenberg Resolution, 1948	High	Exec	Cong	Yes	No	Long
North Atlantic Treaty, 1947–49	High	Exec	Exec	Yes	No	Long
Korean Decision, 1950	None	Exec	Exec	No	Yes	Short
Japanese Peace Treaty, 1952	High	Exec	Exec	Yes	No	Long
Bohlen Nomination, 1953	High	Exec	Exec	Yes	No	Long
Indo-China, 1954	High	Exec	Cong	No	Yes	Short
Formosan Resolution, 1955	High	Exec	Exec	Yes	Yes	Long
International Finance Corporation, 1956	Low	Exec	Exec	Yes	No	Long
Foreign Aid, 1957	High	Exec	Exec	Yes	No	Long
Reciprocal Trade Agreements, 1958	High	Exec	Exec	Yes	No	Long
Monroney Resolution, 1958	High	Cong	Cong	Yes	No	Long
Cuban Decision, 1961	Low	Exec	Exec	No	Yes	Long

Source: James A. Robinson, *Congress and Foreign Policymaking* (Homewood, Illinois, 1962).

chairman of the Joint Chiefs of Staff. This attempt to abandon responsibility did not succeed, as the years of American involvement demonstrate.

The military. The outstanding feature of the military's participation in making defense policy is their amazing weakness. Whether the policy decisions involve the size of the armed forces, the choice of weapons systems, the total defense budget, or its division into components, the military have not prevailed. Let us take budgetary decisions as representative of the key choices to be made in defense policy. Since the end of World War II the military has not been able to achieve significant (billion dollar) increases in appropriations by their own efforts. Under Truman and Eisenhower defense budgets were determined by what Huntington calls the remainder method: the two Presidents estimated revenues, decided what they could spend on domestic matters, and the remainder was assigned to defense. The usual controversy was between some military and congressional groups supporting much larger expenditures while the President and his executive allies refused. A typical case, involving the desire of the Air Force to increase the number of groups of planes is described by Huntington in the *The Common Defense*:

> The FY [fiscal year] 1949 budget provided 48 groups. After the Czech coup, the Administration yielded and backed an Air Force of 55 groups in its spring rearmament program. Congress added additional funds to aid Air Force expansion to 70 groups. The Administration refused to utilize them, however, and in the gathering economy wave of the summer and fall of 1948, the Air Force goal was cut back again to 48 groups. In 1949 the House of Representatives picked up the challenge and appropriated funds for 58 groups. The President impounded† the money. In June, 1950, the Air Force had 48 groups.

The great increases in the defense budget were due far more to Stalin and modern technology than to the military. The Korean War resulted in an increase from 12 to 44 billions and much of the rest followed Sputnik and the huge costs of missile programs. Thus modern technology and international conflict put an end to the one major effort to subordinate foreign affairs to domestic policies through the budget.

It could be argued that the President merely ratifies the decisions made by the military and their allies. If the military and/or Congress were united and insistent on defense policy, it would certainly be difficult for Presidents to resist these forces. But it is precisely the disunity of the military that has characterized the entire postwar period. Indeed, the military have not been united on any major matter of defense policy. The apparent unity of the Joint Chiefs of Staff turns out to be illusory. The vast majority of their recommendations appear to be unanimous and are accepted by the Secretary of Defense and the President. But this facade of unity can only be achieved by methods that vitiate the impact of the recom-

---

†*Impounded*: a tactic used by the executive branch that prevents the disbursement of funds already authorized and appropriated by the legislature.

mendations. Genuine disagreements are hidden by vague language that commits no one to anything. Mutually contradictory plans are strung together so everyone appears to get something, but nothing is decided. Since it is impossible to agree on really important matters, all sorts of trivia are brought in to make a record of agreement. While it may be true, as Admiral Denfield, a former Chief of Naval Operations, said, that "On nine-tenths of the matters that come before them the Joint Chiefs of Staff reach agreement themselves," the vastly more important truth is that "normally the *only* disputes are on strategic concepts, the size and composition of forces, and budget matters."

Military-industrial.   But what about the fabled military-industrial complex? If the military alone is divided and weak, perhaps the giant industrial firms that are so dependent on defense contracts play a large part in making policy.

First, there is an important distinction between the questions "Who will get a given contract?" and "What will our defense policy be?" It is apparent that different answers may be given to these quite different questions. There are literally tens of thousands of defense contractors. They may compete vigorously for business. In the course of this competition, they may wine and dine military officers, use retired generals, seek intervention by their congressmen, place ads in trade journals, and even contribute to political campaigns. The famous TFX controversy—should General Dynamics or Boeing get the expensive contract?—is a larger than life example of the pressures brought to bear in search of lucrative contracts.

But neither the TFX case nor the usual vigorous competition for contracts is involved with the making of substantive defense policy. Vital questions like the size of the defense budget, the choice of strategic programs, massive retaliation vs. a counter-city strategy, and the like were far beyond the policy aims of any company. Industrial firms, then, do not control such decisions, nor is there much evidence that they actually try. No doubt a precipitous and drastic rush to disarmament would meet with opposition from industrial firms among other interests. However, there has never been a time when any significant element in the government considered a disarmament policy to be feasible.

It may appear that industrial firms had no special reason to concern themselves with the government's stance on defense because they agree with the national consensus on resisting communism, maintaining a large defense establishment, and rejecting isolationism. However, this hypothesis about the climate of opinion explains everything and nothing. For every policy that is adopted or rejected can be explained away on the grounds that the cold war climate of opinion dictated what happened. Did the United States fail to intervene with armed force in Vietnam in 1954? That must be because the climate of opinion was against it. Did the United States send troops to Vietnam in the 1960's? That must be because the cold war climate demanded it. If the United States builds more missiles, negotiates a testban treaty, intervenes in the Dominican Republic, fails to intervene in a dozen other situations, all these actions fit the hypothesis by definition. The argument is reminiscent of those who defined the Soviet Union as permanently hostile and therefore interpreted increases of Soviet troops as menacing and decreases of troop strength as equally sinister.

If the growth of the military establishment is not directly equated with increasing military control of defense policy, the extraordinary weakness of the professional soldier still requires explanation. Huntington has written about how major military leaders were seduced in the Truman and Eisenhower years into believing that they should bow to the judgment of civilians that the economy could not stand much larger military expenditures. Once the size of the military pie was accepted as a fixed constraint, the military services were compelled to put their major energies into quarreling with one another over who should get the larger share. Given the natural rivalries of the military and their traditional acceptance of civilian rule, the President and his advisers—who could claim responsibility for the broader picture of reconciling defense and domestic policies—had the upper hand. There are, however, additional explanations to be considered.

The dominant role of the congressional appropriations committee is to be guardian of the treasury. This is manifested in the pride of its members in cutting the President's budget. Thus it was difficult to get this crucial committee to recommend even a few hundred million increase in defense; it was practically impossible to get them to consider the several billion jump that might really have made a difference. A related budgetary matter concerned the planning, programming, and budgeting system introduced by Secretary of Defense McNamara. For if the defense budget contained major categories that crisscrossed the services, only the Secretary of Defense could put it together. Whatever the other debatable consequences of program budgeting, its major consequence was to grant power to the secretary and his civilian advisers.

The subordination of the military through program budgeting is just one symptom of a more general weakness of the military. In the past decade the military has suffered a lack of intellectual skills appropriate to the nuclear age. For no one has (and no one wants) direct experience with nuclear war. So the usual military talk about being the only people to have combat experience is not very impressive. Instead, the imaginative creation of possible future wars—in order to avoid them—requires people with a high capacity for abstract thought combined with the ability to manipulate symbols using quantitative methods. West Point has not produced many such men.

The State Department.   Modern Presidents expect the State Department to carry out their policies. John F. Kennedy felt that State was "in some particular sense 'his' department." If a Secretary of State forgets this, as was apparently the case with James Byrnes under Truman, a President may find another man. But the State Department, especially the Foreign Service, is also a highly professional organization with a life and momentum of its own. If a President does not push hard, he may find his preferences somehow dissipated in time. Arthur Schlesinger fills his book on Kennedy with laments about the bureaucratic inertia and recalcitrance of the State Department.

Yet Schlesinger's own account suggests that State could not ordinarily resist the President. At one point, he writes of "the President, himself, increasingly the day-to-day director of American foreign policy." On the next page, we learn that "Kennedy dealt personally with almost every aspect of policy around the globe. He knew more about certain areas than the senior officials at State and probably called as many issues to their attention as they did to his." The President insisted on his way in Laos. He pushed through his policy on the Congo against strong opposition with the State Department. Had Kennedy wanted to get a great deal more initiative out of the State Department, as Schlesinger insists, he could have replaced the Secretary of State, a man who did not command special support in the Democratic party or in Congress. It may be that Kennedy wanted too strongly to run his own foreign policy. Dean Rusk* may have known far better than Schlesinger that the one thing Kennedy did not want was a man who might rival him in the field of foreign affairs.

Schlesinger comes closest to the truth when he writes that "the White House could always win any battle it chose over the [Foreign] Service; but the prestige and proficiency of the Service limited the number of battles any White House would find it profitable to fight." When the President knew what he wanted, he got it. When he was doubtful and perplexed, he sought good advice and frequently did not get that. But there is no evidence that the people on his staff came up with better ideas. The real problem may have been a lack of good ideas anywhere. Kennedy undoubtedly encouraged his staff to prod the State Department. But the President was sufficiently cautious not to push so hard that he got his way when he was not certain what that way should be. In this context Kennedy appears to have played his staff off against elements in the State Department.

The growth of a special White House staff to help Presidents in foreign affairs expresses their need for assistance, their refusal to rely completely on the regular executive agencies, and their ability to find competent men. The deployment of this staff must remain a presidential prerogative, however, if its members are to serve Presidents and not their opponents. Whenever critics do not like the existing foreign and defense policies, they are likely to complain that the White House staff is screening out divergent views from the President's attention. Naturally, the critics recommend introducing many more different viewpoints. If the critics could maneuver the President into counting hands all day ("on the one hand and on the other"), they would make it impossible for him to act. Such a viewpoint is also congenial to those who believe that action rather than inaction is the greatest present danger in foreign policy. But Presidents resolutely refuse to become prisoners of their advisers by using them as other people would like. Presidents remain in control of their staff as well as of major foreign policy decisions.

Dean Rusk: Secretary of state (1961–1969) under Presidents Kennedy and Johnson.

HOW COMPLETE IS THE CONTROL?

Some analysts say that the success of Presidents in controlling foreign policy decisions is largely illusory. It is achieved, they say, by anticipating the reactions of others, and eliminating proposals that would run into severe opposition. There is some truth in this objection. In politics, where transactions are based on a high degree of mutual interdependence, what others may do has to be taken into account. But basing presidential success in foreign and defense policy on anticipated reactions suggests a static situation which does not exist. For if Presidents propose only those policies that would get support in Congress, and Congress opposes them only when it knows that it can muster overwhelming strength, there would never be any conflict. Indeed, there might never be any action.

How can "anticipated reaction" explain the conflict over the policies like the Marshall Plan and the test-ban treaty in which severe opposition was overcome only by strenuous efforts? Furthermore, why doesn't "anticipated reaction" work in domestic affairs? One would have to argue that for some reason presidential perception of what would be successful is consistently confused on domestic issues and most always accurate on major foreign policy issues. But the role of "anticipated reactions" should be greater in the more familiar domestic situations, which provide a backlog of experience for forecasting, than in foreign policy with many novel situations such as the Suez crisis or the Rhodesian affair.

Are there significant historical examples which might refute the thesis of presidential control of foreign policy? Foreign aid may be a case in point. For many years, Presidents have struggled to get foreign aid appropriations because of hostility from public and congressional opinion. Yet several billion dollars a year are appropriated regularly despite the evident unpopularity of the program. In the aid programs to Communist countries like Poland and Yugoslavia, the Congress attaches all sorts of restrictions to the aid, but Presidents find ways of getting around them.

What about the example of recognition of Communist China? The sentiment of the country always has been against recognizing Red China or admitting it to the United Nations. But have Presidents wanted to recognize Red China and been hamstrung by opposition? The answer, I suggest, is a qualified "no." By the time recognition of Red China might have become a serious issue for the Truman administration, the war in Korea effectively precluded its consideration. There is no evidence that President Eisenhower or Secretary Dulles ever thought it wise to recognize Red China or help admit her to the United Nations. The Kennedy administration viewed the matter as not of major importance and, considering the opposition, moved cautiously in suggesting change. Then came the war in Vietnam. If the advantages for foreign policy had been perceived to be much higher, then Kennedy or Johnson might have proposed changing American policy toward recognition of Red China.

One possible exception, in the case of Red China, however, does not seem sufficient to invalidate the general thesis that Presidents do considerably better in getting their way in foreign and defense policy than in domestic policies.

THE WORLD INFLUENCE

The forces impelling Presidents to be concerned with the widest range of foreign and defense policies also affect the ways in which they calculate their power stakes. As Kennedy used to say, "Domestic policy . . . can only defeat us; foreign policy can kill us."

It no longer makes sense for Presidents to "play politics" with foreign and defense policies. In the past, Presidents might have thought that they could gain by prolonged delay or by not acting at all. The problem might disappear or be passed on to their successors. Presidents must now expect to pay the high costs themselves if the world situation deteriorates. The advantages of pursuing a policy that is viable in the world, that will not blow up on Presidents or their fellow citizens, far outweigh any temporary political disadvantages accrued in supporting an initially unpopular policy. Compared with domestic affairs, Presidents engaged in world politics are immensely more concerned with meeting problems on their own terms. Who supports and opposes a policy, though a matter of considerable interest, does not assume the crucial importance that it does in domestic affairs. The best policy Presidents can find is also the best politics.

The fact that there are numerous foreign and defense policy situations competing for a President's attention means that it is worthwhile to organize political activity in order to affect his agenda. For if a President pays more attention to certain problems he may develop different preferences; he may seek and receive different advice; his new calculations may lead him to devote greater resources to seeking a solution. Interested congressmen may exert influence not by directly determining a presidential decision, but indirectly by making it costly for a President to avoid reconsidering the basis for his action. For example, citizen groups, such as those concerned with a change in China policy, may have an impact simply by keeping their proposals on the public agenda. A president may be compelled to reconsider a problem even though he could not overtly be forced to alter the prevailing policy.

In foreign affairs we may be approaching the stage where knowledge is power. There is a tremendous receptivity to good ideas in Washington. Most anyone who can present a convincing rationale for dealing with a hard world finds a ready audience. The best way to convince Presidents to follow a desired policy is to show that it might work. A man like McNamara thrives because he performs; he comes up with answers he can defend. It is, to be sure, extremely difficult to devise good policies or to predict their consequences accurately. Nor is it easy to convince others that a given policy is superior to other alternatives. But it is the way to influence with Presidents. For if they are convinced that the current policy is best, the likelihood of gaining sufficient force to compel a change is quite small. The man who can build better foreign policies will find Presidents beating a path to his door.

The Rise
of the Bureaucratic State

James Q. Wilson

During its first 150 years, the American republic was not thought to have a "bureaucracy," and thus it would have been meaningless to refer to the "problems" of a "bureaucratic state." There were, of course, appointed civilian officials: Though only about 3,000 at the end of the Federalist period, there were about 95,000 by the time Grover Cleveland assumed office in 1881, and nearly half a million by 1925. Some aspects of these numerous officials were regarded as problems—notably, the standards by which they were appointed and the political loyalties to which they were held—but these were thought to be matters of proper character and good management. The great political and constitutional struggles were not over the power of the administrative apparatus, but over the power of the President, of Congress, and of the states.

The Founding Fathers had little to say about the nature or function of the executive branch of the new government. The Constitution is virtually silent on the subject and the debates in the Constitutional Convention are almost devoid of reference to an administrative apparatus. This reflected no lack of concern about the matter, however. Indeed, it was in part because of the Founders' depressing experience with chaotic and inefficient management under the Continental Congress and the Articles of Confederation that they had assembled in Philadelphia. Management by committees composed of part-time amateurs had cost the colonies dearly in the War of Independence and few, if any, of the Founders wished to return to that system. The argument was only over how the heads of the necessary departments of government were to be selected, and whether these heads should be wholly subordinate to the President or whether instead they should form some sort of council that would advise the President and perhaps share in his authority. In the end, the Founders left it up to Congress to decide the matter.

There was no dispute in Congress that there should be executive departments, headed by single appointed officials, and, of course, the Constitution specified that these would be appointed by the President with the advice and consent of the Senate. The only issue was how such officials might be removed. After pro-

Reprinted from: James Q. Wilson, "The Rise of the Bureaucratic State," *The Public Interest*, No. 41 (Fall 1975). Reprinted by permission.

longed debate and by the narrowest of majorities, Congress agreed that the President should have the sole right of removal, thus confirming that the infant administrative system would be wholly subordinate—in law at least—to the President. Had not Vice President John Adams, presiding over a Senate equally divided on the issue, cast the deciding vote in favor of Presidential removal, the administrative departments might conceivably have become legal dependencies of the legislature, with incalculable consequences for the development of the embryonic government.

THE "BUREAUCRACY PROBLEM"

The original departments were small and had limited duties. The State Department, the first to be created, had but nine employees in addition to the Secretary. The War Department did not reach 80 civilian employees until 1801; it commanded only a few thousand soldiers. Only the Treasury Department had substantial powers—it collected taxes, managed the public debt, ran the national bank, conducted land surveys, and purchased military supplies. Because of this, Congress gave the closest scrutiny to its structure and its activities.

The number of administrative agencies and employees grew slowly but steadily during the 19th and early 20th centuries and then increased explosively on the occasion of World War I, the Depression, and World War II. It is difficult to say at what point in this process the administrative system became a distinct locus of power or an independent source of political initiatives and problems. What is clear is that the emphasis on the sheer *size* of the administrative establishment—conventional in many treatments of the subject—is misleading.

The government can spend vast sums of money—wisely or unwisely—without creating that set of conditions we ordinarily associate with the bureaucratic state. For example, there could be massive transfer payments made under government auspices from person to person or from state to state, all managed by a comparatively small staff of officials and a few large computers. In 1971, the federal government paid out $54 billion under various social insurance programs, yet the Social Security Administration employs only 73,000 persons, many of whom perform purely routine tasks.

And though it may be harder to believe, the government could in principle employ an army of civilian personnel without giving rise to those organizational patterns that we call bureaucratic. Suppose, for instance, that we as a nation should decide to have in the public schools at least one teacher for every two students. This would require a vast increase in the number of teachers and school rooms, but almost all of the persons added would be performing more or less identical tasks, and they could be organized into very small units (e.g., neighborhood schools). Though there would be significant overhead costs, most citizens would not be aware of any increase in the "bureaucratic" aspects of education—indeed, owing to the much greater time each teacher would have to devote to each pupil and his or her parents, the citizenry might well conclude that there actually had been a substantial reduction in the amount of "bureaucracy."

To the reader predisposed to believe that we have a "bureaucracy problem," these hypothetical cases may seem farfetched. Max Weber, after all, warned us that in capitalist and socialist societies alike, bureaucracy was likely to acquire an "overtowering" power position. Conservatives have always feared bureaucracy, save perhaps the police. Humane socialists have frequently been embarrassed by their inability to reconcile a desire for public control of the economy with the suspicion that a public bureaucracy may be as immune to democratic control as a private one. Liberals have equivocated, either dismissing any concern for bureaucracy as reactionary quibbling about social progress, or embracing that concern when obviously nonreactionary persons (welfare recipients, for example) express a view toward the Department of Health, Education, and Welfare indistinguishable from the view businessmen take of the Internal Revenue Service.

POLITICAL AUTHORITY

There are at least three ways in which political power may be gathered undesirably into bureaucratic hands: by the growth of an administrative apparatus so large as to be immune from popular control, by placing power over a governmental bureaucracy of any size in private rather than public hands, or by vesting discretionary authority in the hands of a public agency so that the exercise of that power is not responsive to the public good. These are not the only problems that arise because of bureaucratic organization. From the point of view of their members, bureaucracies are sometimes uncaring, ponderous, or unfair; from the point of view of their political superiors, they are sometimes unimaginative or inefficient; from the point of view of their clients, they are sometimes slow or unjust. No single account can possibly treat of all that is problematic in bureaucracy; even the part I discuss here—the extent to which political authority has been transferred undesirably to an unaccountable administrative realm—is itself too large for a single essay. But it is, if not the most important problem, then surely the one that would most have troubled our Revolutionary leaders, especially those that went on to produce the Constitution. It was, after all, the question of power that chiefly concerned them, both in redefining our relationship with England and in finding a new basis for political authority in the Colonies.

To some, following in the tradition of Weber, bureaucracy is the inevitable consequence and perhaps necessary concomitant of modernity. A money economy, the division of labor, and the evolution of legal-rational norms to justify organizational authority require the efficient adaptation of means to ends and a high degree of predictability in the behavior of rulers. To this, Georg Simmel added the view that organizations tend to acquire the characteristics of those institutions with which they are in conflict, so that as government becomes more bureaucratic, private organizations—political parties, trade unions, voluntary associations—will have an additional reason to become bureaucratic as well.

By viewing bureaucracy as an inevitable (or, as some would put it, "functional") aspect of society, we find ourselves attracted to theories that explain the growth of bureaucracy in terms of some inner dynamic to which all agencies respond and which makes all barely governable and scarcely tolerable. Bureaucracies grow, we are told, because of Parkinson's Law: Work and personnel expand to consume the available resources. Bureaucracies behave, we believe, in accord with various other maxims, such as the Peter Principle: In hierarchical organizations, personnel are promoted up to that point at which their incompetence becomes manifest—hence, all important positions are held by incompetents. More elegant, if not essentially different, theories have been propounded by scholars. The tendency of all bureaus to expand is explained by William A. Niskanen by the assumption, derived from the theory of the firm, that "bureaucrats maximize the total budget of their bureau during their tenure"—hence, "all bureaus are too large." What keeps them from being not merely too large but all-consuming is the fact that a bureau must deliver to some degree on its promised output, and if it consistently underdelivers, its budget will be cut by unhappy legislators. But since measuring the output of a bureau is often difficult—indeed, even *conceptualizing* the output of the State Department is mind-boggling—the bureau has a great deal of freedom within which to seek the largest possible budget.

Such theories, both the popular and the scholarly, assign little importance to the nature of the tasks an agency performs, the constitutional framework in which it is embedded, or the preferences and attitudes of citizens and legislators. Our approach will be quite different: Different agencies will be examined in historical perspective to discover the kinds of problems, if any, to which their operation gave rise, and how those problems were affected—perhaps determined—by the tasks which they were assigned, the political system in which they operated, and the preferences they were required to consult. What follows will be far from a systematic treatment of such matters, and even farther from a rigorous testing of any theory of bureaucratization: Our knowledge of agency history and behavior is too sketchy to permit that. . . .

BUREAUCRACY AND CLIENTELISM

After 1861, the growth in the federal administrative system could no longer be explained primarily by an expansion of the postal service and other traditional bureaus. Though these continued to expand, new departments were added that reflected a new (or at least greater) emphasis on the enlargement of the scope of government. Between 1861 and 1901, over 200,000 civilian employees were added to the federal service, only 52 per cent of whom were postal workers. Some of these, of course, staffed a larger military and naval establishment stimulated by the Civil War and the Spanish-American War. By 1901 there were over 44,000 civilian defense employees, mostly workers in government-owned arsenals and shipyards. But even these could account for less than one fourth of the increase in employment during the preceding 40 years.

What was striking about the period after 1861 was that the government began to give formal, bureaucratic recognition to the emergence of distinctive interests in a diversifying economy. As Richard L. Schott has written, "whereas earlier federal departments had been formed around specialized governmental functions (foreign affairs, war, finance, and the like), the new departments of this period—Agriculture, Labor, and Commerce—were devoted to the interests and aspirations of particular economic groups."

The original purpose behind these clientele-oriented departments was neither to subsidize nor to regulate, but to promote, chiefly by gathering and publishing statistics and (especially in the case of agriculture) by research. The formation of the Department of Agriculture in 1862 was to become a model, for better or worse, for later political campaigns for government recognition. A private association representing an interest—in this case the United States Agricultural Society—was formed. It made every President from Fillmore to Lincoln an honorary member, it enrolled key Congressmen, and it began to lobby for a new department. The precedent was followed by labor groups, especially the Knights of Labor, to secure creation in 1888 of a Department of Labor. It was broadened in 1903 to be a Department of Commerce and Labor, but 10 years later, at the insistence of the American Federation of Labor, the parts were separated and the two departments we now know were formed.

There was an early 19th-century precedent for the creation of these client-serving departments: the Pension Office, then in the Department of the Interior. Begun in 1833 and regularized in 1849, the Office became one of the largest bureaus of the government in the aftermath of the Civil War, as hundreds of thousands of Union Army veterans were made eligible for pensions if they had incurred a permanent disability or injury while on military duty; dependent widows were also eligible if their husbands had died in service or of service-connected injuries. The Grand Army of the Republic (GAR), the leading veterans' organization, was quick to exert pressure for more generous pension laws and for more liberal administration of such laws as already existed. In 1879 Congressmen, noting the number of ex-servicemen living (and voting) in their states, made veterans eligible for pensions retroactively to the date of their discharge from the service, thus enabling thousands who had been late in filing applications to be rewarded for their dilatoriness. In 1890 the law was changed again to make it unnecessary to have been injured in the service—all that was necessary was to have served and then to have acquired a permanent disability by any means other than through "their own vicious habits." And whenever cases not qualifying under existing law came to the attention of Congress, it promptly passed a special act making those persons eligible by name.

So far as is known, the Pension Office was remarkably free of corruption in the administration of this windfall—and why not, since anything an administrator might deny, a legislator was only too pleased to grant. By 1891 the Commissioner of Pensions observed that his was "the largest executive bureau in the world." There were over 6,000 officials supplemented by thousands of local physicians paid on a fee basis. In 1900 alone, the Office had to process 477,000 cases. Fraud was rampant as thousands of persons brought false or exaggerated claims; as Leonard D. White was later to write, "pensioners and their attorneys seemed to have been engaged in a gigantic conspiracy to defraud their own government." Though the Office struggled to be honest, Congress was indifferent—or more accurately, complaisant: The GAR was a powerful electoral force and it was ably and lucratively assisted by thousands of private pension attorneys. The pattern of bureaucratic clientelism was set in a way later to become a familiar feature of the governmental landscape—a subsidy was initially provided, because it was either popular or unnoticed, to a group that was powerfully benefited and had few or disorganized opponents; the beneficiaries were organized to supervise the administration and ensure the funding of the program; the law authorizing the program, first passed because it seemed the right thing to do, was left intact or even expanded because politically it became the only thing to do. A benefit once bestowed cannot easily be withdrawn.

PUBLIC POWER AND PRIVATE INTERESTS

It was at the state level, however, that client-oriented bureaucracies proliferated in the 19th century. Chief among these were the occupational licensing agencies. At the time of Independence, professions and occupations either could be freely entered (in which case the consumer had to judge the quality of service for himself) or entry was informally controlled by the existing members of the profession or occupation by personal tutelage and the management of reputations. The latter part of the 19th century, however, witnessed the increased use of law and bureaucracy to control entry into a line of work. The state courts generally allowed this on the grounds that it was a proper exercise of the "police power" of the state, but as Morton Keller has observed , "when state courts approved the licensing of barbers and blacksmiths, but not of horse-shoers, it was evident that the principles governing certification were—to put it charitably—elusive ones." By 1952, there were more than 75 different occupations in the United States for which one needed a license to practice, and the awarding of these licenses was typically in the hands of persons already in the occupation, who could act under color of law. These licensing boards—for plumbers, dry cleaners, beauticians, attorneys, undertakers, and the like—frequently have been criticized as particularly flagrant examples of the excesses of a bureaucratic state. But the problems they create—of restricted entry, higher prices, and lengthy and complex initiation procedures—are not primarily the result of some bureaucratic pathology but of the possession of public power by persons who use it for private purposes. Or more accurately, they are the result of using public power in ways that benefited those in the profession in the sincere but unsubstantiated conviction that doing so would benefit the public generally.

The New Deal was perhaps the high water mark of at least the theory of bureaucratic clientelism. Not only did various sectors of society, notably agriculture,

begin receiving massive subsidies, but the government proposed, through the National Industrial Recovery Act (NRA), to cloak with public power a vast number of
industrial groupings and trade associations so that they might control production
and prices in ways that would end the depression. The NRA's Blue Eagle fell before the Supreme Court—the wholesale delegation of public power to private interests was declared unconstitutional. But the piecemeal delegation was not, as
the continued growth of specialized promotional agencies attests. The Civil Aeronautics Board, for example, erroneously thought to be exclusively a regulatory
agency, was formed in 1938 "to promote" as well as to regulate civil aviation and it
has done so by restricting entry and maintaining above-market rate fares.

   Agriculture, of course, provides the leading case of clientelism. Theodore J.
Lowi finds "at least 10 separate, autonomous, local self-governing systems" located in or closely associated with the Department of Agriculture that control to
some significant degree the flow of billions of dollars in expenditures and loans.
Local committees of farmers, private farm organizations, agency heads, and committee chairmen in Congress dominate policy-making in this area—not, perhaps,
to the exclusion of the concerns of other publics, but certainly in ways not powerfully constrained by them. . . .

SELF-PERPETUATING AGENCIES

If the Founding Fathers were to return to examine bureaucratic clientelism, they
would, I suspect, be deeply discouraged. James Madison clearly foresaw that
American society would be "broken into many parts, interests and classes of citizens" and that this "multiplicity of interests" would help ensure against "the
tyranny of the majority," especially in a federal regime with separate branches of
government. Positive action would require a "coalition of a majority"; in the
process of forming this coalition, the rights of all would be protected, not merely
by self-interested bargains, but because in a free society such a coalition "could
seldom take place on any other principles than those of justice and the general
good." To those who wrongly believed that Madison thought of men as acting only
out of base motives, the phrase is instructive: Persuading men who disagree to
compromise their differences can rarely be achieved solely by the parceling out of
relative advantage; the belief is also required that what is being agreed to is right,
proper, and defensible before public opinion.

   Most of the major new social programs of the United States, whether for the
good of the few or the many, were initially adopted by broad coalitions appealing
to general standards of justice or to conceptions of the public weal. This is certainly the case with most of the New Deal legislation—notably such programs as
Social Security—and with most Great Society legislation—notably Medicare and
aid to education; it was also conspicuously the case with respect to post-Great Society legislation pertaining to consumer and environmental concerns. State occupational licensing laws were supported by majorities interested in, among other

things, the contribution of these statutes to public safety and health.

But when a program supplies particular benefits to an existing or newly created interest, public or private, it creates a set of political relationships that make exceptionally difficult further alteration of that program by coalitions of the majority. What was created in the name of the common good is sustained in the name of the particular interest. Bureaucratic clientelism becomes self-perpetuating, in the absence of some crisis or scandal, because a single interest group to which the program matters greatly is highly motivated and well-situated to ward off the criticisms of other groups that have a broad but weak interest in the policy.

In short, a regime of separated powers makes it difficult to overcome objections and contrary interests sufficiently to permit the enactment of a new program or the creation of a new agency. Unless the legislation can be made to pass either with little notice or at a time of crisis or extraordinary majorities—and sometimes even then—the initiation of new programs requires public interest arguments. But the same regime works to protect agencies, once created, from unwelcome change because a major change is, in effect, new legislation that must overcome the same hurdles as the original law, but this time with one of the hurdles—the wishes of the agency and its client—raised much higher. As a result, the Madisonian system makes it relatively easy for the delegation of public power to private groups to go unchallenged and, therefore, for factional interests that have acquired a supportive public bureaucracy to rule without submitting their interests to the effective scrutiny and modification of other interests. . . .

Bureaucracy

Max Weber

1: CHARACTERISTICS OF BUREAUCRACY

Modern officialdom functions in the following specific manner:

I. There is the principle of fixed and official jurisdictional areas, which are generally ordered by rules, that is, by laws or administrative regulations.

1. The regular activities required for the purposes of the bureaucratically governed structure are distributed in a fixed way as official duties.
2. The authority to give the commands required for the discharge of these duties is distributed in a stable way and is strictly delimited by rules concerning the coercive means, physical, sacerdotal, or otherwise, which may be placed at the disposal of officials.
3. Methodical provision is made for the regular and continuous fulfilment of these duties and for the execution of the corresponding rights; only persons who have the generally regulated qualifications to serve are employed.

In public and lawful government these three elements constitute 'bureaucratic authority.' In private economic domination, they constitute bureaucratic 'management.' Bureaucracy, thus understood, is fully developed in political and ecclesiastical communities only in the modern state, and, in the private economy, only in the most advanced institutions of capitalism. Permanent and public office authority, with fixed jurisdiction, is not the historical rule but rather the exception. This is so even in large political structures such as those of the ancient Orient, the Germanic and Mongolian empires of conquest, or of many feudal structures of state. In all these cases, the ruler executes the most important measures through personal trustees, table-companions, or court-servants. Their commissions and authority are not precisely delimited and are temporarily called into being for each case.

II. The principles of office hierarchy and of levels of graded authority mean a firmly ordered system of super- and subordination in which there is a supervision of the lower offices by the higher ones. Such a system offers the governed the possibility of appealing the decision of a lower office to its higher authority, in a definitely regulated manner. With the full development of the bureaucratic type, the office hierarchy is monocratically organized. The principle of hierarchical of-

From Max Weber, "Bureaucracy," in *From Max Weber: Essays in Sociology*, edited and translated by H. H. Gerth and C. Wright Mills. Copyright 1946 by Oxford University Press, Inc.; renewed 1973 by Hans H. Gerth. Reprinted by permission of the publisher.

fice authority is found in all bureaucratic structures: in state and ecclesiastical structures as well as in large party organizations and private enterprises. It does not matter for the character of bureaucracy whether its authority is called 'private' or 'public.'

When the principle of jurisdictional 'competency' is fully carried through, hierarchical subordination—at least in public office—does not mean that the 'higher' authority is simply authorized to take over the business of the 'lower.' Indeed, the opposite is the rule. Once established and having fulfilled its task, an office tends to continue in existence and be held by another incumbent.

III. The management of the modern office is based upon written documents ('the files'), which are preserved in their original or draught form. There is, therefore, a staff of subaltern officials and scribes of all sorts. The body of officials actively engaged in a 'public' office, along with the respective apparatus of material implements and the files, make up a 'bureau.' In private enterprise, 'the bureau' is often called 'the office.'

In principle, the modern organization of the civil service separates the bureau from the private domicile of the official, and, in general, bureaucracy segregates official activity as something distinct from the sphere of private life. Public monies and equipment are divorced from the private property of the official. This condition is everywhere the product of a long development. Nowadays, it is found in public as well as in private enterprises; in the latter, the principle extends even to the leading entrepreneur. In principle, the executive office is separated from the household, business from private correspondence, and business assets from private fortunes. The more consistently the modern type of business management has been carried through the more are these separations the case. The beginnings of this process are to be found as early as the Middle Ages.

It is the peculiarity of the modern entrepreneur that he conducts himself as the 'first official' of his enterprise, in the very same way in which the ruler of a specifically modern bureaucratic state spoke of himself as 'the first servant' of the state.[1] The idea that the bureau activities of the state are intrinsically different in character from the management of private economic offices is a continental European notion and, by way of contrast, is totally foreign to the American way.

IV. Office management, at least all specialized office management—and such management is distinctly modern—usually presupposes thorough and expert training. This increasingly holds for the modern executive and employee of private enterprises, in the same manner as it holds for the state official.

V. When the office is fully developed, official activity demands the full working capacity of the official, irrespective of the fact that his obligatory time in the bureau may be firmly delimited. In the normal case, this is only the product of a long development, in the public as well as in the private office. Formerly, in all cases, the normal state of affairs was reversed: official business was discharged as a secondary activity.

VI. The management of the office follows general rules, which are more or less stable, more or less exhaustive, and which can be learned. Knowledge of these rules represents a special technical learning which the officials possess. It involves jurisprudence, or administrative or business management.

The reduction of modern office management to rules is deeply embedded in its very nature. The theory of modern public administration, for instance, assumes that the authority to order certain matters by decree—which has been legally granted to public authorities—does not entitle the bureau to regulate the matter by commands given for each case, but only to regulate the matter abstractly. This stands in extreme contrast to the regulation of all relationships through individual privileges and bestowals of favor, which is absolutely dominant in patrimonialism, at least in so far as such relationships are not fixed by sacred tradition.

2: THE POSITION OF THE OFFICIAL

All this results in the following for the internal and external position of the official:

I. Office holding is a 'vocation.' This is shown, first, in the requirement of a firmly prescribed course of training, which demands the entire capacity for work for a long period of time, and in the generally prescribed and special examinations which are prerequisites of employment. Furthermore, the position of the official is in the nature of a duty. This determines the internal structure of his relations, in the following manner: Legally and actually, office holding is not considered a source to be exploited for rents or emoluments, as was normally the case during the Middle Ages and frequently up to the threshold of recent times. Nor is office holding considered a usual exchange of services for equivalents, as is the case with free labor contracts. Entrance into an office, including one in the private economy, is considered an acceptance of a specific obligation of faithful management in return for a secure existence. It is decisive for the specific nature of modern loyalty to an office that, in the pure type, it does not establish a relationship to a *person*, like the vassal's or disciple's faith in feudal or in patrimonial relations of authority. Modern loyalty is devoted to impersonal and functional purposes. Behind the functional purposes, of course, 'ideas of culture-values' usually stand. These are *ersatz* for the earthly or supra-mundane personal master: ideas such as 'state,' 'church,' 'community,' 'party,' or 'enterprise' are thought of as being realized in a community; they provide an ideological halo for the master.

The political official—at least in the fully developed modern state—is not considered the personal servant of a ruler. Today, the bishop, the priest, and the preacher are in fact no longer, as in early Christian times, holders of purely personal charisma. The supra-mundane and sacred values which they offer are given to everybody who seems to be worthy of them and who asks for them. In former times, such leaders acted upon the personal command of their master; in principle, they were responsible only to him. Nowadays, in spite of the partial survival of the old theory, such religious leaders are officials in the service of a functional purpose, which in the present-day 'church' has become routinized and, in turn, ideologically hallowed.

II. The personal position of the official is patterned in the following way:

1. Whether he is in a private office or a public bureau, the modern official always strives and usually enjoys a distinct *social esteem* as compared with the governed. His social position is guaranteed by the prescriptive rules of rank order and, for the political official, by special definitions of the criminal code against 'insults of officials' and 'contempt' of state and church authorities.

The actual social position of the official is normally highest where, as in old civilized countries, the following conditions prevail: a strong demand for administration by trained experts; a strong and stable social differentiation, where the official predominantly derives from socially and economically privileged strata because of the social distribution of power; or where the costliness of the required training and status conventions are binding upon him. The possession of educational certificates—to be discussed elsewhere[2]—are usually linked with qualification for office. Naturally, such certificates or patents enhance the 'status element' in the social position of the official. For the rest this status factor in individual cases is explicitly and impassively acknowledged; for example, in the prescription that the acceptance or rejection of an aspirant to an official career depends upon the consent ('election') of the members of the official body. This is the case in the German army with the officer corps. Similar phenomena, which promote this guild-like closure of officialdom, are typically found in patrimonial and, particularly, in prebendal officialdoms of the past. The desire to resurrect such phenomena in changed forms is by no means infrequent among modern bureaucrats. For instance, they have played a role among the demands of the quite proletarian and expert officials (the *tretyj* element) during the Russian revolution.

Usually the social esteem of the officials as such is especially low where the demand for expert administration and the dominance of status conventions are weak. This is especially the case in the United States; it is often the case in new settlements by virtue of their wide fields for profit-making and the great instability of their social stratification.

2. The pure type of bureaucratic official is *appointed* by a superior authority. An official elected by the governed is not a purely bureaucratic figure. Of course, the formal existence of an election does not by itself mean that no appointment hides behind the election—in the state, especially, appointment by party chiefs. Whether or not this is the case does not depend upon legal statutes but upon the way in which the party mechanism functions. Once firmly organized, the parties can turn a formally free election into the mere acclamation of a candidate designated by the party chief. As a rule, however, a formally free election is turned into a fight, conducted according to definite rules, for votes in favor of one of two designated candidates.

In all circumstances, the designation of officials by means of an election among the governed modifies the strictness of hierarchical subordination. In principle, an official who is so elected has an autonomous position opposite the superordinate official. The elected official does not derive his position 'from above' but 'from below,' or at least not from a superior authority of the official hierarchy but from powerful party men ('bosses'), who also determine his further career. The career of the elected official is not, or at least not primarily, dependent upon his chief in the administration. The official who is not elected but appointed by a chief normally functions more exactly, from a technical point of view, because, all other circumstances being equal, it is more likely that purely functional points of consideration and qualities will determine his selection and career. As laymen, the governed can become acquainted with the extent to which a candidate is expertly qualified for office only in terms of experience, and hence only after his service. Moreover, in every sort of selection of officials by election, parties quite naturally give decisive weight not to expert considerations but to the services a follower renders to the party boss. This holds for all kinds of procurement of officials by elections, for the designation of formally free, elected officials by party bosses when they determine the slate of candidates, or the free appointment by a chief who has himself been elected. The contrast, however, is relative: substantially similar conditions hold where legitimate monarchs and their subordinates appoint officials, except that the influence of the followings are then less controllable.

Where the demand for administration by trained experts is considerable, and the party followings have to recognize an intellectually developed, educated, and freely moving 'public opinion,' the use of unqualified officials falls back upon the party in power at the next election. Naturally, this is more likely to happen when the officials are appointed by the chief. The demand for a trained administration now exists in the United States, but in the large cities, where immigrant votes are 'corraled,' there is, of course, no educated public opinion. Therefore, popular elections of the administrative chief and also of his subordinate officials usually endanger the expert qualification of the official as well as the precise functioning of the bureaucratic mechanism. It also weakens the dependence of the officials upon the hierarchy. This holds at least for the large administrative bodies that are difficult to supervise. The superior qualification and integrity of federal judges, appointed by the President, as over against elected judges in the United States is well known, although both types of officials have been selected primarily in terms of party considerations. The great changes in American metropolitan administrations demanded by reformers have proceeded essentially from elected mayors working with an apparatus of officials who were appointed by them. These reforms have thus come about in a 'Caesarist' fashion. Viewed technically, as an organized form of authority, the efficiency of 'Caesarism,' which often grows out of democracy, rests in general upon the position of the 'Caesar' as a free trustee of the masses (of the army or of the citizenry), who is unfettered by tradition. The 'Caesar' is thus the unrestrained master of a body of highly qualified military officers and officials whom he selects freely and personally without regard to tradition or to any other considerations. This 'rule of the personal genius,' however, stands in contradiction to the formally 'democratic' principle of a universally elected officialdom.

3. Normally, the position of the official is held for life, at least in public bureaucracies; and this is increasingly the case for all similar structures. As a factual

rule, *tenure for life* is presupposed, even where the giving of notice or periodic reappointment occurs. In contrast to the worker in a private enterprise, the official normally holds tenure. Legal or actual life-tenure, however, is not recognized as the official's right to the possession of office, as was the case with many structures of authority in the past. Where legal guarantees against arbitrary dismissal or transfer are developed, they merely serve to guarantee a strictly objective discharge of specific office duties free from all personal considerations. In Germany, this is the case for all juridical and, increasingly, for all administrative officials.

Within the bureaucracy, therefore, the measure of 'independence,' legally guaranteed by tenure, is not always a source of increased status for the official whose position is thus secured. Indeed, often the reverse holds, especially in old cultures and communities that are highly differentiated. In such communities, the stricter the subordination under the arbitrary rule of the master, the more it guarantees the maintenance of the conventional seigneurial style of living for the official. Because of the very absence of these legal guarantees of tenure, the conventional esteem for the official may rise in the same way as, during the Middle Ages, the esteem of the nobility of office[3] rose at the expense of esteem for the freemen, and as the king's judge surpassed that of the people's judge. In Germany, the military officer or the administrative official can be removed from office at any time, or at least far more readily than the 'independent judge,' who never pays with loss of his office for even the grossest offense against the 'code of honor' or against social conventions of the salon. For this very reason, if other things are equal, in the eyes of the master stratum the judge is considered less qualified for social intercourse than are officers and administrative officials, whose greater dependence on the master is a greater guarantee of their conformity with status conventions. Of course, the average official strives for a civil-service law, which would materially secure his old age and provide increased guarantees against his arbitrary removal from office. This striving, however, has its limits. A very strong development of the 'right to the office' naturally makes it more difficult to staff them with regard to technical efficiency, for such a development decreases the career-opportunities of ambitious candidates for office. This makes for the fact that officials, on the whole, do not feel their dependency upon those at the top. This lack of a feeling of dependency, however, rests primarily upon the inclination to depend upon one's equals rather than upon the socially inferior and governed strata. The present conservative movement among the Badenia clergy, occasioned by the anxiety of a presumably threatening separation of church and state, has been expressly determined by the desire not to be turned 'from a master into a servant of the parish.'[4]

4. The official receives the regular *pecuniary* compensation of a normally fixed *salary* and the old age security provided by a pension. The salary is not measured like a wage in terms of work done, but according to 'status,' that is, according to the kind of function (the 'rank') and, in addition, possibly, according to the length of service. The relatively great security of the official's income, as well as the rewards of social esteem, make the office a sought-after position, especially in

countries which no longer provide opportunities for colonial profits. In such countries, this situation permits relatively low salaries for officials.

5. The official is set for a *'career'* within the hierarchical order of the public service. He moves from the lower, less important, and lower paid to the higher positions. The average official naturally desires a mechanical fixing of the conditions of promotion: if not of the offices, at least of the salary levels. He wants these conditions fixed in terms of 'seniority,' or possibly according to grades achieved in a developed system of expert examinations. Here and there, such examinations actually form a character *indelebilis* of the official and have lifelong effects on his career. To this is joined the desire to qualify the right to office and the increasing tendency toward status group closure and economic security. All of this makes for a tendency to consider the offices as 'prebends' of those who are qualified by educational certificates. The necessity of taking general personal and intellectual qualifications into consideration, irrespective of the often subaltern character of the educational certificate, has led to a condition in which the highest political offices, especially the positions of 'ministers,' are principally filled without reference to such certificates. . . .

NOTES

1. Frederick II of Prussia.
2. Cf. *Wirtzchaft und Gesellschaft*, pp. 73 ff. and part II. (German Editor.)
3. 'Ministerialen.'
4. Written before 1914. (German Editor's note.)

Regulation: Politics, Bureaucracy, and Economics

Kenneth J. Meier

The study of regulatory policymaking is dominated by two perspectives (Weingast and Moran, 1983).[1] One view holds that regulatory agencies are vested with vast discretion and are the major force in regulatory policy. Among the agency characteristics that affect policy outputs are professional values, policy expertise, bu-

From Kenneth J. Meier, *Regulation: Politics, Bureaucracy, & Economics* (New York: St. Martin's Press, 1985). Copyright © 1985. Reprinted with permission of St. Martin's Press, Incorporated.

reaucratic entrepreneurs, and agency structure (e.g., see Wilson, 1980; Katzman, 1980).[2] A second view suggests that regulatory agencies are dominated by their environment. Interest groups, legislative committees, economic forces, and technological change are among the determinants of policy (e.g., see Stigler, 1971; Lowi, 1969; Mazmanian and Sabatier, 1980).[3] Both views are essentially incomplete. Regulatory policy is a product of both regulatory bureaucracies and environmental forces. This chapter develops an outline of the regulatory process that integrates both these explanations. Although the conceptual framework developed is moderately complex, so is regulatory policy. Little is gained by introducing simple views of regulation that are not linked to the real world.

REGULATORY POLICY OUTPUTS

The study of regulation is important because it is part of the policy process that allocates values among members of society. It is, as Lasswell[4] (1936) described politics, a determination of "Who gets what, when and how." In short, what is important about regulatory policy from a political perspective is, Who benefits from regulation?

Although much regulation literature has focused on who benefits from regulation, this focus has been muddied by relying on the concept of the public interest. Bernstein's (1955)[5] theory that regulatory agencies in the long run were captured by the regulated industries contrasted reality with an ideal standard of regulation in the public interest (see also Stigler, 1971; Peltzman, 1976).[6] Unfortunately, defining the public interest in regulatory policy has been as elusive as it has been in other areas of politics (see Schubert, 1960).[7] Even the most self-serving appeal by a regulated group is now phrased as a quest for the public interest.

In a perceptive essay, Paul Sabatier (1977)[8] proposed an alternative to the public interest theory of regulation; regulatory policy can be arrayed on a continuum from self-regulation (regulation in the interests of the regulated) to aggressive regulation (regulation of one individual in the interests of another).[9] Sabatier's thesis can be divided into two separate dimensions—the degree to which regulation benefits the regulated industry and the degree to which it benefits nonregulated individuals such as consumers. These are two separate dimensions rather than poles on a single continuum.

As figure 1 reveals, the two dimensions of beneficiaries produce four extreme types of regulation. Cell 1 contains policies designed to benefit the regulated but not the nonregulated, the traditional "captured" regulation. Regulation by state occupational regulators is a classic example of cell 1 regulation. Cell 3 contains those policies whereby an industry is regulated for the benefit of another party. Occupational safety and health regulation, for example, restricts industry behavior in an attempt to benefit workers. Cell 4 contains those policies that benefit both the regulated and some portion of the nonregulated. Bank regulation and deposit insurance following the Great Depression benefited both depositors by guaranteeing the safety of their funds and the banks by encouraging the use of banks. Finally, cell 2 includes policies that benefit no one. Current antitrust policy concerning price discrimination appears to harm both businesses that wish to compete and consumers.

Although who benefits from regulatory policy is not always easy to discover, the question provides a focal point for comparing unlike regulatory policies. This text will examine two aspects of regulatory policy—what is the current set of regulatory policies, and who benefits from them? The conceptual framework in this chapter permits us to explain why regulatory agencies act as they do and why regulatory policies benefit whom they do.

SUBSYSTEM POLITICS

Although regulatory policies can be produced directly by legislatures, the chief executive, or the courts, in general, regulatory policy is implemented via bureaucracy. Typically, broad areas of regulatory discretion are granted to a regulatory agency by these political institutions of government. The Interstate Commerce Commission, for example, is charged with regulating interstate commerce with only a vague goal (the "public interest") as a guide. The policymaking activities of bureaucratic agencies can best be understood by examining the subsystem in which these agencies operate.

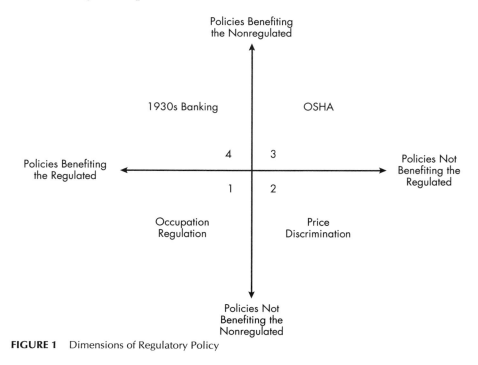

FIGURE 1   Dimensions of Regulatory Policy

That public policy is made in semiautonomous subsystems composed of government bureaus, congressional committees, and interest groups has been a basic tenet of political analysis since the 1950s (see Freeman, 1965; McConnell, 1966).[10] Subsystems exist because the American political system fragments political power (Long, 1962).[11] With its division of federal authority into three branches—executive, legislative, and judicial—each operating with constraints on the other two, political power at the national level is fragmented among numerous political actors. Power is further divided by the federal system and informally kept that way by broker political parties that seek electoral success rather than unified political government. As a result, political power is not concentrated enough to dominate the policy process.

The fragmentation is exacerbated by the numerous policy issues that compete for attention on the policy agenda. Major political institutions must constantly jump from crisis to crisis—social security today, gasoline user fees tomorrow, MX missiles next week. Power in a given issue area flows to those who retain a continuing interest in it. In American politics a continuing interest usually means the permanent bureaucracy, specialized congressional committees, and the interest groups affected by the issue.

Policy subsystems can operate in a relatively independent fashion from the major political institutions *if* the members of the policy subsystem can satisfy each others' needs. The bureaucracy makes policy. It issues the permits, exceptions, and punishments; but to do so it needs resources and legislative authority. Congressional committees can provide the funds and authority needed by the bureau to operate, but the committee members need to be reelected. Reelection requires political support and campaign contributions. The interest groups affiliated with the regulated industry need the outputs that the bureaucracy is creating, especially if the outputs are favorable; and they have the political resources to commit to members of congressional committees. In combination, the members of the subsystem can often supply the needs of the other members. If all the needs of the subsystem members are satisfied, then subsystem members make no major demands on the macropolitical system. In turn, the subsystem is given autonomy.

Although subsystems have been fruitfully applied to numerous areas of political research (see Ripley and Franklin, 1980),[12] recent work suggests that subsystems are not the homogeneous "iron triangles" that they are portrayed to be (see Heclo, 1978; Sabatier, 1983).[13] First, interest groups, even industry groups, rarely agree completely about regulatory policy. Dissension among airline companies permitted deregulation of airline fares in the 1970s (Behrman, 1980);[14] broadcasting interests are fragmented into several groups with vastly different goals, including groups representing networks, independent stations, religious broadcasters, ultrahigh frequency (UHF) stations, frequency modulation (FM) stations, and countless others (Krasnow, Longley, and Terry, 1982).[15] Second, interest groups other than industry groups actively participate in the regulatory subsystem. Consumer groups are active in the auto safety, drug regulation, and consumer products subsystems; labor unions are active in safety regulation and sometimes in environmental regulation. Rarely do industry groups have the opportunity to operate without opposition.

Third, subsystems are often divided among several different subcommittees each with different policy objectives. Environmental protection programs, for example, are under the jurisdiction of seven committees in the House and five in the Senate (Kenski and Kenski, 1984: 111).[16] Even with only a single committee involved in a subsystem, policy conflict occurs. Conflicting positions by the Commerce Committees at different times during the 1970s resulted in a series of policy changes by the Federal Trade Commission (Weingast and Moran, 1982).[17] Fourth, a variety of other actors penetrate the subsystem to urge policy actions, including journalists and scholars who generate important information on policy options. Such issues as acid rain, pesticide regulation, drug safety, and others were placed on the agenda by such actors.

Fifth, one subsystem will sometimes overlap one or more other subsystems, thus adding additional actors to the political battles and creating greater conflict. Environmental protection subsystems collided with energy subsystems following the Arab oil embargo; insurance subsystems and automobile regulation subsystems came into conflict following the Reagan administration's relaxation of automobile safety regulations.

Finally, the subsystems concept ignores the vital role of state and local government officials in the regulatory process. In many areas, federal regulatory programs are implemented by state governments; environmental protection and workplace health and safety are prominent examples. In a variety of other areas such as consumer protection, antitrust, and equal employment opportunity policies, both the federal government and state governments operate programs. Often the policy goals of state regulators can differ significantly from those of federal regulators (see Rowland and Marz, 1982),[18] resulting in policy outputs different from those intended by the federal government. This conflict can result in either more vigorous regulation or less vigorous regulation depending on state objectives. California's aggressive mobile source air pollution regulation in the 1960s and 1970s, for example, often preceded federal efforts, but state-run workplace safety programs lag behind federal-run programs.

In figure 2 an expanded version of the subsystem is shown that includes other (i.e., nonindustry) interest groups, significant others (e.g., researchers, journalists), and state governments in addition to the "iron" triangle. Paul Sabatier (1983) argues that policy subsystems can best be viewed as opposing advocacy coalitions; a coalition of industry and its allies (members of Congress, other groups, and so on) is opposed by other interest groups and their allies. Under such a conceptualization, the traditional iron triangle becomes a special case of a policy subsystem with only one advocacy coalition.

Among the most important aspects of policy subsystems is how open the subsystems are to outside influences via the chief executive, the legislature, and other nonsubsystem actors. Policy subsystems are perceived as fairly consensual, and in areas of distributive politics—health care research, agricultural policy, and

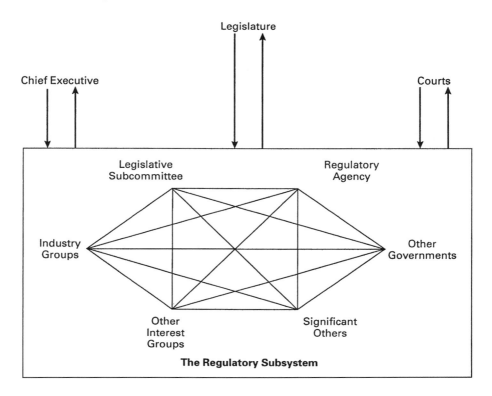

FIGURE 2. The Regulatory Policy System

educational aid—they are (Ripley and Franklin, 1980). The distribution of tangible benefits paid for by general tax revenues ties the members of the subsystems closely together. Consensual subsystems resolve policy issues internally and present a unified front to the larger political system. As a result, consensual subsystems are usually allowed to operate without outside interference.

Regulatory subsystems are not as consensual as those in distributive policy and, therefore, are more likely to be affected by outside influences for several reasons. First, regulatory policy restricts choice so that an industry is likely to see regulation as a mixed blessing. Regulated industries may defend their regulator when it is attacked by other political actors (e.g., the airlines and the Civil Aeronautics Board (CAB) circa 1976), but they are slower to come to the defense and less committed when they do so. Second, members of Congress are likely to be less committed to a regulatory subsystem than to a distributive subsystem. Unlike other policies, regulation often imposes direct costs. A member of Congress from a rural district will receive far more credit from constituents if he or she is on the soil conservation subcommittee distributing benefits than if he or she is on the environmental committee limiting pesticide use. Third, regulatory subsystems are likely to have more nonindustry groups that want to participate in the subsystem. The Federal Communications Commission (FCC), for example, cannot operate in a consensual, autonomous subsystem because numerous interests other than the television industry are also interested in regulating television. Politicians, the movie industry, cable operators, the phone company, and many others see television as important to their interests; accordingly, they will seek to participate in FCC decisions.

REGULATORY AGENCIES: INSIDE THE BLACK BOX

Government agencies are not passive actors pushed along at the whim of other subsystem members. They shape as well as respond to pressures from the subsystem (Rourke, 1984).[19] The U.S. Department of Agriculture (USDA), for example, played a role in creating and developing the American Farm Bureau; Farm Bureau members, in turn, assisted the USDA in crop regulation. The Environmental Protection Agency funds academic research on pollution; such research is then used in debates over environmental protection. In a sense, both agencies helped create a portion of the subsystem. If bureaus can take an active role in structuring their environments, they need not passively respond to subsystem pressures. They can actively seek to influence the forces impinging on regulatory policy. To understand the policy actions of regulatory agencies, two variables—goals and resources—must be discussed.

Agency Goals

Every regulatory agency has goals including policy goals that agency employees wish to attain. Environmental Protection Agency employees seek cleaner air and water; FDA personnel pursue safe and effective drugs. Although this contention may seem trivial, many treatments of bureaucracy either assume an organization's sole goal is to survive or that the bureaucrats' goal is to maximize their income (e.g., see Niskanen, 1971).[20] Both approaches provide a misleading view of regulatory agencies.

This distinction merits some discussion. If we assume, as Niskanen does, that bureaucrats are rational utility maximizers, regulators clearly seek goals other than income maximization. Because incomes are higher in the regulated industry, an income maximizer would choose to work for the regulated industry rather than the regulatory agency. The choice to enter the public sector is not dictated by inferior skills because studies show that public sector employees in jobs similar to private sector ones have greater skills and better training (Guyot, 1979).[21] A public sector bureaucrat, therefore, must be maximizing something other than income; the most logical thing to maximize is policy goals.

Ascribing regulatory policy goals to bureaucrats is consistent with motivation theory (e.g., Maslow, 1970)[22] and empirical evidence. Employees work for the Office of Civil Rights because they believe in racial equality (Romzek and Hendricks, 1982).[23] Individuals work for OSHA because they desire to improve workplace safety (Kelman, 1980).[24] In the long run, most agency employees become advocates of the agency and its goals (Downs, 1967).[25] Those interested in higher incomes or in the goals of the regulated industry will probably leave the agency.

Having policy goals does not mean that bureaucrats would not like to see their organization survive, all things being equal. Survival, after all, is necessary to obtain most policy goals. In some cases, the present Civil Aeronautics Board bureaucrats, for example, are content to accomplish policy objectives that will eventually eliminate the agency. In sum then, regulators regulate because they wish to attain policy goals; without understanding that regulators are goal-seeking and without determining what those goals are, regulatory behavior will appear random to the outside observer.

Also important in terms of regulatory goals is the potential for goal conflict within an agency. Such lack of consensus might result from several different conflicts within the organization: central staff versus field personnel, professionals versus administrators, one profession versus another profession, career staff versus political appointees. The last source of conflict is especially important. Career staff are more likely to identify with the agency and be strongly committed to its programs (Heclo, 1977).[26] Political appointees are more likely to see themselves as the president's representative (Welborn, 1977)[27] and, therefore, hold different views.

Resources

In pursuit of policy goals, regulatory agencies have access to five resources—expertise, cohesion, legislative authority, policy salience, and leadership.[28] Access to such resources determines the value of the agency's participation to other subsystem members. The greater a regulatory agency's resources, the more likely the agency will be able to resist industry pressures for regulation solely in the interests of the industry.

Expertise. Bureaucratic organizations are designed to develop and store knowledge. To a degree greater than legislatures or courts, bureaucracies can divide tasks and gain knowledge via specialization (Rourke, 1984: 16). An EPA employee, for example, could spend an entire career dealing with the intricacies of regulating the pesticide mirex. As part of specialization, American government bureaucracies recruit skilled technocrats as employees, and the agencies become professionalized. A professionalized agency often adopts the values of the predominant profession; the values of safety and health professionals in the Occupational Safety and Health Administration, for example, are the reason why OSHA relies on engineering standards (Kelman, 1980).

Professionalization and specialization permit an agency to develop independent sources of knowledge so that the agency need not rely on the industry (or others) for its information. Although the levels of professionalism and specialization in regulatory agencies cannot rival those of such agencies as the National Institutes of Health, they are a factor. The Nobel laureate Glenn Seaborg's appointment to head the Atomic Energy Commission (AEC; now the Nuclear Regulatory Commission) increased the AEC's reputation for expertise. Similarly, the creation of a separate research arm for the Environmental Protection Agency provided the EPA with expertise it could use in its political battles (Davies and Davies, 1975).[29]

Professionalism does not mean that an agency is dominated by a single profession. At times one or more professions may be struggling for control of the agency. In the Federal Trade Commission (FTC), for example, economists and lawyers have long fought over control of the FTC's antitrust functions. The professional conflict, in fact, has major policy implications. Lawyers prefer cases that can be quickly brought to trial like Robinson-Patman cases. Economists favor either major structural monopoly cases that will significantly increase competition or cases against collusion.

Cohesion. A second resource permitting the agency to affect public policy is the cohesiveness of the bureau's personnel. If agency personnel are united in pursuit of their goals, coalitions opposed to agency actions will need to develop their own sources of information to challenge agency decisions. A cohesive agency is far more difficult to resist than an agency that engages in public disputes over policy direction. Cohesion, in turn, is a function of an agency's goals and its ability to socialize members to accept these goals. Some public agencies such as the Marine Corps or the Forest Service even go so far as to create an organizational ideology for their members. Although no regulatory agency engages in the same degree of socialization that the Marine Corps does, they do seek consciously or unconsciously to influence the values of employees. Bureaucrats in the Environmental Protection Agency, for example, show much greater concern for environmental protection than for compliance costs. The Office of Education in the 1960s was a zealous advocate of school desegregation.

Legislative authority. All regulatory agencies must have legislative authority to operate, but all grants of legislative authority are not equal (see Sabatier, 1977: 424–431). Five important differences in legislative authority exist and contribute to agency resources. First, policy goals as expressed in legislation can be specific or vague. Before 1973, Congress specified agricultural price support levels exactly, leaving little discretion for Agriculture Department regulators. In contrast, the Interstate Commerce Commission regulates interstate commerce with the general goal that regulation should be in the public interest. The more vague the legislative expression of goals, the greater the agency's ability to set regulatory policy. Specific policy goals should be correlated with regulation in the interests of whichever group has the best access to Congress. Consequently, specific goals are associated both with the regulation in the interests of the regulated (e.g., agriculture) and with regulation for the benefit of the nonregulated (e.g., environmental protection; see Marcus, 1980).[30]

Second, legislative delegations vary in the scope of authority they grant. Some agencies have jurisdiction over every firm in the industry (e.g., EPA). Other agencies might be denied jurisdiction over portions of their industry; OSHA's law, for example, exempts small farms. An agency with limited authority cannot affect the behavior of those outside its jurisdiction. The greater the limitations and restrictions on a regulatory agency, the more likely such an agency will regulate in the interest of the regulated industry.

Third, legislative delegations vary in the sanctions permitted to an agency. Bank regulators possess a wide variety of sanctions that can greatly influence the profits and viability of financial institutions. In contrast, the Equal Employment Opportunity Commission (EEOC) has no sanctions and must rely on court action to extract compliance. The greater the range of sanctions available to a regulatory agency, the more likely the agency will regulate in the interests of the nonregulated.

Fourth, regulatory agencies differ in their organizational structure. The two most common structural forms are the department regulatory agency (an agency headed by one person within a larger executive department) and the independent regulatory commission (a multimember board that reports directly to the legislature). Although the different structures do not appear related to performance (see Meier, 1980; Welborn, 1977),[31] often independent regulatory commissions are subjected to other restraints. At the state level, regulatory commissions are often by law composed of members of the regulated industry. When selection restrictions such as this occur, regulation in the interests of the regulated is a given.

Fifth, legislative grants of authority often specify agency procedures. The FTC must follow the lengthy *formal* rule-making process to issue rules, and the Consumer Product Safety Commission was handicapped until recently with a cumbersome "offeror" procedure. Other agencies such as the EEOC and the antitrust regulators are limited further because they must use the courts to set policy and resolve disputes. The more restrictive an agency's procedures are, the less likely the agency will be able to regulate the industry closely.

Political salience.   The salience of a regulatory issue (i.e., its perceived importance by the public) can be used as a resource in the agency's regulatory battles. Regulatory issues vary greatly in salience. Nuclear plant regulation after the Three Mile Island accident was a highly salient issue to political elites and the general public. State regulation of barbers, on the other hand, is rarely salient. Not only does salience vary across issue areas, it also varies across time within an issue area. Banking regulation was highly salient in 1933 but not so in 1973.

According to William Gormley (1983),[32] salience determines the willingness of political elites to intervene in the regulatory process. When issues become salient, the rewards for successful intervention are greater for elected officials. In salient issue areas, therefore, regulators will find their actions closely watched by political elites whereas in nonsalient areas regulatory discretion is likely to go unchecked. A lack of salience should be to the advantage of the regulated industry because it will have little opposition to its demands.

Leadership.   The final regulatory resource is the agency's leadership. Unlike the career bureaucracy, which is fairly stable, leadership positions turn over frequently. Two elements of leadership are important—quality and the leader's goals. Quality of leadership is a nebulous resource that, though difficult to define, is clearly a factor. The leadership abilities of Alfred Kahn as Civil Aeronautics Board chairperson were instrumental in deregulating airlines; the absence of strong leadership in Federal Trade Commission chairman Paul Rand Dixon was often cited as a reason for poor performance by the pre-1969 FTC.

Essential to understanding the impact of leadership are the policy goals of regulatory agency heads. Through the leadership of Caspar Weinberger, Miles Kirkpatrick, and Michael Pertschuk, the Federal Trade Commission became less tied to the interests of the regulated industry and more interested in consumer issues. The appointment of Reese Taylor to head the Interstate Commerce Commission in 1981 signaled an end to the rapid movement toward deregulation of the trucking industry.

Leadership is especially important because the agency head is the focal point for interaction with the subsystem. In such interactions, the agency head is constrained by the expertise, cohesion, legislative authority, issue salience, and policy goals of the agency. An agency head who acts in opposition to the values and normal policy activities of the career staff risks political opposition from within the agency. Anne Burford's effort to alter environmental policy in the 1980s and the response of the EPA career staff is a classic example of this.

Agency Discretion: A Recapitulation

Regulatory agencies, therefore, exercise some discretion in regulatory policy. This discretion is not limitless, however. The amount of discretion accorded an agency is a function of its resources (expertise, cohesion, legislative authority, policy salience, and leadership) and the tolerances of other actors in the political system. Each actor has a zone of acceptance (see Simon, 1957); and if agency decisions fall within that zone, no action will be taken. Because regulatory policy is more important to subsystem actors, the zone of acceptance for subsystem actors is probably narrower than that for macropolitical system actors (e.g., the president). Consequently, subsystem actors will be more active.

As long as the regulatory subsystem produces policies within the zone of acceptance of Congress, the president, and the courts, then these actors will permit the subsystem some autonomy. Actions outside the zone of acceptance will bring attempts to intervene. The size of the zones of acceptance should vary with both salience and complexity (see Gormley, 1983). Salience increases the benefits of successful intervention to a political actor, and complexity increases the costs of intervention. All things being equal, therefore, political actors will be more likely to intervene in policies that are salient but not complex (Gormley, 1983).

NOTES

1. B. Weingast and M. Moran, "Bureaucratic Discretion or Congressional Control? Regulatory Policymaking by the Federal Trade Commission," *Journal of Political Economy*, 91, no. 5 (1983) 765–800.

2. James Q. Wilson, *The Politics of Regulation* (New York: Basic Books, 1980); Robert Katzman, *Regulatory Bureaucracy* (Cambridge, Mass.: MIT Press, 1980).

3. George J. Stigler, "The Theory of Economic Regulation," *Bell Journal of Economics and Management Science*, 2 (Spring 1971), 3–21; Theodore Lowi, *The End of Liberalism* (New York: Norton, 1969); Daniel Mazmanian and Paul Sabatier, "A Multivariate Model of Public Policy-Making," *American Journal of Political Science*, 24 (August 1980), 439–468.

4. Harold Lasswell, *Politics: Who Gets What, When, How* (New York: McGraw-Hill, 1936).

5. Marver Bernstein, *Regulating Business by Independent Commission* (Princeton, N.J.: Princeton University Press, 1955).

6. George Stigler, "The Theory of Economic Regulation," *Bell Journal of Economics and Management Science*, 2 (Spring 1971), 3–21; Sam Peltzman, "Toward a More General Theory of Regulation," *Journal of Law and Economics*, 19 (August 1976), 211–240.

7. Glendon Schubert, *The Public Interest* (New York: Free Press, 1960).

8. Paul Sabatier, "Regulatory Policy Making: Toward a Framework of Analysis," *National Resources Journal*, 17 (July 1977), 415–460.

9. I have taken some liberties with Sabatier's (1977) work here. His intent was to distinguish between managerial and policing types of regulation. His work results in three types of regulation along a single dimension rather than four types along two.

10. J. Lieper Freeman, *The Political Process* (New York: Random House, 1965); Grant McConnell, *Private Power and American Democracy* (New York: Knopf, 1966).

11. Norton Long, *The Polity* (Chicago: Rand McNally, 1962).

12. Randall Ripley and Grace Franklin, *Congress, the Bureaucracy, and Public Policy* (Homewood, Ill.: Dorsey Press, 1980).

13. Hugh Heclo, "Issue Networks and the Executive Establishment," *The New American Political System*, ed. Anthony King (Washington, D.C.: American Enterprise Institute, 1978); Paul Sabatier, "Toward a Strategic Interaction Framework of Policy Evaluation and Learning." Paper presented at the annual meeting of the Western Political Science Association, 1983.

14. Bradley Behrman, "Civil Aeronautics Board," in *The Politics of Regulation*, ed. James Q. Wilson (New York: Basic Books, 1980), pp. 75–121.

15. Erwin Krasnow, Lawrence Longley, and Herbert Terry, *The Politics of Broadcast Regulation* (3rd ed.) New York: St. Martin's Press, 1982).

16. Henry Kenski and Margaret Corgan Kenski, "Congress against the President: The Struggle over the Environment," in *Environmental Policy in the 1980s*, eds. Norman Vig and Michael Kraft (Washington, D.C.: CQ Press, 1984), pp. 97–120.

17. Barry Weingast and Mark Moran, "The Myth of the Runaway Bureaucracy: The Case of the FTC," *Regulation*, 6 (May/June, 1982) 33–38.

18. C. K. Rowland and Roger Marz, "Gresham's Law: The Regulatory Analogy," *Policy Studies Review*, 1 (February 1982), 572–580.

19. Francis Rourke, *Bureaucracy, Politics, and Public Policy* (3rd ed.) (Boston: Little, Brown, 1984).

20. William Niskanen, *Bureaucracy and Representative Government* (Chicago: Aldine, 1971).

21. James Guyot, "The Convergence of Public and Private Sector Bureaucracies." Paper presented at the annual meeting of the American Political Science Association, 1979.

22. Abraham Maslow, *Motivation and Personality* (2nd ed.) (New York: HarperCollins, 1970).

23. Barbara Romzek and J. Stephen Hendricks, "Organizational Involvement and Representative Bureaucracy," *American Political Science Review*, 76 (March 1982), 75–82.

24. Steven Kelman, "Occupational Safety and Health Administration," in *The Politics of Regulation*, ed. James Q. Wilson (New York: Basic Books, 1980), pp. 236–266.

25. Anthony Downs, *Inside Bureaucracy* (Boston: Little, Brown, 1967).

26. Hugh Heclo, *Government of Strangers* (Washington, D.C.: Brookings Institutio.., ... ,.

27. David Welborn, *The Governance of Federal Regulatory Agencies* (Knoxville: University of Tennessee Press, 1977).

28. The section on bureaucratic variables relies heavily on Rourke (1984) and Sabatier (1977). The most applicable parts of the writings of each are used. In some cases, the impact of the variables reflects my interpretation of their work rather than their interpretation.

29. J. Clarence Davies and Barbara S. Davies, *The Politics of Pollution* (2nd ed.) (Indianapolis, Ind.: Pegasus, 1975).

30. Alfred Marcus, "Environmental Protection Agency," in *The Politics of Regulation*, ed. James Q. Wilson (New York: Basic Books, 1980).

31. Kenneth Meier, "The Impact of Regulatory Agency Structure: IRCs or DRAs," *Southern Review of Public Administration*, 3 (March 1980), 427–443; David Welborn, *The Governance*, 1977.

32. William Gormley, "Regulatory Issue Networks in a Federal System." Paper presented at the annual meeting of the American Political Science Association, 1983.

Appellate Courts As Policy Makers

Lawrence Baum

Appellate courts differ from trial courts in their roles as policy makers. The primary task of trial courts is to apply existing legal rules to specific cases. In contrast, appellate courts have more opportunities to establish new rules, to make decisions whose implications extend far beyond individual cases. In this chapter, I will examine what appellate courts do with these opportunities, what kinds of parts they play in the making of government policy.

The chapter's primary concern is the significance of appellate courts as policy makers. As many commentators have noted, appellate courts in the United States are very active as policy makers. Over the past few decades their decisions have transformed government policy on such issues as abortion, civil rights, and compensation for personal injuries. Yet the roles of appelate courts in policy making are limited by judges' own restraint. And when courts do intervene in the making of public policy, the impact of their decisions frequently is narrowed by the reactions of other government institutions and of people outside government.

A secondary concern is the content of the policies made by appellate courts, particularly their ideological direction. At any given time, the decisions of appellate courts are mixed, ranging from some that we would characterize as quite liberal to others that appear to be quite conservative. But the federal and state appellate courts seemed to be predominantly conservative institutions until at least the 1930s; today, in contrast, many appellate courts show strong liberal tendencies.

These concerns and other characteristics of appellate courts as policy makers will be examined in two parts. The first section of the chapter will look at appellate court decisions as government policies. The second will discuss the actual impact of the policies made by appelate courts.

APPELLATE COURT DECISIONS AS POLICIES

We can think of appellate court decisions as having two components, which correspond to the functions of these courts that were discussed in Chapter 8. The first is a review of the way that the lower court treated the parties to the case. The second is the appellate court's judgment about the principles of law that are applicable to the case, a judgment that is expressed in the opinion accompanying the decision. I will consider the policy outputs of appellate courts in terms of these two components of the decision, giving primary attention to the second.

Appellate Review of Lower Court Decisions

In each case that an appellate court hears, its most specific task is to review the treatment of the parties by the court below it. The two levels of appellate courts take somewhat different approaches to this task.

Review by first-level courts. First-level appellate courts—which are intermediate courts in the federal system and in most states—review trial court decisions. They review a fairly high percentage of decisions by major state trial courts and federal district courts because of the general right to appeal adverse trial decisions and the growing tendency to exercise this right.

Most often, they ratify trial decisions by affirming them. It appears that every first-level court approves well over half the trial decisions it reviews. A California court of appeal in the mid-1970s affirmed lower-court decisions 84 percent of the time, and the affirmance rate for the federal courts of appeals in 1987 was also 84 percent.[1] Furthermore, many decisions that are not affirmances (which I will call disturbances of trial decisions) are actually relatively minor modifications of decisions rather than general overturnings. For instance, an appellate court will sometimes eliminate one of several sentences given to a criminal defendant, but in doing so it may not affect that defendant's actual prison time at all.[2]

These high affirmance rates can be explained in three ways.[3] The first is in terms of generally accepted legal doctrines. One of these is the rule that a trial court's interpretation of the facts in a case will not be questioned if there is any *substantial evidence* for that interpretation. On the basis of this rule, appellate courts generally do not take a fresh look at the evidence as a whole in order to weigh it independently; rather, they seek out a basis in the evidence for upholding the trial court's ruling. Another important doctrine is the *harmless error* rule, which holds that even if a trial judge has erred in applying legal rules, an appellate court can still affirm the decision if it concludes the error was harmless, that it probably did not affect the trial court judgment.

High affirmance rates can also be explained in terms of the institutional interests of appellate courts. Frequent reversals of trial court decisions would increase conflict between the two levels of courts, because many trial judges resent reversals as negative reviews of their work. And, more important, to proceed with full and thorough reviews of trial decisions, with no preconceptions, would consume the time and energy of appellate judges at an unacceptable rate, particularly when their work loads have grown in recent years. Moreover, high reversal rates might encourage more litigants to appeal, increasing the burdens of appellate judges even more.

Finally, the past experience of appellate judges also helps to account for their tendency to affirm. Because most appeals in the past have seemed suitable for affirmance, judges expect that this will continue to be true. In combination with the substantial evidence and harmless error rules and with the institutional interests of appellate courts, a judge's past experience tends to create a strong presumption in favor of affirmance. That presumption is reflected in a 1988 opinion by a judge on the federal court of appeals in Chicago; in his view, a decision should not be overturned when it is "just maybe or probably wrong" but only when it is "wrong with the force of a five-week-old, unrefrigerated dead fish."[4]

Affirmance rates are especially high in criminal cases. Thomas Davies' study of a California court of appeal in the 1970s found that only 14 percent of the appeals from criminal convictions resulted in any disturbance of the trial decision, and only 5 percent involved a full reversal. In contrast, 31 percent of the trial decisions in civil cases were disturbed. Similarly, in the federal courts of appeals in 1987, the reversal rate was 8 percent in criminal cases and 18 percent in civil cases.[5]

One reason for this difference lies in patterns of appeals. Civil appeals carry significant monetary costs for most litigants, and civil litigants are ordinarily advised by attorneys. As a result, most appellants probably have fairly strong grounds on which to challenge trial decisions. In contrast, criminal defendants have considerable incentive to appeal when they have received substantial prison sentences, a high proportion of defendants do appeal, and a good many such appeals have little legal basis.

Nevertheless, as Davies has argued, it misses the point simply to assume that most criminal appeals are frivolous, because frivolousness is a subjective concept. Indeed, Davies found in his California study that the court of appeal cited trial court errors in about a quarter of the decisions in which it affirmed convictions.[6] Hence the concept of the frivolous criminal appeal may be as much a justification for affirmance—and for limited judicial scrutiny of trials—as it is an explanation of high affirmance rates.

Of course, the inclination to affirm is linked with the growing use of abbreviated procedures in first-level appellate courts. The establishment of such procedures has been encouraged by the belief that a high proportion of appeals are easy affirmances that staff attorneys can identify and handle. At the same time, when certain cases are labeled as requiring only abbreviated consideration, court personnel are encouraged to treat them as easy affirmances. Thus the use of abbreviated procedures may raise an affirmance rate that already is high.

Review by second-level courts.   Unlike first-level appellate courts, those at the second level disturb lower court decisions in a high proportion of the cases they decide. In its 1987–88 term, for instance, the U.S. Supreme Court affirmed the lower court in only 42 percent of the decisions for which it provided full opinions.[7]

Such a high disturbance rate suggests that second-level appellate courts are quite willing to substitute their own judgments for those of the courts below them. But in this sense, it is quite deceptive. As we have seen, judges on second-level courts are inclined to accept cases for hearings when they think that the lower court has erred in its decision. This means that they approach many of the cases they have accepted with a presumption of reversal, rather than the presumption of affirmance that prevails in first-level courts, and a high reversal rate is virtually guaranteed.

Yet if we take into account all the cases that are brought to the second-level courts, and not just those that are accepted for review, the disturbance of lower-court decisions is in fact quite limited. Of the cases that the Supreme Court receives, for example, it disturbs decisions only in about 5 percent.[8] Thus appellate courts at both levels allow most decisions that they review to remain standing.

Overview.   Because appellate courts uphold most decisions that are brought to them and because some decisions are not appealed, the overwhelming majority of decisions by trial courts and intermediate appellate courts become final. One study indicated that in the late 1960s the federal courts of appeals disturbed only about 4 percent of all the decisions made by the district courts; in turn, the Supreme Court disturbed about 1 percent of all court of appeals decisions.[9] Almost surely, the rates are lower today. Furthermore, if disturbance rates were calculated for the decisions of state trial courts, they would be even lower than those for the federal courts because a relatively small proportion of decisions by minor trial courts are appealed.[10] In this respect, then, appellate courts intervene rather little into the work of the courts below them.

Of course, this is only one aspect of the relationship between higher and lower courts. Even though appellate courts overturn relatively few decisions, the opinions they write influence what the courts below them do in a much larger number of cases. For example, one state supreme court decision on liability rules in auto accident cases can shape hundreds of trial court decisions. For this reason, we must examine the activity of the appellate courts as makers of legal rules and analyze the responses to their decisions in order to get a fuller sense of their roles within the judiciary.

Appellate Court Agendas

Through their opinions, appellate courts lay down interpretations of law that are generally regarded as binding on both lower courts and administrative bodies under their jurisdiction. These interpretations can alter existing legal rules, and they can reshape or even overturn policies made by the legislature and the executive branch. It is primarily through their legal interpretations, rather than through their treatment of individual litigants, that appellate courts exert influence as policy makers.

We can begin to sketch out this role by examining the sets of cases that appellate courts hear and decide with opinions—what I will call their agendas. The more that a court concentrates on cases in a particular field, the greater its potential to shape public policy in that field. As suggested in Chapter 8, the agendas of appellate courts are the products of rules of jurisdiction, patterns of litigation and appeals, and the judges' choices of cases in which to write opinions. The 1987 agendas of three appellate courts at different levels are summarized in Table 1.

The agendas of state supreme courts reflect the work of state courts generally.[11] Thus, because state court litigation is quite diverse, so too is state supreme court business. In recent years, several areas have been frequent subjects of supreme court opinions: torts, particularly cases arising from accidents; criminal law and procedure; contract disputes, most often between debtors and creditors; government economic regulation; and family and estate issues, primarily concerning divorce and inheritance. As a result, state supreme courts make legal rulings in a broad range of policy areas.

The agendas of the federal courts of appeals show both similarities and differences with those of the state supreme courts.[12] Their opinions, of course, are primarily on issues of federal law, but they also deal with a good many state law issues in cases brought under the diversity jurisdiction. The two policy areas that stand out on their agendas are government economic regulation and criminal law and procedure, with regulation cases considerably more numerous than they are in state appellate courts. Also common are torts, tax cases, and contract cases.

The agenda of the U.S. Supreme Court is rather distinctive.[13] Broadly speaking, the Court devotes itself overwhelmingly to public law issues; as the table shows, all other cases account for only a small minority of its opinions. Within this category, the Court is primarily a civil liberties specialist; indeed, in recent years about half its opinions have involved civil liberties issues. The largest number of these cases concern criminal procedure, but the Court also writes a great many opinions on the right to equal treatment under the law and such personal rights as freedom of expression and freedom of religion. Another significant part of the Court's agenda concerns economic regulation by federal and state governments. A third major area, which overlaps the first two, is federalism—that is, the constitutional relationship between national and state governments.

Even this brief discussion suggests two conclusions about the potential roles of appellate courts as policy makers. The first concerns the agendas of appellate courts taken as a whole. While the various state and federal courts cover a broad range of issues, there are some important areas of public policy in which appellate courts are largely inactive. The outstanding example is foreign policy, which state courts barely touch and in which federal courts make relatively few decisions. Even in fields where they are active, the courts may not deal with the most fundamental issues. In economic regulation, for instance, courts focus primarily on the details of regulatory policy rather than on the general form and scope of regulation.

The second conclusion concerns differences among courts. Some issue areas, such as criminal procedure, are important to appellate courts at all levels, but others are concentrated in certain courts. Property disputes and divorce are primarily the domain of state courts, while the Supreme Court gives civil liberties much greater emphasis than does any set of lower appellate courts. Thus different appellate courts have different domains in which to make policy.

Ideological Patterns in Appellate Court Policy

The discussion of agendas indicates the areas to which appellate courts devote the most attention. To get a sense of what they do in these areas, we need to examine the ideological direction and activism of appellate policies.

TABLE 1   Subject Matter of Cases Decided with Published Opinions in 1987, Selected Appellate Courts, in Percentages

Category of Cases[a]	Pennsylvania Supreme Court	Federal Court of Appeals, Sixth Circuit[b]	U.S. Supreme Court[c]
Debt and contract	10.5	11.1	4.1
Real property	4.4	0.4	1.4
Business organization	0.5	3.2	2.1
Torts	18.2	7.9	5.5
Family and estates	7.7	0.0	0.0
Public Law:			
Criminal	34.8	19.8	21.4
Governmental regulation of economic activity	7.7	22.1	19.3
Other	16.0	35.6	46.2

[a]Many cases could have fit into multiple categories; different coding rules would have produced substantially different results. For this reason, the percentages shown should be viewed as illustrations of differences in the agendas of the three courts rather than as exact depictions of each court's agenda.
[b]The time period from which cases were drawn was January–June 1987.
[c]The time period from which cases were drawn was the 1987 term of the Court.

Ideologically, the policies of the appellate courts at any given time are certain to be quite diverse. But diversity is not the same as randomness. During particular periods in American history, liberal or conservative policies have been dominant. In the broadest terms, appellate courts traditionally were fairly conservative in their policies, by the current definition of that term, whereas a strong element of liberalism has developed in the past half century.

The traditional conservatism of appellate courts.   For most of American history, the policies of appellate courts were primarily conservative. Federal and state courts addressed a wide range of legal issues involving the interests of economically powerful groups, and the dominant theme in their decisions was support for those interests.

This theme is fairly clear in the work of the U.S. Supreme Court. In the nineteenth and early twentieth centuries the Court worked to protect property rights and the freedom of business enterprises from restrictions by state and federal governments. As legislation to regulate and restrict business practices proliferated, the Court became increasingly hostile to this legislation, frequently ruling that state and federal laws violated the Constitution. These attacks culminated in the Court's decisions of the 1930s which struck down much of President Franklin Roosevelt's New Deal economic program. Meanwhile, the Court gave little support to the civil liberties of black citizens, unpopular political groups, or criminal defendants. Viewing the Court's record, Attorney General Robert Jackson, who was shortly to join the Court himself, wrote in 1941 that "never in its entire history can the Supreme Court be said to have for a single hour been representative of anything except the relatively conservative forces of its day."[14]

Scholars have disagreed about the historical record of state courts, and this disagreement reflects the diversity in their decisions.[15] But the most important elements in their policies through most of our history were primarily conservative. As the industrial economy developed, state courts did much to protect the business sector from threats to its economic well-being. In the nineteenth century, they devised rules in contract and property law that supported industrial and commercial growth. In their building of tort law in the nineteenth century, state courts created rules that "favored defendants over plaintiffs, businesses over individuals."[16] One example was the contributory negligence rule, which prevented the recovery of money for injuries if the person bringing suit was even slightly negligent. Another was the fellow-servant rule, under which a worker could not sue an employer for injuries caused by another employee. The courts also held that a family could not recover for the death of the person who was their support, because the right to sue had died with the person who was killed.

Of course, there were numerous exceptions to the conservative thrust of judicial policy. Liberal policies and even liberal courts existed throughout the long period when conservatism was predominant. The U.S. Supreme Court, for instance, varied in its hostility to government economic regulation, and some state supreme courts rejected in part or altogether the doctrines that protected businesses against lawsuits. But until fairly recently the general conservatism of appellate courts was pronounced.

This conservatism is not difficult to understand. Judges came primarily from economically advantaged segments of society and were imbued with the values of the elite. Trained in a legal profession in which conservative values predominated, they often embarked on legal careers that involved service to business enterprises. Furthermore, the most skilled advocates who came before their courts generally represented businesses and other institutions with conservative goals. Because of all these factors, it may have been almost inevitable that conservatism became the dominant theme in judicial policy.

A growth in liberalism.   In the past half century, the dominant conservatism of the past has been replaced by an ideologically mixed pattern of policy in which the liberal element often has been more prominent. Across a range of issues, the courts have given more support to the interests of relatively weak groups in society, groups that possess far fewer social and economic resources and far less conventional political power than the business interests that courts tended to favor in the past.

The most visible change has been in the Supreme Court. Beginning in 1937 the Court quickly abandoned its earlier support for business interests that sought protection from government regulation. It also began to provide support for the civil liberties of relatively powerless groups in American society, support that peaked in the 1960s. It applied the constitutional rights of criminal defendants to state proceedings and established new controls on police investigations and trial procedures. It required the desegregation of Southern public schools and protected the rights of racial minority groups in other areas of life. It strengthened freedom of expression both for the mass media and for people who express their views through vehicles such as pamphlets and marches.

In the 1970s and 1980s the Supreme Court supported civil liberties with less consistency. It narrowed the rights of criminal defendants, and it became more reluctant to establish new rights in any area. But, compared with most of its past history, the Court of the past twenty years has remained relatively liberal in its support for civil liberties and its acceptance of government regulation of business.

In the past few decades the federal courts of appeals have differed a good deal in their ideological positions, but in general they too have moved away from their traditional conservatism. The court of appeals for the District of Columbia stood out for its strong liberalism from the 1960s through the mid-1980s, as evidenced in its support for the rights of criminal defendants and the mentally ill, for the interests of consumers, and for protection of the environment. Standing out in another way was the Fifth Circuit Court of Appeals in the Deep South, which gave strong support to black civil rights on school desegregation and other issues in the 1950s and 1960s despite the anti-civil rights pressures in that region.

Early in this century, state supreme courts began to reduce their long-standing support for business in tort law, expanding the ability of people who suffer injuries to recover compensation.[17] This trend gradually gained momentum, as courts increasingly eliminated old rules that had favored defendants. Most dramatically, supreme courts in the 1960s and 1970s largely eliminated the requirement that those who are injured by defective products must prove that the manufacturer was negligent. Some other examples of changes in tort law since the 1950s are shown in Table 2.

State courts were slower to take liberal positions in civil liberties; indeed, in the 1950s and 1960s some supreme courts resisted the Supreme Court's expansions of liberties, interpreting the Court's decisions narrowly. Since the 1970s, however, state courts increasingly have undertaken their own expansions through their interpretations of state constitutions, finding broader rights in those constitutions than the Supreme Court has found in the U.S. Constitution.[18] The largest part of this activity has focused on criminal justice, but it has extended to areas such as freedom of expression and sex discrimination. Not all states have participated in this development, which is concentrated heavily in the West and Northeast, but it has become increasingly widespread.

The relative liberalism of appellate courts in recent years is more difficult to explain than was their traditional conservatism. Undoubtedly the recent liberalism is at least partially rooted in a changing pattern of social values. In this century, support by the general public and political leaders for the autonomy of business enterprises has declined. Meanwhile, some civil liberties—especially those related to equality—have gained more support. This change in values is reflected in judges' own attitudes as well as in the kinds of litigation and arguments that come to the appellate courts.

TABLE 2   Some Changes in Tort Law Doctrine Initiated by State Supreme Courts Since the 1950s

Doctrinal Change	Innovating State	How Many States?
Abolishing the general immunity of municipalities from lawsuits.	Florida, 1957	Many
Allowing parents and children to sue each other for torts.	Wisconsin, 1963	Most
Allowing a person to sue for emotional distress without accompanying physical injury.	Hawaii, 1970	Several
Allowing a person injured by a drug product whose manufacturer is unknown to sue all the manufacturers of that product on the basis of their market shares.	California, 1980	A few

Note: The identity of the state that first adopted a legal doctrine and the number of states that have adopted it are ambiguous for some doctrines.

Sources: Some information obtained from W. Page Keeton, Dan B. Dobbs, Robert E. Keeton, and David G. Owen, *Prosser and Keeton on Torts*, 5th ed. (St. Paul: West Publishing, 1984).

Another source of this ideological change is the kinds of people who become judges. Like judges in the past, members of the current judiciary tend to come from families with high status. But there are more exceptions to this tendency today; as a result, the attitudes of judges on economic and social issues are less likely to be conservative. Furthermore, at the federal level liberal Democratic presidents have sought out appellate judges who shared their liberalism. Franklin Roosevelt's appointments turned the Supreme Court away from its traditional conservatism. Similarly, Roosevelt, Johnson, and Carter all used their appointments to move the lower federal courts in a liberal direction. At the state level, the growing strength of the Democratic party in the North from the 1930s on brought more liberal governors into office; in turn, these governors influenced the direction of state appellate courts with their own appointments.

To some extent, this shift to greater liberalism has been self-reinforcing. The courts' support for civil liberties encouraged interest groups to bring new cases, seeking further expansions of liberties. When the Supreme Court in the 1960s played a strong role in expanding civil liberties, many lawyers gained an appreciation for that role, and those who reached the bench themselves sought to follow it. As I suggested for torts in the state courts, a trend in judicial policy tends to gain a certain momentum of its own.

But this is not to say that the liberal trend is irreversible; unquestionably, it could be reversed, particularly with major changes in the kinds of people who are selected as judges. Indeed, this process is well under way in the federal courts. The appointments by Richard Nixon and Ronald Reagan have turned a strongly liberal Supreme Court into one that could be characterized as moderately conservative by current standards, and appointments by George Bush almost surely would move the Court further to the right. Reagan's numerous appointments to the courts of appeals made some of those courts considerably more conservative, and here too that process is likely to continue. This prospect is a reminder that the ideological stance of the courts, no matter how strong the forces behind it, is always subject to change. . . .

NOTES

1. Administrative Office of the United States Courts, *Annual Report of the Administrative Office of the United States Courts, 1987* (Washington, D.C.: Government Printing Office, 1988), p. 155; Thomas Y. Davies, "Affirmed: A Study of Criminal Appeals and Decision-Making Norms in a California Court of Appeal," *American Bar Foundation Research Journal*, Summer 1982, p. 574. The figure for federal courts was calculated in a somewhat different way from the figure for the California court, so the two are not entirely comparable.

2. Davies, "Affirmed," p. 576.

3. Sources of information for this discussion include Davies, "Affirmed."

4. *Parts and Electric Motors v. Sterling Electric*, No. 88–1609 (7th Circuit 1988), p. 10.

5. Administrative Office of the United States Courts, *Annual Report 1987*, p. 155. The data for civil cases were calculated by the author.

6. Davies, "Affirmed," pp. 582–83.

7. "The Supreme Court, 1987 Term," *Harvard Law Review*, 102 (November 1988), 354.

8. This figure is estimated from the Court's rates of acceptance of cases and of disturbances in the cases it accepts. See "Statistical Recap of Supreme Court's Workload during Last Three Terms," *United States Law Week*, 57 (July 26, 1988), 3074; and J. Woodford Howard, Jr., *Courts of Appeals in the Federal Judicial System: A Study of the Second, Fifth, and District of Columbia Circuits* (Princeton, N.J.: Princeton University Press, 1981), p. 59.

9. These figures are estimated from data in Howard, *Courts of Appeals*, pp. 39, 74.

10. See, for instance, Judicial Council of California, *1984 Annual Report* (San Francisco: Judicial Council of California, 1984), pp. 211, 216.

11. Sources of information for this discussion include Robert A. Kagan, Bliss Cartwright, Lawrence M. Friedman, and Stanton Wheeler, "The Business of State Supreme Courts, 1870–1970," *Stanford Law Review*, 30 (November 1977), 132–51; and Burton M. Atkins and Henry R. Glick, "Environmental and Structural Variables as Determinants of Issues in State Courts of Last Resort," *American Journal of Political Science*, 20 (February 1976), 98–101.

12. Sources of information for this discussion include Howard, *Courts of Appeals*, pp. 315–18; and Lawrence Baum, Sheldon Goldman, and Austin Sarat, "The Evolution of Litigation in the Federal Courts of Appeals, 1895–1975," *Law & Society Review*, 16 (1981–82), 291–309.

13. Sources of information for this discussion include Richard Pacelle, "The Supreme Court Agenda across Time: Dynamics and Determinants of Change" (Ph.D. diss., Ohio State University, 1985), ch. 3.

14. Robert M. Jackson, *The Struggle for Judicial Supremacy* (New York: Alfred A. Knopf, 1941), p. 187.

15. See Lawrence M. Friedman, *A History of American Law*, rev. ed. (New York: Simon & Schuster, 1985); Stanton Wheeler, Bliss Cartwright, Robert A. Kagan, and Lawrence M. Friedman, "Do the 'Haves' Come Out Ahead? Winning and Losing in State Supreme Courts, 1870–1970," *Law & Society Review*, 21 (1987), 403–45; Melvin I. Urofsky, "State Courts and Progressive Legislation during the Progressive Era: A Reevaluation," *Journal of American Law*, 72 (June 1985), 63–91; and Gary T. Schwartz, "Tort Law and the Economy in Nineteenth-Century America: A Reinterpretation," *Yale Law Journal*, 90 (July 1981), 1717–75.

16. Lawrence M. Friedman, *Total Justice* (New York: Russell Sage Foundation, 1985), p. 54.

17. Lawrence Baum and Bradley C. Canon, "State Supreme Courts as Activists: New Doctrines in the Law of Torts," in Mary Cornelia Porter and G. Alan Tarr, eds., *State Supreme Courts: Policymakers in the Federal System* (Westport, Conn.: Greenwood Press, 1982), pp. 83–108.

18. See Ronald K. L. Collins, Peter J. Galie, and John Kincaid, "State High Courts, State Constitutions, and Individual Rights Litigation since 1980: A Judicial Survey," *Publius*, 16 (Summer 1986), 141–61; and Stanley H. Friedelbaum, ed., *Human Rights in the States: New Directions in Constitutional Policymaking* (New York: Greenwood Press, 1988).

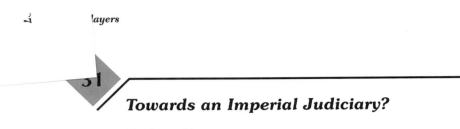

Towards an Imperial Judiciary?

Nathan Glazer

. . . The justices wear black gowns, being not merely the only public officers, but the only non-ecclesiastical persons of any kind whatever within the bounds of the United States who use any official dress.

—The American Commonwealth

A non-lawyer who considers the remarkable role of courts in the interpretation of the Constitution and the laws in the United States finds himself in a never-never land—one in which questions he never dreamed of raising are discussed at incredible length, while questions that would appear to be the first to come to mind are hardly ever raised. This is particularly the case when the concern of the non-professional observer is with social policy rather than with constitutional law as such.

Thus, fine distinctions in the use of evidence in criminal cases are debated at length, and used as a basic test in judging whether a court or individual justices are liberal or conservative; whereas one sees little discussion of why judges may hold up hundreds of millions of dollars in federal payments to states and cities to force them to make numerous civil service appointments, or why judges may require a state or city to provide extensive and specifically defined social services. The original *Brown* decision on school desegregation was properly debated at length by our leading constitutional authorities. But what are arguably the most disruptive decisions ever made by the courts—the requirement that children be bused to distant schools—have excited much less professional interest than popular interest.

One reason for this disparity is that judges and lawyers are trained to see continuity in the development of constitutional law. However far-reaching the actions the courts take, the lawyers who propose such actions and the judges who rule on them are committed by the logic of legal reasoning to insist that they are only unveiling a rule that existed all along in the recesses of the Constitution or the bowels of legislation: Nothing new has been added, they say, even though great consequences follow from their decisions.

Political scientists who study the courts are somewhat freer to see truly original developments in the constitutional law, but they generally do not go beyond interpreting these developments as part of a cycle. If the court changes, to them it

Reprinted from Nathan Glazer, "Towards an Imperial Judiciary," *The Public Interest*, No. 41 (Fall 1975). Reprinted by permission.

2/14 ABC
6:30 pm

MESA MURDERS
HE KILLED 2 PEOPLE
FROM 1 COLLEGE
ECONOMICS - DOW JONES
NASDAQ
CHRYSLER - RETIREMENT
PACKAGE
$35,000 CASH + VEHICLE

SAN FRANCISCO - REVOKING
PRIVATE SCHOOL CHARTER
EDISON CHARTER ACADEMY
SCHOOL BOARD WANTS TO
FIRE EDISON - THEY
THINK THEY CAN
CONTINUE WITH THE SUCCESS

SPACE STATION NEW
SCIENCE LAB
INFRASTRUCTURE - CLOSE LOOK
DALLAS, TX NEIGHBORHOOD
FIBER OPTIC CABLES FOR
FASTER SERVICE
23 CONTRACTORS IN 25 mo
CONGRESS DEREGULATED
PHONE SERVICE
D.C. BANNING COMPANIES
FROM DIGGING UP
STREETS IF PAVEMENT
IS LESS 5 YRS OLD

VALENTINES DAY CELEBRATIONS

REPRODUCTION

changes within a well-understood pattern, in which periods of activism symmetrically contrast with periods of quietism: At some point the Supreme Court, exercising its power to interpret the Constitution and the laws and to overrule the interpretations of legislatures and executives,[1] goes too far—thus, we have the *Dred Scott* decision, or the decisions overruling the actions of the New Deal in the mid-1930's. An explosion then results: as a result of the *Dred Scott* decision, a war; as a result of the anti-New Deal decisions, the court-packing plan. To the political scientist, the court follows not only its own logic but the logic of public opinion. Since it is without the independent power to enforce its decrees, the Court then withdraws. Its withdrawal is assisted ultimately by the appointment power of the President, who is in closer touch with public opinion. A period of quietism thus succeeds a period of activism. This is a reasonable description of the pattern of judicial interpretation, supported by history and by American constitutional arrangements, and this is as far as one of our best-known analysts of the Supreme Court, Robert McCloskey, went.

There is, however, another perspective on judicial interpretation, one which is generally identified with outraged legislators, Presidents, governors, and people: The Court has gone too far, they say, and the return of the quietistic phase of the cycle will not satisfy us, for the Court is engaged in a damaging and unconstitutional revolution that even the cyclical return of a period of quietism cannot curb. The lawyers who must operate within the assumption of continuity are inclined to dismiss such outrage, and the legal commentators who look at the long stretch of history are sure that quietism will replace activism—as it has before— and that the courts will retire from the front pages of the newspapers. Yet in 1975, all the evidence suggests that this third perspective is really the correct one: The courts truly have changed their role in American life. American courts, the most powerful in the world—they were that already when Tocqueville wrote and when Bryce wrote—are now far more powerful than ever before; public opinion— which Tocqueville, Bryce, and other analysts thought would control the courts as well as so much else in American life—is weaker. The legislatures and the executive now moderate their outbursts, for apparently outbursts will do no good. And courts, through interpretation of the Constitution and the laws, now reach into the lives of the people, against the will of the people, deeper than they ever have in American history.

FROM WARREN TO BURGER

These are sweeping assertions, yet the course of the law since 1969 supports them. For in 1969 something was supposed to happen, and didn't. In his first term, President Nixon, who opposed the Warren Court's activism, succeeded in making four appointments, and the period of activism that had begun with the *Brown* decision of 1954 was supposed to come to an end, as the Warren Court was replaced by the Burger Court. Instead, there have been more far-reaching decisions—if estimated by the impact on people and their everyday lives—since 1969 than in 1954–1968, even with four Nixon-appointed Justices. In 1971 the *Swann* decision for the first time legitimated massive busing of children to overcome segregation in a large city; in 1974 the *Keyes* decision for the first time legitimated such massive busing in a Northern city, and in addition legitimated standards of proof for *de jure* segregation that were so loose that it guaranteed that *de jure* segregation could be found everywhere (which meant that the Court's narrow 5–4 decision in *Milliken*–which overturned lower court requirements for the merger of Detroit and its suburbs in order to create, through busing, schools with smaller proportions of black children—could very likely be circumvented by demonstrating that the suburbs, too, were engaged in *de jure* segregation). In 1971 the Court legitimated federal government guidelines for the use of tests in employment that required strict standards of "job-relatedness" if, on the basis of such tests, differing proportions of certain ethnic and racial groups were given employment. This decision has, in effect, declared illegal most efforts by employers, public and private, to hire more qualified employees. Since apparently all tests select differing proportions of one group or another, and few tests can be shown to be job-related by the strict standards of the guidelines, most employee hiring on the basis of tests now can be labeled discriminatory and employers may be required, either by lower court orders or by Department of Justice consent decrees, to hire by racial and ethnic quotas—a practice which is specifically forbidden by the Civil Rights Act of 1964 and (one would think) unconstitutional because of its denial of the "equal protection of the laws." In 1973, the Burger Court ruled in *Roe* and *Doe* that just about all state laws on abortion were unconstitutional and decreed that state laws must treat each third of the pregnancy period according to different standards. In 1975 it spread the awesome limitations of "due process" to the public schools, which now could not restrict the constitutional rights of students by suspending or expelling them without at least something resembling a criminal trial. In 1975 it agreed, in the first of a series of important cases on the rights of mental patients, that harmless persons could not be detained involuntarily in mental hospitals.

The list could be extended. It is true that the Court stayed its hand in other cases that could have had enormous consequences: In particular, it refused to accept the argument that states must ensure that financial support of schools be unaffected by differences in community wealth, and it did not allow a challenge by inner-city residents to suburban zoning ordinances. But in both areas state courts are active, and it is hard to see what is to prevent them from decreeing for their states (as the courts of New Jersey already have) the revolution in equalization of school financing and zoning that the Supreme Court has refused to decree for the nation.

What was most striking is that all of these cases—and many others extending the reach of government, whether it wished it or not, into the lives of people, and of the courts over the actions of legislatures and communities—were made despite the rapid appointment of four Justices by President Nixon. The Nixon Justices either supported the majority in 9–0 decisions (e.g., *Swann*), or split (thus only one of the four dissented from the majority in *Doe* and *Roe*), and only rarely (in *Goss*, on due process for students) voted as a bloc against the majority of five who had served on the Warren Court.

Supreme Court analysts and reporters very often tell a different story from this, because in judging the Court, they tend to focus on the endless details of what is or is not allowed in criminal law—the use of confessions, searches, and the like. Emphasizing the criminal law, they apparently see a retreat where another observer might see a modicum of common sense. But I believe all agree that the Burger Court has been surprisingly like the Warren Court; and this raises the question of why the expected turn has not yet taken place—seven years after Nixon was elected, and after four of his appointees were on the court.

THE END OF A CONSERVATIVE JUDICIARY?

Three characteristics of the Burger Court, and of the Warren Court, have excited less interest than they might have, and would suggest that we must at least consider the possibility that there has been a permanent change in the character of the courts and their role in the commonwealth, rather than simply a somewhat extended activist cycle.

First, the activist cycles of the past have always been characterized by conservative Courts, acting to restrict liberal Congresses, Presidents, or state governments—the Marshall Court, the Taney Court, and the Taft-Hughes Courts. This made sense: The Court, after all, was designed by the Founders to be a conservative institution, a check on popularly elected legislatures and an elected (even if not at the beginning *popularly* elected) President. The Court was appointed, and it held tenure for life. It was, as Alexander Bickel wrote, paraphrasing Hamilton in the 78th *Federalist* paper, "the least dangerous branch." To quote Hamilton: "Whoever attentively considers the different departments of power must perceive, that, in a government in which they are separated from each other, the judiciary, from the nature of its functions, will always be the least dangerous to the political rights of the Constitution; because it will be least in capacity to annoy or injure them. The Executive not only dispenses the honors, but holds the sword of the community; the legislature not only commands the purse, but prescribes the rules by which the duties and rights of every citizen are to be regulated." (As we shall see, however, the legislature no longer controls the purse, if the Court rules otherwise, nor prescribes the rules governing duties and rights—though the sword is still in the hands of the Executive.)

But something extraordinary has happened when a liberal Court confronts a conservative executive and legislature, as the Warren Court did after the election of President Eisenhower: The *natural* expectations, the order of history, have been reversed. It is even more extraordinary when, after 15 years of appointments to the Supreme Court and the subordinate courts by conservative Presidents (against seven years by liberal Presidents), this strange posture still persists.

A second extraordinary feature of the post-1954 activism is a corollary in part of the first: In the past the role of activist courts was to *restrict* the executive and legislature in what they could do. The distinctive characteristic of more recent activist courts has been to *extend* the role of what the government could do, even when the government did not want to do it. The *Swann* and *Keyes* decisions meant that government *must* move children around to distant schools against the will of their parents. The *Griggs* decision meant that government *must* monitor the race and ethnicity of job applicants and test-takers. The cases concerning the rights of mental patients and prisoners, which are for the most part still in the lower courts, say that government *must* provide treatment and rehabilitation whether it knows how or not. Federal Judge Weinstein's ruling in a New York school desegregation case seems to say that government *must* racially balance communities. And so on.

An interesting example of this unwilled extension of governmental action is that of the Environmental Protection Agency (EPA). It did not wish to issue rules preserving pure air in areas without pollution or imposing drastic transportation controls. To the EPA, this did not seem to be what Congress intended; but under court order, it was required to do both. Similarly, the Department of Health, Education, and Welfare (HEW) apparently did not want to move against the Negro colleges of the South, now no longer segregated under law but still with predominantly black enrollments, nor was this in the interests of those colleges, or their students, or indeed anyone else—but Federal judges required HEW to do so.

In these, as in other cases, government is required to do what the Congress did not order it to do and may well oppose, what the executive does not feel it wise to do, and most important what it does not know how to do. How *does* one create that permanently racially balanced community that Judge Weinstein wants so that the schools may be permanently racially balanced? How does one create that good community in Boston public housing that Judge Garrity wants so that vandalism repair costs may be brought down to what the authority can afford? How does one rehabilitate prisoners? Or treat mental patients? Like Canute, the Judges decree the sea must not advance, and weary administrators—hectored by enthusiastic, if ignorant, lawyers for public advocacy centers—must go through the motions to show the courts they are trying.

RECONSIDERING THE CYCLICAL THEORY

A third feature of the new activism which is also extraordinary: The Court's actions now seem to arouse fewer angry reactions from the people and the legislatures. The power of the Court has been exercised so often and so successfully over the last 20 years, and the ability to restrict or control it by either new legislation, constitutional amendment, or new appointments has met with such uniform failure, that the Court, and the subordinate courts, are now seen as forces of nature, difficult to predict and impossible to control. Thus, one may contrast the outburst over the school prayer decisions of 1962–63 with the relative quietude of response to the abortion decisions of 1973. Or, contrast the effort to adopt a constitutional amendment to control the sweep of reapportionment decisions in 1964–66 with the general view in Congress today that any effort to control the Court on busing by means of a constitutional amendment has no chance of succeeding.

This is, of course, not necessarily witness to the strength of the Court as such: What it reflects, in addition, is the agreement of large sectors of opinion—even if it is still minority opinion—with the Court's actions. But this opinion in favor of the Court is shaped by the reserves of strength the Court possesses: the positive opinion of the Court in the dominant mass media—the national television news shows, the national news magazines, and the most influential newspapers; and the bias in its favor among the informed electorate generally, and among significant groups of opinion-leaders. The Court is further the beneficiary of two accidents of political history (or at least they may be accidents): Because he was running against Barry Goldwater, Lyndon Johnson had an overwhelming victory in 1964, and helped bring into office so many liberal Congressmen that the powerful effort to limit the Court on reapportionment was blunted. And because of the Watergate scandal, so many liberal Congressmen were returned to Congress in 1974 that the natural life of the activist cycle in the Court's history was extended at least two years, and perhaps longer. Thus this Congress will not start any amendment process to limit the Court on busing. (It is understood that liberal Congressmen today, as against our previous history, support the power of the Court. If new appointments bring about the expected conservative switch, that position may change.)

The key point, however, is that the major limitation on the Court's power—public opinion, expressing itself through the Presidency and the Congress—has not come into effect to limit this Court. Outrage at its actions was stronger 12 or 13 years ago than it is today, though the intrusive reach of the Court's actions into the daily life of citizens has become much stronger. Ironically, the President who once wanted to impeach Justice Douglas may well find that the Justice who has served longest on the Supreme Court may survive his own Presidential term.

What I am suggesting is that we must reconsider the theory that activist cycles are succeeded by quiescent ones. This belief was based on the view that public opinion in the end controls the Court, which has the power of neither purse nor sword, and that the Court is thus still pretty much where the Founders and Chief Justice Marshall established it, as one of the three coequal branches of government, with great moral authority but little else. In contrast, it appears that the controls on Court power have become obsolescent and that the role of the Court—and courts generally—has changed significantly, such that the most powerful Court and Judiciary in the world have become even more powerful, raising questions of some gravity for the Commonwealth. Of course, any long-range view shortly may be made irrelevant by current events. Two more conservative appointments, one might think, and the Court will revert, only eight years later than one might have expected, to its quietistic phase, and President and Congress will resume their positions of dominance. But there are a number of other factors, which must at least be considered, which would argue that the matter is more serious.

The factors affecting the Court's power transcend, I believe, the question of the individual outlooks and philosophies of the present Justices or their potential successors. It is true that in an institution in which individuality is so dominant that 5–4 decisions on vital matters affecting the nation are common—with no apparent influence that can be exerted on the minority to change its vote so that the nation may accept these decisions with better grace—the character of individual Justices is not a matter to be taken lightly. . . .

THE TRUST OF THE PEOPLE

We may debate whether we have a better society or commonwealth or a worse one as a result. I believe we have a considerably worse one, because a free people feels itself increasingly under the arbitrary rule of unreachable authorities, and that cannot be good for the future of the state. Even the guardians of the "guardian ethic"—the better educated, the establishment, the opinion-makers—are now doubtful of many of the rulings they urged when, unable to institute them through the elected representatives of the people, they made law through recourse to the courts. But in the meantime the great fund of respect and trust by the people for governmental institutions has been drawn down; the courts, trying to create a better society, have increasingly lost the respect and trust of the people—which in the end is what sustained and must sustain the remarkable institution of a supreme judiciary in American life. Even in 1965, McCloskey could write, "'Judicial realism' has eroded the traditional mystique that often lent authority in other days. . . ." That trust is considerably further eroded 10 years later. "To construe the law," Bryce wrote of the Supreme Court, "that is, to elucidate the will of the people as supreme lawgiver, is the beginning and end of their duty." Bryce then adds in a footnote:

> 'Suppose, however,' someone may say 'that the court should go beyond its duty and import its own views of what ought to be the law into its decision as to what is the law. This would be an exercise of judicial will.' Doubtless, it would, but it would be a breach of duty, would expose the court to the distrust of the people, and might, if repeated or persisted in a serious matter, provoke resistance to the law as laid down by the court.

We have seen efforts at resistance: All have failed, and there is little enough now. Some may see this as the triumph of law instituting justice; I suspect it is rather the apathy of cynical and baffled people, incapable of seeing what actions may release them from the toils of the intrusive courts.

A final quotation from Bryce:

In America the Constitution is at all times very hard to change: much more then must political issues turn on its interpretation. And if this be so, must not the interpreting court be led to assume a control over the executive and legislative branches of government, since it has the power of declaring their acts illegal?
There is ground for these criticisms. The evil they point to has occurred and may recur. But it occurs very rarely, and may be averted by the same prudence which the courts have hitherto generally shown.

In 1954 the Court abandoned prudence and for 15 years firmly and unanimously insisted that the segregation and degradation of the Negro must end. It succeeded, and eventually the legislative and executive branches came to its side and the heritage of unequal laws and unequal treatment was eliminated. That was indeed a heroic period in the history of the court. But even heroes may overreach themselves. It is now time for the Court to act with the prudence that must in a free society be the more regular accompaniment of its actions.

NOTES

1 In this article, I do not plan to go into the question of the sources of this power, whether given in the Constitution, or seized by Chief Justice Marshall, or properly or improperly established—it is there, and it is permanent.

News That Matters

Shanto Iyengar and Donald Kinder

Not so very long ago, television was "nothing but a gleam in the entrepreneurial eye" (Weaver 1975, 81).[1] No longer. In just four decades, it has become a comfortable and easy habit, a settled and central institution. As television has moved to the center of American life, TV news has become Americans' single most important source of information about political affairs. The purpose of our effort has been to provide a systematic examination of this new relationship. In this final chapter we summarize our principal results and position them within the context of the broader literature on mass communication and politics. We argue that, for good or ill, television news has become a regular participant in the American political process. Finally, as a means of assessing the normative implications of our results for a democratic society, we discuss the ways in which television news conveys unusual and distinctive views of politics—views that eventually become our own.

RECAPITULATION OF RESULTS

Agenda-setting

Americans' views of their society and nation are powerfully shaped by the stories that appear on the evening news. We found that people who were shown network broadcasts edited to draw attention to a particular problem assigned greater importance to that problem—greater importance than they themselves did before the experiment began, and greater importance than did people assigned to control conditions that emphasized different problems. Our subjects regarded the target problem as more important for the country, cared more about it, believed that government should do more about it, reported stronger feelings about it, and were much more likely to identify it as one of the country's most important problems. Such differences were apparent immediately after conclusion of the broadcasts one day later, and one week later. They emerged in experiments explicitly designed to test agenda-setting and in experiments designed with other purposes in mind; in sequential experiments that drew the viewer's attention to the problem each day for a week and in assemblage experiments that lasted but one hour; and for a broad array of problems: defense, pollution, arms control, civil rights, energy, social security, drugs, and education. Moreover, these experimental results were generally corroborated by our analysis of trends in network news coverage and national public opinion. That we found essentially the same result using different methods strengthens our conclusion that television news shapes the relative importance Americans attach to various national problems.

To our surprise, the basic agenda-setting effect was not generally enhanced by vivid presentations. If anything, dramatic accounts of personal travails chosen to illustrate national problems appear to undermine agenda-setting, particularly when viewers blame the victims for the troubles that have befallen them. We assume that vivid presentations may enhance agenda-setting, provided viewers regard the victims as innocent. For example, intimate, poignant film of Ethiopian children dying of starvation may drive home the meaning of famine in a way that written accounts cannot. Because such children may be widely understood to be blameless victims of a cruel fate, vivid presentations may add to the viewer's conviction that the African famine is a serious problem. Our results, however, showed only that stories of personal suffering, powerfully depicted, generally did not raise the priority viewers assigned to the target problems.

Our experiments showed that the position of a story in a broadcast did affect agenda-setting. Lead stories were generally more influential than nonlead stories. Our analysis of survey data showed that lead stories exerted a much more profound agenda-setting effect than nonlead stories. We suspect that viewers may simply pay more attention to the first story than to stories that appear later on and that disruptions in viewing are especially likely to occur at home. An alternative explanation of the lead story advantage is that the public may perceive lead stories as being particularly newsworthy. Certainly the networks claim to select the lead story on these grounds.

Television news is, of course, not the only source of information people draw on when thinking about the nation's problems. Another is personal experience. Using both experimental and national survey data, we found that people who encountered problems in their everyday lives were more inclined to see these problems as important for the country as a whole than were individuals not so affected. In particular, we found that blacks attached more importance to civil rights than did whites and that the elderly attached more importance to the viability of the social security system than did the young. When people think of themselves as members of a victimized group, they appear to see their own problems as serious and legitimate ones for the country.

Our special interest in personal predicaments was in the possibility that they might serve as predisposing factors making viewers more vulnerable to a particular news agenda. For the most part, that is just what we found. News coverage of civil rights was more influential among blacks than among whites; coverage of unemployment proved more influential among the unemployed than among the employed; and coverage of the possible bankruptcy of the social security system was a more compelling message for the elderly than for the young. The general point here is that television news appears to be most powerful when it corroborates personal experience, conferring social reinforcement and political legitimacy on the problems and struggles of ordinary life.

Overall, we see our results on agenda-setting as a vindication of Lippmann's observations of more than a half-century ago. Although Lippmann was writing with newspapers in mind, his analysis is nevertheless highly relevant to the place of television news in contemporary American society. His observation that citizens must depend on others for their news about national and world affairs—a world they cannot touch themselves—is amply confirmed here. What we have done is to begin to uncover the various and specific ways that television news determines the citizen's conception of the "mystery off there."

Priming

While our agenda-setting results contribute to a long-standing tradition inaugurated by Lippmann and sustained by others, our results in the matter of priming offer a more original perspective. Priming presumes that when evaluating complex political phenomena, people do not take into account all that they know—they cannot, even if they are motivated to do so. Instead, they consider what comes to mind, those bits and pieces of political memory that are accessible. Television news, we supposed, might be a powerful determinant of what springs to mind and what is forgotten or ignored. Through priming (drawing attention to some aspects of political life at the expense of others) television news might help to set the terms by which political judgments are reached and political choices made.

Our results support this claim handsomely. When primed by television news stories that focus on national defense, people judge the president largely by how well he has provided, as they see it, for the nation's defense; when primed by stories about inflation, people evaluate the president by how he has managed, in their view, to keep prices down; and so on. According to a variety of tests, priming is both powerful and pervasive: it emerges in a number of independent tests for arms control, civil rights, defense, inflation, unemployment, and energy; for a Democratic president (Carter) as well as for a Republican one (Reagan); in different experimental arrangements; in response to good news as well as to bad; and in analyses that estimate priming while controlling for the possibility of projection. All this suggests that television news does indeed shape the standards by which presidential performance is measured.

Because our experiments manipulated the attention paid to major national problems, we expected that viewers' judgments of overall presidential performance would be primed more effectively than would assessments of presidential character, whose determinants we assumed were more diverse, an intermixing of the political and the personal. This expectation was confirmed. We also expected that priming would be more pronounced in viewers' assessments of the president's competence than in assessments of his integrity, on the grounds that success or failure in such areas as national defense, inflation, arms control, and the like would reflect more on the president's competence than on his integrity. This expectation was supported in every detail in the case of President Carter but sharply and consistently violated in the case of President Reagan. This unanticipated result suggests that the public may be most susceptible to priming on those aspects of the president's character that are most open to debate. For President Carter, it was a question of competence—was he up to the demands of the job? For President Reagan, it was more a question of trust—did he care for the welfare of all Americans? At a more general level, the aspects of presidential character that the public takes seriously may be determined by the broader political context. Flagrant scandal may underscore trust and integrity, while runaway inflation may feed anxieties about competence and leadership. Should this be so, it would be a case of priming on a historical scale, with potentially historical consequences.

We further found that the power of television news to shape the standards by which presidents are judged is greater when stories focus on the president, and less when stories focus attention elsewhere. When coverage implied that the president was responsible for causing a problem or for solving it, the priming effect increased. When coverage implied that forces and agents other than the president were responsible for the problem, the priming effect diminished. These effects were particularly apparent for problems relatively new to the American political agenda, for which public understanding is perhaps less solidly formed and therefore more susceptible to the way that television news frames the matter of responsibility.

Our final pair of experiments demonstrate that the networks' agenda also primes the choices voters make. First, voters who were shown local news coverage that emphasized the state of the economy, the president's economic policies, and the implications of such policies for the impending midterm elections, relied heavily on their assessments of economic conditions when deciding which congressional candidate to support. In contrast, voters who watched local broadcasts devoted to the congressional candidates themselves—their positions on policy questions, group endorsements, or personal backgrounds—assigned great importance to these qualities in their choices. These results show that television news (*local* television news in this case) can alter the grounds on which elections are contested. Depending on the interests and resources of local television stations, congressional elections can either be a referendum on the president's economic performance, or purely a local contest between two distinct candidates.

The second experiment moved to the presidential level by reconstructing the intensive coverage lavished upon the Iranian hostage crisis in the closing days of the 1980 presidential campaign. The results suggested, in line with the priming hypothesis, that such coverage encouraged viewers to cast their votes on the basis of President Carter's performance on foreign affairs. Because Carter was widely perceived as ineffectual in his dealings with foreign countries, priming in this case may have dealt a final and fatal blow to the President's reelection chances, transforming an election that appeared breathtakingly close on Saturday into a decisive Republican victory on Tuesday.

MINIMAL EFFECTS REVISITED

Our results imply that television news has become an imposing authority, one that shapes the American public's political conceptions in pervasive ways. This conclusion seems to contradict the minimal effects verdict reached by most empirical research on the political consequences of mass media. How can this discrepancy be understood?

Serious and systematic empirical research on mass media and American politics began in the 1930s, motivated both by the spread of fascism abroad and by what many took to be the sinister proliferation of radio at home. But in a brilliant study of the 1940 presidential election described in *The People's Choice*, Lazarsfeld, Berelson, and Gaudet[2] (1948) concluded that media simply strengthen the predispositions that were already in place prior to the campaign. Meanwhile, an extensive and well-controlled series of experimental studies undertaken during World War II found that films designed to indoctrinate new draftees failed rather

spectacularly (Hovland, Lumsdaine, and Sheffield 1949).[3] The avalanche of research on political persuasion that soon followed these path-breaking and ambitious efforts drove home the same point again and again: while propaganda
reinforces the public's preferences it does not, and perhaps cannot, change them.

Political persuasion is difficult to achieve, but agenda-setting and priming
are apparently pervasive. According to our results, television news clearly and decisively influences the priorities that people attach to various national problems,
and the considerations they take into account as they evaluate political leaders or
choose between candidates for public office. Had we been interested in studying
persuasion, we would have designed other experiments and would have written
another book. More likely, we would have written no book at all, since we probably would have had little new to say. That is, had our television news experiments
set out to convert Democrats to Republicans, or pro-choice advocates to pro-life
advocates, we strongly suspect that the results would have demonstrated yet more
evidence in support of minimal effects. Our results on priming in the final days of
the 1980 presidential election suggest that persuasion *is* possible, but only under
very special circumstances: (1) large numbers of voters remain uncommitted in
the closing days of the campaign; (2) late-breaking political events attract considerable media coverage and focus attention on a single aspect of the national condition; and (3) the political developments decisively favor one candidate over the
other. But as a general matter, the power of television news—and mass communication in general—appears to rest not on persuasion but on commanding the public's attention (agenda-setting) and defining criteria underlying the public's
judgments (priming).

We do not mean to suggest that television's power to set the public agenda
and to prime citizens' political choices is unlimited. In fact, our studies suggest
clear limits to television's power, which must be kept in mind as we try to deci-
pher the broader significance of our findings.

One limitation is that the agenda-setting effects detected in our experiments were generally confined to the particular problem featured in the edited
newscasts. Stories about energy affected beliefs about the importance of energy
and energy alone, stories about defense affected beliefs about defense alone, and
so on. Such specificity may reflect both the way that the networks typically package the news—in tight, self-contained bundles (Weaver 1972)[4]—and the way that
most Americans think about politics, innocent of broad ideological frameworks
that might link one national problem with another (Converse 1964; Kinder
1983).[5] Whatever its cause, the specificity of agenda-setting serves to constrain
and channel television's influence. Because of the specific nature of the agenda-
setting effect, Americans are unlikely to be swept away by any coherent vision of
the country's problems. More likely, they will be pushed and pulled in various directions as discrete problems emerge, rise to prominence, and eventually fade
away.

Second, Americans are not without informational resources of their own.
We found that agenda-setting is weakened among those viewers who are most

deeply engaged in public life, presumably because their priorities are more firmly anchored. Because their opinions about the national condition are stronger, they are buffeted less by day-to-day fluctuations in the networks' agendas. We also found that priming is weakened among those who, in effect, are not ready to be primed, by virtue of their partisanship or their tacit theories about national problems. Democrats confronted with news about "Republican" problems, like Republicans confronted with "Democratic" problems, or like viewers whose understanding of national problems is either poorly worked out or does not include links between the president and the problem are, as a consequence, less vulnerable to priming. Television news defines political reality more completely for some Americans than for others.

There is a final and perhaps most important point to make regarding limitations on the power of television news. Each of our experiments on agenda-setting manipulated attention paid to problems that could all plausibly be regarded as relevant to the national interest, each widely understood as having the potential to affect millions of Americans seriously and adversely. Our hunch—unfortunately not tested—is that our experiments could not create concern over *implausible* problems. Had we inserted news stories portraying the discrimination faced by left-handers we very much doubt that viewers would suddenly put aside their worries about unemployment, defense, and environmental degradation. Nor do we think that television news could long sustain a story that was radically at odds with other credible sources of information. In the midst of booming prosperity, could the networks convince Americans that the economy was actually in a shambles? Or, turning the question around, in the depths of a severe recession, could the networks convince the public that times were good? We don't think so, though again we have little direct evidence. We believe that the networks can neither create national problems where there are none nor conceal problems that actually exist. What television news does, instead, is alter the priorities Americans attach to a circumscribed set of problems, all of which are plausible contenders for public concern.

In a parallel way, our experiments on priming reveal that the news reorders the importance viewers attach to various *plausible* standards of political evaluation: our experiments were not designed to test whether network news could induce viewers to apply trivial or irrelevant standards of evaluation to presidents or political candidates. We can only guess that had such experiments been conducted, they would demonstrate that television news cannot induce voters to abandon the traditional standards of evaluation.

In summary, television news shapes the priorities Americans attach to various national problems and the standards they apply to the performance of their government and the qualifications of their leaders. Although subject to limitations (television news cannot create priorities or standards out of thin air) television's power to shape political priorities is nonetheless formidable, as we will see shortly. This view clashes with the romantic ideal of the democratic citizen: one who is informed, skeptical, deeply engaged in public affairs, and thoughtful about the state of the nation and the quality of its leadership. But we know from other evidence that this vision is hopelessly idealistic; in fact, Americans pay casual and intermittent attention to public affairs and are often astonishingly ignorant of the details of contemporary politics (Kinder and Sears 1985).[6]

No doubt a portion of this indifference and ignorance can be attributed to candidates and government officials who practice evasion and deceit, and to the mass media (and especially television news), which operate all too often as if the average American were seven years old. But some of the indifference must be traced to the minor place accorded politics in everyday life. It seems to us highly unreasonable to demand of average citizens that they carefully and skeptically examine news presentations. If politics is ordinarily subordinate to the demands and activities of earning a living, raising a family, and forming and maintaining friendships, then citizens should hardly be expected to spend much of their time and energy each day grappling with the flow of news. How then do Americans "understand" politics?

The answer is that we muddle through. Faced with the enormous complexity and uncertainty of the political world, possessed of neither the motivation nor the wits to optimize, we strike various compromises. We resort to cognitive shortcuts (Tversky and Kahneman 1974)[7] and settle for acceptable solutions (Simon 1955).[8] As a consequence of such compromises, our judgments are often creatures of circumstance. What we think about the federal deficit, turmoil in Latin America, or the performance of our president depends less on what we know in some complete sense and more on what happens to come to mind.

The general moral here is that judgment and choice are inevitably shaped by considerations that are, however briefly, accessible. And when it comes to political judgment and choice, no institution yet devised can compete with television news in determining which considerations come to light and which remain in darkness.

POLITICAL RAMIFICATIONS

Although it was not our purpose to investigate the political ramifications of agenda-setting and priming directly, we nevertheless feel obliged to spell out what we take them to be. In doing so, we are in effect making explicit the assumptions that motivated our research. We undertook the various investigations reported here under the assumption that *if* television news could be shown to be a major force in shaping the viewing public's conception of national life, the political ramifications would be portentous. With the results now in, we believe that through agenda-setting and priming, television news affects the American political process in at last three important ways: first, by determining which problems the government must take up and which it can safely ignore; second, by facilitating or undermining an incumbent president's capacity to govern, and third, by intruding, sometimes dramatically and decisively, upon campaigns and elections.

The Government's Agenda

If television news influences the priorities Americans attach to national problems, and if such priorities eventually shape governmental decision-making, our results on agenda-setting become important for what they reveal about the formation of public policy. The essential question, then, is whether policy makers heed instruction from the general public in selecting which problems to consider and which to ignore.

We believe that public opinion does influence the governmental political agenda. We also agree with V. O. Key,[9] however, that although public opinion influences the focus and direction of government policy, such influence is sharply limited:

> The articulation between government and opinion is relatively loose. Parallelism between action and opinion tends not to be precise in matters of detail; it prevails rather with respect to broad purpose. And in the correlation of purpose and action time lags may occur between the crystallization of a sense of mass purpose and its fulfillment in public action. Yet in the long run, majority purpose and public action tend to be brought into harmony (1961, 553).

The "harmonizing" of government policy and public opinion is loose, and sometimes occurs very gradually, partly because ordinary Americans are indifferent to and uninformed about the details of policy, and partly because of the successful intervention of organized interests whose preferences depart from those of the unorganized public (Edelman 1964; McConnell 1966; Schattschneider 1960).[10] Nevertheless, the national government does appear to respond, if slowly and imperfectly, to the public's wishes (e.g., Burstein 1979; Burstein and Freudenburg 1978; Page and Shapiro 1983; Verba and Nie 1972; Weissberg 1976).[11] Thus, television news must assume a significant role in the intricate process by which citizens' inchoate goals and concerns eventually become government policy.

Presidential Power

Television news may also influence an incumbent president's capacity to govern. As Neustadt (1960)[12] proposed and others have shown (Kernell 1986; Rivers and Rose 1985),[13] presidential power derives partly from public approval. A president who is admired by the people tends to be powerful in Washington. The proliferation of opinion polls has accentuated this connection. Of course, public approval is not the only factor affecting a president's success. But other things being equal, the Congress, the governmental bureaucracy, world leaders, the private sector, and the executive branch itself all become more accommodating to a president who is riding high with the public. As television news shapes the criteria by which the president's performance is measured, so may it indirectly contribute to a president's power.

This point has not escaped presidents and their advisers. Without exception, presidents in the television age have assiduously sought to control the criteria by which they are viewed and evaluated. From the careful staging of news conferences to the manufacturing of pseudoevents, "making news" and "going public" have become essential presidential activities (Kernell 1986). Our findings suggest that presidents would be foolish to do otherwise. To the extent that the president succeeds in focusing public attention on his accomplishments while distracting the public from his mistakes, he contributes to his popularity and, eventually, to the influence he can exercise over national policy.

The Electoral Process

Finally, our results suggest that by priming some considerations and ignoring others, television news can shift the grounds on which campaigns are contested. Priming may therefore determine who takes office—and with what mandate—and who is sent home. Moreover, election results do matter in tangible ways: elected officials pursue policies that are broadly consistent with the interests of their core political constituencies (e.g., Bunce 1981; Cameron 1977; Hibbs 1977).[14] Consequently, insofar as television news contributes, if unwittingly, to the success of one candidate over another, the results on priming we have uncovered here are politically important.

It seems clear to us that television news has become a major force in the American political process. The problems that government chooses to tackle, the president's power over the focus and direction of national policy, and the real and tangible consequences of elections are all affected by the glare of the television camera. Less clear is whether this influence is necessarily undesirable. Whether, as many maintain, television threatens public opinion and menaces democratic government would seem to turn on the question of how faithfully the pictures and stories that appear on the news each night portray what of real consequence is actually happening in the world.

NOTES

1. P. H. Weaver, "Newspaper News and Television News," in *Media Agenda-Setting in a Presidential Election*, eds. D. Cater and R. Adler (New York: Praeger, 1975).

2. P. F. Lazarsfeld, B. Berelson, and H. Gaudet, *The People's Choice* (2nd ed.), (New York: Columbia University Press, 1948).

3. C. I. Hovland, A. Lumsdaine, and F. Sheffield, *Experiments on Mass Communication* (Princeton, N.J.: Princeton University Press, 1949).

4. P. H. Weaver, "Is Television News Biased?" *The Public Interest*, 26 (1972), 57–74.

5. P. E. Converse, "Belief Systems in Mass Publics," in *Ideology and Discontent*, ed. D. E. Apter (New York: Free Press, 1964); D. R. Kinder, "Diversity and Complexity in American Public Opinion," in *The State of the Discipline*, ed. A. Finifter (Washington, D.C.: APSA, 1983).

6. D. R. Kinder and D. O. Sears, "Public Opinion and Political Behavior," in *Handbook of Social Psychology*, Vol. 2 (3rd ed.), eds. G. Lindzey and E. Aronson (New York: Random House, 1985).

7. A. Tversky and D. Kahneman, "Judgement under Uncertainty: Heuristics and Biases," *Science*, 185 (1974), 1124–1131.

8. H. A. Simon, "A Behavioral Model of Rational Choice," *Quarterly Journal of Economics*, 69 (1955), 99–118.

9. V. O. Key, *Public Opinion and American Democracy* (New York: Knopf, 1961).

10. M. Edelman, *The Symbolic Uses of Politics* (Urbana: University of Illinois Press, 1964); G. McConnell, *Private Power and American Democracy* (New York: Random House, 1966); E. E. Schattschneider, *The Semi-Sovereign People* (New York: Holt, 1960).

11. P. Burstein, "Public Opinion, Demonstrations, and the Passage of Anti-Discrimination Legislation," *Public Opinion Quarterly* 43 (1979), 157–172; P. Burstein and W. Freudenburg, "Changing Public Policy: The Impact of Public Opinion, Anti-War Demonstrations, and War Costs on Senate Voting on Vietnam War Motions," *American Journal of Sociology*, 84 (1978), 99–122; B. I. Page and R. P. Shapiro, "Effects of Public Opinion on Policy," *American Political Science Review*, 77 (1983), 175–190; S. Verba and N. H. Nie, *Participation in America: Political Democracy and Social Equality* (Chicago: Harper Collins, 1972); R. Weissberg, *Public Opinion and Popular Government* (Englewood Cliffs, N.J.: Prentice-Hall, 1976).

12. R. E. Neustadt, *Presidential Power: The Politics of Leadership* (New York: Wiley, 1960).

13. S. Kernell, *Going Public* (Washington, D.C.: CQ Press, 1986); D. Rivers and N. L. Rose, "Passing the President's Program: Public Opinion and Presidential Influence in Congress," *American Journal of Political Science*, 29 (1985), 183–196.

14. V. Bunce, *Do Leaders Make a Difference?* (Princeton, N.J.: Princeton University Press, 1981); D. R. Cameron, "The Expansion of the Public Economy," *American Political Science Review*, 72 (1977), 1243–1261; D. A. Hibbs, "Political Parties and Macroeconomic Performance," *American Political Science Review*, 71 (1977), 1467–1487.

Processing the News: How People Tame the Information Tide

Doris Graber

The first major conclusion drawn from this study of information processing is that people tame the information tide quite well. They have workable, if intellectually vulnerable, ways of paring down the flood of news to manageable proportions. When they finish reading their newspapers, two out of every three stories have been excluded. Perusal of the remaining stories is simplified by taking advantage of the inverted pyramid style of news reporting. In this style, the most important information appears in the initial paragraph, allowing the reader to skip the remainder without fear of losing the story's focal point. Nearly half of the stories that people notice are handled through such partial reading. Only 18 percent of the stories in an average newspaper are read in full.

From *Processing the News: How People Tame the Information Tide* 2/e by Doris A. Graber (New York: Longman, 1988). Copyright © 1988 by Longman Publishing Group. Reprinted by permission.

Similar winnowing goes on for televised and radio news. On an average, out of 15 to 18 stories in a television newscast, no more than one is retained sufficiently well to be recalled in any fashion shortly afterward. The total loss of information, however, is not as great as these numbers suggest. Many of the stories are ignored because the audience realizes that they are a repetition of previously reported information. Television and radio newscasts throughout a given day are especially repetitious. If one considers only genuinely new information, the proportion of actual "news" recalled is somewhat higher.

Although the initial news selection process is haphazard, in addition to being stringent, people manage to keep on top of the most important stories. When one focuses only on stories that political elites deem significant, the balance between skipping and paying attention is reversed. People exposed to high-quality news sources recollect to some degree two out of every three prominent stories that are likely to affect the course of politics substantially. The credit for this greater attentiveness to important stories is shared by newspeople. They use a series of prominence cues (for example, story placement, headline size, story length, pictorial treatment, and frequent repetitions) to attract attention to news that political leaders and media gatekeepers deem significant.

In addition to paring down the flow of information by ignoring large numbers of stories, people use a processing strategy that further reduces the amount of information that needs to be stored. This strategy is schematic thinking. It allows individuals to extract only those limited amounts of information from news stories that they consider important for incorporation into their schemata. The schema process also facilitates integration of new information into existing knowledge. Since news sources usually present the news in isolated snippets, without sufficient background, schemata allow the receivers to embed the news in a meaningful context. During relatedness searches, the information extracted from a news story may be integrated into a single schema, or it may be segmented and the segments embedded in several schemata. Alternatively, the whole story may become a part of several schemata. In this way, a single story may be used to broaden substantially an individual's store of knowledge. The schema process also facilitates discarding information by providing criteria for determining that new information is redundant or does not conform to previous knowledge that still appears to be sound.

Although the schema process does well in reducing the danger of information overload, it does not lead to the retention of a large amount of factual data about specific events. Understanding the nature of a problem, rather than rote learning of the reported facts, is the goal. This explains why most people are unable to provide full particulars for news that they have processed. Despite rigorous winnowing, people nonetheless learn some details because many news stories are reported repeatedly with essentially the same information. For instance, most people can provide some details for stories about street crime, unemployment, pollution, and corruption among officeholders. Even when people cannot recall specifics from a particular story, they can make judgments about it. For instance, they know, on the basis of comparisons with familiar information stored in memory, when "nothing new" has been reported. Whenever information needs to be recalled, schemata can provide ready-made nonspecific answers. Schemata can even provide previously stored story details for other stories for which these details have been skipped.

Over time, an individual's fund of generalizations and specific knowledge grows, despite substantial amounts of forgetting. This is not surprising. Several daily lessons about current events, carried on year after year with frequent repetition of the same lesson, are bound to leave their mark, even when learning is purely passive. Since most of these lessons are used to flesh out preformed beliefs, a good deal of systematic error is likely to occur whenever these beliefs are wrong. That is the price people must pay for easing information-processing burdens through the use of schemata.

From the standpoint of average Americans, haphazard news processing is quite satisfactory. Interest in news is comparatively low. Therefore it does not justify great expenditure in time and effort when other things have a higher priority for the individual. But despite lukewarm interest in the news, average Americans want to keep informed because they have been socialized to consider this a civic responsibility. Many of them also want daily reassurance that they are not missing news items that might be personally significant. This combination of normative and personal pressures impels people to give at least cursory attention to news on a regular basis.

Most Americans have also learned to regard news as a form of entertainment. So they try to satisfy two goals simultaneously whenever possible. They scan the news for pieces of information that are important, diverting, and possibly both. The decision to select news or to reject it, therefore, is strongly influenced by an appraisal of the significance and the appeal of a particular piece of news. This fact makes it incumbent upon the media to cover essential stories in ways that capture and hold the public's interest.

IMPLICATIONS FOR AMERICAN DEMOCRACY

The broader political implications of the kind of news-processing behavior that we have depicted need to be considered from two perspectives. The first of these is the capacity of average Americans to acquire enough political information to fulfil the obligations of democratic citizenship. The second perspective requires a look at the implications for democratic living that flow from the substance of currently held schemata as developed and sustained through daily mass media news reports.

The Capacity for Political Learning

The American mass media supply a vast amount of current political information to average Americans throughout the days, months, and years. This news is mixed in with an even larger amount of nonpolitical information. All in all, no single person, even spending all waking hours in news consumption, could begin to pay attention to all of it, let alone absorb it successfully.

Our panelists demonstrated that people from all walks of life, endowed with varying capabilities, can manage to extract substantial amounts of political knowledge from this flood of information. All panelists had mastered the art of paying selective attention to news and engaging in the various forms of relatedness searches. All had acquired schemata into which they were able to fit incoming political information. All were able to work with an adequate array of schema dimensions, and all frequently used multiple themes in their various schemata. All had adopted culturally sanctioned values as the schematic framework into which schemata covering more specific matters were then embedded.

The differences among the panelists in the use of their processing skills were surprisingly minor. Largely, they were matters of degree in the use of various skills, such as segmenting and checking, and differences in coping with highly complex information drawn from settings remote from the individual's life. The high-interest groups generally processed more political information in greater detail and remembered it better than the low-interest groups. But basic choice and processing criteria were similar. Difficulties in access to news led to more selective processing and to combining attention to news with other activities. With some exceptions, interest and motivation to absorb specific information predicted learning better than education or expertise. Some processing differences were linked to needs created by life-style. Insofar as life-style coincides with demographic categories, such as age, sex, and ethnicity, life-style differences take on the appearance of demographic differences.

On balance, the verdict is clear. Average Americans are capable of extracting enough meaningful political information from the flood of news to which they are exposed to perform the modest number of citizenship functions that American society expects of them. They keep informed to a limited extent about the majority of significant publicized events. They also learn enough about major political candidates to cast a moderately thoughtful vote and make some judgments about postelection performance. Our findings show that "no opinion" replies often involved individuals who did have opinions but were afraid to express them until coaxed to do so. Fear of sounding stupid or uncertainty about the merits of particular opinions and the adequacy of their information explained their initial reluctance to reply.

Ideally, one may wish that expectations about the knowledge that citizens need were higher and that the social pressures to keep well informed were greater. One may wonder whether changes in news production and news processing might enhance the quality of citizenship. But answers to such questions are speculative and controversial and generally ignore the fact that people lead complex lives that permit only a peripheral involvement in politics.

Critics of current patterns often question whether people can fulfil citizenship needs adequately when they lack specific knowledge and when they base election choices largely on assessments of the candidates' personal qualities. Shouldn't well-informed people depend more on information about issues for voting decisions? Doesn't effective citizenship require that one remembers the name of one's representative or knows the length of a senatorial term? Isn't it essential for Americans in the 1980s to be able to locate Afghanistan on a map? I believe that the answer is no. One can judge the political qualifications of candidates without knowing their precise positions on issues. One does not have to know the name of one's representative or the length of a senatorial term to understand the role Congress plays in the political process. And one need not be able to locate Afghanistan on a map to be aware that the Soviet Union is intervening militarily in adjacent countries.

Despite lip service to the judgmental criteria advocated by political elites, most people select their political judgment criteria in their own ways. Judged from the perspective of personal efficiency, these criteria appear to work well. Take the example of selecting political leaders largely on the basis of personality. This process makes eminently good sense,

> given the capacities and inclinations of the average voter. Information about personal qualities is the only information which the average layman, remote from the political scene, can appraise intelligently. . . . People may properly feel that a president who is "a good man, capable and experienced" can tackle any kind of problem. At the time of the election it may be uncertain in which areas a candidate's severest test will come. Therefore it may be best to concentrate on general leadership qualities and characteristics of integrity and trustworthiness, rather than dwelling on competence in a variety of areas.[1]

The intellectual abilities of average citizens have also been called into question because social scientists have been unable to find the kind of belief systems for which they were looking. We have indicated that people do have belief systems, although they are not the grand edifices of the researchers' dreams. Broad value principles are the closest thing to an overarching belief structure. Beyond these, people do make causal and other connections among their schemata. The fact that processing involves relatedness searches also shows that there is continual awareness of similarities and connections.

The multiplicity of approaches used in schema construction leads to substantial flexibility and diversity in organizing information. This makes patterns of beliefs far less predictable than the patterns expected as the result of previous belief system research, which envisioned liberalism and conservatism as the cores around which belief structures were built. A multiplicity of organizing principles is intuitively sound. One should not expect to squeeze or stretch the multifaceted problems of the political world into a single Procrustean bed. Taking flexible positions is sensible whenever choices are not clear-cut and present themselves in widely divergent contexts. Rather than worrying about the public's rationality, one may well wonder about "the unwillingness of many political leaders and commentators to accept the public's 'post-ideological' maturity, and their insistence that the public should either endorse the left's traditional affirmation of the state or the right's rejection of it."[2]

The Impact of Schematic Thinking

Since schemata, once created, form the mold into which new information is integrated, previous schemata become extremely important. This highlights the significance of early socialization. The overarching cultural values appear to be internalized early in life. These, of course, are the values that account for the substantial consensus in American politics and for tolerance of a wide variety of views. It is this consensus, coupled with tolerance for a limited range of deviations, that makes a heterogeneous nation like America governable. Early socialization also lays the groundwork for needed diversity. We know that children adopt their party identifications early in life, as well as leanings toward either liberalism or conservatism. These early identifications provide political symbols that have a significant, though limited, influence on subsequent political orientations.

When people fail to learn or create appropriate schemata for certain types of information, that information cannot be readily absorbed. Socialization of average Americans apparently leaves a number of gaps in the schema structure. These gaps have made it difficult to focus public attention on some important problems. News about most foreign countries and news about science are examples. Even when such news is presented in simple ways, much of the audience fails to make the effort to absorb it because appropriate schemata did not form part of past socialization.

One may ask why people learn many new schemata early in life but lose that capacity or inclination as adults. An analogy to language learning may provide the answer. Small children learn new languages with relative ease and without extensive practice in logical thinking. Most adults, despite their greater capacities for logic, find it difficult, and occasionally impossible, to learn new languages and use them for thinking as well as speech. To push the analogy a bit further, just as nearly all people with normal intelligence are able to learn a new language in childhood, so nearly all people with normal intelligence are able to learn schematic thinking during their early years of life. Higher intelligence may permit more sophisticated use of these abilities, but the basic capacities for language learning and for schematic thinking are shared by all. Like language learning, schema development and the creation of new schemata continue throughout life. But as in language learning, the pace becomes much slower, except in the wake of extraordinary events.

The media play a significant part in early as well as later phases of socialization. Because of their pervasiveness and the ready access of all Americans to the same news sources, this socializing role is an important factor in creating a basis for nationwide commonality in thinking. As Lane observed in his Eastport panel, people who take their cues from the media

> reinforce one another's criticisms, they echo each other's solutions, and they share one another's sense of insecurity or of hope. In this they come to evolve common

concepts of industrial and governmental responsibility, of what is appropriate for the individual to do, whether wives should work, whether taxes are driving industry from Eastern States, whether the Republicans should or should not be blamed. And these, arising from more basic views on the proper relationship between social classes, the proper role of government, the proper way to explain a social event of this damaging character, go into the communications network and filter into the political stream. . . .[3]

Regardless of whether people filter their news largely through the eyes of liberals or conservatives, the media to which the average American is exposed have a status quo bias. They legitimize the American system by the deference they pay to its structure, its values, and its elected and appointed officials, in general if not in specific ways.

The fact that the same basic values as well as some specific schemata about the political process are adopted by most Americans during childhood and adolescence means that public political thinking tends toward uniformity and stability. Depending on one's feelings about the substance of consensus among Americans, the uniformity and stability produced by schematic thinking is either a boon or a bane. However, incremental changes do occur fairly readily in the wake of changing circumstances.

Large, abrupt changes in thinking about political issues are rare, except when major upheavals occur or when serious new problems become obvious. When these unusual conditions are widely publicized and involve declarations by well-known opinion leaders, they are apt to shake the confidence of large numbers of people in the continued validity of their existing schemata. Vietnam, Watergate, and the Civil Rights movement are recent examples of events that evidently produced major schema changes in a relatively brief period of time. The growing awareness of pollution, which was heightened by the activities of very visible political action groups, and the impact of the AIDS crisis on sexual mores are other examples. . . .

NOTES

1. Doris A. Graber, "Press Coverage and Voter Reaction in the 1968 Presidential Election," *Political Science Quarterly* 89(1974):96–97.

2. Everett Carll Ladd, "Politics in the 80's: An Electorate at Odds with Itself," *Public Opinion* 5(1983):3.

3. Robert E. Lane, *Political Ideology: Why the American Common Man Believes What He Does* (New York: Free Press, 1962), p. 443.

Parties, the Government, and the Policy Process

Samuel J. Eldersveld

The influence of parties on the policy decisions of governmental leaders is one of the most important questions for democratic societies. It is the "governing function" which affects us all. Does it make any difference how well parties organize, how carefully they recruit candidates, how well they are led, how effectively they campaign, how persuasively they mobilize voters and win elections—for policy outcomes? This is not the only process parties are involved in or the only basic function they perform. Parties engage in a variety of other functions—leadership selection, socialization, communication, agenda setting, government monitoring, and consensus building. But certainly their role in determining policy is a central concern. If they have no policy function, they may still meet other needs of the system, but they could then share, or yield, center stage in the governmental arena to other groups which are important in governmental action. As V. O. Key said, "There are two radically different kinds of politics: the politics of getting into office and the politics of governing."[1]

OBSTACLES TO PARTY INFLUENCE IN THE UNITED STATES

The traditional view is that American parties are too fragmented, dispersed, and undisciplined to have much influence over policy determination. This view argues that if one wants to explain the basis for the legislative decisions of members of Congress, United States senators, state legislators, or local policy makers one cannot explain them primarily on the basis of party influence. Even when strong mayors, governors, or presidents dominate the policy process, it is not their party roles so much as their personal appeals, personal bases of electoral support, and personal attractiveness and expertise which is important in explaining their success in getting new laws adopted. In this traditional view parties are not considered as policy leadership structures which can mobilize support to determine or significantly influence, legislative, executive, judicial, and bureaucratic decisions.

One of the major reasons for this alleged policy impotence of parties, it is argued, is the structural character of the American governmental system. The prin-

From Samuel J. Eldersveld, *Political Parties in American Society* (New York: Basic Books, 1982), chapter 16. Reprinted by permission.

ciples of our constitutional system theoretically do not facilitate a role for parties; indeed, they were designed originally to make it difficult for parties to have such a role. In *The Federalist* James Madison argued that the proposed constitution would make majority control by a party group virtually impossible. The key principles he had in mind, of course, were separation of powers, federalism, and bicameralism. The dispersion of governmental power under these principles constitutes a major challenge to parties seeking to control government for the purposes of policy initiation and innovation. Obstruction is more likely under such principles than the translation of new ideas into new laws. Structural principles, thus, can be critical for the policy process. Our peculiar principles pose a challenge to party leadership seeking to bridge and coordinate the different arenas of governmental authority.

It is not these constitutional principles alone, however, which are obstacles to party influence in the policy process. It is also the fragmentation of authority within the legislative body itself. The United States House of Representatives, up to 1910, was a body with strong leadership, with a speaker who had considerable power. But in that year there was a revolt against Speaker Joe Cannon, and in the seventy years since there has been no return to anything like the centralization of authority which Cannon had. The committee chairmen, the floor leader, the party policy committees, the whips, the party caucus—all these agencies of House operations have divided up the party's power. In addition special groups such as the Democratic Study Group (DSG), with 200 liberal Democrats, or the Republican special group, the "Chowder and Marching Club," have contributed to the decentralization of power in the House and made leadership and policy coordination difficult. Further, as William J. Keefe points out:

> Congress is an institution vulnerable to invasion by others. The three principal external forces that interact with Congress, seeking to move it along lines congenial to their interests, are the chief executive (including the bureaucracy), interest groups, and the constituencies.[2]

Rather than moving in harmony, these actors in the policy process are often in dissonance. There is legislative-executive conflict, a struggle among opposing lobbies, and pressures from different types of constituencies. As Keefe says, on certain issues the party often seems "to fly apart."[3] *It appears* that what we have in the United States—and perhaps want, but certainly tolerate—is "a shared, multiple-leadership form of government."[4]

The traditional model, then, is one which plays down the role of parties in the policy process because constitutional principles disperse power, internal party organization in legislative bodies is not cohesive, and external pressures produce conflicts. The implicit argument is that parties cannot overcome these features of the system—parties as organizations or as leadership groups do not coordinate policy making, parties in fact are secondary to other influences on policy making, and partisan considerations and motivations do not explain policy actions.

This model, further, is usually contrasted to the parliamentary model, such as is found in Britain. It is argued that party plays a much more important role there because there is party discipline in the House of Commons, there is centralized party leadership which determines the party's position on policy questions, there is no dispersion of power as in the American constitutional system (Parliament is supreme), and external pressures play no such negative role (indeed constituency influences facilitate the relevance of party in the policy process). The majority in the party caucus (Labour, Conservative, or Liberal) in the House of Commons selects its leadership, together they decide on policy, defections from these majority decisions are not sanctioned but punished, and thus normally the party as an organization makes policy. There is, thus, *theoretically* a sharp contrast between the United States "fragmentation of party power" model and the parliamentary (British) "party dominance" model.

EVIDENCE OF PARTY INFLUENCE ON NATIONAL POLICY DECISIONS

Despite the negative expectations about the role of American parties on policy decisions, research suggests caution in reaching that conclusion. True, parties are organizationally fragmented, power is dispersed, leadership is not centralized and party discipline of the parliamentary system doesn't exist in the United States. Nevertheless, policies do change as the strength of parties ebbs and flows.

The economic policies of the national government are one important substantive area where it may indeed make a great deal of difference which party wins the election. Edward Tufte has studied this matter and concludes that "the real force of political influence on macroeconomic performance comes in the determination of economic priorities." He then argues, "Here the ideology and platform of the political party in power dominate . . . the ideology of political leaders shapes the substance of economic policy."[5] Indeed, his position is that one can generalize for modern democratic societies, including the United States, as follows: Parties of the Right (including the Republicans) favor "low rates of taxation and inflation with modest and balanced government budgets; oppose income equalization; and will trade greater unemployment for less inflation most of the time." Parties of the Left (including the Democrats) favor "income equalization and lower unemployment, larger government budgets; and will accept increased rates of inflation in order to reduce unemployment." The platforms of the national parties reveal these differences. Thus, in 1976 the Democratic platform pledged "a government which will be committed to a fairer distribution of wealth, income and power." The Republican platform in 1976 pledged "less government, less spending, less inflation." In 1980 the Democratic platform promised to fight inflation but not by increasing interest rates or unemployment. The Republicans said that "our fundamental answer to the economic problem is . . . full employment without inflation through economic growth."

The public's expectations concerning the performance of the two parties are clearly illustrated by their attitudes on the unemployment issue in 1976. When asked to assess the job which President Gerald Ford and the Republicans had done in dealing with unemployment, only 11 percent of the sampling responded that it had been a "good" performance, 57 percent a "fair" job, and 32 percent a "poor" one. Table 1 reveals the results of a study asking which presidential candidate and party would do the best job of reducing unemployment. The public clearly expected Carter to do more about unemployment. Similar results emerged when the sample was asked, "Do you think the problems of unemployment would be handled better by the Democrats, by Republicans, or about the same by both?" The results were: 39 percent Democrats, 10 percent by the Republicans, and 52 percent the same for both parties. The 1980 results were different, however: 19 percent Democrats, 23 percent Republicans, and 58 percent about the same for both parties.

Tufte demonstrates that the actual employment statistics over time reveal a linkage between presidential elections and unemployment and inflation rates. These data point to the following "rules":[6]

1. Both Democrats and Republicans will reduce inflation or unemployment if there is an economic crisis and an election is approaching.
2. If there is no real crisis, the Republicans will do much better in reducing inflation than unemployment; the Democrats will do better in reducing unemployment.

Whether Carter's actions in 1980 supported these observations is an arguable matter!

Another scholar, Douglas Hibbs, has also explored this problem. He concludes that "inter-party differences in government-induced unemployment levels is 2.36 percent"—a sizeable difference in national employment levels as a result of a Democratic or Republican administration. Thus, "the Kennedy-Johnson administration posture toward recession and unemployment stands in sharp contrast to Eisenhower's, . . . the basic economic priorities associated with the Eisenhower era were re-established during the Nixon and Ford administrations" and were "deliberately induced." Hibbs concludes, "The real winners of elections are per-

TABLE 1   Public's Opinion on Which Party Will Best Deal with Unemployment (as a percentage)

Public View	President Ford	Candidate Carter
Candidate will reduce unemployment	31	52
Candidate will not reduce unemployment	46	24
Difference	−15	+28

Source: University of Michigan CPS/NES, 1976.

haps best determined by examining the policy consequences of partisan change rather than simply by tallying the votes."[7]

A study of the policies of our government over the years finds that whichever party is in power for a longer or shorter period of time is crucial for the content of public policy. In an exhaustive study of laws adopted by the United States government from 1800 to 1968 (requiring analysis of 60,000 pieces of legislation) Benjamin Ginsberg was able to determine when the peak points in the adoption of new policies and new laws occurred. He concluded that the peak points were 1805, 1861, 1881, and 1933. These were years after major elections in which a shift in the power of the political parties occurred, called in some instances major "realigning elections." His basic interpretation is that "clusters of policy change" do come as a result of partisan change in electoral choices. He summarized as follows:

> Our findings suggest that voter alignments are, in effect, organized around substantive issues of policy and support the continued dominance in government of a party committed to the principal elements of the choice made by voters during critical eras. . . . Partisan alignments form the constituent bases for governments committed to the translation of the choices made by the electorate. . . . The policy-making role of the electorate is, in effect, a continuing one.[8]

In other words, the voters' decision on what party should govern determines the basic direction of public policy! . . .

NOTES

1. V. O. Key, Jr., *Politics, Parties and Pressure Groups*, 4th ed. (New York: T. Y. Crowell, 1958), p. 702.

2. William J. Keefe, *Congress and the American People* (Englewood Cliffs, N.J.: Prentice Hall, 1980), p. 101.

3. Ibid., p. 105.

4. Thomas E. Cronin, *The State of the Presidency* (Boston: Little, Brown, 1975), p. 107.

5. Edward R. Tufte, *Political Control of the Economy* (Princeton: Princeton University Press, 1980), p. 71.

6. Ibid., pp. 101–102.

7. Douglas Hibbs, "Political Parties and Macroeconomic Policy," *American Political Science Review* 71 (1977): 1486. Other scholars disagree with this position in part, at least the implication of presidential manipulation of the economy for electoral gain. See Thad A. Brown and Arthur A. Stein, "The Political Economy of National Elections," unpublished paper, University of California at Los Angeles, November, 1980.

8. Benjamin Ginsberg, "Elections and Public Policy," *The American Political Science Review* 70, no. 1 (1976): 49.

The Advocacy Explosion

Jeffrey M. Berry

This is not the first period of American history in which an apparent increase in the numbers and influence of interest groups has heightened anxiety.[1] Uneasiness over the power and influence of interest group politics is part of the American political tradition. Yet today's widespread concern contrasts with fairly recent American attitudes. The New Deal, for example, was known for its positive acceptance of interest groups because of the greater role trade associations came to have in the policy making of newly established regulatory agencies. As recently as the 1960s, scholars were arguing that interest group politics contributed to democratic politics.

Currently, a pervasive, popular perception is of an unprecedented and dangerous growth in the number of interest groups and that this growth continues unabated. This view is echoed constantly in the press. *Time* tells us that "at times the halls of power are so glutted with special pleaders that government itself seems to be gagging."[2] Bemoaning the growing lobbying industry, the *New Republic* notes, "What dominates Washington is not evil and immorality, but a parasite culture. Like Rome in decline, Washington is bloated, wasteful, pretentious, myopic, decadent, and sybaritic. It is the paradise of the overpaid hangers-on."[3] The normally staid *Atlantic* thinks things have deteriorated so much that even the First Amendment right to petition the government should not stand in the way of remedial action. "Lobbyists should be denied access to the Capitol," says an *Atlantic* writer, because they are ruining the legislative process.[4]

Journalists might be allowed a bit of literary license, but politicians ring the fire alarm too. After returning to Congress in 1987 after a twelve year absence, Representative Wayne Owens (D–Utah) lamented that "in those twelve years I was gone, basically every group you can think of has developed a Washington office or a national association aimed at presenting their case to Congress."[5] President Jimmy Carter, in his farewell address to the nation, blamed interest groups for many shortcomings of his administration:

> . . . We are increasingly drawn to single-issue groups and special interest organizations to insure that whatever else happens our own personal views and our own private interests are protected. This is a disturbing factor in American political life. It tends to distort our purpose because the national interest is not always the sum of all our single or special interests.[6]

From *The Interest Group Society*, 2/e by Jeffrey M. Berry. Copyright © 1989 by Jeffrey M. Barry. Reprinted by permission of HarperCollins Publishers.

Some scholars find interest groups to be at the heart of this country's problems as well. Economist Lester Thurow states unequivocally that "our economic
problems are solvable," but adds that "political paralysis" stands in the way. The
source of that paralysis, in Thurow's eyes, is an expanding system of effective interest groups that makes it impossible for government to allocate the pain that
comes with realistic economic solutions.[7] Political scientist Everett Ladd blames
special interest politics for our economic woes as well. "The cumulative effect of
this pressure has been the relentless and extraordinary rise of government spending and inflationary deficits."[8]

In short, the popular perception is that interest groups are a cancer, spreading unchecked throughout the body politic, making it gradually weaker, until they
eventually kill it.

Political rhetoric aside, has there really been a significant expansion of interest group politics? Or are interest groups simply playing their familiar role as
whipping boy for the ills of society?

The answer to both questions is yes. Surely nothing is new about interest
groups being seen as the bane of our political system. The muckrakers at the turn
of the century voiced many of the same fears that show up today in *Time* or the
Atlantic. Yet even if the problem is familiar, it is no less troubling. The growth of
interest group politics in recent years should not simply be dismissed as part of a
chronic condition in American politics. Of particular concern is that this growth
took place during a period of party decline. The United States is not just a country
with an increasing number of active interest groups, but a country whose citizens
look more and more to interest groups to speak for them in the political process.

Before addressing the larger problems that arise from this trend, we must
document the increasing number of interest groups. The available statistics show
an unmistakable increase in interest group activity in Washington. Jack Walker's
survey of 564 lobbying organizations in Washington (Figure 1)[9] shows a clear pattern of growth, with approximately 30 percent of the groups originating between
1960 and 1980.[10] The figures do not, however, indicate precisely how many new
groups have been started in different eras because we cannot calculate how many
were started in earlier periods but have since ceased to exist. A second study, by
Kay Schlozman and John Tierney, shows a similar pattern. Their examination of
groups listed in a lobbying directory shows that 40 percent were founded after
1960 and 25 percent after 1970.[11] Both surveys show that citizen groups were the
most likely to have formed recently. In short, we can be confident that the increase in lobbying organizations is real and not a function of overblown rhetoric
about the dangers of contemporary interest groups.

The rate of growth of interest groups seems to be tapering off though. Given
the rather sizable boom in the growth of groups during the 1960s and 1970s, this
is hardly surprising. At some point the market for different types of interest
groups becomes saturated, and new entrants will find it more difficult to gain a
foothold. There will always be new constituencies developing and existing constituencies recognizing that they need greater representation, but rapid expansion

of one sector of an interest group community reduces the amount of available resources for potential new groups. . . .

THE RISE OF CITIZEN GROUPS

The growth of interest group advocacy in different sectors of society comes from many of the same roots. At the same time, the sharp growth in numbers of interest groups also reflects different sectors of society responding to each other. As one segment of the interest community grew and appeared to prosper, it spurred growth in other segments eager to equalize the increasing strength of their adversaries. This spiral of interest group activity began in large part in the civil rights and antiwar movements of the 1960s. . . .

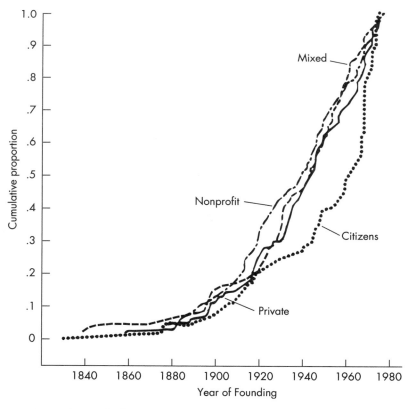

Source: Survey of voluntary associations by Jack L. Walker, "The Origins and Maintenance of Interest Groups in America." *American Political Science Review* 77 (June 1983), p. 395. The "mixed" category represents groups that have members from both the public and private sectors.

FIGURE 1   Interest Groups and Their Year of Origin

DEMYSTIFYING INTEREST GROUP ADVOCACY

The advocacy explosion came from many sources. Different kinds of groups responded to particular events: the growth of adversary groups, changes in the law, and evolutionary changes in the political environment. These stimuli were enhanced by a cumulative learning process as well.

In recent years there has been a "demystification" of interest group politics. A broader segment of the population has come to believe that interest group advocacy has great potential. More and more people have come to understand that interest groups are vital to protecting and furthering their own interests. And more and more people have come to understand how interest groups operate in practice and how new groups could be formed.

Interest group leaders (and prospective organizers) learned by watching other interest groups; lobbying organizations are inveterate copiers. The way in which citizen groups copied the successful civil rights and antiwar organizations is an illustration of this process. Not only did other minorities copy the black civil rights organizations, but new liberal citizen groups were started to appeal to middle-class interests as well.

Conservative citizen groups that arose in the 1970s responded directly to the success of liberal citizen groups. There was a sense that everyone was represented *except* the conservatives. Liberal citizen groups appeared to be enormously successful, with major victories such as establishing regulatory agencies like the Consumer Product Safety Commission and the EPA, the constant media attention given to Ralph Nader and Common Cause, and a stream of successful environmental lawsuits. Most important, liberal groups seemed to have the ear of government and thus were influencing its agenda.

Business in turn was influenced by the liberal citizen groups' growing advocacy. Even though the most direct stimulus was increased regulation, the public interest movement was seen as the primary instigator of "excessive" government regulation. Business has made great use of all major strategies of effective lobbying. It has formed the most PACs and donates the most money, though PACs have multiplied on all fronts. No segment of the interest group population wants to be at a disadvantage in gaining access to congressional offices.

No automatic mechanism in politics exists whereby new groups cause opposing groups to form as a countervailing power; the reality is much more complicated. In recent years, though, proliferation of groups has been facilitated by rapidly increasing knowledge about interest groups. From academic works to the omnipresent eye of the mass media, both laymen and elites have learned how these groups operate. The development of public policy and the interest groups' role in that process have been reported and analyzed in excruciating detail. Thus the costs of acquiring information about interest groups became cheaper. People found it easier to find out what they needed to know to form groups, and once they were formed, what they needed to know to operate them effectively.

More specifically, the growth of interest groups was furthered by increasing knowledge about three subjects.

Organizational maintenance. Interest group leaders have become more effective at raising money and broadening their base of support. Their growing utilization of direct mail is the most obvious example; leaders of newly forming or existing groups can buy lists of likely prospects. Foundations and government became more important sources of money for interest groups during their greatest expansion period. Businesses moved quickly to use the newly acquired right to form PACs to collect money from corporate executives. For interest group leaders who feel they need help in maintaining their organization, many consultants in Washington have expertise in direct mail and how to secure government grants.

Lobbying skills. Through the years, lobbying has had an unsavory behind-the-scenes image of unctuous group representatives using their contacts in government to do the groups' bidding. Yet today's typical lobbyist will often try to gain recognition and publicity for what he or she is doing rather than hide it. Lobbying has quickly become an anyone-can-do-it activity, and little mystery is left as to what successful lobbyists do. One does not have to have close friends in high places (though it certainly doesn't hurt), but other attributes are commonly accepted as vital to effective lobbying. Chief among these is policy expertise. The ability to "network" (form coalitions), to utilize the media, and to develop lasting professional relationships with staffers and policymakers are other well-known fundamentals of lobbying. It is much harder to raise the resources for lobbying than it is to figure out what to do with those resources.

Communications. Lobbying has been furthered by a growing recognition that information is power and that the best lobbyists are the people back home. The Washington newsletter is now a staple of Washington politics. Constituents back home receive frequent mailings on the issues that are being decided by government and what they need to do to influence them. Computerized lists of constituents facilitate mailings to members in key congressional districts when a critical vote is coming. Some groups have special networks of activists, who can be instructed to contact those in government when the need arises.

The growth of interest group politics thus comes in part from learning: Successful groups set the example for others. Washington is really a town of few secrets, and what works for one group is quickly copied by others. Consultants, lawyers, and public relations specialists who work for different clients, the huge Washington media establishment, and the lobbyists who interact constantly with one another make learning about what interest groups do ever easier.

CONCLUSION

By any standard, the amount of lobbying in Washington has expanded significantly. Interests previously unrepresented are now represented before the government by recently formed organizations. Interests that were already represented in Washington tend to be even better represented today.

Although the reasons for lobbying's rise in different sectors of society vary, some common threads appear in the broad movement toward interest group politics. Pluralist theory put forward the idea that interest group involvement in policy making contributed to democratic government. Expanding governmental activity in the 1960s and 1970s, usually at the behest of interest groups, directly affected more and more constituencies and helped catalyze increased advocacy. Finally, as new interest groups form, they stimulate other constituencies to organize because new groups increase awareness about what various interests are doing and, further, their formation threatens their natural adversaries. The success of the public interest movement, for example, resonates through this 1978 plea in the *Wall Street Journal*: "Businessmen of the World Unite." Readers were told that "we need a businessman's liberation movement and a businessman's liberation day and a businessman's liberation rally on the monument grounds of Washington, attended by thousands of businessmen shouting and carrying signs."[12]

While the advocacy explosion created new groups and expanded resources devoted to lobbying, this heightened competition between groups did not bring about a perfect balance of interests represented in Washington. Business was by far the best represented sector of American society before this upsurge in lobbying, and it remains in that position now that the growth in the numbers of interest groups is finally slowing down. Business responded to the challenge of the public interest movement with ample resources and a fierce determination to maintain its advantages in Washington. It now faces potent competition from an array of liberal public interest groups, although its traditional rival, organized labor, is on the decline. . . . It is tempting to make interest groups the scapegoat for the ills of American society, believing that we would have politically acceptable solutions to public policy dilemmas if lobbies didn't exist.[13] However, differing interests will always abound. The attitudes and potential reactions of various constituencies must be considered by policymakers when decisions are made. Yet the organization of interests into an ever-increasing number of lobbying groups adds to the power of those constituencies.

The growth of interest group politics can be applauded for expanding the range of lobbying organizations represented in the political system. A related benefit of this proliferation is that it was instrumental in the replacement of many narrow subgovernments with more open, more participatory, and more conflictual issue networks. If there are to be lobbying organizations, it is best that they be as representative as possible of all segments of American society. Yet it would be naive to assume that interest groups will ever fairly reflect the different interests of all Americans. Upper- and middle-class interests will always be better represented by lobbying organizations.

Government is realistically limited in what it can do to address this imbalance, but it must try to ensure representation for the chronically underrepresented. Financial support for advocacy groups for the poor should be expanded, not decreased, as part of the overall move to cut back government funding of welfare and social services. Such cuts actually create a greater need for this kind of surrogate representation. Citizen participation programs, which have had mixed success, ought to be continued and improved. They make government more accountable to the people it serves and create a potential channel of influence for those who may not be adequately represented by interest groups.[14] The federal government can do little aside from the reforms discussed here, however, to curb the activities of interest groups. Worrisome as the spiraling growth of interest group politics may be, it is not desirable to have the government trying generally to inhibit the efforts of various constituencies to find more effective representation in the political system.

Because government's role will always be limited, prospects for further curbing the influence of faction must come from the political parties. They are the natural counterweight to interest groups, offering citizens the basic means of pursuing the nation's collective will. Only political parties can offer citizens broad choices about the major directions of public policy. Strengthening our parties is a widely shared goal, though there is little consensus over what actions need to be taken to accomplish this.[15] Whatever the future of party renewal, though, interest groups will continue to play their traditional role of articulating this nation's multitude of interests. Interest groups offer a direct link to government on the everyday issues that concern a particular constituency but not the nation as a whole. The role interest groups play is not ideal, but they remain a fundamental expression of democratic government.

NOTES

1. Some arguments here were first published in Jeffrey M. Berry, "Public Interest vs. Party System," *Society* 17 (May/June 1980), pp. 42–48.

2. Evan Thomas, "Peddling Influence," *Time*, March 3, 1986, p. 26.

3. Fred Barnes, "The Parasite Culture of Washington," *New Republic*, July 28, 1986, p. 17.

4. Gregg Easterbrook, "What's Wrong with Congress," *Atlantic*, December, 1984, p. 84.

5. Jeffrey H. Birnbaum, "Congressman Who Returned After Twelve Years Notes Changes Including More Lobbying, Budget Fights," *Wall Street Journal*, June 15, 1987.

6. "Prepared Texts of Carter's Farewell Address on Major Issues Facing the Nation," *The New York Times*, January 15, 1981.

7. Lester C. Thurow, *The Zero-Sum Society* (New York: Penguin Books, 1981), pp. 11–15.

8. Everett C. Ladd, "How to Tame the Special Interest Groups," *Fortune*, October 20, 1980, p. 66ff.

9. Jack L. Walker, "The Origins and Maintenance of Interest Groups in America," *American Political Science Review* 77 (June 1983), pp. 390–406.

10. See an earlier version of the Walker article, similarly titled, presented at the annual meeting of the American Political Science Association, New York, September 1981, p. 14.

11. Kay Lehman Schlozman and John T. Tierney, *Organized Interests and American Democracy* (New York: Harper and Row, 1986), pp. 75–76.

12. Cited in Michael Useem, *The Inner Circle* (New York: Oxford University Press, 1984), pp. 17–18.

13. See Mancur Olson, *The Rise and Decline of Nations* (New Haven: Yale University Press,

1982); and Lester C. Thurow, *The Zero-Sum Society* (New York: Penguin, 1981). See also Robert H. Salisbury, "Are Interest Groups Morbific Forces?," paper presented to the Conference Group on the Political Economy of Advanced Industrial Societies, Washington, D.C., August 1980.

14. See Benjamin Barber, *Strong Democracy* (Berkeley: University of California Press, 1984).

15. For a comprehensive program of party reform, see Larry J. Sabato, *The Party's Just Begun* (Glenview, Ill.: Scott, Foresman/Little, Brown, 1988).

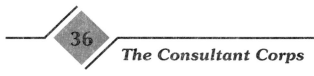

The Consultant Corps

Larry J. Sabato

Controversy is raging about the role and influence of the political consultant in American elections, and properly so. There is no more significant change in the conduct of campaigns than the consultant's recent rise to prominence, if not pre-eminence, during the election season. Political consultants, answerable only to their client-candidates and independent of the political parties, have inflicted severe damage upon the party system and masterminded the modern triumph of personality cults over party politics in the United States. All the while they have gradually but steadily accumulated almost unchecked and unrivaled power and influence in a system that is partly their handiwork.

For a group of political elites so prominent and powerful, consultants have been remarkably little investigated and understood. Indeed, the argument about their role and influence in the electoral system has operated essentially in a vacuum—a vacuum this book attempts to fill. Until now far more misinformation than fact has surfaced in the debate about politicians' use of political consultants, and there are many reasons for this. The consultants themselves make the task of separating fact from fiction and image from reality as difficult as possible. They enhance their own images and increase the fees they can command by keeping their campaign techniques as mysterious and bewildering as possible. Most consultants have been intimately involved with politics for decades, and they know better than most elected officials that, in politics, style is closely intertwined with substance. Fame and fortune—not to mention electoral success—come to those who can adjust the mirrors in just the right way and produce sufficient quantities of blue smoke in the public arena.

In using the blue smoke and mirrors of politics to cloud the view of their profession, consultants have found a valuable ally, the working press. Not only do many journalists fail to understand what it is consultants do and how they do it; those same print and television journalists are responsible in good measure for the glow of expertise and omniscience that surrounds the consultant's every pronouncement. Consultants have become prime and semipermanent sources of information and insight for political reporters, and the election professionals are rewarded with an uncritical press and frequent, beatific headlines.

No one reads these headlines more closely than the prospective candidates, and as a consequence virtually no nominee for public office at any level thinks he can survive without a consultant or two. Remarkably, though, if reporters are ignorant of the consultant trade and technology, candidates are far more so. President Gerald Ford, for instance, would admit almost total ignorance of his 1976 direct-mail operation and even decry "junk mail" after leaving the Oval Office, despite the fact that direct mail had been one of the most successful aspects of his campaign for the Republican presidential nomination. Many other candidates have hired media and polling consultants at great cost without even a superficial comprehension of their techniques or their real worth—taking on faith what they had read and heard about these election wizards, believing all the while that consultants were essential for victory without knowing whether or why the common wisdom was true. Understandably, candidates lack the specialized training in election technology that their consultants possess and have little time to learn in a demanding, pressure-cooker campaign. This leaves the consultant a seemingly indispensable commodity, someone with immense leverage not merely during the election but also after the campaign is over. Few are the politicians who never seek office again, and their relationships with consultants are as permanent as their campaigns. Pollster Patrick Caddell's and media man Gerald Rafshoon's extraordinary alliance with President Carter is by no means exceptional any more.

If a thorough examination of the consultants' profession is in order, so too is an exhaustive study of their much-acclaimed techniques. A glance at any election-year newspaper or political trade journal tells why. In the praise being heaped upon the media masters and soothsayers and direct-mail artists, all sorts of wondrous things are being attributed to them. Upon actually meeting these political wizards, after preparatory reading of hundreds of articles by awe-struck commentators, one inevitably is reminded of Dorothy's disappointment when she unmasked the Wizard of Oz. For, despite their clever public posturings, consultants have no potions or crystal balls, and most of them will admit it forthrightly, at least in private. "If I knew the successful formula," conceded one long-time professional, "I would patent it."

It is reassuring (perhaps deceptively so) to hear one of the most widely experienced generalist consultants, Stuart Spencer, proclaim that "There are good politicians and there are bad politicians, and all the computers and all the research in the world are not going to make the campaign situation any better when bad politicians are involved." Spencer may well be right that consultants cannot turn a sow's ear into a silk purse (although at least a couple of exceptions come to mind). But this book will certainly provide some evidence that a less radical transformation at the consultant's hand is possible, that a black sheep can become a white one upon application of a little dye and a corroded silver dollar can be transformed into a shiny one with a chemical and a bit of polish. Consultants and the new campaign technology have not changed the essence of politics. Politics is still persuasion, still a firm, friendly handshake. But the media of persuasion are no longer the same, and the handshake may be a projection or even an illusion.

Whatever the degree of their electoral influence, consultants—most of them—have talent and enormous experience. One hastens to add that a few well-publicized consultants do not live up even vaguely to their advance billing. As one top professional observed: "The only thing that keeps some of them alive is luck and being in the right place at the right time. They don't really affect anything in a dramatic way because they don't have the political instinct to do it." By and large, however, consultants are hard-working professionals: very bright and capable, politically shrewd and calculating, and impressively articulate. They travel tens of thousands of miles every year, work on campaigns in a dozen or more states simultaneously, and eat, breathe, and live politics. They are no less political junkies than the candidates they serve. For the most part, they are even less concerned with issues, the parties, and the substance of politics than their clients. They are businessmen, not ideologues.

While admired for their abilities and acumen, consultants also suffer an unsavory reputation in some quarters, and certainly among the general public, whose distrust of seamy, "smoke-filled-room" political operatives is traditional and enduring. At best consultants are seen as encouraging the natural instincts of plastic politicians. ("Gripp, Grinn, Waffle, & Faykit" is the sign cartoonist Jeff MacNelly hangs outside his fictional consulting firm.) At worst, consultants are denounced as "hustlers and con men," as Joe Napolitan put it.[1] Consultants bristle at the slightest mention of any unfavorable press, blaming the criticism on the politicians they work for. As media consultant Michael Kaye expressed it:

> People don't like politicians. So no matter how skillfully a political consultant like me does his work, I am a bad guy. I am a packager. I am a manipulator. Now, is it because of what I do, or is it the product that I sell?

Yet widespread doubt about the work of consultants has a basis more thoughtful than Kaye's analysis suggests. That basis is a deep concern for the health and well-being of the democratic process. What consultants seem to forget is that their work cannot be evaluated solely within the context of their profession. "Is this artful media?" or "Is this an effective piece of direct mail?" or "Did this action by a political consultant help to elect candidate X?" are legitimate questions and necessary ones for any judgment of a particular consultant's worth. But the ultimate standard by which the *profession* of political consulting is judged cannot merely be success in electing or defeating candidates. There are much more vital considerations of ethics and democracy to ponder, because electoral politics is the foundation of any democratic society, and important actors in the political sphere must necessarily be the subject of special scrutiny.

This book attempts to provide that scrutiny and to offer an informed discussion of the consequences of the consultant's trade and his new campaign technology. While an observer can reasonably conclude from subsequent chapters that most politicians have been fairly well served by their election professionals, it simply does not follow that the public and the political system have been equal beneficiaries. As the influence of consultants has grown, some very disquieting questions have begun to loom large. Influence peddling, all kinds of financial misconduct, shameful acts of deception and trickery, and improprieties with former clients who are in public office are only a few of the compromising and unethical practices found in far too many consultants' portfolios. At the root of some of the worst offenses is a profit motive unrestrained by ties to party, ideology, or ideals. Sadly, the truth is much as political columnist Jack Germond suggests: "Philosophy and party don't motivate most of the political consultants. Money does, partially, and there is a lot of money to be made if you're any good."

As distressing as they are, the ethical concerns fade by comparison to the democratic effects wrought by consultants. Political professionals and their techniques have helped homogenize American politics, added significantly to campaign costs, lengthened campaigns, and narrowed the focus of elections. Consultants have emphasized personality and gimmickry over issues, often exploiting emotional and negative themes rather than encouraging rational discussion. They have sought candidates who fit their technologies more than the requirements of office and have given an extra boost to candidates who are more skilled at electioneering than governing. They have encouraged candidates' own worst instincts to blow with the prevailing winds of public opinion. Consultants have even consciously increased nonvoting on occasion and meddled in the politics of other countries.

These activities have not occurred in a vacuum. The rules of the political game have been altered dramatically, with consultants clearly benefiting from the changes. The decline of the political parties and the establishment of a radically different system of campaign finance are foremost among the developments that consultants have turned to their advantage. For example, as a direct consequence of the diminution of party strength, a diminution to which consultants have themselves contributed and, in some cases, cheered, consultants have replaced party leaders in key campaign roles.

Yet the power flow from party leaders to political consultants does not have to continue, nor must unethical practices remain unchecked. Consultants and their apologists quite naturally can see no system better than the current one, and they will always have a ready excuse for distasteful doings in their profession. But those who lament the recent technological changes in electioneering have only to look to one of the major parties to see the path of renewal that these same new campaign technologies have made possible. A revitalized national and state Republican party organization, fueled by the marvels consultants had previously harnessed for themselves and monopolized, has provided the model that can tame consultant abuses and develop a healthier, party-based electoral system in the future. This auspicious development and its considerable potential for good will be the object of special examination later. . . .

IMAGES AND ROLES OF POLITICAL CONSULTANTS

The term "political consultant" is bandied about so loosely that any discourse on the subject must begin by attempting to define it. A *political consultant* is a campaign professional who is engaged primarily in the provision of advice and services (such as polling, media creation and production, and direct-mail fund raising) to candidates, their campaigns, and other political committees. Broadly the title can adorn almost any paid staffer on even the most minor of campaigns. Here, however, we shall concentrate on the relatively small and elite corps of interstate political consultants who usually work on many campaigns simultaneously and have served hundreds of campaigns in their careers. They are the sellers, and often the creators, of advanced campaign technology and technique.

There are basically two kinds of consultants. A *generalist* consultant advises a candidate on most or all phases of his campaign and coordinates most or all aspects of the technology employed by the campaign. A *specialist* consultant concentrates on one or two aspects of the campaign and peddles expertise in one or two technological specialties. While almost all of the early consultants were generalists, most consultants today are specialists (who nevertheless often advertise themselves as generalists).

Whether generalist or specialist, the consultant's primary role is the same: to provide services to campaigns. A consultant is hired to conduct a series of public opinion surveys or create a precinct organization or orchestrate a direct-mail fund-raising effort. The secondary roles played by consultants, however, are sometimes more intriguing and just as substantive as the provision of technological services. There is, for example, the "expert" role, a position accorded the consultant by the campaign staff and the candidate because of his wide experience and masterful reputation. (In many campaigns the consultant probably has more influence, and his every word is weighed more carefully than his actual experience or his degree of involvement with the campaign can justify.) Even though he may only visit the campaign once a month or talk with campaign officials weekly, the political professional frequently becomes the grand strategist, designing and supervising the "game plan," orchestrating the press, and selecting the candidate's issues.

Because of the respect he is given as "the expert," the consultant more often than not also seems to assume the role of the candidate's confidant. As media consultant Douglas Bailey has suggested, "Most candidates are hiring outside consultants because within the campaign and within their circle of friends, they don't have anyone whom they feel has the experience or the savvy to satisfy their need for reassurance that they're doing it right or that they can win."

Another media professional, Robert Goodman (who produced advertisements for George Bush's 1980 Republican presidential bid), emphasizes the psychological aspects of the consultant's tour of duty:

> George Bush said to me after four hours with him one day at his house, "Are you a psychiatrist or a filmmaker?" We're really into psychiatry. . . . It is incumbent upon the media guy to really look at the candidate and try to lead him past those personality landmines that will destroy him if he doesn't loosen up and do his thing.

These roles are hardly the only ones in the consultant's repertoire. He often finds himself a trusted postelection adviser when his clients win public office. Most significantly, and regrettably, he and his technological wares are "party pinch hitters," substituting for the weakened parties in a variety of ways.

A BRIEF HISTORY OF POLITICAL CONSULTING

There have always been political consultants in one form or another in American politics, but the campaign professionals of earlier eras were strategists without benefit of the campaign technologies so standard today. Usually, too, consultants were tied to one or a few candidates, or perhaps to a state or local party organization. Before consulting became a full-time profession, lawyers were often assigned campaign management chores since they had a flexible work schedule as well as the personal finances and community contacts to do the job properly.[2] The old-time press agent, usually a newspaperman familiar with the locale,[3] was also a crucial and influential figure in campaign organization. But in most cases these lawyers and press agents were only functionaries when compared to party leaders and organization bosses who wielded far greater authority in political matters.

On a separate track, one supported by the business community, the profession of public relations was developing. As Stanley Kelley, Jr. has stated, "Business was, and is still, the public relation man's most important patron."[4] Businessmen saw image making as a way to counter a rising tide of business criticism. The federal government followed in close pursuit of public relations professionals, expanding their role considerably during the New Deal. State and local governments, charities, religions, and colleges in succession all saw the "P.R. promise."

Dan Nimmo has called political consultants the "direct descendants" of the public relations professionals,[5] and the growth of both groups is clearly related to some similar phenomena, especially the revolution in mass media communications. Yet political consulting has causes all its own. The decline of the political parties has created opportunities for consultants and the tools of their trade. New means of financing campaigns, telling the candidate's story, and getting the candidate's voters to the polls became necessary as the parties' power waned. The new campaign techniques and the development of air travel, television, and the computer combined to give consultants the substitutes candidates desired. The fact that these techniques quickly became too complex for laymen to grasp easily—

consultants themselves were forced to specialize to keep up with changes—and the acknowledged American need for, and trust in, experts, made professionals that much more attractive. Even if false, the belief that consultants' tricks could somehow bring order out of the chaos of a campaign was enormously reassuring to a candidate. And rising campaign costs (and expenditure and contribution limitations) have placed a premium on the wise use of every campaign dollar. All of these alterations of the political map seemed powerful arguments for hiring political consultants, who gradually became an unquestioned essential for serious campaigns. Everyone now needs them if only because everyone else has them.

The consulting movement coalesced first in California.[6] The state's traditionally anemic party system was weakened further in the twentieth century by the addition of new social welfare programs, a broadened civil service system, and a sprawling suburban shift from the central cities matched by the influx of hundreds of thousands of migrants from the East, Midwest, and South. The sheer growth in the size of the electorate made organizing difficult (and redistricting an even more wrenching and enveloping process). Finally, California was in the forefront of the popular initiative and referendum movement, and had an exceptionally long ballot and a multiplicity of elections.

It was during an initiative campaign, in fact, that modern political consultants first had a major effect.[7] In 1933 the California legislature passed a bill authorizing a flood control and irrigation development in northern California (called the Central Valley Project), which the Pacific Gas and Electric Company (PG&E) believed to be a threat to private power. The utility promptly launched a ballot initiative to reverse the decision. The project's proponents hastily enlisted Clem Whitaker, a Sacramento newsman and press agent, and Leone Smith Baxter, a public relations specialist, to mastermind a campaign to defeat PG&E's initiative. On a limited budget of $39,000, and using radio and newspaper appeals, Whitaker and Baxter managed to save the Central Valley Project.

Not only did PG&E hold no grudge, it actually put Whitaker and Baxter on annual retainer! The two consultants incorporated themselves (as Campaigns, Inc., and later as Whitaker and Baxter Campaigns) and eventually married as well.[8] There were two decades of smooth sailing for the firm, operating out of San Francisco, and the lack of extensive competition[9] enabled it to post a 90 percent success rate in seventy-five major campaigns. Eventually, rival California consultants (such as Republicans Stuart Spencer and Bill Roberts and Democrats Don Bradley, Joseph Cerrell, and Sanford Weiner) came to the fore and reduced Whitaker and Baxter's edge and win-loss record.[10]

By the early 1950s it had become obvious that political professionals were playing an increasingly important part in electoral politics, so much so that Neil Staebler, then chairman of Michigan's Democratic party, alarmed a congressional committee with his prediction that " . . . elections will increasingly become contests not between candidates but between great advertising firms."[11]

While Staebler's vision seems a bit exaggerated even today, he was surely right in suggesting a role for consultants far beyond their relatively limited involvement in some statewide and national races in 1952. Political scientist Alexander Heard's survey of state party committees in 1956–1957 showed remarkable growth in a short time. Democratic state party committees in fifteen states and GOP committees in eighteen states employed public relations firms at some point during those years, and in many cases a high proportion of the committees' funds was spent for retainers.[12] Of the 130 public relations firms he contacted, 60 percent had had some kind of political account between 1952 and 1957, and forty firms in fifteen states reported that they could assume complete responsibility for a campaign.

Two decades later political consultants had become a campaign standard across the United States, and not just for major national and statewide contests. State races for lesser offices and U.S. House seats, and elections for local posts and even judicial offices, frequently had the services of one or more consultants. For example, a 1972–1973 survey indicated that 168 of 208 candidates running for state office had hired at least one political professional: sixty-one of sixty-seven U.S. Senate candidates, thirty-eight of forty-two gubernatorial candidates, thirty of thirty-seven attorney general contenders, and even nineteen of thirty-one and twenty of thirty-two aspirants for secretary of state and state treasurer.[13] Most politicians seeking major office attract a small committee of consultants. A *National Journal* review of sixty-seven opposed campaigns for U.S. Senate in 1970 revealed that sixty-two had an advertising firm, twenty-four had a pollster, and twenty secured help from some sort of campaign management firm.[14] Just five candidates made do with no consultants.

Consultants, moreover, rarely miss an opportunity to expand their domain. The judicial field in California is a classic illustration. In Orange County a judge seeking another term was defeated in 1940, and none ever lost again until 1978 when four county judges were beaten simultaneously. Sitting judges became understandably nervous and sought professional assistance. Joseph Cerrell and Associates, which had never done a judicial campaign until 1978, suddenly had nine at once. The agency's candidates, all incumbents up for reelection, made a clean sweep (at $7,500 apiece). Flushed with success, Cerrell sponsored a conference on Judicial Campaigning in 1979, designed for judges of the superior and municipal courts. For a $100 registration fee a judge would be treated to sessions on topics such as "Campaigning with Dignity: Maintaining the Judicial Image."

The number of consultants has skyrocketed along with the demand for their services. As late as 1960 there were relatively few full-time professionals in the field; twenty years later there are hundreds—thousands if local advertising agency executives specializing in politics are counted. In addition, they handle a great deal besides candidates' campaigns. Referenda, initiatives, bond issues, and political action committees (PACs) sustain many firms. Some consultants enjoy overseas work in foreign campaigns or specialize in primary and convention nomination battles as well as general elections. Today the average modern professional manages more campaigns in a year than his predecessors did in a lifetime. . . .

NOTES

1. Napolitan, *The Election Game and How to Win It*, p. 11.

2. W. E. Barnes in *The San Francisco Examiner*, July 25, 1979.

3. Stanley Kelley, Jr., *Professional Public Relations and Political Power* (Baltimore: Johns Hopkins, 1956), pp. 26–30; see also pp. 9–25, 31–38.

4. Ibid., p. 13.

5. Dan Nimmo, *The Political Persuaders: The Techniques of Modern Election Campaigns* (Englewood Cliffs, N.J.: Prentice-Hall, 1970), p. 35.

6. Ibid., pp. 35–37.

7. Barnes in *The San Francisco Examiner*.

8. See Kelley, *Professional Public Relations and Political Power*, pp. 39–66, for a history of the Whitaker and Baxter firm.

9. Baus and Ross of Los Angeles, a rival consulting firm started by one of Whitaker-Baxter's former employees, provided what competition existed. Both firms primarily handled Republicans.

10. Nimmo, *The Political Persuaders*, p. 36, n. 2d. Whitaker and Baxter has now effectively withdrawn from candidate campaigns.

11. Hearings before the Special Committee to Investigate Campaign Expenditures, 1952, House of Representatives, 82nd Congress, 2nd session, p. 76: as quoted in Kelley, *Professional Public Relations and Political Power*, p. 2.

12. Alexander Heard, *The Costs of Democracy* (Chapel Hill: University of North Carolina, 1960), pp. 415–477. Heard notes that his totals were probably understated because of the limitations of his survey.

13. Robert Agranoff, (ed.) *The New Style in Election Campaigns* (2nd ed.) (Boston: Holbrook Press, 1976), p. 8. See also David Rosenbloom, *The Election Men: Professional Campaign Managers and American Democracy* (New York: Quadrangle, 1973). Rosenbloom indicates a 650 percent growth rate in consulting firms overall between 1952 and 1970, an 842 percent increase in consultant involvement in U.S. House of Representatives contests, and a 300 percent increase in their employment for local elections.

14. See *National Journal*, September 26, 1970, pp. 2084–2085.

PART FOUR

The Policy Game

37

Playing the Policy Game

Matthew A. Cahn

The public policy process has been described as a game by several observers.[1] The game analogy is not intended to trivialize the process; rather, it suggests that policy actors must utilize rational strategies to maximize their interests. Earlier I argued that policy actors utilize a variety of resources to maximize their policy interests. Players will increase their chances of winning to the extent that they have knowledge of the policy bureaucracy (bureaucratic knowledge), access to individuals within the bureaucracy (network), citizen backing (size of constituency), money for political contributions, and resources to mount an effective public relations (media) campaign. But these resources are only one part of winning the policy game. It is also necessary to understand the rules and culture of the policy environment. The following discussion explores the context and environment of the policy game, including the constitutional basis of public policy, the culture of policy, maximizing policy strategies, and the problem of policy resources.

RULES OF THE GAME: THE CONSTITUTIONAL BASIS OF PUBLIC POLICY

Legal scholars have long described constitutional law as an arena of conflict resolution that, while not perfect, offers citizens a forum to redress of grievances.[2] While legislation on all levels adds rules to the game at various points, the constitutional basis of policy remains the foundation. For this reason the discourse on constitutional law is of prime importance to policy observers. Rather than focus on specific court decisions, this section is concerned with the constitutional foundations of the policy game.

The classic debate over whose interests are best protected by the Constitution is best illustrated by Charles Beard[3] on the one hand and Forrest McDonald[4] and Robert Brown[5] on the other. Beard's economic interpretation thesis argues that the Constitution was created by the economic elite at the expense of the debtor classes (the disenfranchised and small farmers). McDonald and Brown argue that Beard's historiography is factually flawed. They point to the existence of a large middle class and suggest that all sectors of society benefited from ratification. Further, they argue that while the delegates to the convention were clearly elites, self-interest was not their motivation.

What is of concern to policy scholars is where the dust settled. Rather than quibble over historical detail, contemporary scholars must examine how public law has come to be structured and whether public policy has come to favor specific sectors. Beard's thesis represents one of the most critical interpretations of the U.S. Constitution. Arguing that the Constitution was written by specific elites, for their own self-interest, Beard documents the economic interconnections of the members of the convention in 1787. Further, he explores the specific benefits each received after ratification. Rather than arguing conspiracy theory, Beard sees the framers as representing the dominant elites in American society at the time.[6]

Robert Brown and Forrest McDonald both present critiques of Beard's economic interpretation. Brown disputes Beard's central assertion that the convention delegates shared economic interests that were distinct from the agrarian interests of the debtor classes. Instead, Brown argues that the dominant wealth at the convention was also agrarian, in the form of farmland and slaves, and that the interests of the framers included the interests of society at large. Brown may be correct in his assertion that the interests represented at the Convention included agriculture, but in failing to discuss the obvious distinction between small farmers and early agribusiness—slaveholding agribusiness—Brown fails to consider distinctive class differences present in 1787. McDonald's work fills in the historical details for Beard, drawing a vivid picture of propertied elites interacting to create the Constitution.[7] Similar to Brown, McDonald cites the weight of agrarian interests represented at the convention to disprove Beard. And also similar, McDonald fails to discuss that these economic elites were largely diversified and were thus to benefit from the economic system the Constitution guaranteed. Finally, McDonald fails to comment on the potential coherence of interests represented.

While the delegates of the constitutional convention had economic interests that conflicted in some areas, their interests cohered in key areas: (1) in a strong central government that could protect commerce across state boundaries and control the "passions" of the masses; (2) in the creation of a central currency, protecting creditors from depreciation; (3) in creating protection to creditors for monies loaned at interest—to the distinct disadvantage of the debtor classes represented by people like Daniel Shays.

By failing to discuss the massive propaganda effort, best illuminated by the

Federalist articles, Brown and McDonald gloss over the conflict over ratification. *The Federalist Papers*[8] focused on the structural changes the Constitution would bring, but Hamilton, Madison, and Jay were careful not to discuss the economic implications. While Brown and McDonald may correctly point out the inadequacy in Beard's historiography, it is clear that the framers were elites who stood to benefit from the adoption of the Constitution. In his classic text *The American Political Tradition*[9] Richard Hofstadter points out that to the framers of the Constitution, liberty was tied to property, not democracy. Freedom meant the freedom to own and dispose of private property, not freedom of self-government. The resulting political economy of an urbanized industrial society is the direct manifestation of the framers' principles.

The implications for the policy game are significant. The early Constitution provided for republican government, with only limited citizen participation, resulting in an insulated relationship between elected officials and the populace. This suggests that the framers intentionally sought to protect the Union from "popular passions" through mechanisms such as the electoral college and indirect election of the president, the appointment of senators by state legislators until 1913, single member districts that preclude minority party representation, and the state-imposed gender and property requirements.

Although the American policy process has evolved since the late eighteenth century, the original constitutional framework has had serious policy consequences for those classes who were earlier excluded. African Americans and other people of color, women, the poor, and most recently gays and lesbians have spent the last two centuries fighting an uphill battle for parity. And, as the chapter on "The Players" illustrates, the policy framework continues to provide inherent advantages to economic elites. The following section explores the impact of the cultural legacy of Lockean liberalism on the policy process.

POLITICAL CULTURE AND PUBLIC POLICY

Till there be property there can be no government, the very end of which is to secure wealth, and to defend the rich from the poor (Adam Smith, 1776).[10]

(Property is) that dominion which one man claims and exercises over the external things of the world, in exclusion of every other individual (James Madison, 1792).[11]

All communities divide themselves into the few and the many. The first are the rich and the well-born, the other the mass of the people. . . . The people are turbulent and changing; they seldom judge or determine right (Alexander Hamilton).[12]

Public policy outcomes cannot be divorced from political culture. The assumptions held by a society narrow the scope of viable policy options. As the discussion in the previous section illustrates, and as the comments of Adam Smith, James Madison, and Alexander Hamilton suggest, American political culture reflects a property-oriented legacy.

American political culture is based on the natural or "inalienable" rights of individuals. Drawing from the well of Lockean liberal imagery, the Declaration of Independence clearly sets forth the primacy of individual rights to life, liberty, and property. Yet the primacy of liberal individualism creates a dilemma for public policy: Lockean individualism is nowhere manifested more strongly than in its commitment to individual property rights, and as a result, individual property rights limit the notion of communal rights, creating a problematic definition of communal good.

American liberalism, true to its utilitarian roots, defines the common good as the aggregate sum of individual good. That is, the role of the community is to provide the infrastructure to make individual rights possible. No more, no less. In Lockean terms, the role of the community is to create a stable environment for the acquisition, use, and disposition of private property. Liberal policy is fundamentally organized around economic interaction. The policy implications are twofold: liberal policy seeks to create independent economic actors, and liberal policy demands that any communal need be evaluated in light of individual property rights.[13]

In the classic work in this area, *Capitalism, Socialism, and Democracy*,[14] Schumpeter explains the dilemma of democracy in a capitalist political economy. Stated simply, capitalism defines freedom (rights) on the principle of ownership: one dollar, one vote.[15] Democracy defines freedom (rights) on the principle of one person, one vote. While Milton Friedman[16] and others will argue that there is no conflict here, Schumpeter sees an inherent contradiction. In examining the Schumpeter thesis, Samuel Bowles and Herbert Gintis identify the multiple spheres that make up an individual's life. In *Democracy and Capitalism*[17] Bowles and Gintis point out that liberal society is broken up into two spheres, public and private. The public sphere includes those aspects of society where both liberty and democracy apply, such as government. The private sphere includes those areas where only liberty applies. Bowles and Gintis argue:

> Liberal social theory's arbitrary asymmetric treatment of state and economy stems
> . . . from the untenable notion that the capitalist economy is a private sphere—in
> other words, that its operation does not involve the socially consequential exercise of
> power.[18]

Bowles and Gintis look to the "labor commodity proposition" to explain the antidemocratic tendency within American social culture: if labor were not considered a commodity, to be bought and sold, but rather a partnership, the hierarchical organization of the workplace and the "privacy" of the economy would be untenable. The "market" is a political arena. The feminist notion that the personal is political perhaps is best understood in such a context. Any definition of politics must include the distribution of goods as well as the distribution of power. For all of us, this is regularly played out in our economic relationships.

Bowles and Gintis redevelop the utilitarian argument that people are created by the role they play in society. Our values are tied inextricably to our culture. If liberal society is characterized by limited choice and extensive spheres of domination, the chances of developing democratic values are limited. The economic system produces social values; in short, "the economy produces people."

> The economy produces people. The experience of individuals as economic actors is a major determinant of their personal capacities, attitudes, choices, interpersonal relations, and social philosophies.[19]

The concern Bowles and Gintis have is in the clash of rights inherent in American political culture—property rights conflict with individual rights, economic rights with democratic rights.

Michael Rogin[20] argues that economic domination is only one of the policy implications of American political culture. As a result of the in/out dichotomy of social contract theory, American political culture demonizes cultural and political adversaries. Social contract theory is based on the notion of a society sharing a single set of cultural and political values. That is, one is part of the social contract, either explicitly or implicitly, when he or she accepts the responsibilities of ideological homogeneity. Through a shared concept of civilization, all parties of the social contract are able to live and interact with each other predictably and safely. As they are out of Locke's state of nature, the theoretical state of war is, for the duration of the social contract, over. The implications for anyone outside of the social contract are clear: they are unpredictable, dangerous, and at war with us. Consequently, any individual or group who does not share the dominant cultural and political ideology is, by definition, suspect.[21] The policy implications are that discrimination and inequality are an inherent part of the political and social environment. From the enslavement of African Americans, to the dislocation of Native Americans, to the incarceration of Japanese Americans, to the exclusion of gay and lesbian Americans, Rogin argues that exclusion is a function of American political culture.

Other observers argue that while there are intolerance and antidemocratic tendencies within American society, they are not an integral part of American political culture. Louis Hartz and C. B. Macpherson[22] see the American emphasis on individual economic self-interest as the mechanism for social stability. "Possessive individualism" diverts the passions of men (laziness and self-indulgence) into a drive for economic gain, creating sober, productive citizens. Anthony Downs[23] and other "public choice" scholars see self-interest as the primary motivation of all people. As a consequence, such scholars argue that inequality can, and ultimately will, be addressed within the context of contemporary political culture, albeit with a renewed concern for social and political, if not economic, equality.

MAXIMIZING POLICY STRATEGIES

In *The Prince*[24] Machiavelli presents a blueprint for the effective development and maintenance of power. Machiavelli's notion of *virtu'*—controlling political destiny—is based on the successful manipulation of human circumstances. The virtuous prince is good, merciful, and honest, as long as expediency dictates, yet he must be prepared to be cruel and deceptive. Control is the primary consideration, both of one's populace and of one's neighboring states. *Virtu'*, ultimately, requires successful strategies to maximize policy interests.

In *Presidential Power*[25] Neustadt outlines a Machiavellian strategy for the president. He, like Machiavelli, is overwhelmingly concerned with how a president expands his or her power and maintains it. Because a president lacks the formal power of a dictator, he or she must rely on his or her power to persuade rather than command. In examining Machiavellian influence in American politics, it is necessary to read Neustadt both as prescriptive, as he intended, and as narrative—how presidents *ought* to gain power, and how strong ones do. The presidency, in Neustadt's analysis, is a "clerkship," based on balancing differing interests and keeping in mind the public good.

Presidential virtue is based on the presentation of image; the president must take into account how every decision will be perceived. The reputation of a president, and his or her future power, is greatly dependent on the perception of strength. Charisma is essential for the smooth development of power, as the president must be identified with, respected, and even loved. The president must act quickly and decisively to criticize opponents and reward allies. And, perhaps most important for both Machiavelli and Neustadt, the president must make effective use of the political climate. Only through the successful resolution of crisis can a president truly create dependence and power.

While Machiavelli's Prince can rely on respect or fear, presidents, for the most part, can only rely on respect and the successful manufacture of consent.[26] Through deception, and manipulation of the political climate, a president can essentially create consent. Favorable public opinion, Machiavelli's notion of adulation, is necessary for presidential action, but that public opinion can be manipulated. Drawing on cultural biases, symbols, and traditions a skilled president can maximize his or her power and implement policies as he or she sees fit. The marriage of Locke and Machiavelli becomes clear. Locke's notion of executive prerogative and the cunning of Machiavelli's Prince both influence the successful American president.

The meaning of prerogative, in the context of American liberalism, is that no rights are absolute, no rights are inalienable, regardless of the written law. On the one hand the Constitution promises individual rights; but on the other, it denies those rights at the discretion of the executive. One of the best illustrations of executive prerogative in the United States was the suspension of constitutional protections and collective incarceration of Japanese Americans. By executive fiat, the president of the United States (Roosevelt) authorized the imprisonment of all persons of Japanese ancestry living on the West Coast of the nation.

Murray Edelman[27] similarly argues that those who seek to maximize their policy interests will use deceit and symbolism to manipulate the policy discourse. No one person can possibly experience the entire world, yet everyone has an image or "picture" of the world. Burke suggests that however important that "sliver of reality each of us has experienced firsthand," the overall "picture" is a "construct of symbolic systems."[28] This construct is based on political cognitions that Edelman suggests are "ambivalent and highly susceptible to symbolic cues . . ."[29] Government, Edelman argues, influences behavior by shaping the cognitions of people in ambiguous situations. In this way, government or policy elites help engineer beliefs about what is "fact" and what is "proper."

Maximizing policy strategies is critical for winning the policy game. Each player, regardless of his or her position in the policy environment, seeks to influence policy outcomes. The degree to which players utilize rational strategies, however creative, however slippery, will determine the degree to which policy success can be achieved. This is not to suggest that there are no ethical constraints on players; there are. Rather, the Machiavellian legacy in American political culture recognizes that strategy and cunning are acceptable and necessary components of the policy game.

THE PROBLEM OF POLICY RESOURCES

In *A Preface to Economic Democracy*[30] Robert Dahl redefines his thinking on American democracy. Dahl has long recognized the existence of economic elites and their influence on the policy process. His earlier work[31] argued that these elites compete with one another, creating an equilibrium within which different interests can be represented. This work argues that rather than compete, the interests of these economic elites cohere in specific areas. The result is that democratic processes are dominated by the influence of economic elites—specifically, corporate elites. Domhoff argues that there is a social upper class that effectively operates as a ruling class by virtue of its dominance of economic resources. While there are other political resources—for example, expertise and bureaucratic knowledge—these can be and often are purchased. Thus, Domhoff points out, financial power is often the basis of policy influence.[32]

If it is true that policy influence requires requisite political resources, inequality in resource distribution is tantamount to inequality in political representation. Thus, as Dahl, Domhoff, and many other observers[33] argue, if Americans are serious about creating a truly pluralistic society, it is necessary to democratize political resources, specifically economic resources.

CONCLUSION

This chapter has explored the context of the policy environment. Since public policy cannot be studied apart from the constraints imposed by cultural inheritances, it is necessary to investigate subtle social legacies. This discussion has covered the constitutional basis of the policy process, the culture of policy, policy strategies, and the problem of policy resources.

NOTES

1. See, for example, Peter Navarro, *The Policy Game: How Special Interests and Ideologues Are Stealing America* (Lexington, Mass.: Lexington Books, 1984) and Larry J. Sabato, *The Rise of Political Consultants: New Ways of Winning Elections* (New York: Basic Books, 1981); as well, for a discussion on the competing games individuals play in a democratic society, see Samuel Bowles and Herbert Gintis, *Democracy and Capitalism: Property, Community, and the Contradictions of Modern Social Thought* (New York: Basic Books, 1986).

2. See, for example, Herbert Jacob, *Justice in America: Courts, Lawyers, and the Judicial Process* (4th ed.) (Boston: Little, Brown, 1984).

3. Charles Beard, *An Economic Interpretation of the Constitution of the United States* (New York: Macmillan, 1936).

4. Forrest McDonald, *We the People: The Economic Origins of the Constitution* (Chicago: University of Chicago Press, 1958).

5. Robert Brown, *Charles Beard and the Constitution: A Critical Analysis of "An Economic Interpretation of the Constitution"* (Princeton, N.J.: Princeton University Press, 1956).

6. Charles Beard, *An Economic Interpretation*, 1936.

7. Forrest McDonald, *We the People*, 1958, p. 87.

8. Alexander Hamilton, James Madison, and John Jay. *The Federalist Papers*, ed. Clinton Rossiter (New York: New American Library, 1961).

9. Richard Hofstadter, *The American Political Tradition* (New York: Knopf, 1948), p. 11.

10. Adam Smith, *An Inquiry into the Nature and Causes of the Wealth of Nations* (1776), in *Democracy for the Few* (5th ed.) ed. Michael Parenti (New York: St. Martin's Press, 1988), p. 21.

11. James Madison, "Essay on Property" (1792), in *American Constitutional Law*, eds. Alpheas Mason and D. Grier Stephenson, Jr. (Englewood Cliffs, N.J.: Prentice-Hall, 1987), p. 271.

12. Alexander Hamilton, comments from the Constitutional Convention, in *Records of the Federal Convention, Vol. 1* ed. Max Ferrand (New Haven, Conn.: Yale University Press, 1927).

13. For a fuller discussion on the policy constraints imposed by the liberal legacy, see Chapter 1 of Matthew Cahn, *Environmental Deceptions: The Tension between Liberalism and Environmental Policymaking in the United States* (Albany, New York: SUNY, 1995).

14. Joseph Schumpeter, *Capitalism, Socialism, and Democracy* (New York: Harper Collins, 1942).

15. See also Richard Coe and Charles Wilber (eds.), *Capitalism and Democracy: Schumpeter Revisited* (Notre Dame, Ind.: University of Notre Dame Press, 1985).

16. Milton Friedman, *Capitalism and Freedom* (Chicago: University of Chicago Press, 1972).

17. Samuel Bowles and Herbert Gintis, *Democracy and Capitalism: Property, Community, and the Contradictions of Modern Social Thought* (New York: Basic Books, 1986).

18. Bowles and Gintis, *Democracy and Capitalism*, 1986, p. 67.

19. Bowles and Gintis, *Democracy and Capitalism*, 1986, p. 131.

20. Michael Rogin, *Ronald Reagan the Movie, and Other Episodes in Political Demonology* (Berkeley: University of California Press, 1987).

21. See also Howard Zinn, *A People's History of the United States* (New York: Harper Collins, 1980).

22. Louis Hartz, *The Liberal Tradition in America* (New York: Harcourt Brace Jovanovich, 1955); C. B. Macpherson, *The Life and Times of Liberal Democracy* (New York: Oxford University Press, 1977).

23. Anthony Downs, *An Economic Theory of Democracy* (New York: HarperCollins, 1957).

24. Niccolo Machiavelli, *The Prince*, in *The Portable Machiavelli*, eds. Peter Bondanella and Mark Muse (New York: Penguin Books, 1983).

25. Richard Neustadt, *Presidential Power* (New York: Wiley, 1980).

26. For a complete discussion on American dictatorship, see Clinton Rossiter, *Constitutional Dictatorship* (New York: Harcourt Brace Jovanovich, 1948, 1963).

27. Murray Edelman, *Constructing the Political Spectacle* (Chicago: University of Chicago Press, 1988).

28. Kenneth Burke, *Language as Symbolic Action* (Berkeley: University of California Press, 1966), p. 5.

29. Murray Edelman, *Politics as Symbolic Action* (Chicago: Markham, 1971), p. 2.

30. Robert Dahl, *A Preface to Economic Democracy* (Berkeley: University of California Press, 1985).

31. Robert Dahl, *A Preface to Democratic Theory* (Chicago: University of Chicago Press, 1956) and *Who Governs?* (New Haven, Conn.: Yale University Press, 1961).

32. G. William Domhoff, *Who Rules America Now?* (New York: Simon & Schuster, 1983).

33. In addition to Dahl (1985) and Domhoff, see, for example, C. Wright Mills, *The Power Elite* (Oxford: Oxford University Press, 1956); Michael Parenti, *Democracy for the Few* (New York: St. Martin's Press, 1988); E. Greenberg, *The American Political System: A Radical Approach* (4th ed.) (Boston: Little, Brown, 1986); Bowles and Gintis, *Democracy and Capitalism*; Matthew Cahn, *Environmental Deceptions*.

ADDITIONAL SUGGESTED READING

CAHN, MATTHEW A. *Environmental Deceptions: The Tension between Liberalism and Environmental Policymaking in the United States.* Albany, N.Y.: SUNY Press, 1995.

DOMHOFF, G. WILLIAM. *Who Rules America Now?* New York: Simon & Schuster, 1983.

DYE, THOMAS. *Who's Running America? The Conservative Years* (4th ed.). Englewood Cliffs, N.J.: Prentice-Hall, 1986.

FERRAND, MAX. *Records of the Federal Convention.* New Haven, Conn.: Yale University Press, 1927.

FRIEDMAN, MILTON. *Capitalism and Freedom.* Chicago: University of Chicago Press, 1972.

HOFSTADTER, RICHARD. *The American Political Tradition.* New York: Knopf, 1948.

LASSWELL, HAROLD. *Politics: Who Gets What, When, and How.* New York: St. Martin's Press, 1988.

MACHIAVELLI, NICCOLO. *The Prince,* in *The Portable Machiavelli* eds. Peter Bondanella and Mark Muse. New York: Penguin Books, 1983.

MILLS, C. WRIGHT. *The Power Elite.* Oxford: Oxford University Press, 1956.

PETERS, B. GUY. *American Public Policy: Promise and Performance* (3rd ed.). Chatham, N.J.: Chatham House, 1993.

ROSSITER, CLINTON. *Constitutional Dictatorship.* New York: Harcourt Brace Jovanovich, 1948, 1963.

SMITH, HENDRICK. *The Power Game: How Washington Works.* New York: Ballantine Books, 1988.

ZINN, HOWARD. *A People's History of the United States.* New York: HarperCollins, 1980.

38

An Economic Interpretation of the Constitution

Charles Beard

The requirements for an economic interpretation of the formation and adoption of the Constitution may be stated in a hypothetical proposition which, although it cannot be verified absolutely from ascertainable data, will at once illustrate the problem and furnish a guide to research and generalization.

It will be admitted without controversy that the Constitution was the creation of a certain number of men, and it was opposed by a certain number of men. Now, if it were possible to have an economic biography of all those connected with its framing and adoption,—perhaps about 160,000 men altogether,—the materials for scientific analysis and classification would be available. Such an economic biography would include a list of the real and personal property owned by all of these men and their families: lands and houses, with incumbrances, money at interest, slaves, capital invested in shipping and manufacturing, and in state and continental securities.

Suppose it could be shown from the classification of the men who supported and opposed the Constitution that there was no line of property division at all; that is, that men owning substantially the same amounts of the same kinds of property were equally divided on the matter of adoption or rejection—it would then become apparent that the Constitution had no ascertainable relation to economic groups or classes, but was the product of some abstract causes remote from the chief business of life—gaining a livelihood.

Suppose, on the other hand, that substantially all of the merchants, money lenders, security holders, manufacturers, shippers, capitalists, and financiers and their professional associates are to be found on one side in support of the Constitution and that substantially all or the major portion of the opposition came from the non-slaveholding farmers and the debtors—would it not be pretty conclusively demonstrated that our fundamental law was not the product of an abstraction known as "the whole people," but of a group of economic interests which must have expected beneficial results from its adoption? Obviously all the facts here desired cannot be discovered, but the data presented in the following chapters bear out the latter hypothesis, and thus a reasonable presumption in favor of the theory is created.

Of course, it may be shown (and perhaps can be shown) that the farmers and debtors who opposed the Constitution were, in fact, benefited by the general improvement which resulted from its adoption. It may likewise be shown, to take an extreme case, that the English nation derived immense advantages from the Norman Conquest and the orderly administrative processes which were introduced, as it undoubtedly did; nevertheless, it does not follow that the vague thing known as "the advancement of general welfare" or some abstraction known as "justice" was the immediate, guiding purpose of the leaders in either of these great historic changes. The point is, that the direct, impelling motive in both cases was the economic advantages which the beneficiaries expected would accrue to themselves first, from their action. Further than this, economic interpretation cannot go. It may be that some larger world-process is working through each series of historical events; but ultimate causes lie beyond our horizon.

A SURVEY OF ECONOMIC INTERESTS IN 1787

The whole theory of the economic interpretation of history rests upon the concept that social progress in general is the result of contending interests in society—some favorable, others opposed, to change. On this hypothesis, we are required to discover at the very outset of the present study what classes and social groups existed in the United States just previous to the adoption of the Constitution and which of them, from the nature of their property, might have expected to benefit immediately and definitely by the overthrow of the old system and the establishment of the new. On the other hand, it must be discovered which of them might have expected more beneficial immediate results, on the whole, from the maintenance of the existing legal arrangements.

The importance of a survey of the distribution of property in 1787 for economic as well as political history is so evident that it is strange that no attempt has been made to undertake it on a large scale. Not even a beginning has been made. It is, therefore, necessary for us to rely for the present upon the general statements of historians who have written more or less at length about the period under consideration; but in the meanwhile it can do no harm to suggest, by way of a preface, the outlines of such a survey and some of the chief sources of information.

I. In the first place, there were the broad interests of real property which constituted, in 1787, a far larger proportion of all wealth than it does at the present time. The size, value, and ownership of holdings and their geographical distribution ought to be ascertained. In the absence of a general census, the preparation of such an economic survey would entail an enormous labor, and it could never be more than approximately complete. Neither the census of 1790 nor the assessment for direct taxes under the law of 1798 covers this topic. The assessment rolls of the several states for taxation, wherever available, would yield the data desired, at least in part; but a multitude of local records would have to be consulted with great scrutiny and critical care.

II. In order to ascertain the precise force of personalty in the formation and adoption of the Constitution, it would be necessary to discover not only the amount and geographical distribution of money and public securities; but also the exact fields of operation in which personalty looked for immediate and prospective gains. A complete analysis of the economic forces in the Constitution-making process would require the following data:—

1. The geographic distribution of money on hand and loaned and the names of the holders. It is apparent that much of the material from which evidence on these points may be obtained has disappeared; but an intensive study of the tax returns of the states, the records of the local assessors, wills probated, mortgages recorded, and suits in courts over loans and mortgages, would no doubt produce an immense amount of illuminating information.

2. The geographic distribution and ownership of the public securities. Fortunately the unpublished and unworked records of the Treasury Department at Washington throw great light on this fundamental problem. Shortly after the federal government was established the old debt was converted into a new consolidated, or funded, debt; and holders of public securities, state and continental, brought their papers to their local loan office (one for each state) or to the Treasury to have them recorded and transformed into the stocks of the new government.

The records of this huge transaction (which was the first really great achievement of nascent capitalism in the United States), if they had been kept intact, would constitute, perhaps, the most wonderful single collection on economic history ever possessed by any country. Were they complete, they would form a veritable Domesday Book of the politics during the first years of the new government. But unfortunately they are not complete. The records of Hamilton's administration at the Treasury itself seem to have largely disappeared, and the records of the loan offices in the several states are generally fragmentary, although in one or two instances they are indeed monumental.

A complete set of these financial documents should show: (1) the owners of certificates of the old government as issued, during the Revolution and afterward, to original holders; (2) the transfers of certificates from original holders to other parties; (3) the names of those who held certificates in 1787, when the Convention was called to frame the Constitution; (4) the records of transactions in stocks between the announcement of the Convention's work and the adoption of Hamilton's funding system; (5) the names of those who brought in securities for funding into the new debt; (6) the names of those for whom the brokers, whose names appear on the loan office books, were, in fact, operating.

None of the records preserved at the Treasury Department presents all of the evidence required for the scientific study of a single state. Nearly one-third of the operations were at the Treasury and of these only a meagre fragment seems to have escaped the ravages of time. In the documents of some of the commonwealths, however, it is possible to ascertain the names of hundreds of patriots who risked their money in original certificates or received certificates for services rendered. The books of a few loan offices are so kept that it can be easily discovered who brought in securities to be funded into the new debt and also to whom these securities were originally issued.

In some states the ledgers were carefully preserved and it is possible to find out the names and addresses of the holders of securities funded at the local loan office and the amount held by each person. The ledgers of Connecticut, for example, offer a rich field for the study of the names and geographical distribution of public creditors, and the tracing of these interests through their myriad local ramifications would afford an interesting and profitable undertaking. But unfortunately multitudes of the most significant operations are forever lost; it is to be particularly deplored that the "powers of attorney" for the period are not forthcoming. Unless the Government at Washington follows the example of enlightened administrations in Europe and establishes a Hall of Records, the precious volumes which have come down to us will be worked only with great difficulty, if they do not disintegrate and disappear altogether.[1]

3. The geographic distribution of small mortgaged farms and their connection with various schemes for depreciation of the currency and impairment of the obligation of contract. No doubt work in local records would yield valuable results in this field.

4. Owners and operators in western lands. Speculation in western lands was one of the leading activities of capitalists in those days. As is well known, the soldiers were paid in part in land scrip and this scrip was bought up at low prices by dealers, often with political connections. Furthermore, large areas had been bought outright for a few cents an acre and were being held for a rise in value. The chief obstacle in the way of the rapid appreciation of these lands was the weakness of the national government which prevented the complete subjugation of the Indians, the destruction of old Indian claims, and the orderly settlement of the frontier. Every leading capitalist of the time thoroughly understood the relation of a new constitution to the rise in land values beyond the Alleghenies. This idea was expressed, for example, by Hugh Williamson, a member of the Convention from North Carolina and a land speculator in a letter to Madison. The materials for the study of land operations exist in enormous quantities, largely in manuscript form in Washington; and a critical scrutiny of the thousands of names that appear on these records, in their political relations, would afford results beyond all measure. Here, too, is the work for a lifetime.

5. The geographic distribution of manufacturing establishments and the names of owners and investors. On this important topic a mass of printed and manuscript materials exists, but no attempt has yet been made to catalogue the thousands of names of persons with a view to establishing political connections. To produce the materials for this study, searches must be made in the local records from New Hampshire to Georgia. Wills probated, transfers of property, law suits, private papers, advertisements in newspapers, shipping records, Hamil-

ton's correspondence in the Manuscript Division of the Library of Congress, unclassified Treasury Records and correspondence, and innumerable other sources must be searched and lists of names and operations made.

Pending the enormous and laborious researches here enumerated, the following pages are offered merely as an indication of the way in which the superficial aspects of the subject may be treated.[2] In fact, they sketch the broad outlines of the study which must be filled in and corrected by detailed investigations.

THE DISFRANCHISED

In an examination of the structure of American society in 1787, we first encounter four groups whose economic status had a definite legal expression: the slaves, the indented servants, the mass of men who could not qualify for voting under the property tests imposed by the state constitutions and laws, and women, disfranchised and subjected to the discriminations of the common law. These groups were, therefore, not represented in the Convention which drafted the Constitution, except under the theory that representation has no relation to voting.

How extensive the disfranchisement really was cannot be determined. In some states, for instance, Pennsylvania and Georgia, propertyless mechanics in the towns could vote; but in other states the freehold qualifications certainly excluded a great number of the adult males.

In no state, apparently, had the working-class developed a consciousness of a separate interest or an organization that commanded the attention of the politicians of the time. In turning over the hundreds of pages of writings left by eighteenth-century thinkers one cannot help being impressed with the fact that the existence and special problems of a working-class, then already sufficiently numerous to form a considerable portion of society, were outside the realm of politics, except in so far as the future power of the proletariat was foreseen and feared.[3]

When the question of the suffrage was before the Convention, Madison warned his colleagues against the coming industrial masses: "Viewing the subject in its merits alone, the freeholders of the Country would be the safest depositories of Republican liberty. In future times a great majority of the people will not only be without landed, but any other sort of property. These will either combine under the influence of their common situation; in which case,[4] the rights of property and the public liberty will not be secure in their hands, or, which is more probable, they will become the tools of opulence and ambition; in which case there will be equal danger on another side."[5]

So far as social policy is concerned, however, the working-class problem had not made any impression on the statesmen of the time. Hamilton in his report on manufactures,[6] dismisses the subject with scant notice. He observes that one of the advantages of the extensive introduction of machinery will be "the employment of persons who would otherwise be idle, and in many cases, a burthen on the community, either from bias of temper, habit, infirmity of body, or some other cause, indisposing or disqualifying them for the toils of the country. It is worthy of remark, that, in general, women and children are rendered more useful, and the latter more early useful, by manufacturing establishments, than they would otherwise be. Of the number of persons employed in the cotton manufactories of Great Britain, it is computed that four-sevenths, nearly, are women and children; of whom the greatest proportion are children, many of them of a tender age." Apparently this advantage was, in Hamilton's view, to accrue principally to the fathers of families, for he remarks: "The husbandman himself experiences a new source of profit and support, from the increased industry of his wife and daughters, invited and stimulated by the demands of the neighboring manufactories."

Passing beyond these groups which were politically non-existent, except in so far as those who possessed the ballot and economic power were compelled to safeguard their rights against assaults from such quarters, we come to the social groupings within the politically enfranchised mass. Here we find no legal class distinctions. Social distinctions were very sharp, it is true, as every student of manners and customs well knows; but there were no outward legal signs of special class privileges.

GROUPS OF REAL PROPERTY HOLDERS

Nevertheless, the possessors of property were susceptible of classification into several rather marked groups, though of course they shade off into one another by imperceptible gradations. Broadly speaking, there were the interests of real and personal property. Here, however, qualifications must be made. There was no such identity of interest between the large planters and the small inland farmers of the south as existed in England between the knights and yeomen. The real property holders may be classified into three general groups: the small farmers, particularly back from the sea-coast, scattered from New Hampshire to Georgia, the manorial lords, such as we find along the banks of the Hudson,[7] and the slaveholding planters of the south.

1. The first of these groups, the small farmers, constituted a remarkably homogeneous class. The inland section was founded and recruited by mechanics, the poorer whites, and European (particularly Scotch-Irish) immigrants. It had peculiar social and political views arising from the crude nature of its environment, but its active political doctrines were derived from an antagonism to the seaboard groups. One source of conflict was connected with the possession of the land itself. Much of the western country had been taken up by speculators and the settlers were either squatters or purchasers from large holders. This is illustrated by the situation in Virginia, where, as Ambler points out, "liberality in granting her unoccupied lands did not prove to be good policy. True, large numbers of settlers were early attracted to the state, where they made permanent homes, but much of the land fell into the hands of speculators. Companies were formed in Europe and America to deal in Virginia lands, which were bought up in large tracts at the tri-

fling cost of two cents per acre. This wholesale engrossment soon consumed practically all the most desirable lands and forced the home seeker to purchase from
speculators or to settle as a squatter."[8] As the settler sought to escape from the
speculator by moving westward, the frontier line of speculation advanced.

In addition to being frequently in debt for their lands, the small farmers
were dependent upon the towns for most of the capital to develop their resources.
They were, in other words, a large debtor class, to which must be added, of
course, the urban dwellers who were in a like unfortunate condition.

That this debtor class had developed a strong consciousness of identical interests in the several states is clearly evident in local politics and legislation.[9]
Shays' Rebellion in Massachusetts, the disturbances in Rhode Island, New Hampshire, and other northern states, the activities of the paper-money advocates in
state legislatures, the innumerable schemes for the relief of debtors, such as the
abolition of imprisonment, paper money, laws delaying the collection of debts,
propositions requiring debtors to accept land in lieu of specie at a valuation fixed
by a board of arbitration,—these and many other schemes testify eloquently to
the fact that the debtors were conscious of their status and actively engaged in establishing their interest in the form of legal provisions. Their philosophy was reflected in the writings of Luther Martin, delegate to the Convention from
Maryland, who disapproved of the Constitution, partly on the ground that it
would put a stop to agrarian legislation.

2. The second group of landed proprietors, the manorial lords of the Hudson valley region, constituted a peculiar aristocracy in itself and was the dominant
class in the politics of New York during the period between the Revolution and
the adoption of the Constitution, as it had been before the War. It was unable or
unwilling to block the emission of paper money, because the burden of that operation fell on the capitalists rather than itself. It also took advantage of its predom-
inance to shift the burden of taxation from the land to imports,[10] and this fact
contributed powerfully to its opposition to the Constitution, because it implied a
transference of the weight of taxation for state purposes to the soil. Its spokesmen
indulged in much high talk of state's rights, in which Federalist leaders refused to
see more than a hollow sham made to cover the rural gentry's economic supremacy.

3. The third group of landed proprietors were the slaveholders of the south.
It seems curious at the first glance that the representatives of the southern states
which sold raw materials and wanted competition in shipping were willing to join
in a union that subjected them to commercial regulations devised immediately in
behalf of northern interests. An examination of the records shows that they were
aware of this apparent incongruity, but that there were overbalancing compensa-
tions to be secured in a strong federal government.[11]

Money-lending and the holding of public securities were not confined to
the north by any means; although, perhaps, as Calhoun long afterward remarked,[12] the south was devoid of some of the artifices of commerce which characterized New England. Neither were attempts at relieving debtors by legislative

enactment restricted to Massachusetts and Rhode Island. The south had many men who were rich in personalty, other than slaves, and it was this type, rather than the slaveholding planter as such, which was represented in the Convention that framed the Constitution. The majority of the southern delegates at Philadelphia in 1787 were from the towns or combined a wide range of personalty operations with their planting. On this account there was more identity of interest among Langdon of Portsmouth, Gerry of Boston, Hamilton of New York, Dayton of New Jersey, Robert Morris of Philadelphia, McHenry of Baltimore, Washington on the Potomac, Williamson of North Carolina, the Pinckneys of Charleston, and Pierce of Savannah than between these several men and their debt-burdened neighbors at the back door. Thus nationalism was created by a welding of economic interests that cut through state boundaries.

The southern planter was also as much concerned in maintaining order against slave revolts as the creditor in Massachusetts was concerned in putting down Shays' "desperate debtors." And the possibilities of such servile insurrections were by no means remote. Every slave owner must have felt more secure in 1789 when he knew that the governor of his state could call in the strong arm of the federal administration in case a domestic disturbance got beyond the local police and militia. The north might make discriminatory commercial regulations, but they could be regarded as a sort of insurance against conflagrations that might bring ruin in their train. It was obviously better to ship products under adverse legislation than to have no products to ship. . . .

NOTES

1. A few years ago a negro attendant at the Treasury sold a cart-load or more of these records to a junk dealer. He was imprisoned for the offence, but this is a small consolation for scholars. The present writer was able to use some of the records only after a vacuum cleaner had been brought in to excavate the ruins.

2. See Curtis, *The Constitutional History of the United States*, Book I, Chaps. II-VII; Fiske, *Critical Period of American History*; McMaster, *History of the People of the United States*, Vol. I; Channing, *History of the United States*, Vol. III.

3. Working-men in the cities were not altogether indifferent spectators. See Becker, *Political Parties in New York*. They would have doubtless voted with the major interests of the cities in favor of the Constitution as against the agrarians had they been enfranchised. In fact, this is what happened in New York. See below, Chap. IX.

4. "If the authority be in their hands by the rule of suffrage," struck out in the Ms. See also the important note to this speech in Farrand, *Records*, Vol. II, p. 204, note 17.

5. Farrand, *Records*, Vol. II, p. 203.

6. December 5, 1791. *State Papers: Finance*, Vol. I, p. 126.

7. Roosevelt, *Gouverneur Morris*, pp. 14 ff.

8. Ambler, *Sectionalism in Virginia*, p. 44.

9. Libby has shown the degree of correspondence between the rural vote on paper money measures, designed for the relief of debtors, and the vote against the ratification of the Constitution. *Op. cit.*, pp. 50 ff.

10. The landholders were able to do this largely because New York City was the entry port for Connecticut and New Jersey. The opportunity to shift the taxes not only to the consumers, but to the consumers of neighboring states, was too tempting to be resisted.

11. For a paragraph on nascent capitalism in South Carolina, see W. A. Schaper, "Sectionalism in South Carolina," *American Historical Association Report* (1900), Vol. I.

12. It is not without interest to note that about the time Calhoun made this criticism of New England capitalist devices he was attempting to borrow several thousand dollars from a Massachusetts mill owner to engage in railway enterprise in the south.

The Federalist Papers

Alexander Hamilton, James Madison, and John Jay

NO. 1: HAMILTON

After an unequivocal experience of the inefficacy of the subsisting federal government, you are called upon to deliberate on a new Constitution for the United States of America. The subject speaks its own importance; comprehending in its consequences nothing less than the existence of the UNION, the safety and welfare of the parts of which it is composed, the fate of an empire in many respects the most interesting in the world. It has been frequently remarked that it seems to have been reserved to the people of this country, by their conduct and example, to decide the important question, whether societies of men are really capable or not of establishing good government from reflection and choice, or whether they are forever destined to depend for their political constitutions on accident and force. If there be any truth in the remark, the crisis at which we are arrived may with propriety be regarded as the era in which that decision is to be made; and a wrong election of the part we shall act may, in this view, deserve to be considered as the general misfortune of mankind.

This idea will add the inducements of philanthropy to those of patriotism, to heighten the solicitude which all considerate and good men must feel for the event. Happy will it be if our choice should be directed by a judicious estimate of our true interests, unperplexed and unbiased by considerations not connected with the public good. But this is a thing more ardently to be wished than seriously to be expected. The plan offered to our deliberations affects too many particular interests, innovates upon too many local institutions, not to involve in its discussion a variety of objects foreign to its merits, and of views, passions, and prejudices little favorable to the discovery of truth.

From Alexander Hamilton, James Madison, and John Jay, *The Federalist Papers*, No. 1, No. 10, No. 15, ed. Clinton Rossiter (New York: New American Library, 1961).

Among the most formidable of the obstacles which the new Constitution will have to encounter may readily be distinguished the obvious interest of a certain class of men in every State to resist all changes which may hazard a diminution of the power, emolument, and consequence of the offices they hold under the State establishments; and the perverted ambition of another class of men, who will either hope to aggrandize themselves by the confusions of their country, or will flatter themselves with fairer prospects of elevation from the subdivision of the empire into several partial confederacies than from its union under one government.

It is not, however, my design to dwell upon observations of this nature. I am well aware that it would be disingenuous to resolve indiscriminately the opposition of any set of men (merely because their situations might subject them to suspicion) into interested or ambitious views. Candor will oblige us to admit that even such men may be actuated by upright intentions; and it cannot be doubted that much of the opposition which has made its appearance, or may hereafter make its appearance, will spring from sources, blameless at least if not respectable—the honest errors of minds led astray by preconceived jealousies and fears. So numerous indeed and so powerful are the causes which serve to give a false bias to the judgment, that we, upon many occasions, see wise and good men on the wrong as well as on the right side of questions of the first magnitude to society. This circumstance, if duly attended to, would furnish a lesson of moderation to those who are ever so thoroughly persuaded of their being in the right in any controversy. And a further reason for caution, in this respect, might be drawn from the reflection that we are not always sure that those who advocate the truth are influenced by purer principles than their antagonists. Ambition, avarice, personal animosity, party opposition, and many other motives not more laudable than these, are apt to operate as well upon those who support as those who oppose the right side of a question. Were there not even these inducements to moderation, nothing could be more ill-judged than that intolerant spirit which has at all times characterized political parties. For in politics, as in religion, it is equally absurd to aim at making proselytes by fire and sword. Heresies in either can rarely be cured by persecution.

And yet, however just these sentiments will be allowed to be, we have already sufficient indications that it will happen in this as in all former cases of great national discussion. A torrent of angry and malignant passions will be let loose. To judge from the conduct of the opposite parties, we shall be led to conclude that they will mutually hope to evince the justness of their opinions, and to increase the number of their converts by the loudness of their declamations and by the bitterness of their invectives. An enlightened zeal for the energy and efficiency of government will be stigmatized as the offspring of a temper fond of despotic power and hostile to the principles of liberty. An over-scrupulous jealousy of danger to the rights of the people, which is more commonly the fault of the head than of the heart, will be represented as mere pretense and artifice, the stale bait for popularity at the expense of public good. It will be forgotten, on the one hand, that jealousy is the usual concomitant of violent love, and that the noble enthusiasm of liberty is too apt to be infected with a spirit of narrow and illiberal distrust. On the other hand, it will be equally forgotten that the vigor of government is essential to the security of liberty; that, in the contemplation of a sound and well-informed judgment, their interests can never be separated; and that a dangerous ambition more often lurks behind the specious mask of zeal for the rights of the people than under the forbidding appearance of zeal for the firmness and efficiency of government. History will teach us that the former has been found a much more certain road to the introduction of despotism than the latter, and that of those men who have overturned the liberties of republics, the greatest number have begun their career by paying an obsequious court to the people, commencing demagogues and ending tyrants.

In the course of the preceding observations, I have had an eye, my fellow-citizens, to putting you upon your guard against all attempts, from whatever quarter, to influence your decision in a matter of the utmost moment to your welfare by any impressions other than those which may result from the evidence of truth. You will, no doubt, at the same time have collected from the general scope of them that they proceed from a source not unfriendly to the new Constitution. Yes, my countrymen, I own to you that after having given it an attentive consideration, I am clearly of opinion it is your interest to adopt it. I am convinced that this is the safest course for your liberty, your dignity, and your happiness. I affect not reserves which I do not feel. I will not amuse you with an appearance of deliberation when I have decided. I frankly acknowledge to you my convictions, and I will freely lay before you the reasons on which they are founded. The consciousness of good intentions disdains ambiguity. I shall not, however, multiply professions on this head. My motives must remain in the depository of my own breast. My arguments will be open to all and may be judged of by all. They shall at least be offered in a spirit which will not disgrace the cause of truth.

I propose, in a series of papers, to discuss the following interesting particulars:—*The utility of the UNION to your political prosperity—The insufficiency of the present Confederation to preserve that Union—The necessity of a government at least equally energetic with the one proposed, to the attainment of this object—The conformity of the proposed Constitution to the true principles of republican government—Its analogy to your own State constitution—*and lastly, *The additional security which its adoption will afford to the preservation of that species of government, to liberty, and to property.*

In the progress of this discussion I shall endeavor to give a satisfactory answer to all the objections which shall have made their appearance, that may seem to have any claim to your attention.

It may perhaps be thought superfluous to offer arguments to prove the utility of the UNION, a point, no doubt, deeply engraved on the hearts of the great body of the people in every State, and one which, it may be imagined, has no adversaries. But the fact is that we already hear it whispered in the private circles of those who oppose the new Constitution, that the thirteen States are of too great extent for any general system, and that we must of necessity resort to separate confederacies of distinct portions of the whole. This doctrine will, in all probability, be gradually propagated, till it has votaries enough to countenance an open avowal of it. For nothing can be more evident to those who are able to take an enlarged view of the subject than the alternative of an adoption of the new Constitution or a dismemberment of the Union. It will therefore be of use to begin by examining the advantages of that Union, the certain evils, and the probable dangers, to which every State will be exposed from its dissolution. This shall accordingly constitute the subject of my next address.

PUBLIUS

NO. 10: MADISON

Among the numerous advantages promised by a well-constructed Union, none deserves to be more accurately developed than its tendency to break and control the violence of faction. The friend of popular governments never finds himself so much alarmed for their character and fate as when he contemplates their propensity to this dangerous vice. He will not fail, therefore, to set a due value on any plan which, without violating the principles to which he is attached, provides a proper cure for it. The instability, injustice, and confusion introduced into the public councils have, in truth, been the mortal diseases under which popular governments have everywhere perished, as they continue to be the favorite and fruitful topics from which the adversaries to liberty derive their most specious declamations. The valuable improvements made by the American constitutions on the popular models, both ancient and modern, cannot certainly be too much admired; but it would be an unwarrantable partiality to contend that they have as effectually obviated the danger on this side, as was wished and expected. Complaints are everywhere heard from our most considerate and virtuous citizens, equally the friends of public and private faith and of public and personal liberty, that our governments are too unstable, that the public good is disregarded in the conflicts of rival parties, and that measures are too often decided, not according to the rules of justice and the rights of the minor party, but by the superior force of an interested and overbearing majority. However anxiously we may wish that these complaints had no foundation, the evidence of known facts will not permit us to deny that they are in some degree true. It will be found, indeed, on a candid review of our situation, that some of the distresses under which we labor have been erroneously charged on the operation of our governments; but it will be found, at the same time, that other causes will not alone account for many of our heaviest misfortunes; and, particularly, for that prevailing and increasing distrust of public engagements and alarm for private rights which are echoed from one end of the continent to the other. These must be chiefly, if not wholly, effects of the unsteadiness and injustice with which a factious spirit has tainted our public administration.

By a faction I understand a number of citizens, whether amounting to a majority or minority of the whole, who are united and actuated by some common impulse of passion, or of interest, adverse to the rights of other citizens, or to the permanent and aggregate interests of the community.

There are two methods of curing the mischiefs of faction: the one, by removing its causes; the other, by controlling its effects.

There are again two methods of removing the causes of faction: the one, by destroying the liberty which is essential to its existence; the other, by giving to every citizen the same opinions, the same passions, and the same interests.

It could never be more truly said than of the first remedy that it was worse than the disease. Liberty is to faction what air is to fire, an aliment without which it instantly expires. But it could not be a less folly to abolish liberty, which is essential to political life, because it nourishes faction than it would be to wish the annihilation of air, which is essential to animal life, because it imparts to fire its destructive agency.

The second expedient is as impracticable as the first would be unwise. As long as the reason of man continues fallible, and he is at liberty to exercise it, different opinions will be formed. As long as the connection subsists between his reason and his self-love, his opinions and his passions will have a reciprocal influence on each other; and the former will be objects to which the latter will attach themselves. The diversity in the faculties of men, from which the rights of property originate, is not less an insuperable obstacle to a uniformity of interests. The protection of these faculties is the first object of government. From the protection of different and unequal faculties of acquiring property, the possession of different degrees and kinds of property immediately results; and from the influence of these on the sentiments and views of the respective proprietors ensues a division of the society into different interests and parties.

The latent causes of faction are thus sown in the nature of man; and we see them everywhere brought into different degrees of activity, according to the different circumstances of civil society. A zeal for different opinions concerning religion, concerning government, and many other points, as well of speculation as of practice; an attachment to different leaders ambitiously contending for preeminence and power; or to persons of other descriptions whose fortunes have been interesting to the human passions, have, in turn, divided mankind into parties, inflamed them with mutual animosity, and rendered them much more disposed to vex and oppress each other than to co-operate for their common good. So strong is this propensity of mankind to fall into mutual animosities that where no substantial occasion presents itself the most frivolous and fanciful distinctions have been sufficient to kindle their unfriendly passions and excite their most violent conflicts. But the most common and durable source of factions has been the various and unequal distribution of property. Those who hold and those who are without property have ever formed distinct interests in society. Those who are creditors, and those who are debtors, fall under a like discrimination. A landed interest, a manufacturing interest, a mercantile interest, a moneyed interest, with many lesser interests, grow up of necessity in civilized nations, and divide them into different classes, actuated by different sentiments and views. The regulation of these various and interfering interests forms the principal task of modern legislation and involves the spirit of party and faction in the necessary and ordinary operations of government. . . .

NO. 15: HAMILTON

In the course of the preceding papers I have endeavored, my fellow-citizens, to place before you in a clear and convincing light the importance of Union to your political safety and happiness. I have unfolded to you a complication of dangers to which you would be exposed, should you permit that sacred knot which binds the people of America together to be severed or dissolved by ambition or by avarice, by jealousy or by misrepresentation. In the sequel of the inquiry through which I propose to accompany you, the truths intended to be inculcated will receive further confirmation from facts and arguments hitherto unnoticed. If the road over which you will still have to pass should in some places appear to you tedious or irksome, you will recollect that you are in quest of information on a subject the most momentous which can engage the attention of a free people, that the field through which you have to travel is in itself spacious, and that the difficulties of the journey have been unnecessarily increased by the mazes with which sophistry has beset the way. It will be my aim to remove the obstacles to your progress in as compendious a manner as it can be done, without sacrificing utility to dispatch.

In pursuance of the plan which I have laid down for the discussion of the subject, the point next in order to be examined is the "insufficiency of the present Confederation to the preservation of the Union." It may perhaps be asked what need there is of reasoning or proof to illustrate a position which is not either controverted or doubted, to which the understandings and feelings of all classes of men assent, and which in substance is admitted by the opponents as well as by the friends of the new Constitution. It must in truth be acknowledged that, however these may differ in other respects, they in general appear to harmonize in this sentiment at least: that there are material imperfections in our national system and that something is necessary to be done to rescue us from impending anarchy. The facts that support this opinion are no longer objects of speculation. They have forced themselves upon the sensibility of the people at large, and have at length extorted from those, whose mistaken policy has had the principal share in precipitating the extremity at which we are arrived, a reluctant confession of the reality of those defects in the scheme of our federal government which have been long pointed out and regretted by the intelligent friends of the Union.

We may indeed with propriety be said to have reached almost the last stage of national humiliation. There is scarcely anything that can wound the pride or degrade the character of an independent nation which we do not experience. Are there engagements to the performance of which we are held by every tie respectable among men? These are the subjects of constant and unblushing violation. Do we owe debts to foreigners and to our own citizens contracted in a time of imminent peril for the preservation of our political existence? These remain without any proper or satisfactory provision for their discharge. Have we valuable territories and important posts in the possession of a foreign power which, by express stipulations, ought long since to have been surrendered? These are still retained to the prejudice of our interests, not less than of our rights. Are we in a condition to resent or to repel the aggression? We have neither troops, nor treasury, nor government.° Are we even in a condition to remonstrate with dignity? The just imputations on our own faith in respect to the same treaty ought first to be removed. Are we entitled by nature and compact to a free participation in the navigation of the Mississippi? Spain excludes us from it. Is public credit an indispensable resource in time of public danger? We seem to have abandoned its cause as desperate and irretrievable. Is commerce of importance to national wealth? Ours is at the lowest point of declension. Is respectability in the eyes of foreign powers a safeguard against foreign encroachments? The imbecility of our government even forbids them to treat with us. Our ambassadors abroad are the mere pageants of mimic sovereignty. Is a violent and unnatural decrease in the value of land a symptom of national distress? The price of improved land in most parts of the country is much lower than can be accounted for by the quantity of waste land at market, and can only be fully explained by that want of private and public confidence, which are so alarmingly prevalent among all ranks and which have a direct tendency to depreciate property of every kind. Is private credit the friend and patron of industry? That most useful kind which relates to borrowing and lending is reduced within the narrowest limits, and this still more from an opinion of insecurity than from a scarcity of money. To shorten an enumeration of particulars which can afford neither pleasure nor instruction, it may in general be demanded, what indication is there of national disorder, poverty, and insignificance that could befall a community so peculiarly blessed with natural advantages as we are, which does not form a part of the dark catalogue of our public misfortunes?

This is the melancholy situation to which we have been brought by those very maxims and counsels which would now deter us from adopting the proposed Constitution; and which, not content with having conducted us to the brink of a precipice, seem resolved to plunge us into the abyss that awaits us below. Here, my countrymen, impelled by every motive that ought to influence an enlightened people, let us make a firm stand for our safety, our tranquillity, our dignity, our reputation. Let us at last break the fatal charm which has too long seduced us from the paths of felicity and prosperity.

It is true, as has been before observed, that facts too stubborn to be resisted have produced a species of general assent to the abstract proposition that there exist material defects in our national system; but the usefulness of the concession on the part of the old adversaries of federal measures is destroyed by a strenuous

---

°"I mean for the Union."

opposition to a remedy upon the only principles that can give it a chance of success. While they admit that the government of the United States is destitute of energy, they contend against conferring upon it those powers which are requisite to supply that energy. They seem still to aim at things repugnant and irreconcilable; at an augmentation of federal authority without a diminution of State authority; at sovereignty in the Union and complete independence in the members. They still, in fine, seem to cherish with blind devotion the political monster of an *imperium in imperio*. This renders a full display of the principal defects of the Confederation necessary in order to show that the evils we experience do not proceed from minute or partial imperfections, but from fundamental errors in the structure of the building, which cannot be amended otherwise than by an alteration in the first principles and main pillars of the fabric.

The great and radical vice in the construction of the existing Confederation is in the principle of LEGISLATION for STATES or GOVERNMENTS, in their CORPORATE or COLLECTIVE CAPACITIES, and as contradistinguished from the INDIVIDUALS of whom they consist. Though this principle does not run through all the powers delegated to the Union, yet it pervades and governs those on which the efficacy of the rest depends. Except as to the rule of apportionment, the United States have an indefinite discretion to make requisitions for men and money; but they have no authority to raise either by regulations extending to the individual citizens of America. The consequence of this is that though in theory their resolutions concerning those objects are laws constitutionally binding on the members of the Union, yet in practice they are mere recommendations which the States observe or disregard at their option.

It is a singular instance of the capriciousness of the human mind that after all the admonitions we have had from experience on this head, there should still be found men who object to the new Constitution for deviating from a principle which has been found the bane of the old and which is in itself evidently incompatible with the idea of GOVERNMENT; a principle, in short, which, if it is to be executed at all, must substitute the violent and sanguinary agency of the sword to the mild influence of the magistracy. . . .

Political Repression in the United States

Michael Rogin

Most treatments of the countersubversive mentality . . . disconnect demonology both from major American social divisions and from institutionalized political repression. Most versions of American history, by a complementary set of choices, chart a progress toward freedom and inclusion. To link countersubversive thinking to political repression is to write another history. Such an account hardly stands in for American history as a whole. But if certain familiar patterns recede into the shadows, neglected, dark areas emerge into light.

At the same time, the subject of political repression must not be confined to the suppression of already legitimate political opposition. A history of American political suppression must attend to the repression of active, political dissent. But it must also direct attention to prepolitical institutional settings that have excluded some Americans from politics and influenced the terms on which others entered the political arena. An account of American political suppression must acknowledge the suppression of politics itself. It must notice the relations between politics and private life. Countersubversive ideologies, psychological mechanisms, and an intrusive state apparatus all respond to the fear of subversion in America. . . .

I

"History begins for us with murder and enslavement, not with discovery," wrote the American poet William Carlos Williams. He was calling attention to the historical origins of the United States in violence against peoples of color. He was pointing to America's origins in the origins of a capitalist world system. Indian land and black labor generated a European-American-African trade in the seventeenth century and contributed to the development of commodity agriculture, industrial production, and state power in Europe and the Americas. Karl Marx wrote, "The discovery of gold and silver in America, the extirpation, enslavement, and entombment in mines of the aboriginal population, the beginning of the conquest and the looting of the East Indies, and the turning of Africa into a warren for the commercial hunting of black-skins, signalized the rosy dawn of capitalist production. These idyllic proceedings are the chief momenta of primitive accumulation."[1]

From Michael Rogin, *Ronald Reagan the Movie, and Other Episodes in Political Demonology*. Copyright © 1987 The Regents of the University of California. (Berkeley: University of California Press, 1987), chapters 2 and 5. Reprinted by permission.

By primitive accumulation Marx meant the forcible acquisition by a mixture of state and private violence of land and labor to serve the accumulation of capital. Primitive accumulation made land, labor, and commodities available for the marketplace before the free market could act on its own. The suppression, intimidation, and control of peoples of color supplies the prehistory of the American history of freedom. People of color were important, moreover, not only at the origins of America but also in its ongoing history—through westward expansion against Indians and Mexicans, chattel slavery and the exclusion of emancipated blacks from political and economic freedom, and the repressive responses to Hispanic and Asian workers. The American economy exploited peoples of color, but American racial history is not reducible to its economic roots. A distinctive American political tradition that was fearful of primitivism and disorder developed in response to peoples of color. That tradition defines itself against alien threats to the American way of life and sanctions violent and exclusionary responses to them.

Indians in early America, emblematic of chaos, were not seen through New World lenses. They rather came to embody the masterless men who appeared in Europe with the breakdown of traditional society. "Liv[ing] without government," in the words of one early report, and freed of the restraints of family, church, and village as well, the idle, wandering savages were depicted as engaging in incest, cannibalism, devil worship, and murder. Some European-Americans, to be sure, depicted savages not as monstrous but as noble. Traders, promoters of commercial ventures, settlers no longer threatened by powerful tribes, and humanists drawn to a classical or Christian golden age all imagined peaceful primitives enjoying a state of innocence. But the noble savage and his dark double were joined. Both images of primitivism appropriated Indians for white purposes. Both made the Indians children of nature instead of creators and inhabitants of their own cultures. Both ignored Indian agriculture and depicted a tribalism that menaced private property and the family. Neither the noble nor the devilish savage could coexist with the advancing white civilization. Both images rationalized the dispossession of the tribes.[2]

Indians did not use the land for agriculture, explained Massachusetts Bay governor John Winthrop. Since the wandering tribes failed to "subdue and replenish" the earth, white farmers could acquire their land. Winthrop's principle of expropriation was an accepted tenet of international law by the early eighteenth century. It did not justify the individual acquisition of farming plots, however, but rather state action. First the colonies and the mother country, then the independent states, and finally the federal government expropriated land by making treaties with Indian tribes. George Washington, justifying the treaty method, defended

> the propriety of purchasing their lands in preference to attempting to drive them by force of arms out of our country, which, as we have already experienced, is like driving the wild beasts of ye forests, which will return as soon as the pursuit is at an end,

and fall, perhaps upon those that are left there; when the gradual extension of our settlements will as certainly cause the savage, as the wolf, to retire; both being beasts of prey tho' they differ in shape.[3]

Indians were animals, but fortunately they were men as well. As men they could make contracts, accept money, and consent to the loss of their land. Treaties presented a fiction of Indian freedom to disguise the realities of coerced consent, bribery, deception about boundaries, agreements with one faction enforced on an entire tribe, and the encouragement of tribal debts—real and inflated—to be paid off by the cession of land.

The policy of Indian removal conceived by Thomas Jefferson, employed in his and succeeding administrations, and forced upon the southern Indians by Andrew Jackson, offered Indians the freedom to move west if they relinquished their ancestral holdings. Although removal treaties were forced upon the tribes, the treaty method allowed Indian expropriation to proceed under the color of law. It engaged Indians in consent to their own subjugation.[4]

The federal government abrogated tribal treaty-making rights in 1871. In return for depriving Indians of their collective freedom, the government promised individual freedom. The government had begun to offer freedom to individual Indians early in the nineteenth century to atomize tribes and subject their members to market pressures and state laws. The most important individual freedom offered Indians was freedom from communal land ownership. Some tribal leaders in antebellum America believed that individual allotments were the only way to preserve Indian land, but widespread fraud and intimidation quickly transferred Indian freeholds to white land companies. The Dawes Severalty Act of 1887, which Theodore Roosevelt praised as "a mighty pulverizing engine to break up the tribal mass," offered Indians the opportunity to become free Americans; the freedom that they actually acquired was the freedom to alienate their land. Railroads, mining interests, cattlemen, and land corporations acquired the land allotments granted Indians. Between 1887 and 1934 the tribes lost an estimated 60 percent of their holdings. In 1983 Secretary of the Interior James Watt proposed to grant Indians "freedom" from their "socialistic" dependence on the federal government and on their tribes; Indian spokesmen, in response, denied they were Reds. The freedom offered Indians, from Jackson to Watt, has undermined communal loyalties as sources of political resistance.[5]

American Indian policy from the beginning combined freedom with coercion, the method of the marketplace with the method of the state. Government has shown two faces to the tribes, one of violence, the other of paternal guardianship. Consider the acquisition of land. Whites claimed Indian land not only by right of treaty or proper use but also as the fruits of a just war. Conflicts over land and living space produced a series of Indian wars, beginning with Virginia's war against the Powhatan Confederacy in 1622 and with the New England Pequot War of 1636–37. White expansion provoked most of these wars; savage atrocities were cited to justify them. Wars over living space produced civilian casualties on both sides; but whereas Indian violence was attributed to primitive ferocity, the systematic destruction of Indian crops and villages was defended as a matter of deliberate policy. White victories, it was said, proved the superiority of civilization over savagery. Indian wars were important in the colonies and during the Revolution. They also promoted American continental expansion from the War of 1812 to the closing of the frontier. More than two hundred pitched battles were fought in the West during the Gilded Age, and there was also periodic guerilla warfare in outlying regions.[6] The history of Indian war ended at Wounded Knee, South Dakota, in 1890 with the massacre of two hundred Sioux men, women, and children, including the old warrior, Sitting Bull, after a ghost dance ceremony.

Indians displaced by treaty or defeated in war were offered "paternal guardianship." Indian tribes were "in a state of pupilage," ruled the Supreme Court in *Cherokee Nation* v. *Georgia* (1831); "their relation to the United States resembles that of a ward to his guardian." Since the Cherokees were not a nation, they could not maintain an action in court to protect their autonomy. As the equals of whites, Indians had the freedom to lose their land; as the wards of a paternal government, Indians were confined. The government adopted a reservations policy before the Civil War and enforced it on the western tribes in the late nineteenth century. Confined to reservations, tribes were dependent on government food, clothing, and shelter. Although they were held in protective custody, their land continued to be subject to encroachments from cattle, agricultural, and mineral interests.

Confinement was seen not simply as the opposite of Indian freedom but as the preparation for a new kind of liberty. "Civilized and domesticated," reservation Indians were to be freed from their tribal identities and remade as free men. "Push improvement on them by education, alienation, and individuation," urged an Osage agent in the late nineteenth century. Indian agents encouraged commodity agriculture, ignoring unsuitable topographical and cultural conditions and the presence of rapacious whites. Compulsory government boarding schools regimented children in barracks far from their parents' homes, forced them to abandon tribal dress, and punished them for using their native tongue.[7]

When antebellum Indian Commissioner Thomas McKenney had evoked "their helplessness and their dependence on the President as their father," his intention was more than benevolent description. McKenney wanted to make Indians over into the "children" he described. The passionate, profligate savages imagined at the beginning of American history had given way by the end of the nineteenth century to dependent Indians whose helplessness was the condition of their improvement. Amerigo Vespucci had depicted lascivious savages whose "women, being very lustful, cause the private parts of their husbands to swell up to such a huge size that they appear deformed and disgusting." Four hundred years later a leading Indian reformer, Merrill E. Gates, explained, "We have, to begin with, the absolute need of awakening in the savage Indian broader desires and ampler wants. . . . In his dull savagery he must be touched by the divine angel of discontent. . . . Discontent with the teepee and the starving rations of the Indian camp in winter is needed to get the Indian out of the blanket and into trousers—trousers with a pocket in them, and with *a pocket that aches to be filled with dollars*." (Italics are in the original.) The progress from sex to money had replaced the swollen private parts of Vespucci's Indian with the aching, empty pockets of Gates's.[8]

Aspirations to turn native Americans into passive receptacles for white desires were not wholly fulfilled, however. Reservation tribes maintained some autonomy, thanks in part to varying mixtures of accommodation and resistance and in part to federal recognition (beginning with the New Deal) of Indian rights. Assaults on Indian land, water, and minerals continue, nonetheless, often with the cooperation of the Bureau of Indian Affairs. Dillon S. Myer, for example, as head of the bureau under President Truman, denied tribes the right to hire lawyers to defend themselves against predatory whites. The commissioner accused Felix Cohen, the leading American authority on Indian law and an opponent of Myer's policies, of being a Communist sympathizer.[9] The Eisenhower administration sought to abolish reservations altogether, and although that effort was only partially successful, it shifted considerable land from Indians to whites. Today Indian tribes remain what *Cherokee Nation* v. *Georgia* defined them to be: "domestic, dependent nations" within the United States.

The dispossession of Indians did not happen once and for all in American history. America was continually expanding west, and while doing so it decimated, removed, or confined one tribe after another. That history had major consequences not only for Indian-white relations but also for American history as a whole. It defined America from the beginning as a settler society, an expanding, domestic, imperial power. Expansion guaranteed American freedom, so it was believed, protecting Americans from the crowded conditions and social class divisions of Europe. Although Indian wars actually exemplified state violence, they fed an opposite myth—the myth of the self-made man. Masterless Indians had challenged European institutional restraints at the beginning of American history. Early settlers made Indians a threat to community. By the Age of Jackson, Americans celebrated their own independence, which Indian tribalism threatened to confine. White Americans contrasted their own freedom, disciplined by self-restraint, with the subversive, idle, and violent freedom of the Indians. The self-reliant American gained his freedom, won his authority, and defined the American national identity in violent Indian combat in the West.[10]

With the perceived closing of the continental frontier in the 1890s, the policy of Manifest Destiny was extended to Asia. The suppression of the Philippine independence movement after the Spanish-American war caused hundreds of thousands of deaths. America was, according to those who carried out and defended its Philippine policy, continuing its conquest over and tutelage of primitive tribes. Indian policy also set precedents for twentieth-century interventions in Latin America. The country's expansionist history against savage peoples of color culminated rhetorically and in practice in the war in Vietnam. Counterinsurgent, savage warfare returned in the 1980s to the New World, Central American arena where it had always prospered, as the United States supported death squads in San Salvador and terror bombing and a scorched earth policy in the El Salvador countryside, the torture and murder of Guatemalan Indians, and terrorist attacks by "freedom fighters" on the people and government of Nicaragua. Calling the Nicaraguan contras "the moral equal of our Founding Fathers," President Reagan laid claim to a tradition for which other citizens of the United States might wish to make reparation.[11]

Indian policy also had domestic implications. Indians were the first people to stand in American history as emblems of disorder, civilized breakdown, and alien control. Differences between reds and whites made cultural adaptation seem at once dangerous and impossible. The violent conquest of Indians legitimized violence against other alien groups, making coexistence appear to be unnecessary. The paranoid style in American politics, as Richard Hofstadter has labeled it, goes back to responses to Indians. The series of Red scares that have swept the country since the 1870s have roots in the original red scares. Later countersubversive movements attacked aliens, but the people who originally assaulted reds were themselves aliens in the land. Responses to the Indians point to the mixture of cultural arrogance and insecurity in the American history of countersubversion. The identity of a self-making people, engaged in a national, purifying mission, may be particularly vulnerable to threats of contamination and disintegration. The need to draw rigid boundaries between the alien and the self suggests fears of too dangerous an intimacy between them.[12]

Just as fears of subversion moved from Indians to other social groups, so did techniques of control. The group ties of workers and immigrants were assaulted in the name of individual freedom. State violence, used to punish Indians who allegedly preferred war to labor, was also employed against striking workers. A paternal model of interracial relations developed in slavery as well as in Indian policy. Finally, Indians shared their status as beneficiaries of meliorist confinement with the inmates of total institutions. These arenas—slavery, the asylum, labor relations, and radical dissent—form the major loci of American political suppression. . . .

LIBERAL SOCIETY AND THE INDIAN QUESTION

> Our conduct toward these people is deeply interesting to our
> national character.
>
> *Andrew Jackson, First Annual Message to Congress, 1829*

I

Underneath the "ambitious expansionism" of modern western societies, writes Henri Baudet in *Paradise on Earth*, "with their economic savoir faire, their social ideology, and their organizational talents," lies "a psychological disposition out of all political reality. It exists independently of objective facts, which seem to have become irrelevant. It is a disposition that leads [its adherent] 'to die' rather than 'to do,' and forces him to repent of his wickedness, covetousness, pride, and complacency."[13] The worldly orientation, Baudet argues, points to history and practical consequences, the inner disposition to a primitiveness beyond history. The first is expansive, the second regressive. This regressive, inner disposition, Baudet believes, has fastened on images of the noble savage, the garden of Eden, and paradise on earth.

In America, however, "ambitious expansionism" encountered the "regressive impulse" as a "political reality." This conflict between expansion and regression, I will suggest, is the precise cultural meaning Americans gave to their destruction of the Indians. Their language teaches us some intolerable truths about regression, maturity, and death in liberal America.

In calling America a liberal society, I mean to evoke the unchallenged primacy of propertied individualism across the political spectrum. At the outset the contrast between expansionist, liberal America's self-conception and its image of the Indians seems clear enough. Liberalism insisted on the independence of men, each from the other and from cultural, traditional, and communal attachments. Indians were perceived as connected to their past, their superstitions, and their land. Liberalism insisted upon work, instinctual repression, and acquisitive behavior; men had to conquer and separate themselves from nature. Indians were seen as playful, violent, improvident, wild, and in harmony with nature. Private property underlay liberal society; Indians held land in common. Liberal relations were based contractually on keeping promises and on personal responsibility. Indians, in the liberal view, were anarchic and irresponsible. Americans believed that peaceful competitiveness kept them in touch with one another and provided social cement. They thought that Indians, lacking social order, were devoted to war.

Disastrously for the liberal self-conception, however, its distance from primitive man was not secure. At the heart of ambitious expansionism lay the regressive impulse itself. Indians were in harmony with nature; lonely, independent, liberal men were separated from it, and their culture lacked the richness, diversity, and traditional attachments to sustain their independence. The consequence was forbidden nostalgia, for the nurturing, blissful, and primitively violent connection to nature that white Americans had had to leave behind. At the core of liberalism lay the belief that such human connections to each other and to the land were dreams only, subjects of nostalgia or sentimentalization but impossible in the existing adult world. By suggesting the reality of the dream, Indian societies

I am grateful to Paul Roazen for directing my early reading in psychoanalytic sources, to Leslie and Margaret Fiedler, and to the political theorists once together in Berkeley—Norman Jacobson, Hanna Pitkin, John H. Schaar, and Sheldon Wolin—for providing, with our students, the intellectual setting in which this essay was written.

Portions of a draft of this paper were presented at the University of North Carolina Symposium "Laws, Rights, and Authority," Chapel Hill, 20–22 February 1970, and at the Annual Meeting of the Western Political Science Association, Sacramento, 3 April 1970.

posed a severe threat to liberal identity. The only safe Indians were dead, sanitized, or totally dependent upon white benevolence. Liberal action enforced the only world possible in liberal theory.

The intimate historical encounter with the Indians still further undermined liberal identity. "In the beginning," John Locke had written, "all the world was America."[14] Then men relinquished the state of nature, freely contracted together, and entered civil society. But that was not the way it happened—in America. True, settlers had come to escape the corruption and traditional restraints of Europe, to begin again, to return to the state of nature and contract together. They aimed, as Hamilton put it in the *Federalist Papers*, to build a state based on "reflection and choice" rather than on "accident and force."[15] But while the origins of European countries were shrouded in the mists of obscure history, America had clearly begun not with primal innocence and consent but with acts of force and fraud. Stripping away history did not permit beginning without sin; it simply exposed the sin at the beginning of it all.

In the popular culture of films, Westerns, and children's games, seizing America from the Indians is the central, mythical, formative experience. Its dynamic figures prominently in the Vietnam War, providing symbols for soldiers, names for combat missions, and the framework for Pentagon strategic plans.[16] But historians have ignored the elimination of the Indians and minimized its significance for American development. This was the one outcome American statesmen in the two centuries before the Civil War could not imagine. For the dispossession of the Indians did not simply happen once and for all in the beginning. America was continually beginning again, and as it expanded across the continent, it killed, removed, and drove into extinction one tribe after another. I will focus here on the first half of the nineteenth century and particularly on the "Indian removal" program of Jacksonian democracy.[17]

Expansion across the continent was the central fact of American politics from Jefferson's presidency through the Mexican War. Indians inhabited almost all the territory west of the Appalachians in 1800; they had to be removed. The story is bloody and corrupt beyond imagining, and few American political figures escape from it without dishonor. From 1820 to 1844 one hundred thousand Indians were removed from their homes and transported west of the Mississippi. One-quarter to one-third of these died or were killed in the process.[18] Indian removal was Andrew Jackson's major concrete political aim in the years before he became president; Van Buren later listed it as one of the four major achievements of Jackson's administration, along with the bank war, the internal improvements veto, and the nullification fight.[19] Six of the eleven major candidates for president in the years from 1820 to 1852 had either won reputations as generals in Indian wars or served as secretaries of war, whose major responsibility in this period was relations with the Indians.[20]

How to reconcile the elimination of the Indians with the liberal self-image? This problem preoccupied the statesmen of the period. "The great moral debt we owe to this unhappy race is universally felt and acknowledged," Secretary of War

Lewis Cass reported in 1831.[21] In our relations to the Indians, wrote Van Buren, "we are as a nation responsible *in foro conscientiae*, to the opinions of the great family of nations, as it involves the course we have pursued and shall pursue towards a people comparatively weak, upon whom we were perhaps in the beginning unjustifiable aggressors, but of whom, in the progress of time and events, we have become the guardians, and, as we hope, the benefactors."[22]

Van Buren and the others felt the eyes of the world upon America. They needed a policy and rhetoric permitting them to believe that our encounter with the Indians, "the most difficult of all our relations, foreign and domestic, has at last been justified to the world in its near approach to a happy and certain consummation."[23] They needed to justify—the Puritan word means save for God—a society built upon Indian graves.

The theory and language American statesmen employed cemented the historical white-Indian tie with intimate symbolic meaning. America's expansion across the continent, everyone agreed, reproduced the historical evolution of mankind. "The first proprietors of this happy country"[24] were sometimes said to be the first people on earth. Early in time, they were also primitive in development. Human societies existed along a unilinear scale from savagery to civilization. The early, savage peoples could not coexist with advanced societies; civilization would inevitably displace savagery.[25]

So stated, the theory remained abstract; politicians and social commentators filled it with personal meaning. The evolution of societies was identical to the evolution of individual men. "Barbarism is to civilization what childhood is to maturity."[26] Indians were at the infant stage of social evolution. They were "part of the human family"[27] as children; their replacement by whites symbolized America's growing up from childhood to maturity. Winthrop Jordan writes, "The Indian became for Americans a symbol of their American experience; it was no mere luck of the toss that placed the profile of an American Indian rather than an American Negro on the famous old five-cent piece. Confronting the Indian in America was a testing experience, common to all the colonies. Conquering the Indian symbolized and personified the conquest of the American difficulties, the surmounting of the wilderness. To push back the Indian was to prove the worth of one's own mission, to make straight in the desert a highway for civilization."[28] . . .

NOTES

1. William Carlos Williams, *In the American Grain* (1925; republished, New York, 1956), 39; Karl Marx, *Capital*, 3 Vols. (Chicago, 1906–9), 1:823; Immanuel Wallerstein, *The Modern World System* (New York, 1974).

2. Howard Mumford Jones, *O Strange New World* (New York, 1964), plate 3 and p. 28n; Michael Paul Rogin, *Fathers and Children: Andrew Jackson and the Subjugation of the American Indian* (New York, 1975), 3–11, 113–25; Robert F. Berkhofer, *The White Man's Indian: Images of the American Indian from Columbus to the Present* (New York, 1978); Elemira Zolla, *The Writer and the Shaman* (New York, 1973); Gary B. Nash, "The Image of the Indian in the Southern Colonial Mind," *William and Mary Quarterly* 24 (1972): 201–3.

3. George M. Fredrickson, *White Supremacy* (New York, 1981), 35; Virgil Vogel, ed., *This Country Was Ours: A Documentary History of the American Indian* (New York, 1972), 75–76.

4. Rogin, *Fathers and Children*, 165–247; and chapter 5.

5. Vogel, *This Country*, 193–94; William T. Hagan, *American Indians* (Chicago, 1961), 141–50; *San Francisco Chronicle*, 20 January 1983, p. 24.

6. Alan Trachtenberg, *The Incorporation of America* (New York, 1982), 29.

7. Terry P. Wilson, *The Underground Reservation: Osage Oil* (Lincoln, Neb., 1985), 82.

8. The quotes but not the interpretation of them come from Herman J. Viola, *Thomas L. McKenney, Architect of America's Early Indian Policy, 1816–1830* (Chicago, 1974), 37, 176; Berkhofer, *White Man's Indian*, 8, 173.

9. Cf. Richard Drinnon, *Keeper of Concentration Camps: Dillon S. Myer and American Racism* (Berkeley and Los Angeles, 1986).

10. Cf. Richard Slotkin, *Regeneration Through Violence* (Middletown, Conn., 1973).

11. Richard Drinnon, *Facing West: The Metaphysics of Indian-Hating and Empire-Building* (New York, 1980), 307–467; Eleanor Fuchs and Joyce Antler, *Year One of the Empire* (Boston, 1973); Thomas Sheehan, "El Salvador: The Forgotten War," *Threepenny Review*, no. 22 (Summer 1985): 3–4; *New York Times*, 2 March 1985, p. 8.

12. Richard Hofstadter, *The Paranoid Style in American Politics* (New York, 1965). Cf. Michael Zuckerman, "The Fabrication of Identity in Early America," *William and Mary Quarterly* 34 (1977): 183–214.

13. Henri Baudet, *Paradise on Earth* (New Haven, 1965), 8.

14. John Locke, *Of Civil Government* (London, 1924), *Second Treatise*, 140. For Hobbes and Rousseau, American Indian societies also demonstrated the historical existence of the state of nature. See Hoxie N. Fairchild, *The Noble Savage* (New York, 1961), 23–24.

15. *The Federalist Papers*, Roy P. Fairfield, ed. (New York, 1961), no. 1:33.

16. Cf. Noam Chomsky, "After Pinkville," *New York Review of Books*, 1 January 1970, p. 10, and *American Power and the New Mandarins* (New York, 1969), 279–80; Michael Rogin, "Truth Is Stranger Than Science Fiction," *The Listener*, 7 July 1968, pp. 117–18; Richard Drinnon, "Violence in the American Experience: Winning the West," *The Radical Teacher* (Chicago), 30 December 1969, pp. 36, 45–46.

Hippie and New Left youth identify themselves, and are identified by their enemies, with Indian resistance to American culture. It is fitting that the leading academic defender of American traditions has written an intemperate attack on the "new barbarians" of the New Left. This "rebellion of small groups" is "rude, wild, and uncivilized," "wild and disorganized," demands "infant-instantism," is wholly un-American, and "cannot last, if the nation is to survive" (Daniel Boorstin, "The New Barbarians," *Esquire*, October 1968, pp. 159–62, 260–62).

17. This essay interprets the prevailing cultural myth about Indians in antebellum America. It makes no effort to specify the social basis of that myth—class or mass, popular or elite, frontier or eastern, northern or southern, entrepreneurial or pastoral, speculator or backwoods. These themes are addressed in my *Fathers and Children: Andrew Jackson and the Subjugation of the American Indian* (New York, 1975). The discussion here will indicate that our leading politicians shared the myth and that it was particularly salient to those involved in Indian affairs. I believe that in some form the Indian myth reached deeply into all the social categories enumerated above. But it was sufficiently complex that different social types would stress different aspects. This sort of differentiation is not attempted here.

18. I am indebted to Mark Morris for this estimate. It is derived from Commissioner of Indian Affairs census records and other published sources. The figures in the text are conservative; removal during this period may have caused the deaths of forty thousand Indians.

19. Martin Van Buren, *Autobiography*, American Historical Association Annual Report (1918), 2:275. Cf. Mary E. Young, *Redskins, Ruffleshirts, and Rednecks* (Norman, Okla., 1961), 3–5, passim; Annie Heloise Abel, *The History of Events Resulting in Indian Consolidation West of the Mississippi*, American Historical Association Report of Proceedings (1906). Indians are simply not mentioned at all in perhaps the two major contenders for synthetic interpretations of the Jacksonian period. See Arthur Schlesinger, Jr., *The Age of Jackson* (Boston, 1945); Marvin Meyers, *The Jacksonian Persuasion* (New York, 1960). Thomas H. Benton's biographer largely ignores his important role in

Indian affairs; Lewis Cass's biographer offers the most enormous, elementary, factual errors in his abbreviated account of the secretary of war and Indian removal. See William N. Chambers, *Old Bullion Benton* (Boston, 1956); Frank B. Woodford, *Lewis Cass* (New Brunswick, N.J., 1950), 180–83.

20. "Our Indian Affairs is . . . the most important branch of the war department," Andrew Jackson wrote, offering the secretaryship to Hugh Lawson White (*Correspondence of Andrew Jackson*, John Spencer Bassett, ed., 6 vols. [Washington, D.C., 1926–33], 4:271; hereafter cited as *JC*).

21. *American State Papers, Military Affairs* 4:714. Hereafter cited as *MA*.

22. Van Buren, *Autobiography*, 295.

23. Martin Van Buren, "Second Annual Message," 3 December 1838, in James D. Richardson, ed., *Messages and Papers of the Presidents*, 10 vols. (New York, 1917), 3:500.

24. Secretary of War James C. Calhoun, in *American State Papers, Indian Affairs* 2:190. Hereafter cited as *IA*.

25. Here and throughout I have relied heavily on Roy Harvey Pearce's seminal *The Savages of America* (Baltimore, 1965). See also Winthrop D. Jordan, *White over Black* (Baltimore, 1969), 89–91, 247–48, 477–81; George W. Stocking, Jr., *Race, Culture, and Evolution* (New York, 1968), 26–27, 75–100; Arthur A. Ekirch, *The Idea of Progress in America, 1815–1860* (New York, 1944), 15–46.

26. Francis Parkman, *The Conspiracy of Pontiac*, 10th ed. (New York, 1962), 182–83.

27. General Edmund P. Gaines, in *MA*, 1:684.

28. Jordan, *White over Black*, 90–91.

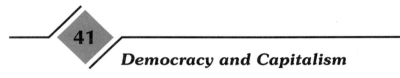

Democracy and Capitalism

Samuel Bowles and Herbert Gintis

This work is animated by a commitment to the progressive extension of people's capacity to govern their personal lives and social histories. Making good this commitment, we will argue, requires establishing a democratic social order and eliminating the central institutions of the capitalist economy. So stark an opposition between "capitalism" and "democracy," terms widely held jointly to characterize our society, may appear unwarranted. But we will maintain that no capitalist society today may reasonably be called democratic in the straightforward sense of securing personal liberty and rendering the exercise of power socially accountable.

"Democratic capitalism" suggests a set of harmonious and mutually supportive institutions, each promoting a kind of freedom in distinct realms of social life. Yet we will show that capitalism and democracy are not complementary systems. Rather they are sharply contrasting rules regulating both the process of human development and the historical evolution of whole societies: the one is characterized by the preeminence of economic privilege based on property rights, the other insists on the priority of liberty and democratic accountability based on the exercise of personal rights.

Our commitment to democracy is thus an affirmation of a vision of a society in which liberty and popular sovereignty govern both learning and history. Democracy, not the interplay of property rights, should provide the fundamental principle ordering the processes by which we become who we are and by which the rules regulating our lives are continually renewed and transformed.

Except to argue that they are feasible and attainable, we will not seek to justify these commitments. Instead we will explore their implications for the way we think about the individual, about society, and about history. Although justification may be unnecessary, clarification of terms is surely in order. In practice we identify democracy with liberty and popular sovereignty. Liberty involves an extensive range of social life over which individuals have the freedom, and where appropriate the resources, to act, and to seek to persuade others to act, as they see fit, without social impediment. Ronald Dworkin has expressed this well:

> Individual rights are political trumps held by individuals. Individuals have rights when, for some reason, a collective goal is not a sufficient justification for denying them what they wish, as individuals, to have or to do, or not a sufficient justification for imposing some loss or injury upon them.[1]

Liberty thus entails freedom of thought and association, freedom of political, cultural, and religious expression, and the right to control one's body and express one's preferred spiritual, aesthetic, and sexual style of life.

By popular sovereignty we mean that power is accountable, and in some sense equally accountable, to those affected by its exercise. But popular sovereignty cannot be unitary. We shall argue that there are multiple centers of power in liberal democratic capitalism and indeed in most social orders, and that this pluralism of powers captures an essential aspect of the conception of a democratic society. We thus reject the concept of a unifying "popular will," and we take sovereignty as ultimately and irreducibly heterogeneous. In effect, democracy requires that both individuals and groups have trumps to play.

We will identify several modifications of social theory implied by a commitment to a democratic society. Our interests, however, are not exclusively contemplative. Our recasting of democratic theory as well as our reading of the tumultuous trajectories of democracy and capitalism over the past two centuries will commit us not to a democratic utopia, but to a broad historical project of making good the long-standing radical but thwarted promise of democracy.

Democratic institutions have often been mere ornaments in the social life of the advanced capitalist nations: proudly displayed to visitors, and admired by all, but used sparingly. The places where things really get done—in such core institutions as families, armies, factories, and offices—have been anything but democratic. Representative government, civil liberties, and due process have, at best, curbed the more glaring excesses of these realms of unaccountable power while often obscuring and strengthening underlying forms of privilege and domination.

But democracy does not stand still. Where democratic institutions have taken root, they have often expanded and deepened. Where a democratic idiom has become the lingua franca of politics, it has often come to encompass unwonted meanings. In the course of its development, democracy thus may challenge, indiscriminately and irreverently, all forms of privilege. The road from the eighteenth-century Rights of Man, which excluded not only women but most people of color as well, to the late twentieth-century civil rights movements, feminism, and the right to a job has been a tortuous one, but the route was amply prefigured even in the discourse of eighteenth-century liberalism.

When democratic sentiments begin to so encroach upon a fundamental social institution as to threaten its ability to function, democratic institutions will find themselves obliged to supplant it or to retreat. This situation precisely captures the present predicament of the liberal democratic capitalist societies of Europe and North America. The beleaguered realm is the capitalist economy itself.*

The post–World War II development of the welfare state and Keynesian economic policy gave notice that profit-making business activities would be monitored and that the capitalist corporation, while permitted a considerable expansion, would be subject to social scrutiny. The striking economic success of the liberal democratic capitalist societies in the postwar era attests to the advantages of this mutual accord of economic elites and citizenry. But the expanding claims of democracy proved to be the accord's undoing. By giving citizens the power to encroach upon the capacity of capital to invest profitably and to discipline its labor force, democratic institutions challenged the basic operations of the capitalist economy and sapped its dynamism.

Yet the welfare state and Keynesian economic policies had been carefully circumscribed; they did not give citizens the power to assume these critical economic functions, nor did they provide the public arena within which citizens could develop their capacities to render economic decision making democratically accountable. Equally important, the postwar system in most liberal democratic capitalist countries gave capital a decisive upper hand in dictating the pattern of organizational innovation and structural change. The result has been an economic and political standoff in which business elites and the citizenry alike have veto power over economic change but share no viable common vision of an economic future.

The political and ideological consequences of this stalemate radically altered political discourse during the 1970s. The Keynesian focus on the state management of total demand for goods and services in the interest of full employment

---

*By liberal democratic capitalist societies we mean those two dozen or so nations whose social life is structured by a limited state that extends civil liberties and suffrage to most adults and an economy characterized by production for the market using wage labor and privately owned means of production. We will return to this characterization in later chapters.

as the key to capitalist prosperity was increasingly seen to be contradictory. The attenuation of economic insecurity brought about by Keynesian policies and the welfare state, it became clear, had compromised an essential basis of capital's power over labor: the threat of unemployment.

Though the architects of the welfare state had not stressed the point, economic stagnation and instability may occur not only because the capitalist class is "too strong" but also because it is "too weak." When the capitalist class is "too strong" it shifts the income distribution in its favor, reducing the ratio of working-class consumption to national income and rendering the economy prone to a failure of total demand. By contrast, when the capitalist class is "too weak" the working class or other claimants on income squeeze the rate of profit and reduce the level of investment (perhaps by inducing investors to seek greener pastures elsewhere).

Capitalist economies regularly experience difficulties of both types. There is much evidence that the Great Depression of the 1930s was a crisis of total demand, brought about in part by the political and economic defeats of the European and North American working classes in the post–World War I era. But the faltering profits in the advanced capitalist economies of the late 1960s and 1970s could hardly be attributed to inadequate demand: the decline in profits coincided with exceptionally high levels of capacity utilization and demand expansion in most countries.[2]

The nature of the crisis of the Great Depression—the deficiency of working-class buying power based on capital's overarching economic power—offered a ready program for labor, social democracy, and progressive groups: the egalitarian redistribution of income would both ameliorate the material situation of labor and end the economic crisis. No such happy coincidence of particular and universal interests is obtained when the crisis has resulted from the capitalist class being "too weak." The economic difficulties experienced by the advanced capitalist liberal democracies in the 1970s and 1980s are not the symptom of inadequate consumption demand; they may be traced more accurately to a collision of capitalist and democratic social relationships. Thus if the immediate economic project of labor and the Left during the last great crisis was first and foremost to redistribute purchasing power so as to alleviate material distress and support a higher level of demand, the task today must be to redistribute power itself in order to provide a new democratic model of production and distribution.

The project of the Right, correspondingly, is to reassert its hegemony in the economy, either through the time-honored methods of using the market to discipline labor and other claimants on income, or through the development of more effective institutions of control.

In this situation, democratic initiatives may either move forward toward rendering investment and production decisions democratically accountable, or they may recede. Should they recede, a strategic withdrawal could easily turn into a massive rout of liberal democratic institutions and a renaissance of authoritarianism. . . .

NOTES

1. Ronald Dworkin, *Taking Rights Seriously* (Cambridge, Mass.: Harvard University Press, 1978), xi.

2. This argument is made more fully in Samuel Bowles, "The Post-Keynesian Capital Labor Stalemate," *Socialist Review* 65 (1982): 45–74; and Thomas E. Weisskopf, Samuel Bowles, and David M. Gordon, "Two Views of Capitalist Stagnation: Underconsumption and Challenges to Capitalist Control," *Science and Society* 49 (Nov. 1985).

Capitalism and Freedom

Milton Friedman

In a much quoted passage in his inaugural address, President Kennedy said, "Ask not what your country can do for you—ask what you can do for your country." It is a striking sign of the temper of our times that the controversy about this passage centered on its origin and not on its content. Neither half of the statement expresses a relation between the citizen and his government that is worthy of the ideals of free men in a free society. The paternalistic "what your country can do for you" implies that government is the patron, the citizen the ward, a view that is at odds with the free man's belief in his own responsibility for his own destiny. The organismic, "what you can do for your country" implies that government is the master or the deity, the citizen, the servant or the votary. To the free man, the country is the collection of individuals who compose it, not something over and above them. He is proud of a common heritage and loyal to common traditions. But he regards government as a means, an instrumentality, neither a grantor of favors and gifts, nor a master or god to be blindly worshipped and served. He recognizes no national goal except as it is the consensus of the goals that the citizens severally serve. He recognizes no national purpose except as it is the consensus of the purposes for which the citizens severally strive.

The free man will ask neither what his country can do for him nor what he can do for his country. He will ask rather "What can I and my compatriots do through government" to help us discharge our individual responsibilities, to achieve our several goals and purposes, and above all, to protect our freedom? And he will accompany this question with another: How can we keep the government we create from becoming a Frankenstein that will destroy the very freedom we establish it to protect? Freedom is a rare and delicate plant. Our minds tell us,

From Milton Friedman, *Capitalism and Freedom.* © 1962, 1982 by the University of Chicago (Chicago and London: University of Chicago Press, 1982), pp. 1–6. Reprinted by permission.

and history confirms, that the great threat to freedom is the concentration of power. Government is necessary to preserve our freedom, it is an instrument through which we can exercise our freedom; yet by concentrating power in political hands, it is also a threat to freedom. Even though the men who wield this power initially be of good will and even though they be not corrupted by the power they exercise, the power will both attract and form men of a different stamp.

How can we benefit from the promise of government while avoiding the threat to freedom? Two broad principles embodied in our Constitution give an answer that has preserved our freedom so far, though they have been violated repeatedly in practice while proclaimed as precept.

First, the scope of government must be limited. Its major function must be to protect our freedom both from the enemies outside our gates and from our fellow-citizens: to preserve law and order, to enforce private contracts, to foster competitive markets. Beyond this major function, government may enable us at times to accomplish jointly what we would find it more difficult or expensive to accomplish severally. However, any such use of government is fraught with danger. We should not and cannot avoid using government in this way. But there should be a clear and large balance of advantages before we do. By relying primarily on voluntary co-operation and private enterprise, in both economic and other activities, we can insure that the private sector is a check on the powers of the governmental sector and an effective protection of freedom of speech, of religion, and of thought.

The second broad principle is that government power must be dispersed. If government is to exercise power, better in the county than in the state, better in the state than in Washington. If I do not like what my local community does, be it in sewage disposal, or zoning, or schools, I can move to another local community, and though few may take this step, the mere possibility acts as a check. If I do not like what my state does, I can move to another. If I do not like what Washington imposes, I have few alternatives in this world of jealous nations.

The very difficulty of avoiding the enactments of the federal government is of course the great attraction of centralization to many of its proponents. It will enable them more effectively, they believe, to legislate programs that—as they see it—are in the interest of the public, whether it be the transfer of income from the rich to the poor or from private to governmental purposes. They are in a sense right. But this coin has two sides. The power to do good is also the power to do harm; those who control the power today may not tomorrow; and, more important, what one man regards as good, another may regard as harm. The great tragedy of the drive to centralization, as of the drive to extend the scope of government in general, is that it is mostly led by men of good will who will be the first to rue its consequences.

The preservation of freedom is the protective reason for limiting and decentralizing governmental power. But there is also a constructive reason. The great advances of civilization, whether in architecture or painting, in science or literature, in industry or agriculture, have never come from centralized government. Columbus did not set out to seek a new route to China in response to a majority directive of a parliament, though he was partly financed by an absolute monarch. Newton and Leibnitz; Einstein and Bohr; Shakespeare, Milton, and Pasternak; Whitney, McCormick, Edison, and Ford; Jane Addams, Florence Nightingale, and Albert Schweitzer; no one of these opened new frontiers in human knowledge and understanding, in literature, in technical possibilities, or in the relief of human misery in response to governmental directives. Their achievements were the product of individual genius, of strongly held minority views, of a social climate permitting variety and diversity.

Government can never duplicate the variety and diversity of individual action. At any moment in time, by imposing uniform standards in housing, or nutrition, or clothing, government could undoubtedly improve the level of living of many individuals; by imposing uniform standards in schooling, road construction, or sanitation, central government could undoubtedly improve the level of performance in many local areas and perhaps even on the average of all communities. But in the process, government would replace progress by stagnation, it would substitute uniform mediocrity for the variety essential for that experimentation which can bring tomorrow's laggards above today's mean.

This book discusses some of these great issues. Its major theme is the role of competitive capitalism—the organization of the bulk of economic activity through private enterprise operating in a free market—as a system of economic freedom and a necessary condition for political freedom. Its minor theme is the role that government should play in a society dedicated to freedom and relying primarily on the market to organize economic activity.

The first two chapters deal with these issues on an abstract level, in terms of principles rather than concrete application. The later chapters apply these principles to a variety of particular problems.

An abstract statement can conceivably be complete and exhaustive, though this ideal is certainly far from realized in the two chapters that follow. The application of the principles cannot even conceivably be exhaustive. Each day brings new problems and new circumstances. That is why the role of the state can never be spelled out once and for all in terms of specific functions. It is also why we need from time to time to re-examine the bearing of what we hope are unchanged principles on the problems of the day. A by-product is inevitably a retesting of the principles and a sharpening of our understanding of them.

It is extremely convenient to have a label for the political and economic viewpoint elaborated in this book. The rightful and proper label is liberalism. Unfortunately, "As a supreme, if unintended compliment, the enemies of the system of private enterprise have thought it wise to appropriate its labe,l"[1] so that liberalism has, in the United States, come to have a very different meaning than it did in the nineteenth century or does today over much of the Continent of Europe.

As it developed in the late eighteenth and early nineteenth centuries, the intellectual movement that went under the name of liberalism emphasized freedom as the ultimate goal and the individual as the ultimate entity in the society. It supported laissez faire at home as a means of reducing the role of the state in economic affairs and thereby enlarging the role of the individual; it supported free trade abroad as a means of linking the nations of the world together peacefully and democratically. In political matters, it supported the development of representative government and of parliamentary institutions, reduction in the arbitrary power of the state, and protection of the civil freedoms of individuals.

Beginning in the late nineteenth century, and especially after 1930 in the United States, the term liberalism came to be associated with a very different emphasis, particularly in economic policy. It came to be associated with a readiness to rely primarily on the state rather than on private voluntary arrangements to achieve objectives regarded as desirable. The catchwords became welfare and equality rather than freedom. The nineteenth-century liberal regarded an extension of freedom as the most effective way to promote welfare and equality; the twentieth-century liberal regards welfare and equality as either prerequisites of or alternatives to freedom. In the name of welfare and equality, the twentieth-century liberal has come to favor a revival of the very policies of state intervention and paternalism against which classical liberalism fought. In the very act of turning the clock back to seventeenth-century mercantilism, he is fond of castigating true liberals as reactionary!

The change in the meaning attached to the term liberalism is more striking in economic matters than in political. The twentieth-century liberal, like the nineteenth-century liberal, favors parliamentary institutions, representative government, civil rights, and so on. Yet even in political matters, there is a notable difference. Jealous of liberty, and hence fearful of centralized power, whether in governmental or private hands, the nineteenth-century liberal favored political decentralization. Committed to action and confident of the beneficence of power so long as it is in the hands of a government ostensibly controlled by the electorate, the twentieth-century liberal favors centralized government. He will resolve any doubt about where power should be located in favor of the state instead of the city, of the federal government instead of the state, and of a world organization instead of a national government.

Because of the corruption of the term liberalism, the views that formerly went under that name are now often labeled conservatism. But this is not a satisfactory alternative. The nineteenth-century liberal was a radical, both in the etymological sense of going to the root of the matter, and in the political sense of favoring major changes in social institutions. So too must be his modern heir. We do not wish to conserve the state interventions that have interfered so greatly with our freedom, though, of course, we do wish to conserve those that have promoted it Moreover, in practice, the term conservatism has come to cover so wide a range of views, and views so incompatible with one another, that we shall no doubt see the growth of hyphenated designations, such as libertarian-conservative and aristocratic-conservative.

Partly because of my reluctance to surrender the term to proponents of measures that would destroy liberty, partly because I cannot find a better alternative, I shall resolve these difficulties by using the word liberalism in its original sense—as the doctrines pertaining to a free man.

NOTE

1. Joseph Schumpeter, *History of Economic Analysis* (New York: Oxford University Press, 1954) p. 394.

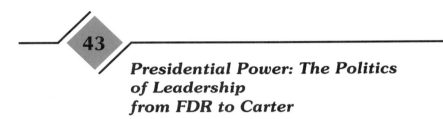

Presidential Power: The Politics of Leadership from FDR to Carter

Richard Neustadt

I

In the United States we like to "rate" a President. We measure him as "weak" or "strong" and call what we are measuring his "leadership." We do not wait until a man is dead; we rate him from the moment he takes office. We are quite right to do so. His office has become the focal point of politics and policy in our political system. Our commentators and our politicians make a specialty of taking the man's measurements. The rest of us join in when we feel "government" impinging on our private lives. In the third quarter of the twentieth century millions of us have that feeling often.

This book is an endeavor to illuminate what we are measuring. Although we all make judgments about presidential leadership, we often base our judgments upon images of office that are far removed from the reality. We also use those images when we tell one another whom to choose as President. But it is risky to appraise a man in office or to choose a man for office on false premises about the nature of his job. When the job is the Presidency of the United States the risk becomes excessive. I hope this book can help reduce the risk.

We deal here with the President himself and with his influence on governmental action. In institutional terms the Presidency now includes 2000 men and women. The President is only one of them. But *his* performance scarcely can be measured without focusing on *him*. In terms of party, or of country, or the West, so-called, his leadership involves far more than governmental action. But the sharpening of spirit and of values and of purposes is not done in a vacuum. Although governmental action may not be the whole of leadership, all else is nurtured by it and gains meaning from it. Yet if we treat the Presidency as the President, we cannot measure him as though he were the government. Not action as an outcome but his impact on the outcome is the measure of the man. His strength or weakness, then, turns on his personal capacity to influence the conduct of the men who make up government. His influence becomes the mark of leadership. To rate a President according to these rules, one looks into the man's own capabilities as seeker and as wielder of effective influence upon the other men involved in governing the country. That is what this book will do.

"Presidential" on the title page means nothing but the President. "Power" means *his* influence. It helps to have these meanings settled at the start.

There are two ways to study "presidential power." One way is to focus on the tactics, so to speak, of influencing certain men in given situations: how to get a bill through Congress, how to settle strikes, how to quiet Cabinet feuds, or how to stop a Suez. The other way is to step back from tactics on those "givens" and to deal with influence in more strategic terms: what is its nature and what are its sources? What can *this* man accomplish to improve the prospect that he will have influence when he wants it? Strategically, the question is not how he masters Congress in a peculiar instance, but what he does to boost his chance for mastery in any instance, looking toward tomorrow from today. The second of these two ways has been chosen for this book.

II

To look into the strategy of presidential influence one must decide at whom to look. Power problems vary with the scope and scale of government, the state of politics, the progress of technology, the pace of world relationships. Power in the Nineteen-sixties cannot be acquired or employed on the same terms as those befitting Calvin Coolidge, or Theodore Roosevelt, or Grover Cleveland, or James K. Polk. But there is a real likelihood that in the next decade a President will have to reach for influence and use it under much the same conditions we have known since the Second World War. If so, the men whose problems shed most light on the White House prospects are Dwight David Eisenhower and Harry S. Truman. It is at them, primarily, that we shall look. To do so is to see the shadow of another, Franklin D. Roosevelt. They worked amidst the remnants of his voter coalition, and they filled an office that his practice had enlarged.

Our two most recent Presidents have had in common something that is likely to endure into our future: the setting for a great deal of their work. They worked in an environment of policy and politics marked by a high degree of continuity. To sense the continuity from Truman's time through Eisenhower's one need only place the newspapers of 1959 alongside those of 1949. Save for the issue of domestic communists, the subject matter of our policy and politics remains almost unchanged. We deal as we have done in terms of cold war, of an arms race, of a competition overseas, of danger from inflation, and of damage from recession. We skirmish on the frontiers of the Welfare State and in the borderlands of race relations. Aspects change, but labels stay the same. So do dilemmas. Everything remains unfinished business. Not in this century has there been comparable continuity from a decade's beginning to its end; count back from 1949 and this grows plain. There even has been continuity in the behavior of our national electorate; what Samuel Lubell nine years ago called "stalemate" in our partisan alignments has not broken yet.

The similarities in Truman's setting and in Eisenhower's give their years a unity distinct from the War Years, or the Depression Era, or the Twenties, or before. In governmental terms, at least, the fifteen years since V-J Day deserve a designation all their own. "Mid-century" will serve for present purposes. And what distinguishes mid-century can be put very briefly: emergencies in policy with politics as usual.

"Emergency" describes mid-century conditions only by the standards of the past. By present standards what would once have been emergency is commonplace. Policy dilemmas through the postwar period resemble past emergencies in one respect, their difficulty and complexity for government. Technological innovation, social and political change abroad, population growth at home impose enormous strains not only on the managerial equipment of our policy-makers but also on their intellectual resources. The gropings of mature men at mid-century remind one of the intellectual confusions stemming from depression, thirty years ago, when men were also pushed past comprehension by the novelty of their condition. In our time innovation keeps us *constantly* confused; no sooner do we start to comprehend than something new is added, and we grope again. But unlike the Great Difficulties of the past, our policy dilemmas rarely produce what the country feels as "crisis." Not even the Korean War brought anything approaching sustained national "consensus." Since 1945 innumerable situations have been felt as crises inside government; there rarely has been comparable feeling outside government. In the era of the Cold War we have practiced "peacetime" politics. What else could we have done? Cold War is not a "crisis"; it becomes a way of life.

Our politics has been "as usual," but only by the standard of past *crises*. In comparison with what was once normality, our politics has been *un*usual. The weakening of party ties, the emphasis on personality, the close approach of world events, the changeability of public moods, and above all the ticket-splitting, none of this was "usual" before the Second World War. The symbol of mid-century political conditions is the White House in one party's hands with Congress in the other's—a symbol plainly visible in eight of the past fifteen years and all but visible in four of the remaining seven. Nothing really comparable has been seen in this country since the Eighteen-eighties. And the Eighties were not troubled by emergencies in policy.

As for politics and policy combined, we have seen some precursors of our setting at mid-century. Franklin Roosevelt had a reasonably comparable setting in his middle years as President, though not in his first years and not after Pearl Harbor. Indeed, if one excepts the war, mid-century could properly be said to start with Roosevelt's second term. Our recent situation is to be compared, as well, with aspects of the Civil War. Abraham Lincoln is much closer to us in condition than in time, the Lincoln plagued by Radicals and shunned by Democrats amidst the managerial and intellectual confusions of twentieth-century warfare in the nineteenth century. And in 1919 Woodrow Wilson faced and was defeated by conditions something like our own. But save for these men one can say of Truman and of Eisenhower that they were the first who had to fashion presidential influence out of mid-century materials. Presumably they will not be the last.

III

We tend to measure Truman's predecessors as though "leadership" consisted of initiatives in economics, or diplomacy, or legislation, or in mass communication. If we measured him and his successors so, they would be leaders automatically. A striking feature of our recent past has been the transformation into routine practice of the actions we once treated as exceptional. A President may retain liberty, in Woodrow Wilson's phrase, "to be as big a man as he can." But nowadays he cannot be as small as he might like.

Our two most recent Presidents have gone through all the motions we traditionally associate with strength in office. So will the man who takes the oath on January 20, 1961. In instance after instance the exceptional behavior of our earlier "strong" Presidents has now been set by statute as a regular requirement. Theodore Roosevelt once assumed the "steward's" role in the emergency created by the great coal strike of 1902; the Railway Labor Act and the Taft-Hartley Act now make such interventions mandatory upon Presidents. The other Roosevelt once asserted personal responsibility for gauging and for guiding the American economy; the Employment Act binds his successors to that task. Wilson and F.D.R. became chief spokesmen, leading actors, on a world stage at the height of war; now UN membership, far-flung alliances, prescribe that role continuously in times termed "peace." Through both world wars our Presidents grappled experimentally with an emergency-created need to "integrate" foreign and military policies; the National Security Act now takes that need for granted as a constant of our times. F.D.R. and Truman made themselves responsible for the development and first use of atomic weapons; the Atomic Energy Act now puts a comparable burden on the back of every President. And what has escaped statutory recognition has mostly been accreted into presidential common law, confirmed by custom, no less binding: the "fireside chat" and the press conference, for example, or the personally presented legislative program, or personal campaigning in congressional elections.

In form all Presidents are leaders, nowadays. In fact this guarantees no more than that they will be clerks. Everybody now expects the man inside the White House to do something about everything. Laws and customs now reflect acceptance of him as the Great Initiator, an acceptance quite as widespread at the Capitol as at his end of Pennsylvania Avenue. But such acceptance does not signify that all the rest of government is at his feet. It merely signifies that other men have found it practically impossible to do *their* jobs without assurance of initiatives from him. Service for themselves, not power for the President, has brought them to accept his leadership in form. They find his actions useful in their business. The transformation of his routine obligations testifies to their dependence on an active White House. A President, these days, is an invaluable clerk. His services are in demand all over Washington. His influence, however, is a very different matter. Laws and customs tell us little about leadership in fact.

IV

Why have our Presidents been honored with this clerkship? The answer is that no one else's services suffice. Our Constitution, our traditions, and our politics provide no better source for the initiatives a President can take. Executive officials need decisions, and political protection, and a referee for fights. Where are these to come from but the White House? Congressmen need an agenda from outside, something with high status to respond to or react against. What provides it better than the program of the President? Party politicians need a record to defend in the next national campaign. How can it be made except by "their" Administration? Private persons with a public axe to grind may need a helping hand or they may need a grinding stone. In either case who gives more satisfaction than a President? And outside the United States, in every country where our policies and postures influence home politics, there will be people needing just the "right" thing said and done or just the "wrong" thing stopped *in Washington*. What symbolizes Washington more nearly than the White House?

A modern President is bound to face demands for aid and service from five more or less distinguishable sources: from Executive officialdom, from Congress, from his partisans, from citizens at large, and from abroad. The Presidency's clerkship is expressive of these pressures. In effect they are constituency pressures and each President has five sets of constituents. The five are not distinguished by their membership; membership is obviously an overlapping matter. And taken one by one they do not match the man's electorate; one of them, indeed, is outside his electorate. They are distinguished, rather, by their different claims upon him. Initiatives are what they want, for five distinctive reasons. Since government and politics have offered no alternative, our laws and customs turn those wants into his obligations.

Why, then, is the President not guaranteed an influence commensurate with services performed? Constituent relations are relations of dependence. Everyone with any share in governing this country will belong to one (or two, or three) of his "constituencies." Since everyone depends on him why is he not assured of everyone's support? The answer is that no one else sits where he sits, or sees quite as he sees; no one else feels the full weight of his obligations. Those obligations are a tribute to his unique place in our political system. But just because it is unique they fall on him alone. *The same conditions that promote his leadership in form preclude a guarantee of leadership in fact.* No man or group at either end of Pennsylvania Avenue shares his peculiar status in our government and politics. That is why his services are in demand. By the same token, though, the obligations of all other men are different from his own. His Cabinet officers have departmental duties and constituents. His legislative leaders head *congressional* parties, one in either House. His national party organization stands apart from his official family. His political allies in the States need not face Washington, or one another. The private groups that seek him out are not compelled to govern. And friends abroad are not compelled to run in our elections. Lacking his position and prerogatives, these men cannot regard his obligations as their own. They have their jobs to do; none is the same as his. As they perceive their duty they may find it right to follow him, in fact, or they may not. Whether they will feel obliged *on their responsibility* to do what he wants done remains an open question. . . .

Constructing the Political Spectacle

Murray Edelman

SOME PREMISES ABOUT POLITICS

The pervasiveness of literacy, television, and radio in the industrialized world makes frequent reports of political news available to most of the population, a marked change from the situation that prevailed until approximately the Second World War. What consequences for ideology, action, and quiescence flow from preoccupation with political news as spectacle? How does the spectacle generate interpretations? What are its implications for democratic theory? Those are the questions addressed in this book.

From Murray Edelman, *Constructing the Political Spectacle*. © 1988 by The University of Chicago and London (Chicago: University of Chicago Press, 1988), chapter 1. Reprinted by permission.

There is a conventional answer that can be captured in a sentence rather than a volume: citizens who are informed about political developments can more effectively protect and promote their own interests and the public interest. That response takes for granted a world of facts that have a determinable meaning and a world of people who react rationally to the facts they know. In politics neither premise is tenable, a conclusion that history continually reaffirms and that observers of the political scene are tempted to ignore. To explore that conclusion is not likely to generate an optimistic book or a reassuring view of the human condition; but I hope this book will provide a realistic appreciation of the link between politics and well-being and a greater chance that political action can be effective.

The spectacle constituted by news reporting continuously constructs and reconstructs social problems, crises, enemies, and leaders and so creates a succession of threats and reassurances. These constructed problems and personalities furnish the content of political journalism and the data for historical and analytic political studies. They also play a central role in winning support and opposition for political causes and policies.

The latter role is usually masked by the assumption that citizens, journalists, and scholars are observers of "facts" whose meanings can be accurately ascertained by those who are properly trained and motivated. That positivist view is accepted rather than defended today. We are acutely aware that observers and what they observe construct one another; that political developments are ambiguous entities that mean what concerned observers construe them to mean; and that the roles and self-concepts of the observers themselves are also constructions, created at least in part by their interpreted observations.[1]

This study is an essay in applying that epistemological principle to politics. Rather than seeing political news as an account of events to which people react, I treat political developments as creations of the publics concerned with them. Whether events are noticed and what they mean depend upon observers' situations and the language that reflects and interprets those situations. A social problem, a political enemy, or a leader is both an entity and a signifier with a range of meanings that vary in ways we can at least partly understand. Similarly, I treat people who engage in political actions as constructions in two senses. First, their actions and their language create their subjectivity, their sense of who they are. Second, people involved in politics are symbols to other observers: they stand for ideologies, values, or moral stances and they become role models, benchmarks, or symbols of threat and evil.

My focus, in short, is upon people and developments with multiple and changing meanings to one another. That perspective offers a difficult analytic challenge because entities do not remain stable while you study them and subjects and objects are continuously evolving constructions of each other. Historical evidence and psychological theory nonetheless support these assumptions. In every era and every national culture, political controversy and maneuver have hinged upon conflicting interpretations of current actions and developments: leaders are perceived as tyrannical or benevolent, wars as just or aggressive, economic policies as supports of a class or the public interest, minorities as pathological or help-ful. It is precisely such differences about the referents of politically significant signs that constitute political and social history.

If political developments depended upon factual observations, false mean-ings would be discredited in time and a consensus upon valid ones would emerge, at least among informed and educated observers. That does not happen, even over long time periods. The characteristic of problems, leaders, and enemies that makes them political is precisely that controversy over their meanings is not re-solved. Whether poverty originates in the inadequacies of its victims or in the pathologies of social institutions, whether a leader's actions are beneficial or dam-aging to the polity, whether a foreign, racial, religious, or ethnic group is an enemy or a desirable ally, typify the questions that persist indefinitely and remain contro-versial as historical issues just as they were controversial in their time. The de-bates over such questions constitute politics and catalyze political action. There is no politics respecting matters that evoke a consensus about the pertinent facts, their meanings, and the rational course of action.

It is just as evident that individuals' opinions on political issues change with transformations in their social situations, with cues about the probable future con-sequences of political actions, with information about the sources and authorita-tive support for policies, and with the groups with whom they identify. The meanings of the self, the other, and the social object are facets of the same trans-action, changing and remaining stable as those others do. Psychological theorists as diverse as Mead, Vygotsky, Marcuse, and Festinger concur on this point with the lesson of historical observation. The radical student who becomes a conven-tional liberal or conservative with graduation to new jobs and new ambition, the dedicated communist who becomes a fervent anticommunist, the liberal who be-comes a neoconservative, the pacifists who support war when their country is about to embark on one, are recurring examples of the principle that political self-definitions and roles reflect the conditions, constraints, and opportunities in which people find themselves: that ideology and material conditions are part of the same transaction. To understand either stability or change, it is necessary to look to the social situations people experience, anticipate, or fantasize.

The incentive to reduce ambiguity to certainty, multivalent people to egos with fixed ideologies, and the observer's predilections to the essence of rationality pervades everyday discourse and social science practice. These premises reassure observers that their own interpretations are defensible. And there is a related rea-son that the conventional view is appealing: its implicit promise that rationality and information will end the uninterrupted record of war, poverty, cruelty and other evils that have marked human history; that rational choice may never be op-timal, but is a central influence in decision making, policy formation, and voting, and is likely to become a stronger one.

The alternative assumption denies a sharp break between the past and the future; the political language that has rationalized privileges, disadvantages, ag-gressions, and violence in the past is likely to continue to do so; the phrase "rational choice" is one more symbol in the process of rationalization rather than the path to enlightenment. Pessimistic conclusions are disturbing but are not reasons for rejecting the premises from which they flow. On the contrary, any political analysis that encourages belief in a secure, rational, and cooperative world fails the test of conformity to experience and to the record of history.

The kinds of empirical observations already mentioned and others to be noted later support the view that interpretations of political news construct diverse realities. Many influential social theories of the twentieth century point to the same conclusion. In his recent books Nelson Goodman has analyzed with impressive rigor and clarity the process of what he calls "making worlds." Goodman sees science, art, and other cultural forms as "ways of worldmaking."[2] So far as politics is concerned, news reporting is a major way as well, complementing scientific claims and works of art. The realities people experience, then, are not the same for every person or for all time, but rather are relative to social situations and to the signifiers to which observers pay some attention. The chapters that follow illustrate that premise.

But relativism is unsettling. It leaves us without a reassuring test of what is real and of who we are; and relativist propositions cannot be verified or falsified in the positivist sense because they pose the Mannheim Paradox problem: observers who postulate that the meanings of observations vary with the social situation or with something else must take the same skeptical and tentative position with respect to their own relativism.

Belief in the verifiability (or falsifiability) of observations, the separability of facts from values, and the possibility of relying upon deduction to establish valid generalizations is a formula for self-assurance, even for dogmatism, as well as for claims to power over others. But if those assumptions are invalid, if knowledge and meanings are in any sense relative to other knowledge and to the observer's social position, then neither precision in observation nor rigor in deductive reasoning will yield acceptable "covering laws" or generalizations. They offer an appearance of doing so as long as attention is diverted from the problematic premises; but reliance upon that conceptual framework for doing social science is rather like looking under the lamppost, where the light is good, for the quarter one dropped in a dark section of the street.

Critics of relativist positions charge that the latter make it impossible to test their own assumptions and conclusions because these conclusions are *also* relative to something else; but that claim should not be mistaken for an affirmation that relativist positions are false. The claim is only that they cannot be conclusively established as true. But the same must be said of the positivist position. There is reason for tentativeness about all forms of explanation. Relativist positions are not uniquely vulnerable with respect to verification or falsification. Reasons for support or for doubt are all mortals can hope for. Final conclusions, like final solutions, are for dogmatists.

There is a moral argument for rejecting relativism as well: the contention that it justifies any kind of behavior at all because it fails to provide an absolute ethical standard. Both logic and historical experience dispute that conclusion. A relativist posture in no way denies the need for a clear moral code; it recognizes, rather, that interpretations of actions do vary with social situations. Acceptance of that variation encourages careful examination of moral claims and tentativeness in applying them in ways that others might find objectionable or harmful; but it neither establishes nor undermines the moral code of an individual or a group.

It is moral certainty, not tentativeness, that historically has encouraged people to harm or kill others. Genocide, racial and religious persecution, and the rest of the long catalogue of political acts that have stained human history can only come from people who are sure that they are right. Only in bad novels and comic books do characters knowingly do evil and boast of it. In life, people rationalize their actions in moral terms, an observation that suggests that relativism is a buttress of the moral life because it encourages a critical and reflective stance toward others' actions and toward one's own.

Some critics contend that anyone who believes that realities are constructed and multiple must also believe that they are equally valid, but that conclusion does not follow. On the contrary, the notion of reality construction implies that some are valid and others not. There are multiple realities because people differ in their situations and their purposes. The reality an impressionist painter constructs respecting a maritime scene is not that of a sailor or that of an atomic physicist. The reality a destitute black person constructs respecting the nature of poverty has little validity for a conservative political candidate or a conservative political scientist or even for the same black when he is trying to achieve high grades in a business school. Every construction of a world is a demanding activity. It can be done well or badly and be right or wrong. To understand the multiple realities are prevalent is liberating, but such understanding in no way suggests that every construction is as good as every other.[3]

Social scientists who deny that there are many worlds cut themselves off from vital modes of observation and interpretation; but they reject their intellectual and moral obligations and their capabilities if they do not also recognize some realities as more valid than others for those who construct them and for social analysts.

Materialism, Idealism, and Indifference

Politicians, officials, journalists whose careers depend on news stories, advocates of causes, and a fair number of people who are continually concerned, shocked, entertained, or titillated by the news constitute an avid audience for the political spectacle. For them there are weekly, daily, sometimes hourly triumphs and defeats, grounds for hope and for fear, a potpourri of happenings that mark trends and aberrations, some of them historic. Political life is hyperreal: typically more portentous than personal affairs.

But most of the world's population, even most of the population of the "advanced countries," has no incentive to define joy, failure, or hope in terms of public affairs. Politics and political news are remote, not often interesting, and for the most part irrelevant. This indifference of "the masses" to the enthusiasms and fears of people who thrive on public attention to political matters is the despair of the latter group. Public indifference is deplored by politicians and by right-thinking citizens. It is the target of civics courses, oratory, and television news shows and the reiterated theme of polls that discover how little political information the public has and how low politics rates among public concerns.

Actions that show resistance to political involvement are even more persuasive than surveys. Nonvoters constitute a larger political grouping in America than the adherents of any political party. Only a small proportion of the population contributes money for political purposes, engages in any other kind of political activity, or pays more than passing attention to political news.[4]

That indifference, which academic political science notices but treats as an obstacle to enlightenment or democracy, is, from another perspective, a refuge against the kind of engagement that would, if it could, keep everyone's energies taken up with activism: election campaigns, lobbying, repressing some and liberating others, wars, and all other political activities that displace living, loving, and creative work. Regimes and proponents of political causes know that it takes much coercion, propaganda, and the portrayal of issues in terms that entertain, distort, and shock to extract a public response of any kind. "The public" is mainly a black hole into which the political efforts of politicians, advocates of causes, the media, and the schools disappear with hardly a trace.[5] Its apathy, indifference, quiescence, and resistance to the consciousness industry[6] is especially impressive in an age of widespread literacy and virtually universal access to the media. Indifference to the enthusiasms and alarms of political activists has very likely always been a paramount political force, though only partially effective and hard to recognize because it is a nonaction. Without it, the slaughter and repression of diverse groups in the name of nationalism, morality, or rationality would certainly be even more widespread than it has been; for the claim that a political cause serves the public interest has often distorted or destroyed concern for personal wellbeing.

Recognition of the power that springs from indifference to political appeals is a precondition for understanding the effectiveness of political symbolism. Symbols, whether language or icons, that have no relevance to everyday lives, frustrations, and successes are meaningless and impotent. They are like the reactions of spectators in a museum to the icons of a culture with which they feel no empathy. In the measure that political advocates resort to appeals that do not touch the experiences of their audience, indifference is to be expected.

Symbols become that facet of experiencing the material world that gives it a specific meaning. The language, rituals, and objects to which people respond are not abstract ideas. If they matter at all, it is because they are accepted as basic to the quality of life. The term "unemployment" may evoke a yawn from an affluent person who has never feared it. It carries a more intense connotation in a depression than at other times even for workers who are always vulnerable to layoffs. A flag may be a garish piece of cloth, a reminder of the repressions and sufferings justified by appeals to patriotism, or an evocation of nostalgia for a land in which one grew up or for the stories about its history one learned as a child. A symbol always carries a range of diverse, often conflicting, meanings that are integral aspects of specific material and social situations. The material condition as experienced and the symbol as experienced stand for each other. The psychological processes by which they come to do so are doubtless subtle and complex and are certainly not fully understood. They may involve the displacement of private affect onto public objects, as Harold Lasswell suggested,[7] or a search for self-esteem[8] or a rational calculation, or a combination of functions. In any case the material basis for the symbol is critical. My references in this book to language or actions or objects that evoke meanings always presuppose that the "evocation" takes place only as a function of a specific material and social condition. Idealism and materialism are dichotomies as abstract concepts, but in everyday life they are facets of the same transaction. Every sign exercises its effect because of the specific context of privilege, disadvantage, frustration, aspiration, hope, and fear in which it is experienced.

The Incoherence of the Subject, the Object, and the Text

These observations about my conceptual framework foreshadow a more general point of view that grows out of the work of George Herbert Mead and Lev Vygotsky and is also explicit in the writings of the French poststructuralists, especially Michel Foucault and Jacques Derrida.

The subject cannot be regarded as the origin of coherent action, writing, or other forms of expression. As just noted, actions and interpretations hinge upon the social situation in which they begin, including the language that depicts a social situation. The language that interprets objects and actions also constitutes the subject. Political leaders, like all other subjects, act and speak as reflections of the situations they serially confront; their diversities and inconsistencies are statements of those situations, not of a persistent "self," for the kind of stability in action that transcends situations with varying political inducements has never existed. Chapter 3, on "political leadership," examines the sense in which that perspective undermines the premise, itself constructed very largely by the term "leader," that identifiable officials are originators of coherent courses of action. That chapter also explores the distortions in analysis implicit in the conventional assumptions about political leaders.[9]

It is probably less jarring to recognize that political objects and events are also discontinuous, sometimes contradictory, entities constituted by the signifiers and contexts that give them meanings, a point of view considered in some detail in chapters 2 and 4. Quite apart from the examples that emerge with every careful examination of a political object, entities are necessarily incoherent because the language that constructs their meaning is inherently discontinuous and in some sense undermines itself.[10] Affirmations bring to consciousness evidence for the contrary position, which the affirmations try to blunt, a form of inversion and sometimes of self deception that is especially pervasive in political language.

When an American official claims that client states like El Salvador or Guatemala are protecting human rights, the statement also reminds those who hear it of evidence that they are not doing so. Every instance of language and action resonates with the memory, the fear, or the anticipation of other signifiers, so that there are radiating networks of meaning that vary with the situations of spectators and actors.

That framework gives political action, talk, writing, and news reporting a different import from that taken for granted in politicans' statements and in conventional social science writing. Accounts of political issues, problems, crises, threats, and leaders now become devices for creating disparate assumptions and beliefs about the social and political world rather than factual statements. The very concept of "fact" becomes irrelevant because every meaningful political object and person is an interpretation that reflects and perpetuates an ideology. Taken together, they comprise a spectacle which varies with the social situation of the spectator and serves as a meaning machine: a generator of points of view and therefore of perceptions, anxieties, aspirations, and strategies. The conventional distinction between procedures and outcomes loses its salience because both are now signifiers, generators of meanings that shape political quiescence, arousal, and support or opposition to causes. The denotations of key political terms become suspect because leaders are not originators of courses of action, problems are not necessarily undesirable conditions to be solved, and enemies need not do or threaten harm. Instead, the uses of all such terms in specific situations are strategies, deliberate or unrecognized, for strengthening or undermining support for specific courses of action and for particular ideologies.

The political entities that are most influential upon public consciousness and action, then, are fetishes: creations of observers that then dominate and mystify their creators. I try here to analyze the pervasive consequences of the fetishism at the core of politics, never a wholly successful enterprise because it is tempting to exorcise a fetish by constructing a rational theory of politics.

NOTES

1. Two recent books, one by an eminent philosopher and the other by an eminent psychologist, expound the conceptual framework I apply here in some detail: Nelson Goodman, *Of Mind and Other Matters* (Cambridge: Harvard University Press, 1983); Jerome Bruner, *Actual Minds, Possible Worlds* (Cambridge: Harvard University Press, 1985).

2. Nelson Goodman, *Ways of Worldmaking* (Indianapolis: Hackett Publishing Co., 1978), and Bruner, *Actual Minds, Possible Worlds*.

3. I discussed this position in *Political Language* (New York: Academic Press, 1978), 5–20. See also Goodman, *Ways of Worldmaking*, 17–22. For a contrary view, see William Connolly's review of *Political Language* in *American Political Science Review* 73 (September 1979): 847.

4. For survey data on the low level of political information among adults see Robert S. Erikson, Norman R. Luttbeg, and Kent L. Tedin, *American Public Opinion*, 2nd ed. (New York: Wiley, 1980), 19.

5. Jean Baudrillard, *In the Shadow of the Silent Majorities* (New York: Semiotext, 1983), 1–64.

6. The term comes from Hans Magnus Enzensberger, *The Consciousness Industry* (New York: Seabury Press, 1974).

7. Harold D. Lasswell, *Psychopathology and Politics* (Chicago: University of Chicago Press, 1930).

8. Paul M. Sniderman, *Personality and Democratic Politics* (Berkeley: University of California Press, 1975).

9. The same lesson applies, of course, to the term "author." In writing this book I also am constituted by a range of disparate sources and inducements, including such contradictory ones as the poststructuralist writers who impress me now and the conventional political scientists I read as a graduate student and whose work I may have learned too well. If the idea that language that depicts discontinuity is itself discontinuous and self-contradictory induces a sense of vertigo, that is preferable to reassuring assumptions that divert analysis from an account of the discontinuities of the social world. The vertigo may stimulate criticism and insight.

10. The point is developed in the work of Jacques Derrida, and also in Kenneth Burke's writing on political rhetoric. See Burke, *The Grammar of Motives* (New York: McGraw-Hill, 1945).

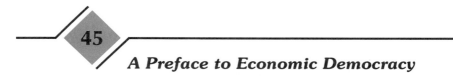

A Preface to Economic Democracy

Robert A. Dahl

Within a generation or so after the Constitutional Convention, a rough consensus appears to have been reached among Americans—among white male citizens, at any rate—that a well-ordered society would require at least three things: political equality, political liberty, and economic liberty; that circumstances in the United States made it possible for Americans to attain these ends; and that, in fact, to a reasonably satisfactory degree these three ends had already been attained in America. Such was the state of mind that Alexis de Tocqueville encountered among Americans in 1831.

At the same time, however, some eminent and philosophically minded observers of the human condition believed that the three goals might very well conflict with one another, quite possibly, indeed, *must* conflict with one another. John Adams, Thomas Jefferson, and James Madison, together with many of Madison's fellow members of the American Constitutional Convention, were deeply concerned that political equality might conflict with political liberty. This possibility forms a major theme—in my view, *the* major theme—of Tocqueville's *Democracy in America*. Echoing an already ancient idea, in the penultimate chapter of his second volume Tocqueville asserts his belief that

> it is easier to establish an absolute and despotic government amongst a people in which the conditions of society are equal, than amongst any other; and I think that if

such a government were once established amongst such a people, it would not only oppress men but would eventually strip each of them of several of the highest qualities of humanity. Despotism therefore appears to me peculiarly to be dreaded in democratic ages. I should have loved freedom, I believe, at all times, but in the time in which we live I am ready to worship it. *(Tocqueville [1835] 1961, 2:385)*[1]

While Tocqueville was mainly concerned with the threat that equality—political, social, and economic—posed for *political* liberty and personal independence, many of the Constitution's framers had been alarmed by the prospect that democracy, political equality, majority rule, and even political liberty itself would endanger the rights of property owners to preserve their property and use it as they chose. In this sense, democracy was thought to menace *economic* liberty as it was then commonly conceived—in particular, that kind of liberty represented by the right to property. Like the conflict between equality and political liberty, this potential conflict between democracy and property was also part of a much older debate. In the United States, the concern expressed at the Constitutional Convention has been frequently voiced ever since.

In considering the threat posed by equality to liberty, Tocqueville, like Jefferson and the Framers before him, observed a society in which it was by no means unreasonable to expect, and hope, that male citizens would be approximately equal in their resources—property, knowledge, social standing, and so on—and consequently in their capacities for influencing political decisions. For they saw a country that was still overwhelmingly agrarian: seven of every ten persons gainfully employed were in agriculture, and the citizen body was predominantly composed of free farmers, or farmhands who aspired to become free farmers. What no one could fully foresee, though advocates of a republic constituted by free farmers sometimes expressed worrisome anticipations, was the way in which the agrarian society would be revolutionized by the development of the modern corporation as the main employer of most Americans, as the driving force of the economy and society. The older vision of a citizen body of free farmers among whom an equality of resources seemed altogether possible, perhaps even inevitable, no longer fitted that reality of the new economic order in which economic enterprises automatically generated inequalities among citizens: in wealth, income, social standing, education, knowledge, occupational prestige and authority, and many other resources. Had Tocqueville and his predecessors fully anticipated the shape of the economic order to come, they probably would have viewed the problem of equality and liberty in a different light. For if, in the older view, an equality among citizens might endanger liberty, in the new reality the liberty of corporate enterprises helped to create a body of citizens highly unequal in the resources they could bring to political life.

The question I want to confront, therefore, is whether it would be possible for Americans to construct a society that would more nearly achieve the values of democracy and political equality and at the same time preserve as much individual liberty as we now enjoy, and perhaps even more. Or is there an inescapable trade-off between liberty and equality, so that we can only enjoy the liberties we now possess by forgoing greater equality? Would therefore the price of greater equality necessarily be less liberty?

More concretely, I propose to explore the possibility of an alternative economic structure that would, I believe, help to strengthen political equality and democracy by reducing inequalities originating in the ownership and control of firms in a system like that we now possess—a system that for want of a better term I call *corporate capitalism*. The last three chapters describe an alternative, explain its justification, and examine some of its problems.

In examining this possibility I have deliberately narrowed the scope of our inquiry into the problem of freedom and equality: first by focusing on *political* equality, then by focusing on the consequences of owning and controlling enterprises. Important as it is, political equality—equality among citizens engaged in governing themselves by means of the democratic process—is not the only relevant form of equality that might serve as a standard for a good society. And owning and controlling firms is not the only source of undesirable inequalities among human beings, or even of political inequalities.

Yet narrowing the focus is, I believe, justified on several grounds. For one, the *general* problem of equality is so complex that perhaps we can deal with it well only by examining parts of it. As Douglas Rae concludes at the end of his masterly analysis of the meaning, kinds, and values of equality:

> Equality is the simplest and most abstract of notions, yet the practises of the world are irremediably concrete and complex. How, imaginably, could the former govern the latter? It cannot. We are always confronted with more than one practical meaning for equality and equality itself cannot provide a basis for choosing among them. The question "Which equality?" will never be answered simply by insisting upon equality. *(Rae 1981, 150)*[2]

Moreover, of the various kinds of equality that might exist in a good society, political equality is surely one of the most crucial, not only as a means of self-protection but also as a necessary condition for many other important values, including one of the most fundamental of all human freedoms, the freedom to help determine, in cooperation with others, the laws and rules that one must obey. In a somewhat similar way, differences in ownership and control of enterprises, while certainly not at the origin of all forms of inequality, are deeply implicated in inequalities of many kinds: in esteem, respect, and status, in control over one's daily life, in income and wealth and all the opportunities associated with them, in life chances for adults and children alike. It seems to me scarcely open to doubt that a society with significantly greater equality in owning and controlling economic enterprises would produce profoundly greater equality than exists among Americans today.

Before considering whether an alternative to corporate capitalism might strengthen political equality without sacrificing liberty, we first need to search for a clearer understanding of the relationships between political equality, political liberty, and economic liberty. In my view these relationships have often been misconceived, or asserted in so general a fashion that we can scarcely judge the truth of statements about them. An enormously influential example of what I believe to be a mistaken view of these relationships is to be found in a very great work by a very great writer—Tocqueville himself, in *Democracy in America.* . . . Tocqueville believed that equality, desirable though it may be, poses a standing threat to liberty. But if self-government by means of the democratic process is a fundamental, even an inalienable right; if the exercise of that inalienable right necessarily requires a substantial number of more particular rights, which are therefore also fundamental and inalienable; and if a certain equality of condition is necessary to the political equality entailed in the democratic process, then the conflict, if there be one, is not simply between equality and liberty. It is, rather, a conflict between fundamental liberties of a special kind, the liberties people enjoy by virtue of governing themselves through the democratic process, and other liberties of a different kind.

Among these other liberties is economic liberty, which Americans have generally understood to include a personal and inalienable right to property. Applied to an economic enterprise, ownership carries with it a right to govern the enterprise, within broad limits, of course, set by the government of the state. Transferred from the operation of farms and small businesses to the large corporation, ownership rights have given legality and legitimacy to undemocratic governments that intrude deeply into the lives of many people, and most of all the lives of those who work under the rulership of authorities over whom they exercise scant control. Thus a system of government Americans view as intolerable in governing the state has come to be accepted as desirable in governing economic enterprises.

I have sketched here an alternative form of government for economic enterprises that holds promise of eliminating, or at least reducing, this contradiction. A system of self-governing enterprises would be one part of a system of equalities and liberties in which both would, I believe, be stronger, on balance, than they can be in a system of corporate capitalism. But whether many Americans will find this vision attractive I cannot say. For we Americans have always been torn between two conflicting visions of what American society is and ought to be. To summarize them oversimply, one is a vision of the world's first and grandest attempt to realize democracy, political equality, and political liberty on a continental scale. The other is a vision of a country where unrestricted liberty to acquire unlimited wealth would produce the world's most prosperous society. In the first, American ideals are realized by the achievement of democracy, political equality, and the fundamental political rights of all citizens in a country of vast size and diversity. In the second, American ideals are realized by the protection of property and of opportunities to prosper materially and to grow wealthy. In the first view, the right to self-government is among the most fundamental of all human rights, and, should they conflict, is superior to the right to property. In the second, property is the superior, self-government the subordinate right.

As a people we are divided among ourselves in the strength of our commitment to these conflicting ideals; and many Americans are divided within themselves. I cannot say whether a people so divided possesses the firmness of purpose and the clarity of vision to assert the priority of democracy, political equality, and the political rights necessary to self-government over established property rights, economic inequality, and undemocratic authority within corporate enterprises.

NOTES

1. Alexis de Tocqueville, *Democracy in America*, 2 vols. (New York: Schocken Books, [1835, 1840] 1961).
2. Douglas Rae, *Equalities* (Cambridge, Mass.: Harvard University Press, 1981).

Who Rules America Now?

G. William Domhoff

INTRODUCTION

Class and *power* are terms that make Americans a little uneasy, and concepts such as *ruling class* and *power elite* immediately put people on guard. The idea that a relatively fixed group of privileged people might dominate the economy and government goes against the American grain and the founding principles of the country. People may differ in their social levels, and some people may have more influence than others, but there can be no ruling class or power elite when power is constitutionally lodged in all the people, when there is democratic participation through elections and lobbying, and when the evidence of upward social mobility is everywhere apparent. If the question is asked, Who rules in the United States? the answer is likely to be in terms of interest groups, elected officials, and the people in general.

Contrary to this pluralistic view of power, it is the purpose of this book to present systematic evidence that suggests there is a social upper class in the United States that is a ruling class by virtue of its dominant role in the economy and government. It will be shown that this ruling class is socially cohesive, has its basis in the large corporations and banks, plays a major role in shaping the social and political climate, and dominates the federal government through a variety of organizations and methods.

The upper class as a whole does not do this ruling. Instead, class rule is manifested through the activities of a wide variety of organizations and institutions. These organizations and institutions are financed and directed by those members of the upper class who have the interest and ability to involve themselves in protecting and enhancing the privileged social position of their class. Leaders within the upper class join with high-level employees in the organizations they control to make up what will be called the *power elite*. This power elite is the leadership group of the upper class as a whole, but it is not the same thing as the upper class, for not all members of the upper class are members of the power elite and not all members of the power elite are part of the upper class. It is members of the power elite who take part in the processes that maintain the class structure. . . .

THE AMERICAN UPPER CLASS

If there is an American upper class, it must exist not merely as a collection of families who feel comfortable with each other and tend to exclude outsiders from their social activities. It must exist as a set of interrelated social institutions. That is, there must be patterned ways of organizing the lives of its members from infancy to old age, and there must be mechanisms for socializing both the younger generation and new adult members who have risen from lower social levels. If the class is a reality, the names and faces may change somewhat over the years, but the social institutions that underlie the upper class must persist with remarkably little change over several generations.

The main purpose of this chapter will be to show that there is an upper class in this institutional, supraindividual sense. This will be accomplished through the presentation of historical, quantitative, questionnaire, and interview data that demonstrate the interconnections among a set of schools, clubs, resorts, and social activities that are the basis of the upper class. The chapter also will attempt through more anecdotal information to describe how these various social institutions provide members of the upper class with a distinctive life-style that sharply differentiates them from the rest of society. The second task is necessary because criteria for the existence of a social class include not only in-group social interaction but a unique style of life.

In addition, marriage patterns within the upper class and the continuity of upper-class families will be discussed, and the wealth, income, and occupations of its members will be examined. The result should be a clear picture of an interacting set of families and social cliques that possesses great wealth and makes up only 0.5 percent of the population. Finally, the chapter will present a lengthy list of indicators of upper-class standing that can be used to study the involvement of upper-class members in the corporate community, the policy planning network, and the government.

The Institutional Infrastructure

Four different types of empirical studies establish the existence of an inter-related set of social institutions, organizations, and social activities that undergirds and defines the upper class. They are historical case studies, quantitative studies of biographical directories, questionnaire studies of knowledgeable observers, and interview studies with members of the upper-middle and upper classes.

The first and most detailed historical study of the upper class was completed in the 1950s by E. Digby Baltzell, a member of the upper class himself. Baltzell drew together all previous historical and anecdotal data on the subject and then turned his attention to the development of the upper class in Philadelphia. He was able to demonstrate in this way that the people of highest status and greatest wealth gradually created a set of exclusive neighborhoods, expensive private schools, restricted social clubs, and such unique social occasions as debutante balls and fox hunts that provided the basis for their day-to-day lives.[1]

Building from his Philadelphia materials, Baltzell was able to show that members of the upper class in that city began in the late nineteenth and early twentieth centuries to frequent the same resorts as the people of highest status in other eastern cities. They also began to send their children to boarding schools in New England and Virginia that catered to the wealthy from other cities across the country, and they joined the social clubs of their counterparts in other cities. Baltzell found that they were listed in great numbers in an exclusive intercity address and telephone book called the *Social Register*, symbolizing the interconnectedness of the families in many different cities.

In effect, then, Baltzell showed the relationships among these institutions and activities through demonstrating that the same few people created and belonged to all of them. To test and extend his findings, we did the same kind of study in an ahistorical and quantitative way. In this particular study we analyzed the information on school attendance and club membership that appeared in 3,000 randomly selected *Who's Who in America* biographies for the late 1960s. We also determined which of these people were listed in the *Social Register*.[2]

The pattern of memberships and affiliations generated by this search were analyzed by means of a statistical technique known as contingency analysis. It provides a means to find out whether or not there is a significant relationship between two or more affiliations by determining whether or not their appearance together is greater than would be expected by chance.[3] The findings of this study fully supported Baltzell's claim that a relationship exists between listing in the *Social Register*, attendance at one of several private high schools, and membership in one or more of several social clubs. In addition, the study added new schools and clubs to those discovered by Baltzell.

A very different method provided further support for these findings and also greatly extended the list of clubs and schools while adding a few new social directories as well. In this study a questionnaire–letter was sent to editors of women's pages and society pages of newspapers in every city in the country with a chapter of the Junior League. This exclusive women's service organization was used as a starting point because it is one of the few nationwide organizations known to have a great many upper-class members. In essence, the question-naire–letter asked if there was a set of high-status schools and clubs in the given city and if the members of those schools and clubs were listed in the *Social Register* or any other social directory. Following these open-ended questions, it asked for an estimate of how many children from that city attended each of eleven boarding schools that were listed on the page.

In all, 128 of the 317 reports were filled out and returned. Some had very little information, but most were quite informative. In twelve cases we received replies from two different newspapers in a city, and in all but one instance there was complete agreement in the reports. The replies of these well-placed ob-servers also produced strong agreement with the findings of Baltzell's historical study and the contingency analysis. For example, the *Social Register* was listed as a useful source on upper-class families by all eight reports from cities covered by it.[4]

A fourth and final method of establishing the existence of upper-class insti-tutions is based on intensive interviews with a cross-section of citizens. The most detailed study of this type was conducted in Kansas City in the 1950s and pub-lished in 1971.[5] The study was concerned with people's perceptions of the social ladder as a whole, from top to bottom, but it is the top level that is of concern here. Although most people in Kansas City could point to the existence of exclu-sive neighborhoods in suggesting that there was a class of "blue bloods" or "big rich," it was members of the upper-middle class and the upper class itself whose reports demonstrated that clubs and other social institutions as well as neighbor-hoods gave the class an institutional existence. . . .

THE CONTROL OF THE CORPORATE COMMUNITY

Most sectors of the American economy are dominated by a relative handful of large corporations. These corporations, in turn, are linked in a variety of ways to create a corporate community. At an economic level, the ties within the corporate community are manifested in ownership of common stock on the part of both families and other corporations, as well as in joint ventures among corporations and in the common sources of bank loans that most corporations share. At a more sociological level, the corporate community is joined together by the use of the same legal, accounting, and consulting firms and by the similar experiences of ex-ecutives working in the bureaucratic structure of a large organization. Then too, the large corporations come together as a business community because they share the same values and goals—in particular, the profit motive. Finally, and not least, the common goals of the corporations lead them to have common enemies in the labor movement and middle-class reformers, which gives them a further sense of a shared identity.

It will be the purpose of this chapter to demonstrate that the most important corporations, commercial banks, investment banks, and law firms at the heart of this corporate community are controlled by members of the upper class and that the corporate community is therefore the primary financial basis for the upper class. Although information presented in the previous chapter showed that upper-class people are heavily involved in financial and business pursuits, such information does not demonstrate automatically that members of the upper class are leaders in the corporate community. It may be that they are involved in smaller businesses, less important sectors of the economy, or in less important positions in large corporations.

In fact, there are a great many pluralists among American social scientists who deny that members of the upper class have control positions within the corporate community. They believe that the growth of the corporation has led to the dispersal of stock ownership on the one hand and the rise in importance of highly trained professional managers with no class allegiance on the other. There has been a "breakup of family capitalism" in the often quoted words of sociologist Daniel Bell, a "separation of ownership and control," in the even more frequently cited words of lawyer A. A. Berle, Jr., and economist Gardner Means.[6] According to this view, the upper class continues to exist as a high-status social group due to dividends from general stock ownership, but this upper class has lost its community of economic interest and its power now that its members no longer control major businesses. By way of contrast, managers of the large corporations are said to have power without property.

The idea that the upper class is cut off from a determinate role in the corporate community is one of the major objections to the claim that the upper class is a ruling class. In order to deal with this issue, this chapter will present four types of information to show that (1) members of the upper class own a majority of all privately held corporate stock in the United States; (2) many large stockholders and stockholding families continue to be involved in the direction of major corporations; (3) members of the upper class are disproportionately represented on the boards of large corporations in general; and (4) the professional managers of middle-level origins who rise to the top of the corporations are assimilated into the upper class both socially and economically and share the values of upper-class owners. . . .

The purpose of this chapter is, first, to describe the ways in which leaders within the upper class and corporate community develop general policies on economic and social issues of concern to them and, second, to show how they attempt to shape public opinion on these issues. It is possible to consider these somewhat different processes at the same time because they both have their origins in the same set of interlocking policy-discussion groups, foundations, think tanks, and university institutes.

The nonprofit organizations concerned with public policy to be discussed in this chapter are necessary features of the corporate landscape because social cohesion and common economic interests are not enough in themselves to lead to agreed-upon policies without research, consultation, and deliberation. Issues of foreign policy are too complex and volatile, and the corporate economy too big and diverse, for the new policies that are often required to be deduced from some storehouse of wisdom on the functioning of corporate capitalism or to arise implicitly from the fact of a common social environment.

The effort to influence public opinion is considered necessary because average citizens do not automatically agree with the corporate community on every policy initiative. Their life situations as wage and salary earners with little or no wealth beyond a house and life insurance often lead them to see things in a light different from the corporate rich. Thus, trade unions, minority organizations, and women's groups, among others, can find independent bases of power within the general populace, and they often suggest policy alternatives opposed to those supported by leaders within the corporate community. To the degree that these groups might be able to hinder the adoption of corporate-favored policy suggestions, to that degree is it necessary for the opinion-shaping network to counter their influence.

However, for all the hundreds of millions of dollars spent each year in the effort to mold public opinion, the importance of public opinion in the functioning of the social system should not be exaggerated. The opinions of the majority on a wide range of issues have differed from those of the corporate elite for many generations without major consequences for public policy. To assume that differences in opinion will lead to political activity does not give due consideration to the fact that people's beliefs do not lead them into opposition or disruption if they have stable roles to fulfill in the society. Routine involvement in a daily round of activities, the most important of which are a job and a family, probably is a more important factor in social stability and acquiescence in corporate-supported policies than any attempts to shape public opinion. Contrary to what many Marxian analysts have claimed, what happens in the economy and in government has more impact on how people will act than what is said in the opinion-shaping process and the mass media.[7]

Members of the upper class and corporate community involve themselves in the policy-planning and opinion-shaping processes in three basic ways. First, they finance the organizations that are at the core of these efforts. Second, they provide a variety of free services for some of the organizations in the network, such as legal and accounting help or free advertising space in newspapers and magazines. Finally, they serve as the directors and trustees of these organizations, setting their general direction and selecting the people who will manage their day-to-day operations.

The nonbusiness trustees and executives of the organizations to be discussed in this chapter, who are not infrequently members of the upper class themselves, join with members of the corporate community in forming the power elite. As stated earlier, the power elite is defined as the leadership group for the upper class as a whole, transcending to some degree the business-oriented perspective of those who are involved only in corporate activities. The core of the power elite is the inner group of the corporate community. Its members sit on the boards of foundations, universities, cultural organizations, and numerous other organizations. However, the policy specialists are an essential complement to members of the inner group in bringing long-range political considerations and issues concerning social stability to their attention.

The Policy-Planning Network

The policy-planning process begins in corporate board rooms, where problems are informally identified as "issues" to be solved by new policies. It ends in government, where policies are enacted and implemented. In between, however, there is a complex network of people and institutions that plays an important role in sharpening the issues and weighing the alternatives. This network has four main components—policy groups, foundations, think tanks, and university research institutes.

The policy-discussion organizations are nonpartisan groups, bringing together corporate executives, lawyers, academic experts, university administrators, and media specialists to discuss such general problems as foreign aid, tariffs, taxes, and welfare policies. In discussion groups of varying sizes, the policy-oriented organizations provide informal and off-the-record meeting grounds in which differences of opinion on various issues can be aired and the opinions of specialists can be heard. In addition to their numerous small-group discussions, these organizations encourage general dialogue within the power elite by means of luncheon and dinner speeches, written reports, and position statements in journals and books. Taken as a whole, the several policy-discussion groups are akin to an open forum in which there is a constant debate concerning the major problems of the day and the best solutions to those problems.

Foundations are tax-free institutions that are created to give grants to both individuals and nonprofit organizations for activities that range from education, research, and the arts to support for the poor and the upkeep of exotic gardens and old mansions. They are an upper-class adaptation to inheritance and income taxes. They provide a means by which wealthy people and corporations can in effect decide how their tax payments will be spent, for they are based on money that otherwise could go to the government in taxes. From a small beginning at the turn of the century, they have become a very important factor in shaping developments in higher education and the arts, and they play a significant role in policy formation as well. The best-known and most influential are the Ford, Rockefeller, and Carnegie foundations.

Think tanks and university research institutes are nonprofit organizations that have been developed to provide settings for experts in various academic disciplines to devote their time to the study of policy alternatives free from the teaching and departmental duties that are part of the daily routine for most members of the academic community. Supported by foundation grants and government contracts, they are a major source of the new ideas that are discussed in the policy-formation groups.

No one type of organization within the network is more important than the others. Nor is any one organization or group the "inner sanctum" where final decisions are made. It is the network as a whole that shapes policy alternatives, with different organizations playing different roles on different issues. . . .

Members of the power elite directly involve themselves in the federal government through three basic processes, each of which plays a slightly different role in ensuring access to the White House, Congress, and specific agencies, departments, and committees in the executive branch. Although some of the same people are involved in all three processes, most people specialize in one or two of the three processes. This is because each process requires slightly different knowledge, skills, and contacts. The three processes are

1. The candidate selection process, through which members of the power elite attempt to influence electoral campaigns by means of campaign finances and favors to political candidates.
2. The special-interest process, through which specific individuals, corporations, and industrial sectors realize their narrow and short-run interests on taxes, subsidies, and regulation in dealing with congressional committees, regulatory bodies, and executive departments.
3. The policy-making process, through which the general policies of the policy-planning network explained in the previous chapter are brought to the White House and Congress. . . .

Conclusion

After all these arguments and counterarguments, what are readers to think? How can they decide what to make of all this disputation? There are many ways in which they might make their own assessments. They could explore the underlying assumptions of each viewpoint further, for example, or they could examine some power question of interest to them to see how well the different perspectives assimilate their findings. In the end, however, I think it comes down to what people think about power indicators and what philosophy of science they find most reasonable.

If wealth and income statistics are accepted as valid indicators of power that reveal the outcomes of ongoing power struggles, then the case for the upper class as a ruling class will be considered a strong one, for those indicators have been very stable throughout the twentieth century in the United States even while income and related inequalities have declined in countries with strong labor unions and cohesive social democratic and socialist parties. However, if these outcomes are seen as a result of general societal structures or various irrational decisions, with only an indirect relation at best to the underlying concept of power, then readers will be less persuaded.

If overrepresentation in corporate, foundation, and government positions is seen as a useful indicator of institutional power, then the argument will be considered fairly strong. But if readers are unimpressed with this indicator because they believe that real power may lie behind the throne of the formal offices, or that government position holders are constrained to follow the will of the majority by a fear of not being reelected, then the evidence will be downgraded.

If influence on specific decisions in a wide range of issue-areas is seen as the only valid indicator of power, as pluralists have insisted, then support for the hypothesis will be viewed as less impressive. Hopefully, though, it will be seen as greatly improved since the 1960s due to the demonstration of a policy-planning network and the articulation of how the special-interest, policy-planning, and candidate-selection processes bring the power elite into direct and very often successful involvement in government.

Beyond the evidence of any one type of indicator, the strength of the argument will be determined by the philosophy of science to which the reader holds. If it is believed that concepts should be studied in terms of multiple indicators, as has been stressed in this book, the evidence for the hypothesis will be seen as very strong, for three very different types of indicators have pointed to the upper class as a ruling class. However, if an approach based upon intervening variables and social traits is rejected in favor of the single-indicator operational definitions advocated by a strict form of scientific positivism, then the case will be seen as less impressive. This is especially so if that single operation consists of adding up influence scores on a wide variety of issues that are picked by pluralists without any regard for the surveyed interests of contending power groups.

Weaknesses in the evidence remain. More work needs to be done on the relationship between the upper class and the corporate community; in particular, little is known in detail about the social and career patterns of the children of upwardly mobile corporate executives. Then, too, more studies need to be done on a wider range of issues within the framework of the policy-planning network, and further information must be developed on if and how the liberal-labor coalition gains concessions from the moderates in the struggle to enact general social legislation.

But if the question is asked once again, who rules America? then on the basis of available evidence the best answer still seems to be that dominant power in the United States is exercised by a power elite that is the leadership group of a property-based ruling class. Despite all the turmoil of the 1960s and 1970s, and the constant chatter about economic crisis that is ever with us, there continues to be a small upper class whose members own 20 to 25 percent of all privately held wealth and 45 to 50 percent of all privately held corporate stock. They sit in seats of formal power from the corporate community to the federal government, and they win much more often than they lose on issues ranging from the nature of the tax structure to the stifling of reform in such vital areas as consumer protection, environmental protection, and labor law. This conclusion is not the be-all and end-all of political sociology, as the gatekeepers of the intellectual world will quickly reassure us. But it must be the starting point for any social inquiry or political analysis that wishes to avoid hopeless irrelevance and embarrassing superficiality from its very outset.

NOTES

1. E. Digby Baltzell, *Philadelphia Gentlemen: The Making of a National Upper Class* (Glencoe, Ill.: Free Press, 1958). See also his *The Protestant Establishment* (New York: Random House, 1964).

2. G. William Domhoff, *The Higher Circles* (New York: Random House, 1970), pp. 11–14.

3. Charles Osgood, "The Representation Model and Relevant Research Methods," in *Trends in Content Analysis*; I. de Sola Pool ed. (Urbana, Ill.: University of Illinois Press, 1959), pp. 55–78.

4. Domhoff, *Higher Circles*, pp. 14–17.

5. Richard P. Coleman and Bernice L. Neugarten, *Social Status in the City* (San Francisco: Jossey-Bass, 1971), chapters 2 and 6.

6. Daniel Bell, "The Break-up of Family Capitalism," in *The End of Ideology*, ed. Daniel Bell (New York: Free Press, 1960); A. A. Berle, Jr., and Gardner C. Means, *The Modern Corporation and Private Property* (New York: Macmillan, 1932); A. A. Berle, Jr., *Power without Property* (New York: Harcourt, Brace, 1959).

7. For a strong argument against an overemphasis by Marxists on ideology and public opinion in explaining the stability of power structures, see Michael Mann, "The Ideology of Intellectuals and Other People in the Development of Capitalism," in *Stress and Contradiction in Modern Capitalism*, ed. Leon N. Lindberg, et al. (Lexington, Mass.: Lexington Books, 1975). For evidence on the differing opinions of elites and underclasses in America, see Richard Hamilton, *Class and Politics in the United States* (New York: Wiley, 1972) and Michael Mann, "The Social Cohesion of Liberal Democracy," *American Sociological Review*, June 1970.